AN INTRODUCTION

METHODS AND MATERIALS OF LITERARY CRITICISM

THE BASES IN AESTHETICS AND POETICS

BY

CHARLES MILLS GAYLEY, A.B.

PROFESSOR OF THE ENGLISH LANGUAGE AND LITERATURE IN THE
UNIVERSITY OF CALIFORNIA

AND

FRED NEWTON SCOTT, PH.D.

JUNIOR PROFESSOR OF RHETORIC IN THE UNIVERSITY OF MICHIGAN

BOSTON, U.S.A.

GINN & COMPANY, PUBLISHERS

The Athenæum Press

1901

PREFACE.

———◦◦◦———

THE temper and conditions of the age encourage the critical habit. Literature is no longer the affair of patron or coterie, but of the public. The public reads for itself and estimates. It is not the scholar alone but the artisan who judges the latest novel, satire, or barrack-room ballad. He weighs, compares, and pronounces judgment. And from the multitude of men that are critics unto themselves, and out of the confusion of conflicting opinions, arises the demand for system and principle.

What obtains for the disinterested reader obtains *a fortiori* for those who attempt to express public opinion or to form the taste of others. The reviewer, the student and the teacher of literature, the investigator of literary history or of literary theory, all who make of criticism a discipline, an aim, or a trade, are interested in whatever tends to simplify the inquiry.

What the inquirer wants is guidance, not dogmatic formulation of principles, but systematic presentation of the problems that must be solved and of the information available for the process. For literary criticism has not yet reached the scientific, still less the ' cocksure ' period of its development. Its present consciousness is dynamic, and its condition transitional. It has outgrown the stage of unquestioning acquiescence in tradition, authority, personal bias or prejudice. But it is not yet fully alive to its possibilities, scope, or aim, — not organized. An appreciative curiosity characterizes the study

acquaintance with literary masterpieces and the history of literature, some knowledge at first hand of art and its history, and a continual study of aesthetics.

While the introduction to each topic here considered is theo-retical, nothing is further from our intent than to encourage *a priori* speculation. The treatment of literary types in the second volume will especially illustrate our conviction concerning this subject. The principles of criticism depend, to a large ex-tent, upon the principles of art. But to institute a vague theo-rizing about the principles of art is as unprofitable as to pursue a criticism grounded on the uncertain bias or prejudice of indi-vidual taste. That music, poetry, and the plastic arts exist implies a reason for their existence. But to arrive at this rea-son and at the characteristics of its various manifestations the student must advance from the particular to the general. So, in seeking the laws of literature, he should naturally first acquaint himself with the history of literature, with the devel-opment of its kinds, and with the peculiarities of the various kinds. He must have material at his command before he spec-ulates upon the ontology of material. Having a fair knowledge of the scope and the evolution of a literary species, he may pro-ceed to an inquiry into the laws that regulate its evolution. For, as we have already said, the forces that impel and the laws that govern literary production are forces and laws that go far to determine the canons by which that production should be judged. To investigate the principles of literary criticism, the student must investigate literature, not by the study of a national literature only, but comparatively. From the study of a specimen he passes to the comparison with others of the same type; he proceeds to the comparison of type with type in characteristics and in growth, of national literature with national literature, and finally arrives at the comparison of literary art with other forms of art. But conjointly with this inductive study of literary art there should be acquired an acquaintance

tory to, the pursuit of other sciences, at the same time that it is correlated with the scientific study of every art.

The plan of study here outlined has been arranged for convenience and comprehensiveness. The objects more directly aimed at in this volume, and that which will shortly follow it, are, first, to give the reader his orientation by showing the relation of literature to art, criticism, aesthetics, and the contributory sciences, and by displaying the solidarity and scope of literature; second, to consider the main types or forms which literature has assumed in the course of its development; third, to trace the movement and determine the law of literary waves or fashions; and, last, to deduce from these considerations the principles which should guide us in critically estimating given literary products.

When possible, each topic has been considered in a twofold aspect, theoretical and historical. Generally, it will be found that, under each of these subdivisions, the first section presents an *analysis* of the subject under discussion, and a statement of the problems involved, with indication of the authorities most necessary to be consulted; the second section consists of a *bibliography* alphabetically arranged, and frequently accompanied by annotations which aim to give the student or the prospective buyer some idea of the content and value of the work in its bearing upon the subject; and the third section, called, for lack of a better name, *General Note*, is an *omnium gatherum*, a receptacle for such references and suggestions as have failed to find lodgment in the preceding sections.

It will not be for an instant imagined that this course of study need be pursued in the order outlined, or that it should be crowded into six months or a year. To each reader and each class are the conditions thereof. Much will depend upon the previous preparation of the reader. The problems presented in the following chapters require for their solution a running application of rhetorical science and psychology, an

to-day; but this confines itself to a few insistent problems, as if unaware of their relativity; and it is vague concerning the processes and materials contributory to the inquiry.

Now this book does not advocate or advance a method, nor does it aim to supply the material necessary for exhaustive investigation of any one department of literary criticism. It seeks to place before those interested a conspectus of the problems to be solved, a review of the methods suggested for their solution, an indication of the materials available with reference to their sources and frequently to their quality.

Such an attempt should be justified in the opinion of those who are unconsciously, as well as of those who are consciously, interested in criticism. For the direct purpose of the study is not to train literary analysts, but rational lovers of literature. And to be a rational lover demands effort ; for while the process of literary enjoyment, like that of literary creation, may appear to be unforced and natural, there are degrees of enjoyment, the highest of which is *criticism;* as there are of creation, the highest of which is *art.* Each of these processes has its reason for existence and its law of development. But the principles which find expression in enjoyment, and ultimately in criticism, have their root in those that underlie the processes of creation. A study of the canons of literary judgment becomes a study of the principles of literature. It is for this reason that lovers of the art are bidden to what may look like a barmecide feast of methods and materials.

But as the principles of literary judgment are akin to all aesthetic principles, are, in fact, only the application in a particular field of the general laws of art, so the methods by which these principles shall be applied in the process of critical appraisement are the adaptation to given conditions, and to a given end, of the critical method that characterizes the larger science of Discrimination. The study, therefore, of the methods of literary criticism is a discipline cognate with, and contribu-

with the critical judgment of the ages concerning art in general, with principles philosophically deduced, as well as with those taught by experience. So also with the best opinion concerning the laws and the development of mind. Hence the necessity of aesthetics and psychology to the student of literary criticism. The results contributed by these studies widen the horizon and intensify the gaze of the literary investigator. They teach him to correlate literature with other arts, and all with the other phenomena by which mind is expressed.

And from this point of view it may appear that this introduction to the Methods and Materials of Literary Criticism is an introduction to aesthetics on the one hand, and on the other to the comparative study of literature.

CONTENTS.

———•◦•———

CHAPTER I.

NATURE AND FUNCTION OF LITERARY CRITICISM.

PART I. — THEORY OF CRITICISM.

CHAPTER II.

PRINCIPLES OF ART.

PART I. — THEORY OF ART.

PART II. — DEVELOPMENT OF ART.

CHAPTER III.

PRINCIPLES OF LITERATURE.

Part I. — Theory of Literature.

Part II. — Comparative Literature.

CHAPTER IV.

THE THEORY OF POETRY.

CHAPTER V.

CHAPTER VI.

CHAPTER VII.

THE PRINCIPLES OF VERSIFICATION.

LITERARY CRITICISM.

CHAPTER I.

NATURE AND FUNCTION OF LITERARY CRITICISM.

PART I. — THEORY OF CRITICISM.

§ 1. DIVISION OF THE SUBJECT AND STATEMENT OF PROBLEMS.

THE study of literary criticism may best be begun by an inquiry into the meaning of the term. The following questions then suggest themselves : What is the nature of the process called criticism ? How many kinds of criticism are there, and what is the principle of classification ? How is literary criticism distinguished from other varieties or types of criticism ?

I. Definitions of criticism. — These may be drawn from the usages of speech and writing, or framed in accordance with some theory ; or, the two methods may be combined, one being used to correct and verify the other. In what follows we shall first consider popular usages of the term, then call attention to its theoretical aspects.

A. USAGE. — The following are some of the meanings commonly attached to the word :

1. Criticism is used in the sense of **fault-finding** or taking exception. The critic is one who takes a hostile attitude.

He is "a carper and a caviller." His business is to discover imperfections. This may be said to be the traditional meaning.

2. Of late years writers like Matthew Arnold have attempted to give criticism a more genial function than it had formerly. Such writers maintain that the business of criticism is less to censure than to **praise**. Some even go so far as to say that the critic ought never to censure. (See Moulton and Taine.) Is not this going too far? May we apply the name critic to a man who sees only the good points of what he is criticising? or who **registers** what he sees without saying whether it is good or bad?

3. Another and more philosophic way of defining criticism is to say that it is a process, or the process, of **passing judgment** upon anything. For this view, support is found in the derivation of the term criticism from κρίνειν, meaning originally to separate and then to judge.

4. Allied to the preceding definition is a fourth, which makes criticism a process of **comparison**. "Criticism," says Mr. Robertson (Essays, p. 1), "is a process that goes on over all the field of human knowledge, being simply comparison or clash of opinion." And Mr. Godkin, in *Forum*, 17: 45, says: "All genuine criticism consists in comparison between two ways of doing something." Does comparison in these cases mean the same as judgment? or as **classifying** with or without ranking? Do these definitions exclude from criticism the exercise of the imagination and the emotions?

5. A famous definition is that which Matthew Arnold gives in his essay, On the Function of Criticism, namely, "to see the object as in itself it really is." To this should be joined another phrase from the same essay, "the endeavor to learn and propagate the best that is known and thought in the world." Do the two definitions come to the same thing? Is not seeing a thing as in itself it really is, the same as judging it? If judging means making a comparison, with what do we compare a thing when we see it as in itself it really is? Again,

what attitude does Mr. Arnold assume towards fault-finding or censuring? May his method be regarded as impartial **appreciation?** and would his definition exclude the destructive kind of criticism? With Mr. Arnold's definition should be compared the idea held by Kant, that criticism is an endeavor to find the principle or common ground which lies back of every difference of opinion. (See § **3,** B 1.)

For other definitions, see Elze, Blass, Urlichs, Moulton, Dowden, Fuller, Brunetière, Ward, Brandes, in § **2,** below.

B. **THEORY.** — Approaching the subject now from a different direction, we may ask :

1. What is the SCIENTIFIC BASIS of criticism? Is criticism a science, or an art, or merely a method? If a science, may it be classed among the exact sciences? Does it belong to the descriptive sciences like psychology, or to the normative sciences like ethics and logic? Is it an inductive or a deductive process?

2. What is the PSYCHOLOGICAL BASIS of criticism? Does criticism proceed from the emotions, or from the intellect? or do both combine in the critical process? If it is purely intellectual, how does it differ from other operations of the intellect, such as imagination and judgment? Is there a critical element in every mental process? If criticism is an act of the judgment, in what way does it differ from other judgments?

3. What is the SOCIAL BASIS of criticism? Is criticism individual or social in its aim? Is the test which it applies an individual or a social test? What part does criticism play in the workings of the social body? How does it affect social progress?

4. What is the PHILOSOPHICAL BASIS of criticism? Where in the division of the field of human knowledge and activity, is the place of criticism? Is it a principal or a subordinate division? Is it a process, or a principle, or is it both? Is it sub-

jective or objective? May it deal with things of nature, or is it concerned only with things of art? Is it abstract or concrete? Is it analytic, or synthetic, or organic? Is it a positive force or a negative force?

II. Criticism and kindred sciences. — *A.* In philology and religion, and sometimes in law, it is customary to distinguish between criticism and hermeneutics (interpretation, exegesis). According to Boeckh (Encykl. d. Phil. Wissensch., p. 77), the purpose of hermeneutics is "to understand the object itself in its own nature," while the purpose of criticism is not to understand an object in and for itself, but "to establish a relation with some other object in such wise that the knowledge of the relation is the end in view" (p. 170). (Cf. Blass, Urlichs, Paul. See also Lieber, who writes on hermeneutics from the legal point of view, and Landerer and Schleiermacher, who write on the same subject from the point of view of the theologian.)

B. How is criticism related to such sciences as ethics, psychology, sociology, politics, anthropology? What is its relation to aesthetics?

III. Kinds of criticism. — Although the difficulties of classification are as great as those of definition, we shall find upon careful examination that much of the confusion is due to the fact that two principles of classification have been commonly employed, one referring to the subject matter of the criticism, the other to the method of procedure.

A. According to the first principle of division, any critical process which deals with the facts of history is called historical criticism, any critical process which deals with science is scientific criticism; and so any critical process which deals with literature is called literary criticism. The kinds of criticism are as numerous as the kinds of subject matter.

B. According to the second principle of division, the name is determined by the method. If the historical method is pursued, the result is called historical criticism. In like manner the application of the principles of science is scientific criticism, and of philosophy is philosophical criticism, whether applied to history, philology, art, or literature.

IV. Types of literary criticism. — *A.* LITERARY criticism,
it will be noticed, is named with reference to its subject matter. It is not a method which can be applied to other subjects. Its method may be scientific, historical, philosophical, psychological, or any other that answers the purpose. Some, it is true, hold that literature is a species of art and that only the methods of criticism appropriate to art are applicable to literature. But is this the case? (Examine the article by J. H. Leuba in *Am. Jl. of Psychology*, 5 : 496 ; The Case of John Bunyan by Prof. Royce in *Psychological Review*, 1 : 22, 134, 230 ; La Psychologie des Auteurs dramatiques by A. Binet and J. Passy in *Rev. Philos.*, Févr. 1894, p. 228.)

B. Two varieties or types of literary criticism which are often contrasted, are judicial criticism and inductive criticism. (See Moulton, Archer, Robertson, Blass, Saintsbury.)

1. THE JUDICIAL METHOD passes judgment on the work of literature, that is, evaluates it or appraises it. Of this class, Jeffrey with his famous "This will never do" (essay on Wordsworth) is a striking example.

2. INDUCTIVE CRITICISM, when employed in its simplicity, busies itself solely with the collection and arrangement of facts. It refuses to evaluate or appraise. (See Moulton, Howells, Taine, Saintsbury.)

Under inductive criticism we may point out two subdivisions. (*a.*) The first occupies itself with the work in hand. It aims to examine the work and in a methodical way to describe the contents. Perhaps Mr. Moulton's method falls in this division. (*b.*) The second kind of inductive criticism sees in the work an expression of external influences, and hence pays most attention to the environment. Its aim is to classify the work, to place it in its proper relation to other works of the same kind and time. Taine and Sainte-Beuve may serve as examples.

C. Many other divisions of literary criticism may be suggested, some of which are perhaps more philosophical than the division into judicial and inductive. Criticism may be divided into personal (or subjective) criticism, such as we find in the writings of Henry James, and impersonal or objective criticism, such as was advocated by Émile Hennequin; it may be classed as analytic and synthetic; as positive and negative; as higher (when it deals with writings as a whole), and lower (when it deals with isolated passages); as internal and external; as static, dynamic, and organic; as scientific, philosophic, ethical, and aesthetic. Possibly no comprehensive and strictly logical classification has yet been made.

An interesting question is whether various types of criticism may not be combined; whether certain types are not complementary to one another. Thus, should not judicial criticism also be inductive? analytical criticism also be synthetic? (See Moulton, p. 22.)

Literary criticism so differs in different countries that it is possible to speak of British, American, French, German, Italian and Russian criticism. (See § **3**, 8.)

On the kinds of criticism, see in general, Patin, Blass, Elze, Urlichs, Saintsbury.

V. Purpose of literary criticism. — The object of criticism should be very closely related to its definition. As there are different opinions on the first point, we may expect to find different opinions on the second. The following are some of the objects which have been advanced as proper to criticism,

(1) Like any other means of obtaining or imparting knowledge, criticism is interesting for its own sake. (2) Since
criticism is a kind of literature, its justification rests on the
same basis as other literary forms. (3) Criticism is a help to
our appreciation of literature. It enhances the impression;
it interprets and makes clear what is obscure in the thing
criticised. (4) It teaches us what in literature is good, and
what is bad, and thus saves our time and mental energy.
(5) It prepares the public for the author. (See Arnold's essay,
On the Function of Criticism.) (6) It shows the author how to
adapt himself to his public. (7) It regulates and disciplines
literary taste. (8) It frees literature from the tyranny of
prejudice or whim. (On this view and the preceding, see
Nisard and Dowden.) (9) It destroys morbidity in the author
or the public. (10) It gives people who have not time to read
the originals information about new books and new ideas.

In connection with this topic the question may be raised
whether in criticism the writer's character is a proper subject
of praise or blame; also, whether the purpose of criticism is to
convince or to persuade.

(See Villemain, Mabie, Bristed, Lowell, Saintsbury, Arnold,
H. James, Stedman, Archer.)

VI. Relation of criticism to creation. — *A.* It has been
often maintained that criticism as a form of intellectual effort
is lower than creation. (See Arnold, Shairp, Macaulay, Posnett,
and Robertson.) If this is so, does the argument apply as
well to inductive as to judicial criticism?

B. The statement has also been made that critics are
naturally hostile to authors and that the history of criticism
has been a history of the triumph of the author over the critic.
(See Moulton, p. 7; Robertson, p. 142; Birrell.) Is such in
fact the case? Does criticism necessarily lag behind creation
(Caine, p. xxx)? Why should it? If it does, is its tardiness

irremediable? or is it merely due to vicious methods of criticism employed by bad critics? Is "the judicial attitude unreceptive"? (Moulton, p. 7.)

C. Again, it is sometimes said that criticism tends to crush out originality; yet according to Mr. Howells (*Harper*, June, 1887) all criticism is futile; the literary movement is "never stayed in the least or arrested by criticism." Which is the sounder view?

D. Another theory, a theory for which Macaulay is often given credit, is that an age of fine creation cannot also be an age of fine criticism. (See Macaulay's essay on Dryden, and compare Burke's On the Sublime and Beautiful, p. 21.) Was this true of the literary history of Greece and Rome? Has it been true in the history of English literature? of the French, and German, and Italian literatures? A corollary is that a good poet cannot be a good critic. Is there anything in the nature of criticism and of creation to make the two incompatible? Have both ever reached a high degree of excellence in the same man? What shall be said of Shakespeare's critical powers (Lewes, Actors and the Art of Acting; Robertson, p. 14)? of Dante's? of Goethe's? of Schiller's? Shenstone (quoted by Robertson, p. 15) thought that "every good poet includes a critic," but he was careful to add, "the reverse will not hold."

E. May not criticism itself be creative? (See Arnold, Robertson, Shairp, Mabie.) May not criticism be even an advance upon the work which is criticised? (Wilde, Posnett, H. James.)

VII. Qualifications of the critic. — Should the critic be in the main a man of intellect or a man of taste? Ought he to be a specialist? (See Saintsbury.) Can he be a good critic if he knows no literature but that of his own nation? Should he be disinterested? (See Arnold.) In general, consult

Wilkinson, Jennings's Curiosities of Criticism, Sainte-Beuve, Allen, Dowden.

VIII. Canons of criticism. — Under this head the question may first be asked whether such things as canons of criticism exist. If they exist and have validity, on what principles, scientific, philosophic, psychological, ethical, or aesthetic, do they rest? Are they relative or absolute? Are they fixed and good for all time, or do they shift with the progress of intelligence and change of taste? (See Saintsbury, Posnett, Moulton, Symonds.) What is the standard of taste? (Begg, Hume.) How far is it alike for all nations? How are individual differences of critical opinion to be accounted for and reconciled? Of what value are the classics as guides in matters of criticism? Are they to be accepted as models? Is it possible to deduce from them all the canons of criticism? (Lewes, Principles of Success, p. 111.) Is it possible for a literary work to violate the canons of criticism and yet be a masterpiece? What value should be attached to consensus of opinion? to the test of time?

Attempts to formulate canons of criticism have been made by some of the authors mentioned in § 2. The validity of such canons may be tested, first, by the success of those who have conformed to them; and, secondly, by comparison with the unformulated rules that may be gathered from the practice of more spontaneous, but perhaps none the less admirable, critics.

§ 2. REFERENCES.

AINGER, A. Charles Lamb. New York: 1882.

In pointing out Lamb's place as a literary critic (pp. 168–182), the author brings into relief some of the fundamental characteristics of criticism, especially the part played by "the higher imagination."

ALLEN, GRANT. *Fortnightly*, 37: 339 Decay of Criticism.

Stimulated by the article of M. Caro (in *Rev. d. D. Mondes*, 1 Févr. 1882) on the Decay of Criticism in France, Mr. Allen looks about him for the causes of a similar decay in England. What he sees, however, is not retrogression, but advance. While the old criticism was very bad indeed, the new, based on the models of Sainte-Beuve and Saint-Marc Girardin, shows signs of improvement. "Just as the critical impulse is dying out in France, it has begun to live in England." Still there are untoward influences, and they correspond in two particulars to those detected by M. Caro in France, namely, the rise of journalism and the growth of specialization. (See *infra* under CARO.)

ARNOLD, M. Essays in Criticism. Boston: 1869.

pp. 1–38 On the Function of Criticism at the Present Time.

Perhaps the most important utterance upon criticism in modern times. The value, practical as well as theoretical, of the definition which is its starting-point — "to see the object as in itself it really is" — cannot well be called in question. The greater part of the essay is occupied with a discussion of the relation between critic and poet: The materials with which the poet works are ideas, the best ideas of his time. He is dependent, therefore, upon the intellectual current of his time, and it is the critic's business to see that the current is broad, and that it moves in the right direction. In the interest of the creative man the critic must help the best ideas prevail. Thus the critic's task may be summed up as "a disinterested endeavor to learn and propagate the best that is known and thought in the world." The essay has given rise to a great deal of discussion, the nature and trend of which are indicated by the following questions : Is Arnold right in subordinating criticism to creation ? Is the critical faculty necessarily lower than the inventive faculty? If Arnold is using 'creative' in the sense of 'original,' may not the critic be as creative as the writer of fiction or drama? If poetry is a 'criticism of life' (see essay on Wordsworth), is not the poetic faculty also a critical faculty? Concerning his definition of criticism, we may ask whether, philosophically speaking, it is possible to see anything as in itself it really is. Things are understood only as they are seen in their relations to other things. More than that, we always see them as they are colored by our personal views and tendencies; the same thing has different meanings for different persons. Again, is it best for the critic to be disinterested? Is he not likely to be indifferent? Is it not better for each critic to have an interest, and allow one extreme to offset the other? (Cf. Goethe's view in Kunst-Aphorismen, II: "I am more and more convinced that, when one has to vent an opinion on the actions or on the writings of others, unless this be done from a certain one-sided enthusiasm or from a loving interest in the person and the work, the result is hardly worth gathering up.") For discussion of Arnold's views, see *Westm.*, 80: 468; *No. Am. Rev.*, 101: 208; *Century*, 14: 184; *No. Brit. Rev.*, 42: 158; Robertson, Essays, pp. 42–44, 144–148.

See also Arnold's article 'Sainte-Beuve' in the 9th edition of the Encyclopaedia Britannica.

BEGG, W. P. The Development of Taste. Glasgow: 1887.

    pp. 140–157 Is there a Standard of Taste?

BERNHEIM, ERNST. Lehrbuch der historischen Methode. Leipzig: 1889.

    pp. 202–390 Kritik ; pp. 395–428 Interpretation.

A comprehensive and methodical treatment of criticism from the point of view of the historical investigator. The task of historical criticism is, positively, to pass judgment upon the truthfulness of the information which has come down from the past, and so to assign to it its proper grade of probability;

negatively, to set aside certain data as untrustworthy. The
form which the criticism takes is a judgment partly upon the
relation of the data to the facts, partly upon the relation of the
facts one to another. Judgments regarding the trustworthiness
of the information as historical evidence make up the lower or
external criticism (niedere oder äussere Kritik); the higher or
internal criticism (höhere oder innere Kritik) consists in judgments regarding the relation of the evidence to the facts.

BLAIR, HUGH. Lectures on Rhetoric and Belles Lettres.
Philadelphia: 1833.

A definition of criticism will be found at the beginning of
Lecture 3.

BLASS, FRIEDR. Hermeneutik und Kritik. (In Iwan Müller's
Handbuch der klassischen Alterthumswissenschaft. Nörd-
lingen: 1886. Bd. 1, pp. 127–272.)

Blass's chapters on hermeneutics and criticism, the "methodology" of Müller's Handbook, are intended as a practical
guide for the investigator in classical philology. Hermeneutics
or interpretation is considered under the three heads, grammatical, historical, and technical. The first is concerned with
matters of grammar (and rhetoric); the second with the kinds,
stages, and limitations of literature; the third with matters of
literary form. Criticism is looked upon as a kind of judgment.
In every judgment, says Blass, there is involved a doubt.
We raise the question whether something is true, or right, or
useful, or beautiful. How is this doubt "resolved" (auf-
gehoben)? By comparing, is the answer, the object to be
judged with another object, regarding which we are not in
doubt. If the two harmonize, there follows a judgment of
truth, or rightness, or beauty, as the case may be. When the
question is one of rightness, or beauty, the object with which
we make comparison is an *ideal* of right or beauty. In philology,

there are two kinds of criticism : historical and aesthetic. The latter is not strictly philological, but the shrewd philologist will be, so Blass thinks, *auch in dieser Weise urtheilsfähig*. In his treatment of the practical aspects of the subject, Blass discusses such topics as the kinds of errors and their origin, causes of critical doubt, conjectural criticism, and criticism of genuineness (Kritik der Echten und Unechten).

BOECKH, A. Encyklopädie und Methodologie der philologischen Wissenschaften. Herausg. von E. Bratuschek. Leipzig: 1877.

> pp. 169–254 Theorie der Kritik.

See the note on Blass, *supra*. Interpretation expounds the object as it is in itself, with reference (1) to objective or (2) to subjective conditions. In the first instance the interpretation may be (*a*) grammatical, that is, it may deal with the meaning of the word in itself ; or (*b*) historical, that is, it may deal with external relations. Subjective interpretation is divided into individual interpretation and interpretation of the species or type (Gattungsinterpretation). Criticism differs from interpretation in that it considers the object not as it is in itself, but as it is in its relations to other objects. Its purpose is to understand the relation rather than the objects themselves. The kinds of criticism are the same as the kinds of interpretation, namely, grammatical, historical, and individual criticism, and criticism of types (Gattungskritik).

A second edition, edited by R. Klussmann, appeared in 1886.

BOURGET, P. Études et Portraits. 2 vols. Paris: 1889.

> Vol. 1, pp. 299–306 Réflexions sur la Critique.

Called out by Caro's article on the decay of modern criticism. (See below.) In a few paragraphs Bourget reviews rapidly but suggestively the progress of modern critical writing. Criticism, he thinks, is not dead, but metamorphosed into psychology.

Brandes, Georg. Die Litteratur des neunzehnten Jahrhunderts in ihren Hauptströmungen. Uebersetzt und
eingeleitet von A. Schodtmann. 5 vols in 3. Berlin:
1872–73.

> Bd. 5, pp. 351–373 Sainte-Beuve; pp. 374–387 Sainte-Beuve und
> die moderne Kritik.

Presents in clear and attractive style the literary life of
Sainte-Beuve and his part in the history of the French Romanticists. Sainte-Beuve reformed criticism by putting it on a
historical and scientific basis (p. 379). See pp. 386, 387 for a
definition of criticism and an estimate of its importance.

Brimley, G. Essays. Edited by W. G. Clark. 3d edition.
London: 1868.

> Pp. 184–203 Poetry and Criticism.

Bristed, C. A. Pieces of a broken down Critic. 4 vols.
Baden-Baden: 1858.

> Vol. 4, p. 34 Purpose of Criticism.

Brockhaus' Conversations-Lexikon. Article 'Kritik.'

The various kinds of criticism are enumerated and briefly
defined.

Brunetière, Ferd. La Critique littéraire. Part of the article
'Critique' in the Grande Encyclopédie.

The article 'Critique' in the Grande Encyclopédie covers
pp. 409–431. Omitting subdivisions irrelevant to our purpose,
we may divide it into six parts, as follows: (1) Philosophy by
L. Dauriac, (2) Philology by A. Waltz, (3) Literature by
F. Brunetière, (4) Music by R. Lavoix, (5) History by A. Giry,
(6) Religious History by M. Vernes. Brunetière's article
covers pp. 411–424. It is divided into two parts, the first
historical, the second systematic. For a notice of the first part,

see § 5. The second and systematic part treats first of the Object and Methods of Criticism; second, of the Function of Criticism. The object in criticism is threefold, (1) to explain, (2) to classify, (3) to judge. By explanation is meant description, analysis, and comment. The critic must explain the author, whose character is not always an analogue of his book, but he must not stop with the author. Others have helped write the book. The author's contemporaries are his collaborators. Other books have influenced him. He lives in a particular moment or phase of the evolution of the *genre* to which his work belongs. A part of the explanation, therefore, consists in placing the work in its *milieu*, national and international. To perform the work of classification criticism needs sound principles of three kinds : 1. *Scientific*, analogous to those of natural history; 2. *Moral*, establishing an ethical hierarchy without identifying morals and art; 3. *Aesthetic*, measuring the work of art by the absolute quantity that it expresses. Furnished with these principles criticism, as a mode of classifying, would become scientific. Finally, criticism is under obligation to pass judgment; for a work of art, while it is a record to be explained and classified, is also a poem or statue better or worse than some other poem or statue. Distinct from the object of criticism is its function. According to Brunetière the function of criticism is to act on public opinion, on authors, and upon the general direction of literature and art. By maintaining literary traditions criticism perpetuates from age to age the literary consciousness of the nation.

Cf. in the same work the article by Alfred Ernst on the Aesthetics of Literature (under Esthétique, p. 409).

BRUNETIÈRE, FERD. L'Évolution des Genres dans l'histoire de la littérature. Tome 1er. Paris : 1890.

Pp. 35–278 L'Évolution de la critique.

In his discussion of the work of the principal French critics

from du Bellay to Taine, M. Brunetière considers the function
of criticism in most of its aspects.   See in particular pp. 35, 36,
on the influence of criticism on literature; pp. 184–6 on the
substitution of the criticism of beauties for the criticism of
defects; pp. 195–201 on dilettanteism and individualism in
criticism, and the chapters on Sainte-Beuve and Taine, *passim*.
For comment on the work, consult § 5.

BRUNETIÈRE, FERD.   Questions de Critique.   Paris: 1889.

> Pp. 297–324 La critique scientifique (on É. Hennequin).

BUCHANAN, ROBT.   Master-spirits.   London: 1873.

> I. Criticism as one of the Fine Arts.

Criticism cannot be reduced to a science, but as an art it is
susceptible of high cultivation.   The old idea of criticism was
the application of tests by which to ascertain the value of the
work ; modern criticism means the impression produced on certain minds by certain products.

BURROUGHS, J.   *Century*, 14 : 185   Matthew Arnold's Criticism.   (Reprinted in Indoor Studies, p. 79.   Boston: 1889.)

The strength of Mr. Arnold's criticism lies in his sincere effort to grasp the totality of life ; its ineffectualness is due to
the unclassical age and people with whom he has to deal.   An
interesting question is raised on p. 190, namely, whether
Arnold's criticism is in line with the movement of individualism which, in Mr. Burroughs's opinion, characterizes the
literature of this century.

CAINE, T. HALL.   Cobwebs of Criticism.   London: 1883.

A contribution to the history of criticism.   Discussions, not
too profound, of critical theory are scattered through its pages.
See, for further notice, § 5.

CAIRD, EDW.   The Critical Philosophy of Immanuel Kant.   2
vols.   Glasgow: 1889.

See vol. 1, pp. 1–20, for a statement of the meaning of criticism in the Kantian sense.

CARO, E.   *Rev. d. D. Mondes*, 1 Févr. 1882 La critique contemporaine et les causes de son affaiblissement.

The kinds of criticism are enumerated, not very logically, and the methods employed by Villemain, Nisard, St.-Marc Girardin, Sainte-Beuve, and Taine, are briefly characterized. Decadence in French criticism is traced to three causes: (1) Absorption of literary talent in the business of politics, which gives rise to partisan hostility; (2) the rise of journalism with its attendant evils; (3) the growth of specialization.   (See, above, Allen's Decay of Criticism, and Bourget's Études et Portraits.)

COAN, T. M.   *Lippincott*, 13 : 355 Critic and Artist.

An interesting and suggestive paper discussing the attitude which the critic should assume toward the artist.   The following are some of the ideas advanced by the author: (1) The theory of evolution, by giving a new aspect to everything in art, has set new tasks for the modern critic.   His business is to see, not to say, new things.   (2) In a work of art the artist himself is a chief object of interest.   Knowledge of his personality is a short cut to knowledge of the work.   Still, from the critical point of view, the character of the artist is not a proper subject for praise or blame.   (3) The critic by a methodical study of himself should determine his personal equation, and when it is determined should make allowance for it. (4) The order of development of the critical faculty is as follows: (*a*) Naïve admiration; (*b*) search for truth; (*c*) interest in the personality of the artist.

DESCHANEL, ÉMILE. Physiologie des écrivains et des artistes, ou essai de critique naturelle. Paris: 1864.

An extreme application, after Sainte-Beuve and Taine, of laws of physiology to the science of criticism. The author shows, by a remarkable assemblage of facts and illustrations, that it is possible to determine by scrutiny of a given piece of literature (1) the period in which it was written, (2) the climate, (3) the nationality of the author, (4) the author's sex, (5) his age, (6) his temperament, (7) his character, (8) his profession, (9) his education, (10) his state of health.

DOWDEN, E. *Fortnightly*, 52:737 Literary Criticism in France.

A careful analysis of the literary theories of Bourget, Sainte-Beuve, Nisard, Taine, and Émile Hennequin. A good introduction to the comparative study of theories.

DROZ, ÉD. La critique littéraire et la science. Paris: 1893.

The purpose of this interesting paper, which was read before a body of scientists at Besançon in 1891, is to show that the scientific method, as understood by men of letters (that is, as misunderstood), has not been of much service to modern literary criticism. The position is supported by an unsparing examination of the pretensions of Sainte-Beuve, Taine, Brunetière, and É. Hennequin. The treatment is admirable in both spirit and style, and especially valuable as showing how the 'scientific' views of the greatest modern French critics strike a man of science.

DRYDEN, J. Works. Edited by Sir Walter Scott. London: 1808.

DRYDEN, J. Dramatic Works. Edited by G. Saintsbury. Edinburgh: 1882.

In the Preface to the State of Innocence Dryden defines criticism as 'a standard of judgment whose purpose is to enable us to observe those excellencies which should delight a reasonable reader.' For other studies of the nature and province of criticism, consult the Essay of Dramatic Poesy, the Essay on Satire, the Defense of Epilogue, the Essay on Translation, the Parallel between Poetry and Painting, the Introduction to Don Sebastian, the Essay on Heroic Plays, and in general the prefatory essays of the plays. (See Wylie's Evolution of English Criticism.)

ELIOT, GEORGE.   Essays and Leaves from a Note-Book. Edinburgh: 1885.

A brief essay, entitled Judgments on Authors, begins on p. 294. George Eliot would make the test of good writing ' the author's contribution to the spiritual wealth of mankind.'

ELZE, KARL.   Grundriss der englischen Philologie.   2d ed. Halle: 1889.
    Pp. 36–99.

Elze agrees with Boeckh in making criticism the art or theory of judgments. He adopts (p. 170) Boeckh's definition of hermeneutics and criticism. The divisions of hermeneutics are (1) lexicological, (2) grammatical, (3) stylistic, and (4) metrical exposition, and (5) exposition of the meaning or content (inhaltliche Exposition). Criticism he divides into textual criticism and aesthetic criticism. Determination of the text rests upon the postulate that every author has a lexicological, grammatical, stylistic, and metrical individuality, in addition to the individuality of his ideas. Aesthetic criticism judges a work in its relation to other works by comparing it with literature of the same kind, and on the basis of such judgment and comparison assigns it to its proper place in literary history. Its value as member of a class is determined by asking how far it corresponds to the canon or class-ideal (Gattungsideal, cf. Boeckh's Kunstregel) laid down by aesthetics.

EMERSON, R. W.　Complete works.　12 vols.　Boston: 1893.
　　　1: 40 Natural History of Intellect (Law of Criticism : " Every
　　　scripture is to be interpreted in the same spirit which gave it
　　　forth "); 2: 252 The Over-Soul (" The supreme critic . . . is that
　　　Unity, that Over-Soul, within which every man's particular being
　　　is contained and made one with all others "); 3: 61 Experience
　　　(The futility of criticism); 243–5 New England Reformers
　　　(Outbreak of critical spirit in New England); 8: 58 Poetry and
　　　Imagination (" The critic . . . is a failed poet ").

FULLER, S. MARGARET.　Papers on Literature and Art.　New
　　　York: 1848.　Pt. 1, pp. 1–9 A short essay on critics,
　　　pp. 11–14 A Dialogue.

Two sketchy but suggestive articles touching the relation of
criticism to creation.　The writer is sure that criticism is a
legitimate thing, but is not clear as to its function.　" The
critic is the historian who records the order of creation."
" The use of criticism in periodical writing is to sift, not to
stamp a work."

HARDY, A. S.　*Andover Rev.*, 14: 522 Letters and Life.

Maintains that each critic is entitled to his independent and
personal judgment, and that the value of his criticism for us
depends on our knowledge of the critic and of his point of
view.

HARRIS, JAS.　Philological Inquiries.　2 vols.　London: 1781.
　　　(Vols. IV and V of the Miscellanies.)

One of the earliest attempts by an Englishman to treat criticism in a scientific manner.　The work is in three parts.　The
first is on the rise, nature, and kinds of criticism ; the second
consists of illustrations of critical principles as they appear in
the writings of distinguished authors, ancient and modern ; the
third is an essay on the taste and literature of the middle ages.
On p. 7 criticism is defined as " a deep and philosophical

search into the primary laws of good writing, as far as they could be collected from the most approved performances." Critics are characterized (p. 38) as "a sort of masters of the ceremony in the court of letters." They are divided into philosophical, historical, and corrective critics.

HENNEQUIN, ÉMILE.　La Critique scientifique.　Paris: 1888.

An attempt, by a follower of Herbert Spencer, to put criticism upon a scientific basis. Hennequin's method, which he terms Esthopsychologie, is in some respects similar to that of Taine. It differs from Taine's in attaching less importance to the race, and in throwing emphasis upon the individuality of the author and his power to create an environment for himself. The purpose of criticism is not to evaluate the work of art, nor yet to determine the means by which it is produced, but to show the relation of the work to the social and psychological characteristics of the artist whom it reveals. See review by L. Arréat in *Rev. Philos.*, 27 : 83; by F. Brunetière in *Rev. d. D. Mondes*, 1 Juillet, 1888, p. 213; and by Dowden in *Fortnightly*, 52 : 752; and the passing notice by J. A. Symonds in *Fortnightly*, 52 : 774 : "His method of criticism may be defined as the science of the work of art regarded as a sign."

HOWELLS, W. D.　Editor's Study.　*Harper's Mag.*, 72 : 321, and each number thereafter to 84 : 643. (The articles dealing with the theory of criticism are reprinted in Criticism and Fiction. New York: 1891.)

The business of criticism is to observe and register. The test of any work of the imagination is, first of all, "Is it true — true to the motives, the impulses, the principles that shape the life of actual men and women?" Criticism, as ordinarily practiced, has no effect on the movements of literature. For comments on Mr. Howells's views, see *Academy*, 40 : 209 ; *Atlantic*, 68 : 566.

HUME, D.   Essays and Treatises on Several Subjects.   2 vols.
    London: 1768.
    Vol. I, pp. 255–281 Of the Standard of Taste.

HUNT, T. W.   *N. Princ. Rev.* 4: 75 Literary Criticism.

A discussion, mainly of Arnold's essay On the Function of
Criticism.

JAMES, HENRY, A. LANG, and E. GOSSE.   *New Review*, 4: 398
    The Science of Criticism.

Intended for the readers of a popular magazine, these entertaining papers do not go very deeply into the subject.   Henry
James, in opening, contrasts French criticism with the criticism
of England, much to the disadvantage of the English.   Among
the writers of Paris criticism is a fine art; the critics disdain to
touch anything except books of the higher class.   In England
they do these things differently.   Mr. James then goes on to
consider the function, or 'programme,' of the good critic, which
he thus characterizes: It is "to lend himself, to project himself and steep himself, to feel and feel until he understands,
and to understand so well that he can say, to have perception
at the pitch of passion and expression in the form of talent, to
be infinitely curious and incorrigibly patient, with the intensely
fixed idea of turning character and history and genius inside
out."   An interesting comparison is made between critic and
novelist.   The critic deals with the swarm of authors, "the
clamorous children of history," as the novelist deals with characters, but his task is harder because he cannot invent and
select — an opinion which gives a new turn to the old question
of the superiority of creation to criticism.

The article is reprinted, with a few curious changes, in the
author's Essays in London (New York: 1893), p. 259.

According to Andrew Lang, the only kind of criticism worth
reading or writing is "that which narrates the adventures of an

ingenious and educated mind in contact with masterpieces."
Its value for us who read it is that it gives acquaintance with
the experiences of another in the same literary world as ourselves.   At its best, however, criticism is a sorry business, and
in the world of letters is likely to do more harm than good.

Edmund Gosse takes a more hopeful view.   He distinguishes
two kinds of criticism.   The first is impersonal and uncompara-
tive, merely a record of books as they are issued; the second,
however, is comparative and composite, and in value falls but
little below creative work.   The function of the critic is not to
praise or to blame, but to analyze.   His necessary qualifications are intelligence, sympathy, and personality.

JOUBERT, J.   Pensées.   2 vols.   Paris: 1880.

See vol. 2, pp. 231, 326, 327, for epigrammatic utterances
upon criticism and critics.   Joubert's definition of criticism
occurs on p. 327 : "La critique est un exercice méthodique du
discernement."

KAMES, HENRY HOME, LORD.   The Elements of Criticism.
New York: 1838.
Introduction.

Criticism is a "regular science governed by just principles."
These principles are valid so far as they agree with human
nature.

KRANTZ, É.   Essai sur l'esthétique de Descartes.   Paris: 1882.

See pp. 1–6 for the relation of criticism to the idea of the
beautiful and to movements in literature.

LESSING, G. E.   Dramatic Notes (Bohn Libr.).   London: 1889.

See Nos. 101–4 for brief but suggestive remarks on the value
and function of criticism.

LEWES, G. H.   Principles of Success in Literature.   2d ed.
Boston: 1892.

See esp. Chap. I, and pp. 110–119.

LIEBER, F.   Legal and Political Hermeneutics.   Boston: 1839.

Although the author writes from the legal and political point of view, the fundamental principles from which he starts, and the analysis which he makes of the subject, may be applied to every field of thought.   Beginning with a discussion of the meaning of words, and the causes of ambiguity in human speech, he defines Interpretation, gives a classification of it, and expounds its principles at length.

LOWELL, J. R.   Prose Works.   6 vols.   Boston: 1890.

Lowell's enunciations on criticism are brief but always characteristic.   The following references indicate a few of the best : 1 : 354 Emerson the Lecturer (on Emerson's criticism); 369 Thoreau (on the inadequacy of Thoreau's criticism); 3 : 28–35 Shakespeare Once More (Need of sympathy *plus* fixed principles; Greek standards still prevail; 55 comparison futile in criticism; 67 criticism destructive and criticism productive); 114 Dryden (Duty of the critic to look on all sides; 140 "the higher wisdom of criticism lies in the capacity to admire"); 332 Chaucer (Criticism of parts misleading; "criticism cleaves to the teleological argument"); 4 : 355 Wordsworth (Necessary to consider failures and defects); 6 : 63 Fielding (No recognized standard in criticism); 71–2 Coleridge (Coleridge's method of criticism); 121–3 Don Quixote (Constructive criticism, " He reads most wisely who thinks everything into a book that it is capable of holding ").

LOWELL, J. R.   *N. A. Rev.*, 66: 358 Literary Criticism.

As introduction to a review of Browning, Lowell reads the critics a lesson on their dullness and incapacity, and lays down the principles by which they should be guided.

LOWELL, J. R.   *Century*, February, 1894 Criticism and Culture.

In this posthumous essay Lowell takes the position that the object of criticism is not to criticise (*i.e.*, to judge), but to

understand.   The critic should look for the strong rather than
for the weak points of the work.

LOWELL, J. R.   Letters.   Ed. by C. E. Norton.   2 vols.   New
    York: 1893.

The occasional brief references to critics and criticism may
be traced by means of the index.   Of especial interest, as bearing on the question of criticism and creation, is Lowell's remark
(vol. II, p. 62) regarding his criticism of himself: " I believe
no criticism has ever been made on what I write (I mean no
just one) that I had not made before, and let slip through my
fingers."

MABIE, H. W.   Short Studies in Literature.   New York: 1891.

See p. 174 for an admirable little essay on the origin, development, and sources of criticism.

MABIE, H. W.   *Andover Rev.*, 15: 583 Significance of Modern
    Criticism.   (Reprinted in Essays in Literary Interpre-
    tation.   New York: 1892.)

Reviewing the development of modern criticism, the writer
shows that through Herder, Goethe, Sainte-Beuve, Coleridge,
Arnold, Emerson, and others, a new form of literature has come
into existence, perfectly adapted to the intellectual methods and
tendencies of the age.   In this new field the creative impulse,
following the scientific method, but in the truest literary spirit,
works with perfect freedom.   " Criticism discloses the law and
the fact of art and life as these final realities are revealed
through literature."

MACAULAY, T. B.   Essays, Critical and Miscellaneous.   New
    York: 1861.

See the essay on Dryden for Macaulay's theory regarding the
relation of criticism and the creative imagination, and the essay
on the Athenian Orators for brief notes on the critics of antiquity.

McLaughlin, Edw. T.   Literary Criticism for Students,
    Selected from English Essays.   New York: 1893.

Selections from Sidney, Jonson, Dryden, Addison, Swift,
Johnson, Wordsworth, Coleridge, Lamb, De Quincey, Carlyle,
Arnold, Lowell, Ruskin, Hutton, and Pater.; with an introduction not so much on criticism as on methods of studying literature.   The author has little sympathy for scientific criticism.
" 'Laboratory work' in literature may be deferred until scientists introduce literary methods into the laboratory."   Literature
will never " yield its best unless we approach it in a spirit not
of fact but of sensibility."   Our first aim, therefore, should
be to acquire the art of sympathy.   This can be done by mus-
ing, at odd times, upon some poem that pleases, and asking
ourselves such questions as, What suggestion can we note of
this or that taste or opinion in the author ?   In what lines does
his heightened style appear at its best ?   When is he most happy
in fancy, or in cadence ?   Later, a wider and more philosophical
study, as of literary development and biography, is, for some,
valuable and interesting, provided they can avoid " the old
danger of mechanical and harshly intellectualized study."
" The most profitable criticism is that broad and philosophical
general discussion which is illustrated by such authors as Coleridge or Arnold."   The function of such criticism is to bring us
in contact with " a more theoretical and aesthetic range of
ideas," and so " to widen our intellectual and artistic world."

Macmillan, 53: 278 Some Random Reflections on Criticism.

Raises the question whether a knowledge of the familiar life
of the author enables us better to criticise his writings.

Macmillan, 61: 73 Principles and Practice of Criticism.

Because there are certain forms of beauty for the appreciation
of which it is not possible to give intelligible reasons, it is hope-
less to expect that a general canon of criticism will ever be framed.

MALLET, L'ABBÉ. Le Critique. (In Encyclopédie Méthodique.)

A brief and formal division of the subject. The name critic is by common use applied to six classes of writers : (1) Those who busy themselves in discriminating between authors and in judging of their styles and deserts ; (2) those who clear up obscure points in history ; (3) those who collate and edit ancient manuscripts ; (4) those who write historical and philological treatises ; (5) those who prepare bibliographies or *catalogues raisonnés ;* (6) those who write commentaries on ancient authors.

MARMONTEL, J. F. La Critique. (In Encyclopédie Méthodique. The same article will be found in his Éléments de Littérature. 3 vols. Paris: 1846. T. I, pp. 344–367.)

The articles of Mallet and Marmontel are chiefly of interest as showing the point of view of the French Encyclopedists. The essay of Marmontel is of considerable length. He takes a broad view of criticism, considering it, first, as the study to which we owe the restoration of ancient literature ; second, as the illuminating examination and equitable judgment of human productions, whether in science, the liberal arts, or the mechanic arts.

MAURICE, F. D. Friendship of Books. London: 1880.
> P. 354 Critics.

The central thought of the chapter is that true criticism aims to discover the things which are true and abiding. (Cf. Symonds.) Historical criticism should not judge other times by the standard of our own, but should try to see ages and men just as they were.

MOULTON, R. G. Shakespeare as a Dramatic Artist. A popular Illustration of the Principles of Scientific Criticism. 2d ed. Oxford: 1888.
> Pp. 1–40 Literary Criticism as an Inductive Science, pp. 265–331 Dramatic Criticism as an Inductive Science.

The author's avowed purpose is to establish literary criticism on a scientific basis. In the development of science there are three stages : (1) The observation of subject-matter; (2) analysis and classification; (3) systematization. The science of literary criticism is still in the second stage. In time it will pass into the third, and then critics will be able to explain the *modus operandi* of literary production, and show how different classes of writing produce their different effects. At present such explanation is mostly of a speculative character. All that the critics of to-day can hope to do is to classify their observations (pp. 266, 267). Such criticism should be called inductive, induction being the universal scientific method. It must be distinguished from judicial criticism. Inductive criticism inquires what is ; judicial criticism inquires what ought to be. Judicial criticism is outside science altogether. It belongs to the creative side of literature (pp. 21, 22), being the expression of individual taste. Inductive criticism rests upon four axioms : (1) interpretation in literature is of the nature of a scientific hypothesis, the truth of which is tested by the degree of completeness with which it explains the details of the work; (2) the function of criticism is to distinguish literary species ; (3) art is a part of nature (and hence may be treated scientifically like any other natural object); (4) literature is a thing of development (hence must always be far ahead of criticism and analysis). The inductive method besides having a scientific interest assists more than any other kind of treatment to enlarge our appreciation of the author.

Prof. Moulton tests his method by applying it, with great wealth of detail and aptness of illustration, to twelve plays of Shakespeare. It will repay the student, while he reads the studies, to observe whether the author does not allow himself at times to use criticism of a judicial character. He may, also, ask himself such questions as these : Are judicial and inductive criticism mutually exclusive ? Is not a kind of criticism possible which shall reconcile the claims of both judge and investigator? Is the inductive criticism real science or pseudo-science? Does Prof. Moulton understand the true relation of art to nature when he says that art is a part of nature? (Cf. Goethe's saying that art is called art because it is not nature, and see Bosanquet, History of Aesthetic, pp. 3, 4.) For comments on Prof. Moulton's theories see Macmillan 54: 45 Criticism as an Inductive Science, by Wm. Archer; Nation 41: 201 A New Inductive Science, by G. E. Wood-berry; and J. M. Robertson's Essays towards a Critical Method, pp. 46–65, 77–9, 83.

NISARD, D.   Histoire de la littérature française.   4 vols.
     Paris: 1844–49.

In vol. I, pp. 1–41, this eminent historian of literature sets forth the principles which have guided him in the composition of the work. The aim of criticism is "to regulate our intel-lectual pleasures, to free literature from the tyranny of the notion that there is no disputing about tastes, to constitute an exact science, intent rather on guiding than gratifying the mind." M. Nisard applies to each work a threefold test: (1) The ideal of the nation, that is, the national type of lit-erature; (2) the ideal of the language; (3) the ideal of human-ity. See Dowden's article, *Fortnightly*, 52: 744.

NISARD, D.   Études de critique littéraire.   Paris: 1858.

Discussing the critical methods of St.-Marc Girardin, M. Nisard finds occasion to distinguish (pp. 147–150) four spe-cies of criticism, as follows: (1) A kind of general history in which authors are the heroes. Of this species the writ-ings of Villemain are examples. (2) A species which is to the first what memoirs are to histories. Each author is looked upon as a type, and the aim of the critic is to present a series of portraits. (3) A treatise, the object of which is to regulate intellectual pleasures, and deliver works from the tyranny of

chacun son goût. This, M. Nisard hints, is the method which
he himself endeavors to put in practice.   (4) Attempts to draw
from literature practical instruction and lessons in morals.

PAGE, G. H.   *Westm. Rev.*, 139: 646 Personality in Art.

The writer seeks to establish four propositions: (1) A critic
should distinguish a writer's method, his creative power, and
his personality; (2) the individuality of the writer is his divergence from the typical man; (3) the personality of the writer may
appear in his work both unconsciously and self-consciously;
(4) the writer may be held accountable for the effect produced by his personality.

PATER, W.   Studies in the History of the Renaissance.   London: 1873.

> Preface.

Approves of Arnold's definition of criticism.   The first step
in aesthetic criticism is to realize one's own impressions clearly.

PATIN, H. J. G.   Études sur les tragiques grecs.

> Vol. II, p. 415 Kinds of Critical Judgments.

Critical judgments are of the following kinds or stages:
(1) Naïve feeling; (2) reflection directed towards beauties and
faults; (3) theories drawn (*a*) from experience, (*b*) from a
speculative view of the means and end of art.   Criticism may
take the form of (1) textual criticism; (2) historic research
directed upon writings or writers.

PAUL, H.   Grundriss der germanischen Philologie.   Strassburg: 1889.

> 1. Lief., III. Abschn., pp. 152–237 Methodenlehre.

Every student of criticism, whether he be a philologist or not,
should have some acquaintance with the methods of research
which philologists pursue.   To such knowledge there is no

better guide than the methodology of this monumental work. The treatise comprises four divisions: (1) General Considerations, including such subjects as Sources, Inferences from Data, the Comparative Method, etc.; (2) Interpretation (p. 170); (3) Textual Criticism (p. 176); (4) Criticism of Evidences (p. 188); (5) History of Language (p. 192); (6) History of Literature. Perhaps the part of most interest to the non-technical reader is that on the history of literature. Paul holds that the business of the historian of literature is not so much to pass a judgment for which he can claim universal validity, as to search for the aesthetic impulse in writer and public through which the work has arisen and has been effective. To accomplish this end the critic should study the impression which the work makes on him and others of his time, and also the impression which it made on the contemporaries of the author. Further, he should compare the effect of this work with that of preceding works, seeking to determine the epoch of taste to which it belongs. If, after such a study has been made, he passes judgment upon the work, his evaluation will rest upon a broad, empirical basis, and be susceptible of historical verification.

PERRY, T. S.   English Literature in the Eighteenth Century.
    New York: 1883.

> Pp. 162–174 Addison's influence upon English criticism.

A scholarly and spirited treatment of an important force in English criticism.

POPE, A.   Essay on Criticism.

Regarded as a treatise on criticism, not as an *ars poetica*, Pope's essay discusses (1) the formation of a critical judgment; (2) the faults of critics; (3) the qualifications of a good critic; (4) the history of criticism.

PORTER, NOAH. Books and Reading. New York: 1876.

Chap. 17, The Criticism and History of Literature, and Chap. 18, The Criticism of English Literature, are reprinted from *New Englander*, 29: 295, where they appeared under the title The New Criticism. This new criticism is said to be of German origin, and its characteristics are given as (1) a more enlarged and profound conception of literature ; (2) a catholic and liberal spirit ; (3) more philosophical methods ; (4) a more generous and genial attitude ; (5) interpretation of the author by means of his times ; (6) interpretation of the times of an author by means of his works.

POSNETT, H. M. Comparative Literature. London: 1886.
Pp. 177-9.

Looking at literature from a strictly scientific point of view, Professor Posnett has no hesitation in ranking criticism as superior, in important respects, to artistic creation. "The true glimmerings of human divinity are visible, not in the creation of the artist, but in the reflection of the critic." The artist, dwelling in his little world of imagination, working for the most part blindly, and unconsciously, limited by particular conditions of space and time, of current language and thought, lives "a life of limitation fancied to be limitless. If he should know and feel his limits, if he should eat of the fatal tree of science and his eyes be opened, the ideas he expresses are likely to be revealed ephemeral in their essence, and his hands are apt to lose their cunning in a craft that has lost its divinity." The critic, on the other hand, by comparing and contrasting divergent social types attains to a scientific freedom of treatment both in idea and language. He loses in enthusiasm but he gains in range and quality of knowledge. He pierces through the veil of appearances, and catches a glimpse of the light which the artist can only imagine.

RENAN, J. E.   Studies of Religious History and Criticism.
   Trans. by O. B. Frothingham.   New York: 1864.

   Pp. 39–43, 215–262, and *passim.*

Detached utterances upon criticism will be found scattered
through these brilliant and attractive studies.   From the suggestive ideas which the author throws out may be selected the
following: " Each order of greatness has its own eminence and
should not be contrasted with another " (p. 40).   ". . . That delicate feeling for shades of thought which we call criticism, without which there is no insight into the past and consequently
no extended understanding of human affairs.   It is surprising
how destitute the English in general are of that gift of historical intuition, so richly bestowed on Germany, so largely possessed by some minds in France, provided the matter in hand
does not involve an antiquity too remote, or an intellectual
state differing too much from our own " (p. 310).   (Is this just
to English critics?   Cf. Arnold's Lectures on Translating
Homer, in Essays in Criticism: " Almost the last thing for
which one would come to English literature is just that very
thing which now Europe most desires — criticism.")   " The
critical sense is not inoculated in an hour; he who has not cultivated it by a long scientific and intellectual discipline will
always find adverse arguments to oppose to the more delicate
intuitions " (p. 217).   " Perhaps our age has overworked the
term spontaneity in explaining phenomena which neither the
experience of the present nor the testimonies of history will
enable us to comprehend; . . . the spontaneous is perhaps
simply the obscure " (p. 262).   " Criticism displaces admiration, but does not destroy it " (p. 263).

ROBERTSON, J. M.   Essays towards a Critical Method.   London: 1889.

The first part of this work deals with science in criticism,
under the four heads: Historic Phases, Recent Nihilism, The

Problem Stated, Principles of Practice.   The *résumé* of the
History of Criticism, while unavoidably condensed and inconclusive, is replete with information concerning the methods of
the science from Aristotle, Horace, and Longinus, down to Vida;
from Webbe, Puttenham, and Sidney, to Pope; from Addison
to Kames and Hume, and so on to Diderot, Lessing, Sainte-
Beuve, Matthew Arnold, Lowell, and Henry James — with side-
glances at, and incisive judgments upon, Rapin, the Abbé
Dubos, Batteux, Rymer, and a great horde of caterpillar critics.
The article is admirable; not so systematic as the lectures of
M. Brunetière in his L'Évolution des Genres dans l'histoire de
la Littérature, but suggestive of the methods of the various
nations.   In Recent Nihilism, pp. 46–65, Mr. Moulton, of the
Inductive School, comes in for as thorough a demolition as
might justly be meted out to a man proposing an inductive
system and (in Mr. Robertson's opinion) practicing methods
largely judicial and deductive.   The Problem Stated, pp. 65–
105, sifts the various theories of a standard of taste, and reviews
the results of the *Fortnightly's* Symposium (Aug.-Nov. 1887).
In Principles of Practice, pp. 105–148, the charge upon the
Inductive School is renewed, and some good-natured advice
about people who live in glass houses is administered to
Mr. W. D. Howells.   The studies of Mr. Robertson do not
build up a method, but they certainly clear the atmosphere and
reveal the possibility of a criticism which may be methodical.
Mr. Robertson's formal definition of criticism is found on p. 6:
"The wording of the active or energizing result of the mental
impression made by books; as all art including verse, and all
literature as apart from criticism is an energizing result of an
impression made by things or actions."   For review of the
work see *Sat. Rev.*, 67 : 673.

SACHER-MASOCH, L. VON.   Ueber den Werth der Kritik.
    Erfahrungen und Bemerkungen.   Leipzig : 1873.

    Controversial and satirical.   The author raises the question

whether modern criticism is of any avail, and answers it by printing numerous critiques upon his own productions, with characteristic comments.   All criticism, he decides, is either adver-
tisement or polemic.

SAINTE-BEUVE, C. A.   M. de Féletz et de la Critique littéraire
    sous l'Empire.   Causeries de Lundi, 25 Févr. 1850.

Sainte-Beuve in this *causerie* takes a somewhat low view of
his art.   Criticism by itself can accomplish nothing.   It succeeds only when it acts in concert with the public and in collaboration with it.   Criticism is the secretary of the public,
divining and expressing every day what the public thinks or
desires.

SAINTE-BEUVE, C. A.   Chateaubriand.   Nouveaux Lundis,
    21, 22 Juillet, 1862, Tome 3ième.   Paris : 1884.

In this double paper Sainte-Beuve expounds in detail his
method of literary criticism.   Starting with the author of the
work, the critic studies him zoölogically, as it were, with reference to his race and his habitat.   He traces his family
history, seeking in the parents (especially the mother), the
brothers and sisters, and even the children, the secret of his
peculiar individuality.   From the family he passes to "le
premier milieu," the group of friends and contemporaries who,
like a literary family, shared in the author's aims and ambitions.
The expressions of his enemies and admirers also furnish clues.
The result of this method of study, which places the author in
his environment of heredity and influence, is the discovery of a
characteristic name by which his peculiar talent may be designated.

Though Sainte-Beuve calls his method naturalistic, he does
not claim for it a place among the exact sciences.   The day
will indeed come, he thinks, when the great families of genius
and their principal divisions shall be accurately determined;

but men in their moral nature are so complex that the critic cannot hope ever to treat them just as he would animals or plants.
Criticism must forever remain an art, demanding like the art
of medicine a special tact or talent in those who practice it
(p. 17). Comments on Sainte-Beuve will be found in *Cornhill*
for July, 1878 (by A. A., presumably Alfred Austin); Robertson's Essays, p. 42–4, 94, 107, 116, 141–3; the article ' Sainte-
Beuve ' in the Encycl. Brit., 9th ed., by Matthew Arnold; Brunetière's L'Évolution des Genres, p. 217–243; Dowden's article
on French Criticism in *Fortnightly*, 46: 737; A. Birrell's Res
Judicatae (London: 1892), p. 271; Brandes's Litteratur des
19ten Jahrh. (see *supra*); P. Deschanel's Figures littéraires
(Paris: 1889), p. 127; R. Flint's Historical Philosophy in
France, p. 621.

SAINTSBURY, G.   Essays on English Literature.   London:
    1891.
        IX. The Kinds of Criticism.

An entertaining essay by an experienced and opinionated
critic. The test of the value of any criticism, according to
Mr. Saintsbury, is the question, What idea of the original would
this criticism give to a tolerably instructed person who did not
know the original?

SCHERER, EDM.   Études critiques sur la Littérature contem-
    poraine.   9 vols.   Paris: 1863–89.

Expositions of critical method are given in M. Scherer's
admirable studies of Nisard, vol. I, p. 171; of Sainte-Beuve,
p. 321; of Taine, vol. II, p. 111; of Shakespeare, p. 137; of
the Portfolio of Sainte-Beuve, vol. IV, p. 114; of the Method
of Taine, p. 253. In vol. I, pp. 239–254, the author treats of
historical criticism.

SCHOPENHAUER, A.   Sämmtliche Werke.   Hrsg. von J. Frauen-
    städt.   6 vols.   Leipzig: 1877.
        Bd. 6, pp. 486–512 Ueber Urtheil, Kritik, Beifall und Ruhm.

SCHOPENHAUER, A.   The Art of Literature.   Trans. by B. Saunders.   London: 1891.

> See p. 87 for translation of Schopenhauer's Essay Ueber Urtheil,
> Kritik, u. s. w.

One of the most readable of Schopenhauer's shorter essays. The author discusses the relation of criticism to the aesthetic sense, the duties of critics, the test of genius, anonymity in criticism, the rarity of critical insight, and numerous related topics. The essay contains acute remarks, such, for example, as the saying that critical taste is the feminine of genius; but it presents no connected theory.

SHAIRP, J. C.   Aspects of Poetry.   Boston: 1882.

> Pp. 31–55 Criticism and Creation (repr. from Macm. 38: 246).

Traverses Arnold's thesis that the critic prepares the way for the poet. The tendency of the critic is to mar the poet. "The critic has had his day; it is time once more the poet should have his" (p. 48).

SNIDER, D. J.   Goethe's Faust.   First part.   Chicago: 1886.

> Pp. 75–101 Critical Standards.

A distinction must be made between the criticism of works of the second or third class and works of the first class. The former may be criticised by rules drawn from models or by native good taste; the latter, the "literary bibles," since they are wholly original and revolutionary, can be judged only by the law of their own being.

STAPFER, P.   Petite Comédie de la critique littéraire, ou Molière selon trois écoles philosophiques.   Paris: 1866.

In the introduction to this entertaining little work, Stapfer divides critics into three schools: first, the dogmatic school, which judges according to literary theories; second, the critical school, which analyzes impressions; third, the historic school, which seeks the causes of the work in its sources and environment. These schools may also be regarded as three stages or movements through which passes the thought of every man who examines the problems of literary criticism. In the dogmatic stage the mind affirms ; in the critical stage it doubts ; in the historic stage it returns to beliefs, principles, and methods. This book is the record of a mind that has passed through the three stages. To illustrate his theory the author examines Molière from the three points of view. The dogmatic school is represented, first, by an essay supposed to be written by a pupil of W. Schlegel; second, by "Thoughts of a Humorist, or Mosaic from the Poetics of Jean-Paul," imitated from Richter ; third, by a "Meditation of a Hegelian Philosopher, or, Picturesque Voyage through Hegel's Aesthetics"; fourth, by a French chorus singing praises of Molière. To represent the critical and the historic schools, no writers can be found; but their places are ingeniously supplied by two characters from Molière's Critique de l'École des Femmes, Dorante, a man of the world, and Lysidas, a pedantic poet. Dorante, who has turned Kantian, criticises the ideas of Lysidas in two essays, "A Criticism of Literary Dogmatism" and an "Essay on Taste." Lysidas, as a representative of the historic school, replies in three essays : "A Critique of Taste," "Doctrine of the Historic School," and "Molière." In his conclusion Stapfer takes a despondent tone, being unable to see how the contradictions of the schools can be reconciled. He inclines to the historic school, but finds it too ferocious and inhuman.

STAPFER, P.   Les Artistes juges et parties.   Causeries parisiennes.   Paris : 1872.

Pp. 1–36 La critique littéraire.

Starting with an idea from Matthew Arnold's essay on the Function of Criticism, Stapfer holds that criticism is inferior to creation, but denies that they are mutually exclusive. The critic may feel some of the joy of the poet. The function of the critic is to take what is best in literature and present it to the public.

STEDMAN, E. C.   Victorian Poets.   Boston: 1876.

In the preface Mr. Stedman sets forth briefly his method of criticism and the principles — "out of fashion just now" — on which he relies.   See, also, pp. 4, 5, for his view of the critic's province, and detached remarks, *passim.*

STEDMAN, E. C.   The Nature of Poetry.   Boston: 1892.

Consult the index for the author's frequent and pointed remarks upon the relation of poetry and criticism, English criticism, the age of criticism, etc.

SYMONDS, J. A.   The Renaissance in Italy.   The Catholic Reaction.   London: 1886.

    Pt. 2, pp. 396–402 Fundamental Principles of Criticism.

The author's view of criticism may be summed up as 'judgment based upon abiding relations between art and human nature.'

SYMONDS, J. A.   Essays Speculative and Suggestive.   London: 1890.

    Vol. I, pp. 84–123 Some Principles of Criticism.

Further development of the ideas brought out in the preceding reference.   Three types of critic are distinguished: The judge, the showman, and the scientific analyst.   The good critic is a combination of the three.

TAINE, H.   History of English Literature.   Trans. by H. Van Laun.   London: 1883.

    Vol. I, p. 1–36 Conditions of Literary Development.

Taine's method of criticism is flatly and frankly scientific. Literature is a natural product whose characteristics are to be investigated and recorded, like those of trees and flowers. Criticism is thus a kind of botany applied to human works, and the efforts of the critic are devoted to determining the literary system or organism which is made up of the productions of a given period or nation.   Within such a system, when it has been found, will be arranged the authors and their works according to the dominant characteristic of each.   The literary activity of any member of such a system is shaped by three influences: (1) The race, or influence of heredity and temperament; (2) the environment, political, social, and physical; (3) the time.   Taine's method can be properly studied only in connection with his general theory of art.

TAINE, H.   Essais de critique et d'histoire.   Paris: 1858.

> Pp. i–xv Préface — De la méthode.

The author explains briefly his method of criticism (see above), which is founded, he says, upon Aristotle and Hegel.

TOBLER, A.   Methodik der philologischen Forschung.   (In Gröber's Grundriss der romanischen Philologie, I, pp. 251–280.)

Similar in purpose to the methodologies of Blass and Boeckh, which are noticed above.   The topics treated by Tobler are as follows: I. Textkritik;   II. Litteraturhistorische Kritik ; III. Hermeneutik.

URLICHS, L. VON.   Begriffsbestimmung und Einteilung der Philologie.   (In Iwan Müller's Handb. der klassischen Altertumswissenschaft.)

> Pp. 7–15 Kritik und Hermeneutik.

Urlichs divides criticism into two classes, lower and higher criticism.   By the term lower criticism he means textual emendation, conjecture, recension, and the like.   The higher criticism, dealing with the work as a whole, is of two kinds : (1) Criticism of the species (Gattungskritik) which judges the work according to the law of its type and its relation to its time; and (2) individual criticism, which attributes a work to a particular author, or pronounces it not to be his. Hermeneutics is similarly divided.

VILLEMAIN, A. F. Cours de littérature française. Paris: 1861.

See vol. III, pp. 197–242, of this standard work, for an account of eighteenth century criticism. Three classes of criticism are distinguished: dogmatic, historic, and conjectural.

VILLEMAIN, A. F. Discours et mélanges littéraires. Paris: 1873.

> P. 29 Discours sur les avantages et les inconvénients de la critique.

Of especial interest on account of the lofty ideal of criticism which it upholds. Villemain believes that criticism may itself be creative. "The good critics cause the differences between the art of judgment and the faculty of production to disappear, or rather by pure force of genius, they carry a kind of creation into their examination of the fine arts. They have the air of inventing that which they observe" (p. 31). Reviewed by W. B. O. Peabody in *N. A. Rev.*, 31: 94.

WARD, S. G. Criticism. (In Eliz. P. Peabody's Aesthetic Papers. Boston: 1849, pp. 5–25.)

An attempt at a philosophical exposition of the subject. The essence of criticism consists in seeing the world from a new point of view, in finding a point from which facts arrange themselves in a new and unexpected manner, so that circumstances before isolated are seen as a part of a new whole. "Such criticism is creative in character."

WESTMINSTER, 80: 468 (p. 215, in Amer. ed.) Aims and Methods of Criticism.

Concerned mainly with the question of criticism and creation apropos of Arnold's essay On the Function of Criticism.

WHIPPLE, E. P. Essays and Reviews. 2 vols. Boston:
    1861.

> Vol. II, p. 208 Shakespeare's Critics (reprinted from *N. A. Rev.*,
> 67: 84).

Criticism has changed from an application of external rules
to an interpretation of inward life.

WILDE, O. *19th Century*, 28: 123, 435 The True Function
    and Value of Criticism. (Reprinted, under the title Critic
    and Artist, in Intentions. New York: 1891.)

An entertaining, though paradoxical and fantastic, argument
upholding the value of criticism as a creative art. Extravagances and affectations aside, it is an article of remarkable
insight and originality.

WILKINSON, W. C. A Free Lance in the Field of Life and
    Letters. New York: 1874.

> Pp. 108–113 Qualifications of the Critic.

The endowment of the critic should include broad knowledge
of his subject and related subjects, sympathetic appreciation,
and standards of judgment which, although not arbitrary, are
yet matters of personal conviction.

WUNDT, WILH. Logik. Eine Untersuchung der Principien
    der Erkenntniss und der Methoden wissenschaftlicher
    Forschung. 2 vols. Stuttgart: 1883.

> Bd. 2 Methodenlehre.

Hermeneutics and criticism (pp. 518–549) are treated as
methods of research employed in the two historical sciences,
philology and history. The function of criticism (p. 529) is (1)
to distinguish the true from the false, and (2) according to the
grade of truthfulness to estimate worth. In discriminating the
various kinds of criticism Wundt follows closely the analysis of
August Boeckh.

Wyzewa, T. de.   *Revue Bleue,* 28 Avril, 1894.   Du rôle de la
   critique dans la littérature de ce temps.

The writer laments that the encroachments of criticism upon
literature have given to France a Taine and a Renan in place
of a Balzac and a Victor Hugo.   In an ideal state of culture
humanity would have no use for criticism, since works of art are
made not to be judged but to be loved.

Such value as modern criticism has it derives from the
originality of the critic's mind.   Most of the so-called critics do
not criticise at all.   Under pretext of writing criticisms they
turn off prose poems, narratives, or philosophical reveries —
graceful transcripts of subtle variations of impression.

Marshall, H. R.   Aesthetic Principles.   New York: 1895.

See pp. 84–111 of this excellent little work for a discussion
of the aesthetic standards of the critic.   Mr. Marshall recognizes a hierarchy of standards ranging from the individual
standard of the moment to which we refer when we make off-
hand judgment, through the "relatively stable individual standard," and the standard of the cultivated man as we conceive
him, up to the ideal aesthetic field of the individual.   Judicious
remarks on the relation of artist to critic, and on the critic's
responsibility, are found on pp. 105–111.

§ 3. general note.

A. **Examination of Critiques.** — The student of criticism, at
the beginning of his course, is advised to read a few recognized
masterpieces of critical workmanship, such as are given below,
asking himself, as he reads, the following questions : (1) Is the
critic's method inductive or judicial ?   (2) If the former, what
factors of literary production does he investigate ?   What
laws of literary growth are stated or implied ?   (3) If the
critic's method is judicial, what standards of evaluation does he

use, and what canons are stated or implied? (4) How closely does he follow Arnold's rule of disinterestedness? (5) What seems to have been the critic's object in writing his critique?

ARNOLD, MATTHEW.   Essays in Criticism.

Essays on Heine, Joubert, and E. de Guérin.

ARNOLD, MATTHEW.   Essays in Criticism.   2d series.

Essays on Milton, Gray, Keats, Wordsworth, Byron, Shelley, Tolstoi, and Amiel.

AUSTIN, A.   The Poetry of the Period.

Critiques on Tennyson, Browning, Swinburne, Arnold, and Morris.

BAGEHOT, W.   Literary Studies.

BRIMLEY, G.   Essays.

Essays on Tennyson, Wordsworth, Patmore, Thackeray, Bulwer, Dickens, and Kingsley.

BIRRELL, A.   Obiter Dicta.

Critique on Browning.

DOWDEN, E.   Studies in Literature.

DOWDEN, E.   Transcripts and Studies.

GIFFORD, WM.   *Quarterly Review* for April, 1818, p. 204.

The famous attack on Keats's Endymion.

GOSSE, E.   Seventeenth Century Studies.

Essays on Lodge, Webster, Herrick, Cowley, Otway.

HOWELLS, W. D.   Editor's Study, in *Harper's Magazine*, beginning in vol. 72.

JEFFREY, F.   Contributions to the *Edinburgh Review*.

See particularly the essay on Wordsworth's Excursion, Nov. 1814; the paper on Keats's Endymion and Eve of St. Agnes,

Aug. 1820; on the Lay of the Last Minstrel, April, 1805; on the Lady of the Lake, Aug. 1810; on Childe Harold, Dec. 1816.

JOHNSON, SAMUEL. Lives of the Poets.

No choice need be indicated here. The Life of Milton should not be overlooked.

LESSING, G. E. The Laokoön, The Hamburg Dramaturgy.

LOWELL, J. R. My Study Windows.

Essays on Swinburne, Chaucer, and Pope.

LOWELL, J. R. Among My Books. 2d series.

MACAULAY, T. B. Essays.

See especially essays on Milton, Dryden, Comic Dramatists of the Restoration, and Robert Montgomery.

MASSON, D. Essays.

Essays on Dryden, Swift, and Wordsworth.

MAZZINI, JOS. Essays.

Essays on Byron and Goethe, Carlyle, and the Minor Works of Dante.

NOEL, RODEN. Essays on Poetry and Poets.

Essays on Shelley, Wordsworth, Keats, Hugo, Tennyson, Browning, and Whitman.

PATER, W. Appreciations.

Essays on Wordsworth, Coleridge, and Lamb.

SCHERER, EDM. Studies in Contemporary Literature.

STEDMAN, E. C. Victorian Poets.

STEPHEN, L. Hours in a Library. 2d series.

SAINTE-BEUVE, C. A. Causeries de Lundi. 3d ed.

See especially the essays in vols. 1, 3, 6, 7, 11, and 13.

WILSON, J. Recreations of Christopher North.

See, for further specimens of criticism, if they are desired, the reviews by Mr. Howells, Mr. Aldrich, and Mr. Scudder, in the *Atlantic Monthly ;* the earlier numbers of the *No. Am. Rev.;* the *Edinburgh, Westminster, Quarterly,* and *Scottish Reviews;* the London *Spectator, Athenaeum, Speaker, Academy,* and *Saturday Review ;* and the articles by Brunetière, Ganderax, and Thérèse Bentzon, in the *Rev. d. D. Mondes.* Goethe's and Lessing's critical essays may be looked up in the complete editions of their works.

The following list is recommended by Prof. Adolfo Bartoli (I migliori libri italiani, Milano: 1892, p. 12) to students who intend devoting themselves to Italian literary criticism : P. Fauriel, Dante e le origini della lingua e della letteratura (Palermo: 1856); A. D'Ancona, Studi di critica e di storia letteraria (Bologna: 1880) ; F. D'Ovidio, Saggi critici (Napoli: 1879); P. Rajna, Le fonti dell' Orlando Furioso (Firenze: 1876); P. Villari, Machiavelli e i suoi tempi (Firenze: 1877); F. De Sanctis, Storia della letteratura italiana (3d ed., Napoli), Saggi critici (3d ed., Napoli), Nuovi saggi critici (2d ed., Napoli); G. Carducci, Poliziano (Preface); D. Comparetti, Virgilio nel medioevo (Livorno). To these should certainly be added Bartoli's own Storia della letteratura italiana (7 v., Firenze).

Brandes, Juan Valera, and Belinski are representative names in Danish-Norwegian, Spanish, and Russian criticism, respectively.

B. **SPECIAL TOPICS.** 1. *Criticism in the Philosophical Sense.*— The term criticism is used in the history of philosophy to designate the philosophical system of Immanuel Kant. The meaning which Kant attached to the term has doubtless had considerable influence in shaping modern views upon the subject ; hence it will be well for the advanced student to gain some acquaintance with the Kantian philosophy. Kant's

three critiques are now available in good translations, and
should, if possible, be read, especially the critique of Judgment (see § **8**); but if they seem too formidable, Wallace's
Kant (Blackwood's Philos. Classics), or the histories of Ueberweg, Erdmann, or Windelband, will give the desired information
in brief compass. Those who care to push their inquiries farther may consult with profit the two volumes of Caird's Critical
Philosophy of Immanuel Kant, especially the first twenty
pages of vol. I. On the critical movement in English thought
see Stephen's History of English Thought in the 18th Century
(2 vols., New York: 1876), vol. I, p. 34.

Discussions of hermeneutics from the philosophical point of
view are contained in Schleiermacher's Ueber den Begriff der
Hermeneutik (in Abhandl. der Berlin. Akad. 1829, and in
Werke zur Philos. 3: 387), and in Wundt's Logik, Bd. 2,
Abschn. IV. Cap. 2 (see § **2**). On philosophical criticism in
general, see Schelling's Ueber das Wesen der philosophischen
Kritik (Sämmtliche Werke, Stuttgart: 1859, I. Abth. 5. Bd.).

2. *Philological Criticism.* — The leading methodologies are
given in § **2**. In addition may be mentioned: Bücheler, Philolo-
gische Kritik (Bonn: 1878); Steinthal, Ueber die Arten und
Formen der Interpretation (in Verhandlungen der 32. Ver-
sammlung deutschen Philologen, Wiesbaden: 1877); H. Paul,
Paul u. Braune's Beiträge, 5: 428 Nibelungenfrage und philo-
logische Methode; O. Froehde, *N. Jahrb. f. Phil. u. Paed.*
147: 433 Begriff u. Aufgabe d. Litteraturwissenschaft; O. Ribbeck, *Rheinisches Museum*, 29: 209 Ueber 'unabhängige' Kritik
mit einem Anhang über gewissenhafte Exegese; Bursian, Archäol. Kritik u. Hermeneutik (in Verhandlungen d. 21. Philo-
logenversammlung zu Augsburg, 1862, p. 55); Levezow, Ueber
archäol. Kritik u. Hermeneutik (in Abhandl. d. Berliner Akad.
1833, pp. 225–248); L. Preller, Grundzüge der archäol. Kritik u.
Hermeneutik (in *Zeitschr. f. Alterthumswiss.* 1845, Suppl. Nr.
13 ff.); G. Bernhardy, Grundlinien zur Encyclopädie der Phi-

lologie, p. 53; C. von Prantl, Verstehen und Beurtheilen (in Münch. Akad. 1877).

3. *Biblical Criticism.* — Exhaustive discussions of this important phase of criticism will be found in the articles by Ebrard and Landerer on 'Kritik' and 'Hermeneutik' in Herzog's Real-Encyclopädie für prot. Theologie. Those who do not read German may consult the lectures of Prof. Tholuck, of Halle, translated by E. A. Park, and published in Bibliotheca Sacra 1: 178, 332, 552, 726. On pp. 353–6 is given an excellent account of the controversy regarding the higher and the lower criticism. A recent work of high character is T. K. Cheyne's Founders of Old Testament Criticism (New York: 1893).

4. *Historical Criticism.* — The most systematic treatise is Ernst Bernheim's Lehrbuch der historischen Methode, Leipzig: 1889 (see § 2). Additional references are: E. B. Andrews, Brief Institutes of General History; Edm. Scherer's Études critiques, vol. I, p. 239–254; E. Dottain, *Rev. contemp.* 1862-II: 452 Nouveau système de critique historique; Floto, Ueber historische Kritik; A. Rhomberg, Die Erhebung der Geschichte zum Range einer Wissenschaft, 1883; H. Sidgwick, *Mind,* 11: 203 The Historical Method; G. Waitz, *Hist. Zeitschrift,* 6: 349 Zur Würdigung von Ranke's historischer Kritik; Ed. Zeller, *Hist. Zeitschr.* 6: 356 Die hist. Kritik und das Wunder; A. Ritschl, *Hist. Zeitschr.* 8: 85 Erläuterungen u. s. w.; Ed. Zeller, *Hist. Zts.* 8: 100 Zur Würdigung der Ritschl'schen Erläuterungen; L. Weiland, *Hist. Zts.* 58: 310 Quelledition und Schriftstellerkritik; C. K. Adams, The Study of History, Introduction to his Manual of Historical Literature (Harpers).

5. *Musical Criticism.* — But a few references out of many can be given on this point. Of value to the general student are Hueffer's Italian Studies, pp. 213–237; Gurney's Power of Sound, chap. 23, and Tertium Quid; R. de Récy's La Critique musicale au siècle dernier, *Rev. d. D. Mondes,* 1 Jan. 1887;

Sat. Rev. 72 : 187; 73 : 332; V. Stanford, *Fortnightly*, N. S., 55 : 826 Musical Criticism in England; J. F. Runciman, *Fortnightly*, N. S., 56 : 170 Musical Criticism and the Critics.

6. *Art Criticism.* — On this head see Colvin, *Fortnightly*, 32 : 210; Fleeming Jenkin, Papers, Literary, Scientific, etc. (London : 1887), vol. I, p. 93; R. St. J. Tyrwhitt, *Contemporary*, 11 : 101; Herder, Werke, Bd. 1, p. 245, Ursprung des Kunstrichter; H. Grimm, *Deutsche Rundschau*, 51 : 398 Bemerkungen über Werth und Wirkung der Kunstkritik; *Atlantic*, 39 : 486 Artists and Art Criticism; *Scribner*, N. S., 9 : 132 Artists as Critics; Jonathan Richardson, Works (London : 1792), II. Essay on the Art of Criticism; Mrs. M. W. Costelloe, *19th Century*, 35 : 828 The New and the Old Art Criticism (favors the scientific study of art); H. Helferich, Kunst für Alle, 1891, pp. 164, 180 Künstler und Kunstkritiker; F. Brunetière, Histoire et littérature (3 vols., Paris : 1884–6), I : 129 La critique d'art au xviie siècle; A. Bougot, Essai sur la critique d'art, ses principes, sa méthode, son histoire en France (Paris : 1877).

7. *Curiosities of Criticism.* — Collections of the mistakes of the critics, being usually made for purposes of entertainment, are as a general thing not very trustworthy. If use is made of them the references should be carefully verified. Among the best of the kind are T. Hall Caine's Cobwebs of Criticism; Jennings's Curiosities of Criticism; Allingham's Varieties in Prose (3 vols., London : 1893), vol. III, p. 313; W. Mathews's Great Conversers, p. 239; A. Repplier's Books and Men (Boston : 1888), p. 125; W. S. Walsh's Paradoxes of Philosophy (Philadelphia : 1889), p. 45; Disraeli's Curiosities of Literature.

8. *National Types of Criticism.* — These are best studied from the original sources by a comparison of the critical essays of Arnold, Lowell, Sainte-Beuve, Goethe, Brandes, De Sanctis, and other representatives of national criticism. The following references may be helpful : AMERICAN : H. H. Boyesen, Ameri-

can Literary Criticism and its Value, *Forum*, 15: 459; C. A.
Bristed, American Criticism, *N. A. Rev.*, 114: 23. BRITISH:
A. H. Everett, Tone of British Criticism, *N. A. Rev.*, 31: 26;
Mrs. M. O. W. Oliphant, Literary History of England (3 vols.,
London: 1882), vol. II, p. 35, English Critics; C. C. Felton,
British Criticism, *N. A. Rev.*, 43: 407; E. P. Whipple, Essays
and Reviews, vol. II, British Critics (also in *N. A. Rev.*, 61:
468); W. H. Prescott, British Criticism, *N. A. Rev.* 49: 325.
FRENCH: H. Harisse, French Criticism, *N. A. Rev.*, 93: 99;
Atlantic, 65: 708 some recent volumes of French Criticism;
J. Levallois, *Correspondant*, N.S., 55 (1873): 904 Critique lit-
téraire en France, sa tradition et ses devoirs; W. Rells, *Vossische
Zeitung*, 1891, No. 21 Die psychologische Kritik in Frankreich;
Atlantic, 43: 650 Zola as a critic; Peschier, Phases de la
Critique en France, *Herrig's Archiv*, 11: 294; *Rev. d. D.
Mondes*, 3: 59, 593 La Critique sous le premier Empire. ITALIAN:
P. Ferrieri, Francesco De Sanctis e la critica letteraria (Milano:
1888); G. Trezza, La critica moderna (2d ed., Bologna: 1880).
GERMAN: G. H. Lewes, Life and Works of Goethe (2 vols.,
London: 1855), vol. II, p. 201 German philosophical criticism
of literature.

(See, also, *supra*, Brunetière, Dowden, Caro, Scherer, and the
references under § **5**.)

9. *Practical Aspects of Criticism.* — Phases of this subject
are touched upon by most of the English and American writers
on criticism whose works are cited above. Additional references are the following: J. C. Adams, Literary Log-Rolling,
Forum, 2: 515; E. Fawcett, Should Critics be Gentlemen?
Lippincott, 39: 163 (reprinted in Agnosticism, New York: 1889,
p. 194); W. Knight, Criticism as a Trade, *19th Century*, 26: 423;
A. J. Church, Criticism as a Trade (reply to Knight's article),
19th Century, 26: 833; A. Lang, Manners of Critics, *Forum*,
4: 58; G. H. Lewes, English Errors and Abuses of Criticism,
Westm., 38: 466; C. Thomas, Ethics of Criticism, *Nation*, 45:

269; Should Critics be Gentlemen? *Sat. Rev.*, 63:41; W. Watson, Critics and their Craft, *National*, 16: 789 (reprinted in Excursions in Criticism, London: 1893, p. 81); *Scribner*, 6:238 Conscience and Courtesy in Criticism, 9: 625 Indecencies of Criticism; *Atlantic*, 53: 578 Ignorant Criticism; R. Blake, Anonymous Criticism (London: 1877).

C. **MISCELLANEOUS REFERENCES ON CRITICISM.** — J. L. Allen, Caterpillar Criticism, *Forum*, 4: 332; H. F. Amiel, Journal intime, vol. II, pp. 72, 238–40, 244; W. Archer, About the Theatre (London: 1886), p. 203 English of Critics; J. C. Bailey, A Plea for Critics, *Murray*, 10: 923; R. Buchanan, The Coming Terror (London: 1891), p. 143 The Modern Young Man as Critic; J. Buckham, Human Element in Criticism, *Critic*, 22: 268; G. R. Carpenter, Literary Criticism, *Harvard Mo.*, 7: 185; M. A. Dodge, Skirmishes and Sketches, p. 399 Critics; Essays from the *Nation* (New York: 1867), II. Critics and Criticism; W. Hazlitt, Table-Talk (2d ed., 2 vols., London: 1824), p. 117 On Criticism (rails at bad critics); W. Hazlitt, Round Table (London: 1884), Commonplace Critics; W. C. Hazlitt, Offspring of Thought (London: 1884), p. 145 Progress of Criticism; W. C. Hazlitt, Sketches and Essays (London: 1839), p. 227 On Taste (the best critic is he who feels to the utmost); A. Helps, Brevia (London: 1871), Critics, How to Bear Criticism, the Slyly-denigrating kind of Criticism (brief notes on criticism, of no great value); A. Helps, Friends in Council (4 vols., London: 1869–72), 1st ser. I. On Giving and Taking Criticism, 2d ser. I. Criticism (principally moral reflection on bad and hasty criticism, etc.); J. G. Holland, Every-day Topics (2 vols., New York: 1892), vol. I, p. 53 Criticism; T. H. Huxley, *Nature*, 27: 396 Art and Science (see p. 397 on the critical element in art appreciation); W. Irving, Biography and Miscellanies (New York: 1866), p. 447 Desultory Thoughts on Criticism (doubts " whether either writer

or reader is benefited by what is commonly called criticism ");
S. S. Kingdon, *Writer*, 2: 222 Rules of Criticism; V. Knox,
Essays (3 vols., London: 1823), vol. I, p. 155 Modern Criti-
cism; A. Lang, *National*, 19:603 A Critical Taboo; *Literary
World* (Boston), 22: 110 Criticism of Books; *Macmillan*, 60:
134 Critics in Court; B. Matthews, *New Rev.*, 3: 455 Whole
Duty of Critics (reprinted in Americanisms, New York: 1892;
draws up " 12 good rules for critics "); B. Matthews, Recent
Essays in Criticism, *Cosmopolitan*, 12: 124; W. Mathews, Lit-
erary Style, p. 100 Folly of Sensitiveness to Criticism; E. S.
Nadal, Essays (London: 1882), p. 261 Newspaper Literary
Criticism; T. Purnell, Literature and its Professors (London:
1867), p. 14 Weight of Criticism; A. Rickett, Modern Criti-
cism, *National*, 21: 717; J. Ruskin, Arrows of the Chace, vol.
II, pp. 235–264; E. F. Wheeler, Critic on the Hearth, *Lippin-
cott*, 43: 755; *Atlantic*, 66: 712 A Critic on Criticism; J. F.
Genung, The Practical Elements of Rhetoric, pp. 302–7 Inter-
pretation, pp. 404–5 Criticism; *Scribner*, 5: 384 Criticism;
Scribner, N.S., 8: 658 Mechanical Criticism; *Atlantic*, 40: 102
A New Kind of Criticism, 44: 257 Change in Criticism, 56:
138 Criticism of a Critic, 59: 283 The Book Notice and the
Criticism; W. James, Principles of Psychology (2 vols., New
York: 1890), vol. 2, p. 365; I. Disraeli, The Calamities and
Quarrels of Authors (London: 1860), p. 51 Influence of Bad
Temper in Criticism, p. 139 Undue Severity of Criticism,
p. 423 Political Criticism on Literary Composition; J. Runci-
man, Side Lights (London: 1893), Colour-Blindness in Litera-
ture (on individual opinion as opposed to received standards,
on sham admiration, etc.); Catharine B. La Monte, *Poet-Lore*,
6: 332 A Brief Defense of Criticism; H. James, *Author*, 3: 67
Literary Criticism; A. Birrell, *New Rev.*, 6: 97 Critics and
Authors; *Blätter f. literarische Unterhaltung*, 1 (1857): 130
Kritik und künstlerisches Schaffen, 183 Kritik und Anti-
Kritik, 262 Zur Kritik (the service of criticism is to cultivate

a sense for good art and prevent dilettanteism); A. Neugr.
Deutsche Zeitung, 7096, Krit. u. Räsonnement; F. Spielhagen,
Aus meiner Studienmappe (Beiträge z. litt. Aesth. und Kritik,
2 Aufl., Berlin: 1891), pp. 1–46 Produktion, Kritik und Publi-
kum (the critic a necessary medium between the artist and his
mixed public); A. Lübben, *Herrigs's Archiv.*, 6: 349 Die
Kritik, besonders die aesthetische Kritik ; *Herrig's Archiv.*,
45 : 35 Ueber die aesthetische-psychologische Beurtheilung der
Poesie ; B. Mazzarella, Della critica (Genova: 1866), vol. I,
pp. 1–33; Necker, *Unsere Zeit,* 1889–II : 273 Werth der Kritik ;
Th. Lipps, *Zts. f. vergl. Litteraturgeschichte,* 5 : 438 Tragik,
Tragödie und wissenschaftliche Kritik ; G. Barzellatti, Nuova
Antologia, 16 Gennaio, 1890 Francesco De Sanctis (see pp. 323,
324, for an exposition after Villari, of De Sanctis' method
of criticism); Chas. de Rémusat, *Rev. d. D. Mondes,* 1 Nov.
1863 L'Art par la critique ; Gustave Planche, *Rev. d. D. Mondes,*
1 Mai 1856 Mœurs et devoirs de la critique ("The aim of the
critic should be to envisage under all its aspects the work of
the poet, the historian, the philosopher "); C. de Mazade, *Rev.
d. D. Mondes,* 15 Juillet 1867, p. 499 Le réalisme dans la
critique (criticism of Taine's methods); Théodore Dupuy,
Mélanges littéraires et historiques (Milan: 1886), I. De la
critique littéraire ; J. Barbey d'Aurevilly, Les ridicules du temps
(2e éd., Paris: 1883), pp. 1–13 La comédie de la critique (written 1867; abuses bad critics, and asserts that criticism is
dead), p. 27 Les chats de la critique (written 1866 ; two
things constitute the essence of criticism : positiveness and
clearness).

The works of Sir Egerton Brydges contain frequent discussions of criticism. The following references are to the Censura
Literaria (10 vols., London: 1805–9): 1 : 349, 2 : 1 Puttenham's
Art of Poesie ; 2 : 275 Webbe's Discourses, 364 James's Essayes
of a Prentise, 234 Notices regarding several old English Poets;
7 : 400 Severity of Fashionable Criticism.   In the Anti-Critic

(Geneva : 1822), pp. 1–4 treat of the character of modern criticism ; pp. 4–29, of modern taste in poetry ; pp. 49–57, of the true principles of poetry.

In Johnson's Cyclopaedia, under 'Critic' and 'Criticism,' in Vapereau's Dictionnaire Universel des Littératures, under 'Critique,' will be found articles of merit. The article in Vapereau is of some length.

On the use of the word κριτικός among the Greeks and Romans, see the citations from classical authors in Prof. A. Gudeman's Outlines of the History of Classical Philology (Boston : 1894), pp. 3, 4.

For further references on criticism, see Gayley and Scott's Guide to the Literature of Aesthetics (Berkeley: 1890): pp. 47–49 Histories of Art; pp. 50–53 Treatises on the Arts in General; pp. 53–72 Special Treatises on the different Arts, — classified under Architecture, Sculpture, Ceramics, Painting, Engraving, Etching, etc., and Music; pp. 73–107 Literature.

Part II. — History of Criticism.

§ 4. Division of the Subject and Statement of Problems.

The history of criticism may be taken to mean either of two things: The history of the practice of criticism, or the history of critical theory. While the two are intimately related, they have not always advanced at the same rate of progress, nor developed along lines which are exactly parallel. For purposes of study and investigation, therefore, they may be regarded as measurably distinct.

I. Development of Criticism as Practice. — *A.* For the **origin of criticism** we must go back to very early times. Expressions of approval or disapproval that may be looked upon as primitive critical utterances, are found in some of the oldest monuments of literature. According to Mr. Bosanquet (History of Aesthetic, p. 12) the following passage from the Iliad (xvii, 548) on the shield of Achilles, is one of the earliest aesthetic judgments in Western literature: "The earth looked dark behind the plough, and like to ground that had been ploughed, although it was made of gold ; that was a marvellous piece of work." (Cf. Egger, pp. 1–5.) Whether the Homeric poems contain criticisms of literature, as well as criticisms of art, is a question the student should investigate for himself. (See Iliad iii, 300, and Mr. Bosanquet's observation on the passage, Hist. of Aesthetic, p. 102.) The Vedas, the Nibelungen Lied, Old-English poetry, the Kalevala, and other early literatures may be examined with the same end in view.

The causes, psychological or social, which give rise to expressions of criticism may also be explored. These may be brought out by questions such as the following: Of what is criticism the outcome? Of curiosity, as held by Mr. Arnold (essay on Function of Criticism)? Of curiosity and self-expression combined, as suggested by Mr. Robertson (Essays, p. 1)? Of egotism? Of wonder? Of admiration? Of the competition of poets or schools of poets? Of a universal spirit of denial or pessimism? Or of "a divine discontent"? An interesting subject for investigation is the question whether criticism in literature, as in philosophy (according to Kant), is preceded by dogmatism and skepticism.

These are questions to be asked in specific cases when the student has the evidence before him.

B. **The principle or law of development** in the practice of criticism should be examined both deductively and inductively.

1. Working deductively, we may inquire whether the nature of criticism is such that in its history a law of evolution, or of progression, or of rhythmical alternation, is likely to be exemplified. Is it not so bound up with its object-matter, literature, that independent development is impossible?

2. Working inductively, we must first determine what shall be regarded as a sign of advance in criticism, whether (*a*) increase in intellectual activity; (*b*) in amount of production; (*c*) in ability to deal adequately with past literature; (*d*) in ability to estimate the value of current literature; (*e*) in ability to forecast the literary future; (*f*) in catholicity of appreciation; or (*g*) in rationality of critical judgment. Furnished with a provisional test of this kind, we may examine in chronological order the critical utterances of a period or a people, noting, as we read, the signs of progress, of retrograde, or of rhythmical ebb and flow. The relation of criticism to the character of the age and the spirit of the people should also receive attention, as well as the influence of a preceding age on a following, and of one people upon another. Questions which should be

kept in view are : Whether the same principle of growth is observed in all countries and at all times ; and whether this principle of growth is independent of, or intimately related to, the principle which determines the growth of literature.

C. **STAGES OF GROWTH.** — Critical practice, if it develops in an orderly way, should exhibit well-marked stages of progression. One kind or phase of criticism should come into being, rise, flourish, decay, and pass into another kind or phase. As a fact, do such stages appear in the history of criticism ? If so, the student should note at what points the lines of demarcation occur, and the reasons why they occur where they do. He should observe whether criticism tends to pass from negative to positive, from abstract to concrete ; and where a succession of stages has been discovered he should endeavor to arrive at the leading characteristic of each. Such orders of succession as are indicated by the terms (1) Synthetic, (2) Analytic, (3) Organic ; or the terms (1) Clan, (2) Individual, (3) Social, may be suggested as helpful ; but the student should not adopt them as working bases without careful, independent research.

It may not be superfluous to suggest the following simple and convenient chronological division : 1. Ancient, including (*a*) Oriental, (*b*) Greek, (*c*) Roman ; 2. Mediaeval ; 3. Renaissance ; 4. Modern.

D. **DIFFERENTIATION OF SPECIES OF CRITICISM.** — A comparison may be made of different countries to determine whether the different kinds of criticism develop everywhere in similar fashion. The student should note whether activity in one kind of criticism is always accompanied by activity in other kinds. The question should also be asked whether the various types of literary criticism, as judicial and inductive, appear contemporaneously. Most writers who touch upon them assume that one follows and grows out of the other, *e.g.*, inductive follows judicial criticism (Moulton). But is this borne out by the facts ?

E. Certain periods in literary history are distinguished as **periods of great critical activity.** Examples are the Alexandrian age of Greek literature, the eighteenth century in English literature, the present century in French literature. They are often set over against periods of great creative activity, such as the age of the tragic poets of Greece and the Elizabethan age of England. An age of criticism is often said to alternate with an age of creation. Matthew Arnold (On the Function of Criticism) holds that critics set in motion the ideas which the creative writer makes use of when his turn comes.

It will be well to examine the critical literature of so-called creative periods, in order to determine the amount and value of it. In some cases it will be found more extensive and of much greater importance than is generally supposed. (See Macaulay, Essay on Dryden ; F. E. Schelling, Criticism of the Reign of Elizabeth ; Egger, Essai sur l'histoire de la critique.)

F. **Relation of the Growth of Criticism to the Growth of Literature.** — This topic presents for consideration two phases : The effect of criticism on the growth of literature, and the effect of literature on the growth of criticism.

1. Criticism, according to some writers (Caine, Arnold, Bascom, Grucker), can hasten, retard, or divert the currents of literary energy. It can get the ear of the public for an author who would otherwise remain obscure ; it can hold back for many years the recognition due to genius ; it can lead or drive a writer into modes of expression which, if he were left to his own impulses, he would not choose to cultivate. By others all these statements are denied. Indeed, the facts that are brought forward by one side to prove the critic's power, are sometimes regarded by the other side as evidences of his impotence. It may be that both extremes are wrong, and that the truth lies somewhere between them. Thus, it may be that different kinds of criticism are of different degrees of effective-

ness. If negative criticism has no deterrent influence, constructive criticism may yet have power to hasten. Inductive criticism may prevail after judicial criticism has spent itself in vain. (See Howells, Robertson, Sainte-Beuve.)

2. Under the second head, the influence of literature on criticism, an interesting question is as to the effect which a new and splendid work of genius exerts upon critical opinion. The effect of Shakespeare's plays, of Milton's Paradise Lost, of Goethe's Faust, of the novels of Scott, Dickens, Thackeray, and George Eliot, upon the movement of European criticism, may be studied in contemporary pamphlets, essays, and reviews. Another question is whether critical practice lags behind literary creation. It has been said that the critic can do no more than convince his generation. (Robertson, Essays, p. 93.) Is this true? Has not criticism at times outstripped creative literature, so called? Has not some critic in each epoch foreseen the course of literary development?

G. **INFLUENCE OF OTHER MOVEMENTS OF THOUGHT UPON CRITICISM.** — How is critical practice affected by movements in religion? In art? In industry? In politics? In science? In education? (On the Puritan element in criticism, see Robertson, Essays, pp. 15, 17.)

II. Development of Criticism as Theory. — By criticism as theory we mean the principles which critics have brought forward as the ground of their judgments or as the basis of their methods of procedure. As grounds of judgment they may or may not be the same as the principles of artistic or literary practice. The critic may work upon one principle, the artist whom he criticises upon another. Again, the critic's practice may not conform to his theory. (This charge has frequently been brought against Taine, as by Brunetière. See, also, Robertson's review of Moulton.)

Most of the questions upon criticism as practice will apply to critical theory as well. The following scheme of study is presented:

1. *First Appearance of a Theory of Criticism.* — (*a*) To be discovered by an examination of early literatures. What writer first gives reasons for his expressions of approval or disapproval? (*b*) What principles underlie the earliest criticisms, and why should these principles get the start of the rest?

2. *Provenience of Critical Theories.* — Where and when did the various principles of criticism come into being? Many of them have been handed down from early times, and transmitted from nation to nation with the progress of culture. Many are known to be of recent origin. Possibly examples may be found of independent rediscovery of old principles.

3. *Law of Development.* — Does the body of critical theory grow by accretion? By the development of contradictions, which, destroying one another, give place to new principles? By the development of specialized forms, or members with specific functions, like a plant or an animal? Where seek for the principle of critical evolution — in psychology, anthropology, philosophy, sociology, or biology? Mr. Robertson (Essays, pp. 95, 96) suggests Herbert Spencer's law of economy (Essay on Style) as a fundamental principle according to which divergent opinions tend to unanimity.

4. *Stages of Growth.* — The stages of development in art-theory outlined in the general histories of aesthetics, such as Schasler's and Bosanquet's, may be applied with little change to the history of criticism. (See § **8**.) The same may be said of the periods or movements indicated in the standard histories of literature. How far do these divisions correspond to the stages of criticism as such?

5. *Relation of Critical Theory to Literature.* — Does criticism lay down laws and principles for literature, or does literature give laws and principles to criticism? (Moulton, Robertson.)

In the works of reputable writers probably every critical theory is exemplified; but which came first, the theory or the work? The question should be answered by a comparative study of the literatures of several periods or of several nationalities.

6. *Influence of Science upon Critical Theory.* — The effect of the scientific spirit upon recent critical theories and methods, as in the case of Taine, Sainte-Beuve, Brunetière, and Moulton, is a striking phenomenon. It will be interesting to note what each of the scientific critics understands by the term science, and the use each makes of it. Are these theories really scientific or only quasi-scientific? Or perhaps pseudo-scientific?

III. Relation of Critical Theory to Critical Practice. — The main question to be asked under this head is the following: In the case of any particular critic, how far is his critical theory adequate to the task which he has undertaken? A similar question may be asked with regard to the critical literature of a given period, or of a nation. (See Bosanquet, Hist. of Aesthetic, pp. 4, 15.)

§ 5. REFERENCES.

ALLEN, G. *Fortnightly*, 37 : 339 Decay of Criticism.
> See § 2.

BAGEHOT, W. Literary Studies. 2 vols. London : 1879.
> Vol. I, pp. 1–40 The First Edinburgh Reviewers.

Mainly concerned with the characteristics of Horner, Jeffrey, and Sydney Smith.

BASCOM, JOHN. Philosophy of English Literature. New York : 1893.
> Pp. 155–209 The Critical Movement from Pope to Johnson.

Beginning with a consideration of the balance existent between creative and critical periods, the author enters upon an inquiry into the causes that induced what he calls the First Critical Period in English Literature. This period he divides into a first and a second phase ; he discusses the relation of the French influence, of the classical influence, of the scientific and political influences of the age to the incipient school of criticism, and exemplifies by a study of Swift, Pope, Addison, and Steele, as critics. Under the second phase are discussed the general influence of theological inquiry, and the special influence of Samuel Johnson upon the literary temper of the age.

BINTZ, J. Der Einfluss der Ars Poetica des Horaz auf die deutsche Literatur des xviii. Jahrhunderts. Progr. Hamburg: 1892.

The text of the Ars Poetica, accompanied by copious footnotes showing by whom and to what purpose the text was cited in German literature of the last century. The author intended an introduction, but died in the midst of his labors.

BOSANQUET, B. History of Aesthetic.

Indispensable to the student of the history of criticism. For notice see § 8.

BORINSKI, K. Die Poetik der Renaissance und die Anfänge der litterarischen Kritik in Deutschland. Berlin : 1886.

An account, interesting, and in the main accurate, of the development of poetical theory and criticism from Opitz to Gottsched.

BOURGOIN, AUGUSTE. Les Maîtres de la critique au xviie siècle. Paris: 1889.

A brief introduction, pp. 5–15, discusses the criticism of the seventeenth century in its general features. The authors selected for treatment in the body of the work are Chapelain, Saint-Évremond, Boileau, La Bruyère, and Fénelon.

BRANDES, G.   Die Litteratur des 19ten Jahrhunderts.

Bd. 5, pp. 374–387 Sainte-Beuve und die moderne Kritik.

An interesting and valuable chapter.   Sainte-Beuve is looked upon as the reformer of modern literary criticism.

BRAITMAIER, FRIEDR.   Geschichte der poetischen Theorie und Kritik von den Discursen der Maler bis auf Lessing. 2 Thl.   Frauenfeld: 1888–9.

Perhaps the best connected account of this period of German criticism.

BRUNETIÈRE, FERD.   La Critique littéraire.   Part of the article 'Critique' in the Grande Encyclopédie.

In the first division of this article M. Brunetière gives in brief outline the history of criticism, ancient, mediaeval, and modern. Ancient criticism began by observation of the development and the laws of literary types; it closed by furnishing the poet a means of imitating models.   Aristotle was the true founder of criticism.   Others of importance in ancient times were Theophrastus, Aristoxenus, Aristarchus, Zoilus, Dionysius of Halicarnassus, Lucius Aelius Stilo, Varro, Horace, Cicero, Tacitus, Quintilian, Plutarch, Dio Chrysostom (whose Olympic Discourse is the first essay in criticism of art), Aristides the Orator, Hermogenes, Lucian, and Longinus.   In the middle ages there was little criticism, because mediaeval man, being a part of his caste or corporation, was not master of his ideas.   The literature of the middle ages is impersonal, universal, anonymous. The only critics of this period are Dante (in his De vulgari Eloquio) and Petrarch (in his philological investigations).   In the Renaissance, philological criticism arose to resume the interrupted work of the Alexandrian school.   In modern times the only country which has had a definite history of criticism is France; she furnishes the scheme for the history of criticism in all other European countries.

In the remainder of this part of his article Brunetière traces
the history of French criticism, following the same plan as in
his L'Évolution de la Critique. (For a notice of the second
division of the article see § 2.)

BRUNETIÈRE, FERD. L'Évolution des Genres dans l'histoire de
la Littérature. Tome 1er. Paris: 1890.

> Pp. 35–278 L'Évolution de la critique depuis la renaissance
> jusqu'à nos jours.

In a series of lectures delivered to the students of the École
normale supérieure, M. Brunetière sketches with a rapid hand
the rise and development of the spirit of modern criticism. He
finds it beginning in Italy in the period of the Renaissance. It
came into existence as the result of two causes: (1) The rediscovery of the classics; (2) (following Burckhardt's Civilization
in Italy) the growth of the sense of personality. The first led
to philological criticism of a pedantic kind, the second to rivalry
and envy, and so to criticism in the sense of fault-finding.
When criticism passed over into France, laying aside its pedantry and its satire it became at first strictly literary, then in turn
aesthetic, philosophical, historical, and scientific.

Beginning with Joachim du Bellay's Défense et illustration de
la langue française, M. Brunetière takes up the principal French
critics in chronological order, and assigns each his proper place.
Du Bellay, by setting up imitation of the ancients as the
standard of the French language and literature, broke with
mediaeval traditions, dissevered national life and national literature, gave the norm to the Pléiade, and laid the foundation of
the classic spirit in France which endures to our day. Scaliger
with his Poetics (1607) set aside Greek models in literature and
criticism, and substituted for them Roman models like the
Aeneid and Horace's Ars Poetica. He introduced also precise
classifications and definitions. With Malherbe criticism became
formal; regularity, order, and correctness were emphasized at

the expense of emotion and imagination. Chapelain was the first to seek principles wider in their application than the personal impression of the critic. He tried, also, to discover the 'law of the type' in the works that he examined, though he fell into the error of confounding 'les lois' with 'les règles.' Boileau represents the reaction of the bourgeois spirit upon the aristocratic spirit in French literature. His critical doctrine is the rational imitation of nature. Because he believed that ancient writers best imitated nature, Boileau taught imitation of the classics. This part of his doctrine was attacked by Perrault in the Parallèle des Anciens et des Modernes, and thus was begun a controversy on the relative merits of classic and contemporary literature which weakened faith in the infallibility of Boileau's principle, and resulted in a great extension of the field of criticism. With Perrault came in the ideas of naturalism and relativity, the first taking form under the hands of Diderot, the second culminating on the one hand in the extreme individualism of Rousseau, and on the other in the comparative and historical methods of Mme. de Staël, Villemain, Sainte-Beuve, and Taine.

BRUNETIÈRE, FERD. Études critiques sur l'histoire de la littérature française. 5e Sér. Paris: 1893.

Contains (p. 111) an admirable study of the criticism of Bayle. The closing essay, on the essential character of French Literature, will be found indirectly helpful.

CAINE, T. HALL. Cobwebs of Criticism. London: 1883.

A popular account of periodical criticism in the early part of this century. The picturesque and dramatic features of the attacks upon Coleridge, Keats, Wordsworth, and the rest are presented in a readable style. Of the history of criticism, in the sense of development, the author has no definite conception. Such statements as "criticism in Shakespeare's day must have been an unknown quantity," and "it was . . . at the beginning of the nineteenth century that English critical literature, properly so called, began," testify to a slender acquaintance with the history of English critical literature. See the comments of Mr. Robertson, Essays, p. 11, note.

CAIRD, E.   The Critical Philosophy of Immanuel Kant.

> Vol. I, Chap. 1 The Idea of Criticism.

See especially pp. 2–8, on the Kantian conception of the way in which the critical stage is reached in the development of philosophical thought.

CARO, E.   *Rev. d. D. Mondes*, 1 Févr. 1882 La critique contemporaine et les causes de son affaiblissement.

Discusses the question whether modern criticism is retrograding.   See § **2**.

CARTON, H.   Histoire de la critique littéraire en France. Paris: 1886.

In a volume of less than two hundred pages the author attempts to cover the history of criticism in France from the earliest times to the present.   Beginning with Marguerite of Navarre and closing with M. Brunetière, he has space for only a few paragraphs upon each author, and as a result his work is scrappy and superficial.   It is of some value as a list of names and works, though the bibliography is far from complete.

CHARPENTIER, J. P.   La littérature française au dix-neuvième siècle.   Paris.

> Pp. 280–297 Critique (le second Empire).

The critics treated of are Sainte-Beuve, Planche, Girardin, De Sacy, Cuvillier-Fleury, Jules Janin, de Pontmartin, Veuillot, Vitet, Patin, and É. Egger.

COAN, T. M.   *Lippincott*, 13 : 355 Critic and Artist.

> See § **2**.

CROUSLÉ, L.   L'Instruction publique, 1888, pp. 22, 68, 116,
     231, 275, 295, 325, 344, 372, 397, 424, 455, 485, 535, 581,
     600, 616, 645, 661, 694, 725 La critique au 19ᵉ siècle.
     Revue de l'histoire de la critique avant le 19ᵉ siècle.

A brief history of French criticism from Voltaire to Sainte-
Beuve.   The principal topics treated of are the following : The
critics of Voltaire's school, — Marmontel and La Harpe ; Voltaire judged by his disciples ; La Harpe as critic of Voltaire ;
M.-J. Chénier ; critics of the classic school ; critics of the
romantic school ; the independents, — Villemain and Sainte-
Beuve.

CRÜGER, JOH.   J. C. Gottsched und die Schweizer.   Berlin :
     1884.

A useful and trustworthy account.

DEMOGEOT, J.-C.   La critique et les critiques en France au xixᵉ
     siècle.   Paris : 1857.

DOWDEN, E.   *Fortnightly*, 52 : 737 Literary Criticism in France.

Treats in an interesting way French criticism in the latter
half of the nineteenth century.   The system and methods of
Nisard, Sainte-Beuve, Taine, Bourget, Brunetière, and Émile
Hennequin are clearly set forth.

EGGER, É.   Essai sur l'histoire de la critique chez les Grecs.
     2ᵉ éd.   Paris : 1886.

Intended as an introduction to a course in Greek literature,
the first edition of this scholarly work, published in 1849, con-
sisted mainly of a translation of the Poetics of Aristotle.   A
sketch of the history of criticism among the Greeks, which it
also contained, was intended merely to throw light upon the
Poetics.   In succeeding editions the history grew in importance until in the last and posthumous edition the translation
disappeared, and the history became the main idea of the
book.

According to the author the term *critique* is used by him in
the sense of *esthétique;* but the work is not, as one might infer
from this statement, a general history of aesthetics ; it is a history only of the aesthetics of literature.   The main divisions
are as follows : Criticism before the Philosophers (the Rhap-
sodes, Homeric Criticism, the Comic Writers); Criticism among
the Philosophers before Aristotle; Aristotle; Criticism after
Aristotle (including the history of the Poetics of Aristotle in
the Middle Ages and among the Arabs).   A conclusion, all too
brief, touches upon the relation of Hellenism to Oriental
thought.   The grace and lucidity of the author's style make
the work delightful reading.

FELLNER, R.   *Deutsche Rundschau,* 75 : 464 Die neuere französische Kritik.

A review and exposition of Tissot's Les évolutions de la
critique française.

GOLDSMITH, O.   Present State of Polite Learning.

In chapter X Goldsmith gives his opinions of the critics and
criticism of his time.

GATES, LEWIS E.   Selections from the Essays of Francis
Jeffrey.   Boston : 1894.

In his introduction the editor shows how Jeffrey developed
ethical criticism, and made use of the historical method.

GRUCKER, ÉMILE.   Histoire des doctrines littéraires et esthétiques en Allemagne.   Paris : 1883.

A voluminous work dealing with Opitz, Leibnitz, Gottsched,
and the Swiss, — Bodmer, Breitinger, Liscow, and Pyra.   The
author's estimate of the work of these critics is summed up as
follows : " The dogmatic and abstract criticism which began
with Opitz and closed with Gottsched, founded on the authority of masters, on the traditions of Latin antiquity and the

Renaissance, on the imitation of French models, accomplished its work. It saved German literature from anarchy and barbarism. It purified, established, and fixed the national tongue. It gave to poetry rules, precepts, and a discipline; it was the first instructress of the German spirit."

HARRIS, JAS.. Philological Inquiries. 2 vols. London: 1781.
> See § 2.

HATZFIELD, A., et GEORGES MEUNIER. Les Critiques littéraires du xixe siècle. Paris: 1894.

Brief notices of leading French critics, with extracts from their writings.

KRANTZ, É. Essai sur l'esthétique de Descartes. Paris: 1882.

On pp. 1–6 the author treats briefly, but suggestively, of the relation of criticism to the development of literature.

MABIE, H. W. *Andover Rev.*, 15: 583 Significance of Modern Criticism.
> See § 2.

MACAULAY, T. B. Essays.
> See § 2.

MAZZARELLA, B. Della Critica libri tre. Vol. I, Storia della critica. Genova: 1866.

A very unsatisfactory book, prolix in style and defective in arrangement; yet noteworthy as almost a solitary attempt at a history of literary criticism from the Greeks to the present time. Having little sense of perspective, the author has given disproportionate space to writers of small moment. He has brought together, however, a mass of curious learning for which other students may be thankful. Two promised volumes, one on the science and the other on the art of criticism, seem not to have been published.

MERLET, G.   *Rev. d. D. Mondes*, 1 Oct. 1883   La critique sous
le premier empire.

To be read in connection with Sainte-Beuve's paper on the
same subject.   The critics treated of are Geoffroy, François
Hoffman, Dussault, and M. de Féletz.

MOULTON, R. G.   Shakespeare as a Dramatic Artist.   2d ed.
Oxford: 1888.

On pp. 7–21 Mr. Moulton maintains the thesis that "the
whole history of criticism has been a triumph of authors over
critics," and to prove it reviews the course of criticism from the
renaissance to the present time, dwelling mainly upon the history of Shakespeare criticism.   The order of progression has
been from judicial to inductive, criticism passing through five
distinct stages.   There was first the idea of judging solely by
classic standards, as in the instance of Rymer's attack upon
Shakespeare.   The second stage was reached when literature
of the modern type was admitted to have merit, though 'contrary to rule'; a third stage when the classics and the moderns
were put side by side, as in the 'Parallels' of Perrault.   In the
fourth stage, illustrated by Addison, the idea of judging, tossed
about between two standards, began to change to the idea of a
search for beauty.   Finally has come the fifth or inductive
stage, when literature, just as it stands, is analyzed for the purpose of discovering its underlying principles.   Inductive criticism (pp. 266, 267) also has its stages : First, mere observation ;
then analysis and topical arrangement ; finally, systematization ;
but the criticism of literature has never gone beyond the second
stage.

For comment, see Robertson's Essays, p. 51 ff.

NETTLESHIP, H.   *Journ. of Philology*, 18: 225 Literary Criticism in Latin Antiquity.

Traces the growth of criticism from Cicero to Quintilian.
An admirable paper.

NISARD, D.   Histoire de la littérature française.   4 vols.
Paris: 1844–9.

See vol. IV, pp. 568–573, for an excellent account of the
criticism of the 18th century.

PATIN, H. J. G.   Études sur les tragiques grecs.
Vol. II, p. 415.

Criticism, as it advances, passes through the following stages:
(1) Naïve feeling; (2) reflection; (3) theories of criticism,
which may be drawn (*a*) from experience, or (*b*) from speculative views as to the means and end of art.

PERRY, T. S.   English Literature in the 18th Century.   New
York: 1883.
Pp. 164–174.

The author writes entertainingly on Addison's criticisms of
Milton, and on the critical spirit of the 18th century in its
relation to Aristotle's Poetics and Horace's Ars Poetica.

PELLISSIER, G.   Le mouvement littéraire au xixe siècle.   2e éd.
Paris: 1890.

A work of unusual merit.   It contains two chapters on the
criticism of the century, of which one (pp. 213–231) treats of
romantic and the other (pp. 305–321) of realistic criticism.
The characteristic of the classic criticism was that it made
rigid application of fixed laws and formulas.   The romantic
criticism, taking the historical point of view, interpreted literature as a picture of society.   Later, the literary work became a
mere 'document' for the study of mankind.

The writers selected for treatment are Mme. de Staël, Villemain, Nisard, Sainte-Beuve, Taine, and Renan.

PESCHIER.   *Herrig's Archiv*, 11: 294 Des Phases de la critique
en France.

A rapid sketch of the history of French criticism in the 17th
and 18th centuries.

Pope, A.   Essay on Criticism.

Lines 643–744 are devoted to a history of criticism and to
characterizations of famous critics of ancient and modern times.
It is interesting to note those whom Pope selected for this
history, and still more interesting to note those whom he
omitted.   " The mighty Stagirite first left the shore," followed
by Horace, Dionysius, Petronius Arbiter, Quintilian and Longinus, who complete the list of ancient critics.   After these
criticism fell into decay, but revived with Erasmus, and reached
a high plane in the Art of Poetry of ' immortal Vida.'   In
France the critical impulse was transmitted to Boileau ; in
England to Roscommon and Walsh.

Porter, N.   Books and Reading.   N. Y.: 1876.

In chapters XVII and XVIII, on the New Criticism, is an
estimate of the influence of German upon English criticism,
and a brief sketch of the course of criticism in England.

Quarterly Review, 175: 102 The Porson of Shakespearian
         Criticism.

Theobald is reinstated in his rights as a master of Shakespearian criticism.   An interesting comparison is made between
him and Bentley, and incidentally light is thrown upon the
course of criticism in the eighteenth century.

Renard, Georges.   Les Princes de la jeune critique.   Paris :
         1890.   (Libr. de la *Nouvelle Revue.*)

The ' princes ' are Jules Lemaître, Ferd. Brunetière, Anatole
France, L. Ganderax, P. Bourget.

Rigault, H.   Histoire de la querelle des anciens et des
         modernes.   Paris : 1856.

The standard history of this famous episode in modern criticism.

ROBERTSON, J. M.   Essays towards a Critical Method.

> See § **2**.

The author suggests (pp. 40–42) that the movement of criticism is rhythmical in character, yet tending to ever greater universality.   Until recent times the aim of critics has been to secure consistency of dictum within a very limited field.   This is illustrated by the systems of criticism evolved in the 17th and 18th centuries.   Collision of dicta, however, the result of differences of taste, induced a general distrust, with the result that men turned from writings about literature to literature itself.   Thus the inductive criticism came into being.   But inductive criticism must give way in time to a new process of judgment, founded on comparative aesthetics and comparative sociology ; in other words, consistency of dictum, which in the eighteenth century could be secured only within a narrow circle, will at some time in the future be secured within a circle of great circumference.   The criterion of consistency is " that universal logic by which facts and principles are settled in natural science."   The reasonable attitude towards criticism is the attitude of research.

SAINTE-BEUVE, C. A.   M. de Féletz et de la critique littéraire sous l'empire.   Causeries de Lundi, 25 Févr. 1850.

> See § **2**.

SAINTSBURY, G.   Essays in English Literature.   London : 1890.

> Pp. 100–134 Jeffrey.

SAINTSBURY, G.   History of Elizabethan Literature.   London: 1887.

On pp. 33–35 Saintsbury refers, in passing, to the remarkable school of critics which sprang up amid the creative activity of the time.

SCHELLING, F. E.   Poetic and Verse Criticism of the Reign of
Elizabeth. Philadelphia: 1891. (Pubs. of the Univ. of Pennsylvania, Series in Philol., Literature, and Archaeol., I, 1.)

A 'plain exposition' of the theories of poetry, and especially
of versification, which were evolved in England between 1507
and 1603, contemporary estimates of poets and poetry being
purposely excluded.   While the order of treatment is mainly
chronological by authors, three classes of criticisms are distinguished: (1) Attempts to apply to English poetry the principles of classical prosody (Ascham, Harvey, Webbe, and Campion); (2) attempts to formulate inductively the rules of existing
English prosody (Gascoigne, James I); (3) treatises on the
wide field of poetical theory (Puttenham, Sidney).   Sidney is
regarded as the sole representative of " that broader criticism
which has founded modern criticism."

SCHERER, EDM.   Études critiques.

See vol. I, p. 171, of these valuable essays, for a study of
Nisard; p. 321 for a study of Sainte-Beuve.   On Taine's place
in the history of criticism, see vol. II, p. 111; vol. IV, p. 253.

STEDMAN, E. C.   The Nature of Poetry.   Boston: 1892.
The passing references to modern criticism may be traced
by means of the index.

STEDMAN, E. C.   Poets of America.   Boston: 1885.

Of value in the study of American Criticism.   See the Index.

STEPHEN, L.   History of English Thought in the 18th Century.
2 vols.   New York: 1876.
Vol. I, p. 34.

Invaluable as a guide to the movements of English thought
which determined the growth of English literary criticism.

SYMONDS, J. A.   Essays speculative and suggestive.   2 vols.
    London: 1890.

In the essay On some Principles of Criticism (vol. I, pp. 84–
123), the author touches here and there upon the history of
critical efforts.   He distinguishes three stages, which he calls
classical, romantic, and scientific criticism (pp. 96–98).   The
passages describing the origin and rise of modern criticism
(pp. 109–114) are of special interest.

SYMONDS, J. A.   Greek Poets.   2d ser.
        P. 303 Greek Criticism.

Gives the attitude of the Alexandrian critics towards Greek
literature.

SYMONDS, J. A.   The Renaissance in Italy.

Contains full and excellent accounts of critics and critical
movements of the Renaissance.   These may be traced by
means of the index.

THÉRY, AUG.   Histoire des opinions littéraires chez les anciens
        et chez les modernes.   Nouvelle éd.   2 vols.   Paris: 1849.

TISSOT, ERNEST.   Les Évolutions de la critique française.
    Paris: 1890.

In some respects an admirable work, though not what its
title would lead the reader to expect.   Purporting to be a history of criticism, it is in reality a classification of critics.
Tissot distinguishes three types of modern criticism: *Literary*,
of which Brunetière and Jules Lemaître are representatives;
moralizing, represented by Barbey d'Aurevilly and Edmond
Scherer; *analytic*, as seen in the writings of Taine, Bourget,
and Émile Hennequin.   Literary criticism judges a work according to set rules or dogmas, without reference to historical
development.   The aim of the moralizing criticism is suggested
by its name, — it judges according to ethical standards.   The

analytic criticism, taking into account both the aesthetic and the sociological aspects of the work, makes special search for the spiritual environment in which it came to birth. Like most attempts at hard-and-fast classifying, Tissot's threefold division breaks down in practical application, but this fact does not greatly diminish its value, which lies in its felicitous characterizations of individual critics.

VILLEMAIN, A. F. Discours et mélanges littéraires. P. 29 Discours sur . . . la critique.

Contains a brief sketch of the history of criticism, with characterization of the most important authors.

VILLARI, P. Nuova Antologia, 1884–III: 73 Francesco De Sanctis e la critica in Italia.

A good account of the work and influence of this leading Italian critic.

WYLIE, LAURA JOHNSON. Studies in the Evolution of English Criticism. Boston: 1894.

This little work, a doctoral thesis, covers the period from 1660 to the close of the first quarter of this century. Its plan and scope may be inferred from the subjects of the chapters, as follows: I. John Dryden; II. The Evolution out of Classicism; III. The German Sources of Coleridge's Criticism; IV. Samuel Taylor Coleridge. In style and method the writer shows the influence, perhaps, of Brunetière's L'évolution de la critique in her fondness for large generalizations and for rhetorical indirectness of statement, but her ideas are, in the main, her own, and her conclusions are based upon much original research. The writer was fortunate in being equipped with a working knowledge of the history of aesthetics.

§ 6. GENERAL NOTE.

In studying the history of a particular period of criticism, the student will of course consult the standard histories of literature as well as monographs upon individual critics. These are too numerous to be cited here. On Methods see Chapter V.

In Chapter VI the names and works of those who are esteemed most important as contributors to critical theory or to critical practice are given in their chronological sequence.

The following references are of less importance than the foregoing, or deal with individual critics :.

On the History of French Criticism. — A. Bettelheim, *Magazin f. d. Litteratur d. In- und Auslandes,* 1888 : 256–258 Neuere französische Kritiker; A. Caumont, La critique littéraire de Sainte-Beuve (*Frankf. Neuphilol. Beiträge* 1–29, Frankfurt a. M.: 1887); Em. Des Essarts, L'Instruction publique 1888 : 675–677 Boileau devant la critique moderne; G. Lanson, *Revue Bleue* 27 Janvier 1894 Critiques d'aujourd'hui : Émile Faguet; G. Pellissier, Essais de littérature contemporaine (Paris : 1893), La doctrine de F. Brunetière; G. Planche, *Rev. d. D. Mondes* 1835 (4e sér., vol. I) : 5 De la critique française en 1835; A. A. J. M. F. de Pontmartin, *Correspondant* N.S., 48 : 5 La critique en 1871; P. Stapfer, *Rev. pol. et lit.* 3e sér. xiv : 297–303 Poètes et critiques du xixe siècle; A. P. Soupé, *Rev. Contemp.* 5 (1868): 496, 6 : 5 Précurseurs de la critique moderne : Grimm; G. Renard, *Nouvelle Revue* 57 : 704–729 Brunetière; J. B. Stiernet, Muséon 10 : 122 L'évolution de la critique (a review of Brunetière's work of the same title); É. Zola, Documents littéraires (Nouv. éd.; Paris : 1894), p. 333 La critique contemporaine (A scathing review of modern criticism); Louis de Loménie, Esquisses historiques de littérature (Paris : 1879), p. 221 Chateaubriand et la critique; G. Larroumet, Études de littérature et d'art (Paris : 1893), p. 347 Brunetière, p. 83 Le

xviiie siècle et la critique contemporaine; C. A. Sainte-Beuve,
Revue d. D. Mondes, Dec. 1835 Bayle et le génie critique ;
J. F. Boissonade, Critique littéraire sous le premier empire
(Paris : 1863); A. de Pontmartin, Derniers Samedis (IIIe sér.
Paris : 1892) Brunetière; É. Faguet, *Revue de Paris*, 1 Févr.
1894 Ferdinand Brunetière (The impersonal element is the most
striking characteristic of Brunetière's criticism); G. Planche,
Revue d. D. Mondes, 1 Janvier 1835 De la critique française en
1835; P. Limayrac, *Revue d. D. Mondes*, 1 Sept. 1847 De
l'esprit critique en France.

An interesting collection of critical judgments, illustrating the
progress of French criticism, will be found in the work of
R. P. Chauvin and G. Le Bidois, La Littérature française par
les critiques contemporains (Paris : 1887). Among the authors
from whom specimens are drawn are Villemain, Sainte-Beuve,
St.-Marc Girardin, Nisard, H. Rigault, Lemaître, Vinet, Taine,
Paul Albert, Brunetière, and Faguet.

On the History of English Criticism. — Fraser, 21 : 190 The
Present State of Literary Criticism in England (1840); Fraser,
28 (1843): 43 Jeffrey and Gifford *vs.* Shakespeare and Milton ;
Blackwood, 2 (1818): 670 Remarks on the Periodical Criticism
of England; H. Hettner, Geschichte der englischen Literatur
(Braunschweig: 1856), p. 415 Die psychologische Aesthetiker,
Burke, Gerard, Home; p. 420 Die Kritik S. Johnson's; *Retro-
spective Review*, vol. I, pt. II, p. 305 Nature and Effects of Mod-
ern Criticism (a review of the writings of John Dennis); H. T.
Tuckerman, Characteristics of Literature illustrated by the
Genius of Distinguished Writers (Philadelphia : 1851), pp. 216–
238 The Critic : Hazlitt.

A collection of criticisms upon noted English writers has
been made by E. Stevenson, under the title Early Reviews of
Great Writers (London : 1890; Camelot series). The extracts
cover the years 1786–1832, and include critiques upon the Vicar
of Wakefield, Burns, and the Lyrical Ballads.

On the History of German Criticism. — O. Wichmann, L'Art poétique de Boileau dans celui de Gottsched (Berlin : 1879); R. Weitbrecht, *Blätter f. litt. Unterhaltung* 1891–II : 625 Kritiker und Dichter. For Gerhard Voss, Opitz, Gottsched, Breitinger, Baumgarten, Sulzer, Eberhard, Solger, Lessing, Schiller, Goethe, Herder, Richter, Tieck, A. W. von Schlegel, and later authorities on criticism and its history, see, below, § **21,** *B* 3, The Development of Poetics in Germany.

On the History of Italian Criticism. — L. Ceci, Ateneo Romagnolo 1882, Nos. 9, 10 Un' occhiata allo svolgimento storico della critica letteraria e politica del seicento (Firenze : 1878); G. Trezza, La critica moderna (2ª ed., con aggiunte, Bologna : 1880); L. Morandi, Antologia della nostra critica letteraria moderna (4ª ed., Città di Castello : 1889); P. Ferrieri, Francesco De Sanctis e la critica letteraria (Milano : 1888). See § **21,** *B* 5.

On the History of Spanish Criticism. — F. F. Gonzalez, Historia de la crítica literaria en España (Madrid : 1867); M. Menendez y Pelayo, Historia de las ideas estéticas en España (5 vols. in 8 ; Madrid : 1883–91). See § **21,** *B* 5.

For brief accounts of Russian and Danish critics, consult Wm. Knight's Philosophy of the Beautiful, Part II (London : 1893), pp. 251–272, and 273–281.

In *De Gids* for April-May, 1891, will be found an able article by Polak on Huet and Potgieter, the two greatest literary critics of Holland.

CHAPTER II.

PRINCIPLES OF ART.

_____

PART I. — THEORY OF ART.

§ 7. STATEMENT OF PROBLEMS; ANALYSIS.

STUDY of the underlying principles of literature leads the student back inevitably to the principles of art. The principles of literature, he finds, are but special applications of the broader principles which lie at the base of all the arts.

It would seem desirable, therefore, that the student early in his course should gain clear and right notions regarding the fundamental conceptions of aesthetics. Familiar with the principles of the broader science, he should be better prepared to work within the limits of the narrower. From a study of writings on the theory of art he should gain a power to discriminate among writings on the theory of literature; he should be enabled to detect the hidden bases of literary principles or precepts; he should be enabled to judge independently of the source and value of traditional literary doctrines.

Aesthetics is a large subject. None but a specialist can hope to master it in all its extent, and but few can hope to keep abreast of the active discussions and investigations that are going on at present. Nevertheless, complex and difficult as the subject appears, its fundamental principles are simple and its main problems few. Further, as in many other branches of knowledge, a thorough study of some one problem or principle will put the student in possession of all the rest. The

following are suggested as some of the important questions
likely to arise in a search for the fundamental principle of art.

I. Fundamental Problems. — (1) What is the relation of Art
to Nature? (2) What is the relation of Art to Imitation?
(3) What is Beauty? (4) Is Beauty subjective or objective, or
both? (5) How is the Beautiful related to the Sublime, the
Ludicrous, the Pathetic, the Comic, and the Tragic? (6) What
is the function of the Imagination in Art? (7) What are the
Aesthetic Emotions? (8) What is the purpose of Art? (9)
What part is played in the theory of Art by Pleasure? By the
Play-impulse? Rhythm? Harmony? Regularity? Economy?
(10) What is the relation of Art to Science, Morals, and Religion? (11) Can Art be useful? (12) What are the principal
classifications of Art? (13) Upon what basis of differentiation
do these classifications rest? (14) If there is a hierarchy of
the Arts, upon what principle does it rest? (15) What is the
function of Taste? (16) What determines the validity and
the limitations of canons of Art?

The answers to these questions may be sought in the authorities mentioned under §§ **8** and **9**.

II. Minute Analysis of Problems. — For those who desire
to go more profoundly into the subject the following analysis is
presented.

The problems of aesthetics may be classified under four
heads: (1) Physiological problems, (2) psychological problems,
(3) speculative problems, (4) social problems. It is not easy,
perhaps not desirable, to keep the four classes wholly distinct;
consequently, in the statement of the problems, some overlap-
ping may be expected.

A. PHYSIOLOGICAL PROBLEMS. — The general problem of physiological aesthetics may be stated in this way : What is the
origin, nature, and physical explanation of the aesthetic thrill?

As the inquiry usually proceeds upon the assumption that aesthetic feeling is a species of pleasurable feeling, the line of research is in the direction of differentiating this kind of sensuous pleasure from sensuous pleasure in general. Thus the following series of subsidiary problems arises :

(1) What changes in the nervous system, resulting from the application of stimuli, produce the sensation of pleasure?

(2) (*a*) What class of objects supply these stimuli? (*b*) What are the attributes of these objects? (*c*) Do dissimilar qualities furnish the same result, or is there some one quality, existing in different forms, in all objects that occasion pleasure?

(3) Is the relation between the stimulus and the pleasurable feeling necessary and invariable, or accidental and mutable?

(4) How are pleasurable feelings related to the vital functions?

(5) (*a*) What quality in the stimulus, or (*b*) what modification of the neural process occasions the aesthetic quality of the feeling?

(6) What are the preëminently aesthetic senses?

Assuming that hearing and seeing are the only, or the preëminently, aesthetic senses, the physiologist may inquire : —

(7) What in the nervous structure and function of the ear corresponds to the relations of tones constituting the musical scale? To the relations of tones constituting harmony or discord?

(8) What are the exact mathematical relations of such tones? (See Helmholtz.)

(9) What are the neural equivalents of rhythm and melody?

(10) What colors and combinations of colors are pleasing to the eye? (See Allen's Color Sense.)

(11) What forms and proportions of objects are pleasing?

(12) What movements of the eye and modifications of its neural processes correspond to pleasing forms and colors of objects?

(13) What are the neural equivalents of contrast, climax, and effective anti-climax?

(14) Is pain a necessary accompaniment, or condition precedent, of aesthetic feeling?

On these problems the student may consult the writings of Allen, Ladd, Sully, Spencer, Helmholtz, and Marshall, and § 9, III. 2.

B. **PSYCHOLOGICAL.** — (See § 9, III. 1.)   Aesthetics as psychology is most obviously concerned with the nature of aesthetic emotions, although it is bound to take into account all facts of consciousness involved in the production of such emotions. Calling, for convenience, all objects that can arouse aesthetic emotion *aesthetic objects*, the psychologist may inquire: —

(1) Does the perception of the aesthetic object differ from that of other objects? And if so, how?

This problem resolves itself into two subordinate problems: —

(*a*) What sensations do the peculiar physical marks of the aesthetic object, as, *e.g.*, color, symmetry, etc., produce?

(*b*) How is this raw material of sensation worked up into consciousness through perception?

(2) What is the nature and function of imagination in so far as it has to do with the aesthetic object?

(3) Are there aesthetic pleasures which are separable from the imagination?

(4) Characteristics of the different kinds of aesthetic imagination?

(5) Are all aesthetic objects (*e.g.*, natural objects) products of the aesthetic imagination?

(6) Can the aesthetic imagination do anything more than combine what has been given it in experience?

(7) Why does the mind take an interest in the aesthetic object? May the same object be at times aesthetic and at other times non-aesthetic?

(8) Characteristics of aesthetic emotion? How related to sensation?

(9) Is pleasurableness the essential characteristic of aesthetic emotion ?

(10) Kinds of aesthetic emotion ?

(11) Relations between aesthetic emotion and other kinds of emotion ?

(12) Are aesthetic pleasures sense-pleasures ?

(13) Is immediacy of pleasure-getting the distinction between ordinary emotion and aesthetic emotion ?   (See Fechner.)

(14) Is all aesthetic emotion the *revival* of pleasurable emotion or of a pleasurable content ?   (See Sully, Marshall.)

(15) What is the nature of the impulse that leads to the production of works of art ?   Is there a difference between ' expression ' and ' discharge of emotion ' ?   (See Bosanquet, *Mind*, N.S. 3 : 153.)

(16) Is the emotional state which is produced by a work of art, passive and receptive, or active ?   (See Allen, Fechner, Guyau, Ladd, and Marshall.)

(17) What is the importance of sub-conscious processes as explanation of aesthetic effects ?   (See Helmholtz.)

(18) Aesthetic function of the Will ?

C. **Speculative Problems.** — The problem of aesthetics as philosophy may be said, in a general way, to be the relation of the subject-matter (whatever that may be determined to be) to human experience.   As suggested by the parenthesis, the nature of the subject-matter is itself a part of the problem. Retaining the convenient term aesthetic object, we may inquire : —

1. What is it about things that makes them aesthetic objects ?

The number of the answers which have been made to this question is very large.   Among the qualities or characteristics posited of the aesthetic object are the following: Truth, Conflict, Reconciliation of Opposites, Repose, Growth, Life, Order,

Symmetry, Fitness, Unity in Variety, Simplicity, Intricacy, Harmony, Usefulness (recognized or unrecognized), Expression, Suggestion, Personality, Novelty, Consistency, Proportion, Freedom, Economy, Rhythm. By most writers these and all similar characteristics are held to be summed up in the comprehensive term *Beauty*.

If it is necessary to posit some particular thing as the essence of the aesthetic object, it would perhaps be better to substitute for the ambiguous term beauty the term *aesthetic value*, which has at least the advantage of suggesting its question-begging character. Adopting this term as a matter of convenience, we may ask:—

2. Is aesthetic value subjective or objective, or both?

3. Kinds of aesthetic value, and relation of one kind to another?

As examples of the different kinds, may be mentioned the Beautiful, the Sublime, the Ludicrous, the Pathetic, the Tragic, the Grotesque, etc.

4. Relation of the work of art to nature?

This question may take on a great diversity of forms, as, for example:—

(*a*) Is art an imitation of nature, and if so, is that all that art is?

(*b*) In what respect does the aesthetic value of art differ from that of nature?

(*c*) Is there a higher and a lower aesthetic value, and if so, which is higher, that of nature or that of art?

(*d*) Does nature, when it takes on aesthetic value, become art?

5. Character of the work of art?

In dealing with the work of art, we may inquire, (*a*) What is its essential principle? Or, taking into account the conditions of its production, may ask (*b*) Why works of art should be produced at all? Or, (*c*) What were the aims and motives of the

producer of a particular work? Or, (*d*) By what processes and
in obedience to what laws he gave embodiment to his idea?
Or, (*e*) In what material he embodied it? Or, (*f*) What are
the laws of the development of art in general? The answer to
the first question will bring before us the theory of art; to the
second, the genesis of art, or the art-impulse; to the third, the
relations of art and the artist; to the fourth, the technique of
art and the nature of genius; to the fifth, the classification of
the arts; and to the sixth, the evolution of art as a historical
growth. For authorities on speculative problems see §§ **8** and
9, II. 1–8.

D. Social Problems. — These are such as relate to the
communal origin and development of the aesthetic impulse,
and the effect exerted upon the community by aesthetic productions.

(*A*) (1) What part has sympathy or altruism played in the
origin and development of aesthetic pleasure? In the production of works of art? Are aesthetic pleasures ever selfish
pleasures?

(2) What part has been played in aesthetic production by
the imitative instinct — the instinct of one man to do what
another has done or is doing?

(3) To what extent does the law of supply and demand govern the production of art?

(4) To what extent is art individual, and to what extent is it
social? Is art the possession of the whole people?

(5) To what extent are the principles of coöperation and
division of labor effective in art?

(6) Place of art in the theory of the State?

(*a*) In what form of government does art best flourish?

(*b*) Does inequality of condition promote or hinder the
healthy development of art?

(7) To what extent is art the expression of pleasure in the
labor of production?

(8) To what extent is freedom of the artist essential to good art?

(9) What part is played by machinery in the production of works of art? Are machine-made articles necessarily bad art?

(10) Does civilization inevitably bring ugliness with it?

(11) Does art go hand in hand with luxury?

(*B*) (1) What effect has art upon social development?

(2) What is the relation of art to morality? May art be non-moral?

(3) Is the best art that which appeals to the people — the masses? Or that which appeals to an aristocracy of intellect and emotion?

(4) What is the service which useful art renders to the community, and how does this differ from the service rendered by fine art?

For information upon the social side of art — as yet but little understood — the student may consult the works of Guyau (L'Art au point de vue sociologique), Wm. Morris, Wilde, De Greef, and Dewey (Outline of Ethics).

§ 8. REFERENCES.

ALISON, ARCHIBALD. Essays on the Nature and Principles of Taste. 2 vols. Edinburgh : 1825.

The student will find in Alison's voluminous essay an interesting defense of the theory that association is the source of the Beautiful. If the association theory is valid, the theory of Beauty as an intrinsic quality in the object will be difficult to maintain. The question will be worth consideration whether the recollection of other objects associated with the one we contemplate is requisite to the awakening of the sense for beauty? Also, whether the Useful is an index to the Beautiful, or *vice versa?* Is Professor Blackie, in the Preface to his Discourses on Beauty, reasonable on the one hand in his denunciation of

Alison, Jeffrey, and the whole school of Scottish philosophers
as half-thinkers, and on the other in his outspoken admiration
of the stand taken by Sir W. Hamilton? For an interesting
essay on Alison's work, see *Blackw.* 13 : 385 Alison explained
by Jeffrey.

ALLEN, G. Physiological Aesthetics. New York: 1877.

Allen is also author of the Color Sense. Among articles
contributed by him to magazines the following are noteworthy :
Mind, 3 : 324 Origin of the Sublime; 4 : 301 Origin of the Sense
of Symmetry ; 5 : 445 Aesthetic Evolution in Man. As developing more fully in a single direction the line of thought followed in psychology by Maudsley, Bain, Spencer, and Sully,
this work on Physiological Aesthetics is of considerable historical value. Grant Allen attempts to translate the aesthetic feelings into terms of neural change and the subjective concomi-
tants of such change. Beginning with an extended analysis of
the two physiological facts of pleasure and pain, he shows that
the first is caused by the normal activity of the tissues, the
second by wasted or arrested activity. To distinguish aesthetic
from non-aesthetic pleasures he adopts Spencer's distinction
between life-serving processes and processes or activities carried on purely for the sake of the gratification they afford.
He thus arrives at the following definition: Aesthetic pleasure
is "the subjective concomitant of the normal amount of activity, not directly connected with the life-serving function, in the
peripheral end-organs of the cerebro-spinal nervous system."
Aesthetic pleasure, Allen holds, differs from play only as a
passive pleasure differs from an active pleasure. On this point
he has been vigorously opposed by Guyau (L'Esthétique Contemporaine), Marshall, and Bosanquet (*Mind*, N.S. 3: 153).
Mr. Marshall notes that Mr. Allen has apparently lost faith in
certain of his own doctrines. (See *Mind*, N.S. 1: 364 and
No. 45.)

ARISTOTLE.　De Arte Poetica (Vahlen's Text), with Translation by E. R. Wharton.　Oxford: 1883.

ARISTOTLE.　The Nicomachean Ethics.　Trans. by F. H. Peters.　London: 1887.

　　Pp. 131–3 Wit; 185–9 Art.

ARISTOTLE.　The Metaphysics.　Trans. by J. H. McMahon. Bohn Libr.　London: 1857.

　　Pp. 4–6, 320.

ARISTOTLE.　The Politics.　Trans. by J. E. C. Welldon.　London: 1883.

　　Pp. 227–249 Music; 245, 246 Purging of the Emotions.

ARISTOTLE.　The Rhetoric.　Trans. by J. E. C. Welldon. London: 1886.

　　Bk. III, chaps. V, VIII.

As a starting-point for the history of aesthetic theories no work is of greater importance than the Poetics.　The student must, however, beware of adopting hastily-formed and careless conclusions concerning Aristotle's meaning.　Of a hundred critics upon Aristotle not more than one has fairly expounded his theory of art in the light of his philosophy as developed in the Rhetoric, the Politics, the Ethics, and the Metaphysics. The student should hold himself unbiased concerning Aristotle's greatest contribution to aesthetics, the theory of Imitation, until he has reconciled on one basis the various statements about art as Imitation scattered through the Poetics.　It should not be assumed without investigation that Aristotle by Imitation meant copying (§ 9, Relation of Art to Nature). Light on this point may be had by comparing Plato's Theory of Imitation and his views on the relation of art to ethics with the corresponding theories of Aristotle.　On such questions as Aristotle's leanings to symbolism, his treatment of the ugly, his

idealism, his view of the relation of art to nature, and other
fundamental problems, see the careful and profound exposition
of Bosanquet (History of Aesthetic, chaps. II–IV, especially
pp. 55–76). Assistance in determining the relation of Aristotle's philosophy of art to the Aristotelian system may be
obtained from Butcher's Aristotle's Theory of Poetry and
Fine Art; Ueberweg's Hist. of Philosophy, vol. I, pp. 177–180;
Erdmann's Hist. of Philos., vol. I, pp. 173–177 ; E. Wallace's
Outlines of the Philosophy of Aristotle; Zeller's Philosophie
der Griechen, Theil 2, Abth. 2, pp. 763–787; Schasler's Krit.
Gesch. Aesth., Theil 1, pp. 120–151.   See, also, references,
under ARISTOTLE, §§ 9, II. *H,* 20, 38, 41, 47.

The following are some of the most important of the numerous monographs on Aristotelian aesthetics :

Twining, Aristotle's Treatise on Poetry (London : 1789);
Pye, Commentary illustrating the Poetic (London : 1792); Tyr-
whitt, De Poetica Liber (Oxford : 1794) ; Raumer, Ueber d.
Poetik (Berlin : 1829); Egger, La Critique chez les Grecs;
Bénard, L'Esthétique d'Aristote (Paris : 1887); and Vahlen,
Teichmüller, Döring, as described in §§ 47, 48; Schrader,
De artis apud Arist. notione ac vi (Berlin : 1843 ; München :
1881); L. Spengel, Ueber κάθαρσις τῶν παθημάτων bei Arist.
(München : 1859); Martin, Analyse critique de la Poétique
d'Aristote (Paris : 1836); Von Wartenburg, Die Katharsis des
Arist. u. d. Oedipus Coloneus d. Sophokles (Berlin : 1866);
Stahr, Aristoteles u. d. Wirkung d. Trag. (Berlin : 1859);
Reinkens, Arist. üb. d. Kunst, besonders üb. d. Trag. (Wien :
1870); A. Dehlen, Die Theorie d. Arist. u. d. Tragödie d.
Antiken Christl. Naturwissenschaftl. Weltanschauung (Göt-
tingen : 1885); E. Jerusalem, Ueber d. Arist. Einheiten im
Drama (Leipzig : 1885); F. Susemihl, *Rhein. Mus.* 18 : 366,
471, 19 : 197, 22 : 217 Studien zur Aristot. Poetik; Th. Sträter,
Zeitschr. f. Philos. N.F., 40 : 219–247, 41 : 204–223 ; F. Ueber-
weg, *Zeitschr. f. Philos.* 50 : 16–39 Die Lehre des Aristoteles

von dem Wesen und der Wirkung der Kunst; G. Zillgenz,
Aristoteles und das deutsche Drama (Würzburg: 1865); Liepert,
Aristoteles und der Zweck der Kunst (Passau: 1862); F. C.
Petersen, Skandin. Litteraturselskab. 16 Om den Aristoteliske
Poetik; Ernst Essen, Bemerkungen zu Aristoteles' Poetik
(Leipzig: 1878); R. Schultz De poetices Aristoteleae princi-
piis (1874); M. Seibel, Zu Arist. περὶ ποιητικῆς (1891); C. Alt-
müller, D. Zweck d. schönen Kunst: Eine Arist. Studie (1873);
R. P. Hardie, *Mind*, July, 1895, The Poetics of Aristotle.

The two essays of J. Bernays which have played so impor-
tant a part in the discussion of the Aristotelian theory of trag-
edy, Grundzüge d. verlornen Abhandlung d. Arist. üb. die
Wirkung d. Trag. (Breslau: 1857), and Ergänzung zu Aris-
toteles Poetik (*Rhein. Mus.* N.F., 8, pp. 561–596), have been
reprinted in one volume under the title Zwei Abhandl. üb. d.
Arist. Theorie d. Dramas (Berlin: 1880).   See, further, Bernays's
Brief an L. Spengel üb. d. trag. Katharsis bei Arist. (*Rhein.
Mus.* N.F., 14: 367, 488), and Zur Arist. Katharsis-Frage
(*Rhein. Mus.* N. F., 15: 606), and Spengel's Zur " tragischen
Katharsis " d. Arist. (*Rhein. Mus.* N. F., 15: 458).

BAIN, ALEX.   The Emotions and the Will.   London: 1859.

> Pp. 65, 91, 92, 117, 143, 153 Laughter, 156, 182, 183, 196, 197, 204,
> 225 Imitation, 246, 247–285 (chap. XIV) The Aesthetic Emo-
> tions.

BAIN, ALEX.   Mental Science.   New York: 1870.

> P. 106 Association in Fine Art, 122, 123 Acquisitions in the Fine
> Arts, 149, 172–4, 289–317 Aesthetic Emotions.

BAIN, ALEX.   The Senses and the Intellect.   2d ed.   London:
1864.

> Pp. 452–454, 543–550, 555, 604, 605, 614–624.

Perhaps no psychologist is more painstaking in gathering
facts, and stating them, than Professor Bain; but his interpretation of the facts must be accepted with caution.   Regarding

aesthetic emotions as a sublimation of the simpler feelings, and distinguishing these aesthetic emotions by the presence of certain characteristics not essential to mere existence, Bain is to be studied with especial profit in connection with Spencer and the physiological school. In a third edition of The Emotions and the Will (London : 1875) changes have been made in conformity with Sully's investigations into the aesthetic emotions ; and the author discusses at some length the bearing of the evolution hypothesis on his premises as hitherto stated. See *Mind* 1: 154.

BEGG, W. P. The Development of Taste and other Studies in Aesthetics. Glasgow: 1887.

A work which, while it cannot be said to advance a new theory of the Beautiful, or of Art, presents with clearness the nature of the theories of the Evolutionists and of the Associationists (chaps. I–IX), and elaborates with enthusiasm the doctrines of Hegel and of the brothers Caird. The chapters on the development of taste among the Assyrians, Egyptians, Hebrews, Greeks, Romans, and Christians — especially in regard to the beautiful in nature — are profitable and of extreme interest. The student will find the distinctions drawn in chap. VIII between the Pretty, the Picturesque, the Beautiful, and the Sublime, suggestive; he should note carefully Begg's answers to the two great questions: What is Beauty? and Is there an absolute standard of Taste? In saying that divine thought immanent in the universe is the supreme cause of Beauty in nature, Begg provokes at once the question: Then how comes the Ugly here? His answer is that of Leibnitz and the Optimists. See review in *Rev. Philos.* 23 : 654.

BELL, SIR CHAS. The Anatomy and Philosophy of Expression as connected with the Fine Arts. 6th ed. London : 1872.

Of considerable importance as a forerunner of the evolutionary and physiological school of aesthetics represented by Bain, Spencer, Sully, and Allen.

BOSANQUET, BERNARD.　A History of Aesthetic.　London :
　1892.

This is the only adequate historico-critical survey of the subject produced outside of Germany.　Aesthetic theory is treated as a branch of philosophy ; but the result is something more than a history of speculation.　The author's appreciation of art, and his sense for the intimate connection between theory and practice, cause him to regard aesthetic theory "as only the clear and crystallized form of the aesthetic consciousness or sense of beauty."　His work is thus at one and the same time a history of aesthetic opinion and a history of the aesthetic consciousness ; and although he has avoided what he calls "the impertinence of invading the artist's domain with an *apparatus belli* of critical principles and precepts," his interpretations of art, and especially of literature (see in particular chap. VII A comparison of Dante and Shakespeare in respect of some Formal Characteristics), are not the least valuable parts of the work.　The point of view is speculative, but ample justice is done to the "exact aesthetic" of Germany and the related investigations in England.　The treatment is by ideas, not by authors.

The appearance of this work was preceded by several studies of aesthetics from the pen of the author.　Among the most important were the essay prefatory to his translation of Hegel, and the following articles in the Proceedings of the Aristotelian Society : Vol. I, No. 2, pp. 77–96 The Part played by Aesthetic in the Growth of Modern Philosophy ; vol. I, No. 3, pt. I, pp. 32–48 The Aesthetic Theory of Ugliness.　Since the History appeared Mr. Bosanquet has published in *Mind*, N.S. 3 : 153, an interesting article entitled On the Nature of Aesthetic Emotion, in which he discusses the relation between emotion and expression.

BROWN, BALDWIN.   The Fine Arts.   London : 1892.

One of the University Extension Manuals, edited by Professor
Knight.   It has the double merit of being scholarly in treatment and fresh and spirited in style.   As an introduction to the
general theory of the arts it has few rivals.

BURKE, EDMUND.   Philosophical Inquiry into the Origin of our
    Ideas of the Sublime and Beautiful.   London : 1821.
    (First published 1756.)

Of much importance historically, and useful to the student
as suggesting a comparison between the physiological theory of
aesthetic which Burke advanced and the theory of associated
ideas maintained by Alison and the Scotch school.   Burke
was one of the earliest writers to emphasize the relation of the
Sublime to the Beautiful.   The validity of his premises calls
for careful examination.   Does the sense for Beauty rest upon
man's impulse toward society, and that for the sublime on the
impulse of self-preservation ?   Cf. Schasler's Geschichte, Bd. 1,
§§ 159–161 ; Bosanquet, Hist. Aesthetic, pp. 203–6.

CARRIERE, M.   Aesthetik.   Die Idee des Schönen und ihre
    Bewirklichg. durch Natur, Geist, und Kunst.   2 vols.
    Leipzig : 1873.   (1st ed. 1859, 3d ed. 1886.)

CARRIERE, M.   Die Kunst im Zusammenhang der Kulturent-
    wickelung, und die Ideale der Menschheit.   5 vols.   Leip-
    zig : 1871–3.   (1st ed. 1862, 3d ed. 1886.)

Carriere is one of the most readable of modern German writers on aesthetics.   He has done as much as any one man, perhaps, to spread a knowledge of the subject among his countrymen.   As regards his philosophical position, he is in essentials
a Hegelian, though he differs with Hegel upon many minor
points.   He calls himself a real-idealist.   The work entitled
Art in Connection with the Development of Culture is a notably successful attempt to write the aesthetic history of human-

ity.   Carriere has also written Das Wesen und die Formen der
Poesie (Leipzig: 1854).   In his Die Sittliche Weltordnung
(Leipzig: 1877), pp. 339–354 deal with art.   A criticism of
Carriere's aesthetics appeared in Bibl. Sacr. 18: 227.

COLVIN, S.   Encycl. Brit.   9th ed.   'Art.'

A somewhat formal discussion of the various meanings of the
word Art, with classification of the arts into useful and fine
arts.

COLVIN, S.   Encycl. Brit.   9th ed.   'Fine Arts.'

The definition, classification, and historical development of
fine art is here handled with great clearness and considerable
accumulation of interesting fact.   The writer makes no pretense to historical insight, but refers in one place and another
to the theories of the important authorities.

COUSIN, V.   Cours de l'histoire de la Philosophie moderne.
1e sér.   5 vols.   Paris: 1846.

> Vol. II, pp. 120–205 Du Beau, 419–428 Du Beau réel et du Beau
> Idéal.

COUSIN, V.   Du Vrai, du Beau, et du Bien.   Paris: 1853.

> Pp. 141–270 Du Beau.

COUSIN, V.   Lectures on the True, the Beautiful, and the
Good.   Trans. by O. W. Wight.   New York: 1860.

> Pp. 123–214.

With Levêque and Jouffroy, Cousin is a member of the
school of *Spiritualistes*.   For him the sense of Beauty is purely
subjective.   His aesthetic is the result of a reaction from the
sensationalism of the 18th century.   His studies were made
first in the wake of Reid and the Scotch philosophers, but after
his visit to Germany in 1817 he became a follower of the
German idealists.   Though calling himself an eclectic spirit-
ualist, he was the most enthusiastic advocate in France of
German philosophy.   Attempting to steer a middle course be-

tween the Scotch philosophy and German Absolutism, he finally
made port with the psychologists.   His work on aesthetics was
produced at this period in his development.

DEWEY. J.   Psychology.   New York: 1887.

See chap. XV on Aesthetic Feeling, and compare with it
chap. VII on Imagination and chap. IX on Intuition.   These
will be found an excellent introduction to the psychology of
aesthetics.   In his Outlines of Ethics (Ann Arbor: 1891) Professor Dewey considers briefly the social aspects of art (pp. 111–
113, 120–127), and develops several highly original conclusions.
Especially noteworthy is his attitude with regard to the relation
of fine and useful art (p. 112).   He holds that the rigid separation of the two in aesthetic theory has no justification.   " Both
are products of intelligence in the service of interests, and the
only difference is in the range of intelligence and the interests
concerned."

DIDEROT, D.   Œuvres Complètes, rev. . . . par J. Assizat.
20 vols.   Paris: 1875–7.

> T. VII, pp. 307–394 De la Poésie dramatique; T. X, pp. 3–42 Sur
> l'Origine et la Nature du Beau, 461–520 Essai sur la Peinture
> (written about 1775); T. XII, pp. 75–133 Pensées detachées sur
> la Peinture, la Sculpture, l'Architecture, et la Poésie; T. X–XII
> Salons ; T. XIII–XVII Dict. Encyclopédique (See articles ' Art,'
> ' Beauté,' etc.).

One of the most penetrating and original of French writers
on art.   His additions to theory, however, are made by way of
suggestion in the course of his art-criticisms, and not in systematic form.

EMERSON, R. W.   Complete Works.   Riverside ed.   11 vols.
Boston: 1883–4.

> Vol. I (Nature), pp. 21–30 Beauty ; vol. II (Essays, 1st ser.), pp.
> 327–343 Art; vol. VI (Conduct of Life), pp. 265–290 Beauty ;
> vol. VII (Soc. and Solitude), pp. 41–59 Art; vol. VIII (Letters
> and Soc. Aims), pp. 9–75 Poetry and Imagination, 151–166 The
> Comic.

May well be laid aside until some progress has been made in the study of aesthetics. The reading of Emerson at an early stage is likely to fill the student's mind with catch-words and epigrams about art, the meaning of which he is not prepared to understand. Emerson's theories of art may best be viewed in the light of his philosophy as a whole. His oracular fragments will then assume a measure of completeness and system.

EVERETT, C. C.   Poetry, Comedy, and Duty.   Boston: 1888.

For this work, as for his Science of Thought, Professor Everett has drawn his inspiration from Schopenhauer and his method from Hegel. The result has been in each case a logical and at the same time a fresh and fascinating treatise. Professor Everett discusses in Poetry, Comedy, and Duty, three sides of life, faces of a prism: The enjoyment of Beauty, the independence of the spiritual life, the obedience to the law of righteousness. The rare interdependence of the three is delicately expressed. Perhaps no writer in America has with equal charm set forth the philosophic connection between Ethics and Art, Art and Imagination, Imagination and the Actual, the Comic and the Tragic, the Beautiful and the Right. The student should consider carefully the ground occupied by both Everett and Schopenhauer (vol. II, pp. 270–284), that the sense of the ludicrous is purely subjective. There is an entertaining article by Professor Everett in the *Andover Rev.*, August, 1890, on the Sublime. Here, again, his views are in sequence with those of Schopenhauer (vol. I, pp. 259–268).

EVERETT, C. C.   The Science of Thought.   Boston: 1882.

This work is an excellent introduction to the study of aesthetics and of criticism. Special attention should be paid to pp. 153–163 Propositions of Beauty, and pp. 221–232 The Logic of Aesthetics.

Eye, A. von. Das Reich des Schönen. Berlin: 1878.

Though outwardly forbidding from its lack of table of contents and index, and its paucity of internal divisions, this work, for one who has the courage to attack it, presents a fairly comprehensive survey of the field of Aesthetic inquiry. A brief review of German Aesthetics begins on p. 38.

Fechner, G. T. Zur experimentalen Aesthetik. Leipzig: 1871.

Fechner, G. T. Vorschule der Aesthetik. Leipzig: 1876.

Fechner's importance lies in his having been among the first to test by actual experiment preferences for outlines, surfaces, and colors. He laid the foundation of modern experimental aesthetics. (See the article by J. Sully in *Mind* 2 : 102, and Bosanquet, Hist. Aesthetic, pp. 381–387.)

Gauckler, Ph. Le Beau et son Histoire. Paris: 1873.

An excellent little manual, covering in a popular style both the theoretical and the historical aspects of aesthetics. On pp. 1–9 the author reviews briefly the important definitions of Beauty. His own is given on p. 14: "The true manifestation in finite phenomena of the unity of being."

Gayley, C. M., and F. N. Scott. A Guide to the Literature of Aesthetics. Berkeley (California): 1890.

This is No. 11 of the University of California Library Bulletins, and can be obtained by librarians by way of exchange.

Goethe, J. W. von. Werke. (Hempel ed.) 36 vols. in 23. Berlin: 1879.

> Bd. II, pp. 175–220 Kunst; Bd. XXVIII Schriften und Aufsätze zur Kunst ; Bd. XXIX Aufsätze zur Literatur. See indexes in Bde. II, XXVIII and XXIX, and index to Bde. I–XXXVI in Bd. XXXVI.

GOETHE, J. W. VON. Sämmtliche Werke. 40 vols. in 20.
Stuttgart : 1840.

> Bd. III, pp. 257–274 Verschiedenes Einzelne über Kunst; Bd.
> XXX Winckelman, Ueber Laokoon, Wahrheit und Wahrschein-
> lichkeit, u. s. w.; Bd. XXXI von Deutsche Baukunst, Verschie-
> denes über Kunst, u. s. w.; Bd. XXXII Deutsche Literatur; Bd.
> XXXIII Auswärtige Literatur und Volkspoesie; Bd. XXXV,
> pp. 333–459 Theater und dramatische Poesie.

GOETHE, J. W. VON, and ECKERMANN, J. P. Gespräche mit
Goethe. 6te Aufl. 3 vols. Leipzig : 1885.

> See Register in Bd. III.

GOETHE, J. W. VON, ECKERMANN, J. P., and M. SORET. Conversations of Goethe. Trans. by J. Oxenford. London :
1875. (Vol. VI of Goethe's Works.)

As in the case of Plato so in that of Goethe, it did not lie
within the purpose of the man to develop a complete system of
aesthetics. But up and down the works of Goethe are scattered thoughts of a finished art-amateur concerning the subject
with which he was most intimate. His opinions are not so
much upon beauty or art in general as upon the peculiar
beauty and the comparative art of this or the other artistic
product. *A propos* of architecture, of the plastic arts, of
Shakespeare, of the French dramatists, of the German Romanticists, Goethe delivers himself frequently and fully. In his
conversations there will be found suggestive passages touching
upon the Unities, the quarrel between Classicism and Romanticism, the theories of Lessing and Winckelmann, the tenets of
various schools of criticism, the necessary principles of art, the
nature of the Beautiful, and the growth of the author's aesthetic convictions. For his definite contribution to the advance
of aesthetic speculation, see Bosanquet, Hist. of Aesth., pp. 304–
316, and § 20 below, under GOETHE.

GURNEY, EDM.   The Power of Sound.   London: 1880.

In the first chapters of this work is outlined a complete system of the Fine Arts as introduction to the treatment of the art
of music.   Gurney is here, as everywhere, clear, straightforward,
and entertaining.

GUYAU, M.-J.   Les Problèmes de l'Esthétique contemporaine.
Paris: 1884.

The problems here discussed are (1) the nature of Art, (2)
the future of art and poetry, (3) the form of poetry, and the laws
of verse.   The author maintains the seriousness of art (cf. Aristotle's and Wordsworth's "high seriousness") as against the
"play" theory of Spencer and Allen.   He deals a hard blow
at the view of aesthetic emotion which makes it a distinctively
passive or receptive attitude of the mind.

GUYAU, M.-J.   L'art au point de vue sociologique.   Introd.
par A. Fouillée.   Paris: 1889.

In this posthumous work M. Guyau presents with great force
and brilliancy of style an interpretation of art in terms of social
relationship.   His doctrine is summed up in the statement that
the function of art is to make all men feel alike, and so to develop social sympathy.   M. Guyau's views are presented appre-
ciatively in Alfred Fouillée's La Morale, l'art et la religion
d'après M. Guyau (Paris: 1889).

HARTMANN, E. VON.   Ausgewählte Werke.   2 vols.   Berlin:
1887.

> 9-12 Hfte. Die deutsche Aesthetik seit Kant ; 13-20 Hfte. Philoso-
> phie des Schönen.

Of these two volumes the first deals with the history of German Aesthetics since Kant, the second presents the author's
system.   In the first volume pp. 1-362 are taken up with a
historico-critical exposition of systems; pp. 363-580 with a consideration of special subjects and problems in aesthetics, such

as the Ugly, the Comic, the Classification of the Arts, etc.
Indexes and tables of contents enhance the value of the work
as a reference book. For those who read German readily this
work is perhaps the best key to modern German aesthetics.
For Von Hartmann's philosophic position see Ueberweg's Hist.
of Philos., vol. II, p. 336; Erdmann, vol. III, pp. 236–248;
Bosanquet's Hist. of Aesth., pp. 424–440.

HEGEL, G. W. F. Werke. 18 vols. Berlin: 1833–48.

> Bd. X, Theile 1–3 Aesthetik. (The three parts of the Aesthetik
> will be referred to as vols. I, II, and III.)

The importance of this work in the history of Aesthetics is
generally recognized, and it is to be regretted that no complete
translation has as yet been made. The Einleitung and Eintheilung (vol. I, pp. 3–114) give an excellent outline of the
whole work, and form the best introduction to it, but give
little idea of the wealth and fertility with which the fundamental conceptions are developed. The remark of Sully that
the German theories of aesthetics "can be adequately estimated and criticised only in connection with the whole system
of thought of which they are a part," is particularly true of
Hegel. A thorough examination of the Aesthetik, preceded
by a review of the Logik and exposition of the Hegelian *Idee*,
may be found in Von Hartmann, Aesthetik, Bd. I, pp. 107–
129. See, also, Schasler, Bd. II, p. 974, and in briefer compass, p. 1084; Lotze's Geschichte der Aesthetik; Ulrici's
Ueber Princip und Methode der Hegelischen Philosophie
(Halle: 1841), pp. 216–244. Ueberweg's and Erdmann's Histories of Philosophy may also be profitably consulted. Exposi-
tory articles are: *Brit. & For. Rev.* 13: 1, *No. Am.* 84: 385,
Church Rev. 46: 372, *Macm.* 16: 441 (Stirling's prefatory note).
Hastie's translation contains a eulogistic preface and a translation of Zeller's summary of the Hegelian philosophy. Best
of all are, for the beginner, the account in Wm. Knight's Phi-

losophy of the Beautiful, pt. I, pp. 70–74, and for the more advanced student the elaborate interpretation in Bosanquet's
Hist. of Aesth., pp. 334–362.

HEGEL, G. W. F.   The Introduction to Hegel's Philosophy of
    Fine Art.   Trans. by B. Bosanquet.   London: 1886.

This fine translation of the Einleitung and Eintheilung should
be in the hands of every student.   The prefatory essay "On
the True Conception of Another World," may be recommended
as an admirable introduction to the reading of Hegel.

HEGEL, G. W. F., and MICHELET, C. L.   The Philosophy of
    Art : An Introduction to the Scientific Study of Aesthetics.
    Trans. from the German by W. Hastie.   Edinburgh:
    1886.

This handy little book contains (1) an appreciative preface
with some remarks on Ruskin and Taine ; (2) a translation of
Zeller's summary of Hegel's Philosophy of Art ; (3) a translation
of pp. 3–30 of Hegel's Einleitung, covering in this volume
pp. 3–34; (4) a translation (not an analysis, as Bosanquet
wrongly assumes) of pp. 105–114 of Hegel's Eintheilung, ex-
tending in this volume to p. 46 ; (5) a translation of pp. 406–
453 of Michelet's System der Philosophie.   While the translation is readable and fairly representative of Hegel's thought, it
falls far below Bosanquet's in point of critical value.   The latter has the great advantage, also, of giving the Einleitung and
Eintheilung entire.

The following are translations of parts of the Aesthetik:
J. Spec. Philos. 1 : 36, 91, 169, 221 ; 2 : 39, 157 ; 3 : 31, 147,
281, 317 Bénard's Exposition of Hegel, translated by J. A.
Martling (see comment in *Mind*, 12 : 599); 5 : 368 ; 6: 125,
252; 7 : 33 Hegel's Philos. of Art — Chivalry, translated by S. A.
Longwell ; 11 : 337 ; 12: 18 Hegel's Symbolic Art, translated
by W. M. Bryant; 12 :145, 277 Hegel's Classical Art, trans-

lated by W. M. Bryant; 12 : 403; 13 : 113, 244, 351 Hegel's
Romantic Art, translated by W. M. Bryant; *Macm.* 16 : 441
Hegel's Symbolism of the Sublime, translated by J. H. Stirling.

HELMHOLTZ, H. L. F. VON.   Sensations of Tone as a Physio-
     logical Basis for a Theory of Music.   Translated and edited
     by A. J. Ellis.   London : 1875.

Upon the physical and physiological problems of music Helmholtz is the highest authority.   In the speculative field, into
which he ventured long excursions (chaps. XIII and XIX), his
opinions do not have and do not deserve so much consideration.   In most points of his aesthetic philosophy Helmholtz is
a close follower of Kant.   " Art," he says, " creates regularly
without conscious law, designedly without conscious aim " —
Kant's " Zweckmässigkeit ohne Zweck."

HERDER, J. G.   Sämmtliche Werke.   Hrsg. von B. Suphan.
     27 vols.   Berlin : 1877–81.

> Bd. I, pp. 43–56 Schönheit, Bd. IV, pp. 1–218 Kritische Wälder
> oder Betrachtungen über die Wissenschaft und Kunst des
> Schönen; Bd. XII, pp. 1–308 Vom Geist der Ebräischen Poesie ;
> Bd. XXII (Kalligone), pp. 3–122 Vom Angenehmen und Schönen,
> pp. 125–224 Von Kunst und Kunstrichterei, pp. 227–360 Vom
> Erhabenen und vom Ideal.

Although of great importance as an independent thinker in
the field of literature, Herder is known in aesthetics chiefly by
his criticisms of the view of Kant.   These will be found in the
Kalligone.

HOGARTH, WM.   The Analysis of Beauty.   London : 1753.

Of especial interest because of its influence upon the course
of modern speculation regarding the standard of taste.   Among
those who are indebted to it are Burke, Lessing, Reynolds, and
Goethe.   Bosanquet in his Hist. of Aesth., p. 208, assigns to
the work a high degree of importance, in that it " represents
the abstract principle of unity in variety on its highest level, so

as to form a point of transition to the analysis of the present century." (See Schasler, Gesch. d. Aesth., Thl. 1, pp. 307–313.)

HUME, D. Philosophical Works. 4 vols. Boston : 1854.

> Vol. II, pp. 30–36 Of Beauty and Deformity ; vol. III, pp. 211–216 Of Simplicity and Refinement in Writing, pp. 237–247 Of Tragedy, pp. 248–273 Of the Standard of Taste, pp. 217–522 Of Essay Writing.

Hume's utterances on questions of aesthetics are brief and fragmentary. They derive their interest partly from their intrinsic value and partly from the fact that they are by Hume. In writing upon Beauty and Deformity (in the Treatise on Human Nature) Hume rests his exposition mainly upon the principle of utility, though the utility of which he conceives is like the Kantian "purposiveness without purpose" and "pleasure without interest," in that it is devoid of selfishness on the part of the spectator. (See Bosanquet, Hist. of Aesth., pp. 178–180.)

JOUFFROY, TH. Cours d'Esthétique . . . Préface par Ph. Damiron. Paris : 1845.

A precise handling of the subject by a somewhat hard-headed disciple of Cousin. The point of view is psychological.

KANT, IMM. Sämmtliche Werke. Hrsg. von C. Hartenstein. 8 vols. Leipzig : 1867–8.

> Bd. II, pp. 227–280 Beobachtungen über das Gefühl des Schönen und Erhabenen ; Bd. V, pp. 205–368 Kritik der Aesthetischen Urtheilskraft ; Bd. VI, p. 386 Von der Aesthetik des Beurtheilsvermögens.

KANT, IMM. Critique du Jugement, suivie des Observations sur le Sentiment du Beau et du Sublime. Trad. par J. Barni. 2 vols. Paris : 1846.

Vol. I, pp. i–xvi Avant-propos du traducteur ; pp. 1–60 Introduction de l'auteur ; pp. 63–340 Critique du Jugement Esthétique (1790); vol. II, pp. 233–320 Observations sur le sentiment du Beau et du Sublime (1764).

KANT, IMM. Kritik of Judgment. Trans. by J. H. Bernard.
     London : 1892.

In the history of modern aesthetics the writings of Kant are
of the very highest degree of importance. In aesthetics, as in
other branches of philosophy, he is a kind of pivot upon which
all later speculation turns. His chief merit is that he attacks
with immense critical power the vital problem of his time. If
he does not succeed in solving the problem, yet he states it
with wonderful clearness, and divines the factors needful for
its solution.

The French translations of Imhoff (1796) and of Keratry and
Weyland (1823) attest the esteem in which this critique was held
by Kant's contemporaries. Barni's translation of the *Observations* is valuable ; the rest of his work is superseded by Bernard's.
For a clear and brief statement of Kant's aesthetical doctrine
of *Zweckmässigkeit ohne Zweck*, and of the position which the
Crit. Judgm. (analyzing phenomena of Feeling) occupies in
relation to the Crit. Pure Reason, and the Crit. Pract. Reason
(analyzing respectively the phenomena of Knowledge and of
Desire), see Bernard's introduction to his translation.

The obscurity of his style, and the difficulty of compre-
hending his philosophical doctrines in their entirety, have
made Kant's writings on aesthetics, except for specialists in philosophy, practically a sealed book. The first obstacle has now
in some measure been removed by the publication of Bernard's
translation of the Critique of Judgment, and the second has
been considerably diminished by the appearance of Caird's
Critical Philosophy of Kant (2 vols.; Glasgow: 1889) and
Bosanquet's History of Aesthetic.

KAMES, LORD. Elements of Criticism. New York: 1838.
     (Published 1761.)

Of interest to the student of the history of aesthetics because
of its influence upon Lessing. Kames's attempt at the discov-

ery of the characteristics of the object which arouse aesthetic
feelings, and at the analysis of these feelings, is, notwithstanding Fr. Vischer's condemnation of his work (Aesthetik, p. 106),
a contribution to the science.   His independence of judgment
and method, and his reference of the source of criticism to the
human soul are specially emphasized in W. Neumann's admirable
dissertation Die Bedeutung Home's für die Aesthetik u. s.
Einfluss auf die deutschen Aesthetiker (Halle: 1894).   Note
the indebtedness of Kames to Gerard's Essay on Taste (Edin-
burg: 1755–6).

KEDNEY, J. S.   The Beautiful and the Sublime.   New York:
    1880.

This is an interesting discussion of some of the leading problems of aesthetics.   The author's aim is to analyze the emotions
of the sublime and the beautiful, and to establish constructively
the objective character of beauty.   A critical supplement reviews the most important theories of the sublime and the beautiful.

KEDNEY, J. S.   Hegel's Aesthetics.   A Critical Exposition.
    Chicago: 1885.

This little work has value as being the only detailed exposition in English of the whole of Hegel's Aesthetik.   Unhappily
the author has followed the plan of substituting his own theories for those of Hegel at every point where he differs with the
latter, and the reader, although warned of the interpolated
matter by the insertion of brackets, cannot be sure whether the
impressions that he carries away from the work are those of the
expositor or the expounded.   Pages 114–181 are to be regarded
as an independent treatise by the author, in which no effort is
made to distinguish between his own views and those of Hegel.
Professor Kedney has called attention to this fact in the preface, but since few students are in the habit of consulting prefaces,

the information should have been repeated at the beginning of Part II. The remaining portion of the work is a fairly successful exposition, although serious errors of interpretation are not wanting. The author's criticism on p. 16 is clearly based upon a misreading of Hegel. (See Aesthetik, vol. I, pp. 58, 59.) The same is true of the bracketed paragraph, pp. 187, 188.

KER, W. P. The Philosophy of Art. (In Seth and Haldane's Essays in Philosophical Criticism. London: 1883.)

A finished and thoughtful paper. The trend of thought is Hegelian.

KNIGHT, WM. The Philosophy of the Beautiful (Part I): being Outlines of the History of Aesthetics. New York: 1891.

KNIGHT, WM. The Philosophy of the Beautiful (Part II): being a Contribution to its Theory, and to a Discussion of the Arts. London: 1893.

By the use of these university-extension manuals the student can lay an excellent foundation for more advanced study. In the first book the writer's aim is not to trace the evolution of aesthetics but merely to give an impartial account of the important theories in chronological order. As a guide to the literature of the subject it is without a superior. The second book undertakes to outline the fundamental principles of art and of the several arts of poetry, music, architecture, sculpture, painting, and dancing. The author's point of view is frankly idealistic, the "meagre doctrine" of the experimentalists receiving in this volume very little notice. Of especial value are the accounts of Dutch, Danish, and Russian aesthetics.

KÖSTLIN, K. Aesthetik. Tübingen: 1869.

Neither the idea of Art (as in Schleiermacher and Hegel) nor the idea of the Beautiful (as in more recent writers) covers the field of aesthetics. The former must be supplemented by the idea of Nature, the latter by that of the Aesthetic Subject in its relation to life. In his correlation of aesthetic form with the concrete world of forms lies Köstlin's contribution to the science.

KÖSTLIN, K. Prolegomena zur Aesthetik. Tübingen: 1889.

For Köstlin's Aesthetics, see *Zeitschrift für Philos.* 87 : 215 ; Von Hartmann's Aesthetik, vol. I, p. 305–317. The Prolegomena, a school-program of 103 pages, forms an excellent brief introduction to the study of Aesthetic. The principal subjects discussed are : Man's Interest in the World, the Meaning and Power of the Agreeable and the Disagreeable, the Beautiful, Taste, the Objectivity and the Relativity of Beauty. The starting-point is psychological. See, also, Köstlin's Ueber d. Schönheitsbegriff (60 pp. Tübingen : 1878).

LESSING, G. E. Werke. 20 vols. in 12. Berlin :

> Bd. VI Laokoon; Bd. VII Hamburgische Dramaturgie; Bd. XI, Abth. 1, 2 Kleinere Schriften zur dramatischen Poesie und zur Fabel ; Bd. XIII, Abth. 2, pp. 249–306 Wie die Alten den Tod gebildet, pp. 332–347 Anmerkungen zu Winckelmann's Geschichte der Kunst.

The Laocoon is indispensable whether as a historic landmark or as the ablest of all discussions of the boundaries of poetry and painting. It has the advantage also over many other German treatises of being perfectly intelligible to the beginner. The student should not hesitate to question the soundness of Lessing's conclusions, and should inquire especially as to the adequacy of the principle upon which he bases his canon of limitations. See Univ. of Mich. Philos. Papers, series II, No. 3 Lessing on the Boundaries of Poetry and Painting, by Professor E. L. Walter; H. Blümner's Laokoon-Studien (Freiburg i. B.: 1881–2); and the long and careful interpretation of Lessing in Bosanquet's Hist. of Aesth., pp. 216–238. The Laocoon has been translated by E. C. Beasley (Bohn Libr.)

and by Ellen Frothingham (Boston: 1890), and edited with notes by A. Hamann (Oxford: 1892). See, also, § **20**, under LESSING.

LEVÊQUE, CH.   La Science du Beau.   2e éd.   2 vols.   Paris: 1872.

This is the most systematic and comprehensive of the French treatises on aesthetics. Like Cousin the author belongs to the school of the *spiritualistes*. Consequently his treatment in many particulars resembles that of Hegel.

LONGINUS, D.   Quae Supersunt Graece et Latine.   Recens. . . . J. Toupius.   Acc. emend.   D. Ruhnkenii.   Editio altera.   Oxford: 1778.

LONGINUS, D.   On the Sublime.   Trans. by H. L. Havell. With an Introduction by Andrew Lang.   London: 1890.

The earliest work in which the Sublime is treated as a distinct aesthetic quality, within or beside the Beautiful. For a discussion of the date and authorship of the treatise, see Egger's Essai, pp. 426–9.

LOTZE, H.   Geschichte der Aesthetik in Deutschland.   München: 1868.

Treats of the German writers from Baumgarten down. The method adopted leads to three different surveys of the same subject-matter: First, with regard to the point of view from which the Beautiful has been discovered; second, with regard to the fundamental problems of aesthetics; third, with regard to the chronological sequence of theories.

LOTZE, H.   Microcosmus.   Trans. by E. Hamilton and E. E. C. Jones.   2 vols.   Edinburgh: 1885.

> Vol. I, pp. 324, 578–586; vol. II, pp. 168, 169 History and Poetry, pp. 398–443 Beauty and Art.

Mainly on types of beauty as conceived in different periods of civilization.

Lotze, H.　Outlines of Aesthetics.　Trans. by T. Ladd.
　　Boston: 1886.

A handy little volume, and easily obtainable, but one from
which the student will not carry away much that is of value unless he has previously acquired some acquaintance with Lotze's
philosophical point of view.　See Erdmann's or Ueberweg's
Hist. of Philosophy.

Marshall, H. R.　Pain, Pleasure, and Aesthetics.　An essay
　　concerning the Psychology of Pain and Pleasure, with
　　special reference to aesthetics.　New York: 1894.

This is, in the main, a reprint of essays published in *Mind*.
The portion dealing directly with aesthetics appeared in vol. I,
N.S., pp. 358–378, 453–469 ; vol. II, N.S., pp. 15–41.

In order to secure a proper basis for his theory, Mr. Marshall first discusses the broad subject of the feelings of pleasure and pain.　In this part of his treatise he makes many
acute criticisms of Allen, Spencer, and other recognized authorities.　Aesthetics is then classified as a division of hedon-
ics, and the following definition of the aesthetic field is proposed : " Each one's field of aesthetic judgment is his relatively
permanent pleasure-field of revival."　The remainder of the
work is largely taken up with an exposition of aesthetic laws,
which are divided into negative and positive.　The handling of
the subject is unusually able and suggestive.

A still clearer exposition will be found in the author's
Aesthetic Principles (New York : 1895).

Menendez y Pelayo, M.　Historia de las ideas estéticas en
　　España.　5 vols. in 8.　Madrid: 1883–91.

The standard work on the history of Spanish aesthetics.　It
includes also valuable chapters on writers of other nationalities,
ancient and modern; thus : Vol. I, pp. 1–156 Greek and Roman writers ; vol. III, pt. I, pp. 1–153 French and German

writers of the 18th century; vol. IV, pt. I German aesthetics of the 19th century; pt. II English and French aesthetics.

The work is as yet unfinished.

MORRIS, G. S.   *J. Spec. Philos.* 10 : 1 Philosophy of Art.

A lecture read before a class who were studying Taine's Philosophy of Art. Besides being a careful criticism of Taine's philosophical position, it is one of the best brief expositions of the philosophy of art anywhere to be found.

MORRIS, WM.   Hopes and Fears for Art.   Boston : 1882.

> Pp. 1–37 The Lesser Arts, pp. 38–70 The Art of the People, pp. 71–113 The Beauty of Life, pp. 114–168 Making the Best of it, pp. 169–217 The Prospects of Architecture in Civilization.

MORRIS, WM.   Lectures on Art.   3d ed.   London : 1883.

MORRIS, WM.   *New Review* 4 : 1 The Socialist Ideal — Art. (See, also, Mr. W. H. Mallock's reply to Morris in *New Review* 4 : 100 The Individualist Ideal.)

Morris is mainly interested in the social aspects of art, a subject which he treats not only with the grace and finish of the literary artist, but also with the insight of the philosopher.

PATER, WALTER.   Studies in the History of the Renaissance. London : 1873.

See especially the Preface, the Conclusion, and the essay on Winckelmann.

PLATO.   The Dialogues of Plato.   Trans. by B. Jowett.   3d ed. 5 vols.   London and New York : 1892.

> Vol. I, Ion, Phaedo, Symposium, Phaedrus ; vol. II, Republic (bk. II, 376–383 ; bk. III, 386–404 ; bk. VII ; bk. IX, 580–591 ; bk. X, 595–608) ; vol. III, Gorgias, Philebus ; vol. IV, Laws (bk. II ; bk. IV, 719 ; bk. VII, 796–803, 811–17 ; bk. VIII, 829). The figures refer to the marginal numbers.

With these dialogues the student of the history of aesthetics may properly begin his reading, and to them he will in the course of his studies return again and again with renewed delight. " Consciously, or unconsciously," says Professor Knight, " all idealism draws its inspiration from Plato." It will be no small part of the student's task to trace the influence of the Platonic doctrine of art — its relation to Nature and the Idea, and its function in Education — upon the aesthetics of the ancients. Its influence, also, upon Goethe, Schopenhauer, Ruskin, and other modern writers, will demand historico-critical investigation. See the treatment of Plato in Bosanquet and Schasler, and the analysis of his Theory of Imitation in § 9 below.

The following are some of the most important monographs on the Platonic aesthetics: Ed. Müller, Ueber das Nachahmende in d. Kunst nach Plato (Ratibor: 1831); A. Ruge, Die Platonische Aesthetik (Halle: 1832); Ch. Lévêque, Platon, fondateur de l'esthétique (Paris: 1857); K. Justi, Die aesth. Elemente in d. Platon. Philos. (Marburg: 1860); Jos. Reber, Plato und die Poesie (München: 1864); M. Remy, Plat. doct. de Artibus liberalibus (Halle: 1864); A. H. Raabe, De Poetica Plat. (Rotterdam: 1866); C. von Jan, Die Tonarten bei Plato (in *Neue Jahrb. f. Philol. u. Paed.*, 95: 815).

PLOTINUS. Opera. Recognovit A. Kirchoff. 2 vols. Leipzig: 1856.

PLOTINUS. Opera Omnia, cura Creuzer. 3 vols. London: 1862. (Creuzer, Moser, Dübner, Paris: 1855, cum Marsilii Ficini interpretatione.)

PLOTINUS. Liber de Pulchritudine (ed. Creuzer). Heidelberg: 1814. (Ennead 1. 6.)

The greatest of the neo-Platonic philosophers. His observations on beauty are scattered through the Enneads; but Ennead 1. 6 (on the Beautiful) and 5. 8 (on Spiritual Beauty) are wholly occupied with the subject. On his aesthetic see R. Volkmann's Die Höhe d. antiken Aesthetik oder Plotin's

Abhandlung vom Schönen (1860); Bosanquet's Hist. of Aesth.,
pp. 111–118 ; E. Brenning's Die Lehre vom Schönen bei Plotin
im Zusammenhang seines Systems dargestellt (Göttingen:
1864); Ed. Müller's Geschichte d. Theor. d. Kunst, vol. II ;
A. J. Vitringa, De egregio, quod in rebus corporeis constituit
Plotinus, pulcri principio (1864); and works cited in A. Richter's
Neu-Platonische Studien (Halle: 1864–7), Hft. 1, pp. 13–15 ;
Hft. 2, pp. iv–vi.   For Richter's exposition of the aesthetics
of Plotinus, see Die Ethik des Plotins (1867).

A French translation of the Enneads by Bouillet appeared in
Paris in 1857–61.   There is a German translation by H. F.
Müller (Berlin: 1878–80).   Thomas Taylor translated Plotinus
on the Beautiful into English, London: 1787 ; Five Books of
Plotinus, London: 1794 ; and Select Works of Plotinus, Lon-
don: 1817.   For other translations see Richter's Neu-Platonische
Studien, as above.   A translation of Ennead 1. 6, by Thomas
Davidson, may be found in the *Platonist.*

REYNOLDS, SIR JOSHUA.   Literary Works.   2 vols.   London ;
     1852 (Bohn Libr.).

     Discourses on Art, and Three Letters to the Idler.

Reynolds reduces our pleasure in beauty to mere force of
custom.   " If we were more used to deformity than Beauty,
deformity would then lose the idea now annexed to it, and take
that of Beauty."   He also advances the idea of a beauty of
typical form — " beauty is the medium or center of all various
forms " — which appeared later under different aspects in
Goethe, Taine, and Ruskin.

RICHTER, JEAN PAUL.   Vorschule der Aesthetik.   3 vols.   Stutt-
     gart: 1813.

Like Schiller and W. von Humboldt, Jean Paul is important
as a popular aesthetician.   Although failing in logical precision
and method he has contributed in an intuitive fashion to
aesthetic theory.   For his distinction between imagination and

fancy, and between the sublime and the comic, see Schasler, pp. 671, 695.

RUSKIN, J.　" A Joy Forever " (And its Price in the Market) : being the Substance (with Additions) of two Lectures on the Political Economy of Art.　Orpington: 1880.

RUSKIN, J.　Arrows of the Chace.　2 vols.　Orpington: 1880.

> Vol. I, pp. 3–252 Letters on Art, 3–50 Art Criticism and Art Education, 53–82 Public Institutions and the National Gallery, 85–114 Pre-Raphaelitism, 117–158 Turner, 161–178 Pictures and Artists, 181–252 Architecture and Restoration ; vol. II, pp. 235–264 Literary Criticism.

RUSKIN, J.　Lectures on Architecture and Painting.　New York : 1856.

RUSKIN, J.　Modern Painters.　5 vols.　Orpington: 1887.

RUSKIN, J.　On the Old Road.　2 vols. in 3.　Orpington: 1885.

> Vol. I, pt. I, pp. 21–132 Lindsay's Christian Art, 133–205 Eastlake's History of Oil Painting, 329–348 Pre-Raphaelitism, 349–400 Architecture ; pt. II, 405–438 Address at Cambridge School of Art, 549–624 Picture Galleries, 643–698 Minor Writings upon Art; vol. II, pp. 3–166 Fiction Fair and Foul, 167–176 Fairy Stories.

RUSKIN, J.　Seven Lamps of Architecture.　New York: 1859.

RUSKIN, J.　Stones of Venice.　3 vols.　New York: 1860.

RUSKIN, J.　The Eagle's Nest.　Ten Lectures on the Relation of Natural Science to Art.　Orpington: 1880.

RUSKIN, J.　The Two Paths : being Lectures on Art, and its Application to Decoration and Manufacture.　Orpington : 1884.

RUSKIN, J.　Aratra Pentelici : Six Lectures on the Elements of Sculpture, delivered at Oxford.　1870.

The reading of Ruskin is a powerful stimulus to the sense for beauty, but a bad propædeutic to the science of aesthetics. Ruskin's dogmatism, eccentricity, and exaggeration are contagious, and make upon the novice impressions from which he

does not readily recover.   A careful study of the relations of
art to ethics, and the acquisition of sound views on the main
questions of political economy, will fortify the student against
Ruskin's most harmful perversities.   Leslie Stephen's article
(*Fraser* 89 : 688) on Ruskin's later works, and a criticism of
the third volume of the Modern Painters by C. C. Everett in
No. Am. 84 : 379, may be recommended.   Milsand's L'Es-
thétique Anglaise is perhaps the most thorough criticism of
Ruskin's Aesthetics as a whole.   See, also, P. Bayne, essays in
Biography and Criticism, 1st ser., pp. 281–333, and Lessons
from My Masters, by the same author, pp. 380–449 ; A. H.
Japp's Three Great Teachers, pp. 187–243 ; and Bosanquet's
Hist. of Aesth., pp. 447–460.   The best of Ruskin is in vols. I–
III of Modern Painters.

SCHASLER, M.   Aesthetik (*Das Wissen der Gegenwart*, Bd. 55).
    1886.

SCHASLER, M.   Das System der Künste aus e. neuen, im Wesen
    der Kunst begründeten Gliederungsprincip. 2. Aufl. Leip-
    zig : 1885.

SCHASLER, M.   Grundzüge d. Wissenschaft d. Schönen und der
    Kunst. 2 vols. 1886.

SCHASLER, M.   Kritische Geschichte der Aesthetik.   2 vols.
    Berlin : 1872.

Schasler's Geschichte is the standard work on the general
history of aesthetics.   On the whole it is remarkably comprehensive, though important names in French and English aesthetics are conspicuously absent.   The place of an index is in part
supplied by a very full table of contents.   For German Aesthetics since Kant, Lotze's and Von Hartmann's histories are more
complete in some ways, the latter bringing the history down to
very recent times.   Schasler's work has not been translated into
English.   For a criticism of certain portions, see Bosanquet's
Hist. of Aesth., pp. 166 ff., 180–182, 246,

SCHELLING, F. W. J. VON. Sämmtliche Werke. Stuttgart:
1856–61.

> Bd. V, Abth. 1, p. 357 Philosophie der Kunst ; Bd. VII, Abth. 1,
> pp. 289–329 Ueber das Verhältniss der bildenden Künste zu der
> Natur.

The objective idealism of Schelling is derived from Kant and
Schiller on the one hand, from Winckelmann on the other.
For his theory of art and its influence upon Hegel, see Bosan-
quet's Hist. of Aesth., pp. 316–334; Watson's Schelling's
Transcendental Idealism (Chicago : 1882), pp. 181–190; von
Hartmann's Deutsche Aesthetik, pp. 27–44 (*abstract* idealism);
Schasler, pp. 827–870.

SCHILLER, J. C. F. Sämmtliche Werke. 12 vols. in 6. Stuttgart : 1847.

> Bd. V, pp. 375–383 Ueber den Gebrauch des Chors in der Tragö-
> die ; Bd. XI, pp. 383–483 ; Bd. XII Aesthetische Schriften.

SCHILLER, J. C. F. The Aesthetic Letters, Essays, and the
Philosophical Letters. Translated, with an Introduction,
by J. Weiss. Boston : 1845.

SCHILLER, J. C. F. Works : Historical Dramas, etc. Trans.
London : 1854.

> Pp. 439–444 On the Use of the Chorus in Tragedy.

Most of Schiller's aesthetic writings, and especially his Aesthetic Letters, are well adapted to the understanding of beginners. Their place in the history of Aesthetics, however, can be
appreciated only when they are read in the light of Kant's
Critique of Judgment, from which their material is principally
drawn. Attention may be called to Schiller's treatment of the
play-impulse (Spieltrieb), and the development of the same idea
by Herbert Spencer. On his theory of Poetry see note under
SCHILLER, § **20.**

Schlegel, A. W. von. Kritische Schriften. 2 vols. Berlin: 1828.

Theil 1, pp. 416–436 ; Theil 2, pp. 145–336.

Schlegel, F. von. The Aesthetic and Miscellaneous Works. Trans. by E. J. Millington. London : 1860. (Bohn Libr.)

Pp. 413–424 On the Limits of the Beautiful. See, also, Index.

On the Schlegels, see Hegel's criticism, Aesthetik, vol. I, pp. 83–90 (Bosanquet's translation, pp. 120–132).

Schopenhauer, A. Sämmtliche Werke. Hrsg. von J. Frauen-städt. 6 vols. Leipzig : 1877.

Bd. II, pp. 197–316 Object der Kunst ; Bd. III, pp. 99–112 ; The-orie des Lächerlichen ; Bd. VI, pp. 447, 448 Metaphysik des Schönen und Aesthetik, 536–586 Schriftstellerei und Stil.

Schopenhauer, A. The World as Will and Idea. Trans. by R. B. Haldane and J. Kemp. 3 vols. London : 1883.

Vol. I, pp. 219–346 The object of Art ; vol. II, pp. 270–284 Theory of the Ludicrous; vol. III, pp. 173–219, 231–244 Aesthetics.

Perhaps the most readable and entertaining of modern writers on aesthetics, but valuable rather for his remarks by the way than for his system as a whole. Indeed, the reader will do well to guard himself against the seductions of Schopenhauer's brilliant logic by some previous study of his philosophical standpoint. Cf. especially his theory of ideas with that of Plato. In his treatment of the ludicrous Schopenhauer has made a real contribution to aesthetic doctrine. See Everett's Poetry, Comedy, and Duty, p. 171 *et seq.*

Shaftesbury, Cooper, A. A., 3d Earl of. Characteristicks. 3 vols. 1749.

Vol. I, pp. 3–38 Enthusiasm, 41–101 Wit and Humor, 105–245 Advice to an Author; vol. III, pp. 5–233 Miscellaneous, 269–279 Art of Design. See, also, index, vol. III, following p. 267.

Shaftesbury is a kind of Christian Platonist on a small scale. He divides the field of experience into the True, the Good, and the Beautiful, but makes confusion by attempting to bring the second division under the third. Bosanquet (Hist. of Aesth., p. 178) points out in Shaftesbury an interesting anticipation of Lessing's Laocoön.

SOLGER, K. W. F.   Vorlesungen über die Aesthetik.   Leipzig: 1829.

For characterization see Schasler, pp. 875–910.   His aesthetic resembles that of Schelling in its symbolic and allegorical tendency.   On Solger's doctrine of the affinity of the *ugly* for certain phases of the beautiful see Bosanquet, pp. 394–397.

SPENCER, H.   The Principles of Psychology.   2 vols.   New York: 1885.

> Vol. I, pp. 272–290 Pleasures and Pains, 472–494 The Feelings ; vol. II, pp. 539–557 Language of the Emotions, 627–648 The Aesthetic Sentiments.

SPENCER, H.   Education.   New York: 1883.

> Pp. 71–84.

SPENCER, H.   Essays: Moral, Political, and Aesthetic.   New York: 1873.

> P. 9, Philos. of Style, 149 Personal Beauty, 312 Gracefulness.

SPENCER, H.   Essays: Scientific, Political, and Speculative.

> Philos. of Style, Origin and Function of Music, Physiology of Laughter.

SPENCER, H.   Illustrations of Universal Progress.   (Repr. of preceding.)

Spencer's starting-point is Schiller's Spieltrieb, which he develops in its physiological and psychological bearings.   His theory of the ludicrous, set forth in the essay entitled Physiology of Laughter, has been much discussed.   His doctrine of economy is, perhaps, his most important contribution to aesthetics.

SULLY, J.   'Aesthetics,' in Encyclopaedia Britannica.   9th ed.

SULLY, J.　Sensation and Intuition: Studies in Psychology and
　　　Aesthetics.　London: 1874.

　　　　Essays: 7–9 Music, 10 Aesthetic Aspects of Character, 11 Char-
　　　　acter in Art, 12 Lessing's Hamburg Dramaturgy, 13 Possibility
　　　　of a Science of Aesthetics.

SULLY, J.　Outlines of Psychology.　London: 1884.

　　　　Pp. 316–329, 531–552.

SULLY, J.　*Mind*, 4: 172 Harmony of Colors.

SULLY, J.　*Mind*, 1 : 479 Art and Psychology.

　　Sully is one of the ablest and clearest of modern writers on
aesthetics.　He is a mild empiricist, a psychologist of the
school of Herbert Spencer, and hence somewhat intolerant of
what he calls "metaphysical speculation."　Essay 13 of Sensation and Intuition, and the first part of the article in the Encyclopaedia Britannica, will be of especial value to those who
are seeking for a statement of the scientific problems of aesthetics.

TAINE, H.　The Ideal in Art.　Trans. by J. Durand.　New
　　　York: 1869.

TAINE, H.　Italy, Florence, and Venice.　Trans. by J. Durand.
　　　New York: 1869.

　　　　Pp. 98–159 Florentine School of Art, 272–327 Venetian Art.

TAINE, H.　Italy, Naples, and Rome.　Trans. by J. Durand.
　　　London: 1867.

TAINE, H.　Lectures on Art.　Trans. by J. Durand.　2d ser.
　　　(Italy, the Netherlands, Greece.)　New York: 1877.

TAINE, H.　The Philosophy of Art.　London: 1867.

　　According to Brunetière, Taine has put in circulation more
new and suggestive ideas upon art than any writer since Hegel.
In two points this statement is open to question.　It may be
doubted whether his ideas were strikingly original, and it may

also be doubted whether they were numerous.   But with regard
to their superior suggestiveness Brunetière is unquestionably in
the right.   Taine's views have aroused more criticism, friendly
or hostile, and set more brains at work upon problems of aesthetics, than the views of any other writer of the time.   For
this reason, if for no other, the student should become familiar
with his writings.

For criticisms of Taine see *J. Spec. Philos.* 10 : 1 ; Colvin's
article on Fine Art in *Encyc. Brit.*, vol. IX, p. 214 ; Brunetière's
L'Évolution des Genres, etc., vol. I, pp. 245–278 ; Edm. Scher-
er's Étude Critique, vol. IV, pp. 253–272 ; Amiel's *Journal
Intime*, vol. II, p. 111 ; J. Fiske's The Unseen World and other
Essays (Boston : 1876), p. 280 ; Sainte-Beuve, Causeries de
Lundi (in Essays of Sainte-Beuve, translated by Eliz. Lee,
London : 1894) ; C. de Mazade, *Rev. d. D. Mondes*, 15 Juillet
1867, p. 499.

VAN DYKE, J. C.   Principles of Art.   New York : 1887.

A brief manual in which will be found clear statements of the
leading problems in art.   See especially pp. 173–199.   The
work is in two parts, the first dealing with art in history, the
second with art in theory.

VERON, E.   Aesthetics.   Trans. by W. H. Armstrong.   London : 1879.

The author was long the editor of *L'Art*, the leading French
art journal, and his treatment of aesthetics is colored largely by
his bent toward pictorial art.   His consideration of other forms
of art, especially of literature, is inadequate to their importance.
The work, as a whole, is rambling and exclamatory, but full of
suggestion drawn from long experience as critic.   The English
translation is good, and easily to be procured.   An interesting
but not altogether trustworthy essay on Plato's Aesthetics forms
an appendix to the volume.

VISCHER, F. T. Aesthetik oder Wissenschaft des Schönen. 3
    vols. Reutlingen: 1846.

The truly German proportions of Vischer's work, and the
juicelessness of his style, are likely to deter any except the
most determined student of aesthetics from examining what is
undoubtedly one of the ablest treatises on the subject in any
language. Fortunately the value of the work lies rather in the
elaboration of the details than in the system, and a full table of
contents, and an astonishingly complete index, enable the student to find whatever topic he desires. (As an example of his
comprehensiveness, see index under Shakespeare.) As Schasler points out, Vischer is particularly fruitful in his treatment
of the beauty of nature. See vol. II, pp. 3–78. For his treatment of the relations of nature to art, see vol. III, pp. 77–86.
A criticism of Vischer may be found in Schasler, vol. II, p. 1040,
or briefer, p. 1087.

XENOPHON. The Anabasis . . and the Memorabilia (Bohn Libr.).

> Pp. 447–450 Socrates on Beauty, 454–456 Painting and Sculpture,
> 499 Beauty.

XENOPHON. Minor Works.

> Pp. 176–178 Banquet, chap. V.

These are the sources for the aesthetics of Socrates. Especial attention should be given to the idea of utility, or purpose, as standard of beauty, presented in the passages of the
Memorabilia referred to above.

§ 9. GENERAL NOTE.

I. Courses of study. — In suggesting a course of study in
the theory of art, as an introduction to the study of literary
criticism, account must be taken of two pretty distinct classes
of students : first, those who prefer to take their opinions from
trustworthy authorities without being put to much expense of

time and trouble ; second, those who, desiring to form for
themselves an independent judgment, are determined to go to
the bottom of the matter at whatever cost.   These two classes,
since their aims are different, will of necessity pursue their
studies in a somewhat different order and according to different methods.

A. GENERAL READING. — 1. Every student, whatever his purpose may be, will do well to learn, at the outset, the limits of
the subject he is to pursue.   He should learn also the most
important problems that are likely to arise in the course of his
study, and should make himself acquainted with the names of
the recognized authorities.   These facts may be gleaned from
the preface (better, from the whole) of Professor Knight's
Philosophy of the Beautiful, Part I,[1] from chapter I of Bosanquet's History of Aesthetic, from Hamerton's Portfolio Papers,
p. 163 ff., or from the articles on Art, Fine Art, and Aesthetics
in the 9th edition of the Encyclopaedia Britannica.   The student who is taking a general survey of the subject, when he
has thus got his bearings in the science, should next try to
gain some familiarity with its psychology and its philosophy.
On the first, such works as Dewey's Psychology, chapters VII
and IX, Sully's Outlines of Psychology, pp. 316–329, 531–552,
and Höffding's Outlines (translated by Mary E. Lowndes,
London: 1891), pp. 274–387, may profitably be consulted ; or,
if these prove too abstruse for the beginner, a gentler approach
is open to him through the first chapter of Everett's Poetry,
Comedy, and Duty, or the article in *Mind* 1 : 479 on Art and
Psychology.

For the philosophical treatment, Knight's Philosophy of the
Beautiful, Part II, and Baldwin Brown's The Fine Arts will be

[1] For details of bibliography, see the references under § **8,** and for further references, if they are desired, consult A Guide to the Literature of Aesthetics, by C. M.
Gayley and F. N. Scott (Berkeley: 1890).

found especially serviceable. Both are admirable in spirit, and so elementary in character that they may be understood and enjoyed by any one. On the same plane is an article by Professor Seeley in *Macmillan's* 16 : 1 Elementary Principles of Art. More difficult to follow, but well worth the extra effort, are the lecture by Professor G. S. Morris in *Jl. Spec. Philos.* 10 : 1 on the Philosophy of Art, and the paper on Art, by W. P. Ker, in Seth and Haldane's Essays in Philosophical Criticism (London : 1883).

The student who has read the foregoing with intelligence and appreciation has made a fair beginning. He has done more, perhaps, than the majority of those who enter upon the advanced study of literature. Should he wish, however, to continue his reading, the following suggestions may be helpful.

2. Of the writings that fill an important place in the history of aesthetics, there are many which can be properly understood only in connection with the philosophical systems of which they form component parts. Though profoundly interesting to the specialist, the casual reader is apt to find them obscure and contradictory. But it sometimes happens that of an abstruse treatise some part is fairly well adapted to the needs of the general reader. Such, for example, is the Introduction to Hegel's Aesthetik. This valuable work is now available in an excellent translation (by Bernard Bosanquet, London : 1886), and should be in the hands of every student. Others of these important contributions to the history of aesthetic are of a semi-popular character throughout. To this class belongs Goethe's Conversations with Eckermann. In this fascinating work almost all the main questions of art-theory are touched upon and rendered luminous. In the same category may be placed Schiller's Aesthetic Letters, which, by their enthusiasm and the charm of their style, carry the student into philosophic deeps that with another companion he might not venture to explore. More readable still are the aesthetic

writings of Schopenhauer, most brilliant and entertaining of modern philosophers, the value of whose works, however, lies rather in remarks by the way than in main conclusions. Lessing's Laocoon is delightful reading, and not less important as a contribution to aesthetics than as a contribution to literature. Cousin's lectures on the True, the Beautiful, and the Good, which at one time enjoyed no little vogue as a text-book, are written in popular form, but cannot be recommended as an adequate presentation of aesthetic theory. Ruskin is, of course, read by every one, and should be; but, by the beginner, he should be read rather for his descriptions than for his philosophy. As a corrective of over-enthusiasm for Ruskin may be read Miss Paget's article on Ruskinism, in Belcaro. In seeking to rectify Ruskin's moral bias, Miss Paget goes far in the opposite direction. A careful yet popular criticism of the third volume of Modern Painters will be found in an article by Professor Everett in *No. Am.* 84 : 379.

3. To make popular expositions of the results of aesthetic speculation has been the aim of many writers. A few of these will be referred to. Miss Paget (Vernon Lee) writes with a capricious self-assurance that makes her occasional essays charming literature. They are interesting, however, rather as recording the shifting moods of a sensitive personality than as constituting careful and connected thinking about art. Belcaro (London : 1886) and Juvenilia (London : 1887), collections of articles upon sculpture, music, and poetry, originally printed in the English magazines, are full of fresh and striking observations. Miss Paget's most ambitious flight is an article on Comparative Aesthetics, in *Contemp.* 38 : 300, a not altogether successful attempt to weld Hegel and Taine. It is an interesting article, and exceedingly suggestive to beginners. The essay on the Value of the Ideal, in Baldwin (London : 1886), defines pretty clearly her philosophical position, in so far as she can be said to have one. Walter Pater's delicacy of

intuition leads him to safe conclusions even where his writings seem mere transcripts of impression. The fundamental principle of his aesthetic is perhaps most clearly set forth in his essay on Style, in Appreciations (London : 1889). In connection with this essay should be read the introduction and conclusion of his Studies in the History of the Renaissance, and the essay on Winckelmann, published in the same volume. Based upon a consistent and easily comprehensible theory of art, are the critical writings of J. A. Symonds. In one or two places the author has stated them with some explicitness; for example, in the Renaissance in Italy, the Catholic Reaction, Part II, pp. 396–402, and Essays, Speculative and Suggestive (London : 1890). Upon the last-named work, see the criticism in *Nation* 51 : 173. [The younger Symonds should not be confused with J. A. Symonds, M.D., author of Principles of Beauty (London : 1857).] Less speculative, and more scientific are the writings of Edmund Gurney, whose magazine articles have been collected in the Power of Sound (London : 1880) and Tertium Quid (2 v. London : 1887). The third chapter of the Power of Sound is an exposition of the author's aesthetics. Sully is not to be mentioned in the category of the merely popular, though the clearness and simplicity of his treatment of difficult matters adapt his writings to the needs of the beginner. His Sensation and Intuition presents the scientific aspect of many important questions.

4. Inquiries are often made by students for some popular compend which shall embrace within its covers all the information about art that any one need acquire. It is hardly necessary to say that all such hopes are vain; no such book exists or ever will exist. Nevertheless, as popular compends have their value, some of the most notable will be briefly indicated. Day's Science of Aesthetics (New York : 1876), being designed for a text-book, deals mainly in formal definitions and classifications. Samson's Elements of Art

Criticism, recently reissued in condensed form, aims at great comprehensiveness, but really does little more than bring into juxtaposition unrelated details. Harris's Theory of the Arts is largely composed of commonplaces grouped about a theory of no great worth or coördinating power. McDermot's Critical Dissertation is clear enough, but antiquated. The popularity enjoyed by Bascom's Aesthetics (New York: 1886) has been deserved by the lucidity and readableness of the text. The prominence given to the author's ethical and theological views may seem to some a trifle obtrusive. Van Dyke's Principles of Art covers much ground, but is restricted by its small compass to a brief treatment of the separate topics. A useful primer of art is Lucy Crane's Lectures on Art and the Formation of Taste (Six Lectures. Illustr. by T. & W. Crane. London: 1882).

Of the French compends, Gauckler's Le Beau is perhaps the simplest and handiest. Veron aims to cover the whole field of speculation, but is exceedingly unsystematic.

In the German language, Lemcke's Populäre Aesthetik, although condemned by Schasler as trivial and conventional, is about the best thing of the kind to be obtained. Other German compends are Stöckel's Allg. Lehrbuch d. Aesthetik (3. Aufl. Mainz: 1889) and Prölss's Katechismus d. Aesthetik (2. Aufl. Leipzig: 1889).

B. **Suggestions for Historical Study.** — 1. For the second class of students, those who desire to make themselves thoroughly at home in this subject, there is no method so satisfactory as the historical. First obtaining a general view of the science in the manner recommended above (§ **9,** *A*), let the student resolutely attack the aesthetic doctrines of *the Greeks.* The theories of Socrates may be gathered from Xenophon's Memorabilia and Banquet. Of Plato's dialogues, the Ion, Phaedo, Symposium, Gorgias, and Philebus should be read

entire, and at least books II, III, VII–X of the Republic.
Jowett's translation of the dialogues is, of course, unrivaled,
except in the case of the Republic, where it shares honors with
that of Davies and Vaughan. Aristotle's Poetics should be
studied, if possible, in the original. Of the translations, Wharton's is by far the best.[1] The passages of the Rhetoric, Metaphysics, and Psychology that throw light on Aristotle's theory
of art, should not escape attention. The writings of Plotinus
and Longinus are important for the history of aesthetics, but if
time presses may be left for later investigation.

2. The *Germans* should next receive attention. In taking
up the German authorities, it is desirable that some acquaintance should first be formed with the theories and results of
Baumgarten (Aesthetica, Frankfurt a. d. Oder: 1750–58), Lessing, and Winckelmann. All of the Laokoon should be read,
and of Winckelmann's History of Greek Art, at least the Introduction. Passing then to Kant, the student should master the
principles of the Kritik der Aesthetischen Urtheilskraft by a
reading of the text in the original or in Bernard's translation,
or by a careful study of Caird's Critical Philosophy of Kant,
vol. II, pp. 420–476. The aesthetic writings of Goethe and
Schiller may next be taken up. Much of Goethe's writing on
aesthetics is still untranslated, as, for example, the Deutsche
Baukunst; but the Conversations, the Correspondence with
Schiller, Wahrheit und Dichtung, and several of the shorter
essays may be had in fair English translations. Schiller may
be read in Weiss's translation or in the Bohn Library edition.
Especial attention should be directed to Schiller's indebtedness
to Kant, and to his advance upon the latter. Schelling's Philosophie der Kunst, of considerable importance in the historical
sequence, must be read in the original, if read at all. With
Hegel's Vorlesungen über die Aesthetik the student should

---

[1] A new translation by Professor S. H. Butcher, which has just appeared (London:
1895), takes rank with Wharton's. See § 20 under ARISTOTLE.

make himself thoroughly at home. If it is too much to ask of
the student that he read the Aesthetik entire — a task which
will amply repay him for his time — let him at least read all the
available translations. Bosanquet's admirable rendering of the
Einleitung and Eintheilung puts in the student's hands the key to
the entire work. Hastie has translated pp. 1–30 of the Einleitung
and pp. 105–114 of the Eintheilung. Kedney's exposition
goes over the whole Aesthetik, but has serious limitations,
which are pointed out above in § **8.** Much translation of
Hegel's Aesthetik, made through the medium of a French paraphrase, will be found in the *Jl. Spec. Philos.* For reference
to it, see § **8,** under Hegel.

Of the remaining German writers Schopenhauer and Lotze
may be read in translation. Then follows a long list of those
whose works have not been translated, and perhaps will never
be translated, such as Ruge (Neue Vorschule d. Aesth. Halle:
1837), Schleiermacher (Vorles. üb. Aesth. Berlin: 1842), Solger, Richter, Weisse (System d. Aesth. als Wissensch. v. d.
Idee d. Schönen. Leipzig: 1830), Vischer, whose monster
treatise is a complete encyclopaedia of aesthetic theory, Krause
(System der Aesthetik. Leipzig: 1882), Zimmermann (Allgemeine Aesthetik. 2 vols.: 1858–65), Carriere (one of the most
popular of German writers), Schasler, Köstlin, Von Kirchmann
(Aesth. auf realistischer Grundl. Berlin: 1869), Horwicz
(Grundl. e. Systems d. Aesthetik. Leipzig: 1869), and Siebeck
(Das Wesen d. aesth. Anschauung. Berlin: 1875). Trahn-
dorff (Aesthetik. 2 vols. Berlin: 1830) has been revived by
Von Hartmann (*Philos. Monatshefte* 22: 59), but hardly seems
entitled to the space allotted to him by the latter in his Aesthetik (I. 129–156). Herbart's wide-reaching influence in psychology makes it desirable to know something of his aesthetics,
in which he includes his ethical theory. Zeising's name (Aesthetische Forschungen. Frankfurt a. M.: 1855) is so identified
with the 'golden section' that his other theories are generally

neglected. Though his standpoint is Hegelian, his aesthetic is influenced by Herbart. The psychophysicist, Fechner, who has verified by elaborate experiment the discovery of Zeising, represents a revolt against the method of speculative aesthetics. The investigations of Helmholtz with reference to the physiology of sound and of light (Optique Physiologique. Paris : 1867) are indispensable to the specialist. Wherever he has expanded his theories in systematic form, Helmholtz has followed the lines laid down by Kant in his Critique of Judgment. The most formidable, and at the same time one of the ablest, of late contributions to aesthetics, is the systematic treatise of Von Hartmann. It is defective in that it gives little or no space to art in its historical aspect.

3. Among the *French writers*, P. André (Traité sur le beau, in Œuvres Philos. Paris : 1843), Buffier (Sur la Nature du Goût, in Cours général et particulier des Sciences. Paris : 1732), Batteux (Les Beaux Arts réduits à un même principe. Paris : 1747), and Diderot, in the last century ; and Cousin, Jouffroy, Pictet (Du Beau dans la Nature. Paris : 1856), Lévêque, Chaignet (Principes de la Science du Beau. Paris : 1860), Prudhomme (L'Expression dans les Beaux-Arts. Paris : 1883), Taine, and Veron, in the present century, have the strongest claim to attention. Of the whole number the treatise of Lévêque is the most systematic. Chaignet is most interested in the psychology of aesthetics. The brilliancy of Taine's style, and the glib simplicity of his system, have made his theories better known in this country than those of any other foreign writer. His *caractère essentiel* should be compared with Herder's Bedeutsame, Hirt's Charakteristische, and Goethe's Bedeutende.[1] (See Schasler's Gesch. d. Aesth., vol. I, pp. 498,

---

[1] For his celebrated formula of the race, the moment, and the environment, Taine was indebted to Hegel's Aesth., vol. I, p. 20 : "Sodann gehört jedes Kunstwerk seiner Zeit, seinem Volke, seiner Umgebung an." Brunetière, who adds to the three conditions specified by Taine the element of individuality (L'Évolution des Genres dans l'Histoire de la Litt., vol. I, p. 22), seems also to have been anticipated by Hegel,

499, Hegel's Aesth., vol. I, pp. 23–26, Bosanquet's translation, pp. 31–37.)

Of late writers who have discussed special topics with ability should be mentioned Bénard, Milsand, Guyau, Séailles, Lechalas, Souriau, Charles Henry, Arréat, Paulhan, and Sorel. All have been frequent contributors to the *Rev. d. D. Mondes*, or the *Rev. Philosophique.* Bénard represents the Hegelian influence. Henry inclines to the mathematical interpretation of aesthetic facts. Sorel is a follower of Fechner. The writings of Guyau throw much light on the social aspect of art.

4. *English aesthetics,* because the science has not been recognized as a department of philosophy, has been slow in taking systematic form. The attitude of the British mind, up to a very late period, is perhaps best indicated by the brief note in the eighth edition of the Encyclopaedia Britannica: —

"Aesthetics. — A term . . . employed by the followers of the German metaphysicians to designate philosophical investigations into the theory of the Beautiful or Philosophy of the Fine Arts, which they are disposed to regard as a distinct science. . . . Aesthetic speculations do not appear to have contributed anything to the improvement of the fine arts, or to our real knowledge of mental phenomena."

Nevertheless the number of British investigators has been large, and their contributions to the science have been of the utmost importance. Bacon, Shaftesbury, Hutcheson, Reid, Hume, Stewart, Lord Kames, Burke, Alison, Jeffrey, and Sir Wm. Hamilton are the most important of the earlier writers. Of the modern contributions, Spencer's chapter on the Aesthetic Emotions in his Psychology, an elaboration of Schiller's doctrine of the *Spieltrieb,* has had most influence on scientific thought;

Aesth., vol. I, p. 45 : " Denn das Kunstwerk, um seiner zugleich materiellen und individuellen Natur willen, geht wesentlich aus besonderen Bedingungen der mannigfachsten Art, wozu vorzüglich Zeit und Ort der Entstehung, dann die bestimmte Individualität des Künstlers und hauptsächlich die technische Ausbildung der Kunst gehören, hervor."

Ruskin's Modern Painters most influence upon the popular consciousness. Grant Allen, in his physiological Aesthetics, has
followed the line of research marked out by Spencer, and has
added much illustrative material. The writings of William
Morris and Oscar Wilde call attention to the social side of art.

5. It may be useful to those pursuing this line of historical
study to mention some of the most important histories and
critical essays. Among the general histories Bosanquet's History of Aesthetic is easily the first. It has the merit of being
a contribution to the history of culture as well as to the history
of aesthetics. Knight's Philosophy of the Beautiful, pt. I,
though much humbler in its aim, deserves honorable mention
in the list. Of the German works, Schasler's Kritische Geschichte should be noted first as the most comprehensive. Zimmermann's Geschichte and Herrmann's Die Aesthetik in ihrer
Geschichte are valuable, but not so complete. Sully's article
in the ninth edition of the Encyclopaedia Britannica, though excellent for reference, does not pretend to be more than a sketch.
Sully's evolutionist inclinations lead him to minimize the results
of German speculation, just as the speculative inclinations of
the philosophical writers often lead them to minimize the results
of the experimentalists. Of the histories of philosophy both
Ueberweg's and Erdmann's histories give generous space to
aesthetics; Windelband's history merely touches the subject in
passing. A short summary of aesthetic theories is given in
Bain's Mental Science, and a fuller account in Lévêque's Science du Beau.

Of authorities on Greek aesthetics, Ed. Müller's Geschichte
der Theorie der Kunst bei den Alten (Breslau: 1834) has as
yet no rival. Egger's Essai sur l'histoire de la Critique chez
les Grecs is admirably clear, but is concerned rather more with
rhetoric and poetics than with aesthetics proper. The first volume of Chaignet's Histoire de la Psychologie des Grecs (Paris:
1887) systematizes the implied psychology of Socrates and

Plato.   For Chaignet's treatment of Aristotle, see his Essai sur
la Psychologie d'Aristote (Paris : 1884).   Zeller's summaries of
Aristotle and Plato (Die Philosophie der Griechen, 3. Aufl.
Leipzig: 1879, and Plato and the older academy. London :
1876) are searching, but have a rigidity peculiar to his mode
of treatment.   The article by Nettleship in Abbott's Hellenica
(Oxford: 1880), though dealing solely with the Republic, contains a fairly adequate exposition of Plato's theory of art.   Less
technical, and therefore of more interest to the general reader,
is Walter Pater's characteristic study of Plato's aesthetics in his
Plato and Platonism (New York: 1893), pp. 24–256.   Jowett's
introductions to the Dialogues are too well known to require
commendation.   The exposition of Plato, which forms the appendix to Veron's Aesthetics, is superficial.   For monographs on
Aristotle see § 8.   Döring's Die Kunstlehre des Aristoteles is
one of the best.   It contains a fairly complete bibliography.
Teichmüller's Aristotelische Forschungen, though hard and dry,
may be recommended for carefulness and minuteness of research.   Bénard's L'Esthétique d'Aristote et de ses Successeurs (Paris: 1890) is done with the author's customary thoroughness.   Bénard is especially severe on those who practice
what he calls *l'Art d'accoucher les grands esprits*, *i.e.*, who read
into Aristotle the results of later speculation.

The standard history of German aesthetics is that of Lotze,
of which an extended exposition may be found in Erdmann's
History of Philosophy (translation), vol. III, pp. 315–322.   A
brief review of German aesthetics will be found in Von Eye's
Das Reich des Schönen (Berlin: 1878), p. 38.   For the lines of
development leading up to Kant, see Fenner's Die Aesthetik
Kants und seiner Vorgänger.   On Kant himself, Caird's exposition of the Critique of Judgment is entitled to particular consideration.   Essays and monographs are numerous.   Among
them may be mentioned as specially worthy of note, Friedländer's Kant in seinem Verhältniss zur Kunst und schönen

Natur, in *Preuss. Jahrb.* 20 (2); H. Cohen's Kant's Begründung der Aesthetik (Marburg: 1889); H. Falkenheim's Die Entsteh- ung d. Kantischen aesthetik (Diss. Heidelberg: 1890).

German writers since Kant are treated with minuteness by Von Hartmann in the first part of his Aesthetik. On the same period Neudecker's Studien zur Geschichte der deutschen Aes- thetik seit Kant (Wurz: 1878), though much condensed, is of no little asssistance to the student. Of especial interest is that portion of Hegel's Aesthetik in which Hegel points out the re- awakening of the science of art that accompanied the reawak- ening of German philosophy in general (Aesth., vol. I, pp. 72– 88; Bosanquet's translation, pp. 107–132). It contains cri- tiques of Kant, Schiller, Lessing, Winckelmann, Goethe, the Schlegels, Fichte, Solger, and Tieck. See, on the same move- ment, Bernard's Bosanquet's masterly paper on The Part Played by Aesthetic in the Development of Modern Philosophy, published in the *Proceedings of the Aristotelian Society*, vol. I, No. 2. For a criticism of some of the most recent German (and other) writers, the student may consult Th. Lipps's Aes- thetischer Litteraturbericht, in *Philos. Monatshefte* 26 : 17, 169, 323.

Of monographs on Schiller, G. Zimmermann's Versuch einer Schillerschen Aesthetik (Berlin: 1889), and K. Berger's Die Entwickelung von Schiller's Aesthetik (Weimar: 1894) are speci- mens of careful research. See, also, L'Esthétique de Schiller, by F. Montargis (Paris: 1890). On Schelling, chap. VII of Watson's volume in the Griggs Philosophical Classics, may be profitably consulted. The limitations of Kedney's Exposition of Hegel are pointed out above. Some assistance may be de- rived from Hastie's somewhat over-enthusiastic introduction to his translation of Hegel and Michelet, and valuable suggestions from Ritchie's review of Bosanquet's translation, *Mind*, 12 : 597. The leading article in vol. XIII of the *British and Foreign Re- view* (by G. H. Lewes) is one of the earliest attempts to introduce Hegel's Aesthetics to English readers.[1] Both Michelet and Ulrici (Princip. u. Methode d. Hegelschen Philos. Halle : 1841, pp. 216–245) have expounded the Aesthetik, but the original will be found in most cases clearer than the exposition.

Schopenhauer's aesthetic doctrines are briefly touched upon by Helen Zimmern in Arthur Schopenhauer, His Life and Philosophy, and by Bowen in his Modern Philosophy, and developed at some length by H. Klee (Grundzüge einer Aesth. nach Schopenhauer) and S. Stransky (Versuch d. Entw. e. allg. Aesth. auf Schopenhauerischer Grundl.). E. Reich's Schopenhauer als Philosoph der Tragödie deals with an interesting feature of Schopenhauer's aesthetic. On Lotze, see T. Kögel's Lotze's Aesthetik, and Röhr's Kritische Untersuchungen über Lotze's Aesthetik. A detailed exposition of Fechner may be found in Erdmann's History of Philos. (translation), vol. III, 296–298.

An excellent monograph on Herbart is O. Hostinsky's Herbart's Aesthetik in ihren grundlegenden Theilen quellenmässig dargestellt und erläutert (Hamburg : 1890).

In *Contemp.* 1 : 279, Professor Dowden discusses French Aesthetics, dealing with Cousin, Jouffroy, Lamennais, and Lévêque. Jouffroy's importance is perhaps over-emphasized. An interesting article by Professor Eaton on Modern French Aesthetics, containing notices of Lévêque, Chaignet, and others, appeared in the *New Englander*, 49 : 246. In the same line is an exhaustive review of Lévêque's La Science du Beau, from the pen of E. Saisset, in the *Rev. d. D. Mondes*, 15 Nov., 1861, reprinted in the latter's L'Ame et la Vie, p. 91. On Taine, see the references given in § 8. For the place of the Cartesian

---

[1] The article contains considerable translation, including a passage from Hegel's Aesthetik, which has since been frequently quoted : " Metre is the first and only condition absolutely demanded by poetry, etc." See the article ' Poetry,' by Th. Watts, in Encyc. Brit., 9th ed., and Gummere's Poetics, Introduction. That this quotation does not accurately represent Hegel's thought will be apparent from a reading of the Aesthetik (vol. III, 280 *et seq.*, especially pp. 227 and 289).

philosophy in the history of aesthetics, the reader may consult Schasler's Geschichte, vol. I, pp. 280, 283, and Krantz's Essai sur l'esthétique de Descartes.

On the aesthetics of Pascal consult the article by Bertrand in *La critique Philosophique*, 1886–I: 228–234; on the aesthetics of Boileau, the article by Brunetière in the *Rev. d. D. Mondes*, 1889–III: 662–685.

II. Investigation of Special Problems. — A few references bearing directly upon leading problems will perhaps be of service to the student who is specializing in this field.

A. THE BEAUTIFUL. — As every writer on aesthetics has something to say on this head, no general references need be given. Blackie's On Beauty (Edinburgh : 1858) is directed against the views of Alison. A great part of the work is taken up by an exposition of the Beautiful according to Plato. Professor Blackie also contributed an article on the Philosophy of the Beautiful to the *Contemp.* 43 : 814. Die Idee des Schönen in der Platonischen Philosophie is the title of the first volume of Sträter's Studien zur Geschichte der Aesthetik (Bonn : 1861). On the Kantian conception of beauty, see Nicolai's Ist der Begriff des Schönen bei Kant consequent entwickelt? (Kiel : 1889), and Blencke's Die Trennung d. Schönen vom Angenehmen in Kant's Kr. d. Urtheilskraft (Leipzig : 1888). Byk's Physiologie des Schönen (Leipzig : 1878) will be found useful to compare with Grant Allen's method of treatment of the same subject. Those who are interested in this phase of aesthetics should not overlook the paragraphs on the Acquisition of Beauty in Darwin's Origin of Species (paragraphs 302–304, 792), and on Ideas of Beauty, in Descent of Man (2d ed., pp. 92, 410–414, 540, 541, 573–585, 595, 596). A consideration of the Beautiful from a speculative point of view will be found in *Jl. Spec. Philos.* 17 : 94 in an article by W. H. Kimball. Köstlin's Ueber d. Schönheitsbegriff will repay perusal. For

the psychological aspects of the question see Dimetresco's Der
Schönheitsbegriff (Leipzig: 1877).

B. **The Ugly.** — Die Aesthetik des Hässlichen, by K. Rosenkranz (Königsberg: 1853), is the most comprehensive work on
this subject. Von Hartmann reviews recent theories of the
Ugly, devoting also considerable space to it in his systematic
aesthetics. See indexes to vols. I and II, under hässliche. A
brief account of German theories will be found in Lotze's Geschichte, pp. 333–342. By far the ablest single article on the
Ugly is Mr. Bernard Bosanquet's paper, The Aesthetic Theory of Ugliness, in *Proceedings of the Aristotelian Society*, No. 3,
pt. I. A full discussion of the subject will be found in the
same writer's History of Aesthetic, and may be traced by
means of the index. Other authorities who have treated it at
length are F. Schlegel, Solger, Weisse, Ruge, Von Kirchmann,
Schasler, and Carriere.

C. **The Sublime.** — A short list of those who have written
upon the sublime, with a rapid sketch of the opinions of each,
will be found in the supplement to Kedney's The Beautiful and
the Sublime (New York: 1880). Arthur Seidl's Zur Geschichte
des Erhabenheitsbegriffes seit Kant (1889) considers with some
fullness Kant and his predecessors (pp. 1–15), and with ex-
haustiveness the writers with whom it is especially concerned.
The list of books (pp. vii–x) that the author has not been able
to consult is rather formidable. A summary of Seidl's conclusions will be found in the article by Professor Everett in *Andover Review*, August, 1890, on the Philosophy of the Sublime.
See, also, index to vol. II of Von Hartmann's Aesthetik,
under Erhabene, Bosanquet's History under Longinus, Burke,
Winckelmann, Kant, Hegel ; Lemcke's Populäre Aesthetik,
p. 94, Vischer's Aesthetik, 1 : 218–333 (see index to vol. V
under Erhabenheit), J. Walter's Geschichte d. Aesthetik im
Altertum (Leipzig: 1893), pp. 86–95, 836–851, and Lotze's

Geschichte, pp. 324–333. A fragment of Kant's writings on the Sublime has been translated by De Quincey (Works, Masson's ed. 14 : 46), and Hegel's chapter, Die Symbolik der Erhabenheit (Aesth., vol. I, p. 454), by Stirling (*Macm.* 16 : 44 Symbolism of the Sublime). With the second, cf. Hegel's Aesth., vol. I, p. 427 *et seq.* The Origin of the Sublime is the title of an article by Grant Allen in *Mind*, 3 : 324. See, also, the treatise by Blencke, cited in the references on the Beautiful.

D. **THE PATHETIC.** —The modern phases of the pathetic have not been fully investigated. Schiller's essay on Pathos deals mainly with the Greek conception. Von Hartmann gives but two pages to Das Pathetische (vol. II, pp. 313, 314), but the entire chapter should be read, especially the paragraphs on Das Rührende, Das Traurige, Das Elegische oder Wehmüthige, etc. See also the works of Lemcke and Vischer.

E. **THE COMIC.** — Only a few references will be given here, since the subject in its whole extent is to be considered under comedy.

Hobbes's often-discussed definition of laughter may be found in his English works (London : 1839–45), vol. III, pp. 45–47 (see, also, vol. IV, pp. 46, 455). For other important theorizings on the subject, see Spencer's Physiology of Laughter, Darwin's Expression of the Emotions (London : 1870), Hecker's Physiol. u. Psychol. des Lachens, L. Dumont's Des Causes du Rire (Paris : 1862), Professor Butcher's article on the Evolution of Humor, in *Harper*, 80 : 898, Marshall's Pain, Pleasure, and Aesthetics, p. 329, J. Dewey in *Psychol. Rev.* 1 : 558–560. A recent work is Masci's Psicologia del Comico (Naples : 1889). For a review of German theories see Lotze's Geschichte, pp. 342–352, Von Hartmann's Aesthetik, vol. I, index, under Anthropologischer. A rather full bibliography of the subject will be found in Regnard's Œuvres Complètes (Paris : 1860).

On the *Tragic*, see §§ **37–48** below.

F. **Genius.** — On the nature of genius the student may consult the following: E. Caro, Mélanges et Portraits (2 vols. Paris: 1888), vol. I, p. 299 (on Séailles); G. Séailles, Essai sur le génie dans l'art (Paris: 1884); C. Lombroso, The Man of Genius, with illustrations (London: 1891); Max Nordau, Entartung (2 vols. Berlin: 1893; tr. Degeneration, N. Y.: 1895), Paradoxes (Engl. tr. Chicago: 1886); R. Falckenberg, *Nord u. Süd*, 56: 376 Künstler und Mensch (Discusses the subject under three heads: 1. What are the characteristics distinguishing the productive from the non-productive man? 2. How does artistic practice react on the artist? 3. What relation is there between the characteristics of the work and the characteristics of the artist?); C. Spitteler, Kunstwart, 1891: 113 Fleiss und Eingebung: Zur Psychologie des dichterischen Schaffens; Karl Bleibtreu, Letze Wahrheiten (Leipzig: 1891), pp. 1–98 Die naturwissenschaftliche Anschauung und das Genie, 99–142 Das Genie an sich, 143–189 Genie, Wahnsinn und Strafgesetz; O. Panizza, Genie und Wahnsinn (München: 1891. *Münch. Flugschriften*, 1. ser. 5–6); Ferd. Brunetière, Histoire et littérature (3 vols. Paris: 1884–6), vol. I, p. 353 Le Génie dans l'art (on Séailles); F. Spielhagen, Produktion, Kritik und Publikum (Berlin: 1891. Thinks genius and work come to the same thing); Grant Allen, Falling in Love, with other essays on more exact Branches of Science (London: 1889), p. 328 The Recipe for Genius; G. H. Lewes, Principles of Success in Literature (2d ed. Boston: 1892. See index under 'Genius'); F. Galton, Hereditary Genius (New York: 1877); Wm. James, Principles of Psychology (see index).

Lombroso, Galton, and Séailles are foremost authorities. The remarks in James's Psychology though brief are extremely good. For a popular and yet accurate characterization of genius, consult Lewes's Principles of Success in Literature.

G. **Rhythm.**— On this fundamental question the student may consult the able study by T. L. Bolton in the *American Jl. of*

Psychol. 6 : 145–238, in which he will find a fairly complete bibliography of the subject.   Of especial interest among recent investigations is E. Meumann's Untersuchungen zur Psychologie und Aesthetik des Rhythmus, in Wundt's Philos. Studien x. pp. 249–322, 393–430.   See also §§ **22,** *A,* and **24,** *C,* below.

H. **THE RELATION OF ART TO NATURE.** — For advanced students pursuing independent research a number of references bearing upon this fundamental question are here brought together.

The relation of art to nature has given rise to a metaphysical discussion ranging all the way from the theory of imitation to that of symbolism.

I) Among the Ancients.

Beginning with Plato's diagnosis of the fine arts as servile imitations and thrice removed from the truth, the speculative criticism of the ancients may be traced through a series of conceptions, such as Aristotle's theory of representation (selective or idealizing imitation), the theory of fantastic symbolism, the theory of mental imitation (which uses penetrative and creative imagination), and finally the theory of adequate symbolism of Plotinus, which, though based upon and read out of Plato's philosophy of ideas, practically destroyed the Platonic doctrine of imitative naturalism.

The *imitative naturalism* of Plato and the Aristotelian theory of *representation* call for serious examination.   They are the historical keys to the situation.   In what follows will be found topical references to these authors which may be useful in first-hand investigation.

A) *Plato's Theory of Art as related to Nature:*

1) The ideal, the phenomenal ; creation and imitation.

a) The ideal and the phenomenal :

Repub. 472–477 ; 485 Lovers of knowledge, and lovers of sights and sounds ; the real beauty compared with its copy ; 509–510, 511, 514–517 the good the prime cause, things on which it shines are visible and knowable, phenomena a stepping-stone to the vision of the ideal good ; the figure of the cave.

b) Relation of the good, the true, the beautiful to the ideal, and to each other :

Repub. 509–511, 514–517 ; 534. Phaedrus 238–258 ; 261–279. Philebus 22–63.

c) Creation :

Sophist, 264–267 : Divine creations are (1) of divine things, (2) of shadows ; human creations are (1) of production for use, (2) of images of things. Images are either likenesses or phantasies. Symposium 196–206 Love as a creator, a maker of poets, an intermediary between the divine and the human. All passage of not-being into being is poetry or making ; the processes of all art are creative ; 210 The grades of beauty which the poet may see and reveal. Timaeus 28 The world created by God after the eternal pattern. Kind of making : Repub. 597 Three kinds : (1) the creation of the divine image, (2) the creation of the visible likeness, (3) the imitation of that likeness.

d) Imitation :

Repub. 393–397 ; 595–607 Imitations three removes from the truth ; indiscriminate, hypocritical, futile, ignorant, inconsistent, provocative of irrational excess. Laws 669–674 How to judge of imitations ; 889 Art produces in play imperfect imitations of natural phenomena (works of fine art) and, in earnest, worthy results equal to those of nature (such as the craft of the statesman). Sophist 219 Imitation as a productive or creative art ; 235–237 Comparison between imitation as practiced by the sophist and by the painter ; 264–267 Imitation a form of creation. Timaeus 19 The poets disgrace their calling when they imitate merely the superficial aspect of life. Cratylus 423 Music and painting imitate color and sound ; words imitate the essence of things. Two kinds of imitation : Sophist 235–237 Copying and fantastic production ; the former makes an image, the latter an appearance; 264–267 The place of imitation among forms of creation; further discussion of likenesses and phantasies. Knowledge required of the imitator: Repub. 402,602. Phaedrus 261–279 Poets, orators, and legislators must understand the soul and how it is affected; *i.e.*, they should be philosophers. Theaetetus: Sense apprehends only the phenomenal, the fleeting; reason grasps the real and permanent.

2) Art:

a) Art coöperates with nature and chance to fulfill the divine purpose: Laws 709, 889.

b) Connotation of Art:

Repub. 342 The word is generally used as including both useful and fine art.

c) Kinds of art (in a general sense):

Repub. 602 There are three arts: (1) that of use, (2) that of making instruments for use, (3) that of imitating these. Statesman 279–286 All arts either causal or coöperative; the latter used by the painter.

3) The metaphysical aspect of the Relation of Art to Nature:

a) The principle of unity in variety:

Phaedrus 261–269 In rhetoric as a prerequisite to poetry and oratory.

b) Art as a medium of ideas:

Statesman 277 The higher ideas seem to require examples as a medium of expression; especially for the enlightenment of dull persons; 286 The highest truths cannot thus be adequately expressed. (See also above the references on Creation and Imitation.)

4) Other aspects of the Relation of Art to Nature which throw light on the metaphysical discussion:

a) The psychological:

Repub. 511. Sophist 264–267 Imagination is opinion expressed under the forms of sense. Phaedrus 238–258 The contrast between opinion, which leads to the best, and desire, which devoid of reason leads to the excessive. The four kinds of madness : prophecy, inspiration, poetry, love. The love that springs from the contemplation of beauty as expressed in sensible form.

b) The aesthetic :

(1) *Art and the love of beauty:*

Repub. 403. Phaedrus 238–258 Love, a form of madness. Its highest enjoyment is in the temperate contemplation of beauty. Symposium 177, 196–205, 210 Love is a poet, a master of poets, an artist, and a creator of order. The truly initiated lover rises to the vision of the eternal reality, of which he may reveal the beauty to the eye of the mind.

(2) *The disinterestedness of art :*

Repub. 342, 346.

(3) *The pleasure proper to art :*

Repub. 581, 582 ; Laws 652–669 Pleasure not a criterion of excellence ; but an attendant ; 700, 701. Statesman 279–289 In art the *fitting* does not primarily produce pleasure. Gorgias 500–513 Pleasure should be sought for the good, and not good for the sake of pleasure. The arts that minister to pleasure only are flattering and false. Philebus, 22, 27, 31, 32, 42, 51–54, 56, 63 The relation of pleasure and pain to knowledge, and the cause of all these ; pure and impure pleasures. The good a union of pure pleasures and knowledge, of which the virtue lies in beauty, symmetry, and truth. Pure pleasure is one of the five good things. Symposium 64, 87–89 The interrelation of pain and pleasure. Order and harmony preventives of disease ; and motion productive of harmony. Gymnastics as a means of purification.

(4) *The aesthetic judgment :*

Laws 652–667 The worth of melodies does not depend upon the pleasure they produce ; 669 Three elements in an aesthetic judgment, — to know that which is imitated, whether the imitation is correct, whether the form is beautiful or well executed; 700, 701 The vicious criterion of pleasure introduced by the poets. Statesman 279–286 Two kinds of measurement of value, — quantitative and qualitative. The qualitative demands a fixed standard: the good, which is the *mean*, any deviation wherefrom is bad. Qualitative arts judge not of mathematical or dynamical conceptions but of the *fitting*, the opportune and the due. Artistic pleasure may attend the *fitting;* but does not primarily spring from it. Repub. 581, 582 The philosopher only is competent to judge of pleasure, whether it be noble or ignoble.

c) The moralistic: •

(1) *The immorality of certain forms of art:*

Repub. 364, 366, 377, 379–386 ; 568 Tragedians to be banished from the Republic; 607 Homer must be expelled; Laws 700–701.

(2) *The educative value of certain forms of art :*

Repub. 397–411 ; 522, 531 ; Laws 662–667 ; 670–674.

(3) *The relative excellence of the arts :*

Statesman 304 Statesmanship dominates the lower arts : music, rhetoric, etc.

(4) *The relation of art to science:*

Statesman 259, 260 The sciences give judgments on matters of theory ; the arts give commands on matters of practice.

5) Poetry and Music :

a) Poetry :

Ion 532–540 The poet either a charlatan or divinely inspired. Phaedrus 238–258 Prophecy, inspiration, poetry, and love as forms of madness. 261–269 Poetry depends upon the principle of unity in variety ; 270–279 When the poet rests upon truth he is a philosopher. Symposium 177–210 It is love that makes the poet, the object of love is birth in beauty, hence immortality. The truly initiated lover is the ideal poet. Timaeus 19 The poets capable of doing better if they were not a tribe of imitators. Protagoras 339 *et seq.* The poets and their interpreters ridiculed. Lysis 204 The poets called fathers and authors of wisdom. Apology 22 The poets write not by wisdom, but by genius and inspiration. Repub. 393 Kinds of poetry.

b) The theory and function of music:

Repub. 397 ; 400–403 ; 409–411 ; 424 ; 442 ; 452 ; 531. Statesman 304. Philebus 27, 31, 32, 41, 51–53, 56. Cratylus 423. Laws 657–669 ; 670–674 ; 700, 701. Symposium 205. Timaeus 47, 87–89.

Of *authorities* on Plato's Theory of Imitation, the best are Ed. Müller, Gesch. d. Theorie d. Kunst bei den Alten,—minute, exhaustive, and critically sound, save that it defers the treatment of Plato's idea of Beauty until after the discussion of his philosophy of art ; Schasler 1: 89–97 ; 134, 135; 2: 1159–1166, 1171, of historical and bibliographical value ; Zeller's Philosophie der Griechen, in its historical development,— the Platonic philosophy is regarded as an artistic creation, but the treatment of the theory of imitation is practical and broad-minded ; Zimmermann's Geschichte d. Aesthetik, — following close in the wake of Müller; A. Ruge's Platonische Aesthetik, — furnishing ample material in the way of reference to the originals, but lacking interpretative insight; Egger 144–148, admirably clear ; Bosanquet, Hist. Aesth., 43–55 ; Butcher's Greek Genius, 257–260, and 287–290, and corresponding chapters in his Aristotle's Theory of Poetry and Fine Art; Walter Pater, Plato and Platonism, Chap. 4 Plato's Aesthetics. Written with his usual subtlety is the Pulchri Artis notione, pt. I (apud Platonem, Aristotelem et Plotinum. Diss. 1850) of Prof. R. Haym. This dissertation is one of the best comparative treatments of the fundamental aesthetics of the three philosophers. See also Ritter's Analyse u. Kritik d. von Plato in seiner Schrift vom Staate aufgestellten Erziehungslehre (Prog. 1881); and Lévêque, Justi, Reber, Remy, Raabe as given above, authorities on Greek Aesthetics.

B) The Aristotelian Theory by References to the Works of Aristotle :

In the Poetics of Aristotle no words are more liable to mis-interpretation than μίμησις (imitation), the correlative parts of speech (μιμεῖσθαι, etc.), and the words and phrases more or less nearly synonymous with these. The student should collate all passages in which such words occur, with a view to determining what Aristotle meant by μίμησις in respect of the material used by the artist, the form inspiring him, the purpose inciting, and the result produced; what he meant by the *Nature* that art imitates, whether imitation of a real thing or of an ideal, — and whether imitation implies truth to nature as an object or as a process ; whether Aristotle was what some would now call a 'realist,' — what distinction he would make or does make between copying, representation, and imaginative creation or idealization, to what extent the theories of selection, illusion, and suggestion are involved, whether the work of art may sur-pass nature ; what he considers to be the relative values of his-torical fidelity and imaginative probability, what aesthetic worth he might, for instance, have attached to photography ; what was his theory of the impulse to imitation, of the aesthetic value of the beautiful, the wonderful, the sublime, the awful, the horrible, the ugly, the loathsome ; what are the respective pecu-liarities of imitation by lyrical poetry, by drama, by epic, etc.,— by music, by dancing, and the plastic arts. Misconceptions of Aristotle's doctrine frequently arise from the various and im-perfect nomenclature of translations of the Poetics. Twining, Pye, Butcher, and Wharton are recommended to English readers ; but scholarly and satisfactory work can be done only with the original. Shades of signification depend upon the context. For μίμησις in the sense of *copying* see 1 : 4 ; 3 : 2 ; (imitate persons acting and doing) ; 4 : 1–5 (*delineation*), — and other passages. For μίμησις as representation see 1 : 5 ; 6 : 2 ; 6 : 4 ; 6: 6, and other passages. For the signification of *selective and imaginative* creation, or idealization see 2 : 2 ; 4 : 9 ; 5 : 1 ; 9 : 1–9 ; 15 : 8, and other passages.

Before attempting to formulate the Aristotelian theory of 'imitation' and to compare it with the aesthetic theories of Plato and Plotinus among the ancients, or of Bacon, Words-worth, Hegel, Goethe, Arnold, Austin, Ruskin, and others among the moderns, the meaning and bearing of the words *nature, art, imitation,* etc., in the Aristotelian writings other than the Poetics should be ascertained. Many popular and ordinarily respected expositions of the theory in question are worthless because the originators of them were ignorant of the connection between Aristotle's Poetics and his general philosophical system.

The following topical references, though by no means in-tended to be exhaustive, may be of assistance.

1. Nature.

ἡ φύσις : Nature is opposed to accidental spontaneity (τὸ αὐτόματον) and chance (ἡ τύχη). As self-producing and self-determined it is opposed to art, in that while art is an originating principle in something outside itself, nature is so within itself. [Wallace, Outlines of the Philos. of Aristotle, pp. 34, 35.] Consult Phys. 2 : 1, 192^b 14 ; 2 : 2, 194^a 28 ; 2 : 8, 199^b 15 ; 2 : 1, 193^a 28 ; Meta. 11 : 3, 1070^a 6 ; 4 : 4, 1015^a 7 ; Polit. 1 : 1, 1252^b 30 ; De Coel. 3 : 2, 301^b 17.

ἡ φύσις is a continuous development from plants to animals, through animals to man, De Part. Anim. 4 : 5, 681^a 12. It must never be mistaken for the appearance, or face, of the visible universe.

ἡ φύσις works always toward an end, De Coel. 1 : 4, 271^a 33, and makes the best of her material, De Coel. 288^a 2 ; De Part. Anim. 4 : 10, 687^a 15 ; Phys. 2 : 8, 199^b 31. In some of her works she excels the possibilities of art, De Part. Anim. 1 : 1, 639^b 19 ; —

but she is sometimes baulked of her intent, matter (ὕλη) overcoming her, Gen. Anim. 4 : 4, 770^b 16 ; Phys. 2 : 9, 200^a 14, —

and she sometimes makes mistakes, Phys. 2 : 8, 199^a 33.

2. Art, in general.

ἡ τέχνη : Phys. 2 : 8 199^a 15, ὅλως τὲ ἡ τέχνη τὰ μὲν ἐπιτελεῖ ἃ ἡ φύσις ἀδυνατεῖ ἀπεργάσασθαι, τὰ δὲ μιμεῖται. *In general, art on the one hand com-*

pletes what nature is unable to carry through, on the other hand it imitates.
According to Butcher (Aristot. Theory of Poetry and Fine Art), the
distinction is not between useful and fine art, but between two aspects
of useful art. On the one hand useful art satisfies those needs of man
for which nature has not fully provided, on the other hand *its processes
are those of nature.* It imitates τὴν φύσιν (the productive principle). If
the two clauses do not "respectively mark the end and the method of
useful art," they may indicate two methods by which art (in general)
realizes the idea of nature (1) by assisting natural processes, (2) by
imitating them. Compare, for instance, Meteorol. 4 : 3, 381ᵇ 6. The
process of cooking is similar to the physical process of digestion : Ὄπτησις
μὲν οὖν καὶ ἕψησις γίνονται μὲν τέχνῃ, ἐστι δ᾽, ὥσπερ λέγομεν, τὰ εἴδη
καθόλου ταὐτὰ καὶ φύσει· ὅμοια γὰρ τὰ γινόμενα πάθη, ἀλλ᾽ ἀνώνυμα·
μιμεῖται γὰρ ἡ τέχνη τὴν φύσιν. ἐπεὶ καὶ ἡ τῆς τροφῆς ἐν τῷ σώματ
πέψις ὁμοία ἑψήσει ἐστίν. . . . Here not only is *Nature* to be explained as
the process of nature, but *Art* is to be construed as useful art — though
not assisting nature in her processes, but imitating her processes for the
material benefit of man.

Art and education supply the deficiencies of nature, Pol. 7 : 17, 1337ᵃ ;
Art assists natural processes, Met. 6 : 7, 1032ᵇ 6, by the skill of the physi-
cian ; it imitates the order of nature and realizes her ends in the useful art
of the politician, Pol. 1 : 2, 1253ᵃ 3, and in the fine arts of painting, music,
poetry, etc., De Mundo 5 : 396ᵇ 12, Poet. 1 : 4 ; 4 : 2–6 ; 6 : 9–18.

According to Eth. Nic. 6 : 4, 1140ᵃ 10, ταὐτὸν ἂν εἴη τέχνη καὶ ἕξις μετὰ
λόγου ἀληθοῦς ποιητική, — art is a faculty which realizes, or produces, in
accordance with a true idea ; and according to Meta. 1 : 1, 981ᵃ 5 and 6,
art comes into being when out of many conceptions of experience one
universal opinion is evolved with respect to similar cases. . . . Experience
is a knowledge of particulars, art of universals. See also Rhet. 1 : 2, 1356ᵇ
29 ; Meta. 6 : 7, 1032ᵃ 32 ἀπὸ τέχνης δὲ γίγνεται, κ.τ.λ. From art are born
those things the forms of which are in the soul (ὅσων τὸ εἶδος). For
explanation of εἶδος, or form, in this context see Meta. 6 : 7, 1032ᵇ 15 ;
Meta. 6 : 9, 1034ᵃ 24 — " For art is form," etc.

3. Imitation.

a) In general.

μιμεῖσθαι : Poetics 4 : 1 " It is innate in men from childhood (1) to imitate
(μιμεῖσθαι) : — in this we differ from the other animals because we are the
most imitative and acquire our first knowledge through imitation, — and (2)
to delight in imitations." Note that here man *shares* the imitative faculty
with other animals, but *excels* them (*a*) in imitative excellence, and (*b*) in

the ability to reason from his attempts at imitation. The original imitative effort is evidently not directed toward the production of images of natural objects; but toward the furtherance of nature's purposes and the satisfaction of man's desires — by the methods of nature.

For imitation among the lower animals, see De Animalibus Historia 8 : 12, 597. Instances of the imitation of natural processes by art are cited from Aristotle by Döring (Die Kunstlehre d. Aristoteles) 49–62, 80–83, 143–188.

Other examples of the general use of the words *imitate, imitation,* etc., are as follows: Rhetorica ad Alexandrum 1 : 13, 1422ᵃ 30, τὸν αὐτὸν τρόπον προσήκει τοὺς υἱεῖς μιμεῖσθαι τὰς τῶν πατέρων πράξεις. *So also it is fitting that sons should imitate the deeds of their fathers.* Meteorol. 1 : 9, 346ᵇ 36 γίνεται δὲ κύκλος οὗτος μιμούμενος τὸν τοῦ ἡλίου κύκλον. Eth. Nic. 9 : 11 Not inferior but superior natures must be imitated; Eth. Nic. 3 : 5 Homer as an imitator; Meta. 987ᵇ 11 The Pythagoreans believed that things subsist by the imitations of numbers. Eth. Nic. 3 : 5, 1113ᵃ 8 Now this is evident from the ancient polities which Homer depicted (ἐμίμειτο). **μίμημα**: Rhet. 3 : 1, 1404ᵃ 21 *Names are the imitations* (μιμήματα) *of things.* Note also the place of the voice in imitation,—Rhet. ad Alexandrum 29, 1436ᵃ 7. On the imitation of ethical qualities in practical life, see Problemata 19 : 10, 951ᵃ 7. **μιμητής**: For the different uses of *imitator,* see Problemata 19 : 15, 918ᵇ 28; Moral. Magn. 1 : 19, 1190. The imitator (painter) is not praiseworthy unless he have an excellent purpose (ἂν μὴ τὸν σκοπὸν θῇ τὰ κάλλιστα μιμεῖσθαι).

b) In particular.

On Aristotle's conception of Imitation as involved in art, especially in the fine arts, the following references may be consulted:

μιμητικαί: Poetics 8 : 4 χρὴ οὖν, καθάπερ καὶ ἐν ταῖς ἄλλαις μιμητικαῖς ἡ μία μίμησις ἑνός ἐστιν, οὕτω καὶ τὸν μῦθον, ἐπεὶ πράξεως μίμησίς ἐστι, μιᾶς τε εἶναι ταύτης καὶ ὅλης, κ.τ.λ. *As in other mimetic arts one imitation is of one object, so the plot since it is an imitation of action must be of one complete action.* See also De Animalibus Historia 8 : 12, 597.

Synonyms for the "imitative arts" (μιμητικαὶ τέχναι) are given by Butcher as μιμήσεις, *modes of imitation,* and ἐλευθέριοι τέχναι, *liberal arts.*

μίμησις: The term occurs in the following passages: Pol. 8 : 5 "Ἔτι δὲ ἀκροώμενοι τῶν μιμήσεων γίγνονται πάντες συμπαθεῖς καὶ χωρὶς τῶν ῥυθμῶν καὶ τῶν μελῶν αὐτῶν. *Besides, when men listen to imitations all their feelings are aroused in sympathy even though there be no rhythm or melody.* Some commentators supply "of the feelings" after "imitations." Poetics 1 : 2 Epic Poetry and Tragedy, and also Comedy and the Dithyramb and most' flute and guitar playing are all of them, to speak generally, imitations (μιμήσεις); also, Rhet. 1 : 11, 1371ᵇ, painting and sculpture; also, Poet. 1 : 5, dancing. Architecture is not mentioned in the list of fine arts, save in so far as it is adorned by sculpture. Poet. 9:9 ὅσῳ ποιητὴς κατὰ τὴν μίμησίν ἐστι, μιμεῖται δὲ τὰς πράξεις. *Since the poet is a poet (maker) by means of his imitation, and he imitates action.*

The following passages, also, throw light upon the connotation of the words "imitative arts." Problemata 19:15, 918ᵇ 28, On the skill necessary to imitation in music. Note especially the context of ὁ μὲν γὰρ ὑποκριτὴς ἀγωνιστὴς καὶ μιμητής, ὁ δὲ χορὸς ἧττον μιμεῖται. Pol. 8:5 ἐν τοῖς μέλεσιν αὐτοῖς ἐστὶ μιμήματα τῶν ἠθῶν, κ.τ.λ., — On the place of music in education, and as an imitation of moral qualities. Music has a greater ethical influence than painting or sculpture, which do not produce *imitations* but *signs* of moral habits; whereas in mere melodies there is an imitation of character, and the various melodies and rhythms have ... various ethical effects. Pol. 8 : 6, 7. Ethical melodies and passionate melodies. The former are preferable in education, but the latter have their uses in affecting and then relieving natures prone to religious frenzy, pity, fear, enthusiasm, and other emotions, in excess. These chapters 8 : 5–8 are valuable also for the light they throw on the tragic catharsis, Poetics 6.

4. Aristotle's conception of artistic 'imitation' is liberally developed and illustrated by his use of *parallel words* such as ὁμοίωμα, a likeness; σημεῖον, a symbol or sign; εἰκών, an image; φαντασία, imagination; φάντασμα, a mental impression.

ὁμοίωμα: De Interp. 1. τὰ αὐτὰ παθήματα τῆς ψυχῆς, καὶ ὧν ταῦτα ὁμοιώματα, πράγματα ἤδη ταῦτα. Polit. 8 : 5, 1340ᵃ 33 συμβέβηκε δὲ τῶν αἰσθητῶν, κ.τ.λ.; 8 : 5, 1340ᵃ 18 In rhythms and melodies we have imitations (ὁμοιώματα) of anger and mildness, etc. Also 8 : 5 Figures and colors are not likenesses (ὁμοιώματα) but signs (σημεῖα) of moral habits. Probl. 19 : 27, 919ᵇ 26 ὅμως ἔχει ἦθος, and 19 : 29, 920ᵃ 3 τὰ μέλη φωνὴ οὖσα ἤθεσιν ἔοικεν (ἔχει ὁμοιότητα) the ability of musical sound to convey likenesses of moral and emotional feelings. Physiognom. 1 : 2, 806ᵃ 28.

σημεῖον or σύμβολον: De Interp. 1:1, 16ᵃ 3; 2 :16ᵃ 27; Polit. 8 : 5.

εἰκών: Topics 6 : 2, 6 An image produced by imitation. De Part. Anim. 1 : 5, b 45, a 5. See also reference to the De Mem. in Teichmüller 2 : 149.

φαντασία: On the meaning of this word J. Freudenthal has thrown considerable light in a compact pamphlet entitled Ueber den Begriff des Wortes φαντασία bei Aristoteles. Diss. 1863.

According to De Anim. 3 : 3, 429ᵃ 1, phantasy, or imagination, is the movement which results upon an actual sensation (Wallace, Outlines, p. 43). De Anim. 3 : 3, 427ᵇ 17–20 ; 3 :10, 433ᵃ 10. See also Rhet. 1:11, 1370ᵃ 28 ; De Somno 1 :459ᵃ 17, 1 :454ᵇ 28, 1 :458ᵇ 25, and numerous passages in the De Insomn. 458–462, and the De Sensu. Aristotle's Psychology (De

Anima), Bk. 3, chap. 3, treats in detail of the imagination. This chapter
must be mastered before a just conception of Aristotle's theory of imitation
can be formed. Wallace, in his Introd. to the Psychology, sums up the
materialistic character of A.'s conception thus : " The pictures which imagination, either in our waking moments or in our dreams, presents to us are
simply the result of a physiological process, in which the movement of the
organ of sensation continues the impression which either originally excited
it, or might at least have originally done so." But Professor Wallace
reminds us that the materialistic aspects of the process do not exhaust
Aristotle's theory of image-making. There is always the background of
the ψύχη as the reality of body.

φάντασμα : De Anim. 3:7, 431ᵃ 14, De Memor. 449ᵇ 31 *The pictures
representative of external objects* furnished by the phantasy form the materials upon which reason (τὸ νοεῖν) (τῇ δὲ διανοητικῇ ψυχῇ) works. On morbid
excitement of the senses and the resulting phantasms, see De Insomn. 460ᵇ
25. For other references, see Teichmüller 2 : 148.

5. General considerations.

a) On the pleasure produced by art, for artist or percipient, and on the
end or purpose of fine art, see Butcher's Aristotle's Conception of Fine
Art and Poetry (Aspects of Greek Genius, pp. 253–289), Döring, Teichmüller and Ed. Müller. The discussion bears in many ways upon the
theory of 'imitation.'

b) For the source of the pleasure derived from artistic representation
of objects (καὶ τὰ τοιάδε ἀνάγκη ἡδέα εἶναι οἷον τό τε μεμιμημένον, ὥσπερ
γραφικὴ καὶ ἀνδριαντοποιία καὶ ποιητική, κ.τ.λ.), see Rhet. 1:11, 1371ᵇ 6. This
passage throws light upon Poetics 4:5 "The reason that we delight in
seeing likenesses is that by viewing them we can learn and conclude what
each is, *e.g.*, that 'this is so and so.' " On the pleasure afforded by metaphors, see Rhet. 3:10, 2 ; and *cf.* 3:8, 2 ; 3:9, 2, and 2:9. Compare also
Probl. 30 : 6, 956ᵃ 14. "Is man the most trustworthy of animals because
he is the most imitative, and hence best able to learn ?" and 19 : 5 where
the pleasure produced by music is similarly explained. On the pleasure
derived from the imitation even of disagreeable objects, see De Part. Anim.
1 : 5, b 45, a 5.

c) On the universal element in art, its tendency to the philosophic,
Poet. 9 : 3, see Teichmüller 2 : 178, and Butcher's Theory of Poetry.
Teichmüller and Butcher translate the passage comparing poetry and
history : Poetry is more philosophic and of *higher worth* (σπουδαιότερον)
than history,— for it *approaches nearer to* the universal (μᾶλλον τὰ καθόλου)
while history deals with particulars.

d) According to Teichmüller, Forschungen 2 : 142–157, the fine arts realize the ideal of nature not by assisting natural processes, or imitating them and their results for practical purposes, as do the useful arts, nor by producing a symbolic representation of nature's moods, processes, and ends, but by completing in a likeness (freed from all material uncertainty) forms which shall express her universal meaning. Butcher in this respect closely follows Teichmüller.

For the standard *texts and translations* of the Poetics, Ethics, Metaphysics, Politics, Rhetoric, Psychology, and other works of Aristotle necessary to this investigation see § 8 ARISTOTLE, and the Bibliography appended to this volume.

Among the more noteworthy and available *critiques* on the Aristotelian ' Imitation' may be mentioned Carl Altmüller's Der Zweck der schönen Kunst, a painstaking Aristotelian study (Doctor's dissertation at Jena ; Cassel : 1873). Ch. Bénard, L'Esthétique d'Aristote et de ses Successeurs (Paris : 1889), gives a brief résumé ; theoretical and historical, pp. 28–39, 53, 145–151. F. Biese (Die Philosophie des Aristoteles, Berlin : 1842) in his chapter on Aristotle's Aesthetics, pp. 661–723, discusses the essential relationship of the arts as based upon the idea of imitation (667 *et seq.*), and compares Aristotle's theory with that of Plato. Cf. Plato, Repub. 3, 394 c, imitation in poetry, with the broader connotation and denotation of μίμησις in the Poetics. Bosanquet's treatment (Hist. Aesth. Lond.: 1892) involves a catholic view of the Aristotelian system of thought. Chapters 1–5 are essential to the discussion, though it may be doubted whether full justice is done to the idea of μίμησις, since the theory which construes μίμησις in terms of a *process* is not considered. One of the most valuable of recent contributions is Prof. S. H. Butcher's treatise in Some Aspects of the Greek Genius (Lond.: 1891), pp. 234–394 Aristotle's Conception of Fine Art and Poetry. From the author's synopsis of the chapters on Useful Art and Fine Art, the End of Art, the Meaning of " Imitation " as an Aesthetic Term, Poetry as an

Imitation or Expression of the Universal, and from the text itself,
may be gathered the outline of his argument: "The saying
'Art imitates Nature' is specially applied in Aristotle to Useful
Art, which *follows nature's methods* and supplies her defects.
Fine art is imitation in another sense. A work of art is not
a servile imitation of an original as it is in itself, nor a symbolical representation of it, but a copy of the original as it is
presented to the 'phantasy.' Fine Art, in poetry, reproduces
under sensuous form the universal elements in human life, ...
is an idealized image of character, emotion, action. In her
structural faculty lies nature's perfection. Useful art, employing
nature's own machinery, aids her in her effort to realize the
ideal in the world around us, so far as man's practical needs
are served by furthering this purpose. Fine art sets practical
needs aside . . . By mere imagery it reveals the ideal form at
which nature aims in the highest sphere of organic existence,
— in the region namely of human life where her intention is
most manifest, though her failures too are most numerous . . . .
Plato saw in Fine Art an illusion as opposed to the reality:
Aristotle saw in it the image of a higher reality. The end is
pleasure for the spectator or hearer: not the recreation
(ἀνάπαυσις), nor the pastime (παιδιά) which may be afforded
by the lower arts to the weary or to children, but rational
enjoyment (διαγωγή), the delight which comes from the ideal
employment of leisure." Professor Butcher gives copious
references to the original. He has made an exhaustive study
of Döring and Teichmüller, but is by no means dependent on
them. All of these ideas and many others have now been
embodied in Butcher's latest work, Aristotle's Theory of Poetry
and Fine Art (with a critical text and a translation of the Poetics.
Lond.: 1895). This book takes rank as the most complete
apparatus in English for the study of Aristotle's aesthetics. One
of the most profoundly critical studies of the subject has been
made by A. Döring, Die Kunstlehre des Aristoteles (Jena:

1876).   Chapter 1 considers the Aesthetics in its broader
sense and in relation to the Aristotelian system; Chapter 2,
Aesthetic and Imitation in the limited aspects of the discussion.   Döring falls foul of Teichmüller (see below), at nearly
every step of the discussion, and on the whole makes good
his critical position.   The work is a storehouse of bibliographical reference and supplementary material.   É. Egger,
Essai sur l'Histoire de la Critique chez les Grecs (2e éd. Paris:
1886), is of unquestioned worth.   The translation of Aristotle's
Poetics which appeared in the first edition has been omitted from
the second to make way for a large amount of new material in
the way of criticism and exposition.   The student will find the
Essay, if not the most profound, one of the most lucid and comprehensive treatises on Greek aesthetics and rhetoric (both are
included in the term *critique*) available in any language.   For
theories of imitation see pp. 144–148, 199, 238–245, 336.   J.
Frohschammer's Ueber die Principien der Aristotelischen Philosophie (München: 1881) is of the systematic order.   Apposite to
this subject are pp. 98–106 Die Kunst als allgemeine Analogie
in der Aristotelischen Welterklärung.   More closely bearing upon
the discussion is F. Heidemann's inaugural dissertation De doc-
trinae artium Aristotelicae principiis (Halle: 1875).   Masson in
Theories of Poetry (Essays, Biographical and Critical) attempts
to distinguish sharply between the Aristotelian 'imitation' and
the Baconian 'creation' — but bases his argument upon a
misconception of Aristotle's philosophy.   See §§ 19, 20.   Ed.
Müller in Ueber das Nachahmende in der Kunst nach Plato
(Ratibor: 1831), and the Geschichte der Theorie der Kunst bei
den Alten (Breslau: 1834) has given us the most learned
treatises on Greek aesthetics.   One of the clearest and most
discriminating expositions of the theory of Imitation is to be
found on pp. 359 *et seq.* of the Geschichte.   An elementary but
still comprehensive and careful study has been recently issued
by Prickard: Aristotle on the Art of Poetry.   See pp. 19–35

and 65–68. "When he says that poetry is imitation, Aristotle
is asserting its power to set forth a special and an elevated kind
of truth . . . . After allowing for the power which lies in mere
eloquence and rhythm, and for the subtler charm of association,
is it not still the simple elementary feelings upon which the epic
poet plays, reproducing and imitating them?" (p. 65). Among
English scholars, Pye and Twining though not broadly philosophical are to be regarded as authorities on the Poetics. In
the first volume of Modern Painters, Ruskin treats of Ideas of
Imitation, placing them lowest in the scale of art-ideas. His
definition of imitation is arbitrary, but has the merit, if it be
one, of restricting the term to a definite range of aesthetic effects.
Reinkens, Teichmüller, and Ueberweg have made special study
of the Poetics. The first in his Aristoteles über Kunst, besonders über Tragödie (Wien : 1870) ; the second in his Aristotelische Forschungen (3 v. in 1, Halle : 1867–9), which is the best
general commentary on the Poetics. Vol. I consists of running
annotations on the text ; vol. II is a dissertation on Aristotle's
philosophy of Art. Chapter 1 of the second volume treats of the
common nature of the fine arts, or of the meaning of imitation.
On the different significations of the word Imitation see pp. 143–
145. Section 1, pp. 145–155 elaborates the important thesis :
Works of Fine Art are reproductions (Ebenbilder) of reality as it
is given in (exists for) the Phantasy (Imagination). Teichmüller
distinguishes between *symbol* and *likeness ;* shows that the arts
furnish likenesses of *reality ;* explains the relation of the likeness in the imagination to the work of art, and asserts that his
proposition, as above enunciated, holds good for poetry — the
highest of the arts. In chapter 2 he considers the object
imitated by art; shows that nature and art have the same ideal,
and attempts to prove that the object of the imitation is determined by the laws of truth and beauty. On pp. 200–207 he
explains the aim and effect of imitative art. For an unsympa-
thetic handling of his premises, Döring should be consulted.

Ueberweg's Aristotelis Ars Poetica (Griechisch und Deutsch) is valuable for the Anmerkungen, pp. 47–91. Anmerkung 2 develops briefly the thesis that Aristotle by the term artistic imitation meant not a slavish copying (Nachbildung) of the particular object, but a representation (Darstellung) which expresses reality and law in concrete form. See also under Anmerkungen 23, 25, 39–41. With these notes may be read pp. 177–180 of the author's Hist. Philos. volume I — although the passage deals rather with catharsis than with imitation ; and also his Die Lehre d. Aristot. von d. Wesen und d. Wirkung d. Kunst (*Zeitschr. f. Philos.* 36 : 260–291 ; 50 : 16–39). Of a more general character are the appropriate sections in M. Schasler's Kritische Geschichte der Aesthetik ; and E. Zeller's Die Philosophie der Griechen (3te Aufl. Leipz.: 1879). In the former, see vol. I, pp. 120–203 for exposition of Aristotle ; especially pp. 136–146, on imitation. Schasler interprets Aristotle's μίμησις as the clothing of the idea according to laws of natural form, or the representation of nature according to the laws of the idea. In the latter see Theil 2, Abth. 2, Aristoteles und die alten Peripatetiker, pp. 763–770 Die Nachahmung. The author bases his statement of Aristotle's theory on passages from the originals, principally the Poetics, which are cited in full, and shows how Plato's conception of art (mere copy of sensible phenomena, worthy of contempt as untrue and worthless) falls below the Aristotelian conception.

E. Wallace's Outlines of the Philosophy of Aristotle (Oxford and Lond.: 1880) is useful as furnishing in brief and lucid form, and with appropriate references, the general information requisite for a systematic study of Aristotle's theory of art. The same writer's Aristotle's Psychology, in Greek and English, with Introduction and Notes (Cambridge: 1882), is even more serviceable. Pp. lxxxvi–xcvii of the Introduction, on Imagination, Dreams, Memory, furnish a trustworthy outline of the theory of Images. This section should be read in connection with Bk. III, chap. 3 of the Psychol. (de Anima). J. C. van Dyke discusses 'Imitation' in a semi-popular style, in the opening chapters of Parts 1 and 2 of his Principles of Art ; and E. Véron makes occasional, not extremely profitable, reference to the subject in his Aesthetics.

In *Mind* for July, 1895, Mr. R. P. Hardie expounds certain doctrines of the Poetics with special reference to the interpretations of Bosanquet, Prickard, and Butcher. He thinks that the great advance of Aristotle upon Plato is the former's introduction of the conception of ὕλη, 'medium.' "This conception necessarily modifies in an important way the meaning of μίμησις . . . . When it is recognized that two things having the same εἶδος may differ in respect of ὕλη, there is no longer any reason why the copy should be regarded as an attempt to rival reality. The imitation is simply the solution of an artistic problem : — Given *xy* when *x* is εἶδος and *y* ὕλη, to express *x* in terms of a new medium *y'*. The relation of *xy'* to *xy* is naturally expressed by 'imitation,' or μίμησις in its ordinary meaning. We may call the other relation, that of *xy'* to *x* (or of *xy* to *x*), 'expression.' . . . Now both Plato and Aristotle use μίμησις of the latter relation as well as of the former. In the case of Plato this is due to the fact that in his theory *x*, the ἰδέα, is merely *another concrete* reality, over and above, and somehow external to *xy'*. But the case of Aristotle is different. He must have been aware, to some extent at least, of the perpendicular relation, so to speak, of *xy'* to *x* as distinct in kind from the horizontal relation of *xy'* to *xy*."

Many of the *critical expositions* of the Poetics are mentioned in §§ **8, 20, 38, 47** (under Aristotle), and in the bibliography of editions, Appendix to this volume. Especially valuable to the investigator of the topic now under consideration are Spengel (in Abh. d. k. bayer. Akad. der Wiss., philos.-philolog. Cl., II, 1837, und XI, 1867); Vahlen in his Beiträge zu Arist. Poet. (Sitzungsberichte der philos.-hist. Cl. der

k. Akad. d. Wiss.   Wien: 1865–6); F. Ritter, Arist. Poet.,
Köln: 1839; Barth. St. Hilaire, Poet. Arist., Paris: 1858;
J. A. Hartung, Lehren d. Alten über die Dichtkunst, Hamb.:
1845; a profound treatise of 115 pages by F. L. G. von Raumer,
Ueber die Poetik des Aristoteles u. sein Verhältniss zu den
neuern Dramatikern (Berlin Akad. Wiss. Abh. 1828); and Vermischte Schriften, vol. 2; Ernst Essen, Bemerkungen zu
Aristoteles' Poetik; H. Martin, Analyse critique de la poétique
d'Aristote (1836. Thèse); W. Schrader, De Artis apud Arist.
notione ac vi, Berlin: 1843, München: 1881; F. Susemihl,
Studien zur Aristot. Poetik (*Rhein. Mus.* 18: 366, 471;
19: 197; 22: 217); F. C. Petersen, Om den Aristoteliske
Poetik (in Skandin. Litteraturselskab. vol. XVI); J. Lemaître,
Corneille et la poétique d'Aristote, Paris: 1888, and the *Rev.
d. Deux Mondes*, 1888, IV: 830; Ch. Bénard, L'Esthétique
d'Aristote et de ses successeurs, Paris: 1889. As stated above
(Plato's Theory of Art), the De Pulchri atque Artis notione of
R. Haym, sets forth with remarkable clearness the respective
theories of Plato, Aristotle, and Plotinus.

C) *The Post-Aristotelians on Imitation:*

For theories of the relation of art to nature in the suc-
cessors of Aristotle such as Chrysippus, Poseidonius, Seneca,
Philodemus, Dionysius of Halicarnassus, see Bosanquet, Hist.
Aesth. 99–103. For Theophrastus περὶ μουσικῆς, see Zeller's
Aristoteles, 867–869, and Egger's Hist. Crit. 345; also
Plutarch, Symp. lib. 1, Quaest. 5, who cites Theophrastus'
three principles of the origin of music (pain, pleasure, and
enthusiasm). For Aristoxenus, another disciple of Aristotle,
see Zeller and Egger. A French translation of Aristoxenus'
On Music has been made by M. E. Ruelle (Paris: 1870). On
theories of imitation, representation, and symbolism among the
Peripatetics, Stoics, and Epicureans, see Schasler 1: 204–210.
Among the Eclectics, Cicero and Plutarch have contributed to
the discussion. Cicero, in the following passages: Orator 71

We must be content with the probable in all things since the truth is hidden ; De Inventione 2: 12 Art works by selection from particulars ; De Officiis 1 : 1, 27–36 and Orator, chaps. 2, 3. Plutarch, in De Audiendis Poetis 2, Symp. 5, Quaest. 1, and Symp. 7, Quaest. 5.

Of the critical grammarians and rhetoricians, Dionysius of Halicarnassus and Dio Chrysostom have made contributions to the theory in question. For Dionysius see Schasler 1 : 219, 220, and Professor Nettleship's Literary Criticism in Latin Antiquity (*Journ. Philol.* 18 : 230). Dio Chrysostom's conception of legitimate symbolism in art and of the boundaries between poetry and the formative arts (cf. Lessing's Laokoon) will be found in the De Dei Cognitione Oratio 12 (pp. 400 *et seq.* of Reiske's edition; the passage is translated by Egger and Bosanquet). Commentary on Chrysostom will be found in Schasler p. 222, Bosanquet p. 108, and Egger pp. 440–455.

The writings of Plotinus as developing the possibilities of Plato's aesthetic beyond the narrow theory of imitation, and definitely propounding a doctrine of symbolism, are more important than any other contribution to the subject since the death of Aristotle. The best guides to Plotinus' writings on Beauty, which are included in his Enneads, are Ed. Müller 2 : 285–315, Schasler 1 : 233–251, Bosanquet 111–119, Egger 474, 475. The standard edition of his works is by Creuzer. The Enneads are translated by H. F. Müller (Berlin : 1878) — Ennead 1, Bk. 1, chap. 6 Das Schöne ; and by others cited in § **8,** PLOTINUS.

In Philostratus the Elder (Flavius), Vita Apoll. vi. 19 (circa A.D. 210), φαντασία is distinguished from μίμησις. The former is of a higher grade than the latter. Φαντασία creates that which it has not seen, μίμησις reproduces what it has seen. The statues of the gods by Phidias and Praxiteles are therefore productions of the φαντασία. Butcher, Greek Genius, p. 279, considers this the nearest approach in Greek literature to the idea of imagination as a creative faculty. Cf. Philostratus, Imagines 1 : 15, and

see Schasler 1 : 249, 250 for the relation between the theories of
Philostratus and Plotinus ; consult, also, Egger 511–515, Bosanquet 109, Overbeck, Schriftquellen zur Geschichte der bildenden
Künste 801, and Ed. Müller 2 : 317 *et seq.* The treatise on
the Sublime, attributed to Longinus, is discussed by Bosanquet, pp. 104–106, by Andrew Lang in his introduction to
Havell's translation, and by Egger, pp. 476–484; but, except in
one or two passages, quoted by Bosanquet, the essay on the
Sublime does not touch upon the aesthetic theory of imitation.
In James Drummond's Philo Judaeus (London : 1888), 2 : 97,
will be found an instructive passage on the oneness of art under
all its manifestations. " Perfect art," concludes Philo, "being
an imitation of nature, seals all materials with the same idea."

The utterances and the practice of the Roman poets are of
indirect rather than of positive value in the discussion. The
Ars Poetica of Horace is historically, if not critically, helpful.
See Bishop Hurd's notes. For the best known of Horace's poetic
canons see Ars Poetica, 333, 334, 343 ; Epist. Lib. II, 1 : 126,
138. By far the most fruitful of recent articles on aesthetic
theory among the Romans is Nettleship's Literary Criticism in
Latin Antiquity (*Journ. Philol.*, vol. 18, p. 230, to which reference has already been made ; and F. Barta's Ueber die auf d.
Dichtkunst bezüglichen Ausdrücke bei den römischen Dichtern;
1 Dichten u. Dichter, Prog. Linz a. D.: 1889 ; 2 Gedicht, 1890).

To the relation of allegorical representation to natural and
traditional symbolism in the formative art and the architecture of the ancients, Bosanquet, referring to Overbeck, Carriere,
Wm. Morris, and other authorities, devotes an interesting and
suggestive section of chapter 5, Hist. Aesth. Concerning
theories of the relation of art to nature in the Early Christian
and the Middle Ages, something of value may be gathered from
Egger, 524–570; Schasler, 1 : 250, 251 ; Bosanquet, 120–150;
Carriere, Die Kunst in Zusam. d. Culturentwickelung, 3 : 77–
138. The names of St. Augustine, Gregory the Great, Abelard,

Scotus Erigena, St. Francis of Assisi, and Thomas Aquinas will indicate the line of investigation to be pursued.

II) Among the Moderns.

For references to the works of modern authorities, Schasler, Bosanquet, and Von Hartmann may be consulted. Shaftesbury considers art to be the construction of material according to the standard of Beauty. Lord Kames limits natural beauty and consequently the representation of it to the objects of vision. Batteux (Traité des Beaux Arts) thinks that he is inculcating Aristotle's theory of imitation while he is more nearly advocating Plato's, and draws a distinction between mechanical, fine, and ornamental art which, although mistaken, still obtains in certain quarters of French criticism. Diderot (Essais sur la Peinture) also makes imitation the principle of his aesthetics, but while he appears to understand that nature should be imitated, according to Aristotle, not as an object, but as a process, he falls into the grievous error of attributing infallibility to natural processes : " Nature," he says, " makes nothing that is incorrect," a radically non-Aristotelian thesis. He does well, however, in insisting upon the imitation of the characteristic in nature. By confusing *actuality* with *truth*, Baumgarten in his Aesthetica comes to a conclusion like that of Diderot concerning the perfection of natural objects presented to perception, deducing therefrom the dictum : " The whole duty of the artist lies in the exact imitation of nature." Karl Philipp Moritz in his pamphlet, Ueber die bildende Nach-ahmung des Schönen, Braunschweig : 1788, advances a theory of imitation as emulation of the model given in nature, which, although his argument ends in the air, is at least suggestive of the truth.

Winckelmann, through all his writings, his Ueber den Geschmack der griechischen Kunst, his Ueber die Ergänzung der alten Statuen, his Kunst-Geschichte, his critique of his own work Ueber die Nachbildung der Alten, emphasizes and reiterates the well-known proposition, that there is but one art, that of the Greeks, and that would-be artists of modern times must draw from this well of inspiration. By this statement he meant not that modern artists must imitate the creations of the ancients, but that they must practice the ancient manner of imitation. He distinguishes between the servile copying and the selective imitation of nature, and by nature he means the ideal beauties revealed in nature. It is hardly necessary to remind the student of the Laokoon and the Hamburgische Dra-maturgie of Lessing, and of the important distinction which that critic makes between the kinds of imitation appropriate to poetry and to painting. Herder (Kritische Wälder u. s. w., Riga : 1769 ; Plastik u. s. w., Riga: 1778 ; Kalligone) appears to narrow art to the imitation of natural beauty, but his identifica-tion of the Beautiful with the True and the Good again extends the scope of the artist. On Kant and the opinions of writers who succeeded him, Goethe, Schiller, Jean Paul, W. von Hum-boldt, Friedrich Schlegel, Adam Müller, Solger, and others of that period, the student must be referred to Bosanquet and Schasler, whence the step to the originals (see § **8**), is easily made. For Schelling's opinions Ueber das Verhältniss der bildenden Künste zu der Natur, see the Sämmtliche Werke, Bd. 7, Abth. 1, 289–329. Hegel's arraignment of the theory of imitation as the end of art is brief, but conclusive. See Aesthetik, vol. I, pp. 55–61; Bosanquet's Trans., pp. 79–87 ; Kedney's Exposition, pp. 15–18. The superfluousness of Kedney's criticism on p. 16 will be seen by reference to the original, esp. p. 58 of the Aesthetik, — p. 84 of Bosanquet's Trans. Cf. Aesthetik, p. 5, Bosanquet's Trans., pp. 4, 5. In F. T. Vischer's Aesthetik, and in Schopenhauer's World as Will and Idea (Haldane and Kemp), vol. I, pp. 219–346, and vol. III, 173–219, 231–244, will be found valuable material, as also in Von Hartmann's Aesthetik. For Von Hartmann's exposition of Deutinger's views on imita-tion, see vol. II, pp. 184–187; of Kirchmann's, see pp. 256–259;

of Zimmermann's, pp. 270, 271. On the interesting question, how architecture is to be regarded as a kind of imitation, see the author's discussion of Schelling, pp. 466, 467. For Von Hartmann's view of imitation as one of the three preliminary stages of artistic activity, see vol. II, pp. 523–526. The subject is touched upon in several other places; see index under Nachahmung.

The best modern exposition is that of Bosanquet in his paper, The Part played by Aesthetic in the Growth of Modern Philosophy (Proc. Arist. Soc. I. 2, pp. 77–96), with which cf. his History of Aesthetic.

The following authors have been selected for brief mention: Professor Bain, Emotions and the Will, pp. 156, 182, 183, 196, 197, 204, 225 ; Beckenstedt, Die Nachahmung der Natur in der Kunst ; Baldwin Brown, The Fine Arts (an excellent introduction to the subject); Ch. Bénard, L'Esthétique contemporaine: La Mimique dans le Système des Beaux-Arts (*Rev. Philos.* 28 : 225. Bénard advocates a psychological and physiological basis for the investigation of the arts as members of an organism. The utility of a theory which predicates a system of united arts, is, however, called in question by Lotze); Walter Borman, Kunst und Nachahmung (Stuttg.: 1892); E. S. Dallas, The Gay Science, vol. I, pp. 97–111 ; Diderot, The Paradox of Acting, translated by W. H. Pollock, with a Preface by Henry Irving (London : 1883); C. C. Everett, Poetry, Comedy and Duty (the object of Prof. Everett's chapters on The Philosophy of Poetry, pp. 50–97, is to reconcile Aristotle's definition of poetry as imitation and Milton's specification that it should be "impassioned"[1]); Alexander von Humboldt, Cosmos (transl. Otté), vol. 2, pp. 1–105; The description of nature in poetry and painting; Kawczinski, (see § **23**), pp. 17, 18, 20, 30 Imitation ; Professor Knight,

---

[1] Milton's word is "passionate." See the Tractate on Education, and Mod. Lang. Notes 5 : 230.

Philosophy of the Beautiful, vol. II, pp. 56–65 (the author concurs with Goethe in his maxim "Art is art, precisely because it is not nature"); J. F. Marmontel, Éléments de Littérature (for Imitation see vol. I, Action; vol. III, Unité); D. Masson, Essays Biographical and Critical, pp. 408–424; G. S. Morris, Philosophy of Art, *J. Spec. Philos.* 10: 1; J. F. Pici, De imitatione libellus, 1530; Quatremère de Quincy, An Essay on the Nature, the End, and the Means of Imitation in the Fine Arts, transl. by J. C. Kent (an elaborate if somewhat conventional discussion); B. Riccii, De imitatione libri tres, Venetiis: 1541; J. J. Rousseau, De l'imitation théatrale (Œuvres Complètes, vol. III, pp. 183–191, a rather superficial contribution to the subject); P. Stapfer, Petite comédie de la critique littéraire (Paris: 1866), pp. 366–368; Wm. Main, Expression in Nature (Lond.: 1894); E. du Bois-Reymond, Relation of Natural Science to Art (Smithsonian Reports, 1891); Victor Cherbuliez, *Rev. d. D. Mondes* 15 Juin, 1 et 15 Juillet, 1 et 15 Août 1891 L'art et la nature; K. Biederman, *Nord u. Süd,* 1883, p. 95 Die Natur als Gegenstand poetischer Empfindung und Darstellung; Ernst Hallier, Aesthetik der Natur (Stuttgart: 1890); R. Vischer, *D. Rundschau* 76: 192 Ueber aesthetische Naturbetrachtung; Adam Smith, Of the Imitative Arts (Works, vol. V, p. 241).

I. **GROWTH OF THE FEELING FOR NATURE.**—In presenting the literature of this important topic, we may distinguish between writings intended for the general reader and writings intended for the specialist. To the first class belong such works and articles as the following: J. Veitch, The Feeling for Nature in Scottish Poetry (2 vols. Edinb.: 1887. The introductory chapters treat nature-feeling in general); E. Dowden *Contemp.* 2: 535 Poetical Feeling for Nature (an article of unusual interest); E. Dowden, Studies in Literature (Lond.: 1889), chapter on The Scientific Movement in Literature; Hamerton, Portfolio Papers (Notes on Aesthetics); Symonds, Essays

Speculative and Suggestive, vol. II, pp. 78–149 (on Landscape
and Nature-myths) ; Victor de Laprade, Histoire du Sentiment
de la Nature (Paris : 1883).

Among those of the second class attention may be drawn
first to the highly original paper by Bosanquet on The Part
played by Aesthetic in the Growth of Modern Philosophy
(Proc. Arist. Soc. I. 2, pp. 77–96) and to the observations scattered through the same author's History of Aesthetic. With this philosophical treatment, compare the
"scientific" views of Posnett presented in the latter's work
on Comparative Literature (see index under Nature). Still
more profound are the voluminous writings of the Germans,
among whom A. Biese takes a foremost place. The following
are the most important of Biese's contributions : Die Entwickelung des Naturgefühls bei den Griechen (Kiel : 1882);
Die Entw. d. Naturgefühls bei d. Römern (Kiel : 1884) ; Die
Entw. d. Naturgefühls im Mittelalter und in der Neuzeit (Leipz.:
1888); Das Metaphorische in d. dichterischen Phantasie ;
Zeits. f. Völkerpsychol. 20 : 245 Die poetische Naturbeseelung
bei den Griechen (1890); *Zeits. f. d. deutschen Unterricht* 5.
Jahrg. pp. 822–839 Die Naturlyrik Ludwig Uhland's und
Eduard Mörike's ; *Zeits. f. vergleich. Litteraturgeschichte*
N.F. 7 : 311 Zur Litteratur der Geschichte des Naturgefühls
(reviews at length previous contributions to the literature of
this subject). A few other German writers have ventured to
discuss nature-feeling in both its ancient and its modern aspects,
as K. K. Hense in his article Ueber das Naturgefühl in alter
und neuer Poesie (*Zeits. f. vergl. Litteraturgesch.* N.F. 1 : 182),
and Winter, in his Beiträge zur Geschichte des Naturgefühls
(Harburg : 1883) ; but the majority have so far specialized in
this field as to restrict their researches either to its ancient or
to its modern aspects.

Of those who have discussed nature-feeling among the
ancients, the following are especially worthy of note : Ad.

Gerber, Naturpersonification in Poesie und Kunst der Alten
(Bes. Abdr. aus d. XIII. Supplementbande d. *Jahrb. f.
klass. Philol.*, pp. 241–317); Grosse, Ueber Naturanschauung
d. alten griechischen und römischen Dichter (Progr. Ascher-
leben: 1890); O. Koerner, Ueber d. Naturbeobachtung im
homerischen Zeitalter (Frankfurt a. M.: 1886. Sonder-Abdr.
aus d. Bericht üb. d. Senckenberg. Naturforsch. Gesellschaft
in Frankf.); H. Planck, Die Entwickelung des Naturgefühls im
Alterthum (Stuttgart: 1891. Beilage des *Staats-Anzeigers für
Würtemberg*, pp. 145–148); L. Schmidt, Die Ethik der Alten
Griechen (2 vols. Berlin: 1881–2, Bd. 2, p. 80 Der Mensch im
Verhältniss zur Naturumgebung); Chr. Semler, Jahrb. d. öffentl.
Handelslehranstalt zu Dresden, 1891, pp. 3–26 Die Gleichnisse
Homers aus der Natur und ihre Bedeutung f. den Unterricht
und die Erziehung; W. Straub, Der Natursinn der alten
Griechen (Progr. Stuttgart: 1889); Ed. Voss, Die Natur in
der Dichtung des Horaz (Düsseldorf: 1889) ; L. Friedländer,
Das Interesse für Natur und das Naturgefühl überhaupt, Die
Entwickelung d. Gefühls für d. Romantische in d. Natur im
Gegensatz zum antiken Naturgefühl (Sittengeschichte Roms,
5th ed. 3 vols. Leipz.: 1881, vol. II, pp. 170–243. An admirable analysis of the emotions aroused in ancient Roman tourists
by objects of natural scenery).

Of German writers who have touched upon the *modern*
aspects of nature-feeling may be mentioned the following:
W. Dilthey, Arch. f. Geschichte d. Philos. 1889–II : 45 Zu
Goethe's Philosophie d. Natur ; H. Drees, Die poetische
Naturbetrachtung in den Liedern der deutschen Minne-
sänger (Festschr. Wernigerode: 1888); V. Hehn, Gedanken
über Goethe (Berlin: 1887), pp. 277–307 Naturphantasie;
Ludw. Kaemmerer, Die Landschaft in der deutschen Kunst
bis zum Tode Albrecht Dürer's (Beitr. z. Kunstgeschichte,
N.F. 4: 107. Leipz.: 1886); Max Kuttner, Das Naturgefühl
der Altfranzosen und sein Einfluss auf ihre Dichtung (Diss.

Berlin: 1889); O. Lüning, Die Natur, ihre Auffassung und poetische Verwendung in der altgermanischen und mittel-hochdeutschen Epik bis zum Abschluss der Blütezeit (Zürich: 1889) ; K. Marold, *Zeits. f. deutsche Philol.* 23: 1 Ueber die poetische Verwertung der Natur und ihrer Erschein-ung in den Vagantenliedern und im deutschen Minnesang ; Th. Urbach, Zur Geschichte des Naturgefühls bei den Deutschen (Progr. Dresden: 1885).

III. Methods of Research. — 1. *Psychological.* —

Of value in the investigation of psychological methods are the following books and articles : L. Arréat, Psychologie du Peintre (Paris: 1892); Bain's various writings (§ **8**); H. Cohen, Die dichterische Phantasie und der Mechanismus d. Bewusstseins (Berlin: 1869); J. Dewey, Psychology (New York: 1887) ; C. D. Dimetresco, Der Schönheitsbegriff (Leipzig: 1877); E. Dreher, Kunst in ihrer Beziehung zur Psychologie u. zur Naturwissenschaft (Ber-lin : 1878); O. D. Ernst, *Mag. f. Litt. d. In- und Auslandes,* 60: 56 Gedankenwerkstatt des Dichters ; M.-J. Guyau, *Rev. d. D. Mondes,* 15 Août, 1881 Le Plaisir du Beau et le Plaisir du Jeu; C. Hermann, Aesthetische Farbenlehre (Leipzig: 1876); H. Höffding, Outlines of Psychology; Max Jahn, Psychologie als Grundwissenschaft der Pädagogik (Leipzig: 1883), pp. 96–103; W. James, Principles of Psychology (New York: 1890. The subject of aesthetic is purposely excluded, but the chapters on Imagination and Feeling are rich in suggestions); Robt. Jardine, Elements of the Psychology of Cognition (London: 1874), pp. 172–179 ; Lazarus, Das Leben d. Seele (2 vols. Berlin : 1875–8); Ch. Lévêque, *Rev. d. D. Mondes,* 1 Sept. 1873 Le Sens du Beau chez les bêtes, le Darwinisme psycholo-gique et la Psychologie comparée ; H. R. Marshall, Pain, Pleas-ure, and Aesthetics ; J. C. Murray, Handbook of Psychology (London: 1885), pp. 223–235, 387–390; F. Paulhan, *Rev. Philos.* 19 : 652 Sur l'émotion esthétique ; Th. Ribot, English

Psychology (Translation.   New York: 1874), pp. 231–237 ;
S. Rubinstein, Psychologisch-aesthetische Essays (Heidelberg :
1878); P. Souriau, L'Esthétique, La Suggestion dans l'art
(Paris : 1892); P. Souriau, L'Esthétique du mouvement (Paris :
1889); J. Sully, Outlines of Psychology (London : 1884); D. G.
Thompson, A System of Psychology (2 vols.   London : 1884),
vol. I, pp. 585–594 ; J. Baldwin, Psychology, vol. II.

For an outline of study consult the Syllabus of Lectures on
the Psychology of Pain and Pleasure, published by B. I. Gilman in the *Am. Jl. Psychol.* 6 : 1.

2. *Physiological and Psycho-Physical.* — As the subjects are
now studied, there is much difficulty in drawing the line between
this method and the preceding.   Many of the writings cited
under the former head might also be called studies in physiology, or in physiological psychology.   Among undoubted investigators in this field are Spencer, Allen, Zeising, Fechner, Helmholtz, Wundt, and Ladd.   The following are a few of the recent treatises : E. Brücke, Principes scientifiques des beaux-
arts (Paris: 1893.   Together with Helmholtz's L'optique et
les Arts); G. Hirth, Aufgaben der Kunstphysiologie (München:
1891; also as Physiologie de l'art, translated from the German by L. Arréat.   Paris: 1892); Th. Lipps, Aesthetische
Faktoren der Raumanschauung (Beiträge zur Psychologie und
Physiologie der Sinnesorgane.   Hamburg u. Leipzig : 1891, pp.
219–307) ; P. Montegazza, Epikurische Physiologie d. Schönen
(translated by R. Teuscher.   Jena: 1891); L. Witmer, Philos.
Studien, ix. 1 : 96–144, 2 : 209–263 Zur experimentalen Aesthetik einfacher räumlichen Formverhältnisse ; A. Binet, La
Psychologie Expérimentale (Paris : 1894) ; Chas. Pékar, *Rev.
Philos.* 40: 186 Astigmatisme et esthétique (maintains that
certain hitherto inexplicable aesthetic preferences are due to
what is known as 'regular astigmatism.'   Reference is made
to a forthcoming work of the author's entitled Esthétique
physiologique et psychologique, of which the first part ap-

peared in 1890 in the *Athenaeum*, a philosophical review published by the Hungarian Academy).

An interesting article by Sorel on psycho-physical contributions to the study of aesthetics will be found in *Rev. Philos.* 29: 561, 30: 22.

3. *Sociological.* — In this promising field the laborers are few and the method of work is as yet but ill defined. Among those whose writings will be found helpful as guides, may be mentioned the following : A. Comte, The Positive Philosophy (Translation. N. Y.: 1854), vols. 2, pp. 213–220, 297–8, 392–405 ; H. Spencer, First Principles, and Principles of Sociology ; G. de Greef, Introduction à la sociologie (2 vols. Bruxelles et Paris : 1886–9), vol. 2, pp. 148–188 Fonctions et organes artistiques (unusually suggestive); A. Schäffle, Bau und Leben des socialen Körpers (4 vols., Tübingen: 1881, Index under Kunst). (The brief but numerous references touch upon a great variety of problems); L. F. Ward, Dynamic Sociology (2 vols. N. Y. : 1883, Index under Aesthetic and Art) ; M. J. Guyau, L'Art au point de vue sociologique (Paris: 1889) ; Von Hartmann, Aesthetik, vol. 2, pp. 425–492 Die Stellung des Schönen im menschlichen Geistesleben und im Weltganzen. See also § 11 under these names, and under Morris; and § 8 under Guyau, Dewey, Morris, and Wilde.

IV. Miscellaneous. — English. — W. H. Beard, Action in Art (New York : 1893. The author thinks that a knowledge of the laws governing action will guide the natural feeling of artists who represent action; by means of instantaneous photographs he shows what actions are possible of representation); A. L. Frothingham, Sr., *Amer. Jl. of Archaeology*, 9 : 165 The Philosophy of Art (traverses the whole field of aesthetic, using the divisions : 1. Personality of the artist; 2. Place of Art in civilization ; 3. Philosophy of Art ; 4. Aesthetic Dualism ; 5. Psychology of Art; 6. Art Ideals and Standpoints of Thought ;

7. Definition of Art — "the universal organon for the representation of the total ideality of existence"; 8. Mission of Art);
A. W. Holmes-Forbes, The Science of Beauty, an Analytical
Inquiry (London : 1889); W. Holman Hunt, *New Rev.* 4 : 420
The Ideals of Art; G. L. Raymond, Art in Theory, an Introduction to the Study of Comparative Aesthetics (New York:
1874. The preface advances the curious idea that art is not
the expression of the age. The best thing in the book is an
appendix by Professor Baldwin, who defines the sense of
beauty as an "emotional state arising from progressive psycho-
physical accommodation to mental objects"); A. Wolf, The
Truth about Beauty (New York: 1894); B. Bosanquet, E. W.
Cook, and D. G. Ritchie, The Relation of the Fine Arts to
one another (a Symposium. In Proc. of the Aristotelian Soc.,
vol. I, No. 3, pt. 2, p. 98); P. N. Waggett, Beauty (in Proc.
of Aristotelian Soc., vol. 1, No. 3, pt. 2, p. 129).

French. — E. Blémont, Esthétique de la Tradition (Paris :
1891); A. de Chambrun, Une étude d'esthétique (Paris : 1891);
Victor Cherbuliez, L'Art et la Nature (Paris : 1892. Repr.
from *Rev. d. D. Mondes*, 106 : 5, 242, 481, 721); Maurice
Griveau, Les éléments du beau: Analyse et synthèse des faits
esthétiques d'après les documents du langage (Paris : 1893);
E. Ledereq, Philosophie de l'enseignement des beaux-arts
(Paris-Verviers : 1891); A. Magnard, *Revue de Paris*, 15 Sept.
1894, p. 424 La synthèse des arts; É. Rabier, Leçons de Philosophie (3e éd. Paris : 1888), vol. I, Psychologie, pp. 623–643
Notions d'esthétique, pp. 644–653 De l'art.

The article Esthétique, in the Grande Encyclopédie, is divided
into four parts : C. Adams contributes a history of aesthetics ;
Henri d'Argés, a follower of Taine, writes on the plastic arts
and literature ; Alf. Ernst writes on Music.

German. — H. Fleischer, Ueber die Möglichkeit e. normativen
Aesthetik (Breslau: 1891. An attack on W. Scherer); Ernst

Grosse, *Gegenwart*, 40 : 70 Der erste Baustein zu einer ethnolo-
gischen Aesthetik (with reference to Hein's Die bildenden
Künste bei d. Dayaks auf Borneo.   Wien : 1891); E. Grosse,
Die Anfänge der Kunst (Freiburg : 1894); G. Hauck, *Preuss.
Jahrb.* 46 : 126 Ueber die Stellung der Mathematik zur Kunst
und Kunstwissenschaft ; Anna Holz, Die Kunst, ihr Wesen
und ihre Gesetze (Berlin : 1891. 'Modern' in tone, but not
genuinely scientific) ; H. Kratz, Aesthetik : Grundzüge einer
Lehre von der Gefühlen (Gütersloh : 1891); H. Marbach, Das
Mysterium d. Kunst (Leipzig : 1890); E. Kühnemann, *Philos.
Monatshefte*, 27 : 442 Bericht über neuere Erscheinungen aus
dem Gebiete der Geschichte der Aesthetik ; N. M. Pichtos, Die
Aesthetik Aug. W. von Schlegels in ihrer geschichtlichen
Entwickelung (Berlin : 1893); Alex. Raciborski, Die naturwissen-
schaftlichen Grundlagen unserer aesthetischen Urtheile (translated from the Polish.   Of slight value); H. Stein, Die Entstehung der neuern Aesthetik (Stuttgart : 1886) ; O. Voigt, Das
Ideal der Schönheit und Hässlichkeit in den altfranzösischen
Chansons de geste (Marburg : 1891); R. Wahle, Das Ganze
der Philosophie und ihr Ende (Wien : 1894), pp. 396–426 Das
Schöne ; K. Werner, Zur Metaphysik des Schönen (*Sitzungsb.
d. Akad. d. Wiss.*   Wien : 1874, p. 737); B. Wille, *Freie Bühne
f. mod. Leben*, 1891, p. 467 Tendenz in d. Poesie (distinguishes
four methods of normative aesthetics : 1. The postulating
method, "I want so-and-so"; 2. The metaphysical, proceeding
from a philosophical system ; 3. The authoritative, taking its
law from the work of an artist ; 4. The psychological, which
observes the effects of the work, notes uniformities [laws] of
effect, and establishes a norm); J. Wohlgemuth, Henry Home's
Aesthetik (Rostock : 1894); Theobald Ziegler, *Zeitschr. f. vergl.
Litteraturgesch.*, N.F. 7 : 113 Zur Genesis eines aesthetischen
Begriffs.

Italian. — Salvatore di Pietro, Sul Bello (Palermo : 1882);
G. S. Ferrari, Sul Bello (Verona : 1882); Maria Pilo, Estetica

(Milano: 1893); L. Leynardi, La Psicologia dell' arte nella Divina Commedia (Torino: 1894).

A review of Italian writers of this century may be found in K. Werner's Idealistische Theorien des Schönen in der italienischen Philosophie des XIX. Jahrhunderts (*Sitzungsb. d. Akad. Wiss.* Wien: 1884, p. 645), and in L. Ferri's Essai sur l'histoire de la philosophie en Italie au XIX. siècle (1869).

On Dutch, Danish, and Russian aesthetics, see Wm. Knight's Philosophy of the Beautiful, parts I and II.[1]

---

[1] A pamphlet entitled Aesthetics, its Problems and Literature (by F. N. Scott), published at Ann Arbor in 1890, but now out of print, has been drawn upon for some portions of this chapter.

Part II. — Development of Art.

§ 10. Statement of Problems.

THE term history of art is used in a variety of senses. In the writings of one author it means biographies of painters; in the writings of another, descriptions, chronologically arranged, of famous monuments of architecture; a third employs it to designate an account of the arts of form, viz. architecture, sculpture, and painting. In this chapter the term will be employed in a large and general sense. Art we shall interpret broadly to mean products of aesthetic activity. History of Art will designate a record of the development of this activity, whenever and wherever and however it may have taken place. The histories of the several arts will be conceived as integral parts of this great record, segregated for purposes of convenience.

For this organic conception of art-history the student may consult the following references: Hegel's Introduction to the Philosophy of Fine Art, in Bosanquet's Translation; Bosanquet's History of Aesthetic, pp. 345–352; Wm. Knight's Philosophy of the Beautiful, pt. II, p. 68; and Miss Paget's article on Comparative Aesthetics in *Contemp.* 38: 300. Of a universal history of art such as this view demands, Carriere's Die Kunst im Zusammenhang der Culturentwickelung und die Ideale der Menschheit is the unique example.

The objections to the organic conception should be considered impartially. See Colvin's article, 'Fine Arts,' in the Encycl. Brit., 9th ed., for a clear statement of the reasons why architecture, sculpture, and painting should be regarded as one group, and music and poetry receive independent treatment.

It will be convenient to consider the problems of art-evolution under two principal heads : (1) problems concerning the history of art in general; (2) problems concerning the several species or sorts of arts.   Under each head it will be necessary to consider origins, principles and stages of growth, and influences.

I. Art in General. A. The ORIGIN OF ART should receive attention first.   Under what circumstances, in response to what stimulus, in obedience to what instinct, did art first make its appearance?   The following hypotheses should be carefully examined :

1. *Art is the Outgrowth of an Imitative Instinct.*—The oldest of all theories of art, this is also the most persistent, having been revived recently by both psychologists and sociologists.   For the views of Plato and Aristotle, see the references in § 7 above, pp. 140–150.   For more recent views, see pp. 160–163. To these references may now be added G. Tarde's La logique sociale (Paris : 1895), chap. IX, and J. M. Baldwin's Social and Ethical Interpretations of Mental Development (N. Y.: 1897), pp. 147–153.   It may not be amiss to observe that by adopting this view of the origin of the art-impulse, the student does not necessarily commit himself to an imitation-theory of modern art.

2. *Art is the Outgrowth of an Instinct for Self-Expression.* — This appears under a great variety of forms, being often combined with other theories.   For a statement of the point of view, see Bosanquet's History of Aesthetic, chap. I, and the article by the same writer in *Mind*, N. S. 3: 153.

3. *Art is the Outgrowth of the Play-Impulse.* — This will be recognized as the view of Schiller, which Spencer in his Psychology and Grant Allen in his Physiological Aesthetics, have elaborated into a system.   The student should observe that Spencer combines this theory with the theory of imitation.

Play, he says, is the result of superfluous energy, accumulated in periods of inactivity ; but it is the instinct for imitation that causes the expenditure of this energy to take the form of mimic chasing, fighting, killing, etc., leading to the dance, to rude forms of drama, and to the beginnings of the graphic arts.

4. *Art is the Outgrowth of an Instinct for Order.* — Under the guise of rhythm, measure, proportion, harmony, and other similar terms, this principle of aesthetic origins has been a favorite. By Professor Baldwin Brown it is ingeniously united with the preceding. There are, he says, "two elements that must combine for the production of even the simplest form of art. (1) There must exist a certain raw material in the form of a movement, an act, a process, which may be the mere instinctive throwing off of superfluous nervous energy, or may possess more or less pronounced emotional or intellectual character, and (2) this material must be disciplined into a certain distinctness of form by the principle of 'Order' till it becomes a rational product." (The Fine Arts, p. 12 ; the idea is elaborated in pp. 10–19.)

5. *Art is the Outgrowth of an Instinct to Attract Others.* — This idea is used by Darwin to explain the colors of animals and the adornments of primitive peoples. For references to the Origin of Species and Descent of Man, see *supra*, p. 135. The reader should also consult G. Semper's Der Stil in den technischen und tektonischen Künsten (2 vols. München : 1878–9), and Brown's The Fine Arts, pp. 20, 21. In H. R. Marshall's Pain, Pleasure, and Aesthetics, the theory is used effectively and given wide application.

6. *Art is the Outgrowth of an Attempt to Repel or Terrify.* — This is a counterpart of the preceding. It is used, in connection with other theories, by De Greef, Introd. à la sociologie, vol. II, pp. 148–188. Adopting the Spencerian view of art as the outcome of superfluous energy, De Greef says that such energy finds expression in two forms : (1) in the decorations

with which warriors adorn their persons to render them more
terrible or imposing; (2) in the pleasing embellishment of
arms and utensils. The same idea is advanced by Sully in
Mind, N. S. 2 : 404.

7. *Art is the Outgrowth of an Impulse to Communicate.* —
This theory has been developed mainly in its application to the
origin of language, on which see § **13.** From writers on art
it has not received the attention to which it would seem
to be entitled. The student will do well to give it serious
consideration.

8. *Art is the Outgrowth of Festal or Ceremonial Celebrations.*
— Properly considered, this origin is secondary rather than
primary. The festal occasion merely supplies a channel for
the overflow of some one of the impulses enumerated above.
For a brief treatment of this view, see Brown's The Fine Arts,
p. 23.

9. *Art is the Outgrowth of a Desire to Obtain an Image of the
Intangible or Spiritual Part of Man.* — Seemingly akin to the
imitation-theory, but in reality very different. The best statement of this view is that of Professor Giddings, Principles of
Sociology (N. Y.: 1896), pp. 247, 248 : "There was one class
of phenomena in which a living self, ordinarily united with the
body though separable from it, seemed to the primitive man to
be already partly separated or in the act of separation. Walk-
ing in the sunlight, he always saw a shadow that moved as he
moved or was motionless when he stood still, but which never
completely detached itself from him. What could this be but
a conscious self, belonging to the bodily self and usually
merged in it, but capable of going away, to live alone? Looking in the pool, he saw the shadow self more distinctly, and
it behaved as before. When he called aloud to his comrades,
his voice came back from the mountain. His double then
could be far away and invisible, and yet speak and preserve
the identity of his proper tone.

"Here were data for curious inferences. The shadow and the echo were parts of one's intangible self. Words, then, and names must be a part of the spiritual self, and to know a man's name must be to have a part of his essential personality in one's possession and therefore to have a mysterious control over him. This belief is found among savages in every quarter of the world to-day. Possibly before it arose some one had traced with a stick the outlines of a shadow on the sand, and rude drawings may have been used as written names. Whether so or not, the thought would arise that to have an image of any object conceived as personal, would be to possess an essential part of that object and to have its name. Words and images then were charms, in themselves, and mediately, as names. Through words and images one could come into subtle relations with the very spirit of another, could feel the stirrings of a spiritual life external to his own. The aesthetic sense was born. Here were the vital origins of writing and literature, and of all the plastic arts of expression."

See also *supra*, p. 86, *D*.

One fundamental question about origins should not be overlooked : Is art something inherent and ineradicable in man's nature, so that in some form it will be found at all stages of his development ? or, on the other hand, is it an acquisition which he makes only when in the struggle upward he reaches a certain point ? In other words, is there in man's history a pre-artistic stage ? See Brown's The Fine Arts, pp. 3–11. A comparison of the aesthetic products of men and animals is held by some to throw light upon this problem. See Brown's The Fine Arts, pp. 12–16.

B. **PRINCIPLE OR LAW OF DEVELOPMENT.**—Principles of artistic evolution may be roughly classified as : (1) speculative or philosophical, and (2) scientific.

1. *Speculative Principles.* — Under this head, for convenience, may be classed all schemes of ideal evolution, whether simple

or elaborate.   As an example of a simple (and formal) scheme may be mentioned that which Winckelmann expounds in the opening chapter of his History of Art, viz. that art begins with the necessary, culminates in the beautiful, and closes with the superfluous.

Of elaborate systems, that of Hegel is the most eminent example.   Indeed it is not going too far to say that, positively or negatively, it has shaped the views of all succeeding writers upon art.   It behooves the student, therefore, to make himself thoroughly at home in the general principles of Hegel's Aesthetik, as they are set forth in the Einleitung (Introd. to the Philos. of Fine Art, Bosanquet's Trans. and Appendix to Bosanquet's History of Aesthetic).   Although the Hegelian law of progression can be better understood from Hegel's own language than from the exposition and comments of his critics, yet help may be derived from the excellent analysis in Bosanquet's History of Aesthetic, pp. 334–354, especially p. 335.

The student should not accept the Hegelian view of art-evolution without careful scrutiny of the bases on which the conception rests.   He should inquire whether Hegel in his theorizings did violence to the artistic materials then accessible to him, and also whether his theories are consistent with the facts of art-history as they have been brought out by later research.   A question of no less interest is whether according to the Hegelian principle art at the present day is in a period of decline, "tending to pass out of the strictly artistic region" and "not possessing in modern civilization the same sole supremacy that it claimed in the Periclean age or in the first flush of the Renascence."   On this question, see Von Hartmann's Aesthetik, vol. I, p. 127, Bosanquet's History of Aesthetic, pp. 343, 344, 354, and Laprade's Essais de Critique idéaliste.

For other philosophic principles of art-evolution, see HENRY, LOTZE, CARRIERE, and VISCHER.

2. *Scientific Principles.* — The application of scientific theories of evolution to the facts of art-history has resulted in a variety of principles, which may be roughly classed as (*a*) biological and (*b*) social.

a. By the first is meant a principle of growth more or less exactly analogous to that which governs the life-history of a plant or animal. According to this analogy, art during a certain period of years is born, comes to the fulness of its strength, grows old, and dies. Although in one form or another this view goes back to very ancient times, Winckelmann was perhaps the first to employ it with a distinct appreciation of its value. "The history of art," according to Winckelmann, "is intended to show the origin, progress, change and downfall of art." (Preface of Winckelmann's History of Ancient Art, p. 107.) How the principle is used by Winckelmann the student should learn for himself by a reading of the History.

A semi-scientific elaboration of this idea is made by Mr. J. A. Symonds in an essay entitled On the Application of Evolutionary Principles to Art and Literature, published in Essays, Speculative and Suggestive (Lond. : 1890), vol. I, p. 42. With it should be compared Miss Paget's article on Comparative Aesthetics, in *Contemp.* 38:300.

Reference should be made at this point to the famous theory of Taine, which also rests upon a biological metaphor. The object of Taine's formula, however, is not so much to furnish a law of progression as to account for the condition of art at any given epoch.

Brunetière in his recent work, L'évolution des genres dans l'histoire de la littérature, supplementing the formula of Taine by a special application of Spencer's theory of evolution, proposes to establish the law of artistic development on a scientific foundation ; but his theories, if sound, are as yet too vague to be susceptible of criticism.

b. Social theories of art-evolution, so far as they have

been developed, appear to be of two kinds : (1) those which
simply posit a connection between certain stages of artistic
development and corresponding stages of social development;
(2) those which endeavor to determine the place and function
of art as a factor in the evolution of society.   For information
on these types of theory and for illustrations of them, the
student may consult the writings referred to on p. 168 above,
and the works of Herder, Comte, Spencer, Ward, Guyau, De
Greef, and Giddings (§ 11).   See especially Ernst Grosse's
The Beginnings of Art (N. Y. : 1897), chaps. II and IX.   A
satisfactory treatment of art-evolution from the social point of
view is, however, still to seek.

In investigating scientific principles of art-development the
student should keep in view such questions as the following :
How far may one trust an analogy with any other set of
phenomena to reveal the essential principle of artistic growth ?
What warrant have we for comparing art with a plant or an
animal ?   Why should we not seek the principle of development
in the nature of art itself rather than in things which resemble
or accompany art ?

For questions touching particularly the social aspects of art,
see above, pp. 86, 87.

C. STAGES OF GROWTH. — Hegel's division into Symbolic,
Classic, and Romantic art, or, what is the same thing, into
Eastern, Greek, and Christian art, is still accepted as the
simplest and most practicable.   These broad divisions have
been variously subdivided.   Miss Paget in *Contemp*. 38: 300
proposes to divide each main period into three stages, viz.
heroic, dramatic, idyllic.   Most of the divisions proposed by
others are chronological, as for example, the division of Christian Art into Early Christian, Renaissance, and Modern.   They
may or may not be based upon a philosophical or scientific
theory of art-evolution.

If the student is able to make extended research he will
find it profitable to inquire into the correspondence of the
stages of art-development in different and isolated countries,
— in Egypt and in Chaldea, for example. The labors of
Perrot and Chipiez have made the sources for such studies
easily accessible.

D. **INFLUENCES.** — The student should inquire as to the influence of climate, religion, science, industry, morals, education, and
politics upon the growth of art. See TAINE, HENNEQUIN, and
GROSSE. He may also inquire how the art of one country has in
general affected the art of another. See MÜLLER, and PERROT
and CHIPIEZ. How the art of any single nation has been
influenced by the materials at hand and by local customs, as,
for example, the art of Greece by the presence of marble in
her soil and love of athletics in the minds of her citizens, is
also a profitable inquiry. See WALDSTEIN and WINCKELMANN.

II. The Several Arts. — *A*. With reference to the ***origin
of the several arts,*** the following theses should be examined :
(1) All art was originally one, and the several arts have come
into being by a process of differentiation. (2) The arts of form,
viz. architecture, sculpture, and music, were originally combined; the other arts had an independent origin. (3) Each
art arose in independence of every other. (4) The arts arose
in different ways and at different relative periods in different
countries. See SPENCER, COLVIN, and KNIGHT. On the origin
of architecture, consult Lübke's History of Art, chap. I, Lübke's
and Fergusson's histories of Architecture, and Brown's The
Fine Arts, pp. 24–33. On the origin of sculpture, see Lübke's
History of Sculpture, and Grant Allen's Physiological Aesthetics, pp. 232–242. On the origin of painting and the graphic
arts generally, see Brown's The Fine Arts, pp. 19–24, Miss
Simcox's Primitive Civilizations, vol. I, p. 4, Middleton's article,

'Schools of Painting,' in the Encycl. Brit., 9th ed., Lübke's History of Art, vol. I, p. 243 *et seq.*, Grant Allen's Physiological Aesthetics, pp. 222–232, and especially Hamerton's Drawing and Engraving (Lond.: 1892: repr. from the Encycl. Brit., 9th ed.), pp. 6–18. For an interesting controversy regarding the origin of music, see Darwin's Descent of Man, vol. II, p. 336, Spencer's essays On the Origin and Function of Music (Essays, Scientific, Political, and Speculative), and On the Origin of Music (*Mind*, October, 1890), Gurney's Power of Sound, chap. XXII, J. F. Rowbotham's essay on the Origin of Music (*19th Century*, October, 1880), and Richard Wallaschek's Primitive Music (Lond.: 1893). The origins of poetry and prose will be discussed in following chapters.

On the origin of all of these arts and also of dancing, see the chapters on the general arts in Wm. Knight's Philosophy of the Beautiful, pt. II, pp. 85–250.

B. **PRINCIPLE OF DEVELOPMENT AND STAGES OF GROWTH.** — For the sake of brevity these topics may here be considered together. The student should inquire whether the various arts in their development pass through similar stages, whether for example the history of architecture in its principal features has been the same as the history of sculpture, whether in painting there is a sequence corresponding to the drum, pipe, and lyre stages in music. He may also compare the course of any one art as it has developed in different countries, *e.g.*, the history of sculpture in Egypt and Assyria. The stages of evolution in the minor arts, such as engraving and ceramics, may be profitably compared with the stages of evolution in the greater arts. See the references cited above, and also J. F. Rowbotham's History of Music (Lond.: 1885).

An interesting though difficult question is as to an art's seeming disappearance. When an art declines and passes away, does it, we may ask, really die as a plant dies? Is it

not rather transformed into some other species, and is not
the art-germ in changing shapes thus perpetuated forever?
Ingenious though unsatisfactory speculations touching this
question will be found in Brunetière's L'évolution des genres
dans l'histoire de la littérature.   Consult also Fergusson's
History of Architecture.

The question has also been raised, especially in the discussion of the Wagnerian Opera, whether through the modern differentiation of artists art has advanced or retrograded.   See
Colvin's ' Fine Arts ' in the Encycl. Brit., 9th ed.

The part played by convention in the development of certain
of the arts is worthy of careful consideration.   On the conven-
tions of architecture and sculpture, see Brown's The Fine Arts,
pp. 244–258.

C. **Influences.** — The student should inquire regarding the
influence which one art exerts upon another, such as the influence of dancing on sculpture, of the textile arts on painting.
See Brown's The Fine Arts, pp. 23, 46, 50, 52, 75.   He may
also ask how the history of an art in one country has operated
upon the same art in another country, either contemporaneously
or successively.   See Perrot and Chipiez, Introd. to History of
Ancient Egyptian Art.   The influence of the environment, and
of movements in religion, science, education, etc., upon the
several arts is a profitable question for discussion.   See in
general, Ruskin, Taine, Macaulay, Waldstein.

The influence of guilds, schools, factions, academies, prizes,
and publications devoted to art, upon the development of the
several arts, awaits the attention of the investigator.

§ 11.   REFERENCES.

Begg, W. P.   The Development of Taste, and other Studies
  in Aesthetics.   Glasgow : 1887.
      See § 8.

BROWN, B.   The Fine Arts.

Especially useful in the study of the origin and connection of the arts.

CARRIERE, M.   Die Kunst im Zusammenhang der Cultur-entwickelung und die Ideale der Menschheit.   5 vols. Leipz.: 1871–73.

CARRIERE, M.   Die sittliche Weltordnung.   Leipz.: 1877.
 Pp. 339–354 Die Kunst.

Following the line of thought which he had so eloquently expressed in his Religious Discourses, that of a God self-conscious and eternally revealing himself in Nature, Carriere, in his celebrated work on Art in its Connection with the Development of Civilization, traces, from the point of view of Ideal-realism, the development of the idea of the Beautiful and its gradual realization in life and art.   Vol. I treats of The Beginning of Civilization, and the Oriental antiquity in Religion, Poetry, and Art; vol. II of Greece and Rome in their Religion, their Wisdom, Poetry, and Art; vol. III (1) of Christian Antiquity and Mohammedanism; vol. III (2) of the Middle Ages in Europe; vol. IV of the Renaissance and the Reformation ; vol. V, of the Period of the Ascendancy of Spirit.   For comment, see article in *Bib. Sac.* 18: 227.

COLVIN, S.   Encycl. Brit., 9th ed.   'Fine Arts.'

Pt. III of this excellent article is upon the History of Art. It is principally an analysis and criticism of the views of Hegel, Spencer, and Taine.

COMTE, AUG.   The Positive Philosophy.   Trans. by Harriet Martineau.   2 vols.   N. Y.: 1854.
 Vol. II, p. 195 Relation of Fetichism to the Fine Arts; pp. 213–220 Polytheistic Art; pp. 297–298 Catholic Art; pp. 392–405 Aesthetic Development; p. 432 Modern Art; pp. 454–455 Recent Aesthetic Progress; pp. 559–561 The Aesthetic Action.

According to the social philosophy of Auguste Comte, man
in his evolution from a lower to a higher plane passes through
three stages or 'states.' There is first the theological state,
within which are the three phases, fetichism, polytheism,
monotheism ; then the metaphysical state ; finally the positive
state. In each of these periods, art as "an ideal and sympathetic representation of human sentiment, — personal, domestic,
and social," conforms to the stage of civilization. "The best
way, therefore, of ascertaining its state at any particular time
is, not by regarding it by itself, but by looking at those characteristics of modern civilization with which it is incorporated, to
ascertain its share in them, and observe what new properties it
may have disclosed " (p. 218). This Comte attempts to do in
the passages indicated above.

The results of this method of treatment are highly interesting and valuable, and will always be suggestive to those who
are seeking to establish a theory of art-evolution upon a
sociological basis ; but at the same time, it must be remarked
that Comte's sweeping generalizations rest upon data which he
appears not always to have verified. It would be a mistake,
therefore, for the student to accept his conclusions and especially
to use them as a basis for further investigation, without subjecting them to careful scrutiny.

CROWE, J. A. and CAVALCASELLE, G. B.   A New History of
      Painting in Italy from the Second to the Sixteenth Century.
      3 vols.   Lond. : 1864–66.

CROWE, J. A. and CAVALCASELLE, G. B.   A History of Paint-
      ing in North Italy. . . .   From the Fourteenth to the
      Sixteenth Century.   2 vols.   Lond. : 1871–74.

The authors of A New History of Painting in Italy have
added to the information furnished by Vasari and Lanzi much
that has been drawn from the direct comparison of works of

art with each other and much that has hitherto been buried in
rare and inaccessible archives.   Towards forming a theory of
the evolution of art in general, perhaps the following chapters
will most contribute : vol. I, chap. I, Art to the Close of the Sixth
Century; chap. II, Italian Art from the Seventh to the Thirteenth
Century; chap. V, Decline of Painting in Central Italy in the
Thirteenth Century ; chap. XII, Giotto's Influence on the Sculp-
tors of his Time; chap. XXVI, Religious Art in Convents; vol.
II, chap. II, Fundamental Difference between Sienese and
Florentine Art; also chaps. VI, VIII, XI, XIII–XVII; vol.
III, chap. III, Decline of the School of Siena; chap. IV,
Rise of the Perugian School.

Crowded with information as is the History of Painting in
North Italy, it is not so suggestive of theories as directly to
benefit the student.

EASTLAKE, SIR C. L. [ed.] Handbook of Painting. The
Italian Schools. Based on the Handbook of Kugler.
4th ed. Revised . . . by Lady Eastlake. 2 vols. Lond.:
1874.

In the preface to this work will be found a brief but somewhat useful reminder of the dependence of art upon religion,
social and political relations, circumstances of climate and of
place, the character of a nation, a school, and an individual.
Otherwise the scope of this work is beside the present purpose
of the student.

FERGUSSON, JAMES. A History of Architecture in all Countries,
from the Earliest Times to the Present Day. 2d ed.
4 vols. Lond.: 1874.

In vol. I, pp. 52–84, of this standard work will be found an
interesting chapter on ethnography as applied to architecture.
The main conclusions, so far as concerns the principle of
artistic development, appear in brief in the following sentence :

"Progress among men, as among the animals, seems to be
achieved not so much by advances made within the limits of
the groups, as by the supersession of the less finely organized
beings by those of a higher class ; — and this, so far as our
knowledge extends, is accomplished neither by successive creations, nor by the gradual development of one species out of
another, but by the successive prominent appearances of
previously developed, though partially dormant creations."

GAUCKLER, PH.   Le beau et son histoire.

A chapter on the Influence of Religion, pp. 60–78, contains original ideas regarding the relation between the development of art and the development of religious thought.   Other
passages bearing upon this and cognate topics are scattered
through the work.

GREEF, GUILLAUME DE.   Introduction à la sociologie.   2 vols.
     Brussels et Paris : 1886–89.
          Vol. II, pp. 148–188, Fonctions et organes artistique.

A work of high standing.   The chapter on the social aspects
of art, though less satisfactory than other portions of the work,
is valuable by reason of its suggestiveness.   Art for De Greef,
as for Spencer and Allen, is the product of superfluous energy,
finding vent, at times of leisure, in simulated and idealized
activity.   The part which it has played, in its various forms,
in the growth of the individual and the evolution of society, is
sketched, if too rapidly, yet clearly and firmly.

GROSSE, ERNST.   The Beginnings of Art.   N. Y. : 1897.

An attempt to find a scientific basis for the theory and
history of art.   Grosse connects the rise of art with methods
of securing food and makes the form of production depend on
geographical and meteorological conditions.   Of especial interest is his distinction of social art, belonging to primitive
stages, and individual art, belonging to later stages.

Guyau, M.-J.   L'Art au point de vue sociologique.

   See § 8.

   The author does not deal directly with the development of art, but by connecting in his theory the growth of aesthetic feeling with the growth of the social instinct, he suggests to students of art-evolution an interesting line of research.

Hegel, G. W. F.   Werke.   18 vols.   Berlin : 1838–48.   Bd. X, Theile 1–3, Aesthetik.

   The importance of this work has already been affirmed in § 10.   It is at once the most elaborate and the most profound of all attempts to philosophize about the history of art.   Nor is it all pure speculation.   Its conclusions are based upon observations both wide and minute, and the keenness of Hegel's criticisms upon particular types and specimens of art is acknowledged by all who have read them.

   The greater part of the Aesthetik, and in some respects the most interesting part, is still untranslated, but those portions which deal especially with the principles of the history of art are now accessible in English.   The following references bear especially upon the historical aspect: Aesthetik, vol. I, pp. 387–547 ; vol. II, pp. 3–240 (Bosanquet's Trans., pp. 133–156, Kedney's Exposition, pp. 114–150, Hastie's Trans., pp. 34–46, and the translations by Bryant and Miss Longwell in *J. Spec. Philos.*). Notice Hegel's application of the terms Symbolic, Classic, and Romantic to the particular arts as well as to the stages of Art, and his reasons therefor.   In connection with the original should be read the exposition and comment in Bosanquet's History of Aesthetic.   In the course of an article on Ruskin, *No. Am.* 84 : 385, Prof. Everett presents a clear exposition of Hegel's theory of Art-evolution.

Henry, Ch.   *Rev. Philos.* 22 : 81.   La loi d'évolution de la sensation musicale.

Evolution has taken place from the objective to the subjective side of experience. This is shown by the fact that sensations of pitch among the Greeks were given an objective interpretation, being associated with the distance of the sonorous body from the hearer ; whereas in modern times pitch is associated with the purely subjective conception of upward and downward direction.

LANZI, L. The History of Painting in Italy : from the period of the Revival of the Fine Arts to the end of the Eighteenth Century. Trans. by Thos. Roscoe. 6 vols. Lond. : 1828.

The author's purpose was threefold : to mark the successive stages of the history of painting in Italy, to contribute to the advancement of the art, and to facilitate the study of the different styles of painting. His treatment of the subject is captivating, and in so far as he has indicated the relation between the political and social history of Italy and the art of the country he is of advantage to the student of aesthetics. Many questions pertinent to the evolution of art are touched upon in Lanzi's preface to vol. I. Since Lanzi died in 1810, it will be advisable for the student to revise his statements with the aid of more recent investigation.

LOTZE, H. Microcosmus. Trans. by E. Hamilton and E. E. C. Jones. 2 vols. Edinb. : 1885.

Vol. II, pp. 398–443, Beauty and Art.

An account of the characteristic forms of beauty and art in ancient and modern times. Readable but not always trustworthy.

LAPRADE, VICTOR DE. Essais de Critique idéaliste. Paris: 1882.

Pp. 49–77 De l'idée de progrès appliquée a l'histoire des arts ; pp. 337–365 Les origines du réalisme.

In these entertaining essays the author presents views of the development of art based upon the theories of Hegel. Starting from Hegel's statement that the age of art is past, he arrives at the conclusion that the idea of illimitable progress, though illustrated in other branches of human activity, is wholly inapplicable to the arts. Art is destined to run its course ; when its season is past a new development is inconceivable. Science can furnish it means of facile execution and of rapid multiplication of copies, but not a single principle of original creation or veritable progress. The Parthenon, the cathedrals, the music of Beethoven are the highest ideals in art. To surpass them is impossible. Laprade constructs a "ladder of the arts," which he epigrammatizes as follows : "God is architectural, the half-god, hero, or saint is sculptural, man is pictorial, external nature is musical." At the present time, he says, through the pursuit of realism, the arts are breaking up into little *genres;* nature is vanquishing man. (Cf. Bosanquet, Hist. of Aesth., p. 343 ff., esp. the footnote on p. 344.)

MACAULAY, T. B. Critical, Historical and Miscellaneous Essays.

> Vol. II, pp. 208–211 (Milton) Poetry and Civilization; pp. 325–351 (Dryden) Laws of Progress of the Fine Arts. See also Index under Art.

MIDDLETON, J. H. 'Schools of Painting.' In Encycl. Brit., 9th ed.

A sketch of the development of painting from the earliest times to the present.

MÜLLER, C. O. Ancient Art and its Remains. With additions by F. G. Welcker. Trans. by John Leitch. Lond. : 1852.

As the first general history of ancient art to appear in Germany, this work may be said to have laid the foundation for a comparative study of art. Müller understood and presented with great clearness the connection between the art of Greece and the art of Rome; but since in his time the study of Oriental art was still in its infancy, he failed to comprehend, or at least did not present, the intimate connection which exists between Greek art and the art of more ancient civilizations.

OVERBECK, J. Geschichte der griechischen Plastik. 3. Aufl. 2 vols. Leipz.: 1881–82.

Overbeck esteems it the duty of the historian of art not to accumulate disconnected facts, nor to indulge the vice of arbitrary classification, but " to seek in the multiplicity of works of art that which is universal and conformable, for it is only by such method that he can attain to a comprehension of the inherent continuity of development." The Einleitung is well worth reading in its entirety.

PAGET, VIOLET (Vernon Lee). *Contemp.* 38 : 300, Comparative Aesthetics.

Follows Hegel in calling the grand divisions of art-history Symbolic, Classic, and Romantic Art, but makes under each division three subdivisions corresponding to the rise, the culmination, and the decline of the art-impulse. These subdivisions she terms the heroic, the dramatic, and the idyllic stages.

PERROT, G., and C. CHIPIEZ. History of Art in Ancient Egypt. 2 vols. Lond.: 1883.

PERROT, G., and C. CHIPIEZ. A History of Art in Chaldea and Assyria. 2 vols. Trans. by W. Armstrong. Lond.: 1884.

PERROT, G., and C. CHIPIEZ. A History of Ancient Art in Phoenicia and its Dependencies. 2 vols. Lond.: 1885.

PERROT, G., and C. CHIPIEZ. A History of Ancient Art in Sardinia, Judaea, Syria, and Asia Minor. Lond.: 1890.

PERROT, G., and C. CHIPIEZ. A History of Ancient Art in Persia. Lond. : 1892.

PERROT, G., and C. CHIPIEZ. A History of Ancient Art in Phrygia, Lydia, Caria, and Lycia. Lond. : 1892.

PERROT, G., and C. CHIPIEZ. A History of Mycenian Art. 2 vols. Lond. : 1894.

Both in substance and in form these are works of the highest order of merit. The several volumes which are enumerated above are to be regarded as a single work having for its aim "to trace the cause of the great plastic evolution which culminated in the age of Pericles and came to an end in that of Marcus Aurelius." In the Introduction to the volumes on Ancient Egyptian Art, M. Perrot speaks out boldly for the evolutionary point of view in the study of art. He asserts that the conception of an isolated Greek art held by Karl Müller and others is no longer tenable : "Our age is the age of history ; it interests itself above all others in the sequence of social phenomena and their organic development, an evolution which Hegel explained by the laws of thought. It would be more than absurd in these days to accept Greek art as a thing self-created in its full perfection, without attempting to discover and explain the slow and careful stages by which it arrived at its apogee in the Athens of Pericles." He also attacks and skillfully confutes the popular theory that Egyptian art underwent no change. On this point see the valuable chapter entitled, "That Egyptian Art did not escape the law of change, and that its history may therefore be written " (Egyptian Art, p. 70).

REBER, F. VON. History of Ancient Art. Trans. and augm. by J. T. Clarke. Lond. : 1883.

This handbook is one of the most available for the student of Ancient Art. Its trustworthiness is guaranteed by the fact of von Reber's original authorship ; its usefulness as a compend of the results of recent investigations is enhanced by the collaboration of Mr. Clarke, who was director of the explorations at Assos. The discoveries made at Olympia and Pergamon are considered. The scope of the work, embracing art in Egypt, Chaldea, Babylonia, Assyria, Persia, Phoenicia, Palestine, and Asia Minor, Hellas, Etruria, and Rome, would render it invaluable to the student, had only the author or translator seen fit to interpolate an occasional chapter containing criticisms upon the art as a whole of any one of these countries, or a comparison of the art of one country with that of another.

RUSKIN, J.　Stones of Venice.

A principal thesis of this work is that corruption of art accompanies and corresponds to degradation in religion and public morality.

SCHÄFFLE, A. E. F.　Bau und Leben des Socialen Körpers. 4 vols.　Tübingen : 1881.

Contains a large amount of interesting fact and speculation on the history of art and its relation to the development of the social organism.　See especially vol. III, p. 129 ff.　For the sections bearing upon art, consult the Index under Kunst.

SCHNAASE, KARL J. F.　Geschichte der bildenden Künste. 2te verb. u. verm. Auflage.　Unter Mitwirkung des Verfassers bearb. von C. von Lützow.　8 vols.　Düsseldorf u. Stuttgart : 1866–79.

This formidable work attempts to survey the history of art from its origin to the present century in all important countries, except China and Japan.　The author's hold upon the evolutionary thread is not very firm, and at times, casting aside this clue, he follows the uncertain guidance of chronology or mere geographical association.

Spencer, H.   First Principles.

> Chaps. XIV–XVI The Law of Evolution.

The progress of the arts and their differentiation is used to illustrate the law of evolution.

Spencer, H.   The Principles of Sociology.   3d ed.   2 vols. N. Y. : 1893.

This work is cited for the sake of one brief passage on p. 431 of vol. I, in which Spencer brings the study of art within the scope of sociology.

Symonds, J. A.   Studies of the Greek Poets.   First Series.

> Pp. 219–222 Law of Sequence in Art.

The law of inevitable progression in art is "from the severe and animated embodiment of an idea to the conscious elaboration of merely aesthetic motives and brilliant episodes." Three stages of progress are distinguished, corresponding to those described by Miss Paget in her article on Comparative Aesthetics (*q. v. supra*). The law is illustrated from poetry, sculpture, and painting.

Symonds, J. A.   The Renaissance in Italy.

> Vol. II, pp. 395–401, The Catholic Reaction.

A brief statement of the principles of art-development. The idea is the same as in the preceding work.

Symonds, J. A.   Essays, Speculative and Suggestive.   2 vols. Lond. : 1890.

> Vol. I, pp. 42–83, On the Application of Evolutionary Principles to Art and Literature.

The course of the writer's thought is the same as in the passage from the Studies of the Greek Poets, referred to above, but the idea is elaborated with greater fulness, and illustrated from the drama and from architecture. The following sentences contain the substance of Mr. Symond's theory : "A type of art, once started, must, according to my view, fulfill itself, and bring to light the structure which its germ contained potentially. As this structure is progressively evolved, it becomes impossible to return upon the past. No individual man in the age of Scopas could produce work of Pheidian quality, albeit his brain throbbed with the pulse of Marathonian patriotism. Original- ity has to be displayed by eliciting what is still left latent in the partially exhausted type. To create a new type, while the old one is existent, baffles human ingenuity, because the type is an expression of the people's mind, and has its roots deep down in the stuff of national character. . . . After meridian accomplishment, a progressive deterioration of the type becomes inevitable and cannot be arrested " (pp. 76, 77).

TAINE, H. History of English Literature. Trans. by H. Van Laun. 4 vols. Lond. : 1883.

> Vol. I, pp. 1–36, Conditions of Literary Development.

TAINE, H. The Ideal in Art. Trans. by J. Durand. N. Y. : 1869.

TAINE, H. The Philosophy of Art. Lond. : 1867.

Taine's formula of the race, the moment, and the environment is most clearly expounded in the Introduction to his History of English Literature. For criticisms, see references under § **8.**

VAN DYKE, J. C. Principles of Art.

> Pt. I Art in History.

A rapid outline of the development of art, mainly of sculpture and painting, from primitive times to the present. An excellent introduction to more comprehensive histories. The art of the three chief periods treated is designated as : (1) imitative, decorative, and symbolic ; (2) classical and symmetrical ; (3) emotional, intellectual, and individual.

Vischer, F. T.   Aesthetik oder Wissenschaft des Schönen.
    3 vols.   Reutlingen : 1846.

Vischer treats of the historical development of art at great
length, — at too great length for most readers to follow him.
Beginning at p. 403 of the second volume, he first traces the
history of the ideal through the ancient, mediaeval, and modern
periods. In vol. III, pp. 134–138, he deals with the development
of style ; pp. 265–330, the history of architecture ; pp. 468–496,
the history of the plastic arts ; pp. 692–755, the history of painting ; pp. 1122–1151, the history of music.   Though the history
of poetry is not taken up separately, Vischer's views upon the
principles of its development may be found in vol. III, pp. 1194–
1198.   The reasons for this change of method in the treatment of poetry are stated at the end of § 861, vol. III, p. 258.
    The trend of thought is throughout Hegelian.

Waldstein, Chas.   Essays on the Art of Pheidias.   Cam-
    bridge : 1889.

Two of these fascinating and scholarly essays the reader
cannot by any means afford to pass by : they are that on the
province, aim, and methods of the study of classical archaeology ; and that entitled the Spirit of Pheidias, in its Relation
to his Age, Life, and Character.   As a valuable contribution to
the study of the evolution of art should also be consulted the
article in the appendix, p. 394 : The Influence of Athletic
Games upon Greek Art.

Ward, Lester F.   Dynamic Sociology.   2 vols.   N. Y. :
    1883.

In this important work some attention is given to the sociological aspects of art, but the references are scattering and
the treatment tentative.   Consult the index under the terms
Aesthetic Forces, Aesthetic Sentiments.   References under Art

are to the industrial or useful arts, to which the author devotes
a great deal of space.   Cf. the same author's more recent
Outlines of Sociology (N. Y. : 1898).

WINCKELMANN, J.   The History of Ancient Art.   Trans. by
       G. H. Lodge.   2 vols.   Boston : 1880.

This work is the earliest of its kind worthy of mention, for such
treatises as Winckelmann himself knew of, Monier's History of
Art, for instance, and Turnbull's Ancient Painting, lack breadth
of knowledge and artistic acumen.   Winckelmann's especial
merit is that he was the first to apply the historic method to the
study of the Fine Arts.   His revelations concerning the principles of Greek Art had an influence that did not stop with
Lessing and Goethe ; it has extended even to our time.   But
the student, though he may gain infinite information and suggestion from this great critic, should remember that Winckelmann's conclusions are drawn rather from the study of Greek
art — and even with that his acquaintance was limited — than
from the study of art in general.   Hegel, Aesthetik, vol. I,
p. 81, says of him : " Winckelmann was inspired by the contemplation of the ideals of the ancients to such a degree that
he has awakened a new sense for the appreciation of art, has
removed such appreciation from the point of view of common
aims and a mere imitation of nature, and has set us to seeking the
idea of art in the works and history of art.   Winckelmann is to
be regarded as one of the men who have been able in the realm
of art to open for the spirit a new organ and entirely new
fashions of contemplation."   The student's attention is especially called to vol. I, pp. 285–320, On the Causes of the Superiority of Greek Art, and on the essential of Art ; pp. 133–167,
On the Origin of Art.   Cf. also the interesting preface to the
Monumenti Inediti (2 vols.   Rome : 1867), in which Winckelmann explains with care the method of his History.

WOLTMANN, A., and WOERMANN, K.   History of Painting.
Trans. by Clara Bell.   2 vols.   Lond. : 1887.

Dr. Alfred von Woltmann, who had been professor of Art at
Prague and afterwards at Strassburg, lived after undertaking
this great work only long enough to complete that part on
Christian and Mediaeval art which occupies the latter half of
the first volume, and the sections in vol. II on the Renascence
in the North, the first chapter on the Renascence in Germany,
and the History of Italian art in the 15th century (as far as
p. 380).   Nearly all the rest of the history : Painting in the
Ancient World, and the latter chapters of vol. II on the Painting
of the Renascence, is the result of the labor of Dr. Karl
Woermann.   The sections on the attitude of the early Christians toward Art, vol. I, p. 151 ; and the general remarks on
pp. 201, 207, 221, 251, 324, 423, 492 ; and in vol. II, pp. 3–7,
61, 93, 124, 253, 270, 459, will give the reader an idea of the
theory underlying the volume.   Professor Colvin, writing in
1880 the preface to the first volume of this work, says that the
narrative now set before the reader will be found to be the
most complete and trustworthy history of painting yet written.

LÜBKE, W.   Ecclesiastical Art in Germany during the Middle
    Ages.   Trans., with appendix, by L. A. Wheatley.   Lond. :
    1870.

LÜBKE, W.   History of Sculpture.   Trans. by F. E. Bunnètt.
    2 vols.   Lond. : 1872.

LÜBKE, W.   Geschichte der Architectur von den ältesten
    Zeiten bis zur Gegenwart dargestellt.   1875.

LÜBKE, W.   Outlines of the History of Art.   Trans. and ed.
    by C. Cook.   2 vols.   N. Y. : 1878.

It will be seen from the following synopsis of the Outlines of
the History of Art, how extended is the scope of this famous
work : vol. I, pp. 1–16, Origin and Beginnings of Art; pp. 17–

121, The Ancient Art of the East : Egypt, Central Asia, Western Asia, Eastern Asia, India ; pp. 121–337, Classic Art : Greek, Etruscan, Roman ; p. 337–vol. II, p. 121, Mediaeval Art : Early Christian, Mohammedan, Romanesque, Gothic; pp. 121–640, Art of Modern Times : Modern Architecture, Plastic Art in Italy and in the North.

Lübke has in a clear, noble, and scholarly manner attempted to trace a progressive development of ideas in the course of art, wherever art has had beginning, has flourished, and has died. He studies this universal language of mankind in its primitive stammering when not the individual but the law behind him seems to speak, and in its mature eloquence when the differences of minds stand out conscious and clear. The rise of the intellectual movement and its expression in the later Romanesque style is of absorbing interest, and from the beginning of the second volume the growth of the spirit of liberty attracts attention with every broadening symptom of art. While the chapter opening on p. 121 of this volume gives a remarkably comprehensive view of the characteristics of modern art, it is, perhaps, a matter of regret that Lübke has seen fit to crowd English Art in the nineteenth century into a page, American Art into a paragraph, and to omit all reference to French contributions to reproductive art. However, this work is, on the whole, a great authority on the evolution of art.

§ 12. GENERAL NOTE.

A. **A SHORT COURSE OF READING** in the history of art should cover at least the following classes of works :

(1) A good representative of the philosophical or speculative treatment of art-evolution, as Hegel's Introduction to the Philosophy of Fine Art (Bosanquet's Translation).

(2) A good representative of the scientific treatment of the same subject, as Baldwin Brown's The Fine Arts.

(3) Some standard history of a single art or a single group of arts, as Lübke's History of Art, or Perrot and Chipiez's History of Ancient Egyptian Art, or Woltmann and Woermann's History of Painting, or Hamerton's Drawing and Engraving. For further references, see Sturgis and Krehbiel's Bibliography of Fine Art (Boston : 1891).

Longer courses of reading have been sufficiently indicated in the references in §§ **9, 10.**

B. **ADVANCED STUDENTS,** who wish to form an independent judgment upon the principles of the history of art, must of course go to the sources — study for themselves not only the scientific histories of Art, but also the history which, growing up day by day out of the investigations of archaeologists and students of the arts, finds a record in such publications as the *American Journal of Archaeology*, *L'Art*, *Die Archaeologische Zeitung*, the bulletins, annals, and memoirs of the Instituto Archeologico, etc.

C. **COLLATERAL AIDS.** — (1) A succinct statement of the evolutionary theories on which the history of art is sometimes based, may be found in Huxley's article 'Biology' in the Encycl. Brit., 9th ed. (2) For sociological principles the reader may be referred to Professor Giddings's Principles of Sociology (N. Y. : 1896), in the opening chapter of which is a brief statement of many theories, including the author's own ; to Vincent's The Social Mind (N. Y. : 1897) ; and to Ward's Outlines of Sociology (N. Y. : 1898).

CHAPTER III.

PRINCIPLES OF LITERATURE.

PART I. — THEORY OF LITERATURE.

§ 13. STATEMENT OF PROBLEMS; ANALYSIS.

In this chapter we shall consider questions relating to literature as a whole, reserving for succeeding chapters questions relating to special classes, epochs, or phases of literature.

1. Nature and Scope of Literature. — The student may begin by comparing a few notable definitions. The following are especially worthy of examination : " All knowledge that reaches us through books is literature " (Matthew Arnold, Discourses in America, p. 90). "The written thoughts and feelings of intelligent men and women, arranged in a way that shall give pleasure to the reader" (Brooke, English Literature, 1st ed., p. 5). "By letters or literature is meant the expression of thought in language, where by 'thought' I mean the ideas, feelings, views, reasonings, and other operations of the human mind" (Newman, Idea of a University, p. 291). "The representation . . . of a specific personality in its preference, its volition and power. Such is the matter of imaginative or artistic literature — this transcript, not of mere fact, but of fact in its infinite variety, as modified by human preference in all its infinitely varied forms" (Pater, Appreciations, pp. 6, 7). "Literature consists of all the books . . . where moral truth and human passion are touched with a certain largeness, sanity, and attractiveness of form " (J. Morley, On the Study of Litera-

ture, pp. 39, 40).   "We may be content to set out with a rough
definition of literature as consisting of works which, whether in
verse or prose, are the handicraft of imagination rather than
reflection, aim at the pleasure of the greatest possible number
of the nation, rather than instruction and practical effects, and
appeal to general rather than specialized knowledge" (Posnett,
Comparative Literature, p. 18).   "Literature is the effort of
man to indemnify himself for the wrongs of his condition"
(Emerson, paper on Walter Savage Landor, *The Dial*, 2 : 262).
"Literature, more especially poetic and dramatic literature, is
the expression in letters of the spiritual, coöperating with the
intellectual, man, the former being the primary, dominant
coefficient" (H. Corson, The Aims of Literary Study, p. 24).[1]

For other definitions the following sources may be consulted :
Dowden, Transcripts and Studies, pp. 237–240 ; Nettleship,
The Moral Influence of Literature; J. Morley, Voltaire,
pp. 13–15 ; Sherman, Analytics of Literature, chap. I ; Bascom,
Philosophy of English Literature, Lecture I ; Thos. Arnold,
Manual of English Literature, pp. 341–342 ; Lewes, Prin-
ciples of Success in Literature, chap. I ; De Quincey, Brevia
(Posthumous Works), pp. 300–305 ; Mabie, Short Studies in
Literature, p. 5 ; Brother Azarius, The Philosophy of Litera-
ture ; Wendell, Stelligeri, and Other Essays, pp. 93–107 ;
Carlyle, On Heroes and Hero-Worship (the Hero as Man of
Letters) ; H. Paul, Grundriss der Germanischen Philologie, Bd.
I, p. 216 ; Gerber, Die Sprache als Kunst, Bd. I, pp. 43–122 ;
Boeckh, Encyklopädie und Methodologie der Philol. Wissen-
schaften, p. 614 ; Joh. Scherr, Allgemeine Geschichte der
Litteratur, Bd. I, p. 1 ; The article ' Litteratur ' in Brockhaus'
Conversations–Lexikon ; G. Körting, Encyklopädie u. Metho-
dologie d. Romanischen Philologie, pp. 63, 64, 73.

---

[1] Although these quotations will be found interesting and valuable in
themselves, the student should bear in mind that they can be rightly interpreted only when they are studied in their proper context.

An attempt should be made to group these definitions in accordance with some principle or system. In one class may be put definitions which assume that literature is one of the fine arts, in another class definitions which do not make this assumption. Definitions may also be grouped accordingly as they survey literature from the aesthetic, the psychological, and the social point of view ; or they may be arranged in a descending scale, from the most to the least comprehensive.

The following questions will be found suggestive when any definition is under examination : Does the definition recognize a unity in all literature ? Does it include all recognized literary movements ? Does it include compositions transmitted by word of mouth ? Does it apply equally well to all nationalities ? Does it throw emphasis equally upon prose and poetry ? Does it include all literary types ? Does it set forth or imply some standard of literary value ?

II. Relation of Literature to Art. — Upon this interesting question the authorities differ widely. Four opinions may be distinguished, as follows : (1) Literature is a variety of fine art, coördinate with music and painting. (2) A single branch of literature, namely, poetry, may be classed with the fine arts ; prose is not fine but useful art. (3) Either poetry or prose may be classed as fine art, provided it is an embodiment of the beautiful ; otherwise it is useful art. (4) Literature is not an art at all, but is a product, *sui generis*, of the mind of man, touching art at one or two points.

The evidences of the artistic character of literature are ably and clearly set forth in an article on Principles of Criticism, by E. R. Sill in the *Atlantic*, 56: 665, and in the opening chapter of Crawshaw's Interpretation of Literature. The same conception underlies Pater's essay on Style, and Newman's Lecture on Literature, in The Idea of a University. The student may also consult Mabie's Short Studies in Literature, Higginson's

Atlantic Essays, pp. 23–47, and Vernon Lee's article on Literary Construction in *Contemp*. 68: 404.   For a conception in which art is set aside or is relegated to a minor office, see Posnett's Comparative Literature, and H. Paul's Methodenlehre in his Grundriss der germanischen Philologie.

The following questions may be found suggestive : If literature is an art, how is it differentiated from architecture, painting, sculpture, music, etc., in point of medium and content ? What ideas may be expressed in literature that cannot find expression in the other arts ?   (See Stricker's Du langage et de la musique, Watts's article ' Poetry ' in the Encycl. Britannica, and Bosanquet's History of Aesthetic, pp. 460–462.   The questions raised by Lessing in the Laocoon, concerning the boundaries of poetry and painting, may profitably be considered at this point.   See Lessing, § 8, and the references there given ; also Hazlitt, Offspring of Thought, pp. 130–144.)   What is the relation of literary form to literary content?   How is literary art related to nature?   What is the fundamental principle of literary art — is it life, expression, personality, unity ? (See *supra*, pp. 84, 85.)

III. Relation of Literature to Science and Philosophy. —

On the relation of literature to science the student may consult Huxley's Lecture on Literature and Science in *Nature*, 22 : 545 (also in *Pop. Sci. Mo.* 18 : 159) ; Matthew Arnold's Discourses in America, pp. 72–137 ; Huxley's Liverpool Lecture, in *London Jnl. of Education* for March, 1883 (see abstract in *Nature*, 27 : 396) ; Brackett's essay on the Relation of Modern Science to Literature, in *Pop. Sci. Mo.* 15 : 166 ; Burroughs's Indoor Studies, p. 43 ; Bishop Thirlwall's Essays, Speeches, and Sermons, pp. 284–311 ; and the discussion by O. L. Triggs and L. A. Sherman, in *Poet-Lore*, 6 : 113, 323, on Literature and the Scientific Spirit.   One phase of the question is touched upon in an interesting way in Woodrow Wilson's essay on Mere Literature, in the book which bears the same title, and in A. S. Cook's address on the Province of English Philology (Pubs. of the Mod. Language Assoc., N. S. vol. VI, No. 2). See also Knight's article on Poetry and Science : Their Contrasts and Affinities, in *University of Chicago Record*, 3 : 9.

On the connection between literature and philosophy, see J. Dewey's Poetry and Philosophy, *Andover Review*, 11 : 92, and B. C. Burt's Some Relations between Philosophy and Literature.

IV. The Elements of Literature. — These are commonly distinguished as *content* and *form*. Regarding the relation of the two much has been written, but the most interesting questions refer to the influence of one upon the other and the degree to which they may be separated by analysis. See on this point the opening paragraphs of De Quincey's essay on Style and the closing paragraphs of his essay on Language ; Steinthal, *Zeitschrift f. Völkerpsychologie*, 4 : 465, Zur Stylistik ; Brunetière, Histoire et littérature, p. 31 *et seq.* For detailed analyses of the elements of literature, see Crawshaw, Boeckh, Körting, Paul, ten Brink.

A. **CONTENT.** — The following are some of the leading questions to be asked upon this point :

Has literature a distinctive subject-matter ? (See Bagehot, Literary Studies, vol. II, p. 341. Some of the subject-matters that have been proposed are, experience, humanity, nature, aspiration, life, God, the relation of man to God, society.)

What is the relative value of the thought-element and the emotional-element in literature ? (See Bascom's Philos. of English Literature, p. 344 ; Crawshaw's Interpretation of Literature, pp. 44–50.)

Must every literary work have an ethical content ?

In what sense may the personality of the author be said to be subject-matter of his literary work?

Is literature restricted to the presentation of objects possessing beauty? ideality? universality?

Is unity of subject-matter essential to a work of literary art?

B. **Form.** — The problems relating to literary form are numerous and perplexing. Only those will be mentioned which concern literature in its broader aspects. For a treatment of the details of rhythm, metre, structure, and so forth, see the following chapters.

1. **The Nature of Language.** — This is an abstruse subject, and one, moreover, which is so overlaid by controversy that many of its profounder aspects must remain, for all except specialists, hopelessly obscure. Nevertheless, some insight may be gained, even by the general reader, into the fundamental principles of the science of language; and these, once mastered, become powerful weapons of attack upon certain questions of style that otherwise must remain insoluble, or be only vaguely apprehended. The old quarrel as to the origin of language, though now generally abandoned by philologists,[1] will always remain interesting reading. A *résumé* of the most important speculations may be found in Whitney's article 'Philology' in the Encycl. Brit., in Max Müller's Lectures on the Science of Language, 1st Series, p. 343, and in Ellis's article on the Relations of Thought to Sound, in Trans. of the English Philol. Society, 1873–74, pp. 10–15. More to the present purpose is the question, What is the relation of thought and language? A suggestive discussion of this problem occurs in Jowett's Translation of Plato's Dialogues, 3d ed. vol. I, pp. 281–321. More scientific treatment is

---

[1] The increasing interest in the study of the language of children seems likely to revive speculation on this question.

given in Whitney's Language and the Study of Language, pp. 403–407, Life and Growth of Language, chaps. II and XIV, the article ' Philology' in the Encyclopaedia Britannica, and Max Müller's Science of Thought. For those who care to pursue the subject further, Paul's Principles of the History of Language may be unhesitatingly recommended. The introduction and pp. 1–19 of the main body of this valuable work may be read with profit even by the general reader. The peculiar theory enunciated by Max Müller (the identification of thought and language) is developed at great length in his Science of Thought. For a more popular exposition, see his Three Introductory Lectures on the Science of Thought, first published in the *Open Court.* The questions raised by the philologists have been pursued with great zeal by writers on psychology. Brief statements of the psychological function of language are given in Dewey's Psychology, pp. 211–214, and in Sully's Outlines of Psychology, pp. 337–351. James's Principles of Psychology, vol. I, pp. 236, 241, 245, 251–283, vol. II, pp. 356–358, 364, is unusually fertile in suggestions. See also the article by G. J. Romanes in the *Monist,* Oct., 1891, on Thought and Language. The more technical points involved in the discussion may be traced through Bruchmann's Psychologische Studien, 2. Theil ; Victor Egger's La parole intérieure ; Ballet's Le langage intérieur ; Bateman's On Aphasia, chap. V ; Lemoine's Physionomie de la parole ; Rabier's Leçons de philosophie, I, pp. 596–622 ; Paulhan's article Le langage intérieur in *Revue Philos.* 21 : 26; and A. Kussmaul's Strörungen der Sprache (Leipz.: 1877). The interesting article, ' Thought and Language,' by G. F. Stout (in *Mind,* 16 : 181) does not treat of language as a means of communication, but as " a means by which a man is enabled to understand himself." The comparison of words to algebraic symbols, often quoted in these discussions, will be found in Lewes's Problems of Life and Mind, 3d Ser., Prob. 4, chap. V. For a suggestion as to

the light which studies of the nature of language may throw
upon questions of style, see Posnett's Comparative Literature,
pp. 44–52, Whitney's Life and Growth of Language, pp. 301, 302,
Campbell's Philosophy of Rhetoric, Bk. II, chap. VII, Spencer's
Philosophy of Style, Gerber's Die Sprache als Kunst, and
Santayana's The Sense of Beauty, pp. 167–174.

2. **STYLE.** — Upon the threshold of his inquiry the student will
encounter the great problem of style, which in the hands of
some writers is made to swallow all other problems, whether
of literature or of criticism. To answer the question, What
is style? the student who reads German may get help from
Rumohr's Italienische Forschungen, where the different meanings attached to the term are carefully discriminated, or from
the article ' Stil ' in Brockhaus' Conversations–Lexikon, in
which Rumohr's views are summarized. On the relation of
originality, style, and manner he may read Hegel's Aesthetik,
vol. I, pp. 365–374, and compare with it Matthew Arnold's
Mixed Essays, p. 200. The definition of style enunciated by
Buffon will be found in the Discours sur le style. The question
as to what Buffon meant by it is discussed briefly in Lewes's
History of Philosophy, chapter on Hobbes, Note, in Saintbury's
French Literature, p. 500, and in Modern Language Notes,
vol. V, pp. 179–180. De Quincey's essay on Style, long-
winded though it is, must be carefully studied by all who
would understand the history of thought on this subject. With
it should be read his essay on Rhetoric. Coleridge's remarks
on Style (in vol. IV of his Complete Works, pp. 337–343) should
not be overlooked. Ruskin's peculiar theories about the grand
style (in Modern Painters, vol. III, and in Fiction, Fair and
Foul) should be compared with those of Matthew Arnold as
set forth in the essay on Translating Homer. Selections from
both, with an interesting preface, will be found in A. S. Cook's
Touchstones of Poetry. In the case of Arnold, the question

should be asked, Can extracts from one class or one period of literature be made to serve as tests for literature of another class or another period?   Other essays and books dealing with certain phases of style are Spencer's Philosophy of Style, Pater's essay on Style, Stevenson's essay On Style in Literature, Joubert's Pensées, and Bourget's chapters on Flaubert and the brothers de Goncourt, in Essais de psychologie.   Those who desire to go more deeply into the philosophy of style may consult Von Hartmann's Aesthetik, vol. II, references in Index under Stil ; Vischer's Aesthetik, references under Stil, Stylgegensatz, Stylgesetz, and Stylisirung ; Richter's Aesthetik, vol. II, pp. 601–656 ; Schopenhauer's Sämmtliche Werke, vol. VI, pp. 536–581; Steinthal's article in *Zeitschrift für Völkerpsychologie*, 4: 465 ; and Veron's Aesthetics, references in Index under Style.

The following questions will be found useful as guides in the study of this somewhat difficult topic : (1) Meaning of the term style as applied to art in general? (2) Its special use, or uses, as applied to literature ? (3) Relation of style to individuality ? (4) Relation of style to manner ? (5) In what sense is the style the man ? (6) Can style be preserved in translation from one language to another (see Posnett's Comparative Literature, pp. 44–49 ; Newman's Idea of a University, pp. 285–290 ; Lewes's Life of Goethe, Bk. VI, chap. VII ; Boswell's Life of Johnson, Index, under Translation) ? (7) Characteristics of national styles? (8) Relation of style and idea ? (9) Tests of style ? (10) Are the tests the same for all literature and all kinds of literature ? (11) Is Lewes's threefold principle of Vision, Sincerity, and Beauty exhaustive ? (12) Will Spencer's principle of Economy account for all literary values ?

3. **FIGURES.** — The following outline of study is submitted. The references are to the bibliography of figures in § **15.** .

a. Nature of figures.

(1) Relation of figures to images? to plain statements? to concrete terms? See LEWES, BUCK, DARMSTETER, SCOTT and DENNEY, GENUNG.

(2) Are figures deviations from the ordinary forms of speech? See DU MARSAIS, QUINTILIAN, WHATELY, BAIN, GUMMERE.

(3) What part has analogy in the composition of figures? What part has resemblance? identification? union, or reconciliation, of opposites? contrast? See D. J. HILL, BAIN, BUCK, SHERMAN.

b. The effectiveness of figures.

(1) In what sense are figures 'ornaments' of discourse? See GENUNG, TOMPKINS.

(2) How do figures contribute to force? to clearness? to beauty of style? See WENDELL, SPENCER, GREENE, HALE, BATES.

c. Classification of figures.

(1) What is the simplest and most natural basis of classification — origin, effectiveness, kind of image aroused, association, etc.?

(2) Value of the division into figures and tropes? See QUINTILIAN, MINTO, GUMMERE.

Schemes of classification are numerous and varied. For specimens of them, see De Mille. Interesting attempts at re-classification have been made by C. B. Bradley, Hale, Greene, Buck, Hart, Sherman, and others. See in general, KOHFELDT, BIESE, GERBER, WACKERNAGEL.

4. **RHYTHM.** — See the sections on Poetry and Versification, **19-24,** below.

C. **PURPOSE.** — The purpose (tendency, aim, object, end, meaning, message) of a literary work is by some writers subsumed under the content, by others regarded as a distinct literary element. Its various meanings should be carefully distinguished. Thus it may mean : (1) the theme of the work ;

(2) the guiding impulse of the author; (3) the effect which the work is expected to have on the public ; (4) the extra-artistic element in the work.

V. The Author. — (1) What distinguishes the man of letters from other kinds of artists, as the musician, the painter, and the sculptor ? What elements in his organization are akin to theirs ? See GIRARDIN. (2) Is it true historically that in great authors the artistic impulse has been the strongest incentive to literary work ? (3) Is the literary artist helped or hindered by a strong moral purpose ? (4) To what extent have authors been conscious of their own methods of work ? (See Bainton, Art of Authorship.) (5) Is it necessary that an author, in order to write effectively, should feel the emotions he depicts ? (See Horace, Ars Poetica, l. 102 ; Diderot's Paradox of Acting ; Lewes's Principles of Success in Literature, p. 91 ; and the *Critic* for March 24 and March 31, 1888.)

VI. The Public. — (1) To what extent and in what sense is the success of a work the test of its real value ? (See Lewes's Principles of Success in Literature, pp. 23–30.) (2) What is the influence of any given mode of publication upon the character of literature ? (See De Quincey, Essay on Style, pt. IV.) (3) To what extent have great works of literature been shaped or influenced by public demand or by the author's consciousness of a public ?

Consult, in general, on this topic the able work of A. Beljame, Le public et les hommes de lettres en Angleterre au dixhuitième siècle. Paris : 1883.

VII. The Classification of Literature. — Most authorities agree in dividing literature into two principal kinds, poetry and prose. The basis of the division is sometimes held to be form, sometimes content, sometimes both form and content. For a careful treatment of the subject in its most important

phases, see the article ' Poetry,' by Watts, in the Encycl. Brit.,
9th ed.; Bosanquet's History of Aesthetic, pp. 460–462 ; and
Crawshaw's Interpretation of Literature, pp. 25–28.   For objections to this division, see Masson, § **20**, *infra*, who proposes
(after Coleridge) a division into poetic and scientific literature ;
and cf. Moir's article on Poetry in the 7th ed. of the Encycl.
Brit. (reprinted in Poetry, Romance, and Rhetoric, Edinb. :
1851), and Bain's On Teaching English, p. 254.   See also L. A.
Sherman's Analytics of Literature, p. 5 *et seq.*

De Quincey's division into the literature of power and the
literature of knowledge will be found in his essay on Pope and
also in Letter III of Letters to a Young Man.

Other divisions that have been proposed are : (1) creative,
(2) critical; (1) instrumental, for the ends of business, (2)
artistic, for the ends of pleasure ; (1) narrative, (2) subjective,
(3) dramatic, (4) descriptive (Crawshaw, Interpretation of
Literature, p. 41).

A division into good literature and great literature is proposed
by Walter Pater at the close of his essay on Style.

For the subdivisions of the two great branches of literature,
see § **15**, **4**, and the following chapters ; and for the classification of literary theory, — ' stylistic,' rhetoric, poetics, metric,
— see §§ **15**, **5**, and **19**.

§ 14. REFERENCES.

ARNOLD, M.   Discourses in America.   Lond.: 1885.

   Pp. 72–137 Literature and Science.

Arnold makes a distinction between literature and belles-
lettres (p. 90), and maintains, against Professor Huxley, the
educative value of letters, on the ground that they furnish (as
science does not) nourishment for the sense for beauty and the
sense for conduct.   For Huxley's lecture, see *Nature*, 22: 545, or
Pop. Sci. Mo. 18:159.   Huxley touches on the same theme (but

with somewhat more liberality towards letters) in his Liverpool Lecture (*London Jnl. of Education*, March, 1883; abstract in *Nature*, 27 : 396).

ARNOLD, M.   Essays in Criticism.   Boston : 1869.

In his lectures On Translating Homer, pp. 284–367, Arnold twice touches upon the nature of the "grand style" in literature.   See especially pp. 330–333, 392–396 ; but the lectures should be read in their entirety.   Cf. A. S. Cook's Touchstones of Poetry.

ARNOLD, M.   Mixed Essays.   N. Y. : 1879.

See p. 200 for interesting remarks on Addison's style and the relation of style to manner.   The essay on Wordsworth contains the paradoxical statement that Wordsworth, when at his best, had no style at all.

ARNOLD, M.   Introduction to Ward's English Poets.   4 vols. Lond.: 1883.

Pp. xxv–xxix.

Arnold here, as in his lectures On Translating Homer, gives passages which may be applied as " an infallible touchstone for detecting the presence or absence of high poetic quality, and also the degree of this quality, in all other poetry which we may place beside them."

ARNOLD, THOS.   A Manual of English Literature, historical and critical.   With an appendix on English metres. Boston : 1891.

See pp. 341–343 for definition and classification of literature.

AZARIAS, BROTHER.   Philosophy of Literature.   6th ed.   N. Y. : 1890.

In these thoughtful and suggestive essays the author's starting-point is a theory of the beautiful that is equally applicable to art and letters. Literature is defined as the expression of humanity. Its origin, functions, and relations to society are entertainingly discussed.

BAGEHOT, W. Literary Studies. Ed. by R. H. Hutton. 2 vols. Lond. : 1879.

A plea for the use of the term *literatesque* to mean what is available for purposes of literary art, will be found in vol. II, p. 341.

BAIN, ALEX. On Teaching English. With detailed examples, and an Enquiry into the Definition of Poetry. Lond. : 1887.

A brief consideration of the kinds of literature will be found on p. 254.

BALLET, G. Le langage intérieur et les diverses formes de l'aphasie. Paris : 1886.

An interesting and valuable work treating of the psychology of language processes.

BASCOM, J. Aesthetics : or the Science of Beauty. N. Y. : 1872.

Lecture 16 is on the aesthetics of literature.

BATES, ARLO. Talks on Literature. Boston : 1897.

Discusses the simpler fundamental questions.

BOECKH, AUG. Encyklopädie und Methodologie der philologischen Wissenschaften. (See § 2.)

This is a work which every earnest student of literature may consult with profit ; for whether he adopts Boeckh's system in its entirety or not, the book will get him in the way of thinking of literature as an organic whole, and will furnish him with an instrument of analysis for approaching literature at any point.

In order to understand Boeckh's philosophy of literature in its entirety one should read at least pp. 124–156, but something may be gleaned from a reading of pp. 142–147. A definition and a classification of literature will be found on pp. 614–616.

Bourget, P. Essais de psychologie contemporaine. 4ᵉ éd. Paris : 1885.

See pp. 156–173 of the essay on Flaubert.

Bourget, P. Nouveaux essais de psychologie contemporaine. Paris : 1886.

See pp. 180–198 of the essay on MM. de Goncourt.

These books contain valuable contributions to the psychology of style.

Burroughs, John. Indoor Studies. Boston : 1889.

See p. 43 for an entertaining discussion of the relation of science and literature. The interests of the two, according to the author, are widely different, but not hostile nor mutually destructive.

Brackett, W. *Pop. Sci. Mo.* 15 : 166 Relation of Modern Science to Literature.

Maintains the inferiority of literature to science in usefulness and permanence.

Brooke, S. A. English Literature. (Literature Primers.) Lond. : 1878.

In the opening paragraph is an often-quoted definition of literature: "The written thoughts and feelings of intelligent men and women arranged in a way that will give pleasure to the reader." The definitions and classifications in the following paragraphs are simple but carefully worded. See Matthew Arnold's review of the work, in Mixed Essays, pp. 180–204.

BRUNETIÈRE, FERD. Histoire et littérature. 3 vols. Paris:
 1884–86.

> Vol. I, p. 31 Théorie du lieu commun.

M. Brunetière holds the view that in the substance of literature invention plays no part; all is commonplace. Originality
inheres only in the form. The thesis is maintained with spirit,
and is supported by a great number of illustrations.

BUFFON, G. L. L., Comte de. Discours sur le style. — Notes
 d'Antoine Rondelet. Paris: 1883.

A curious example of a piece of literature that has become
famous by a single phrase, *le style c'est l'homme,* — a phrase,
moreover, that Buffon never wrote, his own expression being,
le style est de l'homme même. Buffon makes the point that style,
unlike subject-matter, is individual, and therefore non-transfer-
able. Contrary to the theories of modern rhetoricians, he
prefers general to specific terms.

BURT, B. C. Some Relations between Philosophy and Literature. *Univ. of Mich. Philos. Papers,* No. 4.

In part a criticism of Matthew Arnold.

CARLYLE, THOS. On Heroes, Hero-Worship, and the Heroic.
 N. Y.: 1846.

> Lect. 3 The Hero as Poet; Lect. 5 The Hero as Man of Letters.
> See p. 151 for Carlyle's characterization of literature.

CHAIGNET, A.-Ed. La rhétorique et son histoire. Paris: 1888.

> Pp. 413–539 Théorie du style.

CHRIST, W. Geschichte der Griechischen Litteratur. (In
 Iwan Müller's Handbuch der Klassischen Altertumswissenschaft. Bd. VII. München: 1890.)

An outline of the divisions of literature will be found on
pp. 1–8. The author closely follows Boeckh.

COLERIDGE, S. T.   Complete Works.   Ed. by Prof. Shedd.
7 vols.   N. Y. : 1853–54.

> Vol. III, Biographia Literaria, chaps. III–IV, X–XXII; vol. IV,
> pp. 19–22 Definition of Poetry, pp. 22–46 Drama, pp. 328–336
> Poesy as Art, pp. 337–343 Style, pp. 368–370 Taste, pp. 370–
> 373 Beauty, pp. 387–388 Wonderfulness of Prose.

Although Coleridge nowhere presents his conception of
literature in systematic form, his occasional definitions and
discussions are always suggestive.

CORSON, H.   The Aims of Literary Study.   N. Y.: 1895.

See p. 24 for a definition of literature.

CRAWSHAW, W. H.   The Interpretation of Literature.   N. Y.:
1896.

An admirable little work, treating in a clear and readable
style of the elementary principles of literary theory.

DE QUINCEY, T.   The Collected Writings.   Ed. by D. Masson.
14 vols.   Edinb.: 1890.

> The Letters to a Young Man, the essays on Style and on Rhetoric,
> and one of the essays on Language are in vol. X; the essay on
> the Poetry of Pope is in vol. XI; the remaining essay on Language
> is in vol. XIV.

DE QUINCEY, T.   Essays on Style, Rhetoric, and Language.
Ed. with Introduction and Notes by F. N. Scott.   Boston:
1893.

De Quincey's dissertation on Style consists mainly of a history of Greek style and numerous digressions on other national
styles.   As Renton points out, De Quincey has occasional
flashes of insight that make this essay in some respects the
most notable contribution to the theory of style after Aristotle.
See Renton's Logic of Style, Introduction.   Cf. also De Quincey's Essay on Rhetoric and the concluding paragraphs of the

Essay on Language. For De Quincey's distinction between
the literature of knowledge and the literature of power, see
his essay on the Poetry of Pope (the passage is reprinted in
the Appendix of this edition, pp. 238–240), and Letter III
of his Letters to a Young Man.

DEWEY, J. Psychology. N. Y.: 1890.

See p. 3 and pp. 211–213 on the psychology of language.

DRAKE, N. Essays, Biographical, Critical, and Historical.
Illustrative of the Tatler, Spectator, and Guardian. 2d ed.
Lond.: 1814.

Vol. II, pp. 1–116 On the Progress and Merits of English Style.

EGGER, V. La parole intérieure. Paris: 1881.

A valuable discussion of the relation of thought and language.

ELLIS, A. J. *Trans. of English Philological Society*, 1873–74,
pp. 3–34 Relations of Thought to Sound as the Pivot of
Philological Research.

See pp. 10–15 of this able paper for a statement of theories
concerning the origin of language.

ELSTER, ERNST. Prinzipien der Literaturwissenschaft. Bd. I.
Halle: 1897.

· The author attempts to construct a systematic theory of
literature upon psychological, aesthetic, and philological foundations, drawing his underlying philosophy mainly from Wundt
and his philology (very properly) from Paul. The work is in
eight chapters, of which four and a part of the fifth are in the
first volume. The subjects of the chapters are as follows: I,
The Poetic Conception of Life; II, Imaginative and Intellectual
Activity of the Poet; III, Poetic Feeling and Intuition; IV,
Aesthetic Conceptions; V, Style; VI, Modern German Metres;
VII, Kinds of Poetry; VIII, The Various Aims of the Science
of Literature.

EMERSON, R. W.   Complete Works.   Boston: 1883–93.

See the Index in vol. XII, under Literature, for suggestive utterances on the meaning, value, and uses of works of literary art.   Perhaps the best single essay is Thoughts on Modern Literature, in Natural History of Intellect, p. 171 (from *The Dial*, 1: 137).

FERRI, E.   Les criminels dans l'art et la littérature.   Paris: 1897.

A study of art and literature from the point of view of criminology, by a leading criminologist.

FEUILLÉE, A.   Education from a National Standpoint.   Lond.: 1892.

See Bk. V, chap. IV, for a discussion of the relations of literature and aesthetics.

FROEHDE, O.   *Neue Jahrb. f. Philol. und Paedagogik*, 147: 433 Der Begriff und die Aufgabe der Literaturwissenschaft.

An attempt to supplement the methodology of Boeckh.

GAUCKLER.   Le beau et son histoire.   Paris: 1873.

Gauckler calls literature in general *l'art de la parole*, and treats it under the three heads, *la poésie*, *l'art oratoire*, and *la prose écrite*.   See pp. 178–197.

GERBER, G.   Die Sprache als Kunst.   2 vols.   Bromberg: 1871.

Pp. 43–122 of Bd. I give in brief the author's views upon the 'speech-art.'

GERUZEZ, E.   Cours de littérature, rhétorique, poétique, histoire littéraire.   Paris.

An excellent manual, intended for beginners.   Part II, dealing with literature, has passed through about thirty editions.

GIBBON, EDWARD.   Essai sur l'étude de la littérature.   (In
Miscellaneous Works.   3 vols.   Lond.: 1796.   Pp. 449–
495.)

The student will find this famous essay interesting because
it was written by Gibbon rather than because it contains ideas
that he can use in his researches.   Nevertheless, some of the
remarks on the relation of literature to science and philosophy,
and on the interconnection of literary thought and national life,
are worth pondering.

GILMAN, B. I.   *American Journal of Psychology*, 6: 1 Syllabus
of Lectures on the Psychology of Pain and Pleasure.

   Pp. 48–50 Literature.

GIRARDIN, ST. MARC.   Essais de littérature et de morale.
2 vols.   Paris: 1876.

   Vol. II, p. 143 De la profession d'homme de lettres.

GREEF, G. DE.   Introduction à la sociologie.   2 vols.   Bruxelles
et Paris: 1886–89.

See vol. II, pp. 187, 188, for a brief treatment of the social
aspects of literature.

GROSSE, ERNST.   Die Literaturwissenschaft, ihr Ziel und ihr
Weg.   1887.

The author's aim in this doctoral thesis is to formulate a
theory of literature based on the methods of the natural
sciences.

HARTMANN, E. VON.   Aesthetik.   2 vols.   Berlin: 1887.

See vol. II, pp. 139–143, 554–556, for style in general.

HEGEL.   Aesthetik.   (See § **8**, p. 101.)

   Vol. III, pp. 220–282.

Like most writers on aesthetics, Hegel has chosen poetry instead of literature as the representative of the speech-art. His remarks on literature are, therefore, incidental to his remarks on poetry.

HIGGINSON, T. W. Atlantic Essays. Boston: 1871.

> Pp. 23–47 Literature as an art.

The author, in the capacity of mentor to young writers, lays down the essential requirements of good literature, which he finds to be simplicity, freshness, choice of words, thoroughness.

HUNT, T. W. Studies in Literature and Style. N. Y.: 1890.

The main object of the author is to present the characteristics of literature as determined by the personality of the writer. Style is considered under eight heads: intellectual, literary, impassioned, popular, critical, poetic, satirical, humorous. For a definition of literature, see p. 7.

JAMES, W. The Principles of Psychology. 2 vols. N. Y.: 1890.

See vol. I, pp. 236, 241, 245, 251–283; vol. II, pp. 356–358, 364, 407, for suggestive remarks on the relations of thought and language.

JONSON, BEN. Timber, or Discoveries made upon Men and Matter. Ed. by F. E. Schelling. Boston: 1891.

Observations, generally brief, upon a great variety of subjects pertaining to literature and style. They are characterized by acuteness and good sense. See § **21**, *B* 2.

JORDAN, ALFRED. Literature in Relation to Science. Lond.: 1891.

An attempt, fairly successful, to combine the definitions of Brooke and Posnett.

JOUBERT, J. Pensées. 2 vols. Paris: 1880.

> Pp. 263–272 De la poésie, 273–300 Du style, 300–341 Des qualities de l'écrivain, 342–390 Jugements littéraires.

Contains suggestive thoughts on many topics of literary theory.

KAMES, LORD. Elements of Criticism.

> See §§ **2, 8.**

KÖRTING, G. Encyklopädie und Methodologie der Romanischen Philologie. Heilbronn: 1884.

> Erster Theil, pp. 63–82 Die Litteratur; zweiter Theil, pp. 296–311 Die Stylistik.

The broad fields of literature and style are here mapped out for the student in an instructive, if rigid and over-minute, fashion. Körting's treatment may profitably be compared with that of Boeckh and of Paul.

KRANTZ, É. Essai sur l'esthétique de Descartes. Paris: 1882.

The opening chapter points out the conditions of literary growth which make a philosophy of literature possible.

LAURIE, S. S. Lectures on Language and Linguistic Method in the School. Cambridge: 1890.

For an excellent discussion of language as literature, from the teacher's point of view, see pp. 81–104.

LECLERQ. L'art est rationnel. Bruxelles.

For a rambling essay on literature as an art, see pp. 211–218.

LEWES, G. H. The Principles of Success in Literature. Ed. with Introduction and Notes by F. N. Scott. 2d ed. Boston: 1892. (Originally appeared in *Fortn.* 1 : 85, 185, 572, 687; 2 : 257, 689. Reprinted by A. S. Cook, San Francisco, 1885, and by W. D. Armes, San Francisco, 1891.)

An admirable discussion of the fundamental principles of literature.

Lewes, G. H. Problems of Life and Mind. 3d Series. 2 vols.
    Boston: 1879–80.

> See Probl. 4, chap. V, for relations of thought to language.

Lewes's writings are especially adapted to the needs of
persons who are beginning the study of literary theory and
criticism.   They combine the merits of soundness, lucidity,
and interest.

Long, G.   An Old Man's Thoughts about Many Things.   2d
    ed.   Lond.: 1872.

> Pp. 92–161 Style.

This essay is more profitable as an example than as an
exposition of style, but some old truths are so freshly stated as
to have the force of new ones.

Longinus, Dionysius.   On the Sublime.   Trans. by H. L.
    Havell.   Lond.: 1890.

The enthusiasm and catholic taste of the author, whoever he
may be, of this little treatise have made a lasting place for it in
the history of criticism.   Its chief value at the present time,
when its most notable passages have become rhetorical commonplaces, is that it shows us how the classic literatures appealed
to the literary sense of the ancients.   On the meaning of the
Greek περὶ ὕψους, see De Quincey's Essay on Milton, and Minto's
Manual of English Prose, p. 19, note.

Lytton, Sir E. B.   Caxtoniana.   2 vols.   Edinb.: 1863.

See vol. II, pp. 129–169, for some interesting remarks On
Certain Principles of Art in Works of the Imagination.

Lotze, H.   Microcosmus.   Trans. by E. Hamilton and E. E. C.
    Jones.   2 vols.   Edinb.: 1885.

See pp. 618–639 for a discussion of the relations of thought
and language.

McCORMICK, W. S.   Three Lectures on English Literature.
Lond.: 1889.

The opening chapter, on English Literature and University
Education, is a criticism of Professor Freeman's article in
Contemp. 52 : 549.

MABIE, H. W.   Short Studies in Literature.   N. Y.: 1891.

The author announces that his purpose is to study books not
as fragments, but as illustrations of the art of literature ; but,
owing to the brevity of the treatment, the underlying principles
of this art are nowhere worked out in detail.   They seem,
however, to be sound.   See p. 5 for a definition of literature,
p. 29 for a discussion of literary form, and p. 35 for remarks on
personality in literature.

MARMONTEL, J. F.   Éléments de littérature.   3 vols.   Paris:
1846.

> Tome I, pp. 1–51 Essai sur le goût, pp. 204–219 Beau, pp. 306–319
> Comédie, pp. 319–324 Comique, pp. 344–367 Critique; T. II,
> pp. 100–121 Épopée; T. III, pp. 90–104 Pathétique, pp. 137–
> 208 Poésie, poëte, poétique.

This work is a kind of encyclopaedia of literature, the topics
being arranged in alphabetical order.   An excellent index at
the end of each volume makes of it as perfect a reference book
as the character of its contents will permit.   The treatment of
the topics is conventional.

METHNER, JUL.   Poesie und Prosa, ihre Arten und Formen.
Halle: 1888.

MINTO, WM.   Manual of English Prose Literature.   Boston:
1889.

MINTO, WM.   Characteristics of the English Poets from Chaucer
to Shirley.   Boston: 1891.

See the introduction to the Manual of Prose and the remarks
passim in the Characteristics.

Moir, Geo. Poetry, Romance, and Rhetoric. Edinb.: 1851. (From the 7th ed. of the Encycl. Brit.)

Moir classes fiction with poetry rather than with prose.

Morley, H., and Tyler, M. C. A Manual of English Litera- ture. N. Y.: 1880.

See the Introduction for a definition of literature.

Morley, J. On the Study of Literature. Lond.: 1887.

This is a lecture in Morley's best style. It should be read by every student of literature. See pp. 38, 39, for definitions by various writers, and p. 40 for Morley's own definition.

Morley, J. Voltaire. N. Y.: 1872.

See pp. 13–15 for a definition and classification of literature.

Müller, Max. The Science of Thought. 2 vols. N. Y.: 1887.

Sets forth the writer's well-known theory of the identity of thought and language.

Nettleship, H. The Moral Influence of Literature; Classical Education in the Past and Present. Two popular addresses. Lond.: 1890.

Newman, J. H. The Idea of a University Defined and Illustrated. Lond.: 1891.

Cardinal Newman's Lecture on Literature (pp. 268–294) treats the subject in a refreshingly broad and liberal spirit. That style is the effluence of character, and not merely an external decoration, is the writer's principal contention.

Pallen, Condé B. The Philosophy of Literature. Freiburg: 1897.

PATER, W. Appreciations; with an Essay on Style. Lond.: 1889.

The essay on Style, with which this volume opens, was first published in *Fortn.* 50: 728. Structural unity pervading all the elements of composition, from the largest to the smallest, is the requirement upon which the author most strenuously insists. For the quotations from Flaubert, see Flaubert's Correspondence, 1 Ser. 1830–50 (Paris: 1887). On Flaubert's theory of art, cf. Bourget's Essais de psychologie contemporaine, pp. 156–173.

PAUL, H. Grundriss der Germanischen Philologie. Methoden-lehre. (See § 2.)

Under the heading Litteraturgeschichte Paul writes ably of such subjects as the meaning and scope of literature, its classi-fications, its elements, its relations to other fields of culture, etc. A work of the first importance.

PAUL, H. Principles of the History of Language. Trans. from the 2d ed. by H. A. Strong. N. Y.: 1889.

Every student of literature should make himself familiar at least with the Introduction and first two chapters of this admirable work.

RALEIGH, WALTER. Style. Lond.: 1897.

A brilliantly written, novel, and suggestive treatment of the subject.

RENAN, E. The Future of Science. Boston: 1893.

Chaps. VIII–XIV, although they profess to deal with the science of philology, abound in striking and suggestive thoughts on many aspects of literary theory.

ROBERTSON, J. M. New Essays towards a Critical Method. Lond.: 1897.

Contains in the opening essay a forcible and sympathetic exposition of the method of Hennequin.

RENTON, W. The Logic of Style, being an Introduction to
Critical Science. Lond.: 1874.

This is an able examination, from a philosophic standpoint,
of some of the leading questions of style. The abstract character of the reasoning, however, and the highly technical
language in which it is expressed, make the work hard reading
for any save advanced students.

RICARDOU, A. La critique littéraire: étude philosophique.
Avec une préface de M. F. Brunetière. Paris: 1896.

See pp. 161–271 for a readable discussion of the fundamental
principles of literary art.

RUSKIN, J. Modern Painters. 5 vols. Orpington: 1887.

RUSKIN, J. On the Old Road. 3 vols. Orpington: 1885.

Ruskin's remarks on the grand style, in the opening chapters
of vol. III of Modern Painters, apply as well to literature as to
painting, and in chap. I the illustrations are drawn from the
former. In Fiction, Fair and Foul (in On the Old Road, vol.
II, pp. 3–166, reprinted from *19th Century*, 7: 941, 8: 195, 394,
748, 10: 516), the tests of good style are formulated (pp. 87–
92) in six canons: self-command, brevity and simplicity, emphatic
and clear utterance, spontaneity, melody, spiritual content. To
illustrate these canons, Ruskin, with characteristic willfulness,
has chosen passages of Shakespeare which few besides himself
would think of commending. See A. S. Cook's Touchstones
of Poetry, pp. vii–ix, 12–16.

SAINTE-BEUVE, C. A. Causeries du Lundi. 3ᵉ éd. 15 vols.
Paris: 1857–62.

Sainte-Beuve's contributions to the theory of literature must
be extracted from the Causeries by a process of inference.
Only in three or four instances does he stop the steady flow of
criticism to enlighten the reader upon his methods and his
working basis. One of these pauses occurs in vol. III, pp. 38–

55, where a classic is defined (see for translation, Morley, On the Study of Literature, pp. 38, 39) ; another is in vol. XV, p. 345, where the relations of art and ethics are referred to ; and still another is p. 356 of the same volume, at which point the authority of tradition in literature is briefly discussed.   In vol. III of the Nouveaux Lundis, in the articles on Chateaubriand, Sainte-Beuve sets forth his system of procedure at some little length ; but naturally he is more concerned here with a theory of criticism than with a theory of literature.   See Dowden's article on Literary Criticism in France, *Fortn.* 52 : 737, esp. p. 740 (reprinted in New Studies in Literature, Lond. : 1895, p. 388).

SALT, H. S.   *New Review*, 4 : 19 The Socialist Ideal : Literature.

The writer's main contention is that the evils of modern literature grow out of an individualistic form of society.   The ideal of equality will put new life into literary expression.

SCHÄFFLE, A. E. F.   Bau und Leben des socialen Körpers. 4 vols.   Tübingen : 1881.

Bd. I, p. 398 ff.; Bd. IV, p. 70 ff., p. 129.

An original treatment of the social function of literature.

SCHERR, JOH.   Allgemeine Geschichte der Literatur.   2 vols. Stuttgart : 1881, 1882.

See pp. 1, 2, for a definition and classification of literature.

SCHOPENHAUER, A.   Sämmtliche Werke.   6 vols.   Leipz. : 1877.

Bd. VI, pp. 536–581 Ueber Schriftstellerei und Stil.

SCHOPENHAUER, A.   The Art of Literature.   Ed. by F. B. Saunders.   Lond. : 1891.

Contains readable, often brilliant, essays on authorship, style, men of learning, genius, etc.

SHERMAN, L. A.   Analytics of Literature.   A Manual for the
   Objective Study of English Prose and Poetry.   Boston:
   1893.

An attempt to apply " scientific methods " to the study of
the elements and sources of power in English literature.   The
results of the author's investigations as applied to prose possess
undoubted value; it is not so clear that he has made substantive
additions to the theory of poetry.   Chap. I deals with literature
and its divisions.

SILL, E. R.   *Atlantic*, 56: 665 Principles of Criticism.

A valuable paper.   Assuming that literature takes rank among
the fine arts, the writer seeks for principles broad enough to
include artistic manifestations in any medium.   Art is defined
as the expressed power and activity of the human spirit.   Like
other arts, literature gives delight because it satisfies man's
aspiration for full and abounding life.   The forms of literature
must be ranked according to their expressiveness.

SPENCER, H.   The Philosophy of Style.   Together with an
   Essay on Style by T. H. Wright.   Ed. by F. N. Scott.   2d
   ed.   Boston: 1894.   (First published in *Westm. Rev.*, October,
   1852; republished in Essays: Moral, Political, and Aesthetic,
   and Essays: Scientific, Political, and Speculative.)

One of the most important of modern contributions to the
theory of style.   Spencer attempts to explain the effect of both
prose and poetry upon the principle that that language is most
forcible which best economizes the mental energies and the
mental sensibilities.   In order to a correct understanding of
the essay some acquaintance with the Spencerian psychology
is necessary.   (See References, § **8**.)   For a criticism of
Spencer's theory of style, see the essay by T. H. Wright
(*Macmillan*, 37: 78, reprinted in the edition cited above), and
Hiram M. Stanley's Studies in the Evolutionary Psychology

of Feeling (Lond.: 1895), chap. XVIII The Psychology of Literary Style.

SPENCER, H.   *Contemp.* 68 : 228 (also in *Pop. Sci. Mo.*, September, 1895) Orator and Poet, Actor and Dramatist.

A brief and inadequate consideration of the part played in society by writers and actors.

STAËL, MME. DE.   De la littérature considerée dans ses rapports avec les institutions sociales.   Paris: 1845.

> Pp. 213–221 Préface de la seconde édition; pp. 222–240 Discours préliminaire.

The purpose of the work, as stated by the author, is to examine the influence of religion, manners, and laws on literature, and the reciprocal influence of literature on religion, manners, and laws.   The portions indicated above deal with the subject in a theoretical way.

STANLEY, HIRAM M.   Studies in the Evolutionary Psychology of Feeling.   Lond.: 1895.

Chap. XVIII, on the Psychology of Literary Style, is mainly an examination of Spencer's Philosophy of Style, which the writer endeavors to supplement at certain points.   The treatment is able and highly suggestive.

STEINTHAL, H.   *Zeitschrift für Völkerpsychologie*, 4: 465 Zur Stylistik.

A thoughtful article, written from the point of view of the 'folk-psychologist.' The subject is treated first historically, then theoretically, style being defined as a relation between speech and the thing expressed.   The author draws a careful distinction between form and content, and discusses with some fullness the relation of one to the other.

STEINTHAL, H.   *Zeitschrift für Völkerpsychologie*, 6: 285 Poesie und Prosa.

Of this valuable article the most interesting part is the section entitled ' Poetry and Prose according to their Purpose and Content.'

STEVENSON, R. L.   *Contemp.* 47 : 548 On Style in Literature.

As one of the foremost stylists of the century, Stevenson is entitled to speak upon his art with the air of an authority.   His essay will be found readable, and in many ways suggestive; but the student should ask himself whether the author does not emphasize form at the expense of substance.   For a criticism of Stevenson's own style and thought, see the article by Wm. Archer in the *Critic*, 8: 7, 19.

SYMONDS, J. A.   Essays Speculative and Suggestive.   2 vols. London.

Vol. I, pp. 256–331; vol. II, pp. 1–30 Notes on Style.

A fairly comprehensive and consistent theory of style, expounded in the florid and over-strenuous manner characteristic of the writer.

TEN BRINK, B.   Ueber die Aufgabe der Litteraturgeschichte. Strassburg: 1891.

On pp. 1–21 the author outlines clearly and interestingly the elements which constitute a work of literature.   A reading of the whole of this brief address (28 pages) is warmly recommended.

THOREAU, H. D.   Early Spring in Massachusetts.   Boston: 1894.

See p. 301 for a remarkable passage on the social aspects of literature.

VINET, ALEX.   Outlines of Philosophy and Literature.   2d ed. Lond.: 1867.

Pp. 457–639 Literature, Poetry, and Eloquence.

Readable but not especially penetrating remarks upon the philosophical aspects of literature.

WARNER, CHAS. D. Literature and Life. N. Y.: 1897.

Delightfully written essays, of a reflective character, on the worth of literature in the conduct of life, on the relation of literature to the age in which it is produced, and on kindred topics.

WEIL, H. The Order of Words in the Ancient Languages Compared with that of the Modern Languages. Trans. by C. W. Super. Boston: 1887.

A work of the highest authority on the subject of which it treats.

WHITNEY, W. D. Language and the Study of Language. N. Y.: 1867.

Pp. 403–420.

WHITNEY, W. D. Life and Growth of Language. N. Y.: 1877.

Pp. 1–13.

WHITNEY, W. D. 'Philology,' in the Encycl. Brit., 9th ed.

See especially p. 766 *et seq.*

The writings of Professor Whitney, because of the simplicity and charm of their style, furnish an excellent introduction to the study of questions relating to language.

WILSON, WOODROW. Mere Literature and other Essays. Boston: 1896.

The opening essay, which gives the volume its title, is a spirited plea for the study and appreciation of literature as literary art.

WORSFOLD, W. BASIL. The Principles of Criticism. Lond.: 1897.

The following criticism by Dr. F. I. Carpenter in *Nation*,
65: 1691, states very fairly the quality of Mr. Worsfold's book.
It does not, however, deserve the commendation here given for
the historical character of its method. Addison is exalted
altogether out of his place — Ben Jonson, Dryden, Shaftesbury,
Goldsmith, Wordsworth, Coleridge, Carlyle, etc., are wholly or
practically ignored. See § **21**, *B* 2, below. "The book presents
a combination of an analysis of the leading ideas in literary
aesthetics of Aristotle (superfluous in view of the recent work
of Mr. Butcher), Plato, Addison, Lessing, Cousin, Matthew
Arnold, and others, together with a discursive discussion of
current topics of related interest in the review style. The
original 'principles of criticism,' which are the outcome of the
last four chapters, are somewhat obscure and indecisive.

" Mr. Worsfold waives the attempt of German metaphysics
at a 'transcendental' aesthetics, and defends 'psychological'
aesthetics as agreeing both with Greek experience and with
sound philosophy. The truth of art and the truth of logic and
nature are not the same. Art, as Bacon maintained, idealizes
and submits the shows of things to the desires of the mind,
while its peculiar faculty is the imagination, as Addison first
demonstrated. Plato is nearer modern ideas than Aristotle, in
that he emphasizes the test of truth rather than the test of form
in art. Lessing is Aristotelian in concerning himself chiefly
with form and with imitations of the arts. Cousin returns to
the idealist or Platonic aesthetics ; while Matthew Arnold has
been most conspicuous among recent critics in subjecting poetry
to the tests of imagination and of truth, or, in other words, of
the application of moral ideas to the criticism of life. Further
than this there are chapters devoted to the topics of Poetic
Justice, of The Drama as a Composite Art, of The Novel as a
Form of Literature, and of Authority in Literature and Art.
The later chapters are full of a clever young man's confident
modernity of view, while the preceding chapters are soundly

historical in method. The most striking differentiae of the plan of the book as a whole are the historical importance assigned to Addison and to Cousin, and the gaps resulting from neglecting the contributions of other modern writers who are quite as important. Addison is important in the history of applied criticism in England, but in aesthetic theory Mr. Worsfold hardly vindicates the large claims he makes for him. Although the term imagination is little used in critical discussion before his day, the essential idea of the faculty, under the terms 'fancy' (phantasy) or 'wit,' is common enough with the Elizabethan writers, and is regarded by more than one of them as the ground idea of the poetic faculty and function."

§ 15. GENERAL NOTE.

I. Literature and Language. — Additional references under this head are : O. Jespersen, Progress in Language (Lond.: 1894), chaps. I and IX (delightful reading, and a work of the first importance); H. Brunnhofer, *Deutsche Revue*, 1886, III, pp. 83–99 Die Aesthetik der Sprachen ; J. M. Baldwin, *Philos. Rev.* 2 : 385 Internal Speech and Song ; S. Stricker, Ueber die Sprachvorstellungen (Wien: 1880); S. Stricker, *Revue Philos.* 22 : 1 De la parole et des sons intérieurs ; B. Bourdon, L'expression des émotions et des tendances dans le langage (Paris: 1892).

II. Style. — The advanced student who desires to investigate some problem relating to literary style will do well to pursue a course of reading that will take him through the most important of the earlier treatises in their historical order. The list is a very long one and might easily be made formidable, since nearly every writer on aesthetics or rhetoric has touched at least briefly upon questions of style. The following references, however, will perhaps suffice for most students: (1) Plato's

Ion, Phaedo, Symposium, Gorgias; (2) Aristotle's Poetics and
Rhetoric; (3) Cicero's De Oratore, Brutus, and De Inventione
Rhetorica; (4) Horace's Ars Poetica; (5) Quintilian's Institutes;
(6) Longinus on the Sublime; (7) Vida's De Arte Poetica; (8)
Sidney's Apologie for Poetry; (9) Webbe's Discourse of English
Poetrie; (10) Puttenham's Arte of English Poetrie; (11) Jonson's
Discoveries; (12) Boileau's L'Art poétique; (13) Roscommon's
Essay on Translated Verse; (14) Addison's Spectator, Nos. 411–
421; (15) Pope's Essay on Criticism; (16) Voltaire's article on
'Style,' and Montesquieu's article on 'Goût,' in the Encyclopédie
méthodique; (17) Blair's Lectures on Rhetoric; (18) Constable's
Reflections on Accuracy of Style; (19) Johnson's Lives of the
Poets; (20) Lord Kames's Elements of Criticism; (21) Camp-
bell's Philosophy of Rhetoric.

In the discussion of national styles, if it is desired to make
the investigation thorough, information should be sought in such
works as Brownell's Characteristics of the French, Hamerton's
French and English, Baring-Gould's Germany, Present and
Past, Andrew D. White's The New Germany, and similar
monographs; and an attempt should be made to connect literary
characteristics with peculiarities of the social or industrial life
of the people.

The following references on the general subject of Style contain suggestions of greater or less value: H. Liers, *Neue Jahrb.
f. Philol. u. Paed.* 135: 681 Zur Geschichte der Stilarten;
W. Forsyth, Essays Critical and Narrative (Lond.: 1874),
p. 162; W. Wackernagel, Poetik, Rhetorik, und Stilistik (2. Aufl.
Halle: 1888), p. 412 (an excellent handling of the subject);
E. B. Condillac, Œuvres (10 vols. Paris: 1798), vol. VII, pp.
337–424 Du caractère du style, pp. 429–443 Dissertation sur
l'harmonie du style; Sir E. B. Lytton, Caxtoniana (2 vols.
Edinb.: 1863), vol. I, pp. 123–153 On Style and Diction;
K. F. Becker, Der deutsche Stil (3. Aufl. Leipz.: 1884); Em.
Zanella, Lingua e Stile (Roma: 1886); J. Swift, Letter to a

Young Clergyman (contains a famous definition of style) ; Ferd. Loise, Traité de littérature: Les lois du style (Bruxelles : 1887); F. Harrison, *19th Cent.* 43 : 932 On Style in English Prose.

III. Figures. — The following bibliography of figures is taken, with some additions, from Miss Gertrude Buck's Figures of Rhetoric: A Psychological Study (Contributions to Rhetorical Theory, No. 1, edited by F. N. Scott) :

Ancient Writers. — Among the ancients, the observations upon figures of Aristotle, Cicero, and Quintilian outweigh in value those of all the rest. For the views of Aristotle, see the Rhetoric, Bk. III, chaps. X, XI; but cf. also Poetics, chaps. XXI, XXII. Cicero speaks of figures briefly in Orator 27, and more at length in De Oratore 38–43. The remarks of Quintilian will be found in the Institutes, Bk. VIII, chap. VI, and Bk. IX, chaps. I–III. Lesser rhetoricians who wrote treatises on figures are Alexander, Phoebammon, Tiberius, Herodianus, Zonaeus, Tryphon (each the author of a work entitled 'Concerning Figures'); Gregorius Corinthius, Cocondrius, Georgius Choeroboscus (each the author of a work entitled ' Concerning Tropes'); and Polybius Sardianus, author of a work entitled ' Concerning Schematism.' These are Greek writers and may be consulted in Walz's Rhetores Graeci. For the lesser Latin rhetoricians, Rutilius Lupus, Rufinianus, Aquila Romanus, and others, see Halm's Rhetores Latini Minores.

Modern Writers. — Du Marsais was one of the first to lay stress upon the fact that figures of speech are not ' deviations ' from what is natural or ordinary. " Figures," he says, "removed from the ordinary method of speaking should be regarded as ornamental affectations." Herbert Spencer offered the first adequate scientific explanation of figurative effects. Bain's classification has perhaps been more widely accepted than any other. The remaining writers are too numerous to distinguish, except by an occasional passing comment.

J. Q. Adams, Lectures on Rhetoric and Oratory, vol. II, Lects. 30–34 ; H. Arendt, Die Metaphern in den dramatischen Werken Corneilles (Marburg: 1889); H. Arminius, Die Tropen und Figuren (Innsbruck: 1890); *Atlantic Mo.* 73: 574 American Metaphor; A.

Bain, Engl. Comp. and Rhet., vol. I, pp. 135–232; J. Bascom, Philos. of Rhet., pp. 244–246; Arlo Bates, Talks on Writing English (Boston: 1896), pp. 96–106; J. Bauer, Das Bild in der Sprache (Ansbach: 1878, 1889); Bede, De Schematis et Tropis Sacrae Scripturae Liber; A. Biese, Das Metaphorische in der dichterischen Phantasie; A. Biese, Die Philosophie des Metaphorischen (Hamburg: 1893); *Blackwood's Mag.* 18: 719 On the Use of Metaphors; H. Blair, Lects. on Rhet. and Belles Lettres, Lects. 14–18; C. B. Bradley, *Mod. Lang. Notes,* 1: 140 The Classification of Rhetorical Figures; A. Braun, Versuch über die Tropen (Münnerstadt: 1847); F. Brinkmann, Die Metaphern (Bonn: 1878. Cf. *Herrig's Archiv,* 54: 155, 337, 55: 327, 56: 343, 58: 193) ; F. Brunetière, *Rev. d. D. Mondes,* 1 févr. 1888 Les métaphores de Victor Hugo; G. Campbell, Philos. of Rhet., Bk. III, chap. I; G. R. Carpenter, Exercises in Rhet. (Adv. Course), pp. 196–200; W. Caspers, Ueber die Tropen und Figuren (Recklinghausen: 1873); A. Darmsteter, La vie des mots (Paris: 1887), pp. 45–72 (a highly interesting chapter on the way in which words change in sense from literal to figurative); A. Dathi, Libellus de variis loquendi figuris (Ferrariae: 1471); H. N. Day, Art of Discourse, pp. 313–331; E. Degenhardt, Die Metapher bei den Vorläufern Molières (Marburg: 1888); Jas. De Mille, Elements of Rhet., pp. 87–203 (gives on p. 91 eight schemes of classification); Robt. Dodsley, Rhet. and Poetry (Boston: 1796); F. C. Doyle, Introd. to the Study of Rhet., pp. 80–103; C. C. Du Marsais, Des Tropes (Œuvres, vol. III); J. Earle, English Prose, pp. 234–253; E. Elster, Prinzipien der Litteraturwissenschaft (Halle: 1897), Bd. I, pp. 374–394; D. Erasmus, De Parabolis sive similibus (opera, vol. I, p. 557); H. W. Frost, *Galaxy,* 24: 204 Figures of Speech; J. P. Fruit, *Mod. Lang. Notes,* 2: 251 The Evolution of Figures of Speech; J. F. Genung, Practical Rhet., pp. 85–107; G. Gerber, Die Sprache als Kunst (2 vols. Bromberg: 1871. The greater part of this large work is devoted to figures); O. Goldsmith, Essays, Essay 21 On the Use of Metaphors ; H. E. Greene, Pubs. Mod. Lang. Assoc., vol. VIII (1893. A Grouping of Figures of Speech, based on the Principle of their Effectiveness); P. Gross, Die Tropen und Figuren (Leipz.: 1888. A text-book for use in Greek and Latin classes); F. B. Gummere, The Anglo-Saxon Metaphor (maintains that the metaphor is an earlier form of expression

than the simile); F. B. Gummere, Poetics, pp. 83–132; F. B. Gummere, *Mod. Lang. Notes*, 1 : 83 Metaphor and Poetry; J. A. Guyet,
L'élégance: Dialogue sur l'emploi des figures dans la conversation
(Paris: 1858); E. E. Hale, Jr., Constructive Rhetoric (N. Y.: 1896),
pp. 248–298; J. M. Hart, Handbook of Engl. Comp., pp. 177–
192 (classifies figures as objective and subjective); W. C. Hazlitt,
Offspring of Thought, p. 285; F. H. Hedge, Atheism in Philosophy
and other Essays, p. 306 Irony; Hegel, Aesthetik, vol. I, p. 498, vol.
III, p. 282; H. Henkel, Das Goethesche Gleichnis (Halle: 1886);
Hense, Poetische Personification in griech. Dichtung (Halle: 1868);
A. S. Hill, Foundations of Rhet., pp. 192–196 (on the force and office
of figures); A. S. Hill, Principles of Rhetoric, pp. 87–99 Tropes ; D.
J. Hill, Science of Rhetoric, pp. 203–243; A. Hirzel, Gleichnisse und
Metaphern im Rigveda (Leipz.: 1890); H. Höffding, Outlines of
Psychology, pp. 153–154; J. P. Huber, Zu den platonischen Gleich-
nissen (Passau: 1879); W. James, Lectures on the Figurative Lan-
guage of the Holy Scriptures (Lond.: 1821); Kames, Elements of
Criticism, chap. XX; C. F. Koch, Figuren und Tropen (Jena: 1880);
G. Kohfeldt, *Zeitschr. f. Philos. u. Philos. Kritik*, N. F. 103 : 221
Zur Aesthetik der Metapher (one of the latest and ablest contributions
to the philosophy of metaphor); D. Krupp, Homerische Gleichnisse
(Zweibrücken: 1882); E. Küsel, *Herrig's Archiv*, 53:241 Ueber Schillers Gleichnisse ; H. R. Lang, *Am. Journ. Philol.* 6: 74 On Spanish
Metaphors ; Langen, *Jahrb. f. Philol. u. Paed.* 125: 673, 753 Meta-
pher von Plautus bis Terentius ; G. H. Lewes, Principles of Success
in Literature, pp. 69–78 (principally on imagery, but indirectly of much
value); Lingenberg, Platonische Bilder und Sprichwörter (Köln :
1872); D. N. Lord, Laws of Figurative Language; W. P. Lunt, *Chr.
Examiner*, 68: 390 Figurative Language; K. Maass, Ueber Metapher
und Allegorie im deutschen Sprichwort (Leipz.: 1891); J. G. R.
McElroy, Structure of English Prose, pp. 235–246 ; Magdeburg,
Ueber Bilder und Gleichnisse bei Euripides (Danzig : 1882–88);
Marheineke, *Herrig's Archiv*, 51 : 173 Ueber die Shakespeare'schen
Gleichnisse ; Marmontel, Éléments de littérature, vol. II, p. 185; W.
E. Mead, Elementary Compos. and Rhet., pp. 40, 41, 53, 54; Meyer,
Vergl. und Metapher bei Molière ; Meyer, *Herrig's Archiv*, 20: 174
Begründung d. Redefiguren; W. Minto, Manual of Prose Literature,

pp. 11–14; Max Müller, Lects. on the Science of Language, 2d Ser., p. 351; Max Müller, Science of Thought, vol. II, pp. 481–512; Max Müller, *Fortn.* 46: 617 Metaphor as a Mode of Abstraction; F. Niggli, Ueber die Redefiguren und deren Behandlung in der Schule (Aaran: 1871); R. Noel, *Fortn.* 5: 670 Use of Metaphor and Pathetic Fallacy in Poetry; G. C. D. Odell, Development of Simile and Metaphor from the Ballad Poetry to Shelley (Columbia University, Thesis); H. Paul, Principles of the History of Language, chap. IV, Change in Word-significance (highly suggestive); J. Rappold, Die Gleichnisse bei Aeschylus, Sophokles u. Euripides (1876–78; also, Beiträge zur Kenntnis der Gleichnisse u. s. w., Wien: 1886); W. C. Robinson, Forensic Oratory, §§ 290–298; Röfsler, Beitrag zur Lehre von den Tropen (Budweis: 1853); A. Schopenhauer, The World as Will and Idea, vol. I, p. 305 Allegory; Schürmeyer, Vergl. u. Met. bei Racine (Marburg: 1886); F. N. Scott and Jos. V. Denney, Composition-Rhetoric (Boston: 1897), pp. 219–225 Imaginative Expressions; L. A. Sherman, Analytics of Literature, pp. 60–86, 399, 400 (distinguishes figures based on (1) imaginative processes in which spiritual *identity* is discerned, and (2) imaginative processes in which spiritual *likeness* is discerned); H. Spencer, Philos. of Style, pp. 21–28, 38–40; J. Stirling, System of Rhetoric, containing all tropes and figures necessary to illustrate the classics (Lond.: 1764); Stoessel, D. Bild. d. altprovenz. Lyrik (Marburg: 1886); *Theo. and Lit. Jl.* 3: 613 Objections to Figurative Language, 4: 687 Figurative Lang. of Scripture; A. Tompkins, Science of Discourse, pp. 366–420; K. Tumlirz, Tropen u. Figuren (Prag : 1883); W. Wackernagel, Poetik, Rhetorik und Stilistik (2. Aufl. Halle a. S.: 1888), pp. 501–535; Victoria Welby, *Monist*, 3: 510 Meaning and Metaphor; B. Wendell, English Composition, pp. 245–261 (treats figures, after A. S. Hill, as a means of securing force ; the remarks on the uselessness of the distinction between metonymy and synecdoche are judicious); K. Weyman, Studien über die Figur der Litotes (I. Allgemeiner Theil. München: 1886); Whately, Elements of Rhetoric, pt. III, chap. II, §§ 2, 3; Whitney, Life and Growth of Language, pp. 85–89; H. F. Wilhelmi, Von den Tropen (Heidelberg : 1839); H. F. Wilhelmi, Von den Figuren der Wort-wiederholung (Heidelberg : 1841).

IV. Classification of Literature. — At the close of his essay on Style, Walter Pater suggests a division of literature into great literature and good literature. The basis of the classification is given, but the idea is not developed. To pursue the suggestion further, on philosophical grounds, showing the value of the distinction and illustrating it by examples taken from many literatures, will prove an interesting and profitable task. It will be found to involve questions regarding the ethical value of art which can be answered only by a careful study of the appropriate references under § **8.** See also, on this point, Matthew Arnold's remark on Shakespeare's art, in Mixed Essays, p. 193, and M. Thompson's Ethics of Literary Art (Hartford: 1893).

The methodological works of the German philologists contain interesting attempts at philosophical classification. One of the simplest is that of August Boeckh (Encyklopädie und Methodologie der Philologischen Wissenschaften, pp. 144–146, 614–616). It may be presented in outline as follows:

	Objective.	*Subjective.*	*Subjective-Objective.*
Poetry.	Epic.	Lyric.	Dramatic.
Prose.	Historical.	Philosophical.	Rhetorical.

As a specimen of a more complex and systematic classification, the following outline, much abbreviated, is reproduced from Körting's Encyklopädie und Methodologie der Romanischen Philologie, pp. 63–82.[1]

I. Literature in a wide sense includes the totality of written works produced in a given time and place. According to its

---

[1] For the application of this system to Romance literature, see the amazing list on pp. 444–454, — a highly characteristic product of the Teutonic intellect.

purpose and its content, literature in this sense may be classified as follows :

A. Works whose purpose is to present the real.

1. Compositions whose sole purpose is practice in penmanship and in the written expression of thought, *e.g.* school exercises.

2. Records of facts, including

   a. Writings of a private character not intended for publication, *e.g.* private letters, accounts, diaries, etc.

   b. Writings of a private (personal) character intended for publication, *e.g.* mortuary inscriptions, lampoons, etc.

   c. Writings of an official character not intended for publication, *e.g.* deeds, passports, secret treaties, etc.

   d. Writings of an official character intended for publication, *e.g.* laws, public inscriptions.

   e. Writings of a general character, intended for publication, *e.g.* political and local news, statistics, geographical and historical works (in which the presentation of facts and not of the inner relation of facts is the main purpose), parliamentary reports, etc.

3. Works intended to give instruction about matters of fact, including

   a. Text-books for the schools.

   b. Books on scientific or technical matters designed for the educated public, together with travels, popular histories, etc.

   c. Compendiums for specialists in certain sciences and technical subjects.

4. Works intended to amuse and entertain, as collections of anecdotes, riddles, comedies (without moral purpose), etc.

B. Works whose purpose is to present the ideal.

1. Writings which express and communicate subjective reflections upon the relations of personal life, *e.g.* lyric poems, reflective letters, etc.

2. Criticism, which may be

    a. Direct, as in aesthetic and philosophical critiques, or

    b. Indirect, as in Utopias (so-called), fairy stories, idyls, moralizing novels, and the like, in which the deficiencies of the actual are contrasted with the perfections of the ideal.

    c. Negative, or destructive.

    d. Positive, or constructive.

3. Writings which tend to widen the scope of human knowledge, such as the great contributions to science.

4. Writings which tend to uplift and refine man's moral nature, including

    a. Writings whose purpose is ethical, either

        (1) Directly, or

        (2) Indirectly.

    b. Writings whose purpose is religious, either

        (1) Directly, or

        (2) Indirectly.

II. In a narrower sense literature is the totality of written works produced in a given place and time in which a people have found expression for their thoughts and feelings about the ideal. Taken in this sense, literature may be classified as follows :

    A. Works of the understanding, or scientific works.

    B. Works of the imagination, or poetical works.

Körting also classifies literature according to its form. The form of literature is threefold: (1) *material,* relating to the division and arrangement of the subject-matter; (2) *linguistic,* relating to the choice and syntax of words and the combination of sentences ; (3) *rhythmical,* relating to the musical quality of speech. According to material form, literature may be divided into

    A. Works composed artistically.

B. Works not composed artistically.

According to linguistic form, literature may be divided into

A. Logical discourse.[1]

B. Aesthetic discourse.

According to rhythmical form, literature may be divided into

A. Free, or unmetrical discourse (prose).

B. Metrical discourse (poetry).

Finally, viewing works according to both form and content, four classes of ideal literature may be distinguished :

1. Scientific works in which the material and linguistic form are logical, the rhythmical form free.

2. Scientific works in which the material and linguistic form are aesthetic, the rhythmical form free.

3. Poetical works in which the material and linguistic form are aesthetic, the rhythmical form free, *e.g.* dramas in prose.

4. Poetical works in which the material and linguistic form are aesthetic, the rhythmical form metrical.

The student may also consult H. Paul, Grundriss der germanischen Philologie, Methodenlehre, p. 216 *et seq.;* F. Blass, Hermeneutik und Kritik (in Iwan Müller's Handbuch, Bd. I, pp. 127–272; see § **2**).

V. Classification of Literary Theory.— Before passing, as in §§ **19-24,** to Poetry, Poetics, and Versification, attention must be directed to the necessity of discrimination between the term Poetics and the terms more or less involved in the conception of aesthetics: 'Stylistic,' Rhetoric, Metric, etc. The subject is discussed by Elze (Grundr. d. Engl. Philol., pp. 342–360 Stilistik, 361–362 Metrik) and by Boeckh (Encyklopädie,

---

[1] In the original:

    a. In sachlicher Redeform.

    b. In aesthetischer Redeform abgefasste Litteraturwerke.

By 'logical' discourse is meant discourse that aims primarily at clearness and intelligibility.

p. 810).   The latter had included *Stilistik* (the theory of style)
under grammar, because, in his opinion, it held the same relation to syntax that syntax did to etymology; but Elze proceeds
to show (p. 323) that 'stylistic' is no more closely connected
with syntax than it is with lexicography.   And he concludes
that 'stylistic' should be regarded as a discipline entirely separate from grammar.   Adopting Wackernagel's definition of
style (Poetik, Rhetorik, und Stilistik, p. 112, 2. Aufl. Halle:
1889), "the method of representation possible to language
according to the conditions imposed by the personality of the
artist, and by the content and purpose of the object represented,"
Elze approves of the following distinction: Style is subjective
when it is regarded in its character of individual expression
resting upon individuality (personal peculiarity) of thought, —
though both of these factors are, in turn, influenced by the
general culture and the stylistic temperament of the people and
the period under consideration.   Style is objective in so far as
it is determined by the laws of a literary species, and in so far
as it follows methods dictated by the aim of the species in
question.   These, then, may be called the *Unities of Style*, —
subjective and objective.   Style as represented by these unities
is found in both poetry and prose.

Boeckh, too, had drawn a similar distinction showing the
presence of both unities in both kinds of composition.   In the
following remarks about style and manner the characteristics
assigned to style are rather those of the subjective unity; those
to manner, of the objective: "Style is Nature; it proceeds from
the culture of the period, from circumstances, and from the
character of the individual, but it may be also heightened by
art, as was the case with Herodotus.   Manner, on the other
hand, is the imitation of a by-gone style the conditions of whose
existence no longer exist. . . .   Style springs from an inspiration that is begotten of existing circumstances; manner apes
but is uninspired because the conditions fail, or the author him-

self " (p. 248). With regard to the external limitations of style the same author expresses himself (p. 144 ff., 648) to the effect that the objective unity of the literary production is form, prosaic or poetic, decided in accordance with the psychological faculty to which the author appeals. "The purpose of speech is to express thought ; and thoughts are expressed for comprehension either by the understanding or by the imagination. If by the former, we have prose ; if by the latter, poetry."

But while poetry and prose are the forms of the objective unity of the literary production, the choice between these forms is determined by the quality of the stylist, — that is to say, by the nature of the thought that the author would express. For there are qualities of style, subjective and objective, as well as unities; and these qualities, combined in various proportions, decide the species of objective form, and the subspecies, which shall suit the author's thought. Sometimes this thought is a concept to which sense impression is subordinate, — therefore a thought, impersonal, objective in quality, and demanding impersonal or objective expression. Sometimes the thought is an imaginative or emotive ideal, — therefore personal or subjective in quality, and demanding a symbolic form that may appeal to the imagination of the reader. What the objective unity of the style shall be is a question of proportion depending upon the purpose and the quality of the author's thought. If the purpose is to appeal to understanding, then the objective unity of the style is that of prose ; if to imagination, then poetry. According to the quality of the author's thought, the subspecies vary in prose and in poetry. If, in accordance with the purpose, the objective form is prose, then the subspecies will be historical narrative when the quality of the thought is impersonal, or objective ; and it will be philosophical disquisition when the quality of the thought is of inner or subjective relations. If, in accordance with the purpose, the external unity is that of poetry, then an impersonal or objective quality

of thought will demand the epical subspecies of expression;
but a personal or subjective quality will choose the lyrical.
When the subjective, or personal, conviction or ideal tries to
realize itself by finding expression in the conduct of others,
then there results in prose, oratory; in poetry, the drama.

It is evident, therefore, that the individuality and the purpose of the author, the quality of his thought, and the objective
characteristics of literary species and form, are all of them
factors of style. And it would appear that 'stylistic' should
cover the theory of all kinds of writing — poetic and prosaic.
The ancients, indeed, were inclined to apply the term rhetoric
as a cross-division to many common qualities of poetry and
prose. But the moderns do not generally accept that cross-
division. Elze, Boeckh, Maas, and others arrange the matter
thus: Style is the form and method of expression in language.
'Stylistic' is the general theory of style, and this general theory
divides itself naturally into the theory of prose style (rhetoric,
or, if that have an oratorical or any other special significance,
prosaics) and the theory of poetic style (poetics). This is more
reasonable (Elze, p. 347) than to limit 'stylistic,' or the theory
of style, as Wackernagel does, to the material which lies between
the two realms, on the border land of prosaics and poetics,
but belongs to neither. That would be to make 'stylistic'
coördinate with prosaics and poetics. The theory of style, it
may be held, is no more coördinate with, that is, a category
parallel with, prosaics and poetics, than it is subordinate to
either or both of them. Still, writers on rhetoric and poetics
generally propagate one or the other of these opinions, — in England and America, usually the second; and accordingly we find
style treated as a subdivision of rhetoric, or again of poetics;
both of which may be regarded as subdivisions of 'stylistic.'

As for metric, if it is not a subdivision of poetics, as von
Gottschall, Gummere, and others say, then it must be either
coördinate or distinct; entirely distinct, according to Elze, who

says (p. 348) "it does not belong to poetics because it has nothing whatever to do with style." But that is a rash statement; for, even if metres are to be regarded as purely conventional and mechanical, external to the creative spirit and of no appreciable effect, they still fall within the jurisdiction of form, which is itself determined by the objective unity of the style : their formal rules and regulations affect the utterance of the poet, and combine to govern the finality of his expression (*i.e.* his style) in very much the same way as do the methods and purposes of the literary species in which he chooses to cast his thought. So much, indeed, would seem to be conceded by Elze, for in his chapter on Metrik (p. 361), he tells us that "the style of a poem does not remain unaffected by the selection of verse- and strophe-forms."

Metric, therefore, is not a distinct science; it is much more likely to be coördinate with poetics. If so, the term Poetics ought to be restricted to questions affecting the subjective unity of style in poetry, and metric and technique might be regarded as dividing between them questions affecting the objective unity of the style ; technique dealing with the question of literary species or forms, and metric with that of rhythmic sequences arranged in recurring measures.

But such a connotation of poetics would win the approval of none. Metric does not lie outside of poetics, either as distinct or coördinate; for metres as well as literary species betray in their individual and in their generic development their kinship with, if not their descent from, emotional, physical, and cultural conditions that determine the subjective quality of poetic style. It is, in other words, impossible to sunder the theory of measures — of sounds, verses, and strophes, from the theory of motives from which those measures spring. The motives — psychical, ethical, and physical — underlie the existence of poetry as a whole. The rhythms of metres, though chosen with the ease and indifference of conventionality, have their roots as firmly imbedded in the rhythm of nature and of thought as have other qualities of poetry, whether objective or subjective. Elze's " allein die poetische Stilistik findet die Verse und Strophen vor und hat nichts mit ihrer Bildung und ihrem Bau zu thun " betrays a momentary oblivion of historical method. Has poetic style always found its appropriate measures ready-made ?   Have measures and poetic style, bred in diverse climes and times, managed somehow to run into each other's arms, as if by happy accident ?

The definition and classification of disputed terms may be stated somewhat as follows : ' Stylistic ' is the general theory of style ; the discussion of it should precede that of rhetoric and poetics, and should cover the various elements and qualities of style common to and belonging to both. Rhetoric (or prosaics) is that division of the theory of style which treats of the expression of thought addressed to the understanding, as opposed to poetics, which treats of the expression of thought addressed to the imagination.   The appeal to will and emotion may variously — but in a subordinate degree — enter into both kinds of expression.   Metric, or versification, should be regarded not as a separate discipline, nor as coördinate with poetics and rhetoric, but as subordinate to poetics.   The components of poetics are as follows : the material of the conception (ethical, intellectual, emotional), the technique of construction, the aesthetics of effect.   Technique (or technics) regulates the various processes of construction so as to produce a form that is generic (having the characteristic of a poetical kind or species) and rhythmical (having the requisite qualities of verbal measure and sound).   Metric deals with rhythmic form in the field of poetry.

On this whole matter see Boeckh, Elze, and Wackernagel, as above ; also von Gottschall, Schipper (Metrik), Körting, Gerber (Die Sprache als Kunst), Gummere (Poetics), and further references at the beginning of § **19** below.

PART II. — COMPARATIVE LITERATURE.

§ 16. STATEMENT OF PROBLEMS.

THE term Comparative Literature is here employed, as in Professor Posnett's work of that title, to designate the general theory of literary evolution, the idea that literature passes through stages of inception, culmination, and decline. Unfortunately for those who are not prepared to undertake original research, this is a phase of evolution which has received but slight attention. Histories of literature are, of course, common enough, and the tendency at the present time is to connect in some way the biographical and critical fragments of which they mainly consist with the growth of religious and political institutions ; but to set forth explicitly the nature and value of this connection, to show that the birth, rise, culmination, and decline of literary movements are manifestations of a general law, or to point out " any tolerably permanent principle of social evolution round which the facts of literary growth and decay may be grouped " — this has been the task of but a very few, Posnett, Brunetière, Letourneau, Symonds, and one or two others, none of whom can be said to have been unqualifiedly successful.

In approaching this large subject, the student should hold fast to the clues put into his hands in preceding chapters. Literature has been assumed to be an art. Principles of literary growth will, then, be special applications of the general principles of art-evolution. The first question to be asked is, obviously, (1) What form does the general law of art-evolution assume when it manifests itself in the growth of literature ? If the theory of art adhered to makes growth dependent on conditions of environment, the student will be led to inquire, (2) How have these conditions affected the development of literature ?

(3) What facts of physical, social, political, or religious life
will serve as permanent data to which any stage of literary
growth may be referred?   These questions may be further
differentiated : (4) Why do certain types of literature become
prominent at certain epochs in history? (5) Why should
certain literary forms and ideas persist from generation to
generation, or recur at intervals ?   (6) Is there any law governing the times of such recurrence ?   (7) What signs accompany
the rise, the maturity, and the obsolescence of a given type?
(8) Does one literary type, as epic, ever pass into another, as
drama, by a definite process of transformation ? and, if so,
(9) what are the modifying influences which effect such a
metamorphosis ?   (10) Why are certain literary forms missing
from certain literatures ?   (11) What modifications of environment or national character will account for the broad differences in ancient and modern literature ? (12) in Eastern and
Western literatures ?   (13) What has been the influence upon
literary development of the discovery of printing and (14) of
the rise of the newspaper ?   (15) Which has come first in the
historical development, prose or poetry? (16) On what grounds
may the precedence of either be accounted for ?

Other inquiries which it is profitable to pursue concern the
influence of one nation upon another, as of France upon England in the seventeenth century ; the influence of one author
upon another, as of Dante upon Chaucer; the influence of
literary schools ; and the reflex influence, not to be overlooked,
of literature on social and individual development.

The authorities may be briefly dismissed, since their merits
are discussed in the references that follow. Posnett's Comparative Literature is the only work that can make pretense to
having traced a single principle of evolution through all, or at
least the most noteworthy, literatures of the world. It is a work
which is likely, at a first perusal, to arouse, in many readers,
violent and unreasoning prejudices. Against assuming such

an uncritical attitude of mind the student should be warned at
the outset, and recommended, not indeed to accept the author's
conceptions of literature as the last word on the subject, but,
having gained an exact comprehension of the point of view, to
determine for himself whether or not violence has been done
to the literary material. Whatever may be thought of the
value of Posnett's method, a reading of Greek and Latin literature to verify or overthrow the conclusions arrived at in his
chapter on " Clan Survivals in the City Commonwealth," or a
reading of English authors with a view to filling out the hurried
sketch of Nature in National Literature (Bk. V, chap. XXXI),
will be found at once fascinating and profitable. A similar
process of verification may be urged in the case of the elaborate
theory of Brunetière. The speculations of Symonds, though
easily understood, are too broadly and vaguely stated to be used
as a working basis. They will, however, be found remarkably
suggestive. In connection with these authorities the student
will do well to make a thorough study of Taine, Sainte-Beuve,
M.-J. Guyau, and E. Hennequin, as writers who have endeavored
to explain literary phenomena on purely physical grounds, or to
relate them to social organization.

§ 17. REFERENCES.

BASCOM, J.   Philosophy of English Literature.   N. Y. : 1886.

The author believes that an alternation of creation and criticism can be detected in the history of literature.

BIEDERMANN, WOLDEMAR VON.   *Zeitschrift f. vergl. Litteraturgeschichte*, 2 : 415 Zur vergleichenden Geschichte der poetischen Formen.

A good illustration of the comparative method applied to
primitive forms of literature. The material is drawn from folk-
lore collections, early literary monuments, accounts of savage
life, and the like.

BETZ, L. P.   *Revue de philologie française et de littérature*, X, 4,
   p. 247 Essai de bibliographie des questions de littérature
   comparée.

A classified and fairly comprehensive list of references.

BETZ, L. P.   *Zeitschrift f. französch. Sprache und Litteratur*,
   XVIII, 3, 1896 Kritische Betrachtungen über Wesen,
   Aufgabe und Bedeutung der vergleichenden Litteratur-
   geschichte.

An excellent account of the present status of the subject.

BOUTERWEK, FR.   Geschichte der Poesie und Beredsamkeit.
   2 vols.   Göttingen: 1801–19.

   Vol. I Introduction to modern poetry and eloquence; from the
   thirteenth century down.

BRUNETIÈRE, FERD.   L'évolution des genres dans l'histoire de
   la littérature.   Tome 1er. Introduction; l'évolution de la
   critique depuis la renaissance jusqu'à nos jours.   Paris :
   1890.

The object of this work, as given by the author, is to discover the underlying principles of literary development by
applying the theory of evolution to the study of literature.   The
volume opens with an outline of the author's method, and an
indication of the results at which he hopes to arrive.   The
question of the evolution of literary types (*genres*) resolves
itself into five subsidiary questions : (1) the reality and independence of types ; (2) the differentiation of types ; (3) the
stability of types ; (4) modifying influences ; (5) the transformation of types.   The differences in types correspond to differences in the means and ends of different arts and to diversities in
families of minds.   The principle of differentiation is the same
that operates in nature, namely, the advance, through ' divergence
of character,' from simplicity to complexity, from homogeneity to
heterogeneity.   Under stability of type are discussed questions

regarding the signs of youth, maturity, or decay which the type
exhibits at any given time ; it seems in Brunetière's treatment
of it to be most closely connected with the relations of classicism and romanticism.   In his discussion of modifying influences the author builds upon the theory of Taine.   The main
influences are three : (1) heredity, or the race ; (2) environments, divided into geographical or climatic conditions, social
conditions, and historical conditions; and (3) individuality.
The transformation of types takes place according to principles analogous in their operation to the Darwinian struggle for
existence, survival of the fittest, and natural selection.

The system is ingenious, but the question may be raised
whether Brunetière does not overwork the biological parallel.

BRUNETIÈRE, FERD.   L'évolution de la poésie lyrique en France
au dix-neuvième siècle.   2 vols.   Paris : 1894.

This is a continuation of the preceding work and an application of its theories, the object being to trace in part the
evolution of an important *genre*.   In vol. I, pp. 3–42, the author
dwells upon his method.   The evolution of a *genre* is different
from the history of a *genre :* history comes down the course of
time ; evolution goes back over the stages which have led to
the present form.

BUCKLE, H. T.   History of Civilization in England.   3 vols.
Lond. : 1875.

Buckle maintains the thesis that literature is the product, and
not in any true sense the cause, of civilization.

CARLYLE, THOS.   Lectures on the History of Literature.   Lond.:
1892.

Presents at least one thesis worthy of discussion : "During a
healthy, sound, progressive period of national existence, there
is, in general, no literature at all."

CARRIERE, M.   Die Kunst im Zusammenhang der Culturent-
        wickelung und die Ideale der Menschheit.   5 vols.   Leipz. :
        1871–73.

The opening chapters of vol. I (pp. 7–121) deal with the
early development of poetry.   Scattered through the remaining
volumes are chapters in which is traced the development of
both poetry and prose.   (See § 11.)

CARRIERE, M.   Poesie, ihr Wesen und ihre Formen, mit Grund-
        zügen der vergleichenden Litteraturgeschichte.   2. Aufl.
        Leipz. : 1884.

An application of the Hegelian aesthetic to the history of
poetry.   Written in a charming style.

CHECCHIA, G.   *Rivista di Filosofia Scientifica*, vol. VI, Gennaio,
        1887 Del methodo-evolutivo nella critica letteraria.

The author fits ingeniously the ideas and terminology of the
doctrine of evolution to the phenomena of literature as he
conceives them.   The struggle for existence, natural selection,
survival of the fittest, hereditary transmission, and atavism are
illustrated in literature, he thinks, as clearly as in biology.

COMTE, AUG.   The Positive Philosophy.   Trans. by Harriet
        Martineau.   2 vols.   N. Y. : 1854.

    See § 11.

DEMOGEOT, J.   Histoire des littératures étrangères considérées
        dans leurs rapports avec le développement de la littérature
        française.   2 vols.   Paris : 1880.

A study of the influence of Italian, Spanish, English, and
German literatures on the literature of France.

DE VERE, A.   Essays Literary and Ethical.   Lond. : 1889.

Contains some remarks on the social aspects of literature.

DYER, LOUIS.   Studies of the Gods in Greece.   Lond. : 1891.

See pp. 25, 28, 33, 38, 104, 111 for interesting observations on the relations between Greek religion and Greek poetry.

ELLIS, HAVELOCK.   The New Spirit.   Lond. : 1890.

The book may be taken as an illustration of modern attempts to treat literature from the scientific and sociological points of view.

ELSTER, ERNST.   Die Aufgaben der Litteraturgeschichte. Akademische Antrittsrede.   Halle : 1894.

FALKENHEIM, H.   Kuno Fischer und die litterarhistorische Methode.   Berlin : 1892.

A clear and readable exposition of the methods of criticism employed by the eminent German philosopher whose name appears in the title.

GROSSE, E.   Die Litteraturwissenschaft, ihr Ziel und ihr Weg. (Dissert.)   1887.

GROSSE, E.   The Beginnings of Art.   N. Y. : 1897.

These are the writings of an able and original investigator in the field of literature and aesthetics.   They may be consulted with profit by the advanced student.

GROTH, E.   *Die Grenzboten*, 49 (3) : 540–551 Kulturgeschichte und Litteraturgeschichte.

Groth is a follower of Taine, but, like Brunetière, adds to Taine's formula the principle of individuality.   He holds that the presence of the individual element makes it impossible for us to infer from any given work the general character of the period in which it was written.   The great masters lie outside their age.   The major literary products, therefore, as a source for the history of culture, are inferior to the minor.

A second article by Groth, entitled " Die Aufgabe der Litteraturgeschichte," appeared in *Die Grenzboten,* vol. L, p. 260.

GAYLEY, C. M.   *The Dial,* Chicago, August 1, 1894 A Society
    of Comparative Literature.

The author calls for the organization of a society for the
comparative investigation of literary growths.   His statement
of the need is substantially as follows :

Trustworthy principles of literary criticism depend upon the sub-
stantiation of aesthetic theory by scientific inquiry.   For lack of
systematic effort the comparative investigation of literary types,
species, movements, and themes is not yet adequately prosecuted.   No
individual can, unaided, gather from various literatures the materials
necessary for an induction to the characteristic of even one literary
type.   The time has come for organization of effort.   In the proposed
Society of Comparative Literature (or of Literary Evolution) each
member should devote himself to the study of a given type or
movement in literature with which he is specially, and at first hand,
familiar.   Thus, gradually, wherever the type or movement has existed
its evolution and characteristics may be observed and registered.   In
time, by systematization of results, an induction to the common and,
probably, some of the essential characteristics of the phenomena, to
some of the natural laws governing its origin, growth, and differentiation, may be made.   The history of national criticism and the
aesthetics of sporadic critical theory are, of course, interesting subjects
of study ; but to adopt canons of criticism from Boileau, or Vida, or
Puttenham, or Sidney, or Corneille, or even Lessing and Aristotle, and
apply them to types or varieties of type with which these critics were
unacquainted, is illogical, and, therefore, unhistorical.   To come at
the laws which govern the drama, it is not sufficient to modify by
generally accepted aesthetic principles the canons of any one school
of dramatic critics, even if we revise the results in the light of our
inductions from the drama of the Graeco-Roman-Celto-Teutonic
circle with which we are familiar.   The specific principles of technical
(or typical) criticism must be based upon the characteristics of the
type not only in well-known but in less-known literatures, among

aboriginal as well as civilized peoples, and in all stages of its evolution. The comparative formulation of results would assist us to
corroborate or to renovate current aesthetic canons of dramatic criticism. So, also, with other types, — lyric, epic, etc., — and with the
evolution of literary movements and themes. This work is not yet
undertaken by any English or American organization, or by any
periodical or series of publications in the English language.

GUMMERE, F. B. Old English Ballads. Boston : 1894.

In an admirable introduction prefixed to this collection of
ballads, Professor Gummere discusses at considerable length
the question of the communal origin of popular literature. The
author's reviews of books and articles bearing upon the question, and the bibliographical references in the footnotes will be
of great assistance to the student. Gummere's position is, in
essentials, that of ten Brink.

GUMMERE, F. B. The Ballad and Communal Poetry. Child
  Memorial Volume. Boston : 1897.

For a detailed synopsis of this valuable paper, see § **18, //**.

HALLAM, H. Introduction to the Literature of Europe in the
  Fifteenth, Sixteenth, and Seventeenth Centuries. 4 vols.
  N. Y.: 1870.

Perhaps the most successful of all attempts at a general
history of literature. The preface contains a critical review of
preceding works of this character.

HEGEL, G. W. F. Aesthetik. (See § **8**, p. 101.)

In the chapter on Poetry, vol. III, pp. 220–281, Hegel applies
his principle of development to the various forms of literary
production.

HERDER, J. G. Sämmtliche Werke. Hsgb. von B. Suphan.
  31 vols. Berlin : 1877–89.

> Bd. VIII Ueber die Wirkung der Dichtkunst auf die Sitten der
> Völker in alten und neuen Zeiten.

Herder's writings abound in suggestions of laws of literary growth, as might be expected in the case of one in whom the historical sense was so highly developed, who was indeed the great pioneer of the doctrine of evolution ; but the suggestions are not given systematic form, and consequently the laws are somewhat vague. Of especial interest are his two essays, The Effect of Poetry on Popular Morals (vol. VIII, p. 334), and The Causes of Decay and Corruption of Taste (vol. V, p. 593).

HUMBOLDT, ALEX VON.　Cosmos. Trans. by E. C. Otté. 5 vols.　N. Y. : 1850–62.

The chapter on the Poetic Delineation of Nature (vol. II, pp. 1–105) contains material of much interest to the student of comparative literature.

JACOBOWSKI, LUDW.　Die Anfänge der Poesie.　Grundlegung zu einer realistischen Entwickelungsgeschichte der Poesie. Dresden : 1891.

An ambitious attempt to lay the foundations of all future theories of literary evolution.　Amid a good deal of chaff there are some substantial grains of common sense.

KAWCZYNSKI, M.　Essai comparatif sur l'origine et l'histoire des rhythmes.　Paris : 1889.

In his introductory chapter (Questions préliminaires, especially pp. 10–30) the author makes attack upon the theory of the *autochthonèité* of literature, that is, the theory of the spontaneous origin of literature in each nation.　He holds that there is in literature no *Volksgeist ;* each literary product is first invented by an individual, then imitated by the people.　The chapter also contains valuable observations on the transformation through which literary material passes when borrowed by one nation from another.

KOCH, MAX.　*Zeitschrift f. vergl. Litteraturgeschichte,* N. F., Heft I.　Einleitung.

States the field and purpose of the magazine of which Koch is editor.

KÖRTING, G.   Encyklopädie und Methodologie der Romanischen Philologie.   2. Theil, 4. Buch, Die Litteraturcomplexe.

A comprehensive and philosophical discussion of the underlying principles of literary development, intended for the instruction of students of Romance philology.

LETOURNEAU, C.   L'évolution littéraire dans les diverses races humaines.   Paris: 1894.

An able treatment of the subject by a patient and conservative scientist.   A summary of the author's results is given by D. F. Hannigan in *Westm. Rev.* 141: 400, under the title The Literary Evolution of Man.   See also the Origin of Literary Forms, in *Pop. Sci. Mo.*, September, 1893, p. 675, translated from the article by Letourneau in the *Revue mensuelle de l'école d'anthropologie*.

MACAULAY, T. B.   Essays, Critical and Miscellaneous.   N. Y.: 1861.

See the essays on Dryden and Milton for Macaulay's theory that as civilization advances the literary imagination suffers a decline.

MOBERLY, GEORGE.   Oxford English Prize Essays.   5 vols. Oxford: 1830–36.

> Vol. IV, p. 131 Is a rude or a refined age more favorable to the production of works of fiction?

A readable, though somewhat conventional, treatment of the theme.

MORLEY, H.   English Writers.   Vol. I.   Lond.: 1887.

At the beginning of this volume are brief observations on the methods of the literary historian.   The first hundred pages treat of English literature as affected by the influence of other national literatures.

NODIER, C.   Romans.   Paris : 1850.

> Pp. 7–19 Des types en littérature.

A pleasing though somewhat fanciful essay on the origin of individual and national literary types.

OLIPHANT, MRS. M. O. W.   Literary History of England in the End of the Eighteenth and Beginning of the Nineteenth Century.   3 vols.   Lond.: 1882.

Mrs. Oliphant maintains (vol. I, pp. 7–15) that the development of literature is not subject to the operation of discoverable laws.   The evolution of mind "has been regulated by some spasmodic force which no one has tried to define [a surprising statement!], and which acts by great unforeseen impulses of irregular recurrence, of which no one has succeeded in calculating the times or seasons."   (Cf. the preface to Perry's English Literature in the Eighteenth Century.)

PAUL, H.   Grundriss der germanischen Philologie.   Strassburg: 1889.   I. Lief., III. Abschn., pp. 152–237 Methodenlehre.

> See § 2.

PELLISSIER, GEORGES.   Essais de littérature contemporaine.   Paris : 1893.

Contains an interesting discussion of Brunetière's doctrine of the evolution of literary types.

PERRY, T. S.   English Literature in the Eighteenth Century.   N. Y.: 1883.

In the preface to this work the author considers the views advanced by Mrs. Oliphant in the preface to her Literary History of England.   He dissents from her opinion that "every singer is a new miracle, . . . no growth developed out of preceding poets, but something sprung from an impulse which is not reducible to law," maintaining that law prevails in the progress of literature quite as much as in the growth of society.

The resemblance of the author's conception of literature to that of Posnett is pointed out by W. D. Howells in *Harper*, 73 : 318.

PNIOWER, O.   *Freie Bühne f. modernes Leben*, 1 : 289 Die neue Litteraturgeschichte.

The author draws a distinction between the old method of literary investigation and the new method. The old method made search for the spiritual content, the ethical purpose, the idea of the work. The new method, which owes its existence to recent activity in science and philology, proceeds to an analysis. Working in the spirit of the analytical chemist, it examines the literary compound to discover its constituent elements. As representatives of the new method, Pniower mentions Erich Schmidt, Scherer, and Goedecke.

POSNETT, H. M.   Comparative Literature.   N. Y. : 1886.

In spite of many obvious defects and limitations, this work is a remarkable production. It is the first serious attempt, in English, to apply to the history of literature the results of the researches of Herbert Spencer, Sir Henry Maine, and others who have written on the development of social organizations. Beginning with the lowest orders of expression, Posnett traces the evolution of literature to its present complex forms, the stages being : clan literature, literature of the city common-wealth, world literature, national literature. The advance is marked by the widening and deepening of the elements of personality.

Attempting to treat so large a subject within somewhat narrow limits, the work as a whole makes upon the reader an impression of haste and incompleteness. Many facts essential to the argument are perforce omitted. Sweeping inductions are drawn not infrequently from examples that are conspicuous by their fewness. The value of the work is further lessened by its blind, uncritical adherence to the tenets of the Spencerian philosophy and its consequent inclination to polemics. Moreover, the author's sympathies are so engrossed with the social conditions from which he conceives literature to have sprung that he turns somewhat grudgingly to literature itself.   Notwithstanding these drawbacks, the book may be heartily recommended to the student of literature.   If it does nothing more, it will at least upset some of his literary superstitions, and lead him to question seriously the validity of conventional ideas about literary periods and classifications.

The book is sympathetically reviewed by W. D. Howells in *Harper*, 73 : 318, and more rigorously handled in *Nation*, 43 : 143.

PUTNAM, GEO. H.   Authors and their Public in Ancient Times. N. Y. : 1894.

Traces the history of literature from the earliest recorded times to the invention of printing, with a view to determining the development of the idea of literary property.   A useful bibliography is given at the beginning of the book.

RENAN, Ernest.   Essais de morale et de critique.   2e éd. Paris : 1860.

> Pp. 375–456 La poésie des races celtiques.

RICARDOU, A.   La critique littéraire : étude philosophique.   Avec une préface de M. F. Brunetière.   Paris : 1896.

See pp. 32–94 for an outline of the principles of literary evolution.   Ricardou follows Taine, Brunetière, and Hennequin.

REVUE CELTIQUE.   18 vols.   Paris : 1897.   Ed. by D'Arbois de Jubainville.

This and *Die Keltische Zeitschrift*, ed. by Kuno Meyer and Chr. Sterne (Halle and London), should open the field of Irish literary origins to the student.

SALT, H. S.   *New Review*, 4 : 19 The Socialist Ideal : Literature.

See § 14.

SCHERER, WM.   Poetik.   Berlin : 1888.

Scherer finds a place here because of his part in the con-
troversy with Jacob Grimm over the communal origin of poetry.
Scherer holds that early poetry is individual in origin.   (Cf. his
Jacob Grimm, p. 146.   2. Aufl.   Berlin : 1885.)

SCHERR, JOH.   Allgemeine Geschichte der Literatur.   2 vols.
    Stuttgart : 1881–82.

See vol. I, pp. 1–14, for the plan on which this universal
history is composed.

SCHLEGEL, F. VON.   Lectures on the History of Literature.
    Bohn Libr.   Lond. : 1876.

Important as illustrating a conception of literary development
that in its time exercised great influence.

SCHMIDT, ERICH.   Charakteristiken.   Berlin : 1886.
    Pp. 480–498 Wege und Ziele der deutschen Litteraturgeschichte.

In this spirited and scholarly address the author passes in
review the German historians of literature, and expounds at some
length his views of the object and methods of literary research.
The opinions expressed have had considerable influence among
German scholars.

SPENCER, H.   First Principles.   Lond. : 1862.
    See pp. 162–167 on the evolution of literature.

As an example which " vividly illustrates the multiplicity and
heterogeneity of the products that in course of time may arise
by successive differentiations from a common stock," Spencer
sketches the evolution of literature, from the exclamations of
savages and the picture-writing of the Egyptians and Mexicans,
to " the placards inside the omnibus " and " the copy of the
Times lying upon the table."

STAËL, MME. DE.   De la littérature considérée dans ses rapports avec les institutions sociales. Paris : 1845.

    See § **14.**

STAPFER, PAUL.   Des réputations littéraires : essais de morale et d'histoire. 1e Sér. Paris : 1893.

    P. 361 L'avenir de la littérature.

An interesting discussion of the laws of literary evolution, with critical remarks on the system of Brunetière. Stapfer believes in what may be called persistence of literary energy. He holds that it is inaccurate to speak of decadence in literature. What seems decline is merely transformation into some other form.

STEINTHAL, H.   *Zeitschrift f. Völkerpsychologie*, 5 : 1 Das Epos.

Steinthal upholds the theory of a communal origin of literature as the outcome of common feeling and sentiment in the clan.

SYMONDS, J. A.   Essays Speculative and Suggestive. 2 vols. Lond. : 1890.

In his essay on the Application of Evolutionary Principles to Art and Literature, Symonds endeavors to formulate a law that will account for literary growth, culmination, and decay. The results, as might be expected from a writer whose 'science' exists principally in the form of feeling and imagination, are interesting, but vague. See comments in the *London Acad.*, August 30, 1890, p. 166 ; *London Athenaeum*, August 30, 1890, p. 279 ; *Nation*, 51 : 173.

TAINE, H.   History of English Literature. Trans. by H. Van Laun. Lond. : 1883.

Taine is the most prominent, if not the most important, figure in the history of literary methodology. His celebrated formula of the race, the environment, and the moment, the three constituting the conditions of literary development, is presented in vol. I, pp. 1–36, of this history.   The remark has often been made that the author in the body of the work neglects the principles which he enunciates in the preface.   For a careful, though unfriendly, criticism, see Robert Flint, Historical Philosophy in France (N. Y. : 1894), pp. 631–636.

TEN BRINK, B.   Ueber die Aufgabe der Litteraturgeschichte. Strassburg : 1891.

Of special interest as setting forth theoretically the methods of literary history successfully practiced by the author in his works on English literature.

TEXTE, JOS.   *Revue de philologie française et de littérature*, X, 4, p. 241 L'histoire comparée des littératures.

A sketchy but suggestive introduction to the bibliography of L. P. Betz, in the same number.

THOMPSON, ROBT.   Treatise on the Progress of Literature and its Effects on Society.   Edinb. : 1834.

Literature is characterized as the "mirror of society."   Its effects are removal of prejudice, increased security of social rights, education of the manufacturing classes, and the discouragement of war.

UHLAND, LUDW.   Schriften zur Geschichte der Dichtung und Sage.   Stuttgart : 1866.

WATTS, THEODORE.   Encycl. Brit., 9th ed.   ' Poetry.'

In a discussion of the epic and the lyric, pp. 265–272, Watts touches upon the relation between the growth of philosophical conceptions and the growth of literature.

WETZ, W.   *Kritischer Jahresbericht über die Fortschritte der romanischen Philologie*, I, Heft II, 1890, 1894 Litteraturwissenschaft.

WETZ, W.   Ueber Litteraturgeschichte.   Eine Kritik von ten
    Brink's Rede ' Ueber die Aufgabe der Litteraturgeschichte.'
    Worms: 1891.

>   See especially pp. 31–65.

WETZ, W.   Shakespeare vom Standpunkte d. vergleichenden
    Litteraturgeschichte.   Bd. I Die Menschen in Shakes-
    peares Dramen.   Worms: 1890.

>   Pp. 1–43 Einleitung : Ueber Begriff und Wesen der vergleichen-
>   den Litteraturgeschichte.

The author proclaims himself a follower of Taine, whose
theories he endeavors to develop.   He believes that a science
of literature is possible, which shall attain to the rank of an
exact science and ultimately rival the other exact sciences in
completeness of method and precision of results.

WOLFF, EUGEN.   Das Wesen wissenschaftlicher Litteratur-
    betrachtung.   Kiel und Leipz. : 1890.

WOLFF, EUGEN.   Prolegomena d. litt.-evolutionistischen Poetik.
    Kiel : 1890.

WOLFF, EUGEN.   *Hamb. Correspondent,* 1891, Nos. 913, 916
    Litteraturgeschichte rückwärts.

The author belongs to a school of German writers who are
making strenuous (and at times frantic) efforts to base the
history of literature upon natural laws, especially upon the law
of evolution.   According to Wolff, research should be carried
on along three principal lines : historical, psychological, and
aesthetic.   The method proposed seems to be a mixture of the
theories of Taine, Sainte-Beuve, and Wm. Scherer.

§ 18. GENERAL NOTE.

I. Collateral Aids. — Investigations in the philosophy of history (see Flint's Philosophy of History in France and Germany for references), in the doctrine of biological evolution (consult Darwin, Spencer, Haeckel, Wallace, Romanes), and in the principles of sociology (see De Greef's Introduction à la sociologie and Giddings's Principles of Sociology), are urged upon those who would make original contributions to this subject. On the comparative method in general, see the exhaustive treatise of Ernst Bernheim, Lehrbuch der historischen Methode, and Freeman's essay on the Unity of History, in Comparative Politics (N. Y. : 1874).

For the principles of social evolution necessary to the comparative study of literary origins and development, the reader may examine Spencer's Data of Ethics and Principles of Sociology, Leveleye's Primitive Property, and Sir Henry Maine's Village Communities, Early History of Institutions, and Ancient Law. The various theories of evolution referred to by Brunetière are explained by Huxley in the article ' Biology ' in the Encycl. Brit., 9th ed.

For assistance from the realm of anthropology, see Tylor's Primitive Culture, Anthropology, etc., and the references contained therein. On language, rhythm, religious origins, etc., see references in the next paragraph.

II. The Origins of Poetry. — The inquiry into the origin of the lyric and the epic — the methods and materials of the study — naturally falls under the special consideration of those subjects. Since, however, some introduction to the subject must be given here, it has seemed wise, in addition to the analysis and references of the preceding sections, to subjoin the following *résumé* of Prof. F. B. Gummere's article on Ballad and

Communal Poetry (Child Memorial. Boston : 1897), which is altogether the most lucid and practical presentation of the problem as it now stands. There is at present, according to Professor Gummere, a reaction against the doctrine of Jacob and Wilhelm Grimm to the effect that a song of the people is made by the people as a whole. Grundtvig and ten Brink still held with Grimm, but critics are now of A. W. Schlegel's mind : what we attribute to ages and peoples nearly always resolves itself, on closer inspection, into the characteristics and deeds of individuals ; the method of distribution of popular tales is by borrowing, the cause of their production is the love of amusement. Joseph Jacobs says that " artistry is individual," that Scotch ballads merely "lack the initials at the end," that verse and prose began together ; the *cante-fable* " is probably the protoplasm out of which both ballad and folk-tale have been differentiated," and Newell insists that "folk-tales are a degenerate form amid a low civilization of something which was composed amid a high civilization." J. F. Campbell concedes that " the older the narrator is, the less educated, and the farther removed from the rest of the world, the more his stories " have of the bardic composition in them ; he concedes " the stamp of originality and the traces of many minds, and the precedence of singing," but is evidently on the artist's side. Gummere, on the other hand, holds to the communal authorship, but not as understood by the Grimms. He does not believe in the " song that sings itself," " Steinthal's *dichtender Volksgeist* " ; but, rather, in " a process such as Lachmann implies when he speaks of *gemeinsames dichten.*" He adheres to " the belief in certain spontaneous movements of the human mind, particularly as regards rhythmical expression. But this rhythmical spontaneity furnishes the chief argument for the assumption of early communal song ; and it seems even to make difficulties for those who look upon poetry from the artistic point of view alone " (pp. 47–48). He states the questions at issue as follows : " Does a single artist always make poetry, of whatever sort, or may one allow a concert of individuals in the act of composition ? Is the folk-song brought to the folk, or is it made by the folk ? Is the chorus, the communal song, essentially one with the composed poem as we now know it, — an individual, deliberate, and artistic work ? Is there . . . not a dualism in generative poetics . . . of chorus and solo, of throng and poet, of community and artist ? " That the communal theory is opposed to the drift of modern thought is evident from the writings of modern scholars in widely different fields, — of Paul (Principles of the Hist. of Language), who says that " it never happens that several individuals create anything by working together with united forces and divided functions " ; of W. D. Whitney ; of Gerber (Die Sprache als Kunst), " Sprache nimmt ihren Ausgangspunkt von den Individuen," and so poetry ; of M. Tarde, "Language is originally an invention of the single mind, made lasting by imitation on the part of the throng. . . . In the beginning some anthropoid (some savage of genius in some *famille unique*) *imagined* (invented) the rudiments of a language," and this process is true also of trades and arts, poetry and religion. " Poetry begins always with a book, an epopee . . . the Iliad, the Bible, Dante, some high initial source." So also M. Kawczynski on the Origin and History of Rhythms : " Verse is an art always imitated, borrowed." Ballads are not even a primary imitation; they are a " secondary invention " on the part of " sacristans of the parish," etc. Whence the primary imitation is derived, says Professor Gummere, M. Kawczynski fails to inform us, save that we are never to look to the people. Kawczynski's pet aversion is the "false principle of spontaneity." Everything is borrowed; the Nibelungen Lay, alliteration, Germanic verse, all may be traced by levels more or less numerous to Latin and Greek sources. Neither rhythm nor dancing springs from instinct or natural impulse ; they were both discoveries, inventions.

Turning to a criticism of all this, Professor Gummere cites Renan (De l'Origine du Langage), himself a supporter of the theory of individual authorship, in favor of the principle of spontaneity (" Renan saw spontaneity writ large over the entire life of primitive man "), and proceeds to show that, on any other basis, a logical theory of poetry is impossible. Aristotle's antithesis between the artistic and communal in poetry is a recognition of the " dancing, singing, improvising multitude." Gerber, too, excludes improvisation from poetry, " for he defines poetry as 'deliberation,' added to 'enthusiasm.' " But his theory "breaks down utterly, because he does not recognize this dualism of the artist and the throng. Spontaneous composition in a dancing multitude — all singing, all dancing, and all able on occasion to improvise — is a fact of primitive poetry about which we may be as certain as such questions allow us to be certain. Behind individuals stands the human horde. . . . Aristotle saw such a horde or throng. An insistent echo of this throng [the refrain encroaching steadily upon the artist as we retrace the history of the ballad] greets us from the ballads." How, then, was verse " made in, or even by, this mass of 'enthusiastic' men?" This question leads to the consideration of the folk-soul as opposed to the single soul, and of the rhythmic and emotional expression of a throng. Gummere cites Wundt (Ueber Ziele u. Wege d. Völkerpsychologie) in support of the Gesammtgeist, —" die Volksseele " is " an sich ein ebenso berechtigter, ja nothwendiger Gegenstand psychologischer Untersuchung wie die individuelle Seele,"— and, showing that the earliest poetry had the collective and communal conditions and attributes which distinguished primitive institutions, adds communal poetry to Wundt's three products of the communal mind, — speech, myth, and custom. Communal poetry was distinguished " by a maximum of enthusiasm with a minimum of deliberation. . . . Universality of the poetic gift among inferior races, spontaneity or improvisation under communal conditions, the history of refrain and chorus, the early relation of narrative songs to the dance . . . " are facts so well authenticated that " it is no absurdity to insist upon the origin of poetry under communal and not under artistic conditions." Gummere regards the real difficulty as lying not here, " but with the assertion of *simultaneous composition.* Yet this difficulty is more apparent than real " when one considers *not* an artistic ballad, but a primitive choral dance ; and of the choral dance there is here the question. For " the sentence was the unit of speech, just as the verse was and is the unit of poetry," and " repetition was the chief element in primitive verse. To repeat a sentence was poetry. . . . Add to these the lack of individuality, the homogeneous mental state, . . . the leap or step of the dance, etc., . . ." and " the communal making of verse is no greater mystery than many another undoubted feat of primitive man. . . . Add the great fact of reproduction (ten Brink), as vital in ancient poetry as original production is vital in our own, and the case is yet stronger." According to Donovan (Festal Origin of Human Speech), " the earliest expressions of communal interest were in the play-excitement found in all grades of development, from that of the lowest Australian or American aborigines, up to the choral dance out of which the first glorifying songs of the race and its heroes are found growing." Hence, rhythmic motions, excited cries, out of which come music and speech. " Here, then, was the birth of poetry." With reflection comes individuality, the separation of the singer from the crowd, the addition of thought to emotion. " The sense of individuality . . . and the prevailing intellectual bias in emotion are the chief marks of poetry of to-day."

The authors of this volume look with eager anticipation for the result of Professor Gummere's present investigations into the origins of poetry, and would unhesitatingly commend to the attention of students whatever he may publish upon the subject.

The following references on ballad and communal poetry are from his article in the Child Memorial (pp. 41–56) : A. W. Schlegel, *Heidelb. Jahrbücher*, 1815 (repr. in Schlegel's Werke, vol. XII, p. 383 *et seq.;* against the communal origin, answered by W. Grimm, *Altdeutsche Blätter*, 3 : 370 *et seq.;* see works of Jacob and Wilhelm Grimm in general) ; Joseph Jacobs, *Folk-lore*, 4 : 2, 233 *et seq.*, June, 1893 (no such thing as the folk behind so-called folk song) ; Proceedings of International Folk Lore Congress, under Newell and Jacobs, 1891 ; Joseph Jacobs, English Fairy Tales ; J. F. Campbell, Popular Tales of the West Highlands (new ed. The ballad is "a bit of popular history, or a popular tale or romance, turned into verse which will fit some popular air ") ; F. B. Gummere, Introd. to Old English Ballads (Boston : 1894) ; H. Steinthal, *Zeitschrift f. Völkerpsychologie*, 11 : 30 Zur Volksdichtung (*dichtender Volksgeist*) ; Friedländer, Homerische Kritik von Wolf in Grote (Berlin : 1853. P. viii Lachmann's letter to Lehrs ; speaks of *gemeinsames dichten*) ; Eugen Wolff, Vorstudien zur Poetik (in *Zeitschrift f. vgl. Lit.* 6 : 423 *et seq.*, 1893) ; Hermann Paul, The Principles of the Hist. of Language, Strong's trans. (2d ed. pp. xxiv, xxvi, xliii, and the chapter on Original Creation) ; Paul, Grundr. d. germ. Philol. 1 : 73, 231 ("against the notion of gregarious composition ") ; G. Gerber, Die Sprache als Kunst, 2. Aufl. 1 : 246 ff. (1 : 30 ; 1 : 124 ; 1 : 131 ; 1 : 309 — passages used by Gummere) ; G. Tarde, Les lois de l'imitation (Paris : 1890) ; Renan, De l'origine du langage ; Kawczynski, Essai comparatif sur l'origine et l'histoire des rhythmes (Paris : 1889) ; see rev. in *Am. Journ. Philol.*, vol. XLI ; Herbert Spencer, *Pop. Sci. Mo.* 47 : 433 Orator and Poet, Actor and Dramatist ; Ernst Meumann, in Wundt's *Psychologische Studien*, 10 : 249 *et seq.*, 1894 (an attempt to reorganize the science of rhythms on the basis of psycho-physics) ; Bastian, Masken und Maskereien, in *Zeitschrift f. Völkerpsychologie*, 14 : 347 ; Aristotle, Poetics, on Imitation and Tragedy ; Bielschowsky, Geschichte der deutschen Dorfpoesie im 13ᵗᵉⁿ Jhdt.; Schopenhauer, Welt als Wille u. Vorstellung, 1 : § 51 On Poetry; G. Le Bon, L'évolution des peuples (Paris : 1894. Defense of "the historic race "), and his Psychologie des Foules ; Wundt, *Philos. Studien,* 4 : 1 (1888) Ueber Ziele u. Wege d. Völkerpsychologie (in favor of the Gesammtgeist) ; Reclus, Primitive Folk (" at the outset, collectivism was at its maximum, and individualism at its minimum ") ; R. M. Meyer, *Zeitschrift f. vgl. Lit.* 1 : 34 *et seq.* on the Refrain ; Donovan, in *Mind,* 16 : 498–506 The Festal Origin of Human Speech ; ten Brink's Beowulf (Quellen und Forschungen, 62), p. 105 on the tendency to reproduction in ancient poetry ("On the decrease of individual divergences as one retraces history ") ; Dr. Krejci, Das characteristische Merkmal der Volkspoesie, *Zeitschrift f. Völkerpsychologie,* 19 : 115 *et seq.* (1889); Krohn, La Chanson Populaire en Finlande (in Proceedings International Folk Lore Congress, 1891, p. 143 *et seq.*).

Gummere gives also the following references : Andrew Lang, International Folk Lore Congress, 1891, president's address ; H. Spencer, Sociology (3d ed.), 1 : 702 ; 2 : 289, 311 ; Giddings, Principles of Sociology, p. 262 ; H. Spencer, Origin and Function of Music (in Illustrations of Universal Progress. N. Y. : 1867), p. 223 *et seq.*

Most of the following references have also been kindly furnished by Professor Gummere.

Origins. — Karl Bücher, Arbeit u. Rhythmus, XVII. Bd., No. 5. Abh. d. königl. sächs. Gesellsch. d. Wissensch. (Leipz. : 1896. Interesting collection of labor songs to illustrate his theory that song was instituted to lighten labor ; reviewed briefly by R. M. Meyer in Haupt's *Anzeiger,* 1897, also in the *Deutsche Literaturzeitung,* August 7, 1897 ; the book is stimulating ; considered by some to be epoch-making); Karl Groos, Die Spiele der Thiere (Jena : 1896. See p. 340 for a scheme of the arts) ; Dümmler, in Haupt's *Zeitschrift f. deutsch. Altert.* 17 : 523 On the Refrain ; Fr. Nietzsche, Die fröhliche Wissenschaft (Leipz.: 1887. Interesting theory of the origin of poetry); R. Fritzsche, Die Anfänge der Poesie (Progr. Chemnitz: 1886); F. M. Pagano, Discorso sulla origine e natura della poesia (Milano: 1801); J. Darmsteter, Les origines de la poésie persane (Paris: 1888); David Heinrich Müller, Die Propheten in ihrer ursprünglichen Form (Wien: 1896. Draws an analogy between the Greek chorus and the rhapsodies of the Hebrew prophets; attempts thus to determine the sources of Semitic poetry, and concludes that the prophets were successors to a chorus). On the method of poetic composition, *improvisation*, see Raube, Zur Geschichte d. italien. Poesie. Berlin: 1837.

In the 'thirties' and 'forties' of this century a number of writers devoted themselves to the musico-medical explanation of poetic origins and effects: for instance, B. P. J. Schneider, Die Musik u. Poesie nach ihren Wirkungen historisch-kritisch dargestellt (Bonn: 1835); J. Keble, De poeticae vi medica (2 vols. Oxford: 1844. Praelectiones acad. Oxon. habitae). E. Hanslick, Vom Musikalisch-Schönen, 7th ed., p. 119, tells about this school.

Song and Dance. — Hartt, Geology of Brazil (about p. 600, dances of Botocudos) (Boston: 1870); Karl Groos, Die Spiele der Thiere (Jena: 1896). Groos mentions W. H. Hudson, The Naturalists in La Plata (incipient dance of animals), and Ratzel, History of Mankind (trans. by Butler, Lond.: 1896. Anthropological basis of theory). For latest theories, see, of course, Tylor's Primitive Culture, and Anthropology, and references given by him to standard works and sources.

Folk Song. — Talvj (Fräulein T. A. L. von Jacob, afterwards Frau Robinson), Characteristik d. Volkslieder germanischer Nationen (Leipz.: 1840; a description, with translations and extracts, of folk songs of various nations; discussion of popular poetry; one of the first to discard the idea that lyric is subsequent to

epic; F. B. Gummere, Old English Ballads (Boston : 1894.
Introduction for summary of theories and bibliography of the
ballad.   Rev. in Beibl. to *Anglia*, May, 1896, by Max Förster.
See § **17**); Brugsch, Adonisklage u. Linoslied (see Mannhardt,
Mythologische Quellen und Forschungen, 1884) ; J. Bedier,
Les Fabliaux (Paris : 1893. Publ. par Bibl. de l'école des
hautes études.   Most energetically combats the generally
accepted theory that all the Fabliaux come from the east) ;
Mary Hewitt, Literature and Romance of Northern Europe
(translations of ballads) ; Johnson's Scott's Musical Museum,
ed. by David Laing (Edinb. : 1853. A mine of material) ;
Folk-lore Quarterly Rev. No. 1, 1890 Magic Songs of Finns ;
Rev. de l'hist. de religion (1882), La magie chez les Finnois.
Valuable references to this whole subject of folk song and
magic among the Finns will be found in Comparetti's Kalevala
(1892), p. 22, note; Rosenberg, Nordboernes Aandsliv (valuable on Danish folk song) ; Fétis, Histoire générale de la
musique (collection of ballads in vol. IV) ; L. Hearn, *Atlantic*,
September, 1896 Japanese folk songs ; Gaston Paris, Des
origines de la poésie lyrique en France au moyen âge (Paris :
1892) ; L. Jacobowski, Die Physik der Lyrik, ein Beitrag zu
einer realistischen Poetik (this is an introduction to Die Anfänge
der Poesie).

For other references, see § **17** above, and the bibliographies
of general histories of literature in the next paragraph, and in
§ **21** *A* 5.   On rhythm and metre in this relation see §§ **22-24.**

III. General Histories of Literature. — Among the histories
of literature, besides those already mentioned, in which a
systematic effort is made to show the dependence of literature
on political and social movements, may be mentioned the
following : John G. Eichorn, Geschichte der Litteratur, von
ihrem Anfang bis auf die neuesten Zeiten (6 vols. Göttingen :
1805–12.   2d ed. 1828) ; G. G. Gervinus, Handbuch der

Geschichte der poetischen Nationalliteratur (4th ed. Leipz. :
1849), and Geschichte der deutschen Dichtung (5th ed.
Leipz. : 1871–74) ; K. Goedecke, Grundriss zur Geschichte
der deutschen Dichtung (4 vols. Dresden : 1859–81) ; J. G. T.
Grässe, Lehrbuch einer allgemeinen Litteraturgeschichte
aller bekannten Völker der Welt, von der ältesten bis auf die
neueste Zeit (4 vols. Leipz. : 1837–59) ; Jul. Hart, Geschichte
der Weltlitteratur (2 vols. Berlin : 1893–96) ; K. A. Koberstein,
Grundriss der Geschichte der deutschen Nationallitteratur
(Leipz. : 1827), and Entwickelung der deutschen Poesie
(Braunschweig : 1865) ; Wachler, Handbuch der Geschichte der
Litteratur (3d ed. 4 vols. Leipz. : 1833) ; S. Gätschenberger,
Geschichte der englischen Literatur, mit besonderer Berücksichtigung der politischen und Sittengeschichte Englands (3 vols.
Prag u. Wien : 1859–62) ; F. C. Schlosser, Weltgeschichte für
das deutsche Volk (2d ed. 19 vols. in 10. Oberhausen u. Leipz. :
1876 ; vols. I–II contain a history of the literature and culture
of the eighteenth century). See also § **21**, *A* 5, *infra.*

IV. Studies in Literary Influence.

—The following mono-
graphs may be examined as illustrations of studies in literary
influence, whether the influence of one masterpiece upon another
or of one national literature upon another national literature :
J. Darmsteter, Point de contact entre le Mahâbhârata et le Shâh-
Nâmeh (Paris : 1887); J. A. Démogeot, Histoire des littératures
étrangères (see § **17**) ; E. Kölbing, Beiträge zur vergleichenden
Geschichte der romantischen Poesie und Prosa des Mittelalters
unter besonderer Berücksichtigung der englischen und nordi-
schen Litteratur (Breslau : 1876) ; Th. Süpflé, Geschichte d.
deutschen Kultureinflusses auf Frankreich mit besond. Berücksichtigung d. litterarischen Einwirkung (Bd. II, Abth. I Von
Lessing bis zum Ende der romant. Schule der Franzosen. Gotha :
1888); Italo Pizzi, Le somiglianze et le relazioni tra la poesia
persiana e la nostra del medioevo (R. Accad. delle Scienze.

Torino : 1892); G. Zanella, Relazioni poetiche tra l'Italia e la
Spagna nel secolo XVI (in Nuova Antologia. 2d ser. 39 : 5–20);
Arthur H. Hallam, Remains in Prose and Verse (Boston : 1863) ;
J. C. Dunlop, History of Fiction (2 vols. Lond. : 1888) ;
F. H. O. Weddigen, Lord Byron's Einfluss auf die europäischen
Litteraturen der Neuzeit (Hannover : 1884) ; F. H. O. Weddigen,
Geschichte der Einwirkungen der deutschen Litteratur auf die
Litteraturen der übrigen europäischen Kulturvölker der Neuzeit
(Leipz. : 1882) ; Philareté Chasles, Orient : voyage d'un critique
à travers la vie et les livres (2e éd. Paris : 1865), pp. 405–416
Des rapports du drame grec et du drame hindou; V. Rossel,
Histoire des relations littéraires entre la France et l'Allemagne
(Paris : 1897) ; Jos. Texte, *Revue de Cours*, 15 Mars, 1896 Les
relations littéraires de la France avec l'Allemagne avant le
milieu du xviiie siècle ; Chas. Jaret, La littérature allemande
au xviiie siècle dans ses rapports avec la littérature française
et avec la littérature anglaise (Aix : 1876); E. Egger, L'Hellenisme en France : Leçons sur l'influence des études grecques
dans le developpement de la langue et de la littérature française
(2 vols.   Paris : 1869) ; Ed. Zarncke, Der Einfluss der griechischen Literatur auf die Entwickelung der römischen Prosa
(Leipz. : 1888) ; Albert Lacroix, Histoire de l'influence de
Shakespeare sur le théâtre français jusq'à nos jours ; Jas. B.
Angell, *No. Am. Rev.* 84 : 311 Influence of English Literature
on the German, 86 : 412 Influence of English Literature on the
French ; J. Burroughs, *Critic*, 24 : 177 Greek Influence in Literature (see also a reply by M. Thompson in *Critic*, 24 : 212); Ferd.
Loise, De l'influence de la civilization sur la poésie : le monde
oriental et le monde classical (Bruxelles : 1858), L'Italie et la
France (Bruxelles : 1862) ; Ferd. Loise, Histoire de la poésie
en rapport avec la civilization : La poésie espagnole (Bruxelles :
1868), dans l'antiquité et chez les peuples modernes de race
latine (Bruxelles : 1886), en France depuis les origines jusq'à
la fin du xviiie siècle (Tome II, Bruxelles : 1887).

Worthy of separate mention is C. H. Herford's Literary
Relations of England and Germany in the Sixteenth Century,
Cambridge: 1886.

V. Miscellaneous References. — Brother Azarias, Philosophy of Literature (6th ed. N. Y.: 1890. See § **14**);
A. Biese, *Nationalzeitung*, 1891, Nos. 587, 589 Ueber die Aufgabe der Litteraturgeschichte; A. Graf, Riv. di Fil., Genn.–
Apr. 1877 Considerazione intorno alla storia letteraria, a' suoi
metodi e alle sue appartenenze ; A. Graf, Di un trattazione
scientifica della storia letteraria (Torino : 1877) ; Jos. Kohler,
Zeitschrift f. vergl. Litt. 1 : 117 Aesthetik, Philologie, und vergleichende Litteraturgeschichte ; C. Schlottmann, De reipublicae
literariae originibus (Bonn : 1861) ; Gottlieb Stall, Introductio
in historiam litterariam (Lat. vertit C. H. Langius, Jena : 1728.
See remarks on literary history at the beginning) ; Greenough
White, The Philosophy of American Literature (Boston : 1891);
Lord Lytton, Quarterly Essays (Lond.: 1875), p. 336 Love in
its Influence upon Literature ; C. F. Girard, La Centralization
des Lettres en France (Lausanne : 1866) ; G. Lombroso, Il
commercio e la letteratura (Milano: 1842) ; R. S. Storrs, Jr.,
Relations of Commerce to Literature (Monson Academy Discourses, 1855); Julius Salony, Du progrés de l'idée chrétienne
dans la littérature (Paris : 1861) ; R. Treitschke, Die romanischen Sprachen und ihre Literaturmission : zur Völkerpsychologie (in wissensch. Beilage der Leipz. Zeitg. 1878, Nos. 53,
54); Puymaigre, La société et la littérature (Paris : 1881);
W. Roscoe, On the Origin and Vicissitudes of Literature, Science,
and Art, and their Influence on the Present State of Society
(Liverpool : 1817. Address at opening of the Liverpool Royal
Institute) ; F. Linguiti, Sul nuovo indirizzo degli studi letterari
storici e critici, riguardato nelle cause e nei suoi effetti (Salerno :
1877) ; E. Elster, Die Aufgaben der Litteraturgeschichte (Halle
a. S. : 1894) ; Otto, Ueber die Bestrebung um Begründung

einer Universallitteratur (Braunsberg : 1852) ; J. Nehry, Aus
der Weltlitteratur (Aschersleben : 1890) ; G. Perfranceschi, La
letteratura, la civiltà e la scienza (3ª ed.   Jesi : 1887) ; A.
Schröer, *Deutsches Wochenblatt*, 1891 : 118 Ueber die Aufgabe der Litteraturgeschichte ; F. Lammermayer, *Dioskuren*,
19 : 181 Gedanken über Litteraturgeschichte ; J. J. Ampère,
Mélanges d'histoire littéraire et de littérature (2 vols.   Paris:
1867), vol I De l'histoire de la poésie.

CHAPTER IV.

THE THEORY OF POETRY.

§ 19. STATEMENT OF THE PROBLEM; METHOD OF STUDY.

THE student should determine first the relation of poetics to rhetoric, and of these to what the Germans call 'stylistic.' See above, § 15 *V,* and Elze, Grundr. d. Engl. Philol., pp. 343–360; Boeckh, Encycl. d. philol. Wissensch., pp. 810–812; Wackernagel, Poetik, Rhetorik, u. Stylistik, p. 409 *et seq.;* Adolf Calmberg, Die Kunst d. Rede (2. Aufl. Leipz. u. Zürich: 1885); and the best English authorities, Bain, Minto, Whately, Spalding. The question as to whether metric should be classed under poetics cannot satisfactorily be decided before the laws of poetic form (*I, C* 2, below) have been studied; but an introductory view of the relative positions of metric and poetics may be obtained from the references above, and from Elze, Grundr., pp. 360–363; Gummere, Poetics; Stedman, Nature and Elements of Poetry, pp. 8–27, 60–62; Lanier, Science of Verse; Wordsworth, Prefaces to the Lyrical Ballads, and Appendix; Coleridge, Poe, and others, as given in §§ **20, 23,** below. On the relation of poetics to aesthetics, and therefore of poetry to art in general, Kedney's Hegel's Aesthetics, pp. 263–273; von Hartmann's Aesthetik, pp. 524–580; Boeckh's Encykl., pp. 464–473, 536–553, and references in §§ **8** and **20** may be consulted.

The critical study of poetry as determined by fundamental principles of art may be conducted as follows:

I. **Elementary Conceptions.** — Passing the principal theories
of poetry in review, the student will observe (*A*) that many
definitions mistake the poetic faculty for the art; (*B*) that
some definitions, limiting themselves to its nature, and others
to its aim, fail to distinguish poetry from art in general; (*C*)
that no definition is adequate which does not characterize
(1) the subject of treatment ; (2) the form of expression; and
(3) the process of execution.

A. In the attempt to discriminate between the *poetic faculty*
and *the poetic creation or product*, premises not based upon
psychological principles will be found to be of little worth.   The
psychologies of Dewey, Sully, Baldwin, Murray, and James will
furnish a working conception of the position of poetry among
other modes of expression, and of the nature of the artistic faculty
in general.   It will then be clear that all such expositions of
poetry as the following, — "The universal art of the mind, free in
its own nature, and not tied to expression in sensuous matter "
(Hegel),— have reference to the general artistic imagination, and
not to the special poetic gift, or the poetic product.   They have,
therefore, only an indirect bearing upon the definition of poetry.

B. While distinguishing between the *nature* and the *purpose*
of poetry, the student will notice that some definitions treat of
the one to the exclusion of the other, and are, for that reason,
inadequate.

    1. On the one hand, it is evident that abstract definitions of
the nature of poetry, such as Shelley's "something divine," the
"centre and circumference of knowledge," "the record of the
best and happiest moments of the happiest and best minds,"
fail to show the difference between poetry and the other arts.
This criticism applies to Wordsworth's, " Poetry is the breath,
the finer spirit of all knowledge . . . the impassioned expression . . . in the countenance of all science"; to Bailey's, "It
is itself a thing of God " (Festus) ; and to a host of similar
sympathetic but vague evaluations.

2. An examination, on the other hand, into the aim or function of poetry involves the vexed question of all arts: Is its purpose aesthetic or ethical, or both? Materials for the answer to this question are furnished above, §§ 7-9 and 13-15. If it be determined that the purpose is purely aesthetic, an array of specific questions confronts the student. What, for instance, is the *history* of the aesthetic exposition of poetry? (See Bosanquet, Schasler, or Knight, and other references in §§ 9 and 15, for the development of aesthetic interest before Kant.) The statement is made that Hegel is the most pronounced exponent of the purely aesthetic theory of poetry. But Burke and Kaimes in the purgation theory of tragedy, Kant with his demarcation of aesthetic consciousness in the Kritik der Urtheilskraft (1790), Schiller with his doctrine of aesthetic culture and his development of the Kantian theory in the doctrines of aesthetic semblance and the play-impulse, Goethe with his belief in the characteristic as the excellent in art, and Schelling with his treatment of the ideal nature of poetry, had prepared the way for Hegel's definition of the aesthetic purpose of poetry as of all art; and it will be observed that Wordsworth ("the end of Poetry is to produce excitement in coexistence with an overbalance of pleasure," Preface to Lyrical Ballads, 1800), Coleridge in his antithesis between poetry and science, Sir Henry Taylor, Dallas, and Pater, follow in the steps of these masters.

In the next place, the value of current conceptions of the aesthetic function of poetry may be considered. *First*, of the more popular, those, for instance, presented by Poe in his Poetic Principle; by Theodore Watts in his article in the Encycl. Brit.; by Shelley in his Defense of Poetry; by Leigh Hunt; by Principal Shairp (the aim of poetry is to express the glow of emotion, the thrill of joy); by Goldsmith (poetry is "so contrived and executed as to soothe the ear, surprise and delight the fancy, mend and melt the heart, elevate the mind,

and please the understanding "); by Ruskin (it is "the present-
ment in musical form, to the imagination, of noble grounds for
the noble emotions "); by F. W. Newman (it moves "the affections through the imagination "); and by others whose works
are cited in the following section. It will be noted that most of
these definitions are as appropriate to the genus art as to the
species poetry. *Second*, the value of the more scientific explanations may be considered : for instance, the aesthetic effect of
poetry as defined by Dallas ; the theories advanced by Herbert
Spencer in his Philosophy of Style ; by Butcher (Aristotle's
Art of Poetry), Gurney (Power of Sound and Tertium Quid),
Humboldt (Poetic Description of Nature), Grant Allen (Physiological Aesthetics), and the luminous exposition by J. S. Mill
in his Dissertation on Poetry and its Varieties.

As with the aesthetic, so with the frequently asserted ethical
function of poetry, a systematic inquiry can be prosecuted only
when a clear understanding has been reached concerning the
ideas and materials with which poetry deals, the manner of its
procedure, and the form inherent in it. Careful consideration
may show that the supposed ethical function is not a function,
but an after-effect contingent upon the training and temper of
the reader. Ruskin would appear to lean to the didactic rather
than to the aesthetic side of the question, and with varying
fitness the same may be said of Plato, Horace (Ars Poetica),
Lessing (in his theory of the tragic catharsis), Carlyle (Essay
on Goethe), Emerson (Poetry and Imagination), Matthew
Arnold, and many others cited in § **20.**

C. No definition is adequate which does not characterize
(1) the subject of treatment ; (2) the form of expression ; and
(3) the process of execution.

1. The *subject of treatment* consists, first, of a *theme* or *idea*
(the glorification of a god, a hero, a country, a mistress ; the
discharge of emotion, the portrayal of life or character, the
description of nature, the utterance of the meaning of things),

and secondly, of *materials* (actual or imaginative). For theories
of the idea or theme appropriate to and inspiring poetic expression, see Hegel, Carriere, Schiller, Goethe, Coleridge, J. S.
Mill, Watts, and Everett; on the materials, see Paul, Grundr. d.
german. Phil., vol. I, p. 141. Since, however, certain themes and
materials respectively seem to be adapted to poetic treatment
in one period rather than in another, — since, for instance,
the phenomena of natural life, the element of the mysterious,
romantic incidents, and machinery seem to possess no poetic
capability in one age, but are poetically productive in the ages
immediately preceding and succeeding, it would appear that the
'poetical' resides not in the theme and material which constitute the subject of treatment, but rather in the poet's *conception*
of that subject. (See Courthope's Liberal Movement, and the
Bowles and Byron controversy concerning Pope.) If it be
conceded that this is so, the characterization of the *subject of
poetry* implies a theory of *poetic conception,* and must depend for
its success upon a consideration of the third topic of this analysis, — the *process of poetic execution.* But if this be not conceded, the question is very much, perhaps too much, simplified ;
and it will be found that, so far as the theory of poetry turns
upon the definition of the subject-matter (without consideration
of modification by the poetic process), it does not admit of any
great difference of opinion. Hegel, Lessing, Jean Paul, and
Carriere, for whom poetry "speaks out the inner thought that
lies in things," may be classed not only with Sir Philip Sidney,
for whom poetry is a "learning so universal that no learned
nation doth despise it nor no barbarous nation is without it,"
but with Schopenhauer, who makes it the highest objectification
of the idea of man ; and Schopenhauer will agree with Schiller,
for whom poetry expresses "humanity as completely as possible."
Advancing, then, to recent critics, — though Gurney, Austin,
and Arnold may quarrel about the poetic process, do they not
still agree with reference to its subject-matter ? And does not

this subject-matter — life and thought — include that "spontaneous overflow of the feelings," that "imaginative passion,"
which in the opinion of Wordsworth, Hazlitt, Leigh Hunt,
J. S. Mill, Keble, and Principal Shairp, are the prime stuff of
poetry? In fine, if we eliminate all reference to the poetic
process, is it absurd to conceive of materialists, associationists,
and idealists adopting a common definition?

It must be remembered that theories of this kind, treating of
the content of poetry, presuppose the aesthetic form appropriate
to the content, even when they do not explicitly mention it.
Emerson, when he calls poetry "the only verity, the expression
of a sound mind speaking after the ideal, not after the apparent,"
Hegel, when he says broadly that it is the art of the mind
"expatiating in the inner space and in the inner time of the
ideas and feelings," Carlyle, when he weighs it as "musical
thought," Rowland Hazard, when he uses the term as "synonymous with the language of ideality," — none of these forget that,
while it conveys the ideal, poetry is uttering the beautiful, for
in their view the ideal and the beautiful are complements one
of the other. Careful discrimination must, therefore, be made
between these theories and those which, attempting to sever
form from content, make an abstraction of the form and emphasize
its beauty. Such expositions would define poetry as mere form,
"any composition in verse" (Whately), or as any language
capable of producing an *illusion* on the imagination : "the art of
doing by words what the painter does by means of colors"
(Macaulay). Are the latter definitions at all? May we thus
ignore the claims of thought to individuality of expression?
Can different artistic, or even poetic, forms convey the same
aesthetic idea? Does form alone constitute poetry? Do all
arts produce an illusion upon the imagination? or does all
poetry?

2. *The Form of Expression.* — Though definitions which
confine themselves to the form of poetry are one-sided, no

definition can be complete that does not cover the technique of the art (rhythm ; verse ; diction ; type — lyric, epic, dramatic ; species — tragedy, comedy, sonnet, hymn). The scientific study of poetic form involves, first, an examination of the treatises which discuss it from the physical and physiological side, — for example, Grant Allen's Physiological Aesthetics, Spencer's First Principles, Fiske's Cosmic Philosophy, Alexander von Humboldt's Cosmos (Poetic Description of Nature), Gurney's Power of Sound ; second, of more technical works on versification, such as those by Lanier, Schipper, Mayor, Guest, Paul, Sievers, etc., mentioned and discussed in §§ **22-24** below ; third, of the history of language especially as an instrument of poetry ; fourth, of the history and technique of the various literary types.

3. *The Process of Execution.* — The consideration of the manner is as important as that of the subject or of the form. It is the question of the *how*.   How are theme and material, on the one hand, literary type or species, language, rhythm, and metre, on the other, so combined and modified as to produce a result which is not the sum, but the fusion of the two ? What is the nature of the faculties exercised by the poet, the nature of the faculties to which he appeals, the nature of the appeal itself ?   For the investigation of the nature, stages, and operation of imagination, its relation to the processes of knowledge, to other operations of the intellect and other modes of mental activity, see Dewey's Psychology, chap. VII ; Cohen's Dichterische Phantasie ; Sully's Psychology, chap. VIII ; Maudsley's Physiology of Mind, pp. 522–533 ; Lewes's Problems of Life and Mind, 3d series, pt. II, pp. 445–463 ; Frohschammer's Die Phantasie, pp. 73–141 ; Everett's Poetry, Comedy, and Duty, p. 92 ; Shelley's Defense ; Masson ; Courthope, p. 30 ; Austin's Introduction to the Human Tragedy ; Coleridge (on Fancy and Imagination); Ruskin ; J. H. Newman ; Hazlitt, etc., as in § **20** below.   Note especially the psychological distinction

between fancy and creative imagination. For studies of the
quality and function of the aesthetic feelings, the value and
meaning of illusion, and the nature of that "indirectness"
which Keble, Mill, Gurney, and others consider a prime quality
of poetic expression, see Lemcke's Populäre Aesthetik ; Kant's
Critique of Judgment (transl. by Bernard); Grant Allen's Phys.
Aesth. ; Sully's Sensation and Intuition, pp. 186–245 ; Bain's
Emotions and Will, pp. 247–270 ; Siebeck's Wesen d. aesthetischen Anschauung ; and other works referred to in §§ 8 and 9
above.

No more lucid essays on the general bearings of the questions
involved in this analysis of poetry can be found than Theodore
Watts's Poetry (Encycl. Brit., 9th ed.), and E. C. Stedman's
Nature and Elements of Poetry.

As was stated under the paragraph on the subject of treatment, many critical controversies have turned on the question
of the poetic conception, that is, the question whether the poetical lies in the subject itself or in the process by which the
subject is worked up. The most famous is the controversy
between the so-called Aristotelians and the so-called Baconians.
According to the former, poetry is imitative ; according to the
latter, creative. For an introduction to the subject, the student
is referred to the study of Plato and Aristotle (on Imitation)
in § 9, *II,* 8, above ; especially, also, to Butcher's Aristotle's
Theory of Poetry and Fine Art. It being determined what
Aristotle means by "poetry is imitation," Poetics, 1 : 2, the interpretations suggested by his followers should be passed in
review ; for instance, Longinus, Horace, Dryden, Boileau,
Dr. Johnson (" Poetry is a mirror of manners and of life "),
Wordsworth (poetry is "the image of man and nature. . . .
The spontaneous overflow of powerful feelings : it takes its origin
from emotion *remembered* in tranquillity ") ; Landor, Hazlitt,
Colvin (poetry "represents everything for which verbal signs
have been invented "). On the other hand, turning to Bacon,

who appears to adopt unequivocally Plato's teaching that
poetry is the product of inspiration, the student must determine (1) whether the creative character of poetry as emphasized by him and his followers may not be gathered from the
teachings of Aristotle as well, and (2) whether poetry according
to the theory of Plato and Bacon does or can free itself of the
element of imitation as emphasized by Aristotle. " Poetry,"
says Bacon, "is (in respect of matter) nothing else but *feigned
history.*" That is to say, it is creative ; but is not "feigned
history" at the same time an imaginative *imitation ?* And
when Bacon says, " Poesy feigneth acts and events greater
and more heroical (than doth history), . . . it doth raise
and erect the mind by submitting the shows of things to the
desires of the mind," does he uphold the creative character of
poetry any more decidedly than Aristotle, who says, " Poetry is
superior to, and more philosophic than history," and " It is
not a poet's business to relate what occurred, but what might
occur " ?   Among writers who espouse the creative as opposed
to the imitative theory are Plotinus, Emerson, Carlyle, Browning,
Goethe (" Art is art because it is not nature "), Shelley, Leigh
Hunt, Dallas, and Masson. Sir Philip Sidney's Defense of
Poesy combines in one flawless masterpiece the ideality of
Plato's theory and the necessity of Aristotle's.

In connection with this question, the controversy between
Bowles and Byron concerning the merits of Pope deserves
attention. The points upon which it turned were, first, the
relative value of images drawn from nature and images drawn
from art ; and second, the relative value of subject and execution. (See the famous papers in the *Pamphleteer*, 17 : 73 ;
18 : 331, 571 ; and Courthope, p. 6.)

Of great importance to English poetry was the classic-roman-
tic dispute originating with Wordsworth's Preface to the Lyrical
Ballads. It can be followed through Jeffrey's articles in the
Edinburgh Review, and the contributions to *Blackwood's*, the

Quarterly, Fraser's, etc., as cited under Wordsworth, § **20** below. See also Bagehot's Edinburgh Reviewers and Caine's Cobwebs of Criticism. In these controversies the question at issue depended for its solution upon a definition of the imaginative process. The distinctions drawn by Wordsworth and Coleridge between imagination and fancy, and poetry and science, pointed the way to a more profitable discussion of the subject.

In recent times we come to the triangular contest between Arnold, Austin, and Swinburne, which originated with Arnold's dictum, " Poetry is at bottom a criticism of life," and centered about the respective poetic merits of Wordsworth, Byron, and Shelley. (For references, see under Austin and Swinburne, § **20.**) This discussion has resulted in the formulation of various canons of judgment as a basis of criticism ; for instance, Austin says that poetry must *transfigure* life ; Bain, that it must *assimilate* it ; Shairp, that it must *penetrate ;* Masson, that it must *produce a new and artificial concrete ;* Swinburne, that it must do nothing that can be formulated, it must simply *elude ;* and with him Gurney may be said to concur. On the course of poetics in England, see § **21,** 2. For the history of these and similar critical movements in Germany and France, see § **21,** *B* 3, 4.

For the psychology of imitation and invention, and the relation between the two, see Baldwin's Social and Ethical Interpretations of Mental Development, and Professor Royce's article on the Psychology of Invention, in *Psychological Review,* 5 : 113.

II. Scheme of Investigation. — As a foundation for constructive work the following scheme is submitted :

A. **The Historical Side of the Subject.** — 1. *The Evolution of Poetry.* (See §§ **16–18,** and **21,** *A,* for suggestions.) 2. *History of Theories of Poetry.* (See § **21,** *B,* for suggestions.)

B. **THE THEORETICAL SIDE.** — 1. *The Relation of Art to Science, Philosophy, Ethics, and Religion.* — The distinction between poetry and the other arts ; the boundaries of poetry and painting ; of poetry and music, etc. The distinction between poetry and history. Aristotle, Poetics, 9 ; Sidney, Defense of Poesy (Cook's ed., p. 18) ; Bosanquet, Hist. Aesth., p. 59 ; Butcher, Aristotle's Theory of Poetry, chaps. III and XI. Is poetry a term applicable to all the arts ? (Plato, Aristotle, Lessing, Kant, Schiller, Coleridge, Wordsworth, Mill.) Is not the distinction between poetry and other literature of power that of the absolute and the relative, prose and verse being less or more appropriate instruments of poetry, and poetry (or absolute literature) being the emotive expression or suggestion of an aesthetic interpretation of things, by means of the rhythmical and imaginative language *proper to the subject?*

2. *The Materials of Poetry.* — (*a*) *Of Idea* (Aristotle, Poetics, 9 ; 15 ; 18 : 6 ; 24 ; 25. Butcher's Aristotle's Theory of Poetry, chapters on Poetic Truth and Universality. Kant's Critique of Judgment, Schiller's Aesthetic Letters, Eckermann's Conversations of Goethe (Bohn), p. 258, Coleridge, Biographia Literaria, 2 : 41).

(*b*) *Of Form.* The word basis, the sentence basis, the rhetorical and logical bases ; pitch, stress, quantity, and tone ; rhythm ; speech-tunes ; cadences ; rhythms of nature ; imagery and verse, which the more essential ? The sensuous element in relation to the imaginative. (See §§ **22-24.** Lanier, Ellis, Schipper, Gurney, Kawczynski.)

(*c*) *Of Organism.* Whether the organic structure contains elements not present in the materials either of idea or form. If the organism is not the sum, is it the product of idea and form ?

3. *How the Materials are Manipulated.* — The question should be looked at from ; (*a*) the physical point of view ; (*b*) the psychological ; (*c*) the ethical ; and the following

subjects will demand consideration : (1) the faculties aroused
and employed by the poetic impulse ; (2) the effect of mood
and imaginative training upon the appreciation of poetry;
(3) the relation of poetic truth, beauty, and 'accent' to other
truth, beauty, and 'accent' (Arnold) ; (4) the signification
of proportion, harmony, aesthetic economy (Spencer, Dewey),
and rhythm ; (5) the relation of rhythm to idea ; (6) the
relation of metre and rhythm to each other and to language ;
(7) the difference between rhythmical prose and rhythmical
verse ; (8) whether verse is a quality of poetry, or an instrument ; whether rhythmical prose may be used by poetry, and
whether unmetrical or unrhythmical verbal expression could be
so used ; (9) the difference of effect between imaginative
verse and imaginative prose (Gurney), and whether the charm
of rhythm and metre lies in the illusion that they create ;
(10) whether poetry is imaginative language *plus* metrical
form ; or whether the effect is the product of the ear pleasure
and the mind pleasure (Gurney) ; (11) whether poetry is a
"heightened form of prose " ; (12) whether poetry can be turned
into prose, still retaining the poetic flavor, or be translated, as
poetry, from one language into another ; (13) whether poetry
is representative or presentative, imitative or creative, penetrative, 'magical' (Gurney), or suggestive. See Plato, Aristotle,
Plotinus, etc., on Imitation, § 9 above, Kant, Lessing, Goethe,
Schiller, Hegel, Wordsworth, Arnold, Austin, Gurney, Everett,
and others ; (14) whether all theories of poetry may be
reduced to the creative-imitative classification.

4. *The Purpose of Poetry.* — (*a*) *Aesthetic.* Whether the
pleasure conveyed by poetry is essential to the purpose, or accidental. Does the pleasure of the reader lie in the momentary
relief from worldly care, — from the sense of actuality ? in the
opportunity afforded the emotions to 'discharge' themselves
impersonally ? in the aesthetic contemplation of the significance of life ? Does the author aim at giving pleasure to others,

or, by finding expression in poetry, is he merely fulfilling his own play-impulse, or duty-impulse, or impulse of idealization ? For further suggestions on this point, see §§ 7–9 and 46–48.

(*b*) *Ethical.* Whether the principal aim of poetry is aesthetic or ethical. Is it the purpose of poetry to teach truth and virtue through the medium of imaginative and rhythmical word form ? to ' transfigure' life, be a 'guide' for it, 'criticise ' it, or display the ' seriousness' of it? Compare Matthew Arnold's " high seriousness " with the φιλοσοφώτερον καὶ σπουδαιότερον of Aristotle (Poetics, 9 : 3), with Horace's *Os tenerum pueri balbumque poeta figurat*, etc. (Epist. II, 1 : 126) ; his *Carmine di superi placantur, carmine manes* (Epist. II, 1 : 138) ; his *Aut prodesse volunt, aut delectare poetae, Aut simul et jucunda et idonea dicere vitae* (Ars Poetica, 333, 334); his *Omne tulit punctum* (Ars Poetica, 343) ; with Butcher's Theory of Poetry, chaps. IV and V, and with Wordsworth's " Its object is truth, general and operative."

5. *The Effect of Poetry upon the Percipient.* — (*a*) *Physiological.* The immediate effect of poetry, read or heard, upon the senses of sight and hearing.

(*b*) *Psychological.* (1) Is the effect unanalyzable ; and if it be, shall we call the unknown quantity non-reasonable (Gurney), or non-reasoned ? It will be necessary to distinguish precisely between the sensuous, the intellectual, and the aesthetic feelings. (2) Consider the effect upon the emotions of the unselfish pleasure awakened by art. (3) What is the effect of poetic illusion? (4) of the presentation to the mind of ideal values ? and (5) of the universal appeal to the sympathies which is claimed as a prerogative of poetry ? (6) Discriminate between kinds of images — as visual, auditory, tactile, etc. — summoned to the mind by poetic presentations. See the psychologies of James, Dewey, Spencer, Sully, Titchener ; also Ferrier's Functions of Imagination in his Human Mind, Maudsley's Physiology of Mind, Azam's Hypnotisme et Double Conscience,

Galton's Inquiries into Human Faculty (also in *Fortn.* Sept.,
1880, and *Mind*, 4 : 551, and 5 : 301); Binet's articles on ' Mental
Images' in *Rev. Philos.* 23 : 473, and 27 : 337 ; Paulhan's
Le langage intérieur in *Rev. Philos.* 21 : 26 ; articles in the
same periodical, 18 : 685, and 22 : 1, by Stricker.   (7) What
effect does the predominance in the poet of a certain kind of
imaginative power, as the visual, have upon the character
of his poetic imagery ?   (8) Does Tennyson, for instance, incline
to visual or to auditory imagery ?   (9) The imagery of the
following poets should be examined : Homer, Aeschylus,
Dante, Marlowe, Shakespeare, Swinburne, Rossetti, Wm. Blake,
Coleridge, Wordsworth.   (10) Examine the imagery of poets
blind from infancy, as Blacklock ; of those who have lost
their sight in youth or in mature years, as Milton or Philip
Bourke Marston.   (11) To what faculties does poetry appeal ?
(12) Compare poetic imagination with scientific.   (13) What
part do the emotions of the reader play in determining his
poetic sensitiveness ?

(*c*) *Ethical.* Whether the moral effect is direct, or indirect
(by way of emotional and imaginative effect).   Whether such
expositions as the following do not depend for their appli-
cability upon the imaginative and moral condition of the
individual who reads or hears the poetry in question : " Poetry
was the first philosophy that ever was known, whereby men
from their childhood were brought to the reason how to live
well, learning thereby not only manners and natural affections,
but also the wonderful works of Nature, mixing serious matter
with things pleasant " (Sir Thos. Elyot, about 1531) ; " For he
(our poet) doth not only show the way, but giveth so sweet a
prospect into the way as will entice any man to enter into it "
(Sidney, Defense of Poesy) ; cf. 4 *b* above, references to
Horace.

6. *Whether Didactic Verse may be Classed as Poetry.* — Discuss Pope's Essays on Man and on Criticism, Virgil's Georgics,

Hesiod's Works and Days, Horace's Ars Poetica, Boileau's
L'Art poétique, Browning's La Saisiaz, Sordello, Fifine, and
Parleyings, the Phenomena of Aratus, Darwin's Botanic Garden,
Drayton's Polyolbion, Phineas Fletcher's Purple Island, Words-
worth's Excursion, the poems of Langland and Gower, Young's
Night Thoughts.

7. *General Considerations. — Discussion of Inadequate Definitions and of the Principles Underlying Them.* — Is it a reasonable or a profitable business to compare poets in respect
of excellence ?   Should poets of form, of color, of sound, be
classified in the same list?   Can we classify the poet's poet
with the people's poet ?   Is Arnold's theory of poetical touchstones of practical value ?   What is the ultimate test of such
'touchstones' ?   See Gurney's Tertium Quid, and Alfred Austin,
as in § **20**.

C. **DIVISION OF THE SUBJECT.** — On the relation of literature
to the other arts, see §§ **7–9**; also Boeckh, Encykl. d. philol.
Wiss., p. 468.   Boeckh, as already shown (§ **15**, 4, above, and
further discussed, § **15**, 5), divides literature into two principal
kinds, poetry and prose, and these respectively into epic,
lyric, drama, and historical, philosophical, and rhetorical
prose.   (See his Encykl., pp. 28, 144, 255, 648, 684, 743, for a
learned presentation of the subject.)   For other opinions, see
Wackernagel, Poetik, Rhetorik, und Stylistik ; Elze, Grundr.
d. engl. Philol., pp. 233, 347–348, who discusses Boeckh and
Wackernagel ; Körting, Encykl. d. roman. Philol. 1 : 74, 78 ;
2 : 443–454 ; Schmitz, Encykl. d. neueren Sprachen, 1 : 65–67 ;
also, Wordsworth, Hegel, Baumgart, Gottschall, M. Arnold,
and T. Arnold.

§ 20. REFERENCES.

ALLEN, GRANT. Physiological Aesthetics. N. Y. : 1877.

Chap. II Poetry.

For Allen's point of view, see § **8**.

ARISTOTLE. Poetics.

For editions, see Appendix. A trustworthy and inexpensive translation (with the original) is Wharton's (Parker and Co., Oxford, 1883). Professor Bywater's text has just appeared, and is excellent. The commentary is promised presently (Clarendon Press, Oxford). Altogether the best student's edition is Butcher's Aristotle's Theory of Poetry and Fine Art (London : 1895), of which a new and improved edition has recently appeared. In Poetics, 1–5, will be found the statements concerning 'imitation' and 'rhythm' in poetry which have been *cruces* from that day to this. The student is referred to the examination of these terms made in § **9**, where it is attempted to show that Aristotle did not mean by μίμησις what we ordinarily mean by *copying*. It is sometimes forgotten that in Poetics, 4: 6, Aristotle calls music and measure, as well as imitation, natural to man. It should therefore be considered whether it is not in this association of μίμησις with music and rhythm that the meaning of Aristotle's theory of poetry is to be sought. Compare with the passage in 4: 6 that in 1: 4, which enumerates rhythm, language, and harmony (music) as the means of imitation.

The following questions concerning the treatment of poetry in general will arise: whether (in 3: 1) the division of poetry into dramatic narrative (epic), pure narrative (including lyric), and the drama, is orderly and exhaustive; whether Aristotle means to include the lyric under "narration where the poet retains his individuality"; where in this classification

other literary kinds could fall, such as the idyl, the metrical
romance, the modern novel, the elegy, didactic poetry (De
Rerum Natura, the Georgics, etc.), philosophical satire (Horace,
Juvenal, Swift's Voyage to the Houyhnhnms, etc.), and how
this classification bears comparison with others, such as Wordsworth's in Preface to Poems (1815), — narrative, dramatic, lyrical, idyllium, didactic, philosophical satire. (See M. Arnold's
Essay on Wordsworth, concerning the Greek classification of
poetry.) A difficulty presents itself (in 4 : 1–5) in the determination of the "two causes" from which poetry is said to
spring, — whether Wharton's interpretation is correct, (1) the
instinct of imitation, (2) the delight in imitation ; or Butcher's,
(1) the instinct of imitation, (2) the instinct for harmony and
rhythm ; or, yet again, this : (1) the instinct of imitation and
(2) the desire to learn (4: 4). The historical descent of epic
and tragedy on the one hand, from the imitation of noble
actions by noble poets, and of satire and comedy on the other,
from the imitation of the actions of meaner persons by the
more trivial poets (4 : 7), is especially noteworthy when considered in connection with the implication (5 : 3) that the latter
style approaches the former in poetic value in proportion as
it *generalizes* its themes and plots. The study of poetic truth
(chaps. IX and XXV) involves the discussion of the statement,
"Poetry, therefore, is a more philosophical and a higher thing
than history ; for poetry tends to express the universal, history
the particular" (9: 3). It will be necessary to distinguish
between probability, possibility, and actuality ; between the
world of imagination and the world of experience ; between
what looks like chance and what looks like necessity ; and it
will be noted that Aristotle agrees with Bacon that the poet
must be a maker of that which has either *probable* or *necessary*
independence and unity (9 : 9, 10). On the subject of poetry
and the errors to which the poet is liable, see chap. XXV ; on
poetical diction, chaps. XXI, XXII.

Compare Bacon's theory of poetry in the Advancement of
Learning.   See note on Masson's Theories of Poetry, and consult in general notes and comments in the edition of Pye,
Twining, Susemihl; Butcher (Theory of Poetry, chaps. I–V, XI)
and the critical studies of Aristotle's Theory of Art mentioned
in § 8, especially Döring, Die Kunstlehre des Aristoteles (Jena :
1870) ; Teichmüller, Aristotelische Forschungen (Halle : 1869) ;
Reinkens, Aristoteles Ueber Kunst (Wien : 1870) ; and E.
Müller's Geschichte der Kunst bei den Alten (Breslau : 1834).
Aristotle on the Epic will be discussed in § 32, on Tragedy,
§§ 37, 40–42, 46–48, on Comedy, §§ 49–51, in vol. II of this
work.

ARNOLD, M. Essays in Criticism. 2d Series. Lond. : 1888.
      Pp. 1–55.

The Essays on Translating Homer, on the Study of Poetry,
on Wordsworth, Byron, and Shelley, have stirred up a controversy as keen, as entertaining, and so far as inconclusive, as
that between Bowles and Campbell on the merits of Pope.
Matthew Arnold's position rests upon three assumptions : first,
that poetry is at bottom a criticism of life, — " The greatness of
a poet lies in his powerful and beautiful application of ideas to
life — to the question : How to live " (On Translating Homer) ;
second, that there exist generally recognized laws of poetic
beauty and poetic truth ; third, that the relative greatness of
a poet depends upon the soundness of his criticism and the
completeness of his surrender to the laws of poetic beauty and
truth.   By references to these canons of criticism, Arnold
succeeds in placing Wordsworth above Byron, and Byron above
Shelley.   It may, however, be questioned whether he has
distinguished between the criticism of life and its representation ; whether he has demonstrated the universality of his laws
of poetic beauty and truth ; whether, indeed, he has anywhere
logically defined the beauty and truth in dispute ; and, in fine,

whether he understands criticism always in the same sense. Compare, for instance, the uses of the word in the essay on Wordsworth and in the essay on the Function of Criticism. For the controversy with Austin and Swinburne, see under those names below.

Arnold defines poetry with reference to its form, as follows : " Poetry is simply the most delightful and perfect form of utterance that human words can reach. Its rhythm and measure, elevated to a regularity, certainty, and force very different from that of the rhythm and measure which can pervade prose, are a part of its perfection " (The French Play in London).

ARNOLD, M.   The Touchstones of Poetry.   Selected from the
     writings of Matthew Arnold and John Ruskin ; with Intro-
     duction by A. S. Cook.   San Francisco : 1887.

Useful for those who have not access to the originals, namely, Arnold's Last Words on Translating Homer, and Ruskin's Fiction, Fair and Foul.   In the Introduction, Professor Cook points out Arnold's indebtedness to Joubert.   His main indebtedness is, however, to Wordsworth and Goethe.   The aesthetic principle underlying the touchstones quoted by Arnold is not discussed by Professor Cook.   It would appear to be the rhythmical expression of the significant as presented by the synthesis of antithetical manifestations.

AUSTIN, ALFRED.   The Human Tragedy.   Rev. ed.   Lond. :
     1889.
          Introduction, pp. i–xlii.

AUSTIN, ALFRED.   Prince Lucifer.   2d ed.   Lond.: 1887.
          Introduction, pp. vii–xxi.

AUSTIN, ALFRED.   *Contemp.* 40: 884 ; 41: 124 Old and New
     Canons of Criticism of Poetry.

The article introductory to Prince Lucifer, on the End and Limits of Objective Poetry, is rather a defense of that tragedy

than a discussion of the subject announced.   The author asserts
with force the poet's right to use "moral perplexity" as an
agent or cause for the 'epic' drama, although he may desire
to solve no moral problem, to settle no spiritual controversy.
Such agnosticism cannot pass unchallenged; for those who
have best accomplished the aesthetic purpose of poetry have
best understood the ethical relations of the subject that they
treat.

In the articles on the Canons of Poetical Criticism (*Contemp.
Rev.*), Austin combats Arnold's definition of poetry.   The
reader cannot but suspect Austin of putting too restricted an
interpretation upon Arnold's criticism of life.   Can there be,
as Austin says, "no consensus about the criticism of life"?
And is it true that the more a critic the poet is, the more he
injures his poetry?   On the other hand, even if Arnold's definition be inadequate, does it follow that Austin's is satisfactory?   See his article on the Position and Prospects of Poetry,
Introduction to the Human Tragedy, p. xxii : "Poetry is a
transfiguration of life ; in other words, an imaginative representation of whatever men perceive, feel, think, or do."   Or
again : "Poetry, which is a glorified representation of all that is
seen, felt, thought, or done, by man, perforce includes Religion
and Philosophy among the materials reflected in its magic
mirror.   But it has no mission to replace them; its function
being not to supersede, but to transfigure."

Does this definition find room for subjective presentations
such as the Divine Comedy and Rossetti's Blessed Damosel?
Is every imaginative representation, even though in words,
poetry ; for instance Gulliver's Travels, Bowles's Spirit of Discovery, Dr. Syntax in Search of the Picturesque?   Does the
definition indicate the relation of thought to expression?

In the Introduction to the Human Tragedy the discussion of
the novel and the narrative poem leads the author to an interesting forecast of the course of poetry.   For the condensed state-

ment of Mr. Austin's canons, see *Contemp.* 41 : 135, 138.   As
tested by these canons, Byron comes first, Wordsworth second,
Shelley third.

BACON, FRANCIS.   Works.   Ed. by Spedding and others.   15
    vols.   N. Y. : 1869.

> Vol. II, pp. 186–188, 220–226 ; vol. IV, pp. 225–232 ; vol. VI,
> pp. 182, 183, 202–206, 337, 418, 419 ; vol. VII, pp. 285–287 ;
> vol. VIII, pp. 407–409, 439–444 ; vol. IX, p. 220 ; vol. X,
> pp. 403–405.

As in the case of Aristotle, one cannot expect to understand
Bacon's exposition of poetry out of relation to his tenets
touching art.   See Professor Masson's Essays below, and
Kuno Fischer's Francis Bacon und seine Nachfolger (2. Aufl.
Leipz. : 1875. pp. 269–283 Bacon's Poetik).   See also § **21,** *B* 2.

BAGEHOT, W.   Literary Studies.   2 vols.   Lond. : 1879.

In his articles on the First Edinburgh Reviewers (vol. I,
p. 27), Bagehot places in sharp contrast the analytic understanding of Jeffrey, and the mysticism, the religious imagination,
of Wordsworth.   Finding a mythical element in religion as in
art, he naturally adopts the Wordsworthian side of the controversy.   The attack upon the Whig critic is resumed with effect
in the paper (vol. II, p. 338) on Wordsworth, Tennyson, and
Browning.   Here will be found the striking analogy of the
picturesque and the ' literatesque.'   The assertion that the
poet's business is with types, and that those types are mirrored
in reality, should be compared with the similar theories of
Schopenhauer, Hegel, and Plato.   While the division of poetry
into the pure, the ornate, and the grotesque, is plausible, it
may be questioned whether it cover all stages of the art.   The
remarks (2 : 351) on rhythm in verse and in prose are of weight.

BAIN, A.   On Teaching English, with . . . an Inquiry into the
    Definition of Poetry.   Lond. : 1887.

> Pp. 207–256.

After discussing inadequate methods of defining poetry, the author passes in review the definitions of Aristotle, Bacon, Wordsworth, Arnold, Austin, etc., and advances to moot points of criticism, such as the function of language, the relation of poetry to science, to oratory, to morality, the choice of subjects, and the ideal in poetry. He emphasizes the aesthetic aim and effect of poetry, and would, in that respect, appear to sympathize with Austin rather than with Matthew Arnold. The work is a useful discussion of the question, Is Poetry 'imitative,' or is it 'effusive?' According to Bain, poetry neither interprets nor penetrates the natural, but assimilates it with some aspect of humanity. The definition on p. 257, " Poetry is a fine art, operating by means of thought conveyed in language," requires for its interpretation a definition of fine art, and for its validity, a theory of the relation of rhythmical language to aesthetic thought.

BATTEUX, L'ABBÉ CHARLES. Des quatre poétiques d'Aristote, d'Horace, de Vida, et de Despréaux. 2 vols. Paris : 1771.

See § **21,** *B* 4, below for a list of the other French poetics of the century.

BAUMGART, H. Handbuch der Poetik. Stuttg. : 1887.

One of the most learned, trustworthy, and exhaustive of the recent contributions to the science. It should have a place in the library of every critic.

BAYNE, PETER. Two Great Englishwomen . . . with an Essay on Poetry. Lond.: 1881.

    Pp. i–lxxviii.

As the author's object is to make a definition of poetry that will give Mrs. Browning the highest claim to consideration, he immediately falls foul of Mr. Arnold's criticism of life. Lyric poetry is for Mr. Bayne " the essential poetry."

Bénard, Ch.　Hegel : La poétique, précédée d'une préface et suivie d'un examen critique.　2 vols.　Paris : 1855.

The most important, indeed the only special, edition of Hegel's Die Poesie.　In addition to the admirable commentary on Hegel, the author gives a selection of the most important passages on poetry to be found in Schiller, Goethe, Richter, and others.

Biedermann, Woldemar von.　*Zeitschrift f. vergl. Litteraturgeschichte*, 2 : 415 Zur vergleichenden Geschichte der poetischen Formen.

An interesting study of primitive forms.　The author makes use of the material gathered by the folklorists and the anthropologists.

Bodmer, Johann Jakob.　Vom Wunderbaren in der Poesie. Zürich : 1740.

　　See § **21,** *B* 3.

Bodmer, Johann Jakob.　Betrachtung ueber die poetischen Gemählde der Dichter.　Mit einer Vorrede von J. J. Breitinger.　Zürich : 1741.

　　See § **21,** *B* 3.

Boileau, Despréaux N.　L'Art poétique.　(Pp. 91–109 of his Oeuvres Complètes.　Publ. par P. Chéron.　Paris : 1875. Pp. 188–220 of the edition by M. Amar.　Paris : 1851.)

For reprint with translation by Soame, see Cook's Art of Poetry ; see also, Batteux, Les quatres poétiques.　Consult below, § **21,** *B* 4, on Boileau, and read O. Wichmann, L'Art Poétique de Boileau dans celui de Gottsched (Berlin : 1879).

Bosanquet, B.　History of Aesthetic.

After a discussion of Ruskin's penetrative imagination, the author offers (pp. 460–462) an answer to the question, What is the material of poetry? In its full development, poetry, he decides, unquestionably demands metre. As distinguished from the other arts, its material is metrical or rhythmical language, and always a particular language. Bosanquet thus differs with those who hold imagination to be the material of poetry, though he looks upon the penetrative imagination, with its attendant depth of ideal feeling, as necessary to complete his definition. Poetical prose, so called, he would regard as rhetoric, "a thing scarcely compatible with poetical quality."

BOURGET, P. Études et portraits. 2 vols. Paris : 1889.

> Vol. I, p. 189 Science et poésie ; p. 329 L'Emploi des vers au théâtre.

BREITINGER, JOHANN JAKOB. Kritische Dichtkunst. 2 vols. Zürich : 1740.

> See § **21,** *B* 3.

BRIMLEY, GEO. Essays. Lond. : 1882.

> Pp. 184–203 Poetry and Criticism.

An inquiry into the fundamental properties of poetry. Brimley was one of the earliest to prophesy the future greatness of Tennyson.

BROWN, JOHN. Spare Hours. New ed. 3 vols. Boston : 1892.

> Vol. I, pp. 313–352 On Vaughan's Poetry.

The doctor opens with a witty page-and-a-half recapitulation of great critics, disagrees with all, and develops a genial theory of his own.

BROWNING, ROBERT. On the Poet Objective and Subjective . . . on Shelley as Man and Poet. 2d ed. (Browning Soc. Papers, No. 1.) Lond. : 1881.

About 1851 certain letters of Shelley — afterwards shown to be spurious — were published by Moxon, with an introductory essay by Browning. This essay is republished with notes and headings by Mr. F. J. Furnivall. As Mr. Furnivall says, it makes no difference whether the Shelley letters were genuine or not — we are indebted to them for an admirable formulation of Browning's poetic creed. The distinction made between the objective poet — the fashioner — and the subjective poet — the seer — leads (p. 6) to an exposition of the aim of the latter : 'Not what man sees, but what God sees — the Ideas of Plato, seeds of creation lying burningly on the Divine Hand, it is toward these that he struggles.' The remarks on the relation of the poet's life (p. 10) and of his moral purpose (p. 9) to his work are direct and sound. The subjective-objective style of poetry forecast by the youthful Browning has found its best illustration in his own dramatic monologues. Carlyle and Landor take the same view as Browning of poetry : the expression of ideas impressed on man's mind by the Creator.

BRYANT, W. C. Prose Writings. Ed. by Parke Godwin. 2 vols. N. Y. : 1884.

> Vol. I, pp. 3–44 Lectures on Poetry ; pp. 57–67 On Trisyllabic Feet in Iambic Measure; pp. 147–160 Poets and Poetry of the English Language.

The Romantic conception of poetry. It is a suggestive rather than an imitative art, employing purely arbitrary symbols instead of visible or tangible representation. The elements of poetry lie in natural objects and in the experiences, emotions, and relations of human life.

BUCHANAN, R. A Poet's Sketch-Book : Selections from the prose writings of Robert Buchanan. Lond. : 1883.

In the essay on the Poet or Seer (pp. 3–31) we find a characterization of the poet which is excellent as far as it goes. The poet is he who sees life newly, assimilates it emotionally, and contrives to utter it musically. (See also David Gray and Other Essays on Poetry. Lond. : 1868. Pp. 3–60.)

Burke, Edmund.   Essay on the Sublime and Beautiful. Lond. :
     1821.

Poetry cannot be called an art of imitation, save in so far as
it describes the manners and passions of men in the language
which directly expresses them.   But even descriptive poetry is
not strictly imitative, for it operates chiefly by substitution, by
means of sounds which through custom have come to produce
the effects that result from the reality.

(See §§ **8** and **21**, *B* 2.   A cheap edition of the Essay may
be found in Cassell's National Library, N. Y.)

Butcher, S. H.   Aristotle's Theory of Poetry and Fine Art.
     Lond. : 1895.

This volume is a revision and an enlargement of the author's
Some Aspects of the Greek Genius (see § **9**).   It contains a
list of editions, translations, and commentaries on the Poetics of Aristotle, an analysis of that treatise, the Greek text
with an admirable translation into English, and an essay on
the theory of poetry there presented.   The author reads the
Poetics in the light of Aristotle's other writings, connects the
theory of art with the Aristotelian philosophy as a whole, and
gives the vital term ' imitation' its full aesthetic content.   He
holds, undoubtedly with good reason, that the clue to Aristotle's
theory is to be found in the conception that poetry is an expression of the universal element in human life.   The chapters
on the theory of tragedy contain material not included in the
author's earlier work.   The chapters on Art, Nature, ' Imitation' as an Aesthetic Term, Poetic Truth, The End of Fine
Art, Art and Morality, the Generalizing Power of Comedy, and
Poetic Universality in Greek Literature, are of prime importance
to the student of the poetic principle.   It may unhesitatingly
be asserted that this is the best critical edition of Aristotle's
Poetics for English workers.   It is a hundred years later than

Tyrwhitt's, and gathers up all that is best in the Aristotelian criticism of the hundred years.

CARLYLE, THOMAS.   Heroes and Hero-Worship (Lect. 3 The
    Hero as Poet; Lect. 5 The Hero as Man of Letters). N. Y.:
    1846.

CARLYLE, THOMAS.   Critical and Miscellaneous Essays. 4 vols.
    Lond. : 1857.

> Vol. I Richter, State of German Literature, Goethe, Burns, Vol-
> taire, and Signs of the Times ; Vol. II Novalis, History,
> Richter, Schiller, Early German Literature, Historic Survey of
> German Poetry, Biography; Vol. III Goethe's Works, Diderot,
> Sir Walter Scott.

CARLYLE, THOMAS.   Lectures on the History of Literature.
    Lond. : 1892.

As a teacher of the philosophical in poetry and criticism, Carlyle is one of the most important figures of the century. His own masters were Kant, Fichte, Jean Paul, and Goethe. For his position in English poetics, see § **21**, *B* 2.

CARRIERE, M.   Das Wesen und die Formen der Poesie.
    Leipz. : 1854.

> See § **8**.

COLERIDGE, S. T.   Complete Works.   Ed. by W. G. T. Shedd.
    7 vols.   N. Y. : 1853–54.

> Vol. III Biographia Literaria, chaps. III, IV, X–XXII; vol. IV,
> pp. 19–22 Definition of Poetry, pp. 22–46 Drama, pp. 275–285
> The Ludicrous, pp. 328–336 Poesy as Art, pp. 337–343 Style,
> pp. 368–370 Taste, pp. 370–373 Beauty, pp. 387, 388 Wonderful-
> ness of Prose; vol. VI, p. 433 (Table Talk) Meaning and
> Music in Poetry.

COLERIDGE, S. T.   Literary Remains.   Ed. by H. N. Coleridge.
    4 vols.   Lond. : 1836–39.

> Vol. II, pp. 7–12 Definition of Poetry, pp. 12–53 Drama, pp. 372,
> 373 Wonderfulness of Prose ; vol. IV, p. 20 Shakespeare, etc.

"Poetry, or rather a poem, is a species of composition opposed to science, as having intellectual pleasure for its object and as attaining its end by the use of language natural to us in a state of excitement, but distinguished from other species of composition, not excluded by the former criterion, by permitting a pleasure from the whole consistent with a consciousness of pleasure from the component parts; — and the perfection of which is to communicate from each part the greatest immediate pleasure compatible with the largest sum of pleasure on the whole."

The influence of Coleridge upon English poetics of the nineteenth century is incalculable ; not only because of his attempt to base criticism upon aesthetic principles, but because of his liberal eclecticism, which has taught his countrymen to lay under contribution the critical philosophy of Germany while holding to what is best in mediaeval and ancient thought. For the indebtedness of Coleridge to the German romanticists and philosophers, to Kant, Schelling, Schiller, Richter, Lessing, see Brandl's Coleridge ; for his indebtedness to the Neoplatonists and to Plato, to the Mystics and to Spinoza, see the Biographia Literaria, Table Talks, the Friend, *passim*. Miss Wylie's Evolution of English Criticism contains a good study of the sources of Coleridge's criticism. The student may look for a valuable discussion of Coleridge's critical principles in Professor J. M. Hart's forthcoming Selections from Coleridge (Athenaeum Press Series, Boston).

Colvin, S.   'The Fine Arts.'   (In Encycl. Brit., 9th ed.)

A broad and able discussion of poetry — which, as an imitative art, is said to represent by means of verbal signs, arranged with musical regularity, everything for which verbal signs have been invented.

Cotterill, H. B.   An Introduction to the Study of Poetry. Lond. : 1882.

A series of University Extension Lectures, simple in manner and suggestive. Adopting the realistic principles, the author bases his argument upon Plato, but can hardly be said to grasp Plato's conclusions concerning art and poetry. The chapters on Art Creation, The Classical School, and Wordsworth, will be of service to the beginner.

COURTHOPE, W. J.　The Liberal Movement in English Literature.　Lond.: 1885.

> Pp. 3–32 Definition of Poetry, pp. 71–108 Wordsworth's Theory of Poetry, pp. 197–240 Prospects of Poetry.

This work is valuable, even though its judgments are not always trustworthy. Mr. Courthope disavows all intention of prejudicing his argument by the use of political terms, but his treatment of the romantic movement shows that conservatism, whether political or literary, means all that is desirable in civilization. Consequently, although he indicates in his Introductory Chapter, pp. 3–32, the weak point in Bowles's axioms of poetry, he fails to appreciate the general soundness of that poet's criticism upon Pope and the Classical School. The poetic theories of Arnold and Swinburne are criticised with apparent candor, but are disposed of in such a way as to show that the author understands neither of them. Macaulay's dictum concerning the decline of poetry is adopted on altogether insufficient historical proof ; and Wordsworth's theory of poetry is deliberately misstated. It is hard to see that Mr. Courthope recognizes any genuine standard of poetic excellence. His apparently simple definition of poetry (pp. 30, 31), 'the art of producing pleasure by the just expression of imaginative thought and feeling in metrical language,' is invalidated by a dualistic conception of the relation of idea to form. (Cf. his essay in *Nineteenth Century*, 41 : 270 Life in Poetry : Poetical Expression.) The chapter on the Prospects of Poetry is, like the rest of the book, eminently readable, but indicative of the author's

inability to see two sides of a question. The romantic movement is in his opinion an aberration — an obsession — of
poetry.

The author's History of English Poetry, now appearing, will
afford him scope for illustration of these peculiarities.

DALLAS, E. S. Poetics ; an Essay on Poetry. Lond. : 1852.

DALLAS, E. S. The Gay Science. 2 vols. Lond. : 1866.

The Gay Science of the Troubadours was poetry ; of Mr.
Dallas, it is criticism. For, holding with the Troubadours that
the aim of poetry, as of all art, is pleasure, he makes criticism
the science of the laws under which pleasure is produced. He
discusses skilfully, though sometimes inconclusively, the more
notable theories of poetry. His quest for the fundamental
unity of art is scientific in intention, but is vitiated by a misconstruction of Aristotle's theory of imitation, and a radical
misapprehension of Hegel's theory of manifestation ('Art is
the manifestation of the Beautiful'). It may be questioned
whether Mr. Dallas does not also confound the *aim* of poetry
with its *nature*. In vol. I the chapters on the Hidden Soul,
The Play of Thought, and The Secrecy of Art, are decidedly
suggestive. They anticipate in a popular way a theory of art
which is now being worked out scientifically by certain of the
physiological psychologists. His theory of the *unconscious
pleasure* evoked by art requires to be tested by a larger selection from poetry than that adduced to confirm the argument.
According to him, poetry is the imaginative, harmonious, and
unconscious activity of the soul ; the art of giving imaginative
pleasure. Vol. II, chaps. XIII and XIV, and passages in the
section on the Pursuit of Pleasure and the World of Fiction
display to advantage the author's rich and entertaining style.
He asserts that in poetry a synthetic reproduction of truth is
subsumed under the category of poetic imagination. He holds,
therefore, to the Baconian theory.

Many of these theories will be found in Mr. Dallas's shorter and earlier works on Poetics, Masson's review of which will be found in *No. Brit. Rev.* 19 : 297 Theories of Poetry, and in his Essays, as below.

DAVIDSON, JAS. W. The Poetry of the Future. N. Y. : 1888.

" Aims to show that the one essential characteristic of verse — the language of poetry — in English is rhythm."

DE VERE, AUBREY. Essays, chiefly Literary and Ethical. Lond. : 1889.

> P. 10 Definition of Poetry.

DE VERE, AUBREY. Essays, chiefly on Poetry. 2 vols. Lond. : 1887.

" Poetry has ever recognized these two great offices, distinct though allied, — the one, that of representing the actual world ; the other, that of creating an ideal region, into which spirits whom this world has wearied may retire. . . . A perfect poet ought to discharge both these great offices of poetry " (Two Schools of Poetry). De Vere is, in creation and criticism, an ardent admirer and follower of Wordsworth.

DEWEY, JOHN. *Andover Rev.* 16 : 92 Poetry and Philosophy.

A comparison of Arnold and Browning. The author's thesis is that the best poetry is that which is informed by the soundest philosophy.

DIXON, WM. M. English Poetry from Blake to Browning. Lond. : 1894.

> Pp. 1–25 Poetry and its Relation to Life.

The substance of the author's definition (p. 6) is as follows : Poetry is impassioned language, appropriate to higher moods ("intenser spiritual life than the one in which we hourly move "), ordered or marshaled in a rhythmically effective way.

Dryden, J. Works. Ed. by Sir Walter Scott. 18 vols. Lond. : 1808. (Revised and corrected by Geo. Saintsbury. Edinb. and Lond.: 1882–92.)

> Revised Edition, vol. II, p. 291 Defense of an Essay of Dramatic Poesy ; vol. IV, pp. 18–30, pp. 225–247 Defense of the Epilogue, or an Essay on the Dramatic Poetry of the Last Age ; vol. V, pp. 111–124 Preface to the State of Innocence ; the Author's Apology for Heroic Poetry and Poetic License ; vol. XV, pp. 283–377 An Essay of Dramatic Poesy (the author's earliest theories, 1668; 2d ed. and revision, 1684 ; 3d ed. 1693) ; pp. 378–392 Heads of an Answer to Rymer's Remarks on the Tragedies of the Last Age ; vol. XVII, pp. 289–335 A Parallel of Poetry and Painting (Preface to Trans. of Du Fresnoy's Art of Painting).

The critical training of Dryden conspired with his broad literary sympathy and his natural aversion to conventional dogma to make him the most prominent figure in English poetics between Ben Jonson and Coleridge. The articles of his literary belief are simple and easily stated ; and, save for the didactic element natural to his ' milieu,' they will find general acceptance to-day. Poetry, he says, is not a copy, but a lively imitation of nature ; its field is as broad as human life ; the final test of its excellence is its fidelity to that which is essential in nature and in life. Its end is to teach man by way of pleasing him. In other words, instruction is the final cause ; delight, the efficient. The means available to this end are knowledge of nature, justness of imitation, ' equality ' of thought, propriety of expression, and sweetness of numbers.

His opinions concerning dramatic theory and construction, prosody, refinement of language, poetic standards, ancient and modern, the comparative excellence of authors and of literary kinds, and the relations of criticism to creation, are discussed in the following prefaces, prologues and epilogues, epistles and dedications : vol. III Preface to An Evening's Love (on Comedy) ; vol. II Dedication of the Rival Ladies (on blank verse and rhyme); vol. V Dedication of Aurung-Zebe (on heroic characters in tragedy), Preface to All for Love (a justi-fication of Dryden's conception of tragedy as compared with the conceptions entertained by the ancients and by the French School) ; vol. VI Preface to Oedipus (comparison of ancient and modern tragedy), Preface to Troilus and Cressida (criticism of Shakespeare, the imitation of our English dramatists, the grounds of criticism in tragedy), Dedication to the Spanish Friar (on the dovetailing of plots in tragi-comedy and on the dignity of poetic style) ; vol. VII Preface to Albion and Albanius (on the history and theory of the opera), Preface to Don Sebastian (the length of a play, the relation of poetry to history, the three unities) ; vol. VIII Dedication of Love Triumphant (on the undue observance of ancient canons of the drama) ; vol. X Prologues and Epilogues (touching, in many cases, on literary fashions of the day); vol. XI The Epistles — especially those to Lee, Roscommon, Congreve, and Sir Godfrey Kneller ; vol. XII Preface to Trans. of Ovid's Epistles (three ways of trans-lation : metaphrase, paraphrase, and imitation ; the second is preferred by Dryden), Dedication prefixed to Trans. from Ovid's Metamorphoses (an attack upon critics in general, upon the critics of Dryden's time, and Rymer in particular: " the corruption of a poet is the generation of a critic," and a defense of modern drama [British] as against the ancient), the Preface on Translation prefixed to Dryden's Second Miscellany (1685, the appreciation of ancient poets, Theocritus, Lucre-tius, Horace, and Homer, and of their translators) ; vol. XIII Essay on Satire, Dedication of the Pastorals, and the Preface to them (the latter contains rules of the pastoral) ; vol. XIV Dedication of the Trans. of the Aeneis (" The heroic poem is the greatest work which the soul of man is capable to perform ").

For further notice of Dryden, see § **21,** *B* 2.

EMERSON, R. W.   Complete Works.

> Vol. III Essays, 2d Series, pp. 9–45 The Poet ; vol. VIII Letters
> and Social Aims, pp. 9–75 Poetry and Imagination.

In the last of these essays poetry is described as "the only verity — the expression of a sound mind speaking after the ideal, and not after the apparent." "It is the perpetual endeavor to express the spirit of the thing, to pass the brute body and search the life and reason which causes it to exist, to see that the object is always flowing away whilst the spirit or necessity which causes it subsists." The essential mark, or, as Matthew Arnold would say, *accent* of poetry is the activity of mind betrayed in every word, "shown in new uses of every fact and image, in preternatural quickness or perception of relations." Again, "it is a presence of mind that gives a miraculous command of all means of uttering the thought and feeling of the moment." Still again, "poetry is the piety of intellect." Its value is to educate us to a height which it can itself but rarely attain, the subjugation of mankind to order and virtue. It will be noticed that penetrating as these remarks are, and eminently true of the idealistic character and aim of art, they do not attempt to distinguish poetry from the other arts save by the incidental mention of words and images as its material, and of morality as the test of its value. In Emerson's theory of the imagination the student will detect the continual influence of Plotinus and the symbolists.

ENGEL, J. J.   Anfangsgründe einer Theorie der Dichtungsarten aus deutschen Meistern entwickelt.   1783.   (Schriften. Berlin : 1801–06.   Vol. XI, p. 25 ff.)

EVERETT, C. C.   Poetry, Comedy, and Duty.

An excellent introduction to the analytic study of poetry, and especially to German thought upon the subject, is afforded by the first lecture of this work (pp. 1–155), which treats of the Imagination, the philosophy of poetry, the poetic aspect of

nature, and the tragic forces in life and literature. Schopenhauer's best thought on aesthetics pervades the book in solution with much that comes from Hegel. There is none of
Schopenhauer's pessimism ; a good deal of Hegel's healthy
hopefulness. Poetry is defined simply by Professor Everett
(p. 92) as " a process of imagining in speech." For further
criticism, see § **8**, References on the Theory of Art.

GERUZEZ, E.   Cours de littérature, rhétorique, poétique, histoire
litéraire.   Paris.

The first seventy-three pages of pt. I deal with poetics. The
book may be recommended to beginners.

GILDON, CH.   The Complete Art of Poetry.   2 vols.   Lond. :
1718.

> See § **23**.

GOETHE, J. W. VON.   Werke.   (Hempel ed.)   36 vols. in 23.
Berlin : 1879.

> Bd. XXIX Aufsätze zur Literatur.   See indexes in Bde. II,
> XXVIII, XXIX, and index to Bde. I–XXXVI in Bd. XXXVI.

GOETHE, J. W. VON.   Sämmtliche Werke.   40 vols. in 20.
Stutt. : 1840.

> Bd. XXX Winckelmann, Ueber Laokoon, Wahrheit und Wahr-
> scheinlichkeit, u. s. w. ; Bd. XXXI Deutsche Baukunst, Verschie-
> denes über Kunst, u. s. w. ; Bd. XXXII Deutsche Literatur ;
> Bd. XXXIII Auswärtige Literatur und Volkspoesie ; Bd. XXXV,
> pp. 333–459 Theater und dramatische Poesie.

GOETHE, J. W. VON.   Correspondence between Schiller and
Goethe.   Trans. by L. D. Schmitz.   2 vols.   Lond. : 1877.
(Vols. XIII, XIV of Goethe's Works.)

> Vol. I, pp. 321, 322, 324–327 Aristotle, pp. 398, 399, 428–430, 439–
> 460 Epic and Drama ; vol. II, pp. 371–375.

GOETHE, J. W. VON, and ECKERMANN, J. P.   Gespräche mit
Goethe.   6te Aufl.   3 vols.   Leipz. : 1885.

> See Register in Bd. III.

GOETHE, J. W. VON, ECKERMANN, J. P., and M. SORET. Conversations of Goethe. Trans. by J. Oxenford. Lond. :
1875. (Vol. VI of Goethe's works.)

See index.

While Goethe in no place systematically develops a theory of
poetry, the genesis of his theory and the course of his opinions
are not difficult to discover. His aesthetic descent is not, as
Mr. Bosanquet thinks, from Lessing, Winckelmann, and Kant,
by way of Schiller, but rather from Lessing and Winckelmann by
way of Herder. For though Goethe was profoundly influenced
by Schiller's interpretation of Kant's doctrine of the harmony of
the moral and the natural orders in the realm of the aesthetic,
he was rather confirmed in the course of his own development
than converted to any alien way of thinking. As to his utterances on poetics, while his Deutsche Baukunst, his contributions to *Die Horen,* and his Der Sammler und die Seinigen are
in general restricted to the plastic arts, the conclusions there
reached concerning the *characteristic* (typical or significant)
and the *individual* apply as well to music and to poetry. It is
in his Conversations, however, in his Letters, his Wahrheit and
Dichtung, his Sprüche, and occasional poems that the course of
his theory and its relation to details are especially to be sought.
The following outline of his aesthetic growth may be suggestive
to the student :

(1) In his earliest writings he rejects tradition and insists
upon the free utterance of the significant ; the method of utterance being left to the genius. (See Deutsche Baukunst, 1773 ;
Der Schiffer, 1778.) The content of art is furnished by the
artist's interpretation of the harmonies of the universe. " The
world lies before the artist as before its Creator, who, at the
moment when He enjoys his creation, enjoys also the harmonies
by virtue of which he created the world — the harmonies which
constitute its existence." The art, even of the savage, which

acts on what lies around it from inward, single, individual, independent feeling, is characteristic art and is true (Baukunst).
This period of Gothic subjectivity and individualism is succeeded by a revolt to the other extreme.

(2) The necessity of an objective determination of beauty is
recognized, and the poet, influenced by the official routine of
his life in Weimar, and to no slight degree by his reading
of Spinoza, attains a deeper insight into the significance of
reality. "I know God, *rebus singularibus*, through particular
phenomena and through those only" (Letter to Jacobi). Goethe
now rejoices in the contemplation of manifold forms as developed
from primitive and general types, and looks for the meaning
of the individually characteristic in the characteristic of the
universal. "Only by bounds self-set is mastery gained. Law
alone gives liberty." This period of aesthetic reflection and
practice culminates in a Hellenism as severe, formal, and symbolical as the romanticism of the former period was capricious and unrestrained. Before the essential and the typical
of classic art, the arbitrary and the individual fade. In the
masterpieces of Greece "is Necessity: God." The poetic
genius of Goethe did not, however, suffer him to abide in a
passionless atmosphere of Hellenism. While already feeling
his way to an aesthetic position which should transcend the
dualism of his earlier thought, he was led by his intercourse
with Schiller to a more sympathetic understanding of the
doctrines of Kant, and so to the last stage of his aesthetic
theory.

(3) This was a conception of beauty as subsuming both the
significant attribute and the symbolical form; thus revealing
the purpose of the characteristic in the elaboration of the form,
and the individuality of the form in its 'manifestation of the
characteristic. But Goethe does not strive to reduce Beauty to
a definite abstract concept: "Beauty is an ultimate principle
which itself is never revealed to sense, but which is reflected

in a thousand different manifestations of the creative mind —
a reflection as manifold and varied as the universe itself."
" Alles vergängliche ist nur ein Gleichniss." " Law which
manifests itself in freedom and in harmony with its own conditions, produces the objectively beautiful" (Eckermann). For
his theory of the beauty of nature, Eckermann may be consulted
(Oxenford's trans., pp. 244–246 ; pp. 157, 158). An object of
nature is beautiful in so far as it reveals its essential character.
This consists in conformity to the type and the laws of development *plus* the individualizing environment. Beauty in art, on
the one hand, penetrates beneath the actual and the intellectually comprehensible ; on the other, it is dependent upon
the actual phenomena in whose manifestations of beauty that
intangible ultimate must be found. Beauty in art cannot be
defined, but " the artist's work is real in as far as it is always
true ; ideal in that it is never actual." As to the purpose of
art — and this applies to poetry — " its highest achievement is
to give to the rough semblance the illusion of a higher truth "
(Wahrheit und Dichtung). " The work of the poet consists
in presentations to sense. The highest perfection is reached
when the spirit of life informs them, so that they seem to
every one to be concretely present." Poetry at its best appears
to be altogether external and plastic (Sprüche). As to where
the poetical resides, Goethe says to Eckermann, " No material
is, strictly speaking, unpoetical as soon as the poet knows
what to do with it." The poet does not represent scientific, but
artistic concepts. By his imagination the artistic concept of
that which is characteristic (or significant) is embodied in *style*.
The end of art is in art — just as the end of nature is in nature.
Here Goethe agrees with Kant's doctrine of the beautiful, " the
form of purposiveness in an object, in as far as this can be perceived without our referring it to any end " (Bosanquet, Hist. of
Aesth., p. 264). The materials of poetry, as of art, are without
limit : — morals, religion, and science in so far as they possess

general human interest (Eckermann, p. 83).   As to the source
of poetry, "art requires no ennobling purpose, for art springs
from a kind of religious sense, a deep, immutable seriousness"
(Sprüche, 690).   As to the function of poetry, "true poetry
bears this mark, that it is an earthly gospel setting us free, by
an inner serenity and an outward soothing effect, from the
burdens of life ; . . . it lifts us into higher regions and enables
us to obtain a bird's-eye view of the confusion and the perplexi-
ties of earth " (Wahrheit und Dichtung).

The theories of Schiller and Goethe, enriched by reciprocal
suggestion and criticism, have a direct bearing not only upon the
poetics of the philosophers who succeeded them, — Schelling,
Fichte, Hegel, — but upon the poetry of Germany, and indirectly (through Coleridge, Wordsworth, Arnold, and Ruskin)
upon the poetics and the poetry of England.   Since the appearance of Schiller's Ueber naïve und sentimentale Dichtung
(1795–96) and Goethe's Deutsche Baukunst (1773) the dogmatic strife between ancient and modern poetics has given place
to an inquiry into the development of the aesthetic consciousness and its relation to the history of artistic creation.

For other references, see the Goethe-Jahrbuch, 1 : 17 Goethe
und Lessing, 5 : 298 Zu Goethes Aufsätzen über Kunst;
Rosenkranz, Goethe und seine Werke (Königsberg : 1847),
pp. 8–16 Der jetzige Standpunkt der Kritik, pp. 29–36 Die
humanitäre Kritik, pp. 65–78 Goethe als Kunstforscher;
Schubarth, Zur Beurtheilung Goethes (2. Aufl. 2 vols. Breslau :
1820), Bd. II, pp. 48–147 Kunst und Alterthum, pp. 148–200
Poesie und Kritik, pp. 201–425 Aesthetische Aphorismen ; and
Blackie's Wisdom of Goethe (N. Y. : 1884), pp. lxxvii–lxxxiii,
109–147, 201–221.

GOTTSCHALL, R.   Poetik.   Die Dichtkunst und ihre Technik.
    3. verb. Aufl.   2 vols. in 1.   Breslau : 1873.

See, for notice, § **21,** *B* 3.

GOTTSCHED, J. C.   Versuch einer Kritischen Dichtkunst.   1750.

> See § **21**, *B* 3.   And consult Franz Gervoes, Die Poetik Gott-
> sched's u. der Schweitzer (Quellen u. Forschungen, vol. LXI) ;
> and Joh. Crüger, J. C. Gottsched und die Schweitzer (Berlin u.
> Stuttg. : 1884).

GUMMERE, F. B.   A Handbook of Poetics.   Boston : 1885.

A careful outline of the subject adapted to the use of beginners, whom it introduces to problems not only of the older but
of the more modern, especially the German, criticism.   The
work presents in classified form suggestion and example which
the student may elaborate for himself.   The treatment of style
and metre is, perhaps, more satisfactory than that of literary
forms.   The author generally offers a simple but at the same
time philosophic solution of difficulties, and his method of
division is suggestive.   Criticisms of the work, with counter-
criticisms by the author, will be found in Mod. Lang. Notes.
(See § **23**.)

GURNEY, EDMUND.   Tertium Quid.   2 vols.   Lond. : 1887.

In the second volume of this readable collection of essays,
the author discusses the Arnold-Austin-Swinburne controversy.
The essay Poets, Critics, and Class-Lists, enters a complaint
against the practice of ranking poets.   Gurney points out the
fact that rank or grade can be determined only for objects existing
under similar conditions ; that these conditions must be clearly
defined, and the consideration of them conducted upon accepted
principles.   But, if we are to hold with him that there is in
poetry a 'non-reasonable' element, then all attempts, such as
those of Mr. Arnold and Mr. Austin, to analyze poetry and to
rank poets by reasoned discourse must be deemed beside the
question.   The substitution of 'non-reasoned' for 'non-reasonable' would afford a more scientific basis for discussion.
The student should compare with Gurney's 'magical element'

Swinburne's "something at once perceptible and indefinable."
He will note also that while the principles of harmony and of
contrast may promote the pleasurable effects of poetry, they do
not in Gurney's opinion account for the charm of "quintessen-
tially poetic passages." That the musical element does not
account for the charm, and that the poetic whole is the product rather than the sum of the 'mind-pleasure' and the 'ear-
pleasure,' are thoughts worthy of development. In the chapter
on the Appreciation of Poetry the discussion is carried forward
on the same lines : Austin's attempted classification of styles
of poetry is assailed as confused and inadequate ; Arnold's
laws of 'poetic beauty and poetic truth' are, with justice,
pronounced vague. The canon of 'popularity' is treated with
respect, although acknowledged to depend upon incalculable
conditions. And the moral of the whole is that "we should be
chary of attaching too absolute a value to our own orders of
merit, and of measuring poetical achievements by any 'reasonable' considerations."

GURNEY, EDMUND. The Power of Sound. Lond. : 1880.

One of the most suggestive works upon the subject. None,
perhaps, more scientifically and sympathetically discusses the
relation existing between music and poetry. The greater part
of the volume will be of service in the study of versification.
(See § **23**.) For the theory of poetry the opening paragraphs
of chap. XIX, The Sound Element in Verse, should be studied.
The enjoyment of poetry is roughly divided into two kinds,
according as the impressions produced by it could, or could
not, be produced by prose. See also the last pages of the
chapter, especially pp. 448, 449, upon Lessing's Theory of
Poetry.

GUYAU, M.-J. Les problèmes de l'esthétique contemporaine.
    Paris : 1884.

Guyau, M.-J.　L'Art au point de vue sociologique.　Paris :
1889.

The former volume treats, with continual reference to recent
contributions to social and aesthetic problems, of the principle
of art and of poetry, the future of art and of poetry, and the
abiding quality of the laws of verse.　The latter contains a
remarkably acute study of the effect produced by philosophical
and social ideas upon French poetry in this century, and of
the corresponding rôle of poetry in relation to life.

Hartmann, E. von.　Ausgewählte Werke.　Berlin : 1887.

> Bd. IV Zweiter Systemat. Theil, pp. 714–783 Philosophie des
> Schönen.

The analysis of poetry, although apparently logical and
genetic, is evidently forced into conformity with a preconceived
system of aesthetics.　Regarding all poetry as spoken or read,
the author discovers the following progressive classification of
its forms :

A. Spoken. — 1.　*The Epic:* (*a*) the plastic epic, or the pure
epical epic ; (*b*) the picturesque, or lyrical epic ; 2. *The Lyric :*
(*a*) the epical lyric ; (*b*) the pure lyrical lyric ; (*c*) the dramatic
lyric, or the lyric of passion and motivation ; 3. *The Drama :*
(*a*) the lyrical drama ; (*b*) the epical drama ; (*c*) the pure
dramatic drama.

B. Read. — 1.　' Read ' as related to ' spoken ' poetry ;
2. Classification of poetry as read : personal narrative, letter-
poetry, diary-lyrics, the romance, short story, etc.

Haslewood, J.　(Ed.)　Ancient Critical Essays upon English
Poets and Poesy.　2 vols.　Lond. : 1811–15.

> Vol. I Puttenham ; vol. II Webbe, James I, Campion, Daniel,
> Boulton, Letters of Harvey and Spenser.　See §§ 21, *B* 2, and
> 24, *B* 1, 2.

HAZLITT, W. Lectures on the English Poets and English
Comic Writers. Bohn Libr. Lond. : 1876.

> Vol. I, pp. 1–25 Poetry.

His keen and sympathetic appreciation of merit distinguishes
Hazlitt as an author who, though essentially of the romantic
school, could acknowledge the debt owed by English poetry to
the school that had preceded. His paper in the *London
Magazine* on the anti-Pope controversy gave both Bowles and
his opponents their due and settled the dispute. His admiration of Coleridge and the German school of criticism is generally
held in check by a judicial conservatism. The following definitions, given in the chapter mentioned above, are rather of the
poetic faculty than of the art: "Poetry is the language of the
imagination and the passions. Poetry is the universal language
which the heart holds with nature and itself " (p. 1). "Poetry
in its matter and form is natural imagery, or feeling, combined
with passion and fancy " (p. 15).

HEGEL, G. W. F. Werke. 18 vols. Berlin : 1833–48.

> Bd. X, Theile 1–3 Aesthetik, Bd. X, Abthl. 3, pp. 220–581 Die
> Poesie. (See § **8,** p. 101, above.)

See also Bosanquet's Introd. to Hegel's Philos. of Fine Art
(Lond. : 1886) and Kedney's Hegel's Aesthetics (Chicago :
1885), and Bénard, above. No authority can be prescribed
the thorough study of which will be more beneficial. Not that
Hegel's scheme, classification, and theory of poetry are implicitly
to be adopted ; but that they are systematic and profound, and
even through piecemeal translations are the basis of much
recent English and American poetics. There is no complete
rendering into English of the chapters on poetry. Kedney's
work, though sympathetic, is inadequate because of its brevity,
while because of its exegetical nature it is not unmixed Hegel.
Kedney's eighth chapter will, however, be of value to such as

have not a reading knowledge of German.   Bosanquet's close
and luminous translation of the Introduction is the best pro-
paedeutic to the Aesthetik.   It is reprinted as an Appendix to
Bosanquet's History of Aesthetic.   Pp. 171–173 in Bosanquet
furnish a conception of the trend of Hegel's thought, although
the footnote to p. 172 may possibly convey the erroneous
notion that he underrated the function of sound in poetry.
That such was not the case is evident from the Aesthetik,
vol. III, pp. 274, 275.   A truer statement would be that beauty
of sound was not overrated by Hegel.   The report that he
regarded poetic form as a matter of indifference proceeds from
a misinterpretation of an isolated passage on p. 227 of the
same volume.   What he there says about the translatableness
of poetry should be construed in connection with the three
remarks (p. 275) that precede the section entitled Die poetische
Vorstellung.   Another rumor that has got abroad makes Hegel
pronounce metre to be the only condition absolutely indispensable to poetry.   For the correction of this error, see the Aesthetik, vol. III, pp. 234, 235, and 275 The Conditions Demanded
by Poetry.   The passage so often misconstrued, concerning the
value of metre, will be found on p. 289.   It should be translated as follows : "Versified prose gives us not poetry, but
merely verse — just as a purely poetic utterance when sub-
jected to prosaic treatment results in poetic prose ; but, for all
that, metre or rhyme is undoubtedly indispensable to poetry as
the prime and peculiar atmosphere (or fragrance) by which it is
made manifest to the senses ; indeed, metre is more necessary
than picturesque or so-called elegant diction."   On the definition of poetry, see p. 222 *et seq.;* for Hegel's scheme of discussion, p. 235 ; for the material of poetry, p. 236.   For the place
of poetry among the arts, see Schasler, Gesch. d. Aesthetik
(Berl. : 1872), pp. 967, 1003, where will be found a reasonable
criticism of the classification (on the basis of appeal to eye, ear,
or imagination) made by Hegel, Vischer, and Weisse.

HERDER, J. G. VON. Sämmtliche Werke. 31 vols. Hrsg.
    von B. Suphan. Berlin : 1877–89.

> Vol. VIII, p. 334 Ueber die Wirkung der Dichtkunst auf die
> Sitten der Völker in alten und neuen Zeiten.

Herder emphasizes here, as in his Kalligone, the principle,
"The play of mankind, like the play of nature, is thoughtful,
earnest." It is to be remembered that he ranked among the
"free" arts those only that served a purpose ; speech was
one of these "free" arts, but not music or the plastic arts.
Cf. Kant's Kritik d. Urtheilskraft, to which the Kalligone was
written as a reply. Herder represented pre-Kantian principles,
and was consequently unable to appreciate the organic method
of Kant. He defines beauty as the expression of the inner
life, but fails to distinguish between the sphere of beauty
and those of truth and goodness. Hence sprang the didactic
element, which, as shown above, vitiates his classification of
the arts.

HERDER, J. G. VON. Spirit of Hebrew Poetry. Trans. by
    James Marsh. 2 vols. Burlington : 1833.

Especially forcible in the historical treatment of figures.

HOLMES, O. W. Ralph Waldo Emerson. (Am. Men of Letters.)
    Boston : 1885.

> See pp. 312–324 On Emerson's Poems.

HOWISON, G. H. *Overland Mo.*, N. S., 5 : 523 The Essential
    Principle in Poetry. (Repr. San Francisco : 1894.)

A clear and adequate discussion of the theme of poetry, "a
rounded whole of vigorous unity, . . . founded on actual
experience, but transfigured in the light of the ideal borne
within it," of the relation of this ideal to the reality of nature
and the Supreme Ideal, of the conditions determining the
embodiment of the theme, and of the characteristics of the
medium.

HUMBOLDT, ALEXANDER VON. Cosmos. Trans. from the German by E. C. Otté and W. S. Dallas. 5 vols. N. Y. :
1862.

> See the chapter on Poetic Descriptions of Nature, in vol. II,
> pp. 1–105.

HUNT, LEIGH. Selections from the English Poets. N. Y. :
1857.

> Pt. I Imagination and Fancy, pp. 1–49 What is Poetry? pt. II,
> pp. 1–50 Illustrative Essay on Wit and Humor.

" Poetry . . . is the utterance of a passion for truth, beauty,
and power, embodying and illustrating its conceptions by imagination and fancy, and modulating its language on the principle
of variety in uniformity." Hunt distinguishes, as few critics
have done, between the poetic feeling, or faculty, and the
poetic operation of art. He discusses in turn, with simplicity
and directness, imagination, fancy, versification, the classification of poets, poetic truth, beauty, and power. A useful
edition, with introduction and notes, has been prepared by
Prof. A. S. Cook (Boston).

JAMES I OF ENGLAND. The Essays of a Prentice in the
Divine Art of Poesie. . . . Eng. Reprints. . . . Ed. by
E. Arber. Lond. : 1869.

> See, for brief notice, § **24**, *B* 2.

JEFFREY, FRANCIS. Contributions to the *Edinburgh Review.*
N. Y. : 1860.

Containing the famous reviews of Wordsworth and his contemporaries in poetry. A selection from his Essays, " with a
view to illustrating his style and his range and methods as
a literary critic," has been recently edited by Lewis E. Gates
(Boston : 1894). It contains an excellent introduction on the
development of periodical criticism. See also § **21**, *B* 2.

JOHNSON, S. Works. 11 vols. Oxford : 1825.

> Vol. II Rambler: No. 4 Romance, pp. 36, 37 Pastorals, pp. 86, 88, 90, 92, 94 Versification ; vol. III, pp. 139, 140 Samson Agonistes, pp. 156 Tragi-Comedy, p. 168 Poetry; vol. IV Adventurer, p. 58 Criticism and Poetry ; Idler: No. 45 Painting, pp. 60, 61 Criticism, p. 63 Art and Language, pp. 76, 79 Painting, p. 82 Beauty; vol. V, pp. 55–60 Observations of the Tragedy of Macbeth, pp. 118–124 Shakespeare and the Unities, pp. 366–414 Trans. of Brumoy's Dissertations upon the Greek Comedy, pp. 414–430 General Conclusion to Brumoy's Greek Theatre ; vol. VII, pp. 14–16 (Cowley) Wit, pp. 125–142 (Milton) Epic Poetry, pp. 301–307 Dryden as a Critic.

In vols. V and VI will be found the Lives of the Poets, six of which are republished with Macaulay's Essay on Johnson, in Matthew Arnold's edition (Lond. : 1886). Arnold's words, in the Preface to the Lives, concerning Dr. Johnson's literary judgment, hold true for his aesthetic principles at large : " Of poetry he speaks as a man whose sense for that with which he is dealing is in some degree imperfect. Yet even on poetry Johnson's utterances are valuable, because they are the utterances of a great and original man." According to Johnson, " Poetry is the art of uniting pleasure with truth by calling imagination to the help of reason " ; an excellent specimen of the eighteenth-century theory of poetry.

An edition of Selections from Johnson is promised by Professor H. H. Neill (Athenaeum Press Series, Boston).

JORDAN, W. Episteln und Vorträge. Frankfurt a. M. : 1891.

> Pp. 76–156 Bild und Wort.

Reopens the question discussed by Lessing in the Laokoon. Some of the illustrations are new.

JOUBERT, J. Pensées, précédés . . . d'une notice . . . par P. de Raynal. 2 vols. Paris : 1877–80.

> Tome II, pp. 263–272 De la Poésie.

Plato's arraignment, on metaphysical grounds, of art as presenting but a third-hand copy of reality, is answered by Joubert. The poet, he says, does not copy a copy. He clarifies material forms (which are 'impressions' of the idea) and makes of them a cast from the archetype, which shall retain the properties of the archetype. His inspiration springs from the creative quality of imagination ; the product of which — images — are his only symbols. He vitalizes them with ideas. The function of poetry is to enchant the hearer with the changing and inexhaustible delight of beauty, freshness, and meaning ; but the poetic appreciation varies with the sensitiveness of the hearer himself. Therefore, only to the sensitive soul does the real charm of a poem — its invisible and subtle principle — make its full appeal. (Cf. Gurney, Tertium Quid, The Appreciation of Poetry.) The poet need not, however, despair of an audience, for to every man capable of producing an imaginative creation there is provided his *alter ego*, capable of appreciating.

KANT, IMM. Kritik of Judgment. Trans. by J. H. Bernard. Lond. : 1892.

For the study of modern poetics a knowledge of the Critique of Judgment is indispensable. A list of editions and commentaries will be found in § **3,** *B* 1, and § **8.** Three streams of theory converge in this Critique : the English and German aesthetico-critical, — Burke, Kaimes, Reynolds, Hogarth, Baumgarten, Lessing, Winckelmann ; the English abstract-sensationalist and individualist, — Bacon, Locke, Shaftesbury, Berkeley, Hume ; and the continental abstract-rationalist, — Descartes, Spinoza, Leibnitz, Wolff. Kant's aesthetic doctrines were made concrete and popularized by Schiller. Bearing the impress of Schiller and Goethe (who also adapted and modified Kant), the Kantian aesthetic has passed not only into popular poetic theory, but into the dialectic of Schelling and Hegel. See Bosanquet, Hist. of Aesth., and Goethe, above.

KEBLE, J.   Occasional Papers and Reviews.

See particularly the Reviews on Coplestone's Praelectiones and Lockhart's Life of Scott (from *British Critic*, 1838). The following exposition of poetry calls for comparison with Aristotle's view of imitation, and with Mill's associational basis of the poetic art : " Poetry is the indirect expression in words, most appropriately in metrical words, of some overpowering emotion, or ruling taste or feeling, the direct indulgence whereof is somehow repressed." Keble looked upon all poetic expression, therefore, as a species of catharsis, by which the overburdened heart is relieved, imaginatively, of emotions which could not with like decorum find utterance in actual life. See Cardinal Newman's address on Keble, an article in *New Englander*, 56 : 239, on the Poetry of the Tractarian Movement, and the article ' Keble ' in the Encycl. Brit., 9th ed.

KLEINPAUL, E.   Poetik.   9. umg. und verm. Aufl.   Leipz. : 1892.

> Thl. 1 Die Dichtungsformen, Thl. 2 Die Dichtungssprache, Thl. 3 Die Dichtungsarten.   See § **21**, *B* 3, and § **23**.

KNIGHT, WILLIAM.   Studies in Philosophy and Literature. Lond. : 1879.

> Pp. 264–282 A Contribution towards a Theory of Poetry.

A protest, in terms popular but exact, against conventionalism in the art.   It provides a serviceable introduction to the philosophy of the subject.   Same article in *Littell's Living Age*, 116 : 759.

KNIGHT, WILLIAM.   The Philosophy of the Beautiful.   2 vols. Lond. : 1891–93.

> Pt. II, chap. VIII Poetry.

Adapted to the beginner's needs.   Two principles are held to govern all intellectual processes : (1) that a thing is known by its contrast with something unlike it, *e.g.*, the beautiful by contrast with the ugly ; (2) that the free and unimpeded energy of our faculties is always attended by joyful emotion.

KRALIK, R. VON.   Kunstbüchlein gerechten gründlichen Gebrauchs aller Freunde der Dichtkunst.   Wien : 1891.

A work of considerable merit.   The author's views on the relation of poetry and religion excited much comment when the book appeared.

LANIER, S.   The Science of English Verse.   N. Y. : 1880.
    See, for notice, § **23**.

LESSING, G. E.   Werke.   20 vols. in 12.   Berlin.

> Bd. VI Laokoon; Bd. VII Hamburgische Dramaturgie ; Bd. XI, Abth. 1–2 Kleinere Schriften zur dramatischen Poesie und zur Fabel; Bd. XIII, Abth. 2, pp. 249–306 Wie die Alten den Tod gebildet, pp. 332–347 Anmerkungen zu Winckelmann's Geschichte der Kunst.

The Laocoon is, perhaps, the most valuable contribution since the day of Winckelmann to a certain part of the field of aesthetics.   Lessing came to conclusions concerning the boundaries of painting and poetry, the dependence of either art on the medium used and the manner of use, the difference between ancient and modern conceptions of beauty, and the relative places of the ugly, the ridiculous, the grotesque in poetry and painting, which, though in great measure a coördination of preceding aesthetic suggestions, exercised a revolutionary influence upon literary criticism, if not upon the criticism of art in general.

But while the Laocoon deserves the serious attention and admiration of the student, it by no means demands unqualified assent, even to its fundamental doctrines.   By applying the term 'Mahlerey' to the plastic arts without discrimination, Lessing obscures the distinction between painting and sculpture, even though his argument has reference to the function of the latter. His services are to poetics rather than to art-criticism — but still the premises of his literary theory may be called in question. Are actions the only proper objects of poetry? Can successive signs express only objects which are successive, or whose parts are successive? Can poetry avail itself only of a single property of the body presented? To answer the last of these questions in the affirmative is to assert that the imagination has neither the power of retention nor of combination ; that there is no such thing as a resultant of the images presented to the mind by verbal symbols. But the most ordinary visualist can combine the successive properties of an object as rehearsed into a kaleidoscopic image concomitant with and changing with the description. To answer the two former questions in the affirmative is to exclude lyrical, elegiac, idyllic, and reflective poems from the realm of poetry. If the lyric be retained on the ground that it portrays the action of the emotions, what shall be done with L'Allegro, the Deserted Village, the Seasons, the Task, the De Rerum Natura, the nobler philosophical satire, none of which engages in emotional turmoil. Still, although Lessing attempted to restrict the realm of poetry, he enriched its content by justifying the appeal to all aesthetic emotions of which man is capable. His limitation of the realm should be examined in the light of the best English descriptive poetry. The sources of his poetics should be sought in Baumgarten, Burke, Kaimes, Bodmer, Breitinger, Hogarth, Winckelmann, Reynolds, — of course in Aristotle, and to no slight degree in the French School which Lessing combated. (See Bosanquet, Hist. of Aesth., p. 216 *et seq.;* and Schasler, p. 431 *et seq.*) Does Lessing distinguish between poetry and prose? See Gurney's Power of Sound, pp. 148, 149. Consult also in connection with the Laocoon the following works : Jas. Sime, Lessing (2 vols. Lond. : 1877), vol. I, pp. 247–308, vol. II, pp. 1–62, 76–80 ; Helen Zimmern,

Lessing, His Life and Works (Lond.: 1878), chap. XI; A.
Stahr, G. E. Lessing, sein Leben und seine Werke (3. Aufl.
2 vols. Berlin : 1864), Theil I, pp. 168–179, 243–271, 315–
361; Theil II, pp. 26–30; The Life and Works of G. E.
Lessing (Trans. of Stahr's Lessing by E. P. Evans. 2 vols.
Boston : 1866), vol. I, pp. 183–193, 261–289, 337–383, vol.
II, pp. 27–30; E. L. Walter, Lessing on the Boundaries of
Poetry and Painting (Ann Arbor : 1888. Univ. of Mich.
Philos. Papers, 2d Ser., No. 3); H. Blümner, Laokoon-Studien
(Freiburg i. B. : 1881–82. Bears indirectly upon the nature
of poetry, discussing (1) the use of allegory in plastic art, and
(2) the determination of the significant moment and of the
transitory element as propounded by Lessing).

The Laocoon has been translated by Miss Frothingham
(Boston: 1890) and by E. C. Beasley (Bohn Libr.). The
edition of Hamann and Upcott (Oxford : 1892) has helpful
notes. For other notices of Lessing, see §§ **8, 38, 41, 44, 47.**

LOWELL, J. R.   Lectures on the English Poets.   (Lowell Insti-
      tute).

      Lecture I Definition of Poetry.

A statement of the argument for the 'magical' or 'undefin-
able' factor. Cf. Swinburne and Gurney.

LOWELL, J. R.   Literary and Political Essays and Addresses.
      6 vols.   Boston : 1891.

The following essays are especially valuable to the student
of poetry: Vol. I, p. 218 Keats ; vol. II, p. 120 Swinburne's
Tragedies, p. 232 Lessing ; vol. III, p. 1 Shakespeare Once
More, p. 95 Dryden, p. 291 Chaucer ; vol. IV Pope, Milton,
Dante, Spenser, Wordsworth ; vol. VI, p. 68 Coleridge, p. 99
Wordsworth.

MACAULAY, T. B.   Critical, Historical, and Miscellaneous
      Essays.   6 vols.   N. Y. : 1861.

In the essay on Milton, vol. I, pp. 206–211, will be found the argument that the poetic faculty declines as civilization advances. " By poetry," says Macaulay, " we mean not all writing in verse nor even all good writing in verse. Our definition excludes many metrical compositions which on other grounds deserve the highest praise. By poetry we mean the art of employing words in such a manner as to produce an illusion on the imagination — the art of doing by words what the painter does by means of colors." Does Macaulay distinguish clearly between the faculty and the art of poetry? And does he not underestimate the importance of the poetic conception as determining the treatment of the subject? See also the essay on Dryden ; and compare Courthope's Liberal Movement, pp. 24–28.

MASSON, D. Essays, Biographical and Critical — English Poets. Cambr.: 1856.

> Pp. 409–446 Theories of Poetry ; pp. 447–475 Prose and Verse — De Quincey.

An excellent compend of theories. The author refers all definitions of poetry to Aristotle (in the Poetics) or to Bacon (in the Advancement of Learning). On the question whether the ' imitative ' and ' creative ' theories of poetry may be interpreted as two aspects of the same truth, see § **19,** *I, C* 3, above. Masson discriminates between the poetic temperament and the poetic faculty, and defines the latter as the *power of intellectually producing a new or artificial concrete.* Poetry itself he defines as a special mode of intellectual exercise, possible under all degrees of emotional excitement. It is the exercise of the mind " imaginatively or in the figuring forth of concrete circumstances " (On Wordsworth, Shelley, and Keats). An important principle is involved in the proposition that metre holds by original tenure not on poetry but on passion, and that, accordingly, the theories of Wordsworth, etc., are theories of verse not in its origin, but in its character as an existing institution in literature. With this discussion may be compared Dallas's theory (Poetics. London : 1852), which is here criticised.

In the article on the distinction between prose and verse (Essays, pp. 447–475), Professor Masson reverts to Coleridge's opinion, that the line must be drawn not between poetry and prose, but between poetry and science. On the relation of poetry to science, see the article by Professor Thomas in *Open Court*, 3 : 1727.

MILL, J. S.   Dissertations and Discussions.   3 vols.   Boston : 1865.

Vol. I, pp. 89–120 Thoughts on Poetry and its Varieties.

Poetry (as acting upon the emotions) is distinguished first from prose, which appeals to the intellect ; then (as portraying the human soul) from fiction, which gives a picture of life ; lastly (as unconscious of a listener) from eloquence, which holds intercourse with the world. Poetry, says Mill (p. 97), is feeling confessing itself to itself in moments of solitude, and embodying itself in symbols which are the nearest possible representations of the feeling in the exact shape in which it exists in the poet's mind. The distinction between poetry and eloquence obtains, according to Mill, in every art. On p. 106 will be found the principle underlying Mill's exposition : that in poetry emotions are the links of association by which ideas are connected. "What is poetry but the thought and words in which emotion spontaneously embodies itself?" The application of the theory to Wordsworth and Shelley (p. 109 *et seq.*) is worthy of attention. This article is specially commended to the consideration of the student.

MILTON, JOHN.   Prose Works.   Bohn Libr.

Vol. III, p. 462 On Education.

The following is the passage frequently mistaken for an absolute definition of Poetry : " To which [namely, Logic and Rhetoric] poetry would be made subsequent, or, indeed, rather precedent, as being less subtile and fine, but more simple, sensuous, and passionate. I mean not here the prosody of a verse, which they could not but have hit on before among the rudiments of grammar, but that sublime art which in Aristotle's Poetics, in Horace . . . and others, teaches us what the laws are of a true epic poem, what of a dramatic, what of a lyric, what decorum is, which is the grand masterpiece to observe." For further note, see § **21**, *B* 2 Development of Poetics in England.

MONTAIGNE, M. Works. Trans. by W. Hazlitt. Ed. by O. W. Wight. 4 vols. N. Y. : 1859.

> Vol. I, pp. 326, 327 Poetry.

MOON, G. W. What is Poetry ? Trans. Royal Soc. of Lit. 2d Ser., 12 : 173.

A curiosity of literature. The writer illustrates famous definitions of poetry by citations from his own poems.

MORRIS, G. S. British Thought and Thinkers. Chicago : 1880.

> Pp. 80–113 William Shakespeare.

Professor Morris illustrates by a study of Shakespeare the relation of poetry to philosophy. Philosophy is the theory of life ; poetry, the exposition of life. With regard to insight, philosopher and poet are brothers, the former explicitly conscious of the meaning of the vision, the latter not, — a relative difference. The philosopher demonstrates the truth ; the poet envisages. The poet is nature's instrument, a seer, not a creator of new truth. He is universal because he reports the intrinsically real. He creates only the form of that which he tells. He has the substance of the philosopher, but he sings uplifted by his message, not held down by its weight.

NEWMAN, F. W. Miscellanies. 3 vols. Lond. : 1869–89.

> Vol. I, pp. 65–145 Lectures on Poetry. See § 23.

NEWMAN, J. H. Essays, Critical and Historical. 2d. ed. 2 vols. Lond. : 1872.

> Vol. I Poetry with reference to Aristotle's Poetics.

NEWMAN, J. H. Essay on Poetry, with reference to Aristotle's Poetics. Ed. by A. S. Cook. Boston : 1891.

PATER, W. Appreciations. Lond. : 1889.

The theory of poetry advanced by Wordsworth is shrewdly and sympathetically discussed. The articles on Aesthetic Poetry, p. 213, and on Rossetti, p. 228, contain a clever determination of the merits of the pre-Raphaelite School; the Postscript, pp. 243–264, states the *differentiae* of Classicism and Romanticism.

PEACOCK, T. L. Works. 3 vols. Lond. : 1875.

Vol. III, pp. 324–338 The Four Ages of Poetry. The article may also be found in Cook's edition of Shelley's Defense of Poetry. See 'Shelley' below.

PERRY, T. S. English Literature in the Eighteenth Century. N. Y. : 1883.

> Pp. 205, 206 The Definition of Poetry.

PHELPS, W. L. The Beginnings of the English Romantic Movement. Boston : 1894.

PLATO. The Dialogues of Plato.

> See Index to the second edition of Jowett's Translation (by E. Abbott. Oxford: 1875), under *Poetry* and *Poets*. The following passages are of especial interest : Rep. 2 : 363, 377 ; 3 : 392, 394 ; 10 : 595, 605–607; Laws, 2 : 656–669; 3 : 391–398, 682, 700; 7 : 801, 811–817 ; 8 : 568, 801, 829 ; 9 : 858 ; 10: 601–605;

11 : 935 ; 14 : 967 ; Protagoras, pp. 325, 326, 347 ; Ion, pp. 532–
534 ; Laches, p. 183 ; Apology, p. 22 ; Gorgias, p. 502 ; Lysis,
pp. 212, 214 ; Symposium, p. 205. See also under *Plato*, § **9**,
on Imitation, Representation, Creation, etc.

POE, E. A. Works. Ed. by J. H. Ingram. 4 vols. Edinb. :
1875.

> Vol. III, pp. 197–219 The Poetic Principle, pp. 219–265 The
> Rationale of Verse, pp. 266–278 The Philosophy of Composition.

Poe distinguishes between the "poetry of words" and the
general poetic faculty whether merely potential, or expressed
in the other arts. The poetry of words he defines as the "rhythmical creation of beauty." The sole arbiter of poetry is Taste.
The dissertation on the poetic principle is apparently luminous,
but the lights are shifting and uncertain. On the Rationale of
Verse, see below, § **23**.

PRICKARD, A. O. Aristotle on the Art of Poetry. N. Y. :
1891.

The aim of the writer is to present a clear and popular exposition of the contents of the Poetics. The definition of tragedy,
the problem of catharsis, and other mooted points in that
treatise are taken up and handled in a straightforward and
scholarly manner. The notes are of especial value.

PUTTENHAM, GEO. The Arte of English Poesie. Engl. Reprints. . . . Ed. by E. Arber. Lond. : 1869.

> See § **21**, *B* 2, and § **24**, *B* 2.

QUINET, EDGAR. Œuvres complètes. 30 vols. Paris.

> Vol. IX De l'histoire de la poésie.

RAYMOND, G. L. Poetry as a Representative Art. N. Y. :
1886.

ROSENKRANZ, K. Die Poesie und ihre Geschichte. Königsb. :
1855.

> See for notice, § **21**.

Ruskin, J.   Modern Painters.   (See § **8**.)

For the definition of poetry, see vol. III, pp. 10–12, 22 ; vol. V, pp. 163, 166 *et seq*.   Ruskin's peculiar use of the word poetry as common to all the arts is explained in vol. I, p. 8 ; vol. III, p. 13.

Scherer, Edm.   Études critiques sur la littérature contemporaine.   5 vols.   Paris : 1863–89.

> Vol. IV, pp. 25–34 L'avenir de la poésie.

Scherer, Wilhelm.   Poetik.   Hrsg. von R. M. Meyer.   Berlin : 1888.

> See § **21**, *B* 3.

Schiller, J. C. F.   The Aesthetical and Philosophical Essays.   Trans. from the German.   Being vol. VIII of the Cambridge Edition of Schiller's Works.   Boston : 1884.

> Pp. 5–32 Introduction ; pp. 135–148 The Sublime ; pp. 149–174 The Pathetic ; pp. 254–260 The Vulgar in Works of Art ; pp. 261–268 Detached Reflections on Aesthetic Questions ; pp 269–338 On Simple and Sentimental Poetry ; pp. 339–367 On the Stage and on Tragedy.   In general, pp. 33–125 On the Aesthetic Education of Man ; pp. 126–378 Aesthetical Essays.

The Introduction gives a painstaking and profitable though not very lucid outline of Schiller's system of aesthetics and his indebtedness to Lessing, Winckelmann, and Kant.   From the paper entitled Detached Reflections, etc., the student will obtain a fundamental notion of Schiller's theory concerning the relation of the good, the agreeable, the sublime, and the beautiful to Art (adapted from Kant's Kritik der Urtheilskraft).   The special uses of terror and grandeur are illustrated by reference to Greek tragedy.   The essay on the Sublime affirms that if it were not for the beautiful the strife between sense and reason could not be allayed ; if it were not for the sublime, we should be wedded by beauty to the things of this world (for the sublime adds dignity to life) ; if it were not for the pathetic, the sublime could not be elicited, nor tested, nor represented. All these aesthetic values are prerequisite to poetry. In the essay on the Pathetic it is shown that the pathetic has aesthetic value only in as far as it is sublime ; that it requires two conditions, suffering and moral freedom, and that without the latter it becomes cheap. Although the poet may present models of morality, it is not his purpose to inculcate patriotism or temperance or industry, but to affect the heart. Thus he accomplishes by indirection what as an immediate end he would certainly fail of. The limits and use of the commonplace with respect to plastic art and poetry are discussed in the essay on the Vulgar. The best, however, of these essays is that entitled On Simple and Sentimental Poetry. It points out the contrast between the poetry of the child (simple) and the poetry of reflection (sentimental). The former with its realism is the poetry of the Greeks; the latter with its impossible but noble idealism belongs to the Moderns ; and the latter would seem to be more truly in sympathy with nature than the former. Passing to the sentimental poet, the author says that he may represent the impression which objects have made upon him by way either of ridiculing the real aspect of them, or of emphasizing the ideal. The former is satirical poetry ; it reveals the chasm separating the real from the ideal; it includes the satire of pathos or of vengeance (Juvenal, Swift, etc.), and the satire of mirth (Cervantes, Fielding, etc.). The latter is elegiac poetry; it blends nature and the ideal in the product of imagination ; it includes the elegy of sadness, nature lost, the ideal unattained (Ovid, Rousseau, von Kleist, etc.), and the idyl, — nature and ideal realized. The author invests the literary terms here used with the widest possible significance.

For the articles especially devoted to Tragedy, see §§ **38, 41, 47**. For general bibliography the following may be consulted : Sämmtliche Werke (12 vols. in 6. Stuttgart : 1847), Bd. V, pp. 375–383 Ueber den Gebrauch des Chors in der

Tragödie, Bd. XI, pp. 383–483, Bd. XII Aesthetische Schriften;
Sämmtliche Schriften, Hrsg. von R. Köhler (15 vols. in 17.
Stuttgart : 1867–76), Bd. X Aesthetische Schriften, Bd. XIV,
pp. 3–12 Ueber den Gebrauch des Chors in der Tragödie ; The
Aesthetic Letters, Essays, and the Philosophical Letters, Trans.
with an Introduction by J. Weiss (Boston : 1845), pp. 1–338
(see also the Introduction) ; Works : Historical Dramas, etc.
(Trans. Lond. : 1854), pp. 439–444 On the Use of the Chorus
in Tragedy; Jas. Sime, Schiller (Phila. : 1882), pp. 120–126 ;
R. Zimmermann, Versuch einer Schillerschen Aesthetik (Berlin :
1889).

SCHMIDT, J. H. H.   Die Kunstformen d. Griechischen Poesie
    u. ihre Bedeutung.   4 vols.   Leipz. : 1868–72.

SCHOPENHAUER, A.   World as Will and as Idea.   Transl. by
    R. B. Haldane and J. Kemp.   3 vols.   Lond. : 1883.

> Vol. I, pp. 313–340; vol. II, pp. 200–219 The Aesthetics of Poetry.

To appreciate Schopenhauer's conception of poetry it is
necessary to read his statement of the Object of Art, vol. I,
p. 219.   Attempting to base his theory of the Idea as realization of the Will upon Plato and Kant, he proceeds to establish
a hierarchy of the arts as more or less perfect manifestations
of the Idea.   The idea that is objectified in the plastic arts is
the human form ; the idea that is manifested in poetry is human
action.   Poetry is the highest of the arts whose existence
depends upon the manifestation of the Idea.   But the climax
of all art is music, for it presents not ideas but the Will itself
(back of ideas).   Passing to poetry by way of a discussion of
the unsuitableness of allegory in plastic art, and its place in the
art of language, Schopenhauer grades the types of poetry
according to their objectivity.   Tragedy, in which the writer
forgets himself utterly, and, as if " inspired," preaches the " will
to die," is the highest type of poetry.

The remarks on the relation of verse to poetry; of poetry to history; of classic to romantic poetry; and of ancient tragedy to modern, are fresh and suggestive. The reader who picks his way with discrimination through aphorisms and fallacies will find in Schopenhauer no insignificant contribution to poetics.

SCHOPENHAUER, A. The Art of Literature. Trans. by B. Saunders. Lond.: 1891.

SCUDDER, VIDA D. *And. Rev.* 8: 225, 351 The Effect of the Scientific Temper in Modern Poetry.

SELKIRK, J. B. Ethics and Aesthetics of Modern Poetry. Lond.: 1878.

The chapters are principally from *Blackwood's Magazine* and *Cornhill*. They treat somewhat discursively of the position assumed by modern poetry in the face of modern scepticism, modern creeds, modern mysticism, aesthetics, and culture. The poets most carefully considered are Clough, Swinburne, Arnold, Tennyson, and Browning. The author's style is marked by grace and perspicacity.

SHAIRP, J. C. Studies in Philosophy and Poetry. N. Y.: 1872. Lond.: 1878.

SHAIRP, J. C. The Poetic Interpretation of Nature. Lond.: 1877.

SHAIRP, J. C. Aspects of Poetry. Boston: 1882.

The Aspects of Poetry is a very important book. In the chapter entitled The Province of Poetry (pp. 1–30) is a discussion of the unconsciousness of the poetic impulse, of the part played by imagination, and of the purely aesthetic, and indirect ethical, purpose. The author is not in doubt concerning the theory of moral indifference in art. He correlates high poetical effect and high moral ideal. (Cf. Arnold's "criticism of life.") In pp. 56–104, the Spiritual Side of Poetry, and the Poet as a Revealer, the author emphasizes the ethical aspect of the art. Compare Wordsworth's statement of the poetic or prophetic function. The chapter on Style in Modern English poetry must be read as a commentary upon Wordsworth's Prefaces. Compare with it, Bagehot's article on the Pure, the Ornate, and the Grotesque. In Studies in Poetry, the essay on Wordsworth, The Man and the Poet, throws additional light on the bases and functions of poetry. The volume on the Poetic Interpretation of Nature should be read in connection with Professor Veitch's Nature in Scottish poetry. Together they form an admirable introduction to the literary history of the love of nature.

SHELLEY, P. B. Works. Ed. by H. B. Forman. 8 vols. Lond. : 1880.

> Vol. VII, pp. 99–144 Defense of Poetry, pp. 145, 146 Three Fragments on Beauty.

SHELLEY, P. B. A Defense of Poetry. Ed. by A. S. Cook. Boston : 1891. (Contains also Peacock's Four Ages of Poetry.)

A sympathetic and creative rather than a comprehensive or an analytic discussion of the subject. The interest centres upon the educative, legislative, and theological, as well as the artistic function, ascribed to the poet (*vide* p. 104). Consideration should be given to the statement that although poetry has always aimed at a harmonious recurrence of sound, still "the distinction between poets and prose writers is a vulgar error"; also to the explanation (p. 109) of the pleasure which poetry gives to maker as well as auditor ; also to the alleged immorality of poetry, to the poetic quality of Christianity, and to the so-called definition (p. 138), 'Poetry is the record of the best and happiest moments of the happiest and best minds.'

This prose-poem might profitably be read in connection with the Ion, the Philebus, the Phaedrus, and the Symposium of Plato. It should be compared with Peacock's Satirical Four Ages of Poetry, to which, in Shelley's words, it was designed as an antidote.

SIDNEY, SIR PHILIP. Apologie for Poetrie. Engl. Reprints. . . . Ed. by E. Arber. Lond. : 1868.

SIDNEY, SIR PHILIP. The Defense of Poesy. Ed. by Albert S. Cook. Boston : 1890.

SIDNEY, SIR PHILIP. The Defense of Poesy. Ed. by Evelyn S. Shuckburgh. (University Press.) Cambr. : 1891.

As a source for the history of English Criticism, and one of the earliest English essays characterized by philosophical grasp and scholarly grace, this work is of supreme importance (see § 21, *B* 2) ; as an authority on poetry it added little or nothing to what had been said by the critics of Greece and Rome, save where it adapted the theories of contemporary and preceding Italian critics. In connection with the references made to Italian criticism in Professor Cook's edition, see Mod. Lang. Notes, vol. VI, pp. 97–101. While according due homage to Sidney, the poet and chevalier, and due consideration to the idealism of his poetic theory, critics nowadays turn to an aesthetic more scientific than could be known to the Elizabethans — a system based upon psychology and the comparative study of literature and art. For an interesting comparison of Sidney's and Aristotle's poetics, see C. Quossek's Sidney's Defense of Poetry u. d. Poetik d. Arist. (Crefeld : 1880).

SPIELHAGEN, F. Aus meiner Studienmappe. Beiträge zur litt. Aesthetik und Kritik. 2. Aufl. Berlin : 1891.

Pp. 63–76 Wahrscheinlichkeit in der Dichtung.

Thinks that the poet by the exercise of despotic power should compel improbabilities to work his purpose.

STEDMAN, EDMUND C.   The Nature and Elements of Poetry.
    Boston : 1892.

Note especially the part played by "Melancholia" in modern
poetry.   Careful discrimination is made between poetry which
expresses the self-consciousness of the author, and that which
represents life and thought apart from his individuality.   The
noblest poetry is impersonal.   Poetry is defined as "rhythmical,
imaginative language expressing the invention, taste, thought,
passion, and insight of the human soul."

SUTERMEISTER, O.   Leitfaden der Poetik.   2. verb. Aufl. Zürich:
    1874.

    See for notice, § **21**, *B* 3.

SWINBURNE, A. C.   *19th Century*, 15 : 583, 764 Wordsworth
    and Byron.

A combatant in the Wordsworth-Byron-Shelley controversy,
"who desires above all things to preserve in all things the
golden mean of scrupulous moderation"; who mildly characterizes the poetic inspiration of Byron as a "drawling, drag-
gle-tailed drab of a Muse, moderately censures his "gasping,
ranting, wheezing, broken-winded verse," — "bristling with
every sort and kind of barbarism and solecism, not to speak of
its tune which suggests the love-strains of a baboon," — and
with scrupulous courtesy reproaches Matthew Arnold for casting the shield of his authority over such "unutterable rubbish,"
instead of letting it "rot."   The author deems imagination
and harmony the primary elements of poetry ; requires a perceptible but indefinable charm ; and exhorts the reader not to be
a Wordsworthian, — though it is better to be a Wordsworthian
than a Byronite.   As for himself, he prefers the "nebulosity of
Shelley at his cloudiest to the raggedness of Wordsworth at his
raggedest."   With Swinburne's indefinable element in poetry
may be compared Gurney's theory, in Tertium Quid, and

Lowell's definition, in Lecture I of the Lowell Institute Lectures
on the English Poets.   See also Swinburne's William Blake.

THOREAU, H. D.   Concord and Merrimack Rivers.   Boston :
    1894.

See the passage beginning p. 494.   " A true poem," says
Thoreau, " is distinguished not so much by a felicitous expression, or any thought it suggests, as by the atmosphere which
surrounds it."   A division of poetry is suggested.

VIEHOFF, H.   Die Poetik auf der Grundlage der Erfahrungs-
    seelenlehre.   Hrsg. von Victor Kiy.   2 vols. in 1.   Trier :
    1888.

The value of this work is not yet properly appreciated by
English students of aesthetics.   Laying a substantial foundation in the Psychology of Aesthetics (vol. I, Bk. I), the author
constructs a psychological system of poetics.   He describes
skilfully the manner in which poetry satisfies the impulse for
pleasure.   Pleasure he defines as attaining its fulfilment in
the happiness of the species.   Cf. with Viehoff's theory that of
Dallas mentioned above.

While in some respects Viehoff gives his assent to the aesthetics of Fechner, he differs from him in particulars, as, for
instance, on the principle of the aesthetic balancing of opposites (p. 217).

Book II treats of Aesthetic Laws and the Means of Art.
Vol. II, Bk. I, is technical, and treats of the Structure of Verse
and Strophe ; Bk. II, on the Theory of Types in Literature,
most directly concerns the student of poetry.   Especially noteworthy is chap. I, pp. 461–469.

WACKERNAGEL, W.   Poetik, Rhetorik, und Stilistik.   Hrsg. von
    L. Sieber.   Halle : 1873.   See § **21,** *B 3*.

WAGNER, J. J.   Dichterschule.   3. Aufl.   Ulm : 1850.

WARD, T. H. (Ed.) English Poets : Selections, with critical introductions by various authors, and a general introduction by Matthew Arnold. 4 vols. Lond. and N. Y. : 1881.

WARTON, THOMAS. History of English Poetry. Ed. by W. C. Hazlitt. 4 vols. Lond. : 1871.

> See Courthope's Liberal Movement, p. 121.

WATTS, THEODORE. Article ' Poetry ' in Encyclopaedia Britannica, 9th ed.

For a general survey of the history of poetry and of the more important problems of aesthetics involved, this article is especially commended to the student. The following questions are suggested : Is the distinction made by Mr. Watts between relative and absolute vision satisfactory ? Does it mean merely that in degree some men are more poetic than others ? Do the examples cited of egoistic imagination and dramatic imagination emphasize the distinction that Mr. Watts would make ? Does the fact that the *dramatis persona* occasionally expresses sentiments which any one else might express diminish the characteristic of the *dramatis persona* or betoken lack of insight on the part of the dramatist ? Does not one's estimate of the *vision* displayed in a drama or an epic depend upon the relativity or absoluteness of one's own aesthetic vision ?

Mr. Watts's criticism of Hegel's statement of the destiny of art tends to confuse the general with the absolute. But leaving the question of comparative poetic vision on one side, the statement of the nature of poetry, of its relation to music and the other arts, and of the importance of its kinds, can hardly be surpassed for simplicity and clearness.

WEBBE, WM. A Discourse of English Poetrie. Engl. Reprints. . . . Ed. by E. Arber. Lond. : 1870.

> See § **24,** *B* 2.

WOLFF, EUG.   *Zeitschrift f. vergl. Litteratur*, 6 : 423 Vorstudien
    zur Poetik.

Outlines a scheme for an inductive poetics under the following heads: 1. Methodik. 2. (*a*) Theomorphismus; (*b*) He-
roomorphismus; (*c*) Anthropomorphismus, Physiomorphismus
und Ergebnis. 3. Zur Entwickelungsgeschichte des Dramas :
(*a*) Tragödie ; (*b*) Komödie. 4. Wirkung der Poesie.

WORDSWORTH, W. Prose works. Ed. by A. B. Grosart. 3 vols.
    Lond. : 1876.

> Vol. II, pp. 77–214 Essays, Letters, and Notes, elucidatory and
> confirmatory of his Poems.

WORDSWORTH, W.   Prefaces and Essays on Poetry (1798–
    1845). Ed. by A. J. George. Boston : 1892.

Of these articles the more important are the Prefaces to the
Lyrical Ballads (1800, enlarged 1802), Appendix on Poetic
Diction (1802), Preface to Poems (1815, Powers requisite for
the Poet and the Kinds of Poetry), and the Essay supplementary to the Preface of 1815 (Sketch of English Poetry).

The long-continued controversy concerning the doctrine and
practice of Wordsworth in poetry was originated by the preface
to the second edition of the Lyrical Ballads. The student of
modern English poetics should make a careful examination
of Wordsworth's theories in connection (1) with his poetry ;
(2) with the criticism passed by others upon both his poetry
and his theory ; (3) with the poetics of his English and German
contemporaries and successors. Note especially his advocacy
of the poetic use of the language which springs from states of
vivid emotion, his theory of the choice of commonplace subjects
and the way to present them as novel, his remarks concerning
the lethargy of the fashionable mind in matters of imagination,
the soil from which essential passions best spring, and the
poetic necessity of realizing the ideal in nature rather than of
idealizing the real.

The following is a list of the more important contemporary
reviews of Wordsworth's theory of poetry : *Edinb. Rev.* 2 : 283,
6 : 1, 7 : 16, 11 : 214, 19 : 270, 466, 24 : 1, 25 : 355, 27 : 58, 277,
28 : 488, 37 : 449; *Blackw.* 1 : 261, 2 : 201, 5 : 130, 26 : 453;
Quarterly Rev. 14 : 201, 52 : 317 ; *Fraser's* 6 : 607, 42 : 119 ;
Dublin Univ. 5 : 680; *North Am. Rev.* 18 : 356.   See also
Coleridge, Biographia Literaria.

See notes on Arnold, Austin, Bagehot, Courthope, Gurney,
Pater, Swinburne.   See also Brunswick's Wordsworth's Theorie
der Poetischen Kunst (Progr.   Halle : 1884).

Miscellaneous References. — Of magazine articles, not
already mentioned, the following deserve attention : Vida D.
Scudder, *Andover Rev.* 8 : 225, 351 Effect of the Scientific
Temper in Modern Poetry ; *Blackwood*, 6 : 363 Progressive
Changes in Poetical Style, 11 : 153 How far is Poetry an Art ?
27 : 706 Art of Poetry, 38 : 829 Philosophy of Poetry, 132 : 158
Poetry of the Future ; Wm. Knight, *Brit. Q.* (Am. ed.) 57 : 92
A Theory of Poetry ; E. Dowden, *Contemp.* 2 : 535 Poetical
Feeling for Nature (cf. his Studies in Literature); V. Lee,
Contemp. 39 : 682 Morality in Poetry (Repr. in Belcaro) ; F. T.
Palgrave, *Fortn.* 12 : 163 Scientific Study of Poetry ; J. A.
Symonds, *Fortn.* 32 : 686 M. Arnold on Poetry ; P. Bourget,
Fortn. 49 : 568 Science et Poésie; E. Gosse, *Forum*, 7 : 175
What is a Great Poet? *Herrig's Archiv*, 10 : 112 Sprache d.
Poesie u. Poesie d. Sprache, 45 : 35 Ueber d. aesthet.-psychol.
Beurtheilung e. Dichters, 45 : 58 Ueber Wesen u. Zweck d.
Kunst u. d. Poesie ; A. Bettelheim, *Nation* (Berlin), 1891, p. 746
Eine neue Theorie der Dichtkunst ; A. Tilley, *Macm.* 44 : 268
Two Theories of Poetry, 53 : 184 The Poetic Imagination ;
E. A. Sonnenschein, *Macm.* 53 : 5 Culture and Science ; F. T.
Palgrave, *Macm.* 53 : 332 Province and Study of Poetry ; F. T.
Whittaker, *Macm.* 53 : 428 Musical and Picturesque Elements
in Poetry ; M.-J. Guyau, *Rev. Philos.* 17 : 179, 258 L'Esthétique

du vers moderne ; D. Tarrozo, *Rev. Philos.* 18 : 232 A Poesia
Philosophica (Rev. by B. Perez) ; Felix Klein, *Le Correspondant,* 120 : 641 La poésie et le temps présent ; H. Roettiker,
Zeitschrift f. vergl. Litt. 4 : 17 Zur Lehre von den Darstellungs-
mitteln in der Poesie ; Veit Valentin, *Zeitschrift f. vergl. Litt.*
5 : 35 Poetische Gattungen ; Walt Whitman, *No. Am. Rev.*
132 : 195 Poetry of the Future ; C. Thomas, *Open Court,*
3 : 1727 Poetry and Science, *Forum,* 25 : 503 Have We Still
Need of Poetry ?

Most of the following programmes and dissertations are men-
tioned by Hermann Varnhagen in his Systematisches Verzeich-
niss (Anhang to Supplement to Schmitz, Encycl. d. philol.
Studiums), p. 18 : H. Würtzer, De origine et natura poëseos
(Gött. : 1780) ; P. Weierstrass, De poesis natura et partitione
(Deutsche Crone Gymn. : 1851) ; H. Schreiber, Allgemeine
Grundsätze d. Dichtkunst (nach Horaz) (Freiburg i. Br.: 1823) ;
J. J. Dielschneider, Ueber die Poesie (Köln : 1839) ; B.
Piringer, Ueber Wesen u. Bedeutung d. Poesie (Kremsmün-
ster : 1851) ; G. Jauss, Der ideale Gehalt d. Poesie als bilden-
der Element (Oberschützen : 1868) ; Th. Schönborn, Ueber d.
Ursprung d. Naturpoesie (Breslau : 1873); Köster, Kurze
Darstellung d. Dichtungsarten (Barmen : 1837) ; C. N. Sacher,
Die Grundformen d. Poesie, u. s. w. (Brüx.: 1862) ; Valentin,
Der Rhythmus als Grundlage einer wissensch. Poetik (Frank-
furt a. M. : 1870) ; Rud. Eckart, Die didaktische Poesie, ihr
Wesen u. ihre Vertreter (Hannover : 1891).

For a few other definitions of poetry, the following may
be consulted :

W. C. Bryant, Writings (Ed. by Godwin. 2 vols. N. Y. :
1884; vol. I, pp. 3–34 Lectures on Poetry, pp. 57–67 Trisyl-
labic Feet in Iambic Measure), vol. I, p. 6 (Poetry selects and
arranges the symbols of thought in such a way as to excite the
mind most powerfully and delightfully) ; Alex. Bain, Engl.
Comp. and Rhet., p. 257 (Poetry operates by means of thought

conveyed in language) ; H. Blair, Lectures on Rhetoric and
Belles Lettres (Phil.: 1860), p. 421 (Poetry is the language of
passion, of enlivened imagination formed ordinarily into regular
numbers) ; J. Bascom, Philosophy of Rhetoric, p. 33 (Poetry, in
its strictly characteristic form, is emotional conception expressed
in metrical language) ; Sir Redmond Barry, Dublin Afternoon
Lectures : On Music and Poetry, p. 15 (Poetry creates from
intellectual materials by imaginative effort that which arouses
aesthetic emotion of any kind, but it adorns the creation so
that it captivates the senses, surprises the mind, agitates the
passions.   It may impersonate the ideal, or endow with life the
inanimate) ; Byron, Don Juan (Poetry is but passion) ; G. W.
Cook, Poets and Problems, p. 25 (A restatement of the views of
Wordsworth and Coleridge) ; T. Carlyle, Essay on Goethe,
Heroes and Hero-Worship (in the former essay Carlyle shows
that "the true poet is ever, as of old, the Seer,"— a thought
elaborated by Browning in his article on Shelley, — in the
latter essay Carlyle calls poetry musical thought, and explains
music as that which penetrates the harmony of the idea and
expresses it in sound) ; Sir K. Digby, Two Treatises on the
Nature of Bodies and the Nature of Man's Soul (Lond.: 1658.
A quaint and delightful passage on Poetry in the second Treatise, p. 35) ; *Dublin University Mag.* 45 : 471 De Re Poetica
(Poetry is a longing for a more excellent beauty than the things
which are seen can supply, an upward and outward instinct
uttered by gifted persons in musical and modulated words, —
gently delighting itself and others by its creations); H. Heine,
Die Romantische Schule (Trans. as The Romantic School, by
S. F. Fleischmann.   N. Y. : 1882.   According to Heine the
poet understands the symbol of religion and the abstract idea
of philosophy, but the religions and philosophy do not understand the poet.   The poet resembles God in creating characters
after his own image.   See Scintillations, pp. 84, 120 *et seq.*);
Geo. Harris, The Theory of the Arts (2 vols.   Lond.: 1869),

see vol. I, Poetry (It arises by a process of selection from the commonplaces of thought and expression. It excels in suggestion; painting in representation. Its object is to inform and to delight) ; R. G. Hazard, Essays on Language, p. 30 (Poetry is regarded as the 'language of ideality') ; Sir John Lubbock, Essay on Poetry (Poetry lengthens life by creating for us Time, which is the succession of ideas, not of minutes) ; Longfellow, Essay on the Defense of Poetry, in his Prose Works (Poetry, a longing for the ideal; the spirit of the age itself embodied in the forms of language and addressing the external as well as the internal sense) ; E. R. Sill, *Atlantic*, 56 : 665 Principles of Criticism (Poetry is the expression in rhythmic language of some serious thought by the suggestion of that thought through the imagination) ; E. P. Whipple, Essays and Reviews, vol. I, p. 300 *et seq.* (Poetry is the protest of genius against the unreality of actual life. It perceives what is real and permanent. It actualizes real life for the imagination in forms of grandeur and beauty corresponding to the essential truth of things. It is the record left by the greatest men of any of their aspirations after a truth and reality above their age) ; E. C. Moyse, Poetry as a Fine Art (Lond. : 1883).

CHAPTER V.

THE HISTORICAL STUDY OF POETRY.

§ 21, *A.*   It is the purpose of this chapter to indicate some of the methods and materials that may be useful in the investigation of poetry in its historical development.[1]   The suggestions made may, with the proper modifications, be applied to the study of literary history in general.

No treatise in English covers this subject.   On the conception of literary history and its boundaries, the student should consult Paul's Grundriss der germanischen Philologie, 1 : 215–217, and Boeckh's Encyklopädie der philologischen Wissenschaften, p. 648 *et seq.*   The authorities on method are cited in various places in this chapter.

1.   The AIM of the historian is to determine the facts in the division of literature under investigation, and their relation to each other, to discover their characteristics, and record the results obtained (Körting, Encykl. d. roman Philol. 2 : 482). Whatever the historian's conception of poetry, its significance or its boundaries, he must include in his intention the following objects : to determine the literary productions necessary to the complete understanding of the period, type, or movement concerned, and to test the genuineness of these productions ; to interpret each in the light of its special purpose, its author's individuality, and its social and cultural antecedents ; to consider it in its relation to its environment (epoch and country) ;

---

[1] For guidance in the study of the Origins of Poetry, the student is referred to the chapter on Comparative Literature, § **18**, 2, above.

to ascertain its historical position and its influence upon life and thought, especially its influence upon the literary organism of which it is a factor ; to gauge its originality as a work of art, and, finally, to estimate its relative or absolute aesthetic significance.

2. There are three ways of APPROACHING THE SUBJECT : the Chronological (or linear), the Encyclopedic, and the Cyclic. (See Boeckh, Encykl. d. philol. Wiss., pp. 46, 47, for a discussion of the first and third.)   None of these alone is sufficient ; but in its own place, in connection with and dependence upon the others, each is indispensable.   The *first* is the method of experience, the manner in which the investigator would naturally approach an unfamiliar aggregate of materials.   When the subject is a section of literary history, the details — the productions that constitute it — must first, of course, be arranged in chronological order.   And in so far as the student confines his examination of the materials to external criticism, remembers that the order determined is necessarily experimental, and resists the temptation of arguing *post hoc, ergo propter hoc*, the investigation is of fundamental importance.   Ground has been broken, the first stakes have been driven, the element of sequence in time has been established.   But the student will not rest satisfied with this kind of criticism.   If he has noticed the nature and contents of the materials, he detects, or thinks that he detects, resemblances and differences between production and production, characteristics suggestive of a classification according to kinds.   The literature of a nation or of a period appears, for instance, to fall into forms or moulds : epic, lyric, dramatic, etc. The method of approach then becomes *encyclopedic :* a judicial, not an historical, survey of the field ; and it has in view to discover similarities of characteristic, of aspect, or merely of apparent (*a priori*) interrelation, and on that basis to form generalizations concerning the kinds possible, and the laws that govern each as distinct from the others.   Unless such a survey, whether made at first-hand or not, is systematic, the conclusions

will be inadequate, superficial, or confused. But if the review, even when dependent upon guides, *résumés*, and other authorities, is conducted with logical system ; if the materials and hypotheses thus gleaned are frequently tested by inspection of the originals, the results of the study will be useful. They are tentative, but suggestive so far as they go. A first-hand encyclopedic investigation would be preferable, but life is short. The element of resemblance has been recognized, a provisional cross-section of the subject has been made, a method of logical division established ; and it would seem that the characteristics of literary genera might be formulated. But, since the hypotheses of the encyclopedic method are largely *a priori*, and since the process treats the literature of a country or period as a completed or 'static' organism, the characteristics evinced by the several 'fixed' kinds of literature, thus regarded, are neither sufficiently precise nor sufficiently representative to yield criteria or models by which specimens in general may be tested. Criteria drawn, for instance, from the practice of three or four standard ancient poems classified as 'epical' should not be applied to the classification of poems apparently similar but produced under different conditions : as, for instance, when period, or country, or the stage of social, political, or aesthetic development is different. In fact, the linear and encyclopedic methods break down because they are only preliminary. The final and scientific method is the *cyclic*. It does not dispense with the discipline of the two former, nor with the results provided by them, but, proceeding on the principles of rational sequence and organic development, it corrects defective conclusions based upon temporal sequence and formal resemblance. It is dynamic. Beginning with an integral and definite subject, the cyclic method regards this particular as a living organism, studies first the conditions and laws of its existence, advances to the conditions and laws of its environment, and finally interprets the particular in terms of the vital and rational relations by which it is characterized as an individual and, at the same time, as a component of a system. The cyclic method provides from the outset for discipline and progress, for it begins with the unit and by a process of radiation widens the field until it has exhausted the organism.

3. The MATERIALS are twofold : Sources and Guides. The Sources may be classified as absolute and relative. The *absolute* include texts of manuscripts and editions, and original biographical materials pertaining to the subject. The *relative* are contemporary and subsequent notices, oral tradition, and the histories of culture national or general, whether of art, society, religion, or politics, that may illustrate the significance, position, and value of the work under consideration.

Guides are also of two kinds, those that indicate materials and those that indicate methods. To the *former* class belong histories of the subject or of any part of it. These may of course enumerate sources, but they indicate problems as well, and results so far as attained. The *latter* class provides the instruments applicable to the investigation and the means by which we may determine the value and history of each. Guides of this kind are (*a*) those that indicate the methods already prescribed for this investigation or found available in subsidiary or kindred lines, as in the theory of aesthetics, of poetry, of criticism ; methods derived from the consideration of principles, from experience, or from the general science of ' methodology '; and (*b*) those that indicate models of investigation and arrangement : histories of aesthetics, of criticism, of philology.

Bibliographies may be regarded as guides to both materials and methods. (Körting, Grundr. d. rom. Philol. 2 : 488–499; Boeckh, Encykl., pp. 49, 50, 122 *et seq.*, 156, 169–254; Paul, Grundr. d. germ. Philol. 1 : 188, 217–220.)

4. The PROCESS adopted by the historian involves the following Steps : first, the investigation of individual productions ; second, the discovery of the relation existing between each

production and its environment (historical, racial, social, artistic, and personal) ; third, the arrangement of results in an organic whole. But while from the point of view of method the steps should be considered in this order, it will be evident that the first and second cannot be regarded as mutually exclusive divisions, and that the third must be continually present to the mind of the student.

The process involves also the application of Criteria. For as purporting to constitute the literary stock-in-trade of the nationality, period, movement, type, or author in question, the productions must be tested by such methods as may determine their value intrinsic and relative. These methods are the lower or textual criticism, the higher or literary-historical criticism, and the aesthetic criticism. The lower criticism aims to determine in what relation the transmitted wording of the text stands to the wording of the original ; the higher criticism, to determine by whom, at what time, in what place, and under what circumstances the literary work was composed ; the aesthetic criticism, to determine in what degree the literary production satisfies the requirements of the beautiful (Körting, Grundr. 2 : 374–407). In the examination of individual productions the first and second of these methods prevail ; in the determination of relations between productions and environment the second and third are especially in requisition ; but in each stage of the historical process the critic may more or less avail himself of any one of the three methods of criticism.

Let us, then, consider the process by its Steps or Stages.

First: The Investigation of Individual Productions. — *a.* To ascertain the **Authentic Form** of the literary monument, or the most trustworthy copy or edition of it, the various tests of textual criticism must be applied. (For detailed statement, see Paul, Grundr. d. germ. Philol. 1 : 176–188 ; Boeckh, Encykl. d. phil. Wiss., pp. 179–210 ; Körting, Encykl. d. rom. Phil.

2 : 382–399.) Testimony concerning the life of the author, the origin of the work, the dates of composition and publication, the motive of composition and the materials employed, the contemporary and subsequent notices of it, — testimony concerning all in fact that may go to determine the authenticity of the text, — must be collected and sifted. The conclusions of former historians are to be weighed and the evidence of language and of contemporary culture to be considered ; especially so when direct literary proof of the genuine form of the text is lacking. It will be noticed by the student that textual criticism is therefore essential to the later stages of historical work, and that it requires for its proper prosecution accessory and corroborative material derived from the researches conducted in those later stages of the process. (Paul, Grundr. 1 : 188–192 ; Elze, Grundr. d. engl. Philol., pp. 60–82. Cf. the applications of method by the modern school of Shakespearian scholars, and by the writers of the Early English Text Society Papers.)

b. **The Internal History of the Literary Production.** — In order to determine the importance of individual productions with reference to a literary growth, it is necessary to ascertain the comparative independence or originality of each. This is done by analyzing the production into its elements ; and here the higher or literary criticism begins. Concerning the absolute originality of the literary specimen there will frequently be room for doubt, but a relative originality, a novelty of thought, form, or treatment, may generally be conceded. According to Körting (2 : 485–487), the productions of least originality are translations ; next higher come those that reconstruct or ' work over ' a native or foreign original ; next, those that fuse (*contaminare*) two or more existing works into a new whole, such as Molière's L'Avare, Terence's Adelphoe ; next, those that imitate the general thought and plan of an existing original, but are independent in the execution of details ; next, productions

that adapt in a general way the form rather than the contents
of some existing work ; next, those that revive and incor-
porate in modern form materials of national tradition ; next,
those that similarly avail themselves of foreign folklore ; next,
those that derive their material from real life; and, finally, those
that are of independent invention.

Now it will be observed that the materials here cited must be
drawn either from tradition or from an imaginative conception of
nature and human life.   (1) When, as in the case of translations,
reconstructions, fusion, and, to some extent, of imitation and
adaptation, the material is indirectly derived from tradition, the
historian will subject the poem (or other writing) under examination to a comparison with the production upon which it is based,
and a comparison with the " raw " material of tradition.   When,
however, the poem is directly derived from tradition, the historian must fall back upon the original (in its simplest and
most naïve condition) as the basis of comparison.   If there be
more than one original, he will try to determine the indebtedness of the poem to each, and to ascertain the relative aesthetic
capability of the materials chosen.   If there exist various artistic
reproductions of the same oral or written original, the historian
has, of course, increased opportunity of determining by comparison the idealizing power of the poet.   This is, generally
speaking, a mechanical and objective method of analysis.   But
when (2) the materials of the poem are drawn from nature or
the life of man, the procedure of the student becomes more
subjective.   This is the case even when the poet has recorded
an actual experience.   For although the places, persons, events,
and customs described may be identified with some degree of
precision, still the difficulty of personal verification, the untrust-
worthiness of report regarding remote localities and person-
ages of former times, and the impossibility of reconstructing a
by-gone stage of culture are such that the student will be com-
pelled to have more or less resort to the imagination.   And this

subjective characteristic of the study is still further emphasized when the work under examination is one of purely creative imagination. For only by limiting his analysis of the poet's material to the data of psychological and ethical science can the student resist the temptation to indulge in intuitive methods; as soon as he extends his analysis to the criticism of poetic form and treatment, he finds himself within the realm of aesthetics (see Paul, Grundr. 1 : 221, 222).

c. **The Exposition of the Work.** — The historian must characterize the work in hand so that the reader, even though not directly acquainted with it, may understand its contents and appreciate its quality. The essential must be distinguished from the non-essential, the peculiar from the ordinary or purely conventional. The masterpiece should therefore be studied in itself, in the light of the motives which produced it, of the author's life and character, and of his other works; it must be studied in relation to its materials (see *b* above), its literary antecedents, the genus or type to which it belongs, and its historical and cultural value. Most of these suggestions are self-explanatory. In determining the meaning of a work, while note is made of every revelation, unconscious or intentional, of the author's personality, one must be careful not to read into the poet of former days, and through him into his works, the views and culture of the present; while the poet is considered in relation to his age, one must be careful not to make him a mere reflex of that age; while his characteristics are sought not only in the work under consideration but in his complete works, one must be careful not to give him credit for peculiarities which were common to his generation. To characterize a poetic masterpiece, it is also necessary to determine whether it is the outcome of an established literary movement (using traditional materials or following conventional methods), or is reactionary. If it be reactionary, the question will arise whether the poem reverts to natural and social sources of inspiration,

revives a former literary tradition, or domesticates some fashion
from abroad.   This phase of the study implies a knowledge of
literary movements (see under Arrangement of Results, below).
In addition to a knowledge of the materials of the poem (see
under *b*, p. 355), information must be gathered concerning the
poet's preference in respect of types of character, motives,
situations, aesthetic values, ethical ideals, and literary forms,
and his practice should be compared with that of his contemporaries.   The exposition of the poem demands also a technical
acquaintance with the literary genus or species to which it
belongs ; a comparison of the poet's phraseology with contemporary colloquialisms and with conventional poetic diction.
With regard to style and versification similar inquiries must be
instituted.   (Cf. Elze, Grundr. d. engl. Philol., pp. 343–386 ;
Paul, Grundr. 1 : 222–228.   On the extent to which aesthetic
considerations should be regarded while characterizing a masterpiece, see Paul, Grundr. 1 : 228, 229.)   A knowledge of the
poet's relation to his social and national environment, of the
impulses which moved him to write, and of their influence upon
the character of the literary product is likewise essential to the
exposition of the poem ; but an understanding of environments
and of aesthetic worth implies acquaintance with the stage of
the process to be discussed under the next head.   (On interpretation in general, see Boeckh's Encykl., pp. 79–169 ; Blass's
Hermeneutik u. Kritik, pp. 127–232, in Iwan Müller's Handbuch, vol. I.)

*Second : The Relation of the Literary Production to the National
Life.* — The work is the outcome of literary antecedents, of
national culture, and of the author's individuality as affected by
both of them.   The aspects of the question may accordingly be
considered under these and related heads.

a. **Literary Antecedents.** — By following the genealogy of
a production through the series of its literary predecessors, a

critic aims to discover the successive modifications of material, treatment, and form, through which the phenomenon has passed, and to trace it to its source in the national life ; that is to say, to its ultimate objective impulse.   Such literary genealogies of elements, if not of the whole tradition, may frequently be traced beyond the earliest national to a foreign origin. Examine, for instance, Tennyson's Idylls of the King, Spenser's Faery Queene, Chaucer's Canterbury Tales, several of Boccaccio's Tales, Chrestien de Troyes's Le Roman de Cligès, several of Shakespeare's plays and the romantic dramas of his contemporaries, the "Restoration" drama of manners, the Spanish, French, and English novels of the fourteenth, fifteenth, and sixteenth centuries, the drama of the French Classical School, Latin elegiac poetry, etc.   In respect of literary fashions of the purely artificial sort such inherited characteristics can still more readily be traced.   (Cf. Marinism, the 'conceptism' of Quevedo, the 'cultism' of Gongora, the Senecan tragedy in England, the Euphuism of Lyly and the 'preciosity' of l'hôtel de Rambouillet ; and see Körting, 2 : 450.)

b. **National Culture.** — Contemporary and foregoing phases of culture may be regarded as pouring themselves into the literary production through the channels of race, environment, art, and the period.   The work in question must therefore be studied with reference to the history of the people, both institutional (social, religious, and political) and internal (emotional, theoretical, and ethical).   It should, in the second place, be studied as the expression, to a certain extent, of physical and psychical surroundings.   In the third place, it should be regarded not simply as the descendant of a line of literary ancestors, but as related to the arts in general, — to allied arts, such as music, histrionics, and dancing ; to industries, such as printing ; to the history of national art, and especially to existing states of artistic production and of the aesthetic consciousness.   The development of poetry should, indeed, be traced more rigorously

than it generally is, in connection with or in analogy with the
successive stages of the national history of art.   In the fourth
place, the poem should be considered as the offspring of the
moment or period in which it was produced ; and as such it
may, *vice versa*, prove to be an index to some phase or other
of national sentiment.   (Cf. Paul, Grundr. 1 : 216–217 ; Hegel,
Aesth. 1 : 20, 45 ; Taine's formula of aesthetic influences;
Brunetière, L'Évolution des genres, 1 : 22 ; Körting, Encykl.
2 : 455.)

   c. The Personality of the Poet. — It is through the medium
of personality that literary and national antecedents are focused
in the poetic production.   The investigation of the poet's
personality includes, therefore, a study of his relation to the
community, his family, his friends, his important contemporaries, and to the literary, social, religious, and political institutions of his country and of other lands.   Of significance,
moreover, is the extent to which all these in turn modify, or are
modified by, the character of the man — as composed of traits,
personal, moral, and spiritual, inherited and acquired — displayed in the body of his imaginative work and in his life.

   On the comparative value of sources of biographical information, autobiographies, letters, occasional confessions in
the author's works, records, the testimony of contemporaries, oral tradition, subsequent literary reviews, references, allusions, citations, etc., see Paul, Grundr. 1 : 217, 218 ; Boeckh's
Encykl., pp. 124–140, 210–240; Körting's Encykl. 2 : 483,
484.

   From this process of investigation the student will have
acquired the materials necessary for the more exhaustive exposition of the artistic production.   He will also have discovered,
through the medium of the author's personality, the bearing of
the literary work upon national life and culture.   It will be
evident that producer and product together form a component
part of a social organism.

d. But if the historian would properly gauge the importance of the production in the history of national culture (see *b*, p. 359), he must determine its **Aesthetic Worth** as well. For the general consideration of aesthetic values and aesthetic tests, reference may be made to §§ **7–9** of this volume, above ; but for a brief statement of the matter in its literary aspect, see Körting's Encykl. d. roman. Philol. 2 : 399–403 ; Paul, Grundr. 1 : 228, 229 ; Boeckh's Encykl., pp. 240–254 Gattungskritik. Körting, whose sketch of the subject is simple and direct, classifies aesthetic worth as absolute or relative. The *absolute* aesthetic worth of a literary production is decided on its own merits purely, without reference to the stage of culture which it occupies, its artistic environment, or the value of similar productions of the past or present. A work of absolute aesthetic worth has universal import ; it belongs to the literature of the world. The *relative* aesthetic worth of a literary production is determined by comparing it with similar productions of the nation, and especially of the period. A work may stand relatively to the narrow or undeveloped literature of the race very high, but absolutely very low. Aesthetic criticism is always liable to personal bias or prejudice, but the investigator can, in some degree, guard himself against unfair decisions by subjecting the production under examination to the following questions : (1) Is the tendency of the work worthy? (2) Is the material (the subject) worthy and conformable to the tendency already described ? (3) Is the subject fittingly and artistically handled ? *i.e.*, is the technical composition or treatment successful ? (4) Is the style appropriate and artistic ? (5) If the work is a poem, is the rhythmical (metrical) form appropriate and artistic ? (6) If epic or dramatic, does the execution of the story satisfy the requirements of essential probability ? Are the characters psychologically true and consistent ? Do the descriptions (epic) satisfy the requirements of probability ? Other tests will suggest themselves to the critic.

For an elaboration of these, see Körting as above. But all
such tests are reducible to three : Does the work possess qualities of ideal worth, of universal acceptability, of permanent
vitality ?   Now, when this interrogatory can be unreservedly
answered in the affirmative, the production concerned may
safely be esteemed as of absolute aesthetic value ; but when, in
answer to the interrogatory, reference must be had to the
spirit and productions of the people or the period, the work in
question is probably of relative, not of absolute, aesthetic value.
(Cf. M. Arnold, Lewes, Spenser, Ruskin, Stedman, Watts,
Santayana's Sense of Beauty, Gneisse's Schiller's Aesthetische
Wahrnehmung, etc., Gosse, Mod. Engl. Lit., Epilogue.   See, in
general, § **21**, *B* 2, below.)

e. **The Dynamic Relation of the Literary Work to Life and
Thought.** — For this consideration the preceding studies have
cleared the way.   It constitutes the natural transition to the
arrangement of results.   The student has so far regarded the
production under examination as affected by literary, national,
and other influences ; he now regards it as reacting upon its
environment.   (See p. 360, *c*, above.)   He aims to discover
its effect upon the literary life of the nation or the world.   This
effect he may find explicitly estimated by contemporary writers,
recognized informally by them and their successors, or uncon-
fessed but patent in the modification of literary thought and
style.   Its wider influence, aesthetic, religious, social, political, he will find (1) certified by authorities in these fields or
(2) proved, though with an ever waning degree of certainty,
by its bearing upon the concrete institutions of life, by conclusions drawn from inference, or by the uncertain vogue of
tradition.

Third : The Arrangement of Results. — The results of the previous investigation must be arranged with due regard to rationality, continuity, and the interdependence of parts (uniformity) ;

otherwise the growth of the literary period or type will escape observation. Any such organism may be regarded as national or as general (universal).

a. **National Histories of Poetry** (*i.e., of Literary Art*). — The nation, as here understood, is a political and cultural unit, to which identity of race and country, and community of language are more or less contributory. Though the literature of the nation may not be all in one language (cf. the Latin and French literature of the English nation), nor produced by one race (cf. the Irish contributions to English literature), nor — even if produced by one race in one language — confined to one country (cf. the literature of the English colonies and dependencies), still, a national literature is characterized by common political and cultural relations which unite in an unmistakable whole the results of observation, action, feeling, and imagination within their sphere of influence. One is, therefore, justified in regarding a certain body of poetry as national.

As to the proper arrangement of productions within this unit, there is diversity of opinion. Körting (Encykl. 2 : 442, 443) mentions three kinds of relations which may exist between literary works : the External, grouping by authors or schools of authors, by periods of composition, by the localities in which produced ; the Formal, grouping by actual (artistic or non-artistic), linguistic (ordinary or aesthetic), or rhythmical (verse or prose), correspondence of form, or by the method of address (to the individual, the special audience, or the public) adopted by the author ; the Internal, grouping by (1) the tendency of the writings (impersonal, reflective, critical, scientific, moral, religious, etc.) and (2) their composite character, inclusive of the nature of the material (borrowed or invented, elevated or commonplace, popular or learned), the arrangement of the material, the relation of the author to the material (objective or subjective, and — if subjective — sympathetic, ironical, humorous, etc.), and the resulting aesthetic worth. Choosing the internal rela-

tion as a basis of classification, he arranges productions according to the literary kinds or types (Litteraturgattungen) and
literary currents or movements (Litteraturströmungen). Boeckh
(Encykl., p. 648) strongly advocates the arrangement according
to types or species (epic, lyric, dramatic), calling it the generic
or eidographic method; but he appreciates the objection
brought against this method, namely, that though it preserves
the continuity of the type, it ignores or slights the element of
synchronism ; and accordingly he later advocates (Encykl.,
pp. 742–745 Methodologischer Zusatz) a combination of the
eidographic and the synchronistic methods : so as to represent
the mutual relations of contemporary arrangement by periods,
types, movements, and writers.   In his discussion of the merits
of the two methods, he suggests that the general literary development of the period be sketched as an introduction to the
development of individual types within the period.

According to Elze (Grundr. d. engl. Philol., p. 233), the eidographic or generic method, while it may be successfully applied
to the less complex literatures of antiquity with which Boeckh,
for instance, deals, is not adaptable to modern literatures.   And
properly so, for the lines of demarcation between literary kinds
are not so distinct as they formerly were, and the minor species
are in a state of internal modification and mutual flux.   Illustrating the subject, Elze enumerates, with reference to the
history of English literature, the following methods of arrangement, and he advocates a combination to suit the purpose of
the historian : (1) By *countries :* histories of Scottish poetry,
of Irish, American, Australian poetry, etc., *e.g.,* Campbell's
Introd. to the History of Poetry in Scotland (Edinb. : 1779).
(For bibliography, see Elze, Grundr. d. engl. Philol., pp. 244–
246.)   (2) By *political periods :* Anglo-Saxon, Norman, Elizabethan, etc., with subdivisions according to literary periods :
for instance, under the political period entitled modern England
(1688 to the present), literary periods as follows : The Golden

Age of Queen Anne, the Decline of French Taste, the Return
to distinctive National Poetry, the Lake School, etc.; *e.g.*, Stedman's Victorian Poets.   (3) By *kinds or types :* histories of
prose, of poetry, of lyric, epic, etc. ; *e.g.*, Klein's Geschichte des
englischen Dramas (2 vols.   Leipz. :   1876), Collier's or Ward's
histories of the drama.   (4) By *biographies of authors : e.g.*,
English Men of Letters series, Minto's Characteristics of the
English Poets (Chaucer to Shirley).   For a classified bibliography with reference to English literature, see Elze, pp. 244–
249.

Still another method of arrangement is mentioned, but not
with approbation, by Paul (Grundr. d. germ. Philol. 1 : 237),
viz., (5) by *schools :* such as the School of Gottsched, the Swiss
School, Wieland's School, Klopstock's School, — *e.g.*, Gervinus's Gesch. d. deutschen Dichtung and Haym's Romantische
Schule ; or in England the Lake School (cf. Elze's literary
periods), the Classical School, the Romantic School, the Alexandrine poets, the Art School, the Androtheist School, the Realistic School, — *e.g.*, Devey's Comparative Estimate of Modern
Eng. Poets (Lond. : 1873).   If we add to these the arrangement by *movements*, we have six methods in all.   The sixth deals
with such subjects as the pseudo-classical movement in France,
the rise of Classical poetry in England, the romantic movement
in England, — *e.g.*, Heine's Romantic School, Phelps's English
Romantic Movement, Gosse's From Shakespeare to Pope, G.
Sarrazin's La renaissance de la poésie anglaise (Paris : 1889),
Greinz's Die tragischen Motive in d. deutsch. Dichtung seit
Goethes Tode (Leipz. : 1889), Tilley's Literature of the French
Renaissance (Cambr. : 1885), P. Albert's La littérature fran-
çaise au XVIIe siècle (Paris : 1880), Brandes's Romantische
Schule in Frankreich (Leipz. : 1881).

It will have been noticed that the arrangements by countries,
by periods, and by authors — that is to say, the *topographical*,
the *synchronistic*, and the *biographical* methods — deal primarily

with the external relations existing between literary productions ; they are, on that account, severally insufficient. The arrangement by schools — the *magisterial* — is frequently based upon formal relations of style, which, like all fashions, are fleeting ; and even when this arrangement is based upon internal relations, such as tendency, or treatment of material, since the school itself depends upon a master, a locality, or a *coterie* (all external relations), its continuance is uncertain, and its influence limited. There remain, therefore, the arrangements by types — the *generic or eidographic* — and by movements — the *dynamic*. The advantages of the former are adequately set forth by Boeckh, as indicated above (see also Körting, 2 : 443–454). It may be added that the generic arrangement is the outcome of a consideration of internal, and therefore abiding, literary relations (for the epic, lyric, and dramatic forms of expression have psychological reasons for distinct organic existence), and that a proper attention to the development of types implies the study of formal and external literary conditions. But it must always be conceded that implicit adherence to this generic or eidographic method leads to the emphasis of one type at a time, out of relation to others, to a repetition of historical and biographical material, and to neglect of the influence of synchronistic literature. The dynamic method, however, while dealing with the internal relations existent between literary productions, necessitates equally the investigation of movements which lie on the surface (and are formal), and of movements which are altogether external. The study of poetry by its movements requires, therefore, for its instruments the narrower methods already described (by countries, periods, authors, schools), and the method by literary types as well. Because of its vital and genetic character it is especially adapted to afford "that ideal survey" which, as Paul says (Grundr. 1 : 237), "cannot be attained if the historian holds mechanically to any given scheme." It is adapted to the historical presentation of national poetry and of poetry in general. Poetry being a multiple of subject, form, and treatment (see § **19,** *I, C,* above), the dynamic method of arrangement may (1) present the development of any one of these factors : the poetic subject, or form, or process of execution; or it may (2) present movements of complexity involving two or all of these factors (and, therefore, cover the development of a type, epic or lyric, or of a species, such as the historical romance) ; or it may (3) present movements of more restricted scope but of no less persistence, — so that by this means one of the elements constitutive of the poetic *subject* may be traced through a life of centuries (a striking theme or popular plot, for instance ; some rich material of history, nature, or imagination) ; or one of the elements constitutive of poetic *form* may be followed through its various modifications (in style, for instance, in imagery, or diction, or verse) ; or one of the elements constitutive of poetic *procedure* may be shown in its survival or in its revival as a fashion (didactic or hedonic ; idealistic, realistic, or romantic).

Körting (Encykl. d. roman. Philol. 2 : 450–471) divides literary currents (or movements) into Formal and Material. The former proceed from the manner of literary construction : naïve or reflective (consciously artistic); the latter, from the content of the literary production : mystical or rationalistic. The classical (pseudo-classical) movement is primarily reflective (conventional) in form, rationalistic (scientific) in thought ; the romantic is naïve (capricious at times) in form, and given to the mystical and fantastic in conception. For an excellent antithesis of the two movements, see Körting, p. 465 *et seq.*

b. **General Histories of Poetry.**— Any of the previous methods may be employed in the presentation of subjects wider than the national. But, when biographical, the general or universal histories become dictionaries like Vapereau's ; when ethnographical, the element of international continuity, by means of action and reaction, is neglected, as, to some degree, by Scherr in his

Allgemeine Geschichte d. Literatur (2 vols. Stuttg. ; 1875) ;
when periodic, the development of types and movements is
discontinuous, as in Stern's Geschichte d. neuern Litteratur
(6 vols. Leipz. : 1882). The arrangement by schools is open
to the same objection as the biographical. The most feasible
arrangements are therefore those best suited to national histories, the eidographic, as in Klein's Geschichte des Dramas
(13 vols. Leipz. : 1865–76), or the dynamic (genetic), as in
Brandes's Die Litteratur d. neunzehnten Jahrhunderts in ihren
Hauptströmungen (6 vols. Berl. : 1872). Both of these works
avail themselves, however, of the other methods as principles of
cross-division.

5. The LITERATURE OF THE STUDY. — *a.* The student will
find the best *introduction to methods* in the following : Boeckh's
Encykl. d. philol. Wissenschaften, pp. 128, 144, 255, 648, 743 ff. ;
Paul's Grundr. d. germ. Philol., Abschnitt III, Methodenlehre,
pp. 215–238 Literaturgeschichte ; Elze, Grundr. d. englischen
Philol., pp. 232–250 Literaturgeschichte ; Tobler's Methodik
d. philol. Forschung (in Gröber's Grundr. d. romanisch. Philol.),
pp. 251–280, especially the portion entitled Litteraturhistorische Kritik ; Körting's Encykl. d. romanischen Philol., vol. I,
pp. 63–82 Die Litteratur (distinguishes between the " chronistic "
and the " pragmatic " history), and vol. II, pp. 482–505 Die
Litteraturgeschichte.

Other works of general importance are G. Gerber, Die Sprache
als Kunst (Berl. : 1885), vol. I, pp. 50–70 Poesie u. Sprachkunst, pp. 107–115 Andeutungen über die Geschichte d. Sprachkunst, pp. 235–291 Verhältniss der Sprachen der Prosa u. der
Poesie zu d. menschlichen Entwicklung ; vol. II, pp. 501–510
Das Grenzgebiet zwischen Sprachkunst u. Dichtkunst (Gerber's
book is especially useful as furnishing philological principles of
exposition and definition introductory to the historical study
of the subject) ; H. Steinthal, Einleitung in d. Psychologie
u. Sprachwissenschaft (2. Aufl. Berl.: 1881), pp. 32–35 Die

Litteraturgeschichte (of value as providing the psychological basis for exposition) ; and Carriere, Geschichte der Kunst im Zusammenhang d. Culturentwickelung (develops the aesthetic aspect of literary history).

b. To the method of historical procedure in the field of *ancient classical poetry* the following are useful guides : F. A. Wolf, Encykl. der Philologie (Leipz. : 1831, 1845); Schaaff, Encykl. der klass. Altertumskunde (Magdeb.: 1806–1808); Ast, Grundr. d. Philologie (Landshut : 1808); Bernhardy, Grundlinien zur Encykl. d. Philologie (Halle : 1832). Especially worthy of note are the following contributors to Iwan Müller's Handbuch d. klass. Altertumswissenschaften : L. von Urlichs, vol. I, pp. 29–31 Litteraturgeschichte ; Fr. Blass, vol. I, pp. 209–212 Verschiedener Umfang bei d. verschied. Litteraturgattungen (also other portions of the Hermeneutik und Kritik) ; W. Christ, vol. VII, pp. 1–10 Begriff u. Gliederung d. Litteraturgeschichte (follows Boeckh in the classification of methods as synchronistic and eidological, and adopts a combination of the two); M. Schantz, vol. VIII, pt. I, pp. 1–8 Methode u. Entwicklung d. Röm. Litt.-Gesch.; K. Krumbacher, vol. IX, pp. 18–20 on the confusion of literary kinds in Byzantine literature, and the lack of genetic development (cf. on a similar phenomenon G. Knaack's article on Alexandrine Literature in Pauly-Wissowa's Real-Encyclop. d. class. Altertumsw.). But Boeckh's lectures on critical method are the source of most of the subsequent attempts to systematize literary 'kinds.' For general bibliography, see Hübner's Grundr. zu Vorlesungen über d. Gesch. und Encykl. d. class. Philol. (Berl. : 1879).

It is unnecessary to append a list of the histories of classical poetry, since an enumeration has already been made by Boeckh, Encykl., pp. 747–751, and by Christ and Schantz in the Handbuch d. klass. Altertumsw. In the Handbuch the works on Greek literary history which may serve as examples of critical

method, *e.g.*, those of Fabricius, Bernhardy, O. Müller, Fr.
Schöll, Th. Bergk, Nicolai, Sittl, Mure, Mahaffy, Burnouf,
Croiset et Maur, are described in vol. VII, pp. 8, 9 ; the greater
works on Latin literary history, of Schöll, Bähr, Bernhardy, Klotz,
Teuffel, Munk, Sellar, Patin, Ribbeck, Ebert, Nisard, are noticed
in vol. VII, pt. I, pp. 5, 6, and vol. VIII, pt. II, p. 3. For histories
of Greek and Roman literature conjointly considered, see vol.
VIII, pt. I, p. 6.   Further bibliography of Latin literature will
be found in Körting, Encykl. 1 : 131–134 Römische Lit., Kir-
chenlatein, Volkslatein, Mittelalterliches Latein.   An admirable
illustration of the eidographic or generic method of treatment is
offered by Auguste Couat in his La poésie Alexandrine sous
les trois Ptolémées (Paris : 1882).   Professor Couat fulfils the
chronological requirements in his introductory sketch of the
subject ; the body of his work he classifies under elegiac, lyric,
epic, pastoral, and didactic poetry.   (Cf. the twofold method
advocated by Boeckh, Encykl. d. philol. Wissensch., p. 743).
Another excellent instance of the eidographic treatment is
H. Flach's Geschichte d. griech. Lyrik (Tübingen : 1883).

  c. For the treatment of the subject with reference to *modern
poetry in general*, see B. Schmitz, Encykl. d. philol. Studiums d.
neueren Sprachen (2. Aufl.   Berl. : 1876), pp. 63–83 Die Litteratur, pp. 177–186 Französische Litteraturgeschichte, pp. 265–
270 Englische Litteraturgeschichte, p. 303 Vergleichende Litteraturgeschichte (on the whole a wooden production, but it
affords a view of literary methodology, and gives a full but
uncritical bibliography) ; B. Schmitz, Encykl. d. philol. Studiums, 1. Suppl. 1879, 2. Suppl. 1881, 3. Suppl. 1881 ; Anhang:
— Verzeichniss d. auf. d. neueren Sprachen (franz. u. engl.) bezüglichen Programmabhandlungen, u. s. w. (by H. Varnhagen.
Leipz. : 1877).

  d. A later and much more comprehensive edition of the
Verzeichniss, prepared by Johannes Martin (Leipz. : 1893),
covers the field of *romance philology* (as well as of English) and

of philological and pedagogical method.   In Körting's Encykl.
d. roman. Philol., mention is made of the principal works produced on the *history of romance poetry*.   For the masters of
method in Germany, Diez (Leben u. Werke d. Troubadours,
etc.), Tobler (see Gröber's Grundriss), Gaspary, Förster, Neumann, Lemcke, Vollmöller, Suchier, Bartsch, Ebert, Stengel,
Hofmann, Breymann, Gröber, Holland, Mahn, Mätzner, Lücking,
and others, see Körting, 1 : 169–178.   For the contributions to
method by French scholars, such as G. Raynouard, Gaston
Paris, Paul Meyer, Aubertin, L. Gautier, see Körting, 1 : 180–
182.

On literary history, its periods, materials, and methods from
the point of view of the Romance languages, Körting dwells at
length in his Encykl. d. roman. Philol. 2 : 482–505.   No comprehensive scientific history of Romance literature has yet been
written.   For Italy the work has been done best by Tiraboschi
(Modena : 1772–81), for Spain by Ticknor (Boston : 1849),
for Portugal by Braga (Porto : 1875), for the Rhaeto-romanic
race by Rausch (Frankfurt a. M. : 1870).

c. For a *general survey of the history of French poetry*, and
an explanation of the difficulties attending the methodical study
of the subject, the student is referred to Körting, Encykl. d.
roman. Philol. (3 Thle.   Heilbronn : 1884) 3 : 367–421.   Works
which treat of the general history of French literature are
enumerated on pp. 305, 306 ; works on the origins of French
literature, pp. 307, 308 ; histories of special periods, pp. 308–
310 ; an exhaustive bibliography of materials, pp. 310–336 ;
histories of modern French literature, pp. 336–339 ; materials
for middle and modern French literature, pp. 339–367.   A
fair bibliography of the principal histories of French literature,
published between 1830 and 1886, is given in J. Demogeot's
Hist. de la litt. française (22ᵉ éd.   Paris : 1886), pp. 675–
678 ; of materials in poetry, pp. 678–681 ; in drama, pp. 681,
682 ; of sources and works to consult in the study of French

literature, pp. 687–700; origins and sources, p. 690; Middle
Ages, Trouvères and Troubadours, pp. 691–693 ; history of
letters, pp. 695–697 ; poetry, p. 697 ; drama, p. 698.

For *comparative study of method* the student may examine
the following histories (*devoted to poetry* exclusively): Crépet,
Les poëtes français (collection of masterpieces with biograph-
ical and critical notices. 4 vols. Paris : 1861); L. Gautier,
Les épopées françaises (4 vols. Paris : 1878); A. Jeanroy,
Les origines de la poésie lyrique en France au Moyen Âge
(Paris : 1889); G. Paris, La poésie du Moyen Âge (Paris :
1887); Ste.-Beuve, Tableau de la poésie française (in the
16th century — historical and critical. 2 vols. Paris : 1828);
Ch. Aubertin, Les origines de la langue et de la poésie française
(Paris : 1875); Jullien, Hist. de la poésie fr. à l'époque impé-
riale (2 vols. Paris : 1844); Fauriel, Hist. de la poésie pro-
vençale (3 vols. Paris : 1846); Benoiston de Chateauneuf,
Essai sur la poésie et les poëtes fr. aux 12e, 13e, et 14e siècles
(Paris : 1815); Roquefort-Flaméricourt, De l'état de la poésie
fr. dans les 12e et 13e siècles (Paris: 1815); Massieu, La
poésie fr. du 11e au 15e siècle (Paris : 1739).

Continuing the *comparative study of method, histories of French
literature in general* may now more carefully be considered.
Some of these are enumerated under the names of the authors
(Villemain, D. Nisard, Géruzez, Talbot, de Laharpe, Buron,
Demogeot, Roche, Mager, F. Kreyssig, H. Breitinger, Engel,
Kressner, W. König) in Körting's Encykl. 3 : 305, 306. See
Demogeot, pp. 675 and 695, for other authorities, *e.g.*, the
Hist. lit. de la France (by Dom. Rivet, Dom. Taillandier, etc.
24 vols. Paris : 1733–1862); Sismondi, Moke, Théry, Des
Essarts. Dowden's, Van Laun's, and Saintsbury's histories in
English will supply useful outlines. The literary studies of
G. Merlet, Sainte-Beuve, Brunetière, Lenient, Paul Albert, de
Loménie, E. Deschanel, H. Prat, Vinet, Godefroy, Desnoires-
terres, Taine, E. Schérer, Jos. Texte, and the numerous critics

whose articles appear in *Rev. de Deux Mondes, Nouvelle Revue,*
etc., are excellent examples of historical method as applied to
literary biography and literary periods (Körting, Encykl. 3 :
306, 336–339). Descriptions of the studies on periods, authors,
and movements, published by Ampère, Ch. Aubertin, Brunetière,
Feugère, Génin, A. Houssaye, Littré, Ch. Nisard, Paris, Patin,
Pellissier, Planche, St. Marc Girardin, Sayous, are given by
Demogeot (Hist. lit. fr.), pp. 675–677 ; and a still further list
of special studies by Duquesnel, J. Schmidt, Dannon, Le Clerc,
Jolly, Gidel, Fournel, Vinet, Maron, M.-J. Chénier, Nettement,
Callières, Michiels, etc., is given by Demogeot (Hist. lit. fr.),
pp. 695–697.

The *history of literary types* has been cultivated by Frenchmen more than by the English or the Germans. Lists of studies
in the history of the drama are given by Demogeot (pp. 681,
682, 698), and by Körting (3 : 306, 307). On the *epos* and other
types, see Körting, 3 : 310–336. See also the Bibliography at
the end of Professor Dowden's History of French Literature ;
Brunetière, Jeanroy, Lenient, Petit de Julleville, Faguet, Chasles,
le Breton, Morillot, Fournel, etc.

f. The materials for the history of poetry in the *other
Romance languages,* and the bibliography for periods, themes,
authors, and movements, will be found in Körting as follows :
3 : 422–479 Das Provenzalische, 479–501 Das Catalanische,
501–563 Das Spanische, 564–598 Das Portugiesische, 599–751
Das Italienische, 752–783 Das Räto-Romanische, 784–837 Das
Rümanische.

g. Paul's Grundriss, 1 : 129–142, furnishes the necessary
references to methods, advocated or adopted, in the *historical
treatment of German and North European poetry.* The more
important German authorities are the brothers Schlegel, the
brothers Grimm, Lachmann, Uhland (Geschichte d. altdeut-
schen Poesie), Lessing, Schiller, Goethe (Dichtung u. Wahrheit),
Schlosser (Geschichte des 18. Jahrhunderts : 1823) ; Gervinus

(Gesch. d. poetisch. Nationallitteratur d. Deutschen, 1835–42 ;
5th ed., under the title Gesch. d. deutschen Dichtung, Leipz. :
1871–74) ; Koberstein (Entwicklung der deutschen Poesie,
Braunschw. : 1865 ; Vermischte Aufsätze zur Litteraturgesch.
u. Aesthetik, Leipz. : 1858 ; and Grundriss zur Gesch. d. deutsch.
Nationallitteratur., 6th ed., 5 vols., 1884 ff.) ; Vilmar (Gesch.
d. deutsch. Nationallitteratur, 1845) ; Wackernagel (Gesch. d.
deutsch. Litteratur, 1848–55. 2d ed. 2 vols. 1879) ; Goedeke
(Grundriss zur Gesch. d. deutsch. Dichtung aus d. Quellen.
2d ed. 2 vols. Dresden : 1886).

Histories specially devoted to *German poetry* which may be
used as material for criticism by the student of method are
Bohtz (Gesch. d. neuern deutsch. Poesie. Göttingen : 1832);
Cholevius (Gesch. d. deutsch. Poesie. 2 vols. Leipz. : 1854);
Eichendorff (Gesch. d. poetisch. Lit. Deutschl. Paderborn :
1866); Hahn (Gesch. d. poetisch. Litt. d. Deutschen. Berl.:
1888); Loebell (Entwickelung d. deutsch. Poesie, Klopstock
bis zu Goethe. 3 vols. Braunschw.: 1856); Menzel (Deutsche
Dichtung. 3 vols. Stuttg.: 1858); Rapp (Das goldene Alter d.
deutsch. Poesie. Tübingen : 1861); Roquette (Gesch. d. deutsch.
Dichtung. Stuttg.: 1879) ; Waldberg (Deutsche Renaissance
Lyrik. Berl. : 1888).

Of course many of the best known histories, such as Kober-
stein's and Vilmar's, treat of *German literature in general.* It
will suffice to mention a few others worthy of examination :
Brugier (Nat.-Litteratur) ; Götzinger (Deutsche Litteratur,
1844); Hirsch (Gesch. d. deutsch. Litt. 3 vols. 1883); Höfer
(Deutsche Lit.-Gesch., 1885) ; Kluge (Nat.-Litteratur, 1886) ;
Koenig (Deutsche Litt.-Geschichte, 1885); Vogt u. Koch,
Gesch. d. deutsch. Lit. (Leipz. : 1897) ; Kurz (Literatur-Gesch.
4 vols. 1876); Kurz u. Paldamus (Dichter u. Prosaisten. 4 vols.
Leipz.: 1867); Menzel (Germ. Lit., trans. by C. C. Felton.
3 vols. Boston : 1840 ; also trans. by Mrs. G. Horrocks in
Bohn Libr.) ; Scherer (Gesch. d. deutsch. Litteratur. Berl.:

1885 ; trans. by Mrs. F. C. Conybeare. 2 vols. N. Y. :
1886) ; Julian Schmidt (Gesch. d. deutsch. Litt. seit Lessing.
3 vols. Leipz.: 1866) ; Sehrwald (Deutsche Dichter und Den-
ker. 2. Aufl. 2 vols. Altenburg: 1883) ; Barthel (Die deutsche
Nat.-Litt. Gütersloh: 1879); R. von Gottschall (Deutsch. Nat.-
Lit. d. 19. Jahrhs. 4 vols. Bresl.: 1881); Heine (Romantic
School; trans. by S. L. Fleishmann. N. Y. : 1882) ; Hettner
(Gesch. d. deutsch. Lit. im 18. Jahrh. 4 vols. Braunschw.:
1879); Hillebrand (Deutsch. Nat.-Litt. im 18. u. 19. Jahrh. 3 vols.
Gotha: 1875); Horn (Poesie u. Beredsamkeit d. Deutschen von
Luther bis zur Gegenwart. 3 vols. Berl. : 1822). For mono-
graphs on earlier periods, see Paul, Grundriss, 1 : 132–138.

For histories and monographs on *Dutch and Scandinavian
poetry*, see Paul, Grundriss, pp. 139–142.

h. In the *history of English poetry* little that is methodical
has been done by English-speaking writers, and nothing that
is both methodical and exhaustive by the scholars of the Continent. For a full and classified bibliography, see Elze, Grundr.
d. engl. Philol., pp. 243–249. Thomas Warton's History of
English Poetry (3 vols. Lond.: 1774–81. Ed. by W. C. Hazlitt.
4 vols. Lond.: 1871), though a storehouse of learning (to
which the editors, Price and Hazlitt, have materially added),
has no philological basis, begins loosely with the twelfth century and closes with the end of the sixteenth. W. J. Courthope's History of English Poetry (vol. I. Lond. : 1895) is
announced for completion in five volumes by 1900. The first
volume, which discusses the Middle Ages, the influence of the
Roman Empire, the encyclopædic education of the Church, and
the feudal system, leads us to hope for a valuable and lasting contribution to English literary history, although the philological quality of the work has been adversely criticised by
some excellent scholars. Vol. II (Lond.: 1897) treats of the
Renaissance, the Reformation, and the Influence of the Court
and the Universities.

Of *foreign histories of English poetry*, Elze mentions Al.
Büchner (Gesch. d. englisch. Poesie von der Mitte d. 14. bis
zur Mitte d. 19. Jahrhunderts. 2 vols. Darmstadt: 1855)
and S. Gätschenberger (Gesch. d. englisch. Dichtkunst. Lond.:
1874), the latter of which he condemns. *Histories of special
types*, such as Collier's, Ward's, and Klein's of the drama,
will be mentioned elsewhere in this work under the appropriate
heads. *Biographical surveys* of English poetry, such as Phillips's
Theatrum Poetarum (Geneva : 1824) ; Samuel Johnson's Lives
of the most eminent English poets ; Cibber's Lives of the
Poets of Great Britain and Ireland to the Time of Dean Swift
(3 vols. Lond.: 1753. On Robert Shiels's share in the authorship, see references given in Elze, Grundr., p. 248) ; Austin
and Ralph's Lives of the Poets Laureate (Lond. : 1853) ;
Walter Hamilton's Poets Laureate of England (Lond. : 1878) ;
Minto's Characteristics of English Poets from Chaucer to
Shirley (Lond. : 1874) ; Gostwick's English Poets (Lond.:
1875); Masson's Essays, Biographical and Critical, chiefly
on the English poets (Cambr.: 1856) ; and W. M. Rossetti's
Lives of Famous Poets (Lond.: 1878) display in no instance
that combination of continuity and comprehensiveness which is
requisite to a history. The biographical histories of Collier,
Morell, Pryde, Thomas Wright (Biographia Britannica Literaria.
2 vols. Lond. : 1842–46), and the English Men of Letters
series, edited by John Morley, do not treat poetry as a separate
subject. The *biographical treatment of literary periods* has
proved decidedly successful in the hands of such writers as
Gosse (Jacobean Poets, N. Y. : 1894 ; Seventeenth Century
Studies, Lond. : 1885), and E. C. Stedman (Victorian Poets.
Lond.: 1875).

The more important *general histories of English literature*
may be studied as experiments (none entirely successful) in
method, or as indexes to the materials of a history of poetry.
Henry Morley's English Writers (11 vols., beginning 1887 ;

vol. XI entitled Shakespeare and his Time under James I) is
the most ambitious attempt in this field, replete with information and suggestion, but loose-jointed in style and method.
His First Sketch of English Literature deserves examination,
as do the histories (some of them described in Elze, Grundr.,
pp. 243–244) by Chambers, Craik, Welsh, Shaw, Spalding,
Thos. Arnold, Tuckerman, Pancoast. Of more importance
are ten Brink (Gesch. d. englischen Literatur. 2 vols. Berl.:
1877. The Beginnings to the Renaissance, vol. I, trans. by
H. M. Kennedy, N. Y. : 1889 ; vol. II, trans. by W. C. Robinson, N. Y. : 1893); Taine (5 vols. Paris : 1885 ; trans.
by H. van Laun ; new ed. 4 vols., 1883) ; Körting (Grundr.
zur Gesch. d. engl. Lit. Münster : 1887. Unfortunately the
treatment of recent authors lacks discrimination); Scherr (History of Engl. Lit. ; trans. from the German by M. V. Lond.:
1882), and Stopford Brooke (Primer of Engl. Literature).

Of *histories of special periods* no extended list need be
given. The following are the most commendable illustra-
tions of method : Stopford Brooke, Early English Literature
(N. Y.: 1892); R. Wülker, Grundriss zur Gesch. d. ags. Lit.
(Leipz.: 1885); G. Saintsbury, Hist. Elizab. Lit. (Lond.: 1888);
Whipple, Lit. of Age of Elizabeth (Boston : 1871); Hazlitt,
Lit. of the Age of Elizabeth, etc. (Lond. : 1852) ; H. Hettner,
Gesch. d. engl. Lit., 1660–1770 (Braunschw. : 1881) ; A. Beljame, Le public et les hommes de lettres en Anglet. au 18e
siècle (Paris : 1883) ; E. Gosse, Hist. of Eighteenth Century
Literature (Lond. : 1889); Mrs. Oliphant, Lit. Hist. Engl. in the
end of the 18th and beginning of the 19th century (3 vols.
Lond. : 1889) ; Mrs. Oliphant and F. R. Oliphant, The Victorian Age of Engl. Literature (2 vols. Lond. : 1892) ; Saintsbury, History of Nineteenth Century Literature (Lond. : 1896).

i. Of histories of *American literature*, the more important
are Moses Coit Tyler's History of American Colonial Literature
(4 volumes published) ; C. F. Richardson's American Litera-

ture, and E. C. Stedman's Poets of America.   Less pretentious, but useful works are H. A. Beers' Outline Sketch of American Literature ; Brander Matthews' Introduction to American Literature ; White's Philosophy of American Literature ; Nichol's American Literature ; Pattee's History of American Literature ; Pancoast's and Painter's Introductions to American Literature, and Katharine Lee Bates' American Literature.   For various studies of authors and phases, see the notes to the histories by Matthews and Pattee.   The most important contribution to biography is the American Men of Letters series.   Materials are indicated in Whitcomb's Chronological Outlines, in Tyler, in Stedman and Hutchinson's Library of American Literature, in Beers' Century of American Literature, and in the Handbook by Adams and Cleveland.

j. The following are a few of the *histories of poetry in general:* F. A. Hoffmann, Poetry, its Origin, Nature, and History (2 vols. Lond.: 1884); L. Jacobowski, Die Anfänge der Poesie (Dresden : 1891 ; see § 17) ; E. Quinet, De l'histoire de la poésie, in Œuvres complètes, vol. IX (a study of national traditions in poetry. The author treats, in turn, of the Greek *epos,* the Rhapsodists, the influence of the Greek epics on Greek religion and political unity ; of the romance epics, the French epics, Celtic traditions, the Arthuriad, Carlovingian epics, etc. ; of the German epics, the Scandinavian and Slavic. Quinet pays especial attention to Niebuhr's theory of primitive Roman poetry, which he undertakes to confute); Bouterwek, Geschichte der Poesie und Beredsamkeit seit dem Ende des 13. Jahrhs. (12 vols.   Göttingen : 1801–19 ; brought to the present by Brinckmeyer) ; Fritzsche, Ueber die Anfänge der Poesie (Chemnitz : 1855) ; J. D. Hartmann, Versuch einer allgemeinen Geschichte der Poesie von den ältesten Zeiten an (2 vols.   Leipz. : 1797–98 ; comprehensive in intent, but handicapped by limited material and the lack of more modern philological apparatus) ; K. Rosenkranz, Handbuch einer allgemeinen

Geschichte der Poesie (3 vols.   Halle : 1832), and his Die
Poesie und ihre Geschichte (Königsberg : 1855) ; C. Fortlage,
Vorlesungen über die Geschichte der Poesie (Stuttgart und
Tübingen : 1839).   For other authorities reference may be made
to § **17** above, and to Boeckh's Encykl. d. philol. Wissensch.,
p. 751, where will be found most of the titles given above, and
to the *histories of literature in general* of Hallam, Demogeot,
Laharpe, Sismondi, Villemain, Bouginé (Handbuch d. allgem.
Litt.-Gesch. "nach Hermann's Grundriss."   5 vols.   Zürich :
1789–92), Eichhorn, Friedr. Schlegel, Wachler (Handbuch d.
Gesch. d. Litteratur.   4 vols.   Leipz. : 1833), Grässe (Lehrbuch d. allgem. Litt.-Gesch. aller bekannten Völker d. Welt.
3 vols.   Dresden u. Leipz. : 1837–54), Theodor Mundt
(Gesch. d. Litt. d. Gegenwart, von 1789 an.   2. Aufl.   Leipz. :
1853), Fr. von Raumer (Allg. Litt.-Gesch.).   Full titles of
many of these also will be found in § **17,** and in Boeckh,
Encykl., pp. 746, 747, and above.   For further bibliography,
see B. Schmitz, Encyclopädie d. philol. Studiums d. neueren
Sprachen (2. Aufl.   Leipz.: 1876), pp. 76–78.

   See also § **18,** *II, III,* above.

CHAPTER VI.

THE HISTORICAL STUDY OF POETICS.

§ **21**, *B*. The student should first familiarize himself with the poetics of Plato and Aristotle (see §§ **8, 9**, and **20**, above, and, for texts and translations of Aristotle's Poetics, the Appendix to this volume), and especially with such treatises as Butcher's Theory of Poetry and Fine Arts and Bywater's Commentary on Aristotle's Poetics, which, soon to be issued from the Clarendon Press, promises to be of decided worth. The theories of Plotinus, Longinus, Quintilian, and Horace should also find a place in this preliminary study. The influence of Longinus, for instance, is obvious in productions as recent as Shaftesbury's Characteristics and Addison's Pleasures of the Imagination; of Horace's Ars Poetica, the long-continued vitality is in a general way known to every student. The special investigator will naturally desire to follow the course of poetic theory through the Latin treatises (particularly mediaeval and renaissance) devoted to that subject; and for him the following list is inserted. Other students may prefer to turn to the sections dealing with English, French, and German poetics.

1. An exhaustive list of LATIN TREATISES in modern times will be found in Friedrich von Blankenburg's Litterarische Zusätze zu Sulzer's Allgemeine Theorie der schönen Künste (3 vols. Leipz.: 1796–98, article 'Dichtkunst' *passim*, from which much of the following enumeration is taken). Some of the more important authors are as follows: Johannes Garlandia, whose treatise, written in 1260, is of merely antiquarian interest; Dante, the second book of whose De Vulgari Elo-

quio contains observations on Italian verse (concerning their authenticity, see Blankenburg, 1 : 386); Antonio da Tempo, whose Summa Artis Ritmici Vulgaris (about 1332 ; publ. Venet. : 1509) describes contemporary forms of poetry; Raf. Reggius, Horatii Opera, with the commentaries of the scholiasts; Helenius Acron and Pomponius Porphyrion (Pad. : 1481); Marco Girolamo Vida, whose De Arte Poetica (Poeticorum Libri Tres. Cremona : 1520) emphasized the Horatian tradition and exercised an influence on the French classical school (see Batteux, Les quatres poétiques, Paris : 1771 ; and Cook's reprint of Horace, Vida, and Boileau, with translations by Howes, Pitt, and Soame, " The Art of Poetry," Boston : 1892) ; N. B. Campiano, In Artem Poeticam Primordia (Venet. : 1522) ; Janus Parrhasius, whose commentary on the Ars Poetica of Horace appeared in 1531 (Naples; in Paris, 1533); Alex. Paccius, edition of Aristotle's Poetics with notes (Venet. : 1536, Greek and Latin); Franc. Robortelli, Poetics of Aristotle with commentary on Horace's Ars Poetica, and articles on various forms of Poetry (Flor. : 1548 ; Bas. : 1555); Girol. Fracastor, Naugerius (Ven. : 1555) ; A. S. Minturno, De Poetica Libri Sex (Venet. : 1559) ; Vinc. Madius and Bart. Lombardus, an edition of Aristotle's Poetics with explanations and commentary on the poetics of Aristotle and Horace (Venet. : 1550) ; Georg. Fabricius, whose edition of Horace (Bas. : 1555) contains commentaries by several moderns; J. A. Viperani, De Poetica Libri Tres (Antv. : 1558 and 1579), whose commentary, following minutely the divisions of the Epistle to the Pisos, treats but scantily the nature and kinds of poetry in general (Blankenburg, 1 : 387) ; Petr. Victorius, the poetics of Aristotle with a commentary (Flor. : 1560 and 1573, Greek and Latin) ; Julius Caesar Scaliger, whose Poetices Libri Septem is indispensable for the comprehension of classical forms of verse (Gen. : 1561).   The third and fifth books (*Idea* and *Criticus*) abound in conventional classifications of

figures and poetic values, but the sixth, *Hypercriticus*, displays a genuine appreciation of Horace and Ovid, and will
furnish the student with numerous details necessary to the
history of poetics.   Though Scaliger did not possess the high
poetic sense, he was, as regards scholarship and method, the
founder of the early modern school of criticism.   In 1565
Fabricius produced his De Re Poetica, a somewhat independent
and original treatise (Libri Quattuor. Antv. : 1565).   Aldus
Manutius produced a commentary on Horace's Ars Poetica
(Venet. : 1576); Joh. Sturm, a similar commentary (Strasb. :
1576) ; Lor. Gumbara, De Perfecta Poeseos Ratione, etc. (Rom. :
1576); Heinr. Stephanus (Paris : 1577 and 1588), editions of
Horace with treatise on the Ars Poetica ; Ant. Riccoboni, Aristotle's Poetics and Rhetoric with notes (Venet. : 1579.   Note
also his Poetic. Aristotel. per paraphrasin explicans et non-
nullas L. Castelvetry captiones refellens, Vic. : 1584; and his
Praecepta Aristotelis cum praeceptis Horatii collata, Pad. :
1592).   He is followed by Th. Correa, commentary on the Ars
Poetica, and De Antiquit., etc., Poesis (Rom. : 1586) ; Frd.
Ceruto, De Re Poetica (Ver. : 1588) ; Jac. Pontanus, whose
Poeticarum Institutionum Libri Tres (Ingolst. : 1594 and
1597) treats of the nature of poetry and poetic imitation, the
relation of poetry to art, of the grades and kinds of poetry,
and of the material and the purpose of the art ; Ant. Possevin,
Tractatio de Poesi ethica, humana et fabulosa, collata cum
vera, honesta et sacra (Lugd. : 1595) ; Macarius Mutius, De
Ratione scribendi Poemata (published with the preceding);
Dan. Heinsius, edition of Aristotle's Poetics, published with
Heinsius's treatise De Constitutione Tragoediae (Lugd. : 1611
and 1643, Greek and Latin); Paol. Beni, edition of Aristotle's
Poetics with a Commentary (Pad. : 1613) and his Platonis
Poetica (Ven. : 1622); Aelius Donatus, De Arte Poetica Libri
Tres (Rom. : 1631) ; Gerard. Joh. Vossius, De Artis Poeticae
natura et constitutione Liber (Amst. : 1647), and his Poeticarum

Institutionum Libri Tres (Amst. : 1647), both of them influ-
ential in the history of classical criticism, though heavy and
conventional in the treatment of poetic kinds and forms ; Vit.
Bering, De Arte Poetica Natura, etc. (Hafn. : 1650) ; Fdr.
Rappolt, Poetica Aristotelica, seu Veteris Tragoediae expositio
(Lips. : 1679) ; Carlo Renaldini, the third part of the first vol-
ume of whose Philosophia Rationalis (Pad. : 1681) contains,
according to Blankenburg (1 : 388), a tolerable poetics ; Joh.
Jac. Mescolius, Artis Poeticae Institutiones (Flor. : 1692) ;
J. G. Müller, De Natura Media Poes. inter Philos. et Histor.
(Jena : 1707); Jos. Trapp, whose Praelectiones Poeticae (Oxon. :
1716) were the first lectures delivered from the chair of poetry
at Oxford afterwards occupied by Thos. Warton, Spence, Lowth,
Arnold, etc.

2. The Development of Poetics in England.[1]— Since
there is no history of English poetics, the student may, perhaps, best approach the subject by glancing through general
histories of the literature ; histories of literary periods, like
Gosse's Modern English Literature and Saintsbury's Nineteenth Century Literature ; histories of periods of criticism,
like F. E. Schelling's Poetic and Verse Criticism of the Reign
of Elizabeth, P. Hamelius' Die Kritik in der englischen Litteratur des 17. u. 18. Jahrhs. (Leipz. : 1897), and Wylie's Evolution of English Criticism from Dryden to Coleridge ; general
literary discussions of a period, such as C. H. Herford's Age of
Wordsworth (Lond. : 1897) ; and sketches, such as Professor
Vaughan's Introduction to a volume of selections entitled English
Literary Criticism (Lond. : 1896). J. M. Bray's History of English Critical Terms (Boston : 1898), just issued, will be useful.

The Materials and Methods of this investigation are as follows :

(*a*) **Materials.** — Of two kinds : those that yield direct, and
those that yield inferential or circumstantial information.   The

---

[1] The author of this chapter has in preparation, and hopes within a few years to
complete, a history of the subject.

former class includes Theories of Poetry and Histories.   The
Theories take the form of general treatises on the principles :
philosophical, such as Hume's Dissertation on Tragedy, or
literary, such as Sidney's Defense of Poesy, or Stedman's
Nature and Elements of Poetry ; and of special treatises, which
may in their turn be *formal criticisms* of individual poets or
poems, such as Macaulay's Essay on Montgomery, or Addison's
papers on Paradise Lost, or *occasional appreciations*, such as the
numerous 'commendatory verses,' 'recommendatory poems,'
prologues, epilogues, *eulogia*, dedications, and prefaces, and
the replies thereto, that are to be found in any of the standard
collections of English poetry.   In like manner the Histories of
Poetry are general, like Warton's, or special — dealing with
types, movements, periods, schools, or the biographies of poets.
Under the head of biographies would fall, for instance, the
works of our first modern antiquaries, Leland and Bale.[1]

The materials from which we may obtain inferential information are (1) early treatises on the sister art of Rhetoric ;
(2) collections of poetry, as representative of the critical taste
of successive periods, for instance, Tottel's Miscellany (1557) ;
the Paradise of Dainty Devices (1576); · A Gorgious Gallery of
Gallant Inventions (1578) ; A Handefull of Pleasant Delites
(1584) ; the Phoenix Nest (1593) ; England's Helicon (1600) ;
A Poetical Rhapsody (1602) ; or books of 'quotations digested
under a commonplace,' like the Belvidere or the Garden of the

---

[1] Of these, the former (1506–52) left behind him in manuscript five volumes of
Collectanea, the fourth of which (completed about 1545) contains his Commentarii de
Scriptoribus Britannicis, presented in 1632 to the Bodleian Library.   His judgments lack discrimination and historical perspective ; but the facts upon which they
are based were conscientiously and industriously collected and have proved of great
value to succeeding historians.   To this manuscript John Bale (Bishop of Ossory}
was very largely indebted in the preparation of his Illustrium Majoris Britanniae
Scriptorum Summarium in quinque centurias divisum, 1548 (later editions, 1557 and
1559).   The Summary is of historical rather than critical consequence, for, although
based upon the originals consulted by Leland or by Bale himself, it abounds in error
and prejudice.

Muses (1600), to which reference is made in the Return from Parnassus, and so on to the amusing anthology prepared by Goldsmith, and the collections of Campbell, Chalmers, and men of later day ; (3) poetical contributions found available by periodicals of successive ages : the Annuals, the Friendship's Offerings, Forget-me-nots, Literary Souvenirs, Amulets, Keepsakes and Gems of the third decade of this century, and the magazines that have taken their place ; (4) the chronicles of literary clubs,— the Areopagus, the Mermaid, Scribblerus, Turk's Head, so far as accessible, — their rolls of members, their records, and the various evidences of the influence exerted by them upon poetic and critical taste; (5) catalogues of libraries, such as the Edinburgh catalogue of the books bequeathed by Drummond of Hawthornden ; (6) evidence from any source regarding the demand for poetry — a reflex of the poetic consciousness of the day. For instance, the history of editions of the standard poets. The editorial history of Chaucer's works helps in this particular to form a background for the history of poetics.[1]

In addition to these subdivisions of material must be cited another, inferential in general character, but of a negative quality. This is (7) the literary satire, as we find it in the poems of Bishop Hall, Churchill, and Byron, in satiric comedy, such as the Return from Parnassus, the Rehearsal, the Knight of the Burning Pestle, and in the literary lampoon.

Such are the more evident classes of material. The order of investigation should be chronological in respect of individual productions of all these kinds, not in respect of the complete

---

[1] Although there had been printed some half-dozen editions of Chaucer's poems between 1475 (Caxton's) and 1526 (Pynson's), the first collection of his works was not made till 1532, by Thynne. That the interest in Chaucer did not entirely abate during the 16th century, second half, is proved by the fact that two other editors, Stowe and Speght, published editions in 1561 and 1598, respectively. Speght's edition held its own through the 17th century. For the history of poetic appreciation as indicated by the demand for Chaucer's works, see J. W. Hales's article, Chaucer, Dict. Nat. Biog., Skeat's Chaucer, Lounsbury's Studies in Chaucer, ten Brink's Chaucer, etc.

contribution of one author at a time, or of one class of material. But in the presentation of results as a logical whole it will be necessary at times to deviate from chronological arrangement. The following sketch of English poetics aims merely to outline the principal periods and movements of theory and practice ; but it does not pretend to exhaust the bibliography of any one period, nor, so far as secondary materials go, to do more than mention a few.

With regard to the first class of secondary material mentioned above, it will be for the convenience of the student that its earliest specimens should be listed at once. The *rhetorics* of the 15th and 16th centuries have their specific importance for the rhetorician, but for the student of poetics they are useful merely as evidence of a critical movement that was collateral but not intimately related. The following enumeration is prepared from notes principally furnished by Dr. F. I. Carpenter of the University of Chicago.

Early English Rhetorics. — Doubtless the first rhetoric printed in England was that of Traversanus (Fratris laurencii guilelmi de Saona prohemium in novam rhetoricam. Apud villam sancti Albani. 1480. "The first book printed at St. Albans," Brit. Mus. Cat.). Next followed the section on Rhetoric in Hawes's Pastime of Pleasure (written, 1506 ; published 1517). But the first complete rhetoric in the English language was the Arte or Crafte of Rhetoryke, by Leonard Cox, a schoolmaster at Reading, and a friend of Erasmus, Melancthon, Leland, etc. There were two editions, one without date (*circa* 1524 in early bibliographies and in the British Museum catalogue, but more probably *circa* 1530), and one dated 1532. It covers the subject of Invention only, and is mainly a paraphrase of the Institutiones Rhetoricae of Melancthon, 1523, with additions from the De Rhetorica, libri tres, 1519, of the same author, and others by Cox himself. (Result of an investigation made by Dr. F. I. Carpenter, 1897.) This was

followed, but not until 1550, by Richard Sherry's Treatise of
Schemes and Tropes (London).

The next rhetoric in English was that of Thomas Wilson,
The Arte of Rhetorique (1553), ordinarily cited as the earliest English treatise in criticism. It is a sequel to the same
author's Arte of Logique (1551), in the third edition of which
(1553) appears the famous "example of doubtful writing",
taken from Roister Doister. In the Rhetorique the author
does battle for simple, native English as opposed to the corrupt
words and phrases imported by the learned, the travelled,
and the affected. But the work does not vitally affect the
history of poetics. Still less influence in that direction was
exercised by Richard Rainolde's Foundacions of Rhetorike,
"imprinted by Jhon Kingston" ten years later (1563), although
it makes a meagre reference or two to the nature of poetry,
e.g., "that poetes first invented fables," and cites the practice
of Ovid and other classical writers. As a text-book it is significant of the widening literary interests of the period.

After Wilson's Arte several other rhetorics followed in the
second half of the century, all having popular and practical
rather than scientific or critical aims. Such were Richard
Sherry's Treatise of the Figures of Grammar and Rhetoric
(Lond. : 1555 ; English and Latin. A revision of his treatise
of 1550) ; William Fulwood's The Enimie of Idleness: Teaching the maner and stile how to indite, compose, and write
all sorts of Epistles and Letters (Lond. : 1568; and later
editions : the illustrations chiefly borrowed from Cicero and
Latin literature on the one hand, and from Politian, Ficino,
and other Italian scholars of the Renaissance on the other) ;
the Arcadian Rhetorike of Abraham Fraunce (Lond., n. d.,
entered 1588 : restricted to "Eloqution," [style, diction, etc.,]
and "Pronuntiation" [elocution]; short precepts and definitions,
illustrated by examples drawn from Sidney, Spenser, the Greek
and Latin poets, Tasso, Du Bartas, Boscan, and Garcilasso, all

given in the original. Indicative of the interest in foreign literatures at this period).

Next appeared Henry Peacham's Garden of Eloquence, conteyning the Figures of Grammer and Rhetorick (Lond.: 1577, and 1593, revised: a description of figures and tropes, with illustrations from the Bible and the ancient classics ; perfunctory). Of these rhetorics the most interesting, however, was Richard Mulcaster's First Part of the Elementarie which entreateth cheflie of the writing of our English tung (Lond.: 1582 — a treatise on education, an elementary text-book of language-teaching, and a practical rhetoric, all in one). In parts this is valuable and important to the history of poetics. It contains a strong defense of the qualities and possibilities of the English language. See also the same author's Positions wherein those Primitive Circumstances, etc., of earlier date in the century, but intended as the second part of the work of which that above forms the first. (Reprinted, ed. Quick. Lond.: 1888.) Mulcaster's work was followed by an inadequate treatise, Dudley Fenner's (?) The Artes of Logike and Rhetorike (1584, 1588? 1592, etc.): a translation on elocution, style, and pronunciation, dwelling chiefly on figures.

(*b*) **Methods.** — The history of poetics covers the provenience both of *principles of judgment* and *principles of method* in the criticism of poetry : the former being the formulation of poetic theory whether by poet or critic; the latter being the *rationale* of the critical attitude and habit of procedure, whether formulated by the critic or only to be inferred from his practice (see § **4,** *II,* above). In what follows, the development of method, even though only in principle, has been regarded as a contribution to practical poetics, and the general term criticism has been frequently used for the particular, poetic criticism. The historical schools and movements are best differentiated by reference to their theoretical or practical nature : if theoretical, according to the peculiar criteria of judgment adopted (moral, aesthetic, or metaphysical) ; if practical, according to the methods preferred (personal, impartial ; analytic, synthetic ; static, genetic ; historical, comparative ; interpretative, reconstructive). The periods of poetics in England vary according to the basis of division. Symonds calls them Classic, Romantic, and Scientific on the basis of literary influence, and with reference to the source of theory. Vaughan, judging principally by development of method, divides into the period of the Elizabethans and Milton, of which the typical critic is Sidney; the period from the Restoration to the French Revolution, which begins with Dryden and ends with Johnson ; and the period from the Revolution to the present day, beginning with Wordsworth and Coleridge and represented in its earlier phases by Lamb, Hazlitt, and Carlyle. The student would, however, do well to inquire whether more scientific divisions might not result from considering the successive stages of method and theory taken each in relation to the other (the plan adopted in the following outline); or the development of the vehicle of criticism (pamphlet, dedication, essay paper, review, daily newspaper, etc.); or the extension, by social progress, of the audience addressed (academic, histrionic, the "town," the court, the patron, the tea-table, the club, the publisher, and, finally, the country as well as the circle of the 'cultivated'). It may, indeed, be questioned whether anything but convenience is gained from the division into periods — always more or less arbitrary.

(*c*) **The Outline.** — During the *First Period*, if we may call it so, poetics is *chiefly Theoretical and largely Academic.* The first important movement is that in favor of classical versification started by Ascham (The Scholemaster. Bk. II, 1570) and kept in motion by Gabriel Harvey and Spenser (Three Proper and Wittie Familiar Letters, 1579, 1580) and by the Society of the Areopagus to which they belonged. Spenser soon abandoned the attempt at quantitative versification, but the movement was forwarded by the practice of Sidney (in the Arcadia), by the advocacy of William Webbe (Discourse of English Poetrie, 1586), and by Campion's Observations on the Art of English Poesie, 1602. (For most of these earlier treatises, see Haslewood's Ancient Critical Essays, 1815 ; Arber's Reprints ; and Egerton Brydges's Censura Literaria.)

But meanwhile a counter-movement, dating from Gascoigne's Certayne Notes of Instruction concerning the Making of Verse or Rhyme in English, 1575, had been steadily gaining head. In this early protest against traditional conventionality — a protest in itself the forerunner of romantic poetics — the leaders are James VI (Treatise of the Airt of Scottis Poesie : Essays of a Prentise, 1584), and Puttenham (Arte of English Poesie, 1589), who did for the vernacular that in the way of sensible criticism which Nashe (Epistle Prefatory to Greene's Menaphon, 1589, and Pierce Penilesse, 1592) did for the academic affectations of the day. The influence of these men and of Samuel Daniel (Defense of Rhime, 1602) in confirming the native possibilities of our language, style, and prosody cannot be overestimated.

The question of poetic criticism had, however, been approached in these earlier times from the side of morals as well as from that of form. There had been early sermons against Miracle Plays ; and in Northbrooke's Treatise against Dicing, Dancing, Plays, and Interludes (entered for publication, 1577), the question is not whether poetry should wear this or that form, but whether it should exist at all. In 1579 Gosson had published his School of Abuse, a virulent attack upon " poets, pipers, players, jesters," etc., in which he condemned the drama on the ground of its immoral effect. He was answered by Lodge in the Defense of Poetry, Music, and Stage Plays, privately circulated in 1579. But Lodge makes the mistake of accepting his opponent's premise and trying to justify poetry on the ground of its disciplinary value. Not so, Sir Philip

Sidney, who, while insisting upon the moral value of poetry and the drama, transfers the justification of their existence to broader and more philosophical premises. He holds that art is the highest manifestation of nature ; and that to awaken pleasure is an essential of art — an end, not a means to moral instruction. He adjudicates in like manner the strife between the advocates of classical quantitative verse and the dramatic unities on the one hand, and the apostles of the natural movement on the other, by designating the advantages of either practice in its appropriate place. (For a good critique of Sidney's Defense of Poesie, see Vaughan's Lit. Crit. See also editions by Evelyn Shuckbrugh, Cambridge, 1891, and by A. S. Cook, Boston, 1890.) The Defense of Poesie was written between 1581 and 1585, was read in manuscript by many, but not published till 1595. Gosson, to whom answer is made in the Defense, had meanwhile returned to the attack. In 1581 he produced Plays Confuted in Five Actions, and was again met by Lodge in the Address prefixed to the Alarum Against Usurers (1584). Webbe, too, and Puttenham took notice of the moralistic controversy — the latter, however, with the better presentation of the dramatic case. Sir John Harington (Brief Apology for Poetrie, prefixed to the translation of Orlando Furioso. Lond. : 1591) adopts much the same ground as Sidney and Puttenham. From the former, whom he greatly admires, he borrows largely (see *Nation*, 48 : 224) ; of the latter he expresses a qualified commendation. Nash, in his Pierce Penilesse, turns the flank of the anti-dramatic critics by an attack upon the " dunstical sermons " that they would set up as counter-stimulants, and he tries to prove " plays to be no extreme but a rare exercise of virtue." William Vaughan's Golden Grove (completed in 1599, published 1600) has one or two chapters on art and poetry which feebly argue their inferiority to nature, and conclude the immorality of the drama ; but this conclusion is reversed in his Golden Fleece, written a

quarter of a century later.　No attack of the sixteenth century
upon the drama is more bitter than John Rainolde's Overthrow
of Stage Playes, which, published in 1599, arose from a controversy with Dr. Gager and gave birth to one with Dr. Gentiles
concerning the same matter.

Worthy to be mentioned in the same category with Sidney
and Puttenham, because of his noble and catholic conception
of poetry, is Dr. Joseph Hall, Bishop of Exeter, whose satires
demand careful examination.　Books I–III were published in
1597, the remaining books in 1598.　He gives us one of the
earliest descriptions, satirical of course, of a Critic's Club, and
refutes contemporary extravagances in language, versification,
and style.　Ben Jonson appears in 1598 with the defense of
poetry spoken by Lorenzo in Every Man in His Humour; and
even here he sounds a truer note than all but the best before
him.　For the next few years he is engaged in the controversy
with Marston and Dekker, a purely personal affair.　But in
the play just mentioned, as well as in Every Man out of His
Humour, 1599, and The Poetaster, 1601, he takes a more
general view.　He is already an advocate of the classical unities and of the didactic office of poetry ; and he has formed
opinions concerning the nature of idealization and the progressive continuity of dramatic form.　Francis Meres's Comparative
Discourse of our English Poets with Greek, Latin, and Italian
Poets in the Palladis Tamia, 1598, is an attempt at an historical survey somewhat after the manner of Webbe and Puttenham.
The comparative criticism is, of course, crude, but it is of value
in fixing dates and facts.　The author is indebted to Webbe,
Puttenham, Ascham, and Sidney.

The most important contribution to poetics between Sidney's
Defense and Jonson's Discoveries is to be found in the Second
Book of the Advancement of Learning, 1605.　Looking at
poetry from both the ethical and aesthetic sides, Bacon anticipates Wordsworth and Carlyle ; emphasizing the difference

between idealization and actuality, he foreshadows Cowley, Dryden, and Addison; indicating the religious force of poetic thought, he strikes a chord to which Dennis, Wordsworth, Coleridge, and Arnold respond. His ideas of poetic justice are in advance of contemporary theory, and his insistence upon the imaginative appeal as the prime poetic characteristic is in anticipation of Addison. It looks, indeed, as if Addison might have obtained his classification of the qualities productive of imaginative pleasure from Bacon's "more ample greatness, more perfect order, and more beautiful variety." Bacon is also the founder of literary history; he calls for the genetic method of critical study, by cause and effect, movement, influence, relation, change, decay, and revival ; and he suggests the elasticity of literary forms or types ; ideas all essential to the understanding of literature as an historical growth. Just about the same time, 1605, the other great critic of the later Elizabethan Age, Ben Jonson, was pursuing his study of classical criticism and promising a translation of Horace's Ars Poetica (see preface to Sejanus, 1605). That he was busied at this early period with a commentary on the Ars Poetica is a significant fact. For it furnishes a clue to the real beginnings of that Latin-classical conventionalism which exercised so decided an influence on the poetics of the next one hundred and fifty years. The Horatian influence proceeded from Ben Jonson rather than from any other English writer ; not only as regards form, but as regards the didactic motive. On these points consult the prefaces, prologues, epilogues, to his various plays; and his Timber, of which presently.

Minor contributions to poetics before the year 1625 were Edmund Bolton's Hypercritica, parts of which were written, probably, between 1600 and 1603 (Arber dates the work 1620; it contains a comparative estimate of poets by a man who expressly disclaims any of the qualifications of a critic of poetry ; but it is historically useful); Thomas Heywood's Apology for

Actors, 1612 (advances somewhat beyond the moralistic defense
of the drama, advocating art for pleasure's sake ; acknowledges
the critical services of Puttenham and Meres); J. G.'s (John
Green's) Refutation of the Apologie for Actors, 1615 ; Michael
Drayton's Epistle of Poets and Poesy, 1619 ; and Henry Peacham's the Compleat Gentleman, — purloined in large part from
Puttenham (the Bodleian copy is dated 1622).

So far criticism is principally a matter of theory, not yet of
method in application.   But to form a just idea even of the
theory, it is not sufficient to read only such treatises as are
mentioned above.   The student should correct and broaden
the conceptions thus derived by careful comparative study of
the popular taste, as shown by the style of poetry most sought
in that day.   Not only should the works of the greater authors
be studied, but the various poetical collections, such as Tottel's Miscellany, 1557 ; the Paradise of Dainty Devices, 1576 ;
England's Helicon, 1600, etc.   And consideration should be
given to the aesthetic opinions of the poets themselves, so far
as they may be determined from their practice or their informal
utterances.

During the *Second Period* in the history of English poetics,
there is a *Movement toward Practical Criticism*.   The idea of
literary history had been enunciated by Bacon in 1605, and
crude attempts at the practice of it had been made by Webbe,
Puttenham, and others ; but nothing had been accomplished in
the statement of critical method, of the "true office of the
critic," his qualifications, limitations, and aim, before Ben Jonson wrote his Timber, or Discoveries.   Though not printed
till 1641, this work was certainly in course of composition as
early as 1626.   Jonson insists that the critic shall have poetic
potentialities and shall judge of the work as a whole.   His
observations on the essentials of poetry are distinguished by
insight.   His judgments were sometimes prejudiced, but his
doctrines are those of a great critic.   He is the founder of the

English classical school of criticism, but he is by no means responsible for the narrower rules of the latter part of the 17th century, — misinterpreted from Rapin's Reflections sur la poëtique d'Aristotle, and Le Bossu's Traité du poëme epique, — nor for the fixed canons of the 18th, crystallized from André Dacier's commentary on Bossu, and from Boileau's L'Art poétique, 1674. As Rapin and Boileau were much more liberal and constructive than their disciples, so was Ben Jonson. The dignity of his poetic ideal is proved by such poems as the first Ode to Himself ; the didactic quality of his criticism by his defense of comedy in the same ode ; his freedom from formal conventionality by his estimates of contemporary poetry.

During the latter portion of Jonson's life the moralistic attack upon the stage was persistently maintained ; in a less important degree by such pamphlets as A Short Treatise against Stage Plays, 1623, and Lenton's Young Gallant's Whirligig, 1629 ; but with infinitely greater force and ultimate result by Prynne's Histriomastix, 1632, which, at first failing of its object, afterwards produced a progeny of anti-dramatic literature, and was finally efficient in closing the theatres, 1642. Still later, the spirit of Prynne was revived in the Prince de Conti and Jeremy Collier (see below, remarks on the Immorality of the Stage).

We return to legitimate criticism with the Earl of Stirling's (Sir William Alexander) Anacrisis, written 1634, — published with Drummond's Works, 1711, — which, although ordinarily overlooked, contains a statement of theory and methods considerably in advance of the age. This important work is to be found in none of the quartos of Drummond in the Bodleian, but appears in Dr. Charles Rogers's Memorials of the Earl of Stirling (2 vols. Edinb. : 1877), vol. II, pp. 205–210. Stirling is followed by Milton, whose position in poetics, like that of Sidney and of Bacon, is above strife. The poet clothes the spirit of freedom which characterizes our first admirers of the classics, Greene, Marlowe, Peele, and the rest, with the form of restraint, of which Ben Jonson had been the advocate. Although a Puritan, he cuts the ground from under the puritanical objection, by consecrating poetry to the glorification of God and the justification of God's ways toward man ; while, at the same time, he maintains that the vision divine can come only to him who is *purified of passion.* The purification of the passion of the spectator or reader is asserted in the Introduction to Samson Agonistes, 1671 ; the high ideal and function of poetry, in the third contribution to the Smectymnuus controversy, the Reason of Church Government urged against Prelatry, 1642 ; the relation of poetry to rhetoric and logic as means of education, in the Tractate on Education, 1644.

For the parts played by Waller, Denham, and Cowley in the "refinement of English verse" and the promotion of the so-called classical movement, which, originating in its larger features with Ben Jonson, was furthered by Dryden and reached its climax in Pope and Dr. Johnson, reference may be made to Edmund Gosse's From Shakespeare to Pope, his Seventeenth Century Studies, and his Modern English Literature. Waller's rehabilitation of English style and the heroic couplet was begun in 1621. And as late as 1690, in the Preface to the Second Part of his Poems, probably written by Bishop Atterbury, we find his poetic principles acknowledged as they were in the heyday of their youth. The relative significance of Waller and Denham (Cooper's Hill, 1640) in the history of verse is stated by Dryden in the Preface to the Rival Ladies, 1664. For Waller's enunciation of principles the student should study the Verses upon Ben Jonson, On Mr. John Fletcher's Plays, To Mr. George Sands on his translation of some part of the Bible, and In Answer of Sir John Sucklin's Verses. Another herald of coming fashions was Denham's Preface to Sir Richard Fanshaw's Translation of Guarini's Pastor Fido, 1647. Some thirty years later the convictions there expressed were accepted

by the Earl of Roscommon and restated in his more famous
Essay on Translation. Meanwhile Sir William Davenant's
Gondibert, in 1650, furthered by precept and example the mode
of verse adopted by Waller and Denham and the affectation
of Christian themes suggested by the former. The Preface to
Hobbes is a moralistic plea for poetry ; but it has germs of
that poetic estimate of religious subject-matter which Dennis
afterwards emphasized in his Advancement of Poetry. The
Reply to Davenant by Hobbes is even better worth study, for
it contains an attempt at classifying poetry on a new principle,
as well as a philosophical *aperçu* of fancy, imagination, and
imitation, and a study of the relation of poetry to philosophy.
For the aesthetic judgment of Davenant's contemporaries the
student should read the commendatory verses attached to Gondibert and to other poems of the day. Denham's Preface of
1656 to his own Essay on Translation (written much earlier,
1636) states in prose the plea for liberal rendering that he had
already advanced in the verses to Sir Richard Fanshaw, 1647.

With the exception of Milton, Cowley was the writer of
keenest poetic insight between Ben Jonson and Dryden. In
his notes on the Davideis and his Preface to his Works, 1656,
he reverts to the critical principles enunciated by Bacon, and
takes his stand as an advocate of the analytic and historical
methods. While recognizing the poetic possibilities of morals
and religion, he is capable also of a larger view, not utilitarian
nor didactic. Still more striking is the philosophical sympathy
with Bacon which Cowley displays in his Address to the Royal
Society — a species of English Academy to the establishment
of which the poet's Proposition for the Advancement of Learning (1661) had contributed. The Ode or Address, written
between 1662 and 1667, states clearly the relation of philosophy to authority and to reason, the function of philosophy
in respect of nature, and the difference between the poetry of
wit and the poetry of the philosophic imagination. In his

appreciation of nature, her beauty and her significance, the poet distinctly anticipates Wordsworth (see Grosart, Cowley, vol. I, p. civ). Contemporary verses on Cowley's death, 1667, and on Milton's Paradise Lost, which was published in the same year, afford an insight into the literary opinion of the day. On that epic the earliest laudatory criticism was uttered in 1669 by Milton's nephew, Edward Phillips ; and the next by Marvel, in verses written about 1672.

During the interval between Ben Jonson's first attempts in critical method and Cowley's Proposition for the Advancement of Learning, there had been a certain development of practical poetics, but it was marked rather by the greater frequency of applied criticism than by any improvement of the method. With the foundation of the Royal Society, however, which (although its object was the advancement of science) pledged itself to the cultivation of a lucid, forcible, and easy English style, the vehicle of criticism was assured ; and on the ordering and simplification of the style there naturally followed a systematization of principles. Cowley is indirectly the promoter of the refined manner and liberal method which characterize the poetics of Dryden, and he is directly the forerunner of the return to nature and philosophy which characterizes Wordsworth and Coleridge.

The *Third Period* of English poetics, then, beginning with the Foundation of the Royal Society, 1662, and continuing until the publication of the Tatler, 1709, accomplished *the Refinement of Theory and Method*. Its principal representatives are Cowley, Dryden, Mulgrave, Roscommon, Bentley, and Dennis.

To give a complete account of Dryden's contributions to poetics would be impossible in this place. A list of his writings will be found in § 20 above. The first of his "famous prolegomena " was the Dedication to Lord Orrery, prefixed to the Rival Ladies, 1664. Here his desire to improve style and versification found expression in a plea for a literary tribunal like the French Academy. But the preference for rhyme announced in this Dedication being, in 1665, challenged by Howard (Preface to Four New Plays), there was precipitated the discussion which produced Dryden's first great effort in poetics, the Essay of Dramatic Poesy, 1668. This essay, which strives to show that modern drama excels the ancient, displays advance both in method and poetic judgment. In method the discussion proceeds from an accepted definition to the historical application of the same and the analysis of representative examples. In the realm of theory or judgment the emphasis, meanwhile, is laid upon typical idealization, consistency between dramatic content and poetic garb, and the importance of the criterion of imaginative appeal. There is also evident a consciousness of the interpretative function of poetry, and of the value of a wider aesthetic appeal (to many emotions rather than one or two). Even at this stage of his career Dryden displays a catholicity of taste — not merely classical nor romantic, not all didactic, nor hedonistic — that savors of and recalls Bacon, Milton, and Cowley.

In the Defense of the Essay of Dramatic Poesy, 1668, Dryden strengthens his plea for rational idealization by attacking the false principles of personal criticism and unregulated taste advanced by Sir Robert Howard. In the Preface to the Conquest of Granada, 1669–72, the romantic spirit prevails — a sense of the relation between poetry and the age, and a tendency to look at literary productions from the comparative point of view. In the Preface to the State of Innocence, 1674, Dryden expresses his admiration of Paradise Lost, thus early recording the catholicity of his poetic taste. This Preface is of the utmost importance in his career as a critic. It discusses the essence of poetry, the qualifications of the critic, and the methods of criticism. The canons of judgment are considered with reference to nature, imitation, and imagination. The critic must be of poetic temperament, must judge of poetry according to its species, must make organic judgments, and must know when to rely upon authority, when on reason. This essay marks the opening of the second stage of Dryden's criticism. He now abandons the advocacy of rhyme, and begins to feel his way among more difficult problems. In the Preface to All for Love, 1678, he adds to the principles of method already enunciated that of the *milieu*, — a revolt against the authority of foreign criticism (French or classical) in English poetics. In the matter of the *milieu*, he anticipates Hegel, Taine, Brunetière (§ **9,** *I,* *B* 3). Equally revolutionary and equally scientific are not a few of the theoretical principles advanced in this Preface.

Omitting for the present the Preface to Oedipus, 1678, the student may pass to the Heads of an Answer to Rymer (written 1678, but not published till 1711), which displays another change of front and another advance in poetic judgment.

Rymer had in 1678 brought out a work entitled the Tragedies of the Last Age, Considered and Examined by the Practice of the Ancients, and by the Common Sense of all Ages. This essay was a natural sequence of his own translation, made in 1674, of Rapin's Reflections on Aristotle's Treatise of Poesie. In the Tragedies of the Last Age, Rymer, insisting that the Aristotelian laws should be observed by modern tragedy, tests three of Fletcher's plays accordingly, and condemns them for their nonconformity. It happens that on the fly-leaf of a copy of the Tragedies of the Last Age Dryden wrote his Heads of an Answer to Rymer's Remarks. Since these Heads were not intended for publication, we here have Dryden as he was in himself. We find him objecting to the rigor of the ancient classical tradition and formulating his own ideas as to the procedure of criticism. This, indeed, is the beginning of Dryden's third stage of development, a period of widening and deepening in

natural and scientific criticism.   He insists upon a standard of
judgment at once logical and historical, upon the recognition
of development in literary types, upon the principles of *milieu*
and national variety, and upon the adoption accordingly of
criteria which shall make allowance for the modification of
literary conditions.   The Grounds of Criticism in Tragedy, published by him the next year, is much more conservative, but at
bottom maintains the breach with the school of the ancients.
This breach is also evident in the Preface to Oedipus, 1678, and
still more noticeable in the Epistle Dedicatory of the Spanish
Fryar, 1681.   But while Dryden more steadily advocates the
natural development of tragedy, he by no means sanctions lack
of restraint or of propriety.   The advance in historical method
and in analysis of principles is continued until with the Preface
to Don Sebastian the critic may be regarded as entering upon
his last and most profitable period of development.   Before
examining the productions of that period, however, it is necessary to review the course of contemporary criticism.

In 1669 had appeared Edward Phillips's Compendious
Enumeration of the Poets (with praise of Milton's Paradise
Lost), and in 1675 his Theatrum Poetarum.   To 1680 belongs
Roscommon's Translation of Horace's Art of Poetry, which
realized what Ben Jonson had in 1641 attempted, and therefore crowned the movement toward which the glorification of
Horace had since 1605 steadily contributed.   So far as the
style of translation is concerned, Roscommon followed in the
footsteps of Denham (1647, 1656) and Waller.   It must be
remembered, too, that Roscommon had especially at heart
the improvement of the English language and of style ; and
that, during the ' seventies ' he had prosecuted, though without
formal success, a plan for the foundation of an Academy like
that of France, a scheme in which he was seconded by Dryden
and others.   (The history of attempted literary academies in
England is worthy of careful study.)

In 1682 was published the Earl of Mulgrave's (afterward Duke of Buckinghamshire) Essay upon Poetry. This had a decided effect in confirming the " correct taste "; but the author was not, by any means, a mere advocate of Horace and the French models. Roscommon's Essay on Translated Verse followed in 1684, characterized by independence of judgment, observation, and a respect for the English language, and ' wit ' as contrasted with the French. The advocacy of free translation was, however, not new ; nor was the encomium on Paradise Lost the first of its kind.[1]

The publication of the *Athenian Gazette* in 1690, and of La Croze's Works of the Learned, the same year, is significant of the widening interest in critical literature ; also the appearance of the Athenae Oxonienses (2 vols. 1691, 1692) by Antony à Wood, who may be considered to be the founder of modern biography in England. His Fasti, or Annals, followed later. Subsequent authorities on literary and scholastic biography were Hearne, Anthony Hall, and Bishop Tanner, for whom see the Dictionary of National Biography.

Dryden's last and ripest season of critical production dates from the publication of the Preface to Don Sebastian, 1690. This preface marks a growing confidence in an aesthetic large enough to subsume the hitherto mechanical and inflexible law of tradition ; and it reaffirms the best of his conclusions concerning practical and theoretical poetics. The Discourse on the Original and Progress of Satire, 1692, 1693, illustrates his method of literary comparison ; while the Dedication of the Third Miscellany, 1693, reiterates the necessity of regarding literature as a historical growth and of applying criteria suit-

---

[1] Talking of encomia, the flood of verses that deluged the merits of Waller in 1688 is of interest ; it bears upon its bosom many a relic of contemporary criticism. The student, indeed, should make a point of examining all such verses with a view to collating the criteria of poetry as applied in successive ages. As far as Waller is concerned, the literary estimate of his more thoughtful contemporaries is furnished by the Preface to the Second Part of his Poems, 1690.

able to the literary period and habit concerned. The last of these utterances was provoked by the appearance in 1692 or 1693 of A Short View of Tragedy, etc., in which the indefatigable Rymer poured contempt upon the irregularities (from the point of view of ancient dramatic criticism) of Shakespeare, Corneille, and others of a modern cut. A field of criticism still somewhat broader is entered by Dryden in his Parallel of Poetry and Painting, 1695, prefixed to the translation of Du Fresnoy's Art of Painting. Here he looks upon poetry from outside as well as from within, and draws, though in a naïve and speculative fashion, one or two distinctions between literary and plastic arts. This is one of the first attempts, if not the first, at comparative aesthetics, that England had produced.

Meanwhile the moralistic objection to the stage, the last manifestation of which had taken form in Histriomastix some sixty years before, — the moralistic objection was again preparing for expression. It made itself mildly obvious in Richard Blackmore's Preface to Prince Arthur, 1695. This, however, although it attacked Dryden, was not, for some two years, deemed worthy of his notice. But in 1696 John Dennis, who had already proved his ability in the Impartial Critic, of 1693, an answer to Rymer's Short View of Tragedy, and in his Miscellanies in Verse and Prose of the same year, made a vigorous reply to Blackmore, entitled Remarks upon Prince Arthur. This is one of our earliest reviews in the modern critical sense. Dennis was an ardent and judicious admirer of Dryden, — perhaps better equipped to espouse his cause than was any other of his generation. But Dennis's reply has left no mark upon history. For the irritation of the religious-minded was soon to find expression in such condemnation of the Restoration Drama as should render Blackmore's assistance and Dennis's defense equally trivial. In 1698, Jeremy Collier spoke out; and his " Short View of the Immorality and

Profaneness of the English Stage, etc.," prejudiced, unhistorical, uncritical, and unfair, as in many respects it was, put an end to the vices — and to some of the virtues, too — of English drama at one and the same time. It is interesting to note that Collier undoubtedly made use, in the preparation of this work, not only of the manifest English source, Prynne, but of a French adaptation of Prynne, called Traité de la comédie et des spectacles selon la tradition de l'Église, written by Armand de Bourbon, Prince de Conti, and published in 1667. Accordingly, odd as it may appear, the English stage owes something of its reformation to the quarter whence one would least expect reform to proceed. This fact seems not to have been hitherto noticed by the historians. No synopsis of the Short View need be given here, as it is familiar to every student, and, though not reprinted, may be picked up at any secondhand bookseller's in England. For a list of the numerous 'Replies' to this work the student should consult Beljame's Le public et les hommes de lettres en Angleterre au XVIIIᵉ siècle, 1660–1744 (Paris : 1884) ; and for a full enumeration of Collier's rejoinders, the article 'Collier,' Dict. Nat. Biog. Dryden's part in the controversy was all the more dignified, because he acknowledged the justice, in one respect at least, of the attack. (See the Epistle to Motteux, 1698.) His Preface to the Fables, 1700, *apropos* of a fresh provocation from Blackmore, made further reference to the affair. But that is the matter of least interest in the Preface, which, as a whole, sums up what is best in Dryden's poetics and exemplifies what is best in his method. In the same year the poet-critic died. He had outlined the course that criticism was to pursue. Where his own practice failed, the failure is due to the age, the writer's lack of information, the ignorance of the scientific methods necessary for the prosecution of the aesthetic and comparative principles that he had enunciated.

During the last years of the century two movements had gained strength which were to set their mark upon the criticism of the next century, the philosophical and the scientific-classical. The former is represented by two names : that of Locke, to whose doctrine of the association of ideas (Essay concerning the Human Understanding, 1690) Addison refers in his papers on the Pleasures of the Imagination, and whose inquiry into the nature of the mental faculties has influenced subsequent aesthetic speculation ; and that of Shaftesbury, whose rhapsodical teaching of the relation between the good and the beautiful was to color the numerous 18th century treatises on taste, Addison's included, while his advocacy of criticism as an educative agency was to produce the *Virtuosi*, and with them a class of readers able to appreciate the efforts of aesthetic criticism.   Shaftesbury's Characteristics was not published till 1711–14 ; but the papers of which it is composed had appeared at various dates from 1699 on.

The other movement, the scientific-classical, underlies the controversy between modern and ancient learning, and although in appearance it was a mere battle of the books, it in fact laid the foundations of the critical literary scholarship of the present century.   The principal contestants on the side of the moderns were, in France, Fontenelle and Charles Perrault, 1688, as opposed to Boileau for the ancients.   In England, Wotton, 1694, espoused the cause of modern literature, while Sir William Temple, 1692, and later, Swift (Battle of the Books, begun 1699, published 1704), took the other side.   But it was not until the question arose concerning the authenticity of the Letters of Phalaris, which Temple had cited in confirmation of his views, that the quarrel assumed a scientific character.   Boyle, in 1697, made a frivolous attack upon Bentley, who could see nothing classical or even genuine in 'Phalaris.' Bentley's reply, A Dissertation upon the Letters of Phalaris, 1698, is "the earliest model of a new criticism, which by a scientific method was to bring accurate philological knowledge into relation with historical research " (Professor Jebb, 'Bentley,'

Eng. Men of Letters series). In literary criticism Bentley's work is the forerunner of the antiquarian, mediaeval, and Old English researches which have helped to develop historical method during the last one hundred and fifty years.

In 1701 an effort to bring about an understanding between the combatants was made by Dennis, in his Advancement and Reformation of Modern Poetry. He attempts with considerable skill and some success to show that both sides have overlooked the real basis of difference between ancient and modern poetry. He maintains that the excellence of ancient poetry lies in its religious quality, and that it is superior to the modern only when the modern fails to avail itself of the poetic advantages afforded by the superior emotional and moral qualities of Christianity. In this treatise, in his Large Account of the Taste in Poetry and the Causes of the Degeneracy of it, 1702, and in his Grounds of Criticism in Poetry, 1704, Dennis variously anticipates principles of theory and method for the advocacy of which credit is ordinarily given to Addison, Goldsmith, and Wordsworth.

The *Fourth Period* in the history of English poetics begins with the popularization of criticism by the essay-papers, and extends to the foundation of the Reviews, — from the *Tatler*, 1709, to the *Edinburgh*, 1802. It is distinguished by the *crystallization of the older theories and methods, and the preparation for a reaction against their authority*. The general features of criticism after the death of Dryden are known to the student, and the details become too numerous to be comprehended within the limits at our command. What follows is consequently but a summary. For some of the particulars reference may be made to Miss Wylie's work and the more recent treatises of Vaughan and Hamelius.

The history of periodical literature should first occupy the student. *Résumés* will be found in Andrews's History of British Journalism, Grant's History of the Newspaper Press,

Courthope's Addison (Eng. Men of Letters series), and in Miss Bateson's contributions to Traill's Social England. Not only the spread of reading but the development of social life (through coffee-houses, clubs, etc.) tended to alter the relation between critic and public, and so to modify the style of criticism. With the foundation of the *Tatler* and the *Spectator*, for instance, the style became more conversational, and gradually more timely and more direct.

The schools of poetic theory are during this period well defined. That with which the century opened, and which, in spite of growing opposition, maintained its authority till almost the close of the century, was characterized by 'correctness,' classical authority, mechanical and personal method, and fixed canons of judgment. As the contemporaries of Dryden, though not Dryden himself, had followed the system of Rapin, which they themselves had made illiberal, so the contemporaries of Pope and Johnson followed in the path of Boileau, which they themselves made arid and strait. The other school was the romantic, led by Young, Gray, the Wartons, Hurd, and others. It acquired greater strength during the latter half of the century than the historians ordinarily have noticed; such force, indeed, that it is altogether a mistake to regard Wordsworth's Preface to the Lyrical Ballads as the beginning of the romantic movement. It was rather the climax of the romantic revolt which had sprung into significance some sixty years before.

During the earlier years of the period, Steele, in the *Tatler*, started the fashion which Addison followed and confirmed. The papers on Paradise Lost, in the *Spectator* (Dec. 31, 1711 — May 3, 1712), were one of the earliest instances of criticism applied to a single poem; but it is not to be assumed that they were the first, or that no one had appreciated Milton before Addison wrote these papers. Addison's method combines a certain liberality of view with the application of classical canons, but Dryden's had displayed the same characteristic.

The papers on the Pleasures of the Imagination discuss the nature of our delight in poetry more exhaustively than had been done since Dryden's time, but the criterion of Appeal to the Imagination, which Worsfold (Principles of Criticism) considers to be a discovery of Addison's, had been recognized by Bacon, Dryden, Shaftesbury, and Dennis; and the analysis of the qualities productive of pleasure into Grandeur, Beauty, and Novelty may with ease have been derived from Bacon and Shaftesbury. It is not the novelty of Addison's poetics, but the sanity and impartiality of his judgment, together with the facility of his style and the felicity of his method, that makes him one of the greatest of our critics. To the earlier productions of this school of 'correctness' belong also Pope's Discourse on Pastoral Poetry, 1709, the Essay on Criticism, 1711, and various papers in the *Guardian*, 1713. Of the Essay the external stimulus may be found in the revolt against the so-called Gothic and apparently unregulated taste that had for many years obtained on the Continent.

In 1709 appeared Rowe's edition of Shakespeare, the forerunner of a series of editions most important in the history of applied poetics; and in 1710–11 Dennis's Three Letters on the Genius and Writings of Shakespeare, worthy of appreciative examination. These were succeeded by Pope's Essay on Criticism, already mentioned, and that by the quarrel between Pope and Addison on the one hand and Dennis on the other. Swift's Proposal for Correcting the English Tongue, following in the wake of Cowley, Dryden, and Roscommon, strengthened the classical movement. In 1718 appeared Gildon's Complete Art of Poetry, and in 1720 his Laws of Poetry; neither of which was of more than formal quality. In 1719 Addison died. He had without doubt recalled art to a natural basis (as he understood nature), and had " drawn the principles of invention from dispositions inherent in the mind of man " (Johnson, Lives of the Poets). He had done much " to produce a habit of reasoning rightly on matters of taste and criticism " (Courthope), and it must not be supposed that his influence was merely in the direction of formal correctness. He had helped to cultivate the judgment of the public ; so that the generation succeeding him might address its poetry and its criticism to the people and not to the patron. In 1725 appeared Pope's Edition of Shakespeare, with an introductory essay that is not by any means devoid of sound critical judgment. In 1726 Spence wrote his classical essay on Pope's Homer; and in 1727 appeared the treatise on Bathos, by Pope, Swift, and Arbuthnot. The former work displayed true taste, the latter developed a code of negative poetics.

Colley Cibber's Apology for My Life, an excellent review of theatrical performances, was produced in 1740 ; and in 1742–43 he became hero of the Fourth Dunciad. In 1743 Pope died. His malignities in criticism are introductory to the magisterial method of Johnson and the literary personalities of Southey and Gifford. The canons of his school made " poetry prosaic " and undermined the scientific comparative method of criticism in process of construction during the previous century. But his power shows also in his contribution to literary ethics: the establishment of independent authorship and the consequent destruction of the habit of dedications. After him the influence of patronage waned steadily, till with Johnson it expired. Thereafter, the public and the publisher became arbiters of fate in matters both creative and critical.

The philosophers who during Pope's life exercised an influence upon aesthetic theory were Hutcheson and Hume ; the former by his Enquiry into the Original of our Ideas of Beauty and Virtue, 1725, and his Essay on the Passions and Affections, 1728 (a development of Shaftesbury); and the latter by his Treatise of Human Nature, 1739. (On Hume's aesthetics, see Bosanquet, Hist. Aesth., p. 261.) Hume's analytic method was the complement to the aesthetics of Burke, Hogarth, Kames, and Reynolds. Out of the synthesis proceeded several of the cardinal ideas of subsequent critical theory. The later dissertations of Hume are sometimes a working over of the Treatise; but they should all be studied. See § 8.

With Thomson's poem, Edward and Leonora, 1739, and Joseph Warton's Enthusiast, or The Love of Nature, 1740, the Romantic movement began to gather strength. Warton called for a return to sincerity of observation and sanity of description. Dodsley's Collection of Old Plays was published in 1744, and in 1746 Joseph Warton's Preface to Odes on Several Subjects. Poetry was now fairly embarked on the romantic stream. In criticism, too, the Wartons, Goldsmith, Young, Gray, Collins, Cowper, and Hurd were all in the line of transition from the romanticism of Sidney and Bacon to that of Wordsworth. But it must be remembered that not only in these writers, but in Dryden and Dennis, and differently in Addison, are to be found germs of our present critical principles and methods.

Before rehearsing the productions of the Wartons and their followers, we turn again to the older line of thought. Akenside's Pleasures of the Imagination, frigidly constructed upon the basis of Addison and Hutcheson, came out in 1743. In 1744 Samuel Johnson made his appearance with Observations on Macbeth; and in 1747 Warburton produced his unfortunate edition of Shakespeare. In 1755 Johnson's Dictionary saw the light (note the Preface); and from this time the lexicographer was Dictator. His Lives of the Poets did not appear till 1779–81, but his Shakespeare, his articles in the *Rambler*, etc., and the concreteness of his personality enabled him to set his mark upon criticism even before he had substantially exemplified his theories. There is much sound sense in the Lives, and there is the 'grand style'; but they are dominated by the fixed pseudo-Aristotelian principles and the dictatorial method. They are significant in the history of criticism because they summarize not only the approved literary opinion of the day, but the accumulated wisdom of those whose authority as critics had been recognized during a century.

The principal contributions to the Romantic movement in criticism during the ascendency of Dr. Johnson in the Classical school were the following : Spence's Polymetis, 1747 ; the introductory chapters in Fielding's Tom Jones (directed against the belief in the fixity of literary types); Joseph Warton's Prefatory Essay to the Edition of the Georgics and Eclogues, 1753 ; Hurd's dissertations on the Provinces of the Several Species of Dramatic Poetry and on Poetical Imitation, in his edition of Horace's Epistles to the Pisos and to Augustus (2 vols. Lond.), 1753 ; Thomas Warton's Observations on the Faerie Queene, 1754, and in 1757 Joseph Warton's Essay on the Life and Genius of Pope (where for the first time that poet is critically handled); in 1759 some of Goldsmith's suggestions in the Polite Learning and in the *Bee* (where he more than once calls for direct study of the people, for interpretative idealization, and for a historical appreciation of literary and social characteristics); Young's Letter to Samuel Richardson on Original Composition, 1759 ; Gray's Metrum, 1760–61; Macpherson's Fragments of Ancient Poetry, 1760, and the Poems of Ossian, 1762 (which aroused a controversy of great import to romanticism); Hurd's Letters on Chivalry and Romance, 1762; Blair's Critical Dissertation on Ossian, 1763; Thomas Warton's History of English Poetry, 1774–81 (in which he acknowledges the receipt of Gray's outline for the history); in 1781 the second volume of Joseph Warton's Life and Genius of Pope, and in 1797 his edition of that poet's works. These last-mentioned works completed the preliminaries of the attack upon the school of 'correctness.' In 1798 followed the brief and telling preface to the first edition of the Lyrical Ballads, and in 1800 the famous Preface to the second edition, in which Wordsworth, in so far as he does not exploit untenable theories of his own, sets clearly before the world the strength and the claims of the romantic return to imagination and nature; a return that affected the principles and methods of poetics as emphatically as it affected those of poetry.

The student must not fail to estimate the influence meanwhile exercised by the writers of treatises upon aesthetics. Of these the first was Burke, whose Sublime and Beautiful, 1756, told directly upon aesthetic speculation in England, and later indirectly through the influence of Lessing and Kant. For to Burke both of these men were indebted: Lessing in the Laocoon, 1766, and Kant in the Kritik der Urteilskraft, 1790. Other English aestheticians were Kames (Elements of Criticism, 1762), Hogarth (Analysis of Beauty, 1753), Hume (later Dissertations, 1757), and Reynolds (Papers on the Idler, Discourses on Beauty, 1758–59); for whom see § 8 above. Also to be considered is the effect of the impetus given to historical and comparative research by Winckelmann's Geschichte der Kunst des Altertums, 1764, by Stuart's Antiquities of Athens (two years earlier), and by other works on the archaeology, literature, and art of the northern as well as the southern nationalities of Europe. Nor should the return wave of romantic interest from Germany be ignored. The outward movement proceeded from the early work of the Wartons, 1740–60, from the revival of Shakespearian scholarship, Gray's interest in Northern Literature, Macpherson's Ossian, 1762, Percy's Reliques of Ancient English Poetry, 1765. The movement returned from Germany in Bürger's Lenore, in the works of Herder, Jean Paul, Wieland, and, later, of the Schlegels, Tieck, and the Romantiker. That the English romantic revival owes anything to Bodmer (1721) and the German critics of the Swiss school is not probable, for they had no disciples in England; indeed, they themselves drew their inspiration largely from English poetry. Nor did it begin with Rousseau (whose influence shows itself as early as with Goldsmith), for Rousseau's Nouvelle Héloïse did not appear till 1760. It would appear not unlikely that most of this romantic inspiration — later carried by France and Germany into sentimentalism — issued in England from Thomson, 1739, Samuel Richardson, 1740, and Lillo (George Barnwell, 1731) ; in France from Marivaux and Prévost, 1731, — but that both schools had in turn derived it from the Sentimental Comedy of Sir Richard Steele (The Funeral, 1702, The Lying Lover, 1703, The Conscious Lovers, 1722), and of Addison (The Drummer, 1715). The creative literature of the century must, evidently, be studied as a background to poetic theory. The numerous editions of older authors, collections of early poetry and drama, histories of types and periods of art, biographies of authors, translations of and commentaries upon the ancients, as Tyrwhitt's and Pye's editions of Aristotle's Poetics, — the effect of all such upon critical theory and practice must be considered.

This fourth period comprises the tyranny of conventional poetics and the preliminaries of the reaction. By Johnson and his school, on the one side, principles were conventionalized, while method was made systematic and style improved. To be sure, the manner was ponderous and the method personal, dictatorial, and mechanical ; but criticism had learned to set itself an object and to move toward it. The followers of the Wartons had, on the other side, attempted to deepen the study of theory and to widen the courses of method. They had revived the poetic tests of nature, passion, and imagination, and had put into practice the elementary principles of historical method, genetic and comparative.

The present, the *Fifth, Period* in the development of English poetics opens with the present century. So far as theory is concerned, the dominant movement of this period had been gaining momentum ever since 1739 ; it had reached its culmination as a movement of revolt in 1798 ; as a movement of positive and practical influence it still continues. Divisions into periods are arbitrary. The classical and the romantic movements in one form or another are perennial ; they flow through periods. But, viewed synthetically, the 19th century may be called the *Period of Reconstruction.* Its beginning is marked by the organization of criticism which attended the establishment of the Reviews, — in 1802 the *Edinburgh*, and in 1809 the *Quarterly*, — soon to be followed by *Blackwood* and the *London Magazine.* Hitherto criticism had carried the authority of the writer only ; and the labor of criticism was generally an avocation, or, at best, secondary to some regular profession. But the judgments of the *Edinburgh* and the *Quarterly* were known to proceed from one or other of a coterie of acknowledged scholars and men of letters ; to represent the opinions and policy of the coterie and the best ability of the writer. Criticism, accordingly, was, at the beginning of the century, organized as a profession by the *Edinburgh*, under the editorship of Jeffrey, with the collaboration of Sydney Smith, Brougham, Scott, Leslie, etc. ; by the *Quarterly*, under the editorship of Gifford, with the collaboration of Scott, Southey, Lockhart, etc. ; by *Blackwood's Magazine*, under Wilson, Lockhart, Hogg, and Maginn ; and by the *London*, under Lamb, Hazlitt, and De Quincey. (See Traill's Social England, and Saintsbury's Nineteenth Century Literature.)

The history of criticism in the early part of this century may be considered systematically as follows : (1) The Enunciation of the Romantic Principle : Wordsworth, Coleridge's earlier writings, Scott in the *Edinburgh*, etc. (2) The Classical Reaction : the Reviews — Jeffrey, Gifford, Lockhart, Southey, Wilson, etc. But here the student should discriminate between the impressionism and narrow prejudice of Gifford (the nadir of personal criticism) and the reactionary but altogether more catholic and philosophical traditionalism which, in spite of occasional spleen and error, characterizes Jeffrey. *Blackwood* follows, to some extent, the lead of the older reviews, but Wilson's temper frequently prompts to liberal appreciation ; while

Lockhart (even if he did commit the diatribe against Keats) deserves credit as a master of critical biography, and displays neither the caprice of Wilson nor the malignity and retrogressive bigotry of Gifford.

(3) The Establishment of Romantic Criticism.   First, Bowles, whose criticism of Pope's poetry, prefixed to his edition of that poet's works, 1806, gave rise to the controversy with Campbell and Byron (Campbell's Essay on Poetry, 1819; Byron's Letter to John Murray, and Observations upon Observations, 1821; Bowles's Invariable Principles of Poetry, 1819, and Letters to Byron and Campbell, 1822).   Second, Coleridge (Lectures on English Poets, 1808, 1812; Biographia Literaria, 1817).   On Coleridge's relation to Wordsworth's theories, see Traill's Social England; for the source of his criticism, German and English, see Brandl's Coleridge and Miss Wylie's Evolution of Criticism. Third, Campbell (Lectures on Poetry, 1810; Specimens of the British Poets, 1819–1848).   Fourth, Leigh Hunt, in criticism a direct descendant of the Wartons and Spence, in temperament, of Goldsmith; he in turn influenced his contemporaries Hazlitt and Lamb, and probably both Carlyle and Macaulay, the leaders of criticism in the next generation (Critical Essays, 1805; What is Poetry? 1844; Wit and Humor, etc.).   Fifth, Charles Lamb, unique in sympathetic insight, a forerunner of Pater.   Sixth, William Hazlitt, the ally of Coleridge in the contention that poetry should be judged not by some stand-ard of the critics, but by the criterion of poetry—poetry uni-versal and in the abstract (Round Table, 1817; Characters of Shakespeare's Plays, 1817; English Poets, 1818; Eng-lish Comic Writers, 1819; Dramatic Literature of the Reign of Elizabeth, 1821; Table Talk, 1821–22).   Seventh, Shelley, whose Defense of Poetry, 1821, provoked by T. L. Peacock's Four Ages of Poetry, recalls the best of Sidney, Bacon, Words-worth, and Coleridge, and anticipates Carlyle's gospel of poetic significance and Pater's of rational aesthetic delight.

Minor writers during these years were Sir Egerton Brydges (Censura Literaria, etc., 1805–1809), John Nichols (Literary Anecdotes of the Eighteenth Century. 9 vols. 1812–15; and Illustrations of Literary History. 8 vols. 1817–58), Hartley Coleridge (Marginalia, etc.), John Sterling, Baker, Reed, and Jones (Biographia Dramatica. 3 vols. 1812), Genest (Account of the English Stage. 10 vols. 1830).

(4) Attempts at an Historical Method. These began with Henry Hallam, and were continued by Carlyle, De Quincey, and Macaulay. Of Carlyle it may be said that his services are rather in the theory of criticism than the practice; but both in theory and practice his keynote is ' historical': poetry is history vitalized; the poet is the outcome of his own history and the history of the nation. Carlyle taught the significance of poetry, the interpretative function of criticism, and advocated a method of research at once genetic and comparative. His influence in the systematization and limitation of modern criticism has been immense, and has by no means begun to exhaust itself. It affects rather the matter than the manner, and is more a philosophy than an aesthetic of poetry (see Miscellanies, Goethe, etc., Lectures on Heroes, History of Literature, and § **20** above). In their recognition of national literary development and in their familiarity with German literature Carlyle and De Quincey were sympathetic; but as regards the appreciation of German literature De Quincey is more insular than Carlyle, and as regards literary history, while Carlyle would discover the bearing of the poet's ethical significance, De Quincey is concerned with that of his literary characteristic. Macaulay, who knew not Germany, and with all his biographical industry never learned the comparative method, represents the " personal " wing of the historical school. He is judge and advocate combined. He derives from Samuel Johnson, Gibbon, Jeffrey, Hallam, and Hazlitt.

In the latter half of this century a movement is manifest which has for its purpose the Investigation of Principles and the Establishment of a Scientific Basis for poetic and artistic appreciation.   The leaders in this movement are John Stuart Mill (System of Logic, 1843, etc.; Thoughts on Poetry and its Varieties, etc.), Herbert Spencer (Social Statics, 1851; Psychology, 1855, etc.; Philosophy of Style, 1852 ; On Gracefulness, 1854), and G. H. Lewes (Problems of Life and Mind, 1874–79, etc.; Principles of Success in Literature).

By the teachings of these men Morris, Ruskin, and Arnold have been more or less affected.   But Morris and Ruskin have confined themselves principally to the aesthetics and economics of the plastic arts, while the aesthetics and didactics of poetry are the immediate concern of Matthew Arnold.   For the comparative method of literary criticism Arnold has done what Ruskin is doing for that of art-criticism (see Collingwood's Art-Teaching of Ruskin).   A combination and modification of the qualities of Ruskin and Arnold (by the omission of the economics of the first and the didactics of the second) appear in the essays of Walter Pater, who, with Symonds, is regarded as the leader of the hedonistic school.   But Pater's chief characteristic is his desire to interpret and reproduce the author ; Symond's, to show the historical relations of poetry and art. For Ruskin, Arnold, Pater, etc., see §§ **2, 5, 8, 14, 20.**

Most of the other writers on poetry who should be considered in connection with the tendencies that have affected the latter half of the century have been already mentioned in the sections indicated above.   The more important may be classified by the student.   They are such as Spedding (Bacon, and Essays and Reviews) ; William Edmondston Aytoun, whose Firmilian (a verse satire) upset the spasmodic school ; Sir Francis Doyle (Lectures on Poetry. Lond.: 1869. Extremely good reading — especially the Inaugural, in which certain so-called tests, definitions, and laws of poetry are deftly handled; but Doyle does not accept the distinction between fancy and imagination enunciated in various ways by Wordsworth, Coleridge, and

Ruskin); Dallas, Palgrave, Brimley, Robert Buchanan (David
Gray and other Essays, chiefly on Poetry. Lond.: 1868. See
pp. 3–60); Masson ; Minto (Characteristics of the English Poets
from Chaucer to Shirley. Edinb.: 1874); Browning (the luminous Essay on Poetry, referred to in § 20) ; Courthope, Austin,
Stopford Brooke (Primer ; History of Early English Literature;
Theology in the English Poets, N. Y.: 1875 ; and his Tennyson); Bagehot; Gurney ; Myers ; Dowden (especially his constructive and poetic Shakespearian criticism ; his Shelley; and
his Transcendentalism in Poetry, etc., in his Studies in Literature, 1789–1877, Lond.: 1887) ; Wm. Knight (Studies in Philosophy and Literature); Leslie Stephen (numerous articles in
the Dictionary of National Biography and elsewhere); John
Morley; Saintsbury (especially in his History of Nineteenth
Century Literature, and his contributions to Traill's Social
England); Swinburne; Gosse (in addition to works already cited,
his recent History of Modern English Literature, with its admirable Epilogue, in which he calls for the abandonment of 'individualistic' criticism, and the adoption of methods borrowed
from the field of science. He would apply but two criteria to
the poem : (1) Does the poet perform with distinguished skill
what he sets out to perform? (2) What is his place in literary
evolution, and his relation to those of his own kith and kin ?
This is the best word that has been said for many years in regard
to criticism); Robert Bridges (who, in addition to verses which
have placed him among our foremost living poets, has produced
a Prosody of Milton, and an interpretative Essay on Keats,
which entitle him to be regarded as one of our keenest and
most scholarly critics); Patmore (Principles in Art, etc. Lond.:
1890. Sentimental Essays); Roden Noel; Cotterill; W. M. Dixon
(Poetry and its Relation to Life, in his treatise From Blake to
Browning. Lond.: 1894. Attempts to restore the discussion
to the philosophical basis established by Plato and Aristotle);
Worsfold (Principles of Criticism, Lond.: 1897; a fair statement

of the aesthetics of Plato, Aristotle, and Spencer, with an interesting but disproportioned and unhistorical history of poetic theory as traced through Bacon, Addison, Lessing, Cousin, and Arnold); J. M. Robertson (Essays, and New Essays, toward a Critical Method); Alfred Miles (and his coadjutors in the unique and excellent volumes of the Poets and Poetry of the Century).

(*d*) **Present Condition of English Criticism.** — Few English critics, if any, have fulfilled the requirements of both theory and method. Many excel in some particular sphere of criticism, but even the broadest is one-sided. By some the comparative method has been impartially handled, by some the light of art-criticism has been brought to bear, by some the philosophical elements of poetry have been studied, by some the school and age and movement have been considered ; with still others the individuality of the poet is the problem of prime importance, or his conformity to traditional consensus, or his relation to national history. Some analyze and pigeon-hole ; some praise, some condemn, some appreciate; some neither pass judgment nor appreciate, — they register, record, or interpret. Some judge with regard to truth, some with regard to conduct, some with regard to emotion. For one, poetry is the breath of science, for another the criticism of life, for another an art for its own sake. There is neither system nor consensus. Criticism is still largely personal, capricious, traditional, sometimes mechanical, sometimes ignorant, and too frequently unregulated by control of any kind. But the signs of the times indicate a growth of inquiry into the principles of judgment and of method, and a discrimination of the one kind from the other : an inclination to decide the canons of theory with reference to philosophical, comparative, scientific, and aesthetic considerations, not apart but in organic relation, — regarded as genetic, not as static, — and to develop canons of method by adapting methods of scientific research to the old problems and the new mate-

rials. The period of reconstruction is, however, still in its
infancy.

In estimating the present condition of English criticism, it
may perhaps be of service to consider what has been elsewhere
said by the author of this chapter on the condition of literary
science in our universities (*The Dial,* Chicago, July 24, 1894).
Adapted to our present purpose, those remarks would have been
as follows : The present anarchy, sometimes tyranny'of critical
practice is due generally to a deficient analysis of theory and
method, and an incomprehensive view of the function of criticism and the extent of the field.   Hence the uncertainty of aim
with which criticism is frequently reproached.   This lack of
system is, however, indicative only of the fact that literary
science is in a transitional stage ; no longer static, nor yet
organic, but genetic.   The criticism of literature in the sentimental, the formally stylistic, or the secondhand-historical
fashion is out of date.   Scholars in philology have set the new
pace by making of their branch a genetic study ; a study of
sources, causes, relations, movements, and effects.   Students
of literature and criticism are now, as rapidly as may be, adapting progressive methods, whether historical or aesthetic, to
their lines of research.   But each is naturally liable to urge the
method that he favors, or thinks that he has invented.   One,
therefore, advocates ethical and religious exegesis, another aesthetic interpretation, another comparative criticism, another
the placing of the masterpiece in the evolution of the type.
This is to be expected ; and our genetic and frequently sporadic
stage of literary science cannot fulfil its promise until, by elim-
ination, attrition, and adjustment of results, the way has been
prepared for something organic.   Hospitality to ideas and conservative liberality of method will hasten the advent of systematic investigation.   Even now there are those who study the
masterpiece, not only in dynamic relation to author and type,
but also in organic relation to the social and artistic movements

of which author and type are integral factors.   The sum of the methods of any literary inquiry should be exhaustive, so far as circumstances permit.   The exigencies of leisure, space, and purpose are, however, such that due regard in turn for historical criticism (linguistic, textual ; relative to the history of the move-ment, national, social, literary, and artistic), technical criticism (distinctive of the type ; its evolution, characteristic, construc-tion, and function), interpretative criticism (the ethical and intellectual conception, the psychological condition), and aes-thetic criticism (in its narrow acceptation referring to the effect of the masterpiece upon imagination and emotion, but in its broader including with this all previous kinds of criticism), — due regard for each kind can rarely be observed in the study of any one specimen of literature.   But it should be the aim of the critic, availing himself of these instruments of research, to present an impartial interpretation, reproduction, and estimate of the author to the reading public.   With these considerations in mind, it is evident that the attempt to limit the practice or the theory of criticism to one method or one school would end in formalism ; would remand literary science to its static stage. Such limitation, however, is, fortunately, impossible.   For we now understand that criticism cannot be restricted to form alone, or thought alone, or to one kind of form or one kind of thought.   It is of both, and of all kinds of each.   Form and thought are as inseparable in literature as in life ; the expression is inherent in the idea ; and to understand literary expression one must be capable of appreciating all sides of the literary idea.   Social, metaphysical, and ethical themes are within the function of the bellelettrist as soon as, emotional-ized and clad in aesthetic form, they enter the field of letters. Nay, further, the methods of science, historical, chemical, geo-logical, anthropological, or biological, are within his function as soon as their adaptation may assist him to weigh aesthetic values or to trace the development of literary organisms.   It is consequently unwise to contemn efforts at scientific method, even though in the hands of enthusiasts they may appear to countervail aesthetic interpretation and discipline. In periods of transition, monomaniacs are forces. It is for those of far gaze and patient temper to compute results and perform the synthesis.

Among later critics there has been evident a right tendency in theoretic criticism to regard poetry both as absolute and relative ; to test the absolute aesthetic worth by reference to the laws of nature and thought, the poet's own conception of these and of his poetic function in interpreting them, — the poet's aim ; to test the relative worth of a poem by reference not to the standard of some preferred, so-called classical, or romantic school, but with reference to the particular movement of which it was part, and to the social, the inherited, the artistic, and the individual conditions of the age that have contributed to that movement and have affected the individual. And in method the tendency has fortunately been, with the best writers, more impartial, comparative, genetic, psychological, sometimes with a view to recording, sometimes to interpreting, sometimes to teaching. As a result, something like artistic criticism has occasionally been produced. Credit in this regard is especially due to Ruskin, Arnold, Pater, Symonds, Gurney, Stephen, Gosse, and Dowden. In France such men as Sainte-Beuve and his successors are worthy of mention; in Germany, the followers of Lessing and the recent writers of the great histories of literature ; and in Denmark, Brandes, with his Haupt-strömungen and the admirable Study of Shakespeare (2 vols. Lond.: 1897).

3. IN GERMANY. — *First Period.* — If we turn to the history of poetics in Germany, we shall find between the births of Gerhard Voss, 1577, and of Baumgarten, 1714, no writers worthy of more than passing mention. The Prosodia Germania (Frankf.: 1634) of Martin Opitz is representative of this interval

— purely *formalistic*. But a *Second Period* opened when, in 1721, by his Diskurse der Mahler, Johann Jakob Bodmer, of Zürich, pointed out the vanity of the existing French school of German poets and critics, and attacked the accepted authorities on German Art. The tenets of the Swiss writer were adopted by J. J. Breitinger and other gifted young scholars in Germany. It was not till 1740, when Bodmer's Vom Wunderbaren in der Poesie (Zürich) and Breitinger's Kritische Dichtkunst (2 vols. Zürich) appeared, that the Swiss school encountered any organized opposition. In Bodmer's anxiety to revive the worship of classic models and of the older German masters, and to create an appreciation of English poetry, he had found it necessary to censure the teaching of Gottsched and the Saxon school. Critics took sides. Gottsched's heavy artillery was brought to bear in 1750, but without much effect, for his Versuch einer Kritischen Dichtkunst was as old-fashioned and ponderous as the Prosodia of Opitz. See for full bibliography, and an excellent history of poetics in the 18th century, O. Neboliczka's Schäferdichtung und Poetik im 18. Jahrh. (Vierteljahrsch. f. Litteraturgesch. 2 : 22 : 1. Die deutsche Schäferdichtung von Gottsched bis auf die Bremer Beiträge ; 2. J. A. Schlegel's Satire : Vom Natürlichen in Schäferdichten ; 3. Der eigentliche Gegenstand der Schäferpoesie ; 4. Der Fortgang der dichterischen Production bis 1756 ; 5. Gessner u. der Umschwung der Theorie. Beilage : J. A. Schlegel u. Liscow). On Bodmer, Gottsched, etc., see also references under their names in § **20** above.

But while on either side the adherents of Bodmer and Gottsched were exalting for imitation antagonistic models of poetic perfection, it appeared to another critic that both parties misunderstood the nature of the subject. This was Baumgarten, who, by his De Nonnullis ad Poema pertinentibus (1735) and his Aesthetica (2 Bde., 1750–58), exhibited the relation of poetics to aesthetics and established the position of the latter as

an independent science.   Baumgarten was followed by Sulzer
and Eberhard (see F. Braitmaier, Gesch. d. poetisch. Theorie
u. Kritik von d. Diskursen d. Mahler bis auf Lessing.   Frauenfeld: 1888–89), and by Gellert, whose article, Wie weit sich
der Nutzen der Regeln in d. Beredsamkeit und Poesie erstrecke,
thrashes the ancient straw with fine poetic vigor (Sämmtliche
Schriften.   10 vols. in 5.   Bern: 1774–75; Bd. VII, pp. 117–
154).   These were, in turn, followed by the critics of the
Third, the Classical Period : Lessing, Schiller, Goethe, Herder,
and Richter.   The critical tenets of these writers were to
no slight extent influenced by the attitude toward aesthetics
adopted by Kant and Fichte.   For references to the poetics of
Lessing (especially the Laocoon and the Hamburgische Drama-
turgie), Schiller, Goethe, Herder, and Richter, see § **8**, and for
a review of Herder, Th. Wagener's Herder's Forschungen über
Sprache und Poesie (Progr. der Realschule I. O. zu Potsdam:
1875).   J. J. Engel's Anfangsgründe einer Theorie der Dichtungsarten aus deutschen Mustern entwickelt, which appeared
in 1783, could not have exercised any particular influence upon
the course of poetics, for although its conception was sound, no
induction worthy of the effort could be made from German
literature before the greatest works of Goethe and Schiller were
produced.

The movement which succeeded the classical owed its origin
to Solger (Vorlesungen über Aesthetik, 1829), who took as his
theme Fichte's principle of Artistic Irony : "The mood of the
artist, that impels him to represent things eternal in terms of
the phenomenal and evanescent."   Construing this principle
of Irony as dependent upon the caprice of the artist, A. W.
von Schlegel [Kritische Schriften.   2 vols.   Berl.: 1828.   Especially Lectures on Dramatic Literature (Bohn) and Briefe
über Poesie, Silbenmass und Sprache, 1795] and F. von Schlegel (Aesthetic and Miscellaneous Works.   Trans. by Millington.
Lond.: 1860), Tieck, and others established in Germany *the*

Romantic School of Poetics.   This dominates the *Fourth Period.*
The aesthetic teachings of the Romantiker inspired Germany
with a taste for Spanish and English drama as opposed to the
formal and so-called classical productions of France and Italy.
Hence the admirable Shakespearian criticism of the earlier
part of the century. (See Heine's Die romantische Schule :
a brilliant essay on the romantic revival and its characteristics.)

The one-sidedness, however, of the romantic school became
evident under the flood of light poured upon aesthetics by
Hegel. And round Hegel's Die Poesie most subsequent
German writers on poetry, accordant or divergent, revolve.
This is true even of such anti-Hegelians as Schopenhauer
(chapters on object of art, aesthetics of poetry, and of music),
who either borrow their ideas from Hegel or owe their virility
to the intensity of their antagonism. With Hegel's poetics as
presenting the view-point of absolute idealism should be read
F. T. Vischer's chapters on poetry in his Aesthetik, and C. H.
Weisse's statement of theory in his System d. Aesthetik als
Wissenschaft von d. Idee d. Schönheit (Leipz.: 1830). This,
the *Fifth Period* of German poetics, may be called the *historic-
aesthetic ;* it has its philological side, as well as its philosophical,
the former represented by Boeckh, Paul, Elze, etc., the latter by
Brandl, Vischer, etc. See § **21,** *A* 5. Lotze writes on poetry
as well as on philosophy ; but, unfortunately, his chapter on
poetry in the Geschichte d. Aesthetik in Deutschland is inadequate even for an historical sketch. The sections on poetry
in his Outlines of Aesthetics are likewise inconclusive, though
suggestive. Much more valuable from the historical point of
view is J. J. Wagner's Dichterschule (3. Aufl. Ulm: 1850).
The writings of Moritz Carriere are always refreshing and
enthusiastic in matter as in style. Not only his earlier volume,
Das Wesen u. d. Formen d. Poesie (Leipz. : 1854), but Die
Kunst im Zusammenhang d. Culturentwickelung, and Die Aes-

thetik are valuable for the liberal literary material with which
the author's theories, generally Hegelian, are illustrated.

During this period other German writers of more or less importance are Wackernagel, Wilh. Scherer, Rosenkranz, Sutermeister, Kleinpaul, Gottschall, Meyer, and Cohen. Wackernagel's
Poetik, Rhetorik, u. Stilistik (Halle : 1873) indicates the common basis of the three departments mentioned in the title.
The treatment of poetry is historico-philosophical, and happily
avoids the futility of rule-making.   It is an honest effort toward
the discovery of fundamental laws.   The chapter, pp. 16–35,
Das Wesen d. Poesie im Ganzen u. Allgemeinen is a cogent
argument against the imitation theory.   The lectures on poetics (Poetik.   Hrsg. von R. M. Meyer.   Berl.: 1888) by Wilh.
Scherer, delivered shortly before his death, though rambling
and fragmentary, may be called his best piece of work.   In his
discussion of the material of poetry, pp. 205–226, it will be
noticed that he has adopted the classification into the worlds
physical, moral, and imaginative used by Goethe and Schiller
in their correspondence.   Chapter I, Das Ziel, follows the lines
laid down by Hegel.   Pp. 118–147, Ueber den Werth d. Poesie,
are a lucid, if not technically philosophical, exposition of the
subject.   A decidedly less important volume is Otto Sutermeister's Leitfaden d. Poetik (Zürich: 1874); but, in spite
of its pedagogical character, it displays within the compass
of a hundred pages a fruitful application of the theories of
Carriere and Vischer.   Perhaps the most spirited of popular
German monographs on poetry is R. von Gottschall's Poetik :
Die Dichtkunst u. ihre Technik (5. Aufl.   Breslau: 1882).
Von Gottschall is a special pleader ; he writes poetics from a
'modern point of view,' and would have poetry, in Germany at
least, written in the same spirit : " It shall be the utterance of
the *Zeitgeist.*"   But, in spite of von Gottschall's prepossessions,
his work is forcibly and philosophically performed ; and, perhaps because of his nationalism, it has had a remarkable run.

The sketch of the history of poetics, pp. 1–16, is valuable,
especially from the point of view of aesthetics in Germany.
Pp. 19–134, Die Poesie im System d. Künste, and Der Geist d.
Dichtkunst, are an excellent *résumé* of much of the thought
of Hegel, Rosenkranz, and Carriere. The Poesie u. ihre
Geschichte of K. Rosenkranz (Königsb. : 1855) is comprehensive in method and subject-matter. It has the merit of
proceeding on a systematic induction from national literatures.
The groups are sub-classified under the following heads :
(1) the Ethnic Peoples and the Ideal of Beauty ; (2) the
Theistic Peoples and the Ideal of Wisdom; (3) the Christian
Peoples and the Ideal of Freedom, — a division suggestive,
indeed, but easily liable to forced interpretation, since it assumes that the evolution of poetry has proceeded upon lines
determined for the evolution of religion. Pp. 3–31, Einleitung, will especially interest the student of the comparative
method.

Other historical studies of poetry are K. T. Schröer's Die
Deutsche Dichtung des 14. Jahrhunderts (Leipz. : 1875), and K.
Goedeke's Deutsche Dichtung im Mittelalter (Dresden : 1871).
Lange's Deutsche Poetik, Formenlehre d. deutschen Dichtkunst, neu bearb. von R. Jonas, is a useful outline of the subject.
Meyer's little volume (Leitfaden d. deutsch. Poetik. Leipz. :
1869) is noteworthy merely as a compendious German school-
book. It has no critical value. The same may be said of F.
Bachmann's Schusters Lehrbuch der Poetik (3. Aufl. Halle :
1890), of J. Methner's Poesie und Prosa (Halle, A. S.: 1889), and
of R. von Zeynek's Lehrbuch d. deutschen Stilistik und Poetik
(6. Aufl. Graz : 1891). In connection with the theories of
Bacon, Buckle, Vischer, and Schelling, might be read H. Cohen's
clever plea for a psychological study of the conditions of poetry,
Die Dichterische Phantasie u. d. Mechanismus des Bewusstseins (Berl.: 1869. Abdr. aus d. *Zeitschrift f. Völkerpsych.*).
Kleinpaul's Poetik will be referred to under § **23**. It is an

admirable text-book, and may well be studied in connection
with the Populäre Vorträge über Dichter und Dichtkunst of
Ernst Grad (Triest : 1870). In Deutsche Poetik, Umriss d.
Lehre vom Wesen u. von d. Formen d. Dichtkunst, mit einer
Einführung in das Gebiet d. Kunstlehre (Dresden-Striesen :
1891), P. Heinze and R. Goette make pretense to scientific
treatment, but are not very successful. See on recent German
treatises E. Wolff's article in *Archiv f. Gesch. d. Philos.* 4 : 251
Ueber Neuere Beiträge z. Gesch. d. Poetik. A novel but by
no means convincing recent German investigation into the
nature of Poetry is Jacobowski's Die Anfänge der Poesie
(Dresden : 1891), which attempts a physiological as well as
psychical explanation of its origin. See for notice § 17. For
Werner and other authorities on the lyric, and for criticism of
other special types, see the second volume of this book.

In general on the history of German criticism, see the numerous references in §§ **2, 5, 8, 21** *A*, etc., above; and on the
movements of nineteenth century poetics, see Brandes's Hauptströmungen.

4. IN FRANCE. — In the following brief outline the subject
is divided into periods according to development in theory
(principles of judgment). Development in method is incidentally noticed, and the history of dramatic criticism is held apart
from that of poetics in general. It will, however, be understood that details of poetic and dramatic theory — such as the
principle and history of the unities, the function of the drama,
the discussion of literary movements — are here as elsewhere
reserved for the chapters devoted to these subjects.

The *First Period* may be called the *Primitive;* it extends
from the origins of verse-elaboration to the renaissance, from
Thibaut de Champagne to Du Bellay. The first writer of
importance in French poetics was Eustache Deschamps (1328–
1415), who, about 1400, wrote an Art poétique, "a treatise," as
Saintsbury says, "rendered at once necessary and popular by

the fashion of artificial rhyming." The characteristic of poetics in the hands of Deschamps and de Croy is formality.
It deals with the artificial forms of verse, — rondeau, ballade,
virelai, etc., — which had supplanted the earlier romances, pas-
tourelles, chansons d'amour and fabliaux of the trouvères and
troubadours. The tendency is, therefore, didactic. Henri de
Croy's L'Art et science de rhétorique pour faire rimes et ballades was published in 1493, and is of the same rhetorical and
artificial character as Deschamps's treatise.[1]

During this period, the drama evolved no theories of importance. The art was still confined to miracle-plays, mysteries,
and farce.

In the *Second Period* we pass to the literary 'humanism' of
Du Bellay and the Pléiade. This is the period of the *Renaissance*. It extends in poetry from Villon and Marot to Regnier.
In poetics it opens with the Défense et illustration de la langue
française of Joachim du Bellay, 1549, — which is the announce-
ment of intended reforms. Beside Du Bellay, this school, the
Pléiade, counted among its members Ronsard, Daurat, Baïf.
As opposed to the rhetorical and formal characteristic of the
previous period, the purpose of the school is to reform and
enrich the language, the prosody, and the inspiration of poetry,
by assimilation of such elements as were possible from the
classics — especially from the Greek. Du Bellay and Ronsard
(Art poétique, and Preface to the Franciade) advocate and
illustrate in practice the substitution of Latin and Greek metres
for popular artificial forms of verse, and the introduction of a
literary diction largely composed of classical importations and
technical expressions, — the improvement, in short, of the French
tongue for the purpose of literary expression. But while, as

---

[1] An attempt has been made by Ernest Langlois in his De artibus rhetoricae
rhythmicae (Paris: 1890), pp. 51–61, to show that de Croy was a plagiarist, having
claimed for himself a book written by Molinet. See also A. Sarradin, Eustache
Deschamps (Paris: 1879).

children of the Renaissance, these critics retained, with all their scholastic acquisition, the spirit of mediaeval romance, they did not see deep into the meaning of things. Their inspiration is not from nature itself, but from nature hellenized, — by the instrumentality of imperfect antiquarian scholarship, — it is an imitation of a conception that never existed. The attempt at the introduction of classical metres is interesting to the student of English poetics, for it anticipated by some forty years the efforts of Harvey and the Areopagus. Other writers of this period are Scaliger, whose Poetics, in Latin, appeared in 1561 (for notice, see § **21,** *B* 1), and Vauquelin de la Fresnaye (Art poétique française, 1604), the former of whom was the greatest critic of his age, the latter a mere rhetorician.

On the history of French poetics in the 16th century, see Th. Rücktäschl : Einige Arts poétiques aus der Zeit Ronsards und Malherbes (Leipz. : 1889); Georges Pellissier, De sexti decimi saeculi in Francia artibus poeticis (Paris : 1883) ; Sainte-Beuve, Tableau historique et critique de la poésie française au XVIe Siècle ; and E. Egger, L'Hellenisme en France (Paris : 1869).

The Recueil de l'origine de la langue et poésie françoise, ryme et romans, plus les nommes et sommaires des œuvres de CXXVII poètes françoises vivans avant l'an MCCC, by Claude Fauchet, is one of the earliest, if not the earliest of attempts in France to indicate the growth of the literature. It appeared in 1581. A much less conventional and less classical conception of poetry was presented by Étienne Pasquier in his treatise on the Pléiade, "De le grande flotte de poètes que produisit le regne du roi Henri Deuxième," which forms part of his Recherches de la France. Pasquier lived from 1529 to 1615. He wrote also on the earlier history of French poetry — the Provençal. Certain philologists and rhetoricians, whose influence was in general thrown against the Latinizing tendency of the time, are mentioned by Saintsbury (Hist. French Lit.,

p. 237). The linguistic treatises of Henri Estienne, on the relation of French and Greek, on the excellence of French, and on
the Italianized French, indicate the reaction against the Ron-
sardizing of the tongue. A similar protest was uttered by
Geoffroy Tory, also of the 16th century ; and studies in prosody
were conducted by Pelletier and Fontaine, grammarians.
Pierre Fabri, whose Le grand et vrai art de pleine rhétorique
has recently been reëdited by A. Heron (Paris : 1889), must
be added to this list of scholars.

In the drama, meanwhile, the form is scholastic, classical :
and the manner is by rhetorical declamations ; but, even so,
there is evidence that the spirit of mediaevalism still lingers.
With Scaliger appears the principle of the so-called classical
unities of time, place, and action.

The *Third Period* is the *Classical*. It receives its impress
from Malherbe, who led the reaction against the uncritical
innovations of the Pléiade. But in eliminating what was
excessive he managed to eliminate also the genuine romantic
inspiration that was the true life of their poetry. He ejects
the larger number of their classical importations of diction and
prosody ; he ejects as well the Gascon, Provençal, and Italian
forms in style. He devotes himself to the elaboration of the
alexandrine among metres, and of the lyric among species.
The impersonal, the allegorical, the declamatory, and the elegant take the place of the inspiration and feeling that had
colored the verses of Ronsard and the earlier poets of the
Renaissance. This may be called the first division of the
Classical Period. The poetics is mainly concerned with forms
of the lyric — especially the ode.

(1) To this earlier part of the Classical Period belongs the
Foundation of the Academy, an event by which was thwarted
whatever tendency there had been to revive the older freedom
of poetry and drama. Such a tendency was manifested in
Hardy's pastoral plays, in Daniel d'Anchères's drama, Tyr et

Sidon, and in François Ogier's preface to the second edition of
the play, 1628. But the counter-movement toward restraint
of passion and imagination, and in favor of obedience to the
classical unities, had asserted its strength in the Sophonisbe of
Mairet, and in the same author's preface to Sylvanire, 1631.
In 1634 this movement secured the active coöperation of
Richelieu ; in that year the Académie Française held its first
informal meeting, and in 1837 it was officially established.
The avowed purpose of the institution was to ascertain the
vocabulary of the language, fix its grammar, and reform its
style. Two of the earliest academicians to gain distinction
were Vaugelas in lexicography, and Chapelain in criticism. In
1636 there appeared a play which, had it not been condemned
by the new Academy, might have altered the course of French
dramatic literature. This was Corneille's Cid — romantic in
incident and conception, vital in characterization, and natural
in expression. But with Richelieu it did not find favor; nor
with Chapelain, who condemned it in the well-known Sentiments
de l'académie, especially for its violation of the Aristotelian
rules. From that time forth, for two centuries, the dramatic
theory of France was classical. In the Examens to his plays,
Corneille acquiesces in the supremacy of the Unities, but not
with a very sincere heart. Ultimately he stretches them almost
to breaking. On this division and the next of the Classical
Period, see Le Duc de Broglie, 'Malherbe' (Paris: 1897);
Rücktäschl, as above ; Demogeot, Tabl. de la litt. fr. au XVIIe
siècle avant Corneille, etc. (Paris : 1859); Pellisson et D'Olivet,
Hist. de. l'académie fr. (2 vols. Paris : 1858); Bourgoin, Les
maîtres de la critique au XVIIe siècle (1889); E. Deschanel, Le
romantisme des classiques (Paris: 1883) ; Rigault, Hist. de la
querelle des anciens et des modernes (Paris : 1856); G. Lanson,
'Boileau' (1892), and other references in Professor Dowden's
Bibliography, Hist. Fr. Lit.

(2) A second division of the Classical Period begins with

Rapin and Boileau. Réné de Rapin's chief work was the
Réflexions sur la poétique et sur les ouvrages des Poëtes
anciens et modernes (Paris : 1674 ; with many alterations, in the
edition of Paris : 1684, and in vol. II of his Œuvres, Haye :
1725. Translated into English by Rymer, as Reflections on
Aristotle's Treatise of Poesie, etc., 1674, printed for H. Her-
ringman). For the influence of the Réflexions on English
criticism, see Gosse, Modern English Literature, pp. 199–200.
"Rapin has been strangely forgotten ; when he died in 1687,
he was the leading critic of Europe ; and he is the writer to
whom, more than to any other, is due the line taken by English
poetry during the next hundred years. The peculiarity of the
Reflections, which were promptly translated into English, was
that they aimed at adapting the laws and theories of Aristotle
to modern practice. As is often the case, Rapin was less rigid
than his disciples, he frequently develops a surprisingly just
conception of what the qualities of the highest literature
should be." Mr. Gosse calls Rapin the father of 18th century
criticism. Indeed, Rapin stands in somewhat the same relation to the English criticism of Dryden's time as Boileau to
that of Pope's. We find Dryden, as early as 1674, in the
preface to the State of Innocence, citing both Rapin and
Boileau in company with the Italians (Piccolomini, Castelvetro)
as revivers of the classical doctrines of Aristotle, Horace, and
Longinus ; but until Addison and Pope fell under the spell of
Boileau the critical influence in England was that of Rapin.
In France the Réflexions provoked a controversy in which
Vavassor and L'Enfant participated, — the former with his
Rémarques (Paris : 1675) and his Réponse to Rapin of the
same year ; and the latter (L'Enfant) with a Critique des
Rémarques (in the *Nouv. de la Républ. des Lettres*, Mars,
1710). Another French contemporary of Dryden, and a critic
of the same school with Rapin, was Saint Évremond (1610–
1703). He deserves mention here because, like Rapin, he

exercised, though rather by word of mouth than by published theory, a considerable influence over English criticism in the end of the 17th and the beginning of the 18th centuries. During his residence in England he not only cultivated English literature but criticised it; and one in reading his remarks on Ben Jonson's comedy of humors can readily appreciate the salutary effect that his critical opinions must have had upon Dryden. Saint Évremond understood the scientific importance of literary history, and the advantages of the comparative method in criticism (Œuvres publ. par Maizeaux. Amst. and Leipz.: 1739).

But the second division of this period finds its most distinguished representative in N. Boileau-Despréaux, who, adopting Malherbe's reforms in general, reacted against the extravagances of the contemporary Italian influence, and introduced a conception of poetry much more rationalistic and moral than that of Malherbe. The sphere of poetics, which had been practically restricted to lyrical theory by Malherbe, Boileau broadened so as to include that of epic and drama as well. The characteristic of Boileau's poetics is a conventional rationalism, which displays itself in the rejection of modern sentiments and forms, and the adoption of technique and ideals supposed to have been formulated by the ancients. He insisted upon the imitation of nature, just as afterwards his disciples in England, Pope and Akenside, insisted. But his Nature had for its synonym Reason, and his Reason was bounded by the genius of the ancients. The Art poétique of Boileau appeared in 1674. See pp. 91–109 of his Œuvres complètes, publ. Chéron, Paris: 1875, reprinted by Cook. See also 'Boileau' in § **20**. With regard to his influence on English criticism: "He had insisted on inspiration," says Mr. Gosse (Mod. Engl. Lit., p. 206), "on the value of ceaseless variety, on obedience to the laws of language. The preface to the 1701 edition of his works is one of the landmarks of European criticism, and we can scarcely doubt that it wakened a high spirit of emulation in the youthful Pope. In it Boileau had urged that none should ever be presented to the public in verse but true thoughts and just expressions. He had declaimed against frigidity of conceit and tawdry extravagance, and had proclaimed the virtues of simplicity without carelessness, sublimity without presumption, a pleasing air without farce. He had boldly convicted his predecessors of bad taste, and had called his lax contemporaries to account. He had blamed the sterile abundance of an earlier period and the uniformity of dull writers. Such principles were more than all others likely to commend themselves to Pope, and his practice shows us that they did." His influence upon French poetry and criticism was supreme until the days of Madame de Staël, Chateaubriand, and Victor Hugo.

But even during the early dictatorship of Boileau, the supremacy of the ancients was not altogether undisputed. "As early," says Professor Dowden (Hist. French Lit., p. 241), "as 1657 Desmarets de Saint Sorlin had maintained that Christian heroism and Christian faith afforded material for imaginative handling more suitable to a Christian poet than the history and fables of antiquity." To this Boileau had replied in his Art poétique.[1] In 1687 Charles Perrault read a poem before the Academy entitled Le siècle de Louis le Grand, in which he exalted modern poetic genius and performance above that of the ancients. The contention of Perrault was supported by Fontenelle in his Discours sur l'églogue and the Digression sur les anciens et les modernes. (For a review of Fontenelle's Réflexions sur la poésie, see E. Egger's La critique chez les Grecs, p. 271.) From 1688 to 1697 Perrault continued to maintain his thesis in a series of dialogues called Parallèle des anciens

---

[1] The parallelism between movements in English and in French Literature is here, again, of especial interest. This idea of Desmarets, for instance, had been expressed by Davenant in the Preface to Gondibert, just seven years earlier.

et des modernes. The cause of the ancients was meanwhile
espoused by Boileau (Réflexions sur Longin), La Fontaine
(Epître à Huet), La Bruyère (Les caractères), and Andr.
Dacier, who in the Preface to his Poétique d'Aristote (1692)
goes so far as to say of poetry, not merely that the art is unal-
terably established, but that "ses régles sont si certainement
celles qu'Aristote nous donne, qu'il est impossible d'y rëussir
par un autre chemin." The issue was somewhat modified by
Lamotte, who advocated the claim of cultivated (that is, modern)
prose as the best literary form. Against him Mme. Dacier
entered the lists. Finally, Fénelon, toward the close of his
life (1715), "stated the case of the ancients against the moderns, and of the moderns against the ancients, with an attempt
at impartiality; but it is evident that the writer's love was
chiefly given to his favorite classical authors." (See Dowden
for the materials of this account. Hist. French Lit. London:
1897.)

Since the appearance of Boileau's Art poétique, the stream
of similar treatises had steadily been flowing. In 1709 was
issued Le Bossu's Traité du poëme épique. In England it
shared the popularity of Rapin. In 1719 the Abbé J. B. Dubos
produced his Réflexions critiques sur la poésie et la peinture
(3 vols. Paris: 1740), which, according to Professor Dowden,
"anticipates the views of Montesquieu on the influence of
climate, and studies the action of environment on the products
of the imagination." Dubos had a just conception — even if
crude— of the aesthetic catharsis, and a decidedly modern way
of looking at the relation of drama to life. Batteux, who follows
him, in 1746, with Les beaux arts reduits à un même principe,
had a much more liberal conception of the idealizing function of
art than either Boileau or Rapin.

(3) Indeed, Dubos and Batteux might, perhaps, better be
regarded, with Voltaire and Diderot, as representatives of the
third, or philosophical, division of the Classical Period. Beside

the Quatre Poétiques, two other productions of Batteux go to
prove the originality of his view : the Analyse de la poétique
d'Aristote, in vol. XLI, p. 409 *et seq.*, of the Mémoires de
l'Académie des inscriptions, and the Quatre Mémoires (on
the nature and aims of Tragedy and of Comedy ; and on the
Epic compared with Tragedy and History), in vol. XXXIX,
p. 54 *et seq.*, of the same series (also printed together, Gen. :
1781). The character of Voltaire's earlier theories is sufficiently indicated in his youthful Essai sur la poésie épique, and
his Temple du goût (1733). He adopts Christian symbolism,
advocates the introduction of both national and exotic elements, and admires Shakespeare. But with the development of
the scientific spirit and of philosophical criticism he becomes
more conservative, and, though still preferring modern to
ancient poetry, eschews the " savagery " of Shakespeare. A
sample of the formal quality of his later literary opinion is
afforded by his Commentary on Corneille. Another philosophical treatise, Rousseau's Discours sur les sciences et les arts, of
1750, condemning, as it did, civilization on the ground that it
corrupted morals and natural freedom, must have awakened
critics to the advisability of studying art and poetry in their
social relations. Louis Racine's Réflexions sur la poésie is,
on the other hand, a formal treatise, though it appeared two
years later than Rousseau's. But Buffon's Discours de récep-
tion, of 1753, develops an essentially modern and philosophical
argument for the intrinsic individuality of style. Style proceeds
from within, is the expression of the idea, not a mould imposed
upon the idea from without.

The criticism of the encyclopaedists, who constitute the
really philosophical school of the century, is both of drama
and poetry, in the narrower acceptation of the latter term.
D'Alembert's Éloges (D'Alembert, 1717–83. Œuvres. 5 vols.
Paris : 1821–22) are distinguished by impartiality of method.
Diderot, much of whose critical work first appeared in Les

Feuilles de Grimm, makes there, and in the prefaces to his plays (Père de famille and Le fils naturel), an effort toward emancipation from the classical conventionalities. "Everywhere," says Saintsbury (Hist. French Lit., p. 462), "there is to be perceived the cardinal principle of sound criticism; that a book is to be judged, not according to arbitrary rules laid down *ex cathedra* for the class of books to which it is supposed to belong, but according to the scheme of its author in the first place, and in the second to the general laws of aesthetics; a science which, if the Germans named it, Diderot, by their own confession, did much to create." He made the return to nature in his poetics, and attempted to do so in his dramas — giving us not mere types, but actual characters. For the strictly defined tragedy and comedy of the former epoch he substituted the play of the *bourgeoisie* — the *drame* or melodrama. This movement was, of course, assisted by the vogue of Marivaux's *comédie larmoyante*, and by sentimental novels, such as his Marianne. And the same movement was further advanced by J. J. Rousseau's advocacy, in his Lettre à D'Alembert, in 1758, Sur les spectacles, in which he censures the theatre of the day, with its sentimental and imaginative adventures, and insists upon the cessation of spectacles based upon the afflictions of noble and royal characters, upon the introduction of popular interests and individualities, and the manifestation of a desire to teach, to moralize.

In 1786 the historical method in criticism is illustrated by the practice of La Harpe (Lycée lectures — Cours de littérature), but, unfortunately, not by the contemporary essays for the Encyclopaedia written by Marmontel, and collected in 1787, under the title Éléments de la littérature. These adopt an attitude of unreasoning admiration for Boileau, and judge all poetry by the productions and laws of the classical school. As an instance of the contemporary antagonism to the encyclopaedists and philosophers should be read the effusions of Fréron in *L'Année littéraire* (see Villemain, Tabl. de la litt. au XVIIIe siècle. 4 vols., Paris: 1841; Lebasteur, 'Buffon.' Paris: 1888; Desnoiresterres, 'Voltaire,' etc. 8 vols., Paris: 1871–76; Saint-Marc Girardin, 'J. J. Rousseau.' 2 vols., Paris: 1875; Reinach, 'Diderot.' Paris: 1894; Bertrand, 'D'Alembert.' Paris: 1889; and other references in Dowden's Bibliography).

(4) An entirely different movement from these characterizes the poetics of the fourth division of the Classical School. André Chénier (1762–1794) has been called a precursor of the Romantic School; but this, says Saintsbury, is a mistake. His aesthetic was at once imaginative and traditional. Though possessed of a natural idealism, this did not lead him to disregard the models of antiquity. He revived indeed the reforms of Ronsard, but not from any artificial or childish fondness for the ancient — rather from a genuine love of nature and of classical paganism. "A Greek by birthplace, and half a Greek by blood, his tastes and standards were wholly classical. But the fire and force of his poetic genius made the blood circulate afresh in the veins of the old French classical traditions, without, however, permanently strengthening or renovating it" (Saintsbury, Hist. Fr. Lit., p. 402). He knew Greek literature and the Greek language much better than Ronsard, Malherbe, and Boileau had known it. His verse has the Grecian purity. His "humanism" may be called natural as opposed to the literary "humanism" of Ronsard. Chénier's principal contribution to poetics proper was the Poëme de l'invention. It would appear that, all things considered, the Romantic movement was not without obligation to Chenier — but that perhaps his influence is most evident in the practice and theory of the Parnassiens of the present century.

The *Fourth Period* of French poetics is the *Romantic;* and to it the Transition was made by Madame de Staël and Chateaubriand.

(1) Madame de Staël's De la littérature considerée dans

ses rapports avec les institutions sociales (1800) reminds one
of Gibbon's Essay on the History of Literature and of Shaftesbury's doctrine of cosmopolitan culture.   Like the former, the
authoress attempts to show that literature is an affair of the
spirit and can proceed only from conditions of freedom and
progress ; and, like the latter, to encourage her fellow countrymen to assimilate the best that is offered by other nations and
literatures.   By her De l'Allemagne (1813) she introduced
German literature to France as De Quincey and Carlyle were
soon to introduce it to England.   Her influence over Wilhelm
von Schlegel, who "became the interpreter of Germany to her
eager and apprehensive mind," is noticed by Dowden.   Italy
and England also were conquered by her ; and she prepared
the way in no slight degree "for the Romantic movement. . . .
She advanced criticism by her sense that art and literature
are relative to ages, races, governments, environments.   She
dreamed of an European or cosmopolitan literature in which
each nation, while retaining its special characteristics, should
be in fruitful communication with its fellows."   With Chateaubriand we enter upon a revival of mediaeval religious and
aesthetic sentiment, his most important critical work being the
Génie du christianisme (1802).   He calls for a sentimental,
romantic, but spontaneous and modern, treatment of life.   And
it may, indeed, be said that Madame de Staël and Chateaubriand effected the overthrow of the sceptical, atheistic, and
unscientific interpretation of literature and art; they did away
with classical models and abstract rules; they introduced the
appeal to the imagination and the senses; they revived the
spontaneous and artistic characteristics of mediaeval lyricism,
and Christianized nature and man for the purposes of literature.

Various other forces had been working during this season
of transition to hasten the advent of a romantic conception
of the poetic and a comparative method of criticism.   In

1801 Baour-Lormian gave his countrymen the flavor of Macpherson in the Poésies Ossianiques; and later (1812) Creuzé de Lesser produced his Table ronde. In 1799 Sénancour had produced his melancholy Rêveries; and after the death of Joubert, 1825, appeared a collection of that author's prose poems, the Pensées. In 1811 Ginguené published the beginnings of his Histoire littéraire de l'Italie. Historical and philological studies were meanwhile prosecuted by Fauriel and Raynouard, and minor critics were feeling their way toward a comparative and psychological method. "Foreign life and literature," says Dowden, who mentions, in various places, the preceding facts, "lent their aid to the Romantic movement in France — the passion and mystery of the East; the struggle for freedom in Greece; the old ballads of Spain; the mists, the solitudes, the young heroes, the pallid female forms of Ossian; the feudal splendors of Scott; the melancholy Harold; the mysterious Manfred; Goethe's champion of freedom, his victim of sensibility, his seeker for the fountain of living knowledge; Schiller's revolters against social law, and his adventures of court and camp" (Hist. French Lit., p. 364). There were also changes in language and form, "of which Hugo and Sainte-Beuve were the chief initiators."

The way for the poetics of Hugo was still further prepared by Henri Beyle (Stendhal, 1783–1842), whose chief contributions to criticism were his Histoire de la peinture en Italie and the Racine et Shakespeare. His method was comparative and psychological, and in his habit of characterizing the poet by his *milieu* he was the precursor of Taine and Brunetière. "In temperament," says Saintsbury, "religious views and social ideas, he was a belated philosopher of the Diderot school. But in literature he had improved even on Diderot, and very nearly anticipated the full results of the Romantic movement. . . . In his De l'amour and in his novels he made himself the ancestor of what has been called successively realism and naturalism in

France." Stendhal merits the serious attention of the literary investigator.

The history of criticism during the rest of the Romantic period may be conveniently treated under the following heads, of which the first two refer to theory, the other to method:

(2) The Romantic Revolution in the Drama. This was effected by Victor Hugo's Preface to Cromwell, 1828, and his Hernani, 1830. Hugo definitely discards the ' unities,' declines all artificial limitations, and asserts that art should represent the whole truth, no matter what kind of aesthetic emotion may result.

(3) The Philosophical and Comparative Studies of Cousin (1792–1868), whose Du vrai, du beau, et du bien is one of the ablest treatises in aesthetics produced in France ; of Michelet (1798–1874), whose philosophy, like that of Cousin, shows the influence of Herder and Hegel ; and of Edgar Quinet, the bosom friend of Michelet and a sympathizer in his aesthetic views.

(4) The Scientific-Historical Movement, headed by Villemain, who, in his Tableau de la littérature au moyen âge, in the Tableau de la littérature au XVIIIᵉ siècle, and in his lectures, applied a method inclusive of the social, biographical, genetic, and comparative aspects of the subject under discussion. The resulting criticism was characterized by impartiality, sanity, and scientific decisiveness that placed it far in advance of that produced by preceding critics. Villemain was seconded by Saint-Marc Girardin and Sainte-Beuve, the latter of whom was probably the greatest critic of the century. Sainte-Beuve incorporates the romantic, historical, social, and psychological attempts of his predecessors and contemporaries under a new method, at once more logical, more scientific, and more imaginative than theirs — a method which has been justly called the naturalistic. Of his work an admirable estimate will be found in Pellissier's Le mouvement littéraire au XIXᵉ siècle

(Paris: 1891), and in Dowden. The latter says that, "wandering endlessly from author to author in his Portraits littéraires and Portraits contemporaires, Sainte-Beuve studied in all its details what we may term the physiology of each." His long research in "his most sustained work, 'Port-Royal,' led him to recognize certain types or families under which the various minds of men can be grouped and classified." So, also, in his *Causeries du Lundi* and the *Nouveaux Lundis*. "They formed, as it were, a natural history of intellects and temperaments. He did not pretend to reduce criticism to a science; he hoped that at length, as a result of numberless observations, something like a science might come into existence. Meanwhile he would cultivate the relative and distrust the absolute." To estimate a work, he studies the personality of the author, his conditions, his inherited qualities, his education, life — everything that can be ascertained concerning him. Thus he aims to discover the key to the secret of his literary utterances. This is the method, according to Professor Dowden, "which has best served the study of literature in the 19th century." It is largely the method of Matthew Arnold, whose success, however, hardly equaled that of his master, Sainte-Beuve. (For further remarks on Sainte-Beuve, see § 2 above.)

(5) The Reaction against Liberal Methods on the part of Nisard and his followers, who reverted to an abstract, authoritative, and individual standard, and attempted to test the author in question by that. On all these methods, see the concluding chapter of Professor Dowden's excellent History, and refer to the annotations on the several authors in §§ 2, 5, 8, etc., above.

The *Fifth Period* of Criticism includes the movement of art for art's sake, whose representatives, de Vigny, Théophile Gautier, Théod. de Banville, Leconte de Lisle, Sully-Prudhomme, etc., are called the Parnassiens. This movement is characterized by a revolt against the excesses of the Romantic school, and a revival of a more philosophical and rationalistic theory

of inspiration.   It cultivates accuracy in form, and aims in
an aesthetic fashion at sculptural and picturesque effects of
style.   Its doctrines may, in fact, be compared with the much
more refined aestheticism or hedonism of Walter Pater.

The period includes, also, important developments in scientific criticism ; the esthopsychological of Hennequin, the naturalistic (historically objective) of Taine, the national and
eidographic of Brunetière, etc.; for which see above, §§ 2 and
5.   At the present moment especial attention is directed to
Jos. Texte's revival of the comparative or cosmopolitan ideal
advocated by Rousseau, and adopted by Mme. de Staël,
Villemain, and Sainte-Beuve (see Texte's Études de lit.
européenne, Paris : 1898).   Other writers of theoretical and
applied criticism during the century have been frequently mentioned in these pages, or will demand mention in the next
volume of this work.   Some of the more important are Paul
Albert, É. Faguet, Nettement, J. J. Ampère, Jules Lemaître,
Gaston Paris, Edm. Scherer, Anatole France, Petit de Julle-
ville, Bernard Thalès (Hist. de la poésie : 1864), Pellissier,
Aubertin, Léon Gautier, J. Bédier, Lenient, Langlois, Jeanroy,
A. Darmesteter, É. Egger, Vinet, A. Dupuy, Demogeot, Guizot,
Deschanel, Rigault, Lanson, P. Janet, Pellisson, Caro, Sorel,
Desnoiresterres, G. Larroumet, Géruzez.

In dramatic theory and practice, meanwhile, Émile Augier and
Alexandre Dumas have instituted a reaction against romanticism
that is as realistic as that of the Parnassiens is aesthetic.   (See
Brandes, Hauptströmungen, etc. ; Pellissier, Le mouvement
litt. au XIXᵉ siècle, 1891; Th. Gautier, Hist. du romantisme,
1874 ; Brunetière, L'Évolution de la poésie lyrique en France
au XIXᵉ siècle, 2 vols., 1894, and other references in Dowden,
p. 436.)   On the minor French schools of poetry and their theories, les décadents, les symbolistes, etc., see *Rev. Bleue,* 47 :
442, 721 ; *Harper,* 87 : 858 The Decadent Movement in Literature ; J. H. Leuba in the *Am. Journ. Psychol.,* July, 1893.

In the study of the history of French poetics, Saintsbury and
Dowden, to whom reference has been frequently made in this
chapter, will be found very useful ; also Petit de Julleville (Hist.
de la langue et de la littérature franç., and his shorter Hist.
de la litt. franç.) ; Lanson (Hist. de la litt. franç.) ; Körting
(Encykl. d. roman. philol.), and other references as in §§ **21**,
A 5, and **24**, *B* 6.

Of the periodicals the most important to the student are :
*Ausgaben und Abhandlungen aus dem Gebiete der romanischen
Philologie*, veröffentlicht von E. Stengel (Marburg : 1882-89) ;
Französische Studien, herausg. von G. Körting und E. Koschnitz
(Heilbronn : 1881) ; *Romanische Studien*, herausg. von Edward
Böhmer, Halle ; *Revue des langues romanes*, Montpellier et
Paris ; *Revue critique d'histoire et de littérature*, Paris ; *Biblio-
thèque de l'École des Chartes*, Paris ; *Bibliothèque de l'École des
Hautes Études*, Paris ; *Journal des Savants*, Paris ; *Revue de
philologie française et provençale*.

5. IN OTHER ROMANCE LITERATURES. — It is especially a
matter of regret that space does not permit an historical outline
of Italian, Spanish, and Portuguese poetics. Some of the more
important among Italian writers are, however, mentioned in
paragraph (1), Latin treatises, above ; in § **24**, *B* 8, and in the
appendix to this volume (on Aristotle's Poetics). The following
enumeration is principally derived from Blankenburg, and may
be supplemented from him (Literarische Zusätze, 1 : 381-411),
or from any of the histories of Italian literature.

(*a*) *Italian.* — Giov. Gior. Trissino, La Poetica, Divisione
IV (Vicenze : 1529) ; Divis. V e VI (Ven.: 1563) ; Tutte le
Opere (2 vols. in 1. Verona : 1729. The Poetica, although
not responsible, as has been frequently supposed, for the introduction of the laws of the three unities into France, is still
historically of greater importance than most of the formal
' poetics ' produced in Italy during the 16th and 17th centuries) ;
Lud. Dolce, whose translation of Horace's Epistle to the Pisos

(Ven. : 1535 and 1559) is accompanied by a commentary ;
Bern. Danielo, La Poetica (Ven. : 1536); Bernardo Segni, who
published a translation into the Italian of the Poetics and the
Rhetoric of Aristotle (Flor. : 1549); Ben. Varchi, Lezioni
della Poetica e della Poesia (in Lezioni lette publicamente nell'
Acad. Florentina. Flor. : 1549); Const. Landi, Libro primo
della Poetica (Piac. : 1549); Girol. Muzio, Dell' Arte poetica,
Libri Tre (in Rime diverse. Ven. : 1551); Giamb. Giraldi
Cintio, Discorsi intorno all comporre de' Romanzi, delle Come-
die e delle Tragedie, e di altre maniere de Poesie (Vineg. :
1554) ; Giov. P. Capriano, Della vera Poetica, Libro Uno
(Vin. : 1555) ; Bernardo Tasso, Ragionamento della Poesia
(Vin. : 1562, and in his Lettere, vol. 2. Pad. : 1733) ; Ant.
Minturno, L' Arte poetica (Ven. : 1564); Lud. Castelvetro,
the Poetics of Aristotle, text, translation, and commentary
(Vienna : 1570. Most important); Al. Piccolomini, a trans-
lation of Aristotle's Poetics, with notes (Sienna : 1572. Also
scholarly and luminous) ; Giov. Andr. Gilio da Fabriano, La
Topica poetica (Vineg. : 1580); Agnolo Segni, Ragionamento
sopra le Cose pertinente alla Poetica (Flor. : 1581) ; Franc.
Patrici, Della Poetica la Deca disputata (Ferr. : 1586. Suggestive of novel points of view); Torquato Tasso, Discorsi dell'
Arte poetica, e in particolare del Poema eroico (Ven. : 1587.
Three discourses on the choice, the arrangement, and the
handling of material); Gias. de Nores, Discorso intorno a quej
principj, cagione e accrescimenti, che la Comedia, la Tragedia,
e 'l Poema eroico ricevano dalla Filosofia morale e civile, e da'
Governatori delle Republiche (Pad. : 1587), and a continuation of the same, Poetica . . . nella quale per Via di Diffinizione
e de Divisione si tratta, secondo l' Opinione d' Aristotile, della
Tragedia, del Poema eroico, e della Comedia (Pad. : 1588.
The judgments passed upon tragi-comedy and the Pastor Fido
of Guarini led to a literary controversy) ; Giov. Fabbrini da
Fighine, the Ars Poetica of Horace, translation in blank verse,

and notes (in the Opere. Ven. : 1587); Giul. Ces. Cortese,
Avvertimenti nel poetare (Nap. : 1591) ; Franc. Buonamici,
Discorsi poetici in difesa d' Aristotile (Flor. : 1597. Directed
against the position assumed by Castelvetro); Faustino Summo,
Discorsi poetici ne' quali si discorrono le più principali quis-
tioni di Poesia, e si dichiarono molti luoghi dubbj e difficili
intorno all' Arte del poetare, secondo la Mente d' Aristotile, di
Platone, e di altri buoni Autori (Pad. : 1600) ; Giov. Bern.
Brandi, Trattato dell' Arte poetica (in his Rosario di Maria
Vergine. Rom. : 1601); Chiodino da Monte Melone, Specul.
Poet. Aristot. (in his Rhetoric. Ven. : 1613) ; Orat. Marta,
Sposizione della Poetica d' Aristotile (in his Rime e Prose.
Nap. : 1616) ; Cam. Pellegrino, Discorso della Poetica (Ven. :
1618) ; Udeno Nisieli (pseud. for Ben. Fioretti), Proginnasmi
poetici (Flor. : 1620–39) ; Giov. Colle Bellunese, Ragiona-
menti poetici e risposte sopra la Poetica d' Aristotile (in his
Acad. Colle Bellunese. Ven. : 1621); Celso Zani, Poetica
ecclesiastica e civile . . . nella quale si pone in chiaro la Diffinizione della Poesia commune alla Tragedia e all' Epopeja
(Rom. : 1643) ; Flav. Querengo, Trattato della Poesia (Pad. :
1644) ; Loretto Mattei, translation of Horace's Ars Poetica
(Bol. : 1686) ; and Ces. Grazzini, translation of the same
(Ferr. : 1698) ; Bened. Menzini, Arte poetica (Rom. : 1690);
Nic. Cicognari, Discorso di nuova Invenzione disegnato sul' Idee
d' amico e celebre Poeta (Parma : 1696); Giov. Mar. Crescimbeni, La Bellezza della volgar Poesia (Rom. : 1700. Enlarged
in the sixth volume of his Istoria della volgar Poesia. Ven. :
1730); Vinc. Gravina, Della Ragione poetica, Libri Due (Rom. :
1704) ; Lud. Ant. Muratori, Della perfetta Poesia italiana,
spiegata e dimostrata (Moden. : 1706. Crescimbeni, Gravina,
and Muratori are of prime importance to the historian); Pietro
Jac. Martelli, Della Poetica, Sermoni (in his Versi e Prose.
Rom. : 1710); F. Palesi, Della Poetica, Libri Tre (Palerm. :
1734); Scip. Maffei, Discours sur l' Histoire et le Génie des

Poëtes Italiens (in the Bibl. italique, 1 : 223–278; 2 : 176–
324, Gen. : 1728) ; Giov. Salio, Esame critico intorno a varie
Sentenze d' alcuni Scrittori di Cose poetiche (Pad. : 1738) ; Frc.
Quadrio, Della Storia e della Ragione d' ogni Poesia (7 vols.
Bol. e Milan. : 1739–1752. One of the standard treatises —
historical and theoretical) ; Carlo Denina, Saggio sopra la
Letteratura italiana (Tor. : 1762) ; Frc. Maria Zanotti, Dell'
Arte poetica, Ragionamenti cinque (Bologna : 1768); Girol.
Tiraboschi, Storia della Letteratura italiana (Mod.: 1772–1782;
10 vols. in 13 parts, Fir.: 1780). Of later writers on poetics
mention is made in § **24,** *B* 8, below.

(*b*) *Spanish.* — The following list may serve to direct the
student to some of the earlier authorities ; it may be supplemented from Blankenburg (Literarische Zusätze), whence it is
principally derived, and from the histories of Spanish literature.

Enrico de Villena, Libro del arte de trovar, o gaya ciencia
(of which Blankenburg, Lit. Zusätze, I: 394, says that an extract
is to be found in the Origines de la lengua Española of Gregorio
de Mayans y Siscar, vol. II, 321, and mention of it in Warton's
History of English Poetry, vol. III, 349, note x); Juan de la
Enzina, Arte de Poesia Castellana (in his Cancionero. Sev.:
1501; Zarag.: 1516); Ped. Seraphi, De poesia vulgar en lengua
Catalana (Barc.: 1565); Mig. Sanchez de Viana, Arte poetica
Castellana (Alc. : 1580) ; Juan de la Cueva, Egemplar poetico,
o arte poet. Española (a didactic poem, *circa* 1582 ; in the Parnasso Español. Mad.: 1774, vol. VIII, p. 1 *et seq.*) ; Vinc.
da Espinel, a translation of Horace's Epistle to the Pisos (in
blank verse, in Espinel's Rimas. Mad. : 1591, and in the
Parnasso Español, vol. I, p. 1 *et seq.*); Luis de Zapata, a translation of the same Epistle (Lisb. : 1592) ; Juan Garcio Rengifo,
Arte poetica Española (Salam.: 1592); Hier. de Mondragon,
Arte para componer en metro Castellano dividida en dos partes
(pt. I, on verse ; pt. II, the composition of the various kinds of
poetry. Zarag. : 1593) ; Al. Lopez Pinciano, Philosophia anti-

gua poetica. (Mad. : 1596) ; Villen de Biedma, translation of the
Epistle to the Pisos (Gran. : 1599) ; Luis Alonzo de Carvallo,
Cisne de Apolo de las Excelencias y dignidad y todo lo que al
arte poetica y versificatoria pertenece (Med. : 1602) ; Lope da
Vega Carpio, Nueva Arte de hazer comedias en este tiempo
(in his Rimas humanas. Mad.: 1602); Andr. Rey de Artieda,
a Satire on Spanish Comedy (in an Epistle in his Discursos,
Epist. e Epigr. Zarag., 1605, and in Parnasso Español, vol. I,
p. 352); Chr. de Mesa, Compendio de la poetica en versos
(in his Rimas. Mad. : 1607 and 1611); Franc. Cascales,
Tablas poeticas (Murc. : 1617 ; new edition, containing Cascales'
Poetics of Horace by Franc. Cerda y Rico. Mad. : 1779) ;
Ped. Soto de Roxas, Discurso sobra la poetica (in his poem
Desengano de Amor en Rimas. Mad. : 1623); Al. Ordonez,
translation and text of Aristotle's Poetics (Mad. : 1626; new
ed. by Cas. Florez, with the notes of Heinsius and Batteux.
Mad. : 1778); Diego de Colmenares, Censura de Lope da
Vega Carpio, o discurso de la nueva poesia, con una respuesta,
(1630); Jos. Ant. Gonzalez de Salas, Nueva idea de la Tragedia
antigua, o ilustracion ultima al libro singular de poetica de
Aristotiles prima parte ; Tragedia practica y observacion, que
deben preceder a la Tragedia Española intitul. las Troyanas,
parte seg. (Mad. : 1633 ; new ed. by Cerdo y Rico. 2 vols.
Mad. : 1778) ; Jos. Pellicer de Salas de Tovar, Idea de la
Comedia de Castilla (Mad. : 1639) ; Diego Vich, Breve discurso de las Comedias y de su representacion (Valenc. : 1650);
Ignacio de Luzan Claramunt de Suelves y Guerra, La Poetica,
o reglas de la poesia en general y de sus principales especies
(Zarag. : 1737 ; new ed. enlarged by Eug. Llaguno. 2 vols.
Mad. : 1779); Ant. Nasarre y Ferriz, Dissertacion, o prologo
sobre las Comedias de España (before the Comedias di Mig.
de Cervantes Saavedra. 2 vols. Mad. : 1749). For some of
the later authorities, see below, § **24**, *B* 9. Also for references
to Portuguese versification.

6. For the poetics of Northern European Literatures, see brief notice in § **24,** *B* 11–13.

7. For some references on poetics in the Orient, see § **24,** *B* 14–20.

CHAPTER VII.

THE PRINCIPLES OF VERSIFICATION.

§ 22. STATEMENT OF PROBLEMS; ANALYSIS.

THE student will find it necessary at the outset to determine the relation between 'primary' and 'secondary' rhythm, — or, to use the more common parlance, between rhythm and metre, — and to discover what common basis, if any, rhythm and metre have.

I. He should then proceed to the consideration of **Rhythm** as inherent, or manifest, in

A. **THOUGHT.** — See Dewey, Baldwin, Sully, and other writers on the psychology of aesthetics, pp. 166, 167, above.

B. **NATURE.** — See, for instance, Spencer's First Principles, pp. 256, 257; John Fiske's Cosmic Philosophy, vol. I, pp. 297–314; Helmholtz's Sensations of Tone ; Ch. Henry's Rapporteur esthétique ; Lanier's Science of Verse, and the references on pp. 138, 139, above.

C. **ART** (exclusive of music and literature). — See Hegel's Aesthetik (or Kedney's exposition, Hastie's, Bosanquet's, Bryant's translations), and §§ **7-9** above.

D. **MUSIC.** — See Lanier in his Science of Verse, Ruskin in his Prosody, Gurney in his Power of Sound, Schmidt in his Introduction to Rhythmic and Metric, for various theories of the relation between musical and poetical rhythm. More spe-

cial reference on rhythm in music may be made to physiological
treatises such as Helmholtz's Sensations of Tone, or to aesthetic
theory as elaborated by Weber, Schubart, Hauptmann, Bähr,
et al., for whom see Gayley and Scott's Guide to the Literature
of Aesthetics, pp. 70–72.

E. **LANGUAGE.** — See Lanier and Poe for the basis of speech-
rhythm. For more exhaustive treatment of the subject, see
references as given in § **23** to Ellis (Quantitative Pronunciation
of Latin), Guest, Schmidt, Mayor, Abbott and Seeley, Westphal, Gurney, Schipper, and others. For the rhythm of prose,
see §§ **25–27**.

II. The field is now clear for the consideration of *Metre,
or Secondary Rhythm.* — The student is confronted, first, with
numerous conflicting definitions of the well-known terms : foot,
section, pause, caesura, etc. As to the kinds of feet, classical
and modern, he may with profit consult Abbott and Seeley,
Gummere, Schmidt, Ruskin, Lanier, Poe ; as to ratios within
the foot, Hadley, Schmidt, and Gildersleeve. On the section
he will derive enlightenment from Mayor and Ellis, still more
from Fleeming Jenkin. Let him approach Guest with caution,
lest he be mystified. In regard to the various theories of the
pause, — compensating or rhythmical, — the end-pause, run-on
lines, or *enjambement*, the general relation of verse to sentence,
the caesura, etc., Thomas Arnold, Gummere, Abbott and
Seeley, Lanier, and Mayor are trustworthy guides. Attention
may next be turned to the following details :

A. **THE ELEMENTS OF THE VERSE AND FOOT.** — (1) Quantity,
— ancient and modern. — It will be wise to distinguish at once
between the quantity of a syllable and its emphasis, — see
Mayor ; and to inquire into the relative value of syllables in
classical and in modern feet. See Ellis, Gummere, Guest,
Sylvester, Schipper, Jenkin.

(2) Accent. — In Guest will be found a discussion of the verbal, logical, and rhetorical qualities of accent. (See Skeat's edition.) On the hovering and the wrenched accent, see Schmidt and Gummere ; also Mayor, Ellis, Jenkin, Symonds, and Schipper. Questions touching emphatic and unemphatic accents will rise for decision, and others concerning the adjustment of foot-sequence and section in modern verse.

(3) Pitch, — Lanier, Ellis, Schipper, Schmidt.

(4) Stress in word and in metre, — Mayor, Lecky, and Ellis.

(5) Force and weight, — Mayor, Ellis.

(6) Tone and color, — for instance, the colors of vowels and of consonants in assonance, alliteration, and onomatopoeia, — see Bacon, Guest, Lanier, Ruskin, Tolman, Gummere, M.-J. Guyau, Schipper, Stevenson in his essay on style, etc. Symonds treats poetically, though not always critically, of the relation that thought and emotion bear to word-color.

B. **The Historical Inquiry into Metre.** — The student should study first the genesis of metre, its evolution and differentiation in any one literature (Kawczynski, Posnett, Gummere, Jacobowski) ; then the dependence of metrical forms upon linguistic conditions and the modifications of metre that have attended the development of a language. This most interesting investigation will lead to a comparison of the distinctive metres of various nations and a consequent induction may establish certain affinities between national metres and national characteristics. Here also may be studied the connection between special moods or emotions and the metres most frequently used to express them. As a source and at the same time an example of this method, consult Kawczynski's Essai comparatif sur l'origine et l'histoire de rhythme, and Wilh. Meyer's Anfang u. Ursprung d. lateinischen u. griechischen rhythmischen Dichtung.

C. But that consideration leads one, of course, to the threshold of the **Theoretic Inquiry.** Whence, psychologically considered, does the demand for metre spring? From the desire for regularity? From a mechanical impulse to stereotype the relation between unity and variety? From a passion for 'aesthetic economy'? From consideration of the frailty of man's memory? And the delight in metre, does it consist in the consciousness of technical difficulty overcome; or in the sense of expectancy satisfied? What effect, if any, upon the eye, as well as upon the ear or upon the imagination, does metrical arrangement in lines produce? Compare with this the metrical arrangement of bars, and consider the relation of metre to music.

III. The Kinds of Metre. — Mayor, Schipper, Abbott and Seeley, and Schmidt provide the material necessary for a general introduction. Questions concerning metrical license, extra syllables, anacrusis, the 'catch,' truncated metres, 'metrical metamorphoses,' merit especial attention.

A. Selected references for the study of **Classical Metre** will be found in § **23** below; courses of reading for more exhaustive investigation are indicated in § **24.** The beginner cannot choose a better guide than the Rhythmic and Metric of J. H. H. Schmidt (trans. by J. Williams White). The advanced student is referred especially to Schmidt's Kunstformen d. gr. Poesie, and to Rossbach and Westphal. (See § **23.**)

B. Concerning **Modern Metres,** — especially those used in English, — Guest, Schipper, Mayor, Abbott and Seeley, Lanier, Gummere, Hood, and Goold Brown may for most aspects of the study be consulted. As to French, German, Italian, and other modern European systems of versification, see § **24.**

Of strictly modern forms none deserves attention more than English Blank Verse, in its history and its theory. Mayor,

Schipper, Guest, and Masson present the various difficulties attendant upon the determination of the origin and development of this form. They also discuss, as do Symonds, Ellis, Abbott and Seeley, Keightley, and a host of others, the phenomena of pause, section, elision, slurring, substituted foot, hendecasyllable, and show by illustration what changing tones of quantity and accent this organ of many stops has been made to produce. The qualities of English blank verse cannot be better determined than by an induction based upon the usage of Sackville and Norton, Marlowe, Shakespeare, Fletcher, Milton, Wordsworth, Landor, Tennyson, Browning, and Matthew Arnold. The following are a few of the questions suggested by this study : What adaptability has blank verse to the expression of varying moods, and of conception more or less profound? How does its style change with the development of national thought and taste? In what fashion does the 'interweaving' of section and foot reconcile the technique of ancient and of modern verse? What similarity exists between the pause of blank verse and the caesura of hexameter? What special adaptability has blank verse as a vehicle for English characteristic and mental attitude, rather than for those of other nationalities? What, by comparison, is the characteristic of French *prose mesurée*, and of Italian *versi sciolti?* Is blank verse better adapted than rhyme to such a poem as Goethe's Faust? Compare with it the metrical style of Marlowe's Faustus.

The student of modern metre may with profit undertake an investigation into the revival in modified form of certain classical metres, such as the Alcaic, the Sapphic and Adonic, the Hendecasyllabic, the Hexameter, and the Elegiac. On the most important experiment, — the renovation of the hexameter, — let him consult the practice of Goethe, Arthur Hugh Clough, Kingsley, Longfellow, and others as suggested in Schipper ; and the theories of Arnold, Blackie, Cayley, and others mentioned below, § **24**, *B* 5 (*b*). Munby's 'Dorothy' is an excellent example of

English elegiacs not often noticed.　The Elizabethans and other metrists and poets down to the present time have variously illustrated the enormities, as well as the possibilities, of English imitations of classic verse.

IV. Rhyme ; the Refrain, etc. — Under this division of the subject the following questions will demand consideration :

A. HISTORICAL. — What is the origin, and what the evolution, of rhyme ? Why does it prevail in modern verse and not in the classics ? Did it obtain in ancient literatures outside of the Greek and Latin ? Does it obtain in all modern literatures ? What is the custom in the Japanese, the Hebrew, the Basque, the Lappish and Finnish, and other eastern, and western literatures not shaped by Graeco-Latin, Teutonic, or Romance influence ? See § **24**, Disraeli's Amenities of Literature, pp. 272, 273 ; and, as in §§ **23, 24,** Schipper, W. Grimm, C. F. Meyer, Gleditsch, Blass.

B. THEORETICAL. — What purpose is served by rhyme ? What are its advantages, what its aesthetic value, and how are its effects limited ? Under this head see, in addition to the more exhaustive treatises cited below, §§ **23, 24,** Schopenhauer's World as Will and Idea, vol. III The Aesthetics of Poetry ; Spencer's Philosophy of Style ; G. P. Marsh's Lectures on the English Language, pp. xxiii–xxv, and Gummere. Is the best effect of the rhyme produced by one recurrence of the salient sound ? Is it weakened by more frequent repetition ? What of the recurrence in the *terza rima*, the *ottava rima*, the sonnet ? Does the virtue of rhyme lie in the expectancy on the part of the hearer which it arouses and allays ? Does it lie in a heightening of tone, pitch, quality of sound, or in the element of duration and sequence imparted to the verses? Does it serve to emphasize the ideas expressed ? What is the effect of 'deferred' rhymes ? See Gottschall's Poetik; Blass,

p. 210.　On the effect of false rhymes, eye-rhymes, 'allowable' rhymes, and the like, consult the entertaining article An Inquiry as to Rhyme, by Brander Matthews, in *The Bookman*, September, 1898.

C. **The Connection between the Essence and Structure of any Given Tongue and the Extent to which it Avails itself of Rhyme.** — See Marsh, Disraeli, Mac-Carthy's Translation of Calderon (Introd.), and others, as below, § **24.**

D. **The Elements and the Kinds of Rhyme.** — Distinguish between beginning, middle, and end rhymes, — or alliteration, assonance, and rhyme in the modern English sense of the term.　In what languages is alliteration availed of?　what are the respective merits of obvious and concealed alliteration? examples?　Discuss the manner of middle rhyme in Spanish and Portuguese; of tautophony in French.　See Blass (p. 209), Marsh, Gummere, Abbott and Seeley, Skeat, Vetter (Zum Muspilli), Bellanger, Mac-Carthy, Gramont, Ticknor.

E. **The History, Philosophy, and Laws of the Refrain.** — Consult works on modern fixed forms of verse, as in § **24;** and see R. M. Meyer, *Zeitschrift f. vergl. Litteraturgesch.* 1 : 34–47 Ueber den Refrain.

V. The Strophe. — Under this head the student might consider, first, forms distinctively English; secondly, forms derived from foreign literatures; thirdly, foreign forms not domesticated in English.　For English forms he will find Hood, Schipper, and Abbott and Seeley a helpful introduction.　Of 'derived' forms the most important are the ode, the sonnet, and the lately revived French forms of verse, the *rondeau, ballade, villanelle,* etc.　To the nature, the objects, and the history of the sonnet, he will find Sharp's Sonnets of the Century an especially good introduction; but a bibliography of the subject is indicated, § **24.** The following questions may point out the line of examination : Of what kind of burden is the sonnet the best vehicle? What are the technical conditions of excellence? What is the historical connection with the Greek epigram, or with the stornello? What forms has it assumed in the hands of Guittone, Petrarch, Dante, Tasso, Camoëns, Bellay, and the English poets from Wyatt to Mrs. Browning and Rossetti?

On French forms of verse, see references, § **24.**

In general should be considered the evolution of stanzaic and fixed forms of verse, national preferences in fixed forms, and the comparative excellence of fixed and free forms. See Kawczynski and Gottschall.

VI. The History of Metre in Any One Literature.

VII. The Study of Comparative Versification. — These subjects should be attempted only after extensive special research. See T. H. Key, A Partial Attempt to Reconcile the Laws of Latin Rhythm with those of Modern Languages (*Trans. Eng. Philol. Soc.*, 1868–69, pp. 311–351); Harbois de Jubainville, *Romania*, 8 : 145 Des rapports de la versification du vieil irlandais avec la versification romane; and a similar title in *Romania*, 9 : 177. Other references will be found in § **24.** Metric as a comparative study is still in its infancy.

VIII. Métric from the Phonetic Point of View is also a comparatively unworked mine. An abundance of raw material will be found in Sweet's History of English Sounds, Ellis's various writings on phonetics, and Siever's Grundzüge der Phonetik. See especially Lecky's paper in *Proc. of the Eng. Philol. Soc.* for Dec. 19, 1884, on the Phonetic Theory of English Prosody.

§ **23.** REFERENCES.

ABBOTT, E. A., and SEELEY, J. R.　English Lessons for English People.　Boston : 1880.

ABBOTT, E. A.　Shakespearian Grammar.

In English Lessons, Part III, on Metre, is clearly and interestingly written.　§§ 91–151 should be studied.　In treating of Blank Verse the author (Dr. Abbott) clings somewhat too tenaciously to traditional prejudice, but attempts to justify his rules by induction.　Taking the foot and the accent as the bases of metre, he draws a distinction between word-accent and metrical accent.　But does an examination of blank verse confirm his conclusions?　While emphasizing metrical accent, does he not distort the verbal accent, lay abnormal stress upon unemphatic monosyllables, or split them inexcusably in two, in order to avoid trochees, dactyls, anapaests, spondees, and pyrrhics that may not conform to his theory?　Is it not with a similar bias that he sanctions (§ 114) slurred syllables?　Is he justified in ruling out (§ 101) the 'hovering' accent, by so many deemed a valuable mediator between the emphasis of verse and that of prose?　In § 138, under the License of Trochee, he would do well to recognize the 'double trochee' in any part of the line, or else the monosyllabic foot with compensating dactyl.　The sections 115–122 on the Pause, based upon interesting inductions from Pope, Dryden, Shakespeare, etc., will be still more useful to the student if he will compare with Dr. Abbott's results those of Professor Mayor, English Metre, pp. 135–196.　For an admirable review of Abbott's 'rules' (English Lessons, § 98), see Mayor, chap. III.

With the English Lessons should be studied Abbott's Shakespearian Grammar, §§ 452–515, especially § 453 The 'Pause-Accent'; §§ 454–458 on 'Pause-Extra' Syllables and Monosyllables ; § 459 *et seq.* on Contractions ; § 477 *et seq.* on the Lengthening of Words, and § 513 on the ' Amphibious ' Section.

ARISTOTLE.   Poetics (Wharton's trans.).
> Chap. I : 4.

ARNOLD, M.   Three Lectures on Translating Homer.   Lond.:
> 1861.

ARNOLD, M.   Last Words on Translating Homer.   Lond.:
> 1862.

After considering, in the first and second lectures on Translating Homer, the inadequacy to that end of ballad-verse, rhymed verse in general, and of slow, artificial, obscure, or ignoble style, Arnold passes (p. 67) to the discussion of the measures best suited to Epic composition.   These are the heroic, the blank verse, and the hexameter.   The heroic, as rhyming, is eliminated from the consideration.   In Lecture 3 blank verse likewise, after a careful estimate, is deemed unfit for the needs of Homeric translation.   Hexameter (p. 76 *et seq.*) is recommended.   As to the difficulty of naturalizing the hexameter, Arnold's *Solvitur ambulando* is comforting, but scarcely conclusive.   The Last Words are devoted to a " sweet and illuminated " excoriation of Professor Newman ; but with page 36 the discussion of hexameter is again resumed.   Useful information is imparted concerning the nature of the caesura, the pause, accent, quantity.

ARNOLD, THOMAS.   Manual of English Literature.   Boston :
> 1889.   Appendix on English Metres.

AUBERTIN, CH.   La versification française et ses nouveaux
> théoriciens.   Paris : 1898.

A good introduction to recent theories.

BANVILLE, T. DE.   Petit traité de poésie française.   Paris :
> 1881.

BARHAM, THOS. FOSTER.   *Trans. Eng. Philol. Soc.,* 1860–61,
    p. 45 On Metrical Time, or the Rhythm of Verse, Ancient
    and Modern.

BECQ DE FOUQUIÈRES.   Traité général de versification fran-
    çaise.   Paris : 1879.

This book, and that of De Banville cited above, may be
unhesitatingly recommended.

BENLOEW, L.   Précis d'une théorie des rhythmes.   Paris and
    Leipz. : 1862–63.

Part I treats of French and Latin metres ; Part II of Greek
metres.

BINET, A.   Introduction à la psychologie expérimentale.
    Paris : 1894.

BIRT, TH.   Ad historiam hexametri latini symbola.   Bonn :
    1877.

BLASS, F.   Hermeneutik und Kritik.   (In Iwan Müller's Hand-
    buch der Klassischen Altertumswissenschaft. Bd. I. Nörd-
    lingen : 1886.)

> Pt. I, pp. 206–209 Technik d. Zusammenfügung d. Worte; pt. II,
> pp. 209, 210 Figuren d. Gleichklangs u. d. Wiederholung ; pp.
> 210–212 Alliteration u. Reim; pp. 212, 213 Melodie u. Accent ;
> pp. 213–215 Versmass d. Poesie ; pp. 222–225 Die Uebersetz-
> ungen.

Of exceeding value to the metrist.   Intended as an introduction to classical antiquities.

BOHM, H.   Zur deutschen Metrik.   (Progr.)   Berl. : 1890.

The author maintains that the trochee and the amphibrach
are the principal feet in German poetry.   Iambs, he thinks,
can always be read as trochees.

BOLTON, T. L.   *Am. Jour. Psychology,* 6 : 2 Rhythm.

BORINSKI, K.   Deutsche Poetik.   Stuttgart : 1895.

An extremely useful little book, supplying a good bibliography, and handling the subject in accordance with modern scientific method.   Metric is treated in Part III, pp. 50–92.

BORINSKY, F.   Das *Enjambement*.   (Studien zur Literaturgesch. M. Bernays gewidmet.   Hamb. und Leipz. : 1893.)

BOUVY, P.   Poètes et mélodes.   Paris : 1886.

BREWER, R. F.   Orthometry.   N. Y. : 1893.
>   Pp. 827–903 Versification.

A large and pretentious but crude work on versification and the technique of poetry.

BRIDGES, ROBERT.   Milton's Prosody.   Oxford : 1890.

This is "an examination of the rules of the blank verse in Milton's later poems, with an account of the versification of Samson Agonistes."   It is one of the best studies of blank verse in English, written by one who has the qualifications of a poet as well as a critic.   For a review, see *Athenaeum*, No. 3465.

BROWN, GOOLD.   Grammar of English Grammars.   N. Y. : 1873.

BROWNE, W. H.   *Mod. Lang. Notes*, 4 : 97 Certain Considerations Touching the Structure of English Verse.

The writer recognizes but three fundamental genera or 'patterns' of accentual verse-structure : (1) one strong syllable to one weak ; (2) one strong to two weak ; (3) one strong to three weak.

BRÜCKE, ERNST.   Die physiologischen Grundlagen der neuhochdeutschen Verskunst.   Vienna : 1871.

See *Trans. Eng. Philol. Soc.*, 1875–76, p. 469, for description of Brücke's method, which was to utter the syllables, 'pap,' 'bim,' 'bam,' while a wooden lever rested on his lower lip.

CARRIERE, M. Das Wesen und die Formen der Poesie. Leipz. : 1834.

A thoughtful and well-arranged discussion of the historical and aesthetic bases of poetic theory.   The distinctions between literary types are not far different from Hegel's, but they are clearly presented, and with a wealth of illustration.

CAYLEY, C. B.   *Trans. Eng. Philol. Soc.*, 1867, p. 43 Pedigree of English Heroic Verse.

CAYLEY, C. B.   *Trans. Eng. Philol. Soc.*, 1862–63, p. 67 Remarks on English Hexameters.

CHAIGNET, A.-Éd.   Essai de métrique grecque.   Paris : 1887.

CORSON, HIRAM.   A Primer of English Verse.   Boston : 1893.

The treatise illustrates sympathetically and forcefully the principle of inherent form.

DUC, LUCIEN.   Étude raisonnée de la versification française. Paris : 1889.

DÜHR, A.   Ueber Metrik und Rhythmik.   Friedland i. M. : 1885.   (Prog.)

A *résumé* of the contrasting phases of the development of accent and quantity in verse displayed by the classical languages on the one hand and by the modern on the other.   The dissertation furnishes a rapid survey of Greek and Latin metric and metrists.

EICHTAL, E. d'.   Du rhythme dans la versification française. Paris : 1892.

Clear, simple, and trustworthy.

ELLIS, A. J.   Essentials of Phonetics.   Lond. : 1848.

ELLIS, A. J.   Early English Pronunciation.   1869.

ELLIS, A. J.   *Trans. Eng. Philol. Soc.*, 1873–74, p. 113 On the Physical Constituents of Accent and Emphasis.

ELLIS, A. J. *Trans. Eng. Philol. Soc.*, 1875–76, p. 435 Remarks on Professor Mayor's Two Papers on Rhythm.

ELLIS, A. J. The Quantitative Pronunciation of Latin. Lond. : 1874.

On accent, quantity, verse, and prose rhythm, *passim*.

In his Essentials of Phonetics (1848) Ellis first laid down his laws of English heroic verse. His method was inductive, and his conclusion was, in general, that the normal form of iambic pentameter is rarely to be found, that the number of syllables is frequently greater than ten, while the number of accents is generally less than five. In his Early English Pronunciation, pt. I, pp. 333–335, he pointed out the difference between Chaucerian and modern rhythms, and laid down rules for the distribution of stress in modern pentameter. In the article in *Trans. Eng. Philol. Soc.*, 1873–74, on Accent and Emphasis, he pursued still further his inductive inquiry, and in the article of June, 1876, *Trans. Eng. Philol. Soc.*, he elaborated a nomenclature for degrees of force, length, pitch, weight, and silence. This system distinguishes forty-five gradations of stress, ready to the caprice of the poet, the delight of the metrist, and the confusion of the profane vulgar. Ellis's researches (barring the over-minuteness of the system that they have led him to elaborate) are characterized by common sense. But do they throw much light upon the palpable variations of intensity within the foot, or upon the limits of metrical substitution? Mayor (English Metre) criticises the value of Ellis's 'principle of weight'; and with some justice, for the principle must remain at the best "a very complex phenomenon." Shuddering at the Teutonic analysis elaborated by Ellis, Mayor discards all stress distinctions save those of force. (See Mayor, English Metre, pp. 57–74.) Ellis is the chief representative of what Mayor calls the natural, or *a posteriori* system. For a review of Early

English Pronunciation, see Hadley (Essays, Philological and Critical, pp. 240–262).

ELZE, K. Grundriss der englischen Philologie. Halle: 1889.
Pp. 361–386 Metrik.

EVERETT, ERASTUS. A System of English Versification. N. Y.: 1848.

A treatise of the old-fashioned, formal kind, with "pieces," marked "original," by the author of the treatise.

GHIL, RENÉ. Le traité du verbe. Avec avant-dire de Stéphane Mallarmé. Paris: 1886.

Presents in a curious and almost unintelligible jargon the poetical creed of the French *décadents*. According to Ghil, two main principles should guide in the making of verse: (1) symbolism, or the use of words to convey not ideas but merely sensuous impressions ; (2) verbal instrumentation or tone-color. The author's ideas on the latter point are a crude and fanciful anticipation of late psychological research into the phenomenon of 'colored hearing,' so called. Ghil associates *o, oi*, with red, *oû* with black, etc. See *Am. Jour. Psych.* 5 : 503, 504.

GILDON, C. The Complete Art of Poetry. 2 vols. Lond.: 1718.

Vol. I deals in six parts with the nature and use of poetry, the use of rules, the manner and rules of epigrams, pastorals, and odes, the plot and characters of tragedy and comedy, the rules of the epic, and the rules of English numbers, followed by various examples from Shakespeare. Vol. II is devoted to an anthology of poetry, of merely antiquarian interest. Gildon stands in direct opposition to Bysshe, the latter making the Art of Poetry depend upon beauty of coloring, the former on excellence of design.

GILDON, C. The Laws of Poetry. Lond.: 1720.

GLEDITSCH, HUGO.	Metrik der Griechen und Römer.	(Vol.
II, pp. 677–852 of Iwan Müller's Handb. der Klassischen
Altertumswissenschaft.	2. Aufl.)

GOTTSCHALL, R.	Poetik: Die Dichtkunst und ihre Technik.
2 vols. in one.	Bresl.: 1882.

> Vol. I, pp. 208–223 Vers und Reim; pp. 223–249 Die vorzüglich-
> sten Versmasse; pp. 249–262 Altdeutsche, antike, orientalische
> Strophen.	See § **24** for further note.

GRAMONT, F. DE.	Le vers français.	Paris: 1876.

GRIMM, W.	Zur Geschichte des Reims.	Berlin: 1852.	(Ori-
ginally published in *Abhg. d. Akad. zu Berlin*, 1851.)

GUEST, E.	A History of English Rhythms.	2 vols.	Lond.:
1838.

GUEST, E.	A History of English Rhythms.	A new edition,
by W. W. Skeat.	Lond.: 1882.

In Bk. I the parts most necessary to be read are: chap. I, on
the definition of rhythm, on quantity and accent; chap. IV,
on accent, pause accents, slurring, and emphasis; chap. V,
on quantity; and chap. VII, with its famous *dicta* on sections
and pauses.	In Bk. II the account of the origin of English
rhythms and the discussion of their poetical characteristics
(chap. I) will complete what is needful to know of Guest's
system.	Chaps. II–VII are valuable as a garner of apt illus-
trations, of curiosities in verse, and metric *cruces*, but Dr.
Guest's classification of the last is wearisome.	In vol. II
the history of English metres is learnedly done, but is by
no means trustworthy.	It is, for instance, doubtful whether
he understands either the nature or the function of Chaucer's
heroics.	Milton (p. 244) is scored for violating the Doc-
tor's rule about 'middle' and 'final' pauses.	"Versification,"
says the Doctor, "ceases to be a science if its laws may be

thus lightly broken!" The special insufficiencies of Guest's work are that his principle of the section and his laws concerning pauses are drawn from the meagre material of Anglo-Saxon poetry, and that most, if not all, of the rules that he formulates are disregarded by the greatest English poets. The most valuable parts of his work are Bk. III, on Anglo-Saxon literature, and Bk. IV, on various kinds of stanzas or 'staves,' as he calls them. The new edition of Guest, edited by W. W. Skeat, is a thorough revision of the original, with an index and some notes.

GUMMERE, F. B. A Handbook of Poetics. Boston: 1888.

Pt. III of this work is an admirable short treatise on Metric. The work of Child, Ellis, Sweet, and of the Shakespearian verse-scholars, as well as of Schipper, ten Brink, and Westphal, has been carefully studied and assimilated. The chapters on Metres of English Verse (pp. 166–234) evince careful research and discrimination. Gummere does not follow Guest in assigning aesthetic influence to Anglo-Saxon verse. The sixth chapter (pp. 133–166) will give the student an adequate survey of the leading difficulties as to rhythm, accent, quantity. It is probably oversight that a misconstruction of Hegel's statement about metre is allowed to stand (pp. 1 and 133). For Hegel's language see § **20** above, *Hegel*. For a discussion of the principles on which the treatise is based, see the articles by the author and Prof. J. M. Hart in *Mod. Lang. Notes*, vol. I, pp. 17, 18, 35, 36, 83, 84, 102, 103. Professor Gummere (p. 36) gives the following outline of his position : English metres are (1) based on regular time intervals; (2) marked off and determined by accent; (3) regulated but not determined by quantity (Schipper); (4) neither determined nor regulated by pitch; (5) influenced by pauses and slurring; (6) beautified by tone-color; (7) still pervaded to a large extent by rhyme. The test of the individual verse is its movement.

GURNEY, E.　The Power of Sound.　Lond.: 1880.

> See, also, Gurney's Tertium Quid, vol. I, pp. 191–251 The Appreciation of Poetry.

This work is a valuable as well as a delightful contribution to the aesthetics of music.　From the point of view of metric it is of much importance.　Gurney bases his conclusions upon induction.　With Ellis and Mayor he adopts accent (or the noticed regularity of *stimuli*) as the essential of metre, and metre as the fundamental principle of verse.　He holds (p. 429) that there is no necessary connection between the accentuation and the duration of syllables, and would consequently be declared " time deaf " by Professor Sylvester.　Especially noticeable is the assertion that there is nothing to prevent the accented syllable from occupying the smaller portion of the space between ictus and ictus, though generally the long syllable is that which bears the accent.　The student should consider critically the value of p. 109 *et seq.* on rhythm and the pleasure arising from a series of muscular sensations, and of pp. 127–149 on rhythm (stimulation at fixed degrees of time) and pitch (which deals with differences of distance and direction).　Gurney holds (p. 361 *et seq.*) that poetry and music are not differentiated developments of a common germ, but that music is the older type.　On poetry as a representative art, see p. 393.　Chap. XIX, on the sound-element in verse, attempts to prove that metrical rhythm is imposed on, not latent in speech, and that verse arises from the regularity of accents, not from their presence.　See p. 428 for the marking off of lines and stanzas; p. 430 *et seq.* for deviations from the norm in metre, and for distinction between the " pause " and the " foot of silence."　Chap. XX is on song.　In chap. XXI Gurney attacks Spencer's theory concerning the derivation of music from the cadence of emotional speech.

GUYAU, M.-J.　L'esthétique contemporaine.

> Pp. 171–257 L'Avenir et les lois du vers.

According to this able thinker and delightful writer the science of verse, since verse is at the same time a system of vocal sounds or physiological movements and a system of thoughts or emotions, should be based upon the two sciences, physiology and psychology. From this double point of view the author discusses the following topics : Chap. I, Rhythm of language and its origin — formation of modern verse; chap. II, Romantic theories of verse — office of the caesura; chap. III, The new metres — the hiatus ; Chap. IV, La rime riche; chap. V, Thought and verse.

HADLEY, J.   Essays, Philological and Critical.   N. Y.: 1873.
> Pp. 81–109 Greek Rhythm and Metre.

This admirable article is especially a *résumé* and criticism of the conclusions on Greek rhythm and metre arrived at by Rossbach, Westphal, Weil, Caesar, and Susemihl. A sketch is given of the more important ancient writers on verse, and elementary facts and principles, as set forth in their systems, are discussed. The elucidation of the terms "arsis" and "thesis," to the original significance of which Hadley reverts, and the rehearsal of the doctrine of compound feet are a contribution to the science of ancient verse well worthy the attention of the student.

HELMHOLTZ, H. L. F.   Sensations of Tone as a Physiological Basis for a Theory of Music.   Trans. and ed. by A. J. Ellis.   Lond.: 1875.

HELMHOLTZ, H. L. F.   On the Physiological Causes of Harmony in Music.   (In Popular Lectures on Scientific Subjects.   Trans. by E. Atkinson.   Lond.: 1873.)

HENRY, CHARLES.   Rapporteur esthétique.   Paris: 1888.

HOHLFELD, A. R.   Studies in French Versification.   Deprinted from *Mod. Lang. Notes*, vol. VIII, Nos. 1 and 5.   Baltimore: 1893.

HOLMES, O. W. *Boston Medical and Surgical Journal,* Jan. 7,
    1875 Physiology of Versification and the Harmonies of
    Organic and Animal Life.

HOOD, TOM. Practical Guide to English Versification. 3d
    edition. With an appendix on versification; and Bysshe's
    rules for making English verse. Lond.: 1888.

HOOD, TOM. The same, entitled the Rhymester, edited with
    additions by Arthur Penn [Brander Matthews]. N. Y.:
    1882.

Of Hood's work not more need be said than that it is a
practical elementary handbook. It treats in no philosophic,
but in lucid, although frequently dogmatic and *a priori* style,
of classic and modern principles of versification, of feet and
caesuras, of metre, rhythm, and rhymes, of figures, comic verse,
vers de société, and of song writing. The author aims rather at
showing the versifier the 'how' than the 'why' of versification.
He clings to classical terminology and tries (p. 25) to establish
a relation between accent and quantity. For a light and general survey of versification the work may be recommended to
the beginner.

Arthur Penn's Rhymester adds three useful chapters, on the
Sonnet, the Rondeau, Ballade, and other Fixed Forms of Verse,
with Ben Jonson's Fit of Rhyme against Rhyme.

HUMBERT, C. Die Gesetze des französischen Verses. Ein
    Versuch, sie aus dem Geiste des Volkes zu erklären, mit
    besonderer Rücksicht auf den Alexandriner und Molière's
    Misanthrope. Leipz.: 1888.

HUNT, LEIGH. What is Poetry? (In Selections from the Eng-
    lish Poets. N. Y.: 1857.)

Note the remarks on versification which succeed the discussion of imagination and fancy.

JACOBOWSKI, L.   Die Anfänge der Poesie.   Grundlegung zu
    einer realistischen Entwickelungsgeschichte der Poesie.
    Dresden : 1891.

JENKIN, FLEEMING.   Papers, Literary, Scientific, etc.   Ed. by
    S. Colvin and J. A. Ewing.   Lond. : 1887.

A new edition of Guest's Rhythms was issued, under the su-
pervision of the Rev. W. W. Skeat, in 1883.   Three admirable
articles, suggested by the reprint of this work, appeared in the
Saturday Review of February and March, 1883, and are published in abridged form among the Papers, Literary, Scientific,
etc., of Fleeming Jenkin, vol. I, pp. 149–170.   Professor Jenkin
accepts neither the ancient method of scanning English verse
nor the accentual and sectional method of Guest, Goold
Brown, and others.   He traces in English metre the blending
(p. 154) of two independent systems of rhythm, the Anglo-
Saxon and the classical ; and he elucidates (pp. 155–170) a
method of verse-analysis based upon the combination of classic
foot, sectional rhythm, pause, and accent.   The article is cor-
dially commended to the student.

KAWCZINSKI, MAX.   Essai comparatif sur l'origine et l'histoire
    des rhythmes.   Paris : 1889.

This important contribution to the long and involved discussion of the origin of Romance versification contains also by
the way many profound and original remarks upon metrical
questions of a general character.   Of especial interest is his
view that modern metres are inheritances from Greece, not
autochthonous in their origin.   Reviewed by F. M. Warren,
Am. Jour. Philol. 40: 358–371.

KLEINPAUL, E.   Poetik.   8. umg. und verm. Aufl.   Leipz. :
    1879.

A methodical and fairly scientific introduction to the subject.

KLUGE, F.   Zur Geschichte des Reimes im Altgermanischen
   (in Paul und Braune's *Beiträge*, vol. IX, p. 422).

LA GRASSERIE, R. DE.   Études de grammaire comparée.
   Analyses métriques et rhythmiques.   Vannes : 1893.

LA GRASSERIE, R. DE.   Étude de rhythmique.   Essais de
   métrique védique et sanscrite.   Paris : 1893.

LA GRASSERIE, R. DE.   *Le museon*, 10 : 299, 419, 589; 11 :
   38, 191, 307, 389 Essai de rhythmique comparée.

   Examines in succession : (1) the phonic or rhythmic element ; (2) the psychic element ; (3) the union of the two in
the morphology of verse, forming the poetic whole.   The
author holds that the essence of poetry is creation.

LA GRASSERIE, R. DE.   *Bulletin histor. et philol. du comité des
   travaux hist. et scientifiques*, 1893, p. 181 De la strophe
   et du poème dans la versification française, spécialement
   en vieux français.

   According to the ingenious theory of La Grasserie the strophe
arose in a somewhat mechanical way through the efforts of ver-
sifiers to do away with the monorhyme of the epic and to give
to this type of poetry a lyric movement.

LANIER, S.   The Science of English Verse.   N. Y. : 1880.

   The student will thank Lanier for the suggestive history of
English metric supplied by the preface.   He will find, on turning to p. 98, Experimental Test of Accent, that Lanier, with
Sylvester and Poe, posits time-relation as the basis of modern
rhythms.   In this respect, therefore, his system is opposed to
those of Ellis, Abbott, Hale, and Mayor.   He attributes the
theory of the accentualists to their confusion of 'primary
rhythm' (quantity) with 'secondary rhythm' (the arrangement
of pitch and stress).   From such premises naturally follow

Lanier's elaborate classification of rhythms and the musical notation of them. The elements — duration, pitch, and tone-color — suggest the order of treatment adopted : rhythms, tunes, and colors of verse.

Under rhythms, pp. 62–65, 98–109, 119, 120, discriminate between quantity and stress, and between the various kinds of stress. Pp. 89–94, 182–224 treat of blank verse, 'run-on' lines, the 'pause,' the 'rest,' etc. The main division of rhythm into its so-called six orders (p. 95) is lucid and ingenious ; but as dependent upon the time-theory of verse, is it scientific or trustworthy? The chapter on the tunes of English verse should be compared with the scientific treatises of Weil (Order of Words), V. Egger (La parole intérieure), and Gurney. Part III, which takes up without discrimination what Sylvester would call the chromatic and synectic of verse (color, vowel-distribution, rhyme, etc.), is valuable. In chap. XIII Lanier elaborates Sylvester's Phonetic Syzygy, first admiring the aptness of the term. May we not suggest the superior simplicity of some such nomenclature as 'vowel and consonant coördination,' or 'vocal sequences'?

LECKY, J. *Proc. Eng. Philol. Soc.,* Dec. 19, 1884 (Monthly Abstract) Phonetic Theory of English Prosody.

Abstract of a paper read by Mr. James Lecky, in which is proposed a phonetic notation for the scansion of English verse. Provision is made for indicating three degrees of stress and five of length. By beginning each foot with a strong syllable, as proposed by Ellis and Pierson, Mr. Lecky identifies the foot with the "stress-group."

LE GOFFIC, C., and THIEULIN, E. Nouveau traité de versification française. Paris : 1890.

For higher classes in the lycées and normal schools. Treats of origins, value of syllables, elision, hiatus, rhyme, caesura, *en-*

jambement, alliteration, assonance, strophes, and fixed forms. A good introduction.

LUBARSCH, E. O. Französische Verslehre mit neuen Ent-
    wickelungen für d. theoret. Begründung d. französischen
    Rhythmik. Berlin: 1879.

Pronounced by Körting the best handbook of French versification.

MASSON, D. Poetical works of John Milton. 3 vols. Lond.:
    1874. Vol. I, pp. cvii–cxxxii Essay on Versification.

A thorough and liberal inductive examination into Milton's blank verse. Masson scouts the so-called norm of blank verse. "Whatever combinations of accented and unaccented syllables," he holds, "can produce a blank verse which shall be good to the ear, is not a matter for arithmetical computation, but for experience." He approves the use of trochee, spondee, ana-paest, dactyl, and even of tribrach, amphibrach, and antibac-chius. Mayor's criticism (Eng. Metre, pp. 74–79) shows that by the recognition of elision and slurring many of Masson's tri-brachs, amphibrachs, etc., may be reduced to ordinary English feet. With Masson's views Mayor compares those of Keightley (Life, Opinions, Writings of Milton), who also belongs to the inductive school. (See in addition Masson's Essays, Biograph-ical and Critical, pp. 447–475 Prose and Verse, De Quincey.)

MAYOR, J. B. Chapters on English Metre. Lond.: 1886.

Professor Mayor pleads for a scientific treatment of English metre. He defends the principle of routine scansion, believes that, whether poets have respected it or not, there are scientific uses to which it must be put; and as to the classical nomen-clature of prosody, does not see any advantage in giving it up. He states (p. 10) the more important questions demanding con-sideration, and advances to a consideration of the best-known

English metrists.   In chap. II he attacks Dr. Guest's system.
He objects decidedly to the assumption that our verse is to be
judged by the laws of Anglo-Saxon metre and the principle of
the 'section,' and esteems Dr. Guest's approbation of a poet a
dubious compliment.   He is more in accord (chap. III) with the
logical *a-priorism* of Dr. Abbott, but, in chap. VI, especially
applauds the *a posteriori* method of Mr. Ellis.   Symonds, who
argues for an aesthetic disregard of scientific scansion, is not
commended.   The more original and constructive part of Professor Mayor's work is contained in chaps. VI–XII.   The
chapters (pp. 81–123) on metrical metamorphoses and substitutions cover the interesting questions of truncated lines,
catches, pauses, mixed metres, allowable conversions of feet,
etc.   In these chapters the author's judgments are remarkably
clear and sound.   His examination of the metres of Marlowe,
Surrey, Shakespeare, Milton, Tennyson, and Browning are a
genuine contribution to the science of the subject.   All in all,
this is perhaps the best short English treatise on versification.   Ellis's remarks on Mayor's Two Papers on Rhythm are
to be found in *Trans. Eng. Philol. Soc.*, 1875–76, pp. 435–449.
" Single lines cannot be scanned by themselves.   Rhythm
must be taken by paragraphs."

MEYER, W.   Anfang und Ursprung der lateinischen u. griechi-
    schen rythmischen Dichtung.   (*Abhandlg. d. phil.-hist.
    Classe d. bayerischen Akademie d. Wissenschaften*, xvii, ii.)

MEYER, W.   Numerous articles on Versification, especially on
    the origin of Romance Versification.   (See § 24 and, in
    general, Kawczynski, chaps. VII and VIII.)

MINCKWITZ, J.   Lehrbuch der deutschen Verskunst.   3. Aufl.
    Leipz. : 1854.

While this handbook deals professedly with German metric
and prosody, it covers, in a manner too formal indeed, but

scholarly, a large part of the field common to modern versification. According to Minckwitz, syllables in German prosody
are valued in terms of accent, significance of thought, and
sound-relation or vowel-weight. German verse has, then, short,
long, and medium syllables, as well as accent, to deal with ;
and the German tongue has, in so far as comports with its
nature, united the claims of quantity and accent, as was the
case in Greek and Latin verse.

NEWMAN, F. W. Miscellanies. Lond.: 1869. Pp. 65–145
  Four Lectures on Poetry.

Of these lectures, the second (pp. 32–103), on Forms of Poetry,
opens with a distinction between the modern oratorical metre,
which depends on the prose accent, and the ancient musical
metre, which depended on 'equable times.' There is also a
remark to the effect that certain words may be accentually
of one metre and quantitatively of another — *e.g. female,* accentually a trochee, quantitatively a spondee. This is probably
(p. 83) the passage which Professor Sylvester, Laws of Verse,
p. 65, misconstrues into an assertion of the abbreviating effect
of the accent, and elaborately condemns.

PARIS, G. Le vers français. Paris : 1885.

PARSONS, JAMES C. English Versification for the Use of Students. Boston : 1891.

A well-ordered, respectable compilation. Hardly to be called
a contribution to the science.

PAUL, H. Grundriss der germanischen Philologie. Strassburg : 1889.

Students who desire to master Germanic versification, and
who are willing to give to the subject the attention it requires,
will do well to become familiar with this important work. The
treatment of metres occupies pp. 861–1072, and is from the

hands of four eminent specialists.   Pp. 861–898, by Sievers, are taken up with a discussion of Old German metric.   At the beginning the author makes an interesting comparison of the theories of Lachmann, Schmeller, Wackernagel, and himself, regarding alliterative poetry.   The general structure of the normal verse in Old German, as well as of the 'Schwellvers,' is set forth briefly but comprehensively.   A second division deals with old northern metres, such as those of the Edda, the Skalds, etc.; a third with Anglo-Saxon metres, and a fourth with the old Saxon metre, that is, the metre of the Heliand. The essay closes with a few paragraphs on Old High German Metres.   The chapter by Paul, on German versification, which follows (pp. 898–993), is better adapted to the needs of the beginner.   The author first defines the various terms used in the discussion, such as quantity, accent, verse, etc., then passes (p. 903) to a consideration of rhythm in general, which in German he finds to rest upon expiratory accent and quantity.   In the treatment of accent Paul recognizes four degrees of stress : (1) primary accent, (2) strong secondary accent, (3) weak secondary accent, (4) no accent.   A certain minimum of stress is necessary to characterize the principal accent; the other degrees have a relative value and are determined, as suggested by Moriz, by the neighboring syllables.   Thus a syllable is unaccented when its stress is less than that of the preceding and following syllable; it has the strong secondary accent when (without being primary) it (a) rises in stress above the preceding and is followed either by a weaker stress or by a pause, or (b) begins a sentence; it has the weak secondary accent when it follows a primary accent and rises in point of stress above the following syllable.   This idea is applied with considerable detail (pp. 905–907), after which comes a brief discussion of quantity (pp. 907–910).   In the following sections the various periods of German poetry are passed in review with reference to their methods of versification, Paul's treatment of the Volkslied (pp. 941–944) and of modern verse (Kunstdichtung, pp. 947–962) being of especial interest. The chapter closes with sections on rhyme, assonance, alliteration, the refrain, and kinds of verse and strophe. In the next chapter Karl Luick and Schipper write upon English metres, the first treating historically of native English metres; the second, of the introduction of foreign metres into English verse.

PELLISSIER, GEORGES. Essais de littérature contemporaine. Paris: 1893.

    Le vers alexandrin et son évolution rhythmique.

PIERSON, P. Métrique naturelle de langage. Avec une notice préliminaire par Gaston Paris. Paris: 1884.

PLATO. Dialogues.

For Plato's observations on rhythm and metre, see Symposium 187, Cratylus 424, Republic III, 400, Philebus 17, Laws II, 665, Gorgias 502.

POE, EDGAR ALLAN. Works. 4 vols. N. Y.: 1880. Vol. I, pp. 214–258 The Rationale of Verse.

A virulent but virile article. The poets of whom Poe happened to be jealous, the scholiasts of antiquity, and the "Frogpondians" of his own day come in for the abuse of a peevish author. But the theories advanced concerning metre (Poe does not here treat of the whole range of rhythm; not at all of thought in poetry, nor of expression as poetic) deserve painstaking attention; they were new to many of Poe's contemporaries, and they are in many particulars sound. His most notable assertions are that with spondee, dactyl, anapaest, iamb, and trochee, all modern verse may be scanned; that modern feet are of the same length; that the accented syllable is long; that the basis for the measure is time. His system of scansion by units, halves, quarters, etc., is simple and gen-

erally sane; his suggestion of 'run-on' feet, stepping from one
line into the next, may be new to the student, and should be
considered. Is it not because Poe failed to give its full value
to the 'rest,' or 'silent syllable,' that he falls into difficulty
with his monosyllabic feet, spondees, so-called bastard trochees,
bastard iambs, etc.? For the opposing view of the value of the
accented syllable see F. W. Newman's Second Lecture on
Poetry (Miscellanies, p. 83). Poe's system of quantification
(p. 246) will be better understood if instead of the words "accented" and "unaccented" be read "noted" and "unnoted,"
or "designated" and "undesignated." His criticism (p. 223)
of Leigh Hunt's Principle of Variety in Uniformity is a piece
of invidious quibbling.

QUICHERAT, L. Traité de versification française. 2e éd.
     Paris: 1850.

RAYMOND, G. L. Poetry as a Representative Art. N. Y. and
     Lond.: 1886.

Both argument and preface might inspire more confidence if
they were less pretentious. There is nothing novel in the chapters on psychological and speculative aesthetics. The development of the relation between elocution and prosody may,
however, be worth something to the general student. The
nomenclature — initial, median, and terminal measures — is
happy, but the 'median' measure is, *per se*, still as much a
matter of question as is the existence of the amphibrach in
English verse.

RUSKIN, JOHN. Elements of English Prosody. Orpington:
     1880.

While asserting in his usual omniscient manner that 'meas-
ured times of utterance are the basis of verse,' the author, as
an afterthought, also informs us (Preface, p. vii) that 'stress-
accent and quantity are identical.' The volume has, therefore,

no value in the argument beyond what attaches to the author's name. English metres (feet) are enumerated as ten. The classical terminology is preserved. Six metric lines (from monometer to hexameter) are discussed; stanzas also, but meagrely. The usefulness of the book lies in Ruskin's semi-poetic *dicta* concerning the relative significance of metres.

SANDERS, D.   Abriss der deutschen Silbenmessung und Vers-
    kunst.   Berlin: 1891.

Distinguishes three movements in German poetry: (1) Old German; (2) the versification of Opitz on the basis of Romance languages; (3) the versification of Klopstock and J. H. Voss on the basis of Latin and Greek quantity.

SCHERER, W.   Zur Geschichte der deutschen Sprache.   2d ed.

Contains a suggestive chapter on the Origin of Metre.

SCHIPPER, J.   Englische Metrik (in Paul's Grundriss d. ger-
    manischen Philologie, Abschn. IX).

    See H. Paul above.

SCHIPPER, J.   Englische Metrik in historischer. . . . Entwicke-
    lung. . . .   2 vols.   Bonn: 1881–88.

This is the most scientific and exhaustive treatise to be found on English versification. Vol. I traces English metres from the Anglo-Saxon period to the reign of Henry VIII. The second volume, which is of more immediate importance for the student of classic English versification, traces the growth of metres from the beginning of the Renaissance to the present day. The Einleitung (pp. 1–14) supplies the reader with a very useful list of early English metrists; it also (p. 9) describes briefly the movement on the part of some writers of the second half of the sixteenth century toward imitating, *in toto*, classical metres. In chap. II (pp. 15–75) Schipper discusses the rhythm of verse, decides upon the normal line in blank verse, condemns the 'hovering' accent and Shakespeare's 'feminine

endings,' and considers the pause, *enjambement*, and alliteration
in Later English Poetry. His division of the caesura (pp. 24–
32) into *stumpfe, lyrische*, and *epische*, is excellent, though somewhat formal. In the Second Part (pp. 164–464) are considered :
(1) the kinds of verse handed down from Old English, and
(2) (pp. 256–464) the kinds of verse introduced or suggested
by the influence of the Renaissance. The chapter on blank
verse (pp. 256–374) considers the style of the predecessors of
Shakespeare, of Shakespeare (pp. 287–315), of his Elizabethan successors, of Milton (340–347), and of other poets down
to the present time. This is a masterly handling of blank
verse ; and as an historical treatment it is the best available. Pp. 439–448 furnish a *résumé* of the discussion on
hexameters, not so satisfactory as the author's presentation of
blank verse, or of the sonnet. Schipper does not do justice
to Arthur Hugh Clough ; if he has read, he has not understood, the 'Bothie of Tober-na-Vuolich,' which he describes
as a "burlesque sentimental epos." A discussion of the hexameters both of that poem and of Kingsley's Andromeda would
have been in place. Schipper's view of the quantity and accent
question is substantially that of Abbott, not of Ellis. Vol. II
treats of the strophe : (1) of strophes derived from Old English poetry ; (2) of forms imported under the Renaissance influence or later. Pp. 766–835, on the Spenserian stanza and
on ode-forms, should be noted. The chapter on the sonnet
(pp. 835–886) covers the historical and aesthetic sides admirably. In a footnote to pp. 836–837 will be found a fair
bibliography of literature upon the sonnet. Pp. 886–936 are
on other fixed forms of verse. There is as yet, unfortunately, no English translation of this monumental treatise.
In his Grundriss der englischen Metrik (Wien u. Leipz. :
1895) Schipper revises his chapters on the development of
the national metre, and condenses the whole of his former
work.

SCHMIDT, J. H. H.   Introduction to the Rhythmic and Metric
    of the Classical Languages.   Trans. by J. W. White.
    Boston : 1878.

The student of classical versification is especially referred to
this treatise.   Bk. I opens with a general discussion of tone ;
its duration or quantity ; its strength or intonation ; its eleva-
tion or accent.   These introductory considerations are all-
important, for, as Schmidt says, the understanding of the
poetic forms of the classics depends upon the correct articula-
tion of the vowels.   The author considers (Bk. II) the metrical,
rhythmical, and musical factors of song.   He then passes to
the special treatment of classical metres, giving under some six
heads a clear outline of the main principles of ictus, length,
and substitution.   The fundamental forms of the measure,
equal, unequal, and quinquepartite, are arranged according to
numerical and musical equivalents.   Bk. II closes with a useful study of Doric measures (Pindaric Odes and Choruses)
and of Logaoedics.   Bks. III–V are occupied with a treatment
of the rhythmical sentence, of typology and eurythmy.   The
common basis of poetic and prosaic rhythm is discussed in a
manner both instructive and interesting.   In the appendix
(pp. 154–193) are valuable schemes of the lyric parts of the
Medea, of the Antigone, and an index to the metres of
Horace.

This work is a clear and practical presentation of a subject
covered in more scientific fashion by the same writer in Die
Kunstformen der griechischen Poesie und ihre Bedeutung.
4 vols.   Leipz. :   1868–72.   The larger work agrees in the
main with the conclusions of Rossbach and Westphal, but
depends for its value upon painstaking and independent research into the practice of the Greek poets.

SIEVERS, E.   Grundzüge der Phonetik.   3d ed.   Leipz. : 1885.
    §§ 29–35 On Quantity and Accent.

See also under Paul (Grundriss d. germanischen Philologie)
as above; and on Old English Versification Sievers's articles in
Paul and Braune's *Beiträge*, vols. X and XII.

Skeat, W. W.   Essay on Alliterative Poetry.

> See Furnivall and Hales, Bishop Percy's Folio MS., Lond.:
> 1867, vol. III, pp. xxvi–xxviii.

Skeat, W. W.   The Complete Works of Geoffrey Chaucer.
7 vols.   Oxford: 1894–97.

In the Introduction to vol. VI (1895) will be found the most
recent authoritative discussion of Chaucer's versification.   For
criticism of Professor Skeat's position on various matters see
Professor T. R. Lounsbury in the *N. Y. Tribune*, February 24
and March 3, 1895, and compare Lounsbury's treatment of
versification in his Studies in Chaucer.

Souza, Rob. de.   Questions de métrique.   Le rhythme poétique.   Paris: 1892.

Spedding, J.   Reviews and Discussions: Literary, Political,
and Historical, not relating to Bacon.   Lond.: 1879.

> Pp. 316–343 On English Hexameters.   (A review of Matthew
> Arnold's Three Lectures on Translating Homer.)   Reprinted
> from *Frazer*, June, 1861, with corrections and explanations con-
> taining a criticism of a paper read by Mr. Munro before the
> Camb. Philos. Soc., Feb. 13, 1860.

Spedding, J.   *Blackw.* 7: 641 Sweetness of Versification.

Spencer, Herbert.   Philosophy of Style.   Boston: 1892.

Spencer, Herbert.   Illustrations of Universal Progress: A
Series of Discussions.   N. Y.: 1865.

> Pp. 210–238 The Origin and Function of Music.

The essay on the Origin and Function of Music discusses
the relations between emotional speech, music, poetry, recita-
tion, and song.   Note that according to Spencer the cadences

of emotional speech precede the development of music, while
by Darwin, Descent of Man, 2 : 320, the opposite order is
maintained. A later utterance of Spencer is to be found in
Mind, October, 1890. See also his Philosophy of Style for
remarks on metre and rhyme.

STENGEL, EDM.   Romanische Verslehre.   (In Gröber's Grund-
    riss d. romanischen Philologie.   Strassburg: 1893.)

This work, written in 1887 and revised for publication in
1893, is in many respects the best treatment of Romance
versification as a whole. The author holds to the theory that
Romance verse originated in the Latin popular poetry, and
asserts, somewhat dogmatically, that a fixed number of syllables
and not word-accent is the underlying principle. Of especial
value is his discussion of the caesura (for which he substitutes
the term *Reihenschluss*) and of the development of the strophe.

STRAMWITZ, E.   Strophen- und Vers-Enjambement im Altfran-
    zösischen.   Greifswald: 1886, and Leipz.: 1887.

SYLVESTER, J. J.   The Laws of Verse; or Principles of Versi-
    fication, etc.   Lond.: 1870.

The ostensible purpose of this very queer book is to prove
that "the technical part of versification is capable of being
reduced to rules and referred to fixed principles." The actual
purpose of the author seems to be twofold: first, to print his
rhymed translation of Horace, Od. III, 29; and, second, to express at one and the same time his appreciation of the esteemed
friends who "recite his verses," and his contempt of the "ver-
sifiers — highly cried up, betitled, and decorated ones, too —
of the present day, who have no notion, explicit or implicit, of
the law of syzygy!" Professor Sylvester's translation of the
Tyrrhena regum is a neat specimen of scientific versification;
but his other metres, appended for no satisfactory reason to the
Tyrrhena, are, as he appears to apprehend, worth very little.

His methodology of the science of verse, however, if one has the patience to disentangle it from a web of footnotes and divagations, and unravel the snarls of its nomenclature, has the merit of system and practicability.   When the student has conquered the needless pedantry of Syzygies, Synectics, and Anastomoses, he will admit that the division of poetry into idealistic, linguistic, and rhythmic, and of rhythmic into metric, chromatic, and synectic, and each of these, by further trichotomy, into an unending procession of trinities or triplets, should, at any rate, exhaust the subject.   Attention is called to pp. 10–17, 45–49, specially to the footnotes on method and the text on the Alcaic; and to pp. 63–71, Sylvester's approval of Poe's theory of measure.   For a review (of no great value), see *Fortn.* 14: 448, by C. M. Ingleby.

SYMONDS, J. A.   Sketches and Studies in Southern Europe. 2 vols.   N. Y.: 1880.

> Vol. II, pp. 325-382 Appendix : Blank Verse.

This entertaining article consists of (1) a prefatory note on accent and quantity, licenses, pause, and elision, which should be read in connection with Mayor's critique upon the author's aesthetic theory of verse ; (2) a pleasant history of blank verse ; and (3) a treatise on Milton's verse.   Symonds derides the *a priori* criticism of Milton's prosody indulged in by Dr. Johnson, and approves of the more liberal metrical theories of Sir Edgerton Brydges and Keightley.   But he lays himself open, by vague and idealistic speculation concerning matters scientific, to numerous forms of attack.   For an elaboration of "aesthetic intuitivism" see Symonds's Predecessors of Shakespeare, pp. 590–603.   The article by Symonds with which Mayor disagrees is The Blank Verse of Milton, in *Fortn.*, December, 1874.

TISSEUR, CLAIR.   Modestes observations sur l'art de versifier. Lyon : 1893.

> See *Rev. d. l'Hist. Litt.*, 15 Avr. 1894 (Souriau).

TOLMAN, A. H.   *Andover Review*, 7 : 326 The Laws of Tone-
     Color in the English Language.

An attempt to derive the laws of tone-color from the practice of English writers.   A simple and useful statement of the
subject.

VALENTIN, V. Der Rhythmus als Grundlage einer wissen-
     schaftlichen Poetik. Prg. der Handelschule zu Frankfurt
     a. M. 1870.

VERGALO, DELLA ROCCA DE.   Poétique nouvelle.   Paris :
     1880.

The author puts in a plea for verse without caesura or
elision, in which hiatus and alliteration shall be recognized as
essential features.   According to Rodenbach (*Rev. Bleue*, 47 :
422), "Vergalo est, si non l'inventeur, du moins le restaurateur
du vers libre."

VIEHOFF, H.   Die Poetik.   (See § **20**.)

> Bd. 2, chap. I, pp. 241–280 Der Vers ; chap. II, pp. 280–304 Der
> Reim ; chap. III, pp. 321–461 Theorie d. Strophe; p. 357 Von
> den neuern entlehnten Strophenformen; p. 382 Antike Formen.

WESTPHAL, R. [ed.] Scriptores Metrici Graeci.   2 vols.
     Leipz. : 1866.

Westphal's Scriptores Metrici Graeci, which furnishes us with
the text of Hephaestion's Enchiridion, of Proclus's Chresto-
mathia, and of other Greek works on prosody, is the outcome
of a series of critical treatises inspired by Boeckh's famous
essay on the metres of Pindar.   Of these treatises the first
(giving the results of the work of both Westphal and Rossbach
of Tübingen) appeared in 1854, as Griechische Rhythmik, by
A. Rossbach.   In 1856 followed Griechische Metrik, by Westphal and Rossbach.   The authors were laboring in an almost

unknown field, and their work attracted attention. In 1861
was published Westphal's Die Fragmente und Lehrsätze der
griechischen Rhythmiker, the most important volume of the
series ; and in 1863 came the same author's Harmonik und
Melopöie der Griechen. For a lucid statement of Westphal's
contributions to the history and science of Greek prosody see
Hadley's Greek Rhythm and Metre (Essays, Philol. and Crit.,
pp. 81–102). Of Westphal's conclusions the following are
most noteworthy : (1) that the relation of music to poetry was
entirely different in the ages of Greek classical poetry from
what it now is ; (2) that Aristophanes and other ancient
rhythmists worked not theoretically but inductively ; (3) that
these rhythmists based their inductions upon the poetry of the
Golden Age, not of the Age of Decline ; (4) that ancient
rhythmic proves the existence and use of compound feet ;
(5) that the practice of pause and prolongation obtained in
Greek verse.   See also Westphal's Metrik d. indogerman.
Völker, in *Kühn's Zts.* 9 : 437 ; Tradition of Anc. Metre,
Philologus, 20 : 76.   On non-classical metres, see Westphal's
Theorie d. neuhochdeutschen Metrik (Jena : 1877), and his
important work entitled Allgemeine Metrik d. indogerman. u.
semit. Völker auf Grundlage d. vergleich. Sprachwissenschaft,
mit einem Excursus : Der griech. Hexameter in d. deutschen
Nachbildung, von H. Kruse (Berlin : 1892).

§ 24. GENERAL NOTE.

A. CLASSICAL METRES.[1]— 1. It is not our purpose to furnish
an exhaustive bibliography of versification. The literature of
Greek and Latin metres would itself fill a volume. For the

---

[1] Additional material will be found in Sulzer's Allgemeine Theorie der schönen
Künste, and in Blankenburg's Lit. Zusätze, under the titles : *Accent, Dichtkunst*
(Poetik), *Prosödie, Sylbenmaas,* and *Vers.*

general outline of the subject the student should consult the
standard Greek and Latin grammars and such works as Boeckh's
Encyklopädie, Corssen's Aussprache, Vokalismus u. Betonung
d. lateinischen Sprache (2 vols. 2d ed. Leipzig: 1888);
Westphal's Metrik d. Griechen (2 vols. 2d ed. 1867); Iwan
Müller's Handbuch d. klassischen Altertumswissenschaft, especially Blass's chapter on Hermeneutik u. Kritik (see § 23),
and Blass's essay Metrik ; Klotz's Ueber die neueren Erscheinungen auf d. Gebiete d. gr. u. röm. Metrik, in Müller's *Jahresbericht ü. d. Fortschr. d. class. Altertumsw.*, 1886, pp. 26–160 ; W.
Christ's Metrik d. Griechen u. Römer ; and J. H. H. Schmidt's
Introduction to the Rhythmic and Metric of the Classical Languages (trans. by J. W. White. Boston: 1878). Somewhat
antiquated but still *gründlich eingehende* are Munck's Die Metrik
d. Griech. u. Röm., 1834, and Freese's Die griech.-röm. Metrik,
1842. While Bentley was the father of modern metrical criticism, Boeckh, by his great work De metris Pindari, gave that
decisive impulse to inductive study of ancient metric and metrists which has resulted in the treatises of Rossbach, Westphal,
and J. H. H. Schmidt; in the Grundzüge d. griech. Rhythmik
im Anschluss an Aristides Quintilianus, of Julius Caesar, 1861 ;
and in the articles *apropos* of the subject by Weil, Susemihl,
and others, in *Jahn's Jahrbücher*, 1856–63. What light the
scholarly investigation into the metres of Pindar has thrown
upon Greek prosody will be appreciated by the student familiar with Professor Gildersleeve's edition of the Olympian
and Pythian Odes (N. Y.: 1885). The Preface to this work
calls attention to Engelbrecht's contributions to Greek metric ;
M. Schmidt's Ueber d. Bau d. Pindarischen Strophen (Leipz.:
1882) ; Mezger, Thiersch, Cronet, Dissen, Fürtwängler, and
others. Professor Gildersleeve, in his chapter on the metres
of Pindar (pp. lxiii–lxxvi) gives a valuable summary of the
more complicated metrical schemes of J. H. H. Schmidt and
Westphal. Dissen's article, De ratione poetica carminum Pin-

daricorum et de interpretationis genere iis adhibendo, will be
found in his edition of Pindar (1830), pp. xi–xciv. Boeckh's
Kritik d. Ausg. d. Pindar von Dissen is especially valuable;
it is contained in his Kleinere Schriften, 7 : 369. See also
Alf. Croiset's La poésie de Pindare et les lois du lyrisme grec
(Paris : 1880), and O. Riemann and M. Dufour's Traité de
rhythmique et de métrique grecque (Paris : 1894).

As a result of the impulse to metrical research given by
Boeckh and Westphal, treatises have been multiplied on the
metres of the Greek tragedies, epics, and lyrics. For a bibliography of them the student is referred to standard editions of
the various Greek poets.

2. GREEK METRISTS. — To a study of Greek writers on versification Hadley's Essay, recommended § 23 above, Usener's
Altgriech. Versbau (Bonn : 1887), and Dühr's Ueber Metrik
u. Rhythmik will be a good introduction. The student must
turn to J. H. H. Schmidt, to Boeckh's De metr. Pind. and his
Encykl. d. klass. Wissenschaften, p. 547, to Westphal's Fragmente u. Lehrsätze and his Scriptores metrici graeci, as well
as to the commentaries on Greek music, for more intimate and
immediate acquaintance with the rhythmic elements of Aristoxenus, pupil of Aristotle, and, according to Boeckh, *summus
auctor* in the matter of Greek rhythm (the best translation
is Westphal's, Leipz. : 1883 ; see Preface for exhaustive history of the discussion), — with the De composit. verborum of
Dionysius Halicarnassus (1st cent. B.C.), ed. Schäfer, — with
Plutarch's De musica (1st cent. B.C.), and with the treatise on
the same subject by Aristides Quintilianus (2d cent. A.D.).
The Studien zur alten griech. Musik, by Joh. Papastamatopulos
(Bonn : 1878), furnishes other valuable material. Proceeding
to the more formal treatises on metre, there should be noticed,
among the grammarians, Aristophanes of Byzantium (264 B.C.) ;
Dracon of Stratonicea (A.D. 130), whose περὶ μέτρων is edited
by G. Hermann (Leipz. : 1812) ; Hephaestion (*circa* A.D. 150),

author of the Enchiridion of Metres (ed. by Gaisford.   Oxford:
1810 ; and by Westphal, Scriptores metr. graec., vol. I, trans.
by Barham.   Cantab.: 1843) ; Longinus (b. A.D. 213), whose
Prolegomena to Hephaestion's Enchiridion will be found in
Westphal's Scriptores metr. graec. ; Proclus (5th cent. A.D.);
and others.   See Westphal, Scriptores metr. graec., vols. I and
II.   In general, on Greek metres, see Boeckh, Encykl. d. klass.
Wiss., pp. 813, 818, 844.

3. LATIN METRES. — Beside the sections on Metric in
Boeckh, Encykl., pp. 818, 846, 848, and in the standard Latin
grammars, should be consulted the chapters relative to the
subject in the best-known histories of Latin literature.   The
student's attention is called especially to Bähr's Geschichte d.
röm. Litt. (3 vols.   Carlsruhe: 1868–70) ; Barnhardy's Grundriss d. röm. Litt. (Braunschw.: 1869–72) ; Teuffel's Geschichte
d. röm. Litt., Leipzig (trans. by W. Wagner.   2 vols.   Lond.:
1873) ; Munck's Geschichte d. röm. Litt. (3 vols.   Berlin : 1858–
61) ; and to the chapters on literature in Mommsen's History
of Rome.   The works on Latin literature of the Frenchmen
Boissier, Champagny, Diderot, and Nisard may be consulted
ad loc.   For commentaries on the verse of special Latin poets
or of periods of Latin literature see John Wordsworth's Fragments and Specimens of Early Latin (Oxford: 1874); Westphal's Ueber d. Form d. ältesten römischen Poesie ; R. Klotz's
Grundzüge d. altrömischen Metrik (Leipz.: 1890) ; Ribbeck's
Frag. lat. relliquiae (Berlin : 1835) and his Comic. lat. relliquiae ; Ritschl's or Fleckeisen's Plautus ; Vahlen's Ennianae
poëseos relliquiae ;   C. F. W. Müller's Plautinische Prosodie ;
W. Wagner's Terence (Cantab. : 1869) ; L. Müller's Lucilius ;
C. O. Müller's Varro's De lingua latina (Leipz.: 1833) ;
Munro's Lucretius (Cantab. : 1866); Ellis's Catullus (Oxford :
1876) or Simpson's Catullus ; Ribbeck's or Conington's Vergil ;
Orelli's Horace (2 vols.   1850) or Macleane's ed. ; Lachmann's
Tibullus and Propertius (Berlin : 1829) ; Paley's or Postgate's

Propertius; Merkel's Ovid (3 vols. Leipz.: 1851); Haase's
Seneca (3 vols. Leipz.: 1862–71). For commentaries upon
poets of the period of decline see Cruttwell's Hist. Rom. Lit.,
pp. 487–489, from which several of the titles here cited are
taken.

The bibliography of Latin versification arranged according
to the periods of Latin literature may be directly and exactly
obtained by the student who will turn over, page by page, the
admirably executed, but poorly indexed, Bibliographical Clue to
Latin Literature, ed., after Hübner, by Prof. John E. B. Mayor
(Lond.: 1875). On pp. 7–10 will be found most of the authorities on the earliest Latin verse : Schneidewin, Hermann,
Düntzer, Corssen, Westphal, Ribbeck, Bartsch, etc. For Livius,
Ennius, Naevius, and Plautus, see pp. 12–18 under general
list, or sub-title Language and Metres; on Terence, see p. 19;
and so, in chronological order, through this valuable little
volume.

4. LATIN METRISTS. — The bibliography of Cornificius
(Rhetorica ad Herennium) will be found in Mayor's Clue,
p. 43. Quintilian should be consulted (De orat. inst. i : 10;
ix : 4). Caesius Bassus's (before A.D. 90) Fragmentum de
metris will be found in Keil's Scriptores artis metricae, p. 243
et seq. (vol. VI of Grammatici latini. Leipz.: 1874. Bibliography of Bassus, Mayor's Clue, p. 91). Aulus Gellius, Noctes
atticae, xvi : 18, should be consulted. The De litteris, de
syllabis, de metris, of Terentianus Maurus (end of 3d cent.
A.D.), is given in Keil as above, p. 313 *et seq.;* bibliography in
Mayor's Clue, p. 99. For the Fragment, formerly attributed to
Censorinus, on Music and Metres, see Keil, pp. 605–616, and
Mayor's Clue, pp. 161–162. For the Ars Atiliae Fortunatiani
(about A.D. 350), see Keil, p. 278 *et seq.;* for Marii Victorini
artis grammaticae, libri IV (about A.D. 350), see Keil, p. 1
et seq.; for Marii Plotii Sacerdotis artium grammaticarum,
libri tres, see Keil, p. 417 *et seq.;* for Aelius Donatus, see

Keil, Gram. lat., vol. VI, and references in the works of
Marius Victorinus, Max. Victorinus, Rufinus, and others in
Keil, vol. VI; and for bibliography of the foregoing and for the
commentators of Donatus, Flavius Mallius Theodorus, Marius
Servius Honoratus, and Sergius (about A.D. 355), see Mayor's
Clue, pp. 172, 173. The De metris of Theodorus is given by
Keil, vol. VI, pp. 599–601. Of the metrists of the 5th century
Rufinus (De metris comicorum et de numeris oratorum) figures
in Keil, pp. 547–578, and in Mayor's Clue, pp. 173, 174. Keil
(pp. 617–646) appends Fragmenta et excerpta metrica, including the De pedibus and De caesuris of Julius Severus. As
to the metrists of the 6th and 7th centuries, a bibliography of
Aldhelm will be found in Mayor, p. 211, and of Bede, on p. 213.
Bede's De arte metrica will be found in vol. VI, pp. 40–79,
of Bede's Miscellaneous Works, ed. by Giles (12 vols. Lond.:
1843–44). For passages from St. Augustine (De musica), Dio-
medes (Gram. lat.), Charisius (Gram. lat.), see Kawczynski,
pp. 50–52. Consult also Cicero, De oratore, III: 48, and
Orator, 58.

5. ON CLASSICAL ALLITERATION, RHYME, RHYTHM, AND
ACCENT, see Blass (Hermeneutik u. Kritik, pp. 211, 212). —
GREEK : Beer, De arte Aeschyli (Leipz. : 1877); Gustafsson, De
vocum in poemat. gr. consonantia, Acta Soc. Fennicae, xi (1879),
p. 297 *et seq.;* Jacobi, Fr., De usu alliterationis apud Sophoclem
(Göttingen : 1872); Jacob, G., De aequali stroph. et antistroph.
in trag. gr. confirmatione (Berlin : 1866); Holzapfel, *Zeitschrift
für Gymnasialwiss.* 1851, page 1 Ueber den Gleichklang bei
Homer; Isid. Hilberg, Die Princip. d. Silbenwägung u. d. daraus
entspringenden Gesetze d. Endsylben in d. gr. Poesie (Wien :
1879) ; Kiehl, *Mnemosyne,* 1852, p. 202 Correspondierender
Reim bei Aesch. — LATIN : Luc. Müller, De re metrica lat.,
p. 455 ; A. F. Nacke, *Rhein. Mus.* 1829, p. 324 Reime b. d. klass.
Dichtern ; H. Usener, *Jahrb. f. Phil.* 1873, p. 174 Reim in
altlat. Poesie ; E. Wölfflin, *Berichte d. Bayr. Acad.* 1881, 2 : 1

Bei den Dichtern; Landgraf and Wölfflin, *Sitzungsb. d. k. Akad. München*, Ueber d. alliterirenden Verbindungen d. lat. Sprache, 1887; Weil and Benloew, Théorie de l'accentuation latine, in the Philolog. Versamml. in Göttingen, 1852, pp. 66, 240; also H. Weil, *ibid.*, p. 85 *et seq.;* Seelmann, Die Aussprache des Latein; W. Meyer in *Abhg. d. k. Bayr. Acad.*, tome 59: 371. To these references should be added J. B. Greenough's Accentual Rhythm in Latin, in Harvard Studies in Class. Philol. IV: 105–115; and Early Latin Prosody, Harvard Studies, V: 57–71; O. Dingeldein's Gleichklang u. Reim in antiker Poesie (Büdingen: 1888), and Der Reim bei den Grie- chen und Römern (Leipz.: 1892); and W. Grimm's article on rhyme in classical Latin verse in the Proceedings of the Berlin Academy, 1851.

On classical rhythms, see G. Amsel, De vi atque indole rhythmorum quid veteres judicaverint (Vratislaw: 1887), in *Bresl. philol. Abhandlg.* I : 3; K. Deutschmann, De poesis graec. rhythmicae primordiis (Malmedy: 1883. Progr.) and De poesis graec. rhythm. usu et origine (Koblentz: 1889. Progr.); J. A. Hartung, Geschichte der Rhythmenschöpfung in griech. Lyriker (5 vols. Leipz.: 1858); W. Meyer, Anfang und Ursprung d. lat. u. griech. rhythm. Dichtung (München: 1885. *Akad. Abhandlg.*).

On classical alliteration, see C. Bötticker, De alliter. apud Rom. vi et usu (Berlin: 1884); W. Ebrard, Die Alliteration in d. lat. Sprache (Bayr.: 1882. Progr.); H. Habenicht, Allitera- tion bei Horaz (Eger: 1885. Progr.); E. Loch, *Rhein. Museum*, 3 (1829) : 324 De alliteratione serm. lat.

On classical accent, see T. H. Key, *Trans. Eng. Philol. Soc.*, 1873–74, p. 35 Accent a Guiding Principle, not merely of the Old Comic Metres, but generally of Latin Poetry; and first of Virgil's Latin Hexameters; W. Meyer, Ueber die Beobachtung des Wortaccents in d. altlat. Poesie (München: 1884, *Akad. Abhandlg.*).

6. TRANSITION TO ACCENT. On the transition from the principle of quantity in the Latin poetry to that of accent (as in
Latin hymns), see Huemer's Untersuchungen über die ältesten lat. christ. Rythmen (Wien : 1879) and his Untersuchungen über d. jambisch. Dimeter bei d. . . . Hymnendichtern
d. vorkarolingischen Zeit (Wien : 1879. Progr.) ; Zarncke's
Zwei mittelalterliche Abhandlg. über d. Bau rhythm. Verse,
Berichte d. k. sächs. Ges. der Wissensch. 1871, p. 34 ; Du Meril,
Poésie populaire lat. du moyen âge. See also Kawczynski,
chap. VII *et seq.*, for a history of the transition ; J. A. Symonds,
Wine, Women, and Song, pp. 8–14, 181 for materials of Goli-
ardic Literature (rhymed Latin). A standard treatise is Ferd.
Wolf's Ueber die Lais, Sequenzen u. Leiche, . . . Ein Beitrag
zur Gesch. d. rhythm. Formen d. Volkslieder, . . . Kirchen u.
Kunstlieder im Mittelalter (Heidelb. : 1841). See also Ritschl,
Opusc. phil., vol. I, p. 289 Accentuirte Verse, for the treatment
of the same transition in Greek poetry.

7. OF MAGAZINE ARTICLES ON GREEK AND LATIN PROSODY
the name is legion; the painstaking investigator will find specially
useful matter among the following : *Trans. Amer. Philol. Assoc.*
16 : 30 Feminine Caesura in Homer (Seymour) ; 16 : 78 Quantity (Goodell); Am. School at Athens, Papers, vol. IV Greek
Versification in Inscriptions (Allen); *Archiv. f. Philol. u. Paed.*
2 : 268–307 Ueber Hermann's Lehre vom Vortrage d. griech.
u. lat. Vers (Gotthold) ; *Jahrb. f. Philol. u. Paed.* 122 : 65 Theorie d. Versmasses (Hermann); 123 : 753 De Saturnio Versu
(Schweizer-Sidler); 124 : 599 ; 126 : 121, 144 Begriff d. Metr.
(Minckwitz) ; 133 : 451 Kleine Beiträge (Blass); *Journ. Philol.*
4 : 223 Latin Metres in English (Munro) ; 12 : 136 Tragic
Metres (Verrall) ; 18 : 161 Iambic Trimeter (Platt) ; *Kuhn's
Zeitschrift*, 24 : 556 Origin of Homeric Metre (Allen) ; *Philologus*, 1 : 395 Dithyrambos (Hartung); 5 : 85 Zur Metrik (Meiss-
ner); 10 : 1 Choriambus (Meissner) ; 250 Latein. Hexam.
(Crain) ; 11 : 328 Namen d. Füsse (Leutsch) ; 533 De hexam.

lat. (Froehde) ; 12 : 12 Entstehung d. ep. Hexam.'s (Leutsch);
23 : 81 Vom Saturnischen Verse (Spengel) ; 24 : 407 ; 25 : 54
Auflösungen im Trimeter (Rumpel) ; 25 : 471 ; 26 : 241 Griech.
Trag. Metr. (Rumpel) ; 28 : 230 Vom Saturnischen Verse
(Düntzer) ; 425 Griech. Troch. Tetram. (Rumpel) ; 31 : 98
Latein. Ictus, etc. (Langen) ; 193 Griech. Takte (M. Schmidt);
33 : 461 Griech. Pausen (Buchholtz) ; 46 : 27 Pseudo-Plutar-
chus de metro heroico ; *Rhein. Museum* 8 : 529 Iamb. Tetram.
Terent. (Krauss) ; 25 : 232 Metrik u. Musik (Brambach) ; 33 :
509 Varro's Beurtheilung d. römisch. Versmasses (Buchholtz) ;
45 : 236, 385 Latein. Hexam. (Eskuche) ; 41 : 427 Iamb.
Trim. (Kopp). See also file of *Transactions Philol. Society*,
of *Herrig's Archiv*, and of the *Zeitschrift f. deutsch. Philol.*
Note also a dissertation by Johansson on Latin ictus and
accent in the writers of comedy (Upsala, Univ. Dissert., vol.
III).

B. **MODERN METRES.** — 1. To the historical position and
theoretic value of English treatises on versification the best
guides are Schipper, Luick and Schipper in Paul's Grundr. d.
germ. Phil., Guest, and, for a brief historical sketch of English
metric accompanied by an annotated bibliography, Karl Elze's
Grundriss d. englischen Philologie, Halle : 1889, pp. 361–386
Metrik. (See § **23.**)

Nathan Drake's Shakespeare and his Times (2 vols. Lond.:
1817), vol. I, pp. 461–470, has been freely used by Schipper.
Joseph Haslewood's edition of ancient critical essays on English Poets and Poesy (2 vols. Lond.: 1811–15) supplies not
only the texts of the more important Elizabethan works on
poetics, but also, in prefaces and footnotes, most of the information at his time procurable concerning the lives of the authors.
(Arber's reprints of these essays furnish, of course, the results
of later research.) Haslewood himself draws his details largely
from Strype's Annals, Warton's History of English Poetry,

Seward's Anecdotes of Distinguished Persons, Nichols's Queen
Elizabeth's Progresses, and the Censura Literaria. Dr. Schipper in his Neuenglische Metrik, vol. I, pp. 7–12, runs over the
principal features of Elizabethan criticism, basing many of his
judgments upon Haslewood, and upon Haslewood's citations
from Gilchrist in the Censura Literaria. See also F. E. Schelling's Poetic and Verse Criticism of the Reign of Elizabeth
(Publications of Univ. of Penn., vol. I).

2. EARLIER ATTEMPTS AT ENGLISH METRIC. — Of incidental
criticism of English verse before 1570, the most noteworthy
appears in Roger Ascham's Scholemaster, published in that
year, but written probably between 1563 and 1568. Ascham
is distressed that his countrymen will "follow the Goths in
rhyming" rather than "the Greeks in true versifying." To be
sure, "the English tongue does not well receive the Carmen
Heroicum, and the Carmen Hexametrum does rather trot and
hobble than run smoothly," but the Carmen Iambicum is as
well adapted to English as to Greek or Latin. The author
praises Surrey for his unrhymed translation of Virgil. He
rises to real poetic criticism in the condemnation of contemporary English tragedy. (See Arber's Reprint, pp. 145–147.)
The earliest theoretic examination of English verse known to
us is George Gascoigne's Certayne Notes of Instruction concerning the making of Verse or Rhyme in English (Lond. :
1575). It will be found in Haslewood, vol. II, pp. 3–12, is in
the form of a letter thrown off for the benefit of one Master
Edouardo Donati, and treats in an eminently sensible way the
errors that an unskilled versifier is liable to fall into. In § 4
the wrenching of accents is condemned; in § 6 the use of
"rime without reason." In §§ 14 and 16 the Rithme Royal,
the Ballade, the Sonnet, the Verlay, the Poulter's Measure, and
the Ryding Rime are touched upon and tossed to one side in a
right "preposterous order" but with "brevitie." Next on the
list comes the pleasant correspondence of Spenser and Gabriel

Harvey, which appears in Haslewood (vol. II, pp. 255–303)
under the headings, Thrée Proper and Wittie Familiar Letters,
lately passed between two Universitie men : touching the Earth-
quake in Aprill last, and our English refourmed Versifying;
and Two Other very Commendable Letters, of the same men's
writing : both touching the foresaid Artificiall Versifying, and
certain Other Particulars. These are of the years 1579 and
1580; the two latter being prior in composition. They are,
as Chalmers says in his apology, instructive for their criticism
and dignified for their sense. Harvey was an enthusiast for
the introduction of classic metres into English; and Spenser,
though he found that the forced union of quantity and accent
made many a word, like a lame gosling, draw one "legge after
hir," still did not see " why a God's name we may not, as else
the Greekes, have the Kingdom of our owne Language, and
measure our Accentes by the sounde, reserving the Quantitie
to the Verse." The criticism in Harvey's letter of Oct. 23,
1579, on Spenser's iambic trimeters is an amusing piece of
pedantry. The letters throw light on the eminent but still obscure society of the Areopagus. It is probably to these letters and to Gascoigne's Notes of Instruction that King James
refers in his "Schort Treatise conteining some Reulis and Cau-
telis to be observit and eschewit in Scottis Poesie," 1584. For
he prefaces that part of his " Essayes of a Prentise " with
the statement that "mony learnit men, baith of auld and of
late hes already written thairof [of Poetry] in divers and sindry
languages." There is little imaginative force in King James's
treatment of *ryming*, of *fete*, of *flowing*, of *wordis*, of *sentences*,
and of *phrasis* in verse ; but there is a quantum of hard Scots
in his caution concerning *Ryming in Termis*, and the use of
Tumbling Verse ; and in the advice to " put in verse . . . ne
wordis, other than *metri causa*, or zit for filling furth the nom-
ber of fete, bot that they be all sa necessaire . . . as in case ze
were speiking the same purpose in prose. . . . " And that " ze

waie zour wordis according to this purpose." The royal author
uses the word "fute" consistently for verse-syllable. He does
not show any acquaintance with Sidney's Defense of Poesie
(1581–95, see § 21, *B* 2). For Sidney's attitude toward the
revival of classic versification, see Cook's edition, pp. 55–57.
E. Flügel's edition of the Ponsonby text (Halle: 1889) must
not be overlooked. The Preface to William Webbe's Discourse
of English Poetrie, 1586, says that the "Laureat Masters of
England might winne credit to their native speeche . . . if
English Poetrie were truly reformed, and some perfect plat-
forme or Prosodia of versifying were by them ratifyed and sette
downe . . ." after the fashion of the Greeks and Latins. A
large part of the Discourse is occupied with a *résumé* of opinions touching poets, Greek, Latin, and English. Imitators and
translators of the Latin are commended. From p. 54 on
(Haslewood's edition) will be found Webbe's remarks on prosody. The work closes with certain not very commendable
experiments in hexameters, Sapphics, and other classical
metres. In the appendix are "Englished" Horace's "Canons of Poetry" from the scheme of Fabricius Cremnicensis.
Webbe was succeeded by an equally ardent advocate of English hexameters, Abraham Fraunce, whose Arcadian Rhetoricke,
or the Precepts of Rhetoricke made plain by example, Greeke,
Latyne, English, Italyan, and Spanish, appeared in 1588. It
is written in prose and verse, and abounds with metrical experiments by the author. Hake's Touchstone of Wittes, of the
same year, is based upon the Arcadian Rhetoricke. A far abler
critic than Webbe or Fraunce was George Puttenham, concerning whose Arte of English Poetrie, published in 1589, Sir John
Harrington says: "A whole receit of Poetrie is [here] prescribed,
with so manie new-named figures as would put me in great
hope in this age to come would breed manie excellent Poets,
save for one observation that I gather out of the verie same
book; . . . he doth prove nothing more plainly than that

poetry is a gift and not an art." Puttenham's work is on a
large scale ; it discusses in three books Poets and Poesie, Proportion Poetical, and Ornament. His history of poets and his
judgments are valuable. His arrangement of verse in lozenges,
rhomboids, pilasters and eggs, is a whimsical and curious vanity. It is indeed not incredible that 'when he wrote of these
devices he smiled with himself.' But as a treatise on prosody
and on rhetorical figures, the Arte of English Poetrie is of greater
historical and practical importance than any contemporary essay
on criticism. On the cesure, accent, time, stir, cadence, etc.,
see Haslewood, vol. I, p. 61 *et seq.;* on Greek and Latin metres,
p. 85 *et seq.* Puttenham is not an advocate of English versification by quantity. On the subject of versification Sir John
Harrington's Apologie for Poetrie (1591) profits the student
but little. There is, also, little on prosody to be found in the
well-known Comparative Discourse of our English Poets, with
the Greeke, Latine, and Italian Poets (an excerpt from the Palladis Tamia), written in 1598 by Francis Meres. A very important attempt at reforming English verse on the classical basis
was Thomas Campion's Observations on the Art of English
Poesie (1602). "Old customes," says the poet-critic, "if they
be better, why should they not be recald? as the yet florishing
custome of numerous poesy used among the Romans and Gre-
cians." Since then (Haslewood, vol. II, p. 164) "the facilitie
and popularitie of Rime creates as many poets, as a hot summer
flies," . . . "I have studyed to induce a true forme of versefy-
ing into our language: for the vulgar and unartificiall custome
of riming hath I know deter'd many excellent wits from the
exercise of English Poesy." Campion not only declares the
unaptness of rhyme, but shows how the English tongue may
receive eight several kinds of classical numbers. His rules for
quantity in English verse, set down in his tenth chapter, are, if
we should imitate classical metres, truly of great reasonableness
and practicality. But his assault upon rhyme was not to go

unchallenged.   A more easy writer of prose than he, and a
more able controversialist, at once took up the cudgels in defense of the numbers and measures proper to the English
tongue.   This was Samuel Daniel, whose Defence of Rime
appeared in 1603.   In this work, as the author with justice
announces, "is demonstratively proved that Ryme is the fittest
harmonie of wordes that comports with our Language."   The
essay has acquired a merited fame.   It applies itself to the
vindication not only of "symphonious endings," but of the
idiosyncrasy of modern verse: "For as Greeke and Latine
verse consists of the number and quantitie of sillables, so
doth the English verse of measure and accent."   It is as
smoothly and sweetly written a bit of prose as any of the time.
Edmund Bolton's Hypercritica, which followed, *longo intervallo*
(1610–17), is of interest to the prosodist only in the Fourth
Addresse, and there for its curious and critical synopsis of
English poets rather than for information concerning the rules
or history of verse.   Ben Jonson's Fit of Rhyme against Rhyme
(see Penn's Hood's Rhymester) is merely a *jeu d'esprit*.   Davenant's Preface to Gondibert (1650) is of historical worth for its
advocacy of the "interwoven stanza of four" for the purposes
of heroic verse.   Milton's Preface to Paradise Lost is the last
of the famous protests against rhyme in English verse.   The
list of historical productions might, of course, be prolonged;
suffice it, however, merely to call attention to Henry Peacham's
Article on Poetry in the Compleat Gentleman (1634), to certain of Dryden's essays as mentioned in § 21, *B* 2, to the
Tragedies of the Last Age by Thomas Rymer (1692–93), to
the Duke of Buckingham's Essay on Poetry, to Pope's Essay
on Criticism, to John Dennis's Remarks on Pope's Rape of the
Lock (Lond.: 1728), to Dennis's select works (1718), to the
works of Bysshe and Gildon discussed above (§ 23), and to
Warton's History of English Poetry from the twelfth to the close
of the sixteenth century (ed. Hazlitt.   4 vols.   Lond.: 1871).

In this list it has not been deemed advisable to introduce in their chronological order certain works of merely historical interest. Some such are cited by Lanier (Preface to Science of Verse): the Epistola ad Acircium of Aldhelm (700); the De arte metrica of the Venerable Bede ; or, coming down to the last two centuries, Goldsmith's Essay on Poetry, Complete Works (ed. by Prior. 4 vols. Lond. : 1837), vol. I, pp. 250–322 ; pp. 557–566 Preface to the Beauties of English Poetry ; vol. IV, pp. 345–498 Criticism relating to Poetry and the Belles Lettres ; Sheridan's Art of Reading ; Steele's Prosodia Rationalis ; Chapman's Music of Language ; and Harris's Discourse. Mitford's Inquiry into the Principles of Harmony in Language, 1804, is of more value than other treatises of that time. (For criticism, see Lanier, Preface, pp. xii, xiii.) For later authorities, see § 23, and for writers on English poetics, see § 21, *B* 2, above.

3. On Early English Versification, see J. H. Schipper, Altenglische Metrik, as above, § 23; also the bibliography given by him, p. 40 *et seq.* of that work. Schipper makes special reference to Schubert's De Anglo-Saxonum arte metrica ; Vetter's Zum Muspilli und zur germanischen Alliterationspoesie ; K. Hildebrand's Verstheilung d. Edda (Höpfner's u. Zacher's *Zeitschrift*, Ergzbd., pp. 74–139) ; Max Rieger's Alt- und angelsächsische Verskunst (Halle : 1876) ; C. F. Koch's Historische Grammatik d. engl. Sprache (Weimar : 1863), Bd. I, pp. 149–170 ; and to the best English editions of Old English poetry. An essay which has marked an epoch in the history of metrical research is Sievers's Zur Rhythmik d. german. Alliterationsverses, Paul and Braune's *Beiträge*, Bd. X, pp. 209–314, 451–545 (see also Bd. XII). See also Kluge's Geschichte des Reimes im Altgermanischen in Paul and Braune's *Beiträge*, Bd. IX ; W. W. Skeat's Essay on Alliterative Poetry (Percy Folio MS., vol. III, ed. Hales and Furnivall) ; Guest, as in § 23 ; K. Luick, Zur altengl. u. altsächs. Metrik (Schwell-

vers u. Normalvers, Allit. u. Versrhythmus) in Paul and
Braune's *Beiträge*, Bd. XV, p. 441; John Lawrence, chapters on
Alliterative Verse (Lond.: 1893. 1. Metrical Pointing in Cod.
Junius XI : its Relations to Theories of Old English Verse-
Structure ; 2. Crossed Alliteration ; 3. Vowel Alliteration in the
14th cent. compared with that of Beowulf); F. B. Gummere, The
Translation of Beowulf and the Relation of Ancient and Modern
English Verse, *Am. Jour. Philol.*, vol. VII, p. 46.

Beginners are referred to Bright's Anglo-Saxon Reader,
Appendix II (N. Y.: 1891); Cook's First Book in Old English,
pp. 108–120 Prosody (Boston: 1894); O. L. Triggs in Mac-
Lean's Old and Middle English Reader, pp. lxv–lxxiv (Lond.
and N. Y.: 1893).

4. ON THE VERSE OF MIDDLE AND MODERN ENGLISH
POETRY the following authorities may be consulted : Guest,
Sievers, Skeat, Schipper, as in § **23**; ten Brink's Chaucer's
Sprache u. Verskunst ; T. R. Lounsbury's Studies in Chaucer,
His Life and Writings (3 vols. N. Y.: 1892. vol. III,
pp. 296–316 Chaucer's Versification); R. Alscher's Sir Thomas
Wyatt in der Entwickelungsgeschichte d. engl. Lit. u. Vers-
kunst (Wien: 1886. *Wiener Beiträge zur deutsch. u. engl.
Philol.*) ; C. Knaut's Ueber die Metrik Robert Greene's (Dis-
sert. Halle: 1891); H. M. Regel's article Ueber Chapman's
Homer-Uebersetzung in *Eng. Studien*, 5: 349, 350; G. König's
Zu Shakespeare's Metrik (Diss.), 1888 ; W. von Schotten's
dissertation, Metrische Untersuchungen zu John Marston's
Trauerspielen (Halle: 1886) ; Karl Elze's Notes on the Eliza-
bethan Dramatists, 2d Series, pp. 132–140 (Halle: 1884) ;
Schröer's article Ueber die Anfänge d. Blankverses in Engl.,
Anglia, 4 : 1 ; Em. Penner, *Herrig's Archiv*, 85 : 269 Metrische
Untersuchungen zu George Peele ; *Cornh.* 15 : 620 Blank Verse ;
C. B. Cayley's Pedigree of English Heroic Verse, *Trans. Philol.
Soc.*, p. 43 (Lond.: 1862–63) ; Hazlitt's Essay on Milton's
Versification, in The Round Table ; E. Kennedy's Lecture on

the Principles and Uses of Alliteration in Poetry, Dublin Afternoon Lectures on Literature and Art (3 vols. Lond. : 1866),
vol. III, pp. 89–128 ; W. E. Mead's Versification of Pope in its
Relations to the Eighteenth Century (Dissert. Leipz. : 1889);
and other references as under the next head, and in § **23**.

5. SPECIAL ENGLISH FORMS. — (*a*) *Blank Verse.* — In addi-
tion to the discussions under Mayor, Abbott, Guest, and others,
referred to in § **23**, the following may be consulted : Wagner,
The English Dramatic Blank Verse before Marlowe; O. F.
Emerson, The Development of Blank Verse : A Study of
Surrey, in *Mod. Lang. Notes*, vol. IV, No. 8 ; W. S. Walker,
Shakespeare's Versification (Lond. : 1854); Furnivall, Intro-
duction to the Leopold Shakespeare, § 7 ; G. Koenig, Der Vers
in Shakespeare's Dramen, in Quellen und Forschungen zur
Sprach- und Culturgesch. d. germ. Völker, Bd. LXI ; Schröer,
Anglia, 4 : 1 Die Anfänge des Blankverses in England ; Hil-
gers, Der dramatische Vers Shakespeare's (1868); Thos. R.
Price, The Construction and Types of Shakespeare's Verse as
seen in Othello (N. Y. : 1888. Papers of the N. Y. Shakespeare
Soc., No. 8) ; H. C. Beeching, On the Prosody of Paradise
Regained and Samson Agonistes, being a Supplement to the
Paper on the Elements of Blank Verse, which is printed in
the Rev. H. C. Beeching's edition of Paradise Lost, Book I
(Oxford : 1890).

(*b*) *Hexameters.* — Matthew Arnold's On Translating Homer,
see § **23**; J. S. Blackie, Horae Hellenicae (Lond. : 1874.
pp. 278–296) ; Cayley's Remarks on English Hexameters,
Trans. Philol. Soc., pp. 67–85 (Lond. : 1862–63) ; *Herrig's
Archiv*, 2 : 370 ; Preface to Derby's translation of the Iliad ;
prefaces to Crane's and Cranch's translations of the Aeneid.
One of the most exhaustive treatises on the subject is Karl
Elze's Geschichte des englischen Hexameters (Dessau : 1867.
Progr.), upon which Schipper's treatment of the subject
(Neuengl. Metrik, 1. Hälfte, pp. 439–450) is essentially based.

See Schipper, p. 445, for some of the best writers of English
hexameter verse, and Elze, Grundr. d. engl. Phil., p. 375. Also
worthy of notice are Robinson Ellis's Poems and Fragments of
Catullus, translated in the metres of the original (Lond.: 1871),
and C. M. Gayley's Peleus and Thetis of Catullus, translated
in equivalent hexameters (Classic Myths in Engl. Lit. Boston :
1893. pp. 261–266 and 278–281). See also *Mod. Lang. Notes*,
5 : 212 The Inventor of the English Hexameter (Gabriel Harvey), by F. E. Schelling; *Dublin Review*, N. S., 54 : 414; William
Taylor in the *Monthly Magazine*, June, 1796; Lord Lindsay's
Theory of English Hexameters (Lond. : 1862); Fitzgerald
Tisdall, A Theory of the Origin and Development of the Heroic
Hexameter (N. Y.: 1889); and J. Spedding, whose opinion on
hexameters is noticed by Arnold in his Last Words on Translating Homer. On elegiac verse, see *Blackwood*, 59 : 496. On
other English experiments with classic metres, consult again
Schipper, Neuengl. Metrik, 1. Hälfte, pp. 450–464; and on
quantitative verse, Elze, Grundr. der engl. Philol., p. 376.

(*c*) *The Heroic Couplet.* — See, in particular, Gosse's From
Shakespeare to Pope, in which Waller's part in the fashion-
ing of this form of verse is, perhaps, unduly magnified. A
criticism of Gosse's theory is made by Henry Wood in *Am.
Jour. of Philol.* 11 : 55 Beginnings of the Classical Heroic
Couplet in England. Consult also W. E. Mead's Versification
of Pope (Leipz.: 1889); G. L. Larkin's Scansion of the
Heroic Verse (abstract in *Lond. Academy*, December 27, 1890,
p. 617).

(*d*) For *The Sonnet*, see Schipper, Neuengl. Metr., pp. 835–
886 : a most thorough and critical treatment. On pp. 836,
837 will be found Schipper's bibliography of the subject. He
goes carefully into the origin and history of this form of verse,
and (p. 878) classifies it as Italian, specifically English, Spenserian, Miltonian, and Wordsworthian, pp. 879–885. References
will be found in the Guide to the Literature of Aesthetics, pp.

99, 100, to Hunt and Lee's Book of the Sonnet ; David Main's
Treasury of English Sonnets ; M. Pattison's Essay on the Sonnet in his edition of Milton ; W. Sharp's Sonnets of this Cen-
tury ; C. Tomlinson's Sonnet : its Origin, etc. ; S. Waddington's
English Sonnets by English Writers ; and to Rosenkranz's
Poetik, Viehoff's Poetik, etc.   Other standard works on poet-
ics, such as Wackernagel's, Gottschall's, etc., should be con-
sulted *ad loc.*   A monograph by Lentzner, Ueber d. Sonett u. s.
Gestaltung (Halle : 1886), will be useful.   To this list we
append from Schipper, Capel Lofft's Laura, an Anthology of
Sonnets (5 vols. Lond. : 1814) ; French's History of the
English Sonnet, in the Dublin Afternoon Lectures, 4th Series
(Lond. : 1867) ; *Dublin Review,* N. S., vols. XXVII, XXVIII
Critical History of the Sonnet ; also 55 : 174 by E. Elliot ; L.
de Veyrières, Monographie des sonnets (2 vols.   Paris : 1869) ;
Quart. Rev. 134 : 186 The Sonnet ; T. Hall Caine's Sonnets
of Three Centuries (Lond. : 1882).   For a comparative study
of the sonnet, see L. Biadene's Morfologia del sonetto nei
secoli xiii e xiv, reviewed by F. M. Warren in *Mod. Lang. Notes,*
4 : 151 ; Welti's Geschichte des Sonnetts in der deutschen
Dichtung (Leipz. : 1884) ; and R. Bunge's Zur Geschichte des
italienischen Sonetts, in *Magazin f. d. Litt. d. In- und Auslandes,*
1884 : 537, 554, 566, 582.

(*e*) For *Other Fixed Forms of Verse,* see Guide to Lit. Aesth.,
pp. 99, 100 ; and consult especially Theodore de Banville's
Traité de poésie française (Paris : 1881) ; Hood's Rhymester,
ed. by Arthur Penn ; Austin Dobson's Foreign Forms of Verse
(in W. D. Adams's Latter-Day Lyrics.   Lond. : 1878) ; Edmund
Gosse's Plea for Certain Exotic Forms of Verse (*Cornh.*, July,
1877) ; F. de Gramont's Les vers français (Paris) ; and Gleeson
White's Ballades and Rondeaux, etc. (Lond. : 1887).   See
also Schipper's Neuengl. Metrik, p. 886 *et seq.;* and Franz
Hueffer's Troubadours, Ancient and Modern (*Macmillan,* No-
vember, 1880).

6. ON FRENCH VERSIFICATION some of the leading authorities are L. Bellanger's Études historiques et philologiques sur la rime française (Paris et Anjou : 1876. See § **23**) ; Becq de Fouquière's Traité général; F. de Gramont's Les vers français and the works of de Banville, Benloew, Bouvy, Lubarsch, Quicherat, and others cited § **23** above. A discussion of the old French decasyllabic metre, cited by Mayor (English Metre, pp. 47–49), will be found in Gaston Paris's edition of La vie de Saint Alexis (Paris : 1890). See also G. Paris, Étude sur le rôle de l'accent latin dans la langue française (Paris : 1862) ; his Lettre à M. Léon Gautier sur la versification rhythmique and his Le vers français ; and L. Gautier, Les epopées françaises, vol. I, pt. II, p. 310 *et seq.* In Curme's edition of the selected poems of Alphonse de Lamartine, pp. 139–146 (Boston : 1888), will be found a brief but lucid dissertation on French versification. Voltaire, Œuvres complètes (50 vols. Paris : 1877–83), has dropped various formal but really unillumined remarks concerning metres and rhyme, some of which will be found, vol. II, pp. 313–325 ; vol. XX, pp. 371–374, 561–571. Schipper's reference (Altengl. Metrik, p. 88) to Diez's article Ueber d. epischen Vers opens to the student the bibliography of theories regarding the origin of the French Alexandrine. See also on the Alexandrine, Ernst Traeger's Gesch. d. Alexandriners (Leipz.: 1889, 1. Theil, bis Ronsard. Diss.); F. Diez, Altromanische Sprachdenkmäler berichtigt u. erklärt (Bonn : 1846); Bartsch's Altfranzösische Chrestomathie (Leipz.: 1875); and Maurice Souriau, L'Évolution du vers français au XVIIᵉ siècle. In G. Körting's Encyklopädie und Methodologie der romanischen Philologie, III. Teil, pp. 278–301, will be found a concise statement of the principles of French versification, according to Körting, and a bibliography. As a general treatise and as suggestive of further bibliographical material, Adolph Tobler's Vom franz. Versbau (Leipz. : 1883) is recommended.

A commendably systematic and complete history of French
metric prefixed to Bellanger's Étude historique, etc., pp. v–xiv
(see also Additions, pp. 2–4), precludes the necessity of further specification on that subject. Beginning with L'Art de
Dictier of Eustache Deschamps, 1392, and passing by way
of the metrists of the sixteenth century (Du Bellay, the two
Estiennes, Fabri, Dubois, Pelletier, Des Autels, Baïf, Meigret,
Fontaine, Fouquelin de Chauny), then of Bouhours, Corneille,
Marmontel, Malherbe, Voltaire, etc., to Gaston Paris, Pellissier,
and other writers of this century, Bellanger provides abundant
material for research in the history of French versification.
In poetics a similar course has already been outlined above,
pp. 428–445.

Since, however, these books may not be accessible to all, the
following modern treatises are recommended: A. Kressner's
Leitfaden d. französischen Metrik nebst einem Anhange über d.
altfranzösischen epischen Styl (Leipz.: 1880); H. Anderson's
Ueber den Einfluss von Metrum, Assonanz, und Reim, auf die
Sprache d. altfranzösischen Dichter (Bonn: 1874); H. Schu-
chardt's Reim u. Rhythmus im Deutschen u. Romanischen (1873);
Benloew's Précis d'une théorie des rhythmes, pt. I Rhythmes
lat. et franç. (Paris: 1862); E. d'Eichthal's Du rhythme dans
la versification franç. (Paris: 1892); F. Diez's Grammaire des
langues romanes, 3e ed. trad. par G. Paris (5 fasc. Paris:
1873–75); Fauriel, Hist. de la poésie provençale (3 vols.
Paris: 1847); J. Bedier, Les fabliaux; Lamartine, Premières
méditations poétiques (prefaces and commentaries. Paris:
1860); Mémoires de la soc. de linguistique de Paris, tome I
(1869); Gotthold Naetibus, Die nichtlyrischen Strophen-
formen des Altfranzösischen (Leipz.: 1891); Pellissier, La
langue française, etc. (Paris: 1866); R. Sonnenburg, Wie sind
die französischen Verse zu lesen? (Berlin: 1885); K. E. Müller, Ueber accentuirend-metrische Verse in der französischen
Sprache d. 16. bis 19. Jahrhunderts (Rostock: 1882); H.

Rigault, Histoire de la querelle des anciens et des modernes
(Paris: 1859); Sainte-Beuve, Tableau hist. et crit. de la Litt.
franç. et du théât. franç. au xvie siècle (Paris : 1869); J. de
Boisjoslin, Esquisse d'une histoire de la versification française
(Amiens : 1885. Extrait de la *Revue de la société des études
historiques*, Nov.–Dec., 1884). The more general works on
French literature and language by Brachet, L. Gautier, Génin,
Littré, Livet, Marmontel, J. Palsgrave, and Wey, as also the
Histoire littéraire de la France par des bénédictins . . . de St.
Maur et . . . des membres de l'Institut (24 vols. Paris :
1733–1804), and the files of the *Rev. d. D. Mondes*, the *Zeit-
schrift f. romanische Philol.* (ed. by G. Gröber), and of *Romania*
(ed. by Meyer and Paris), should be consulted.

On the burning question of the origin of Romance versification, the following are the leading disputants : Gaston Paris,
Léon Gautier, W. Meyer (Proceedings of the Munich Academy,
1882–86), Ch. Aubertin (La langue et la littérature française
au moyen âge, vol. I, p. 169. Paris: 1883), V. Henry (Des
origines du décasyllabe. Paris : 1886), R. Thurneysen (*Zeitschrift f. romanische Philol.* 11 : 306), P. A. Becker (Ueber
den Ursprung der romanischen Versmasse. Strassburg: 1890),
and Kawczynski. The article of E. Stengel, on Metrik der
romanischen Sprachen, in Gröber's Grundriss, Bd. II., is an
able review of the discussion.

The origin and development of the *vers libre* are ably treated
by P. A. Becker in his Zur Geschichte der *Vers libres* in der
neufranzösischen Poesie (Halle : 1888. Originally appeared
in *Zeitschrift f. romanische Philol.* 12 : 89–125). Becker defines
'free verse' as a non-strophic metrical form, with rhyming
lines of unequal length, both lines and rhymes being arranged
to suit the pleasure of the poet. He traces the history of
the verse from the Greek chorus to the poems of Alfred de
Musset. See also Ch. Comte, Les stances libres dans
Molière.

For further material upon recent phases of French metric,
see H. P. Thieme's indispensable bibliography, La littérature
française du dix-neuvième siècle (Paris: 1897), and the same
author's doctoral thesis, The Technique of the French Alexandrine (Ann Arbor: 1899).

7. ON GERMAN VERSIFICATION. — In addition to the many
authorities mentioned in § 23 the following are of importance:
E. Belling's Beiträge zur Metrik Goethes ; S. Mehring's Deutsche
Verslehre (Leipz.: 1891); R. Gottschall's Poetik, discussed
already, § 21 (see especially his chapters on Technik); A.
Grabow's Ueber Musik in d. deutschen Sprache (Progr.
Lemgo: 1876); T. Vernakken, *Herrig's Archiv*, 4 : 52 Der
deutsche Vers ; H. Viehoff's Poetik, above referred to (Buch
I, pp. 3–451 Vers u. Strophenbau) ; F. W. Rückert's Antike u.
deutsche Metrik (1847) ; J. H. Voss's Die deutsche Zeitmessung
(2te Ausg.: 1831) ; K. Luick's Zur Entstehung der Theorie
der Schwellverse (1887) ; R. Genée's Ueber Rhythmik d.
Sprache u. Vortrag (Dissert. Dresden). Of works on the
German iambic pentameter, one of the most readable and
learned is Zarncke's Der fünffüssige Iambus, which, as being
difficult to obtain in the original, has been wisely appended in
translation by Professor Mayor to his work on English Metre,
pp. 197–202. Zarncke "laments the indifference shown by
German scholars in regard to the metres employed by their
greatest poets," and indicates Koberstein and Diez (Altröm.
Sprachdenkmäler. Bonn: 1846) as the only Germans who have
notably treated of the five-foot iambus. He traces the metre
to the Provençal, from which also was, in his opinion, developed
the Italian hendecasyllabic. He cites (Mayor, p. 200) the
theories of the practice touching metrical substitutions, and
the caesura, of Opitz (d. 1639), Gottsched (1737), J. A. Schlegel (1757), Wieland (1762), of Klopstock, of Herder (1768),
and of Lessing (in his Nathan der Weise, 1778). To this
bibliography of German metrical criticism may be added a list

of authors rehearsed by Minckwitz in his Verskunst (see above,
§ 23), p. vii.   Dr. Ernst Brücke throws light from the scientific side upon the questions of accent and rhythm in his Die
physiologischen Grundlagen der neuhochdeutschen Verskunst
(Wien: 1871), a work which was reviewed by W. Scherer in
his Geschichte der deutschen Sprache (Berlin : 1878).   On this
subject of Neuhochd. Metrik, see Westphal's work, § 23 above ;
W. Scherer's Ueber den Hiatus in d. neueren deutschen Metrik ;
Phillips's Zur Theorie des neuhochdeutschen Rhythmus (Dissert.
Leipz.: 1879) ; Assmuss's Die äussere Form neuhochdeutscher
Dichtung (Leipz. : 1882); Goldbeck-Loewe's Zur Geschichte
der freien Verse in d. deutschen Dichtung (Dissert.   Kiel :
1891) ; P. Remer's Die freien Rhythmen in H. Heine's Nord-
seebildern (Heidelberg : 1889) ; O. Schmeckebier's Deutsche
Verslehre (Berlin : 1886) ; Kräuter's Ueber neuhochdeutsche
und antike Verse (Saargemund : 1873); and the series of stud-
ies by Belling, entitled Die Metrik Schillers (Breslau : 1883),
Beiträge zur Metrik Goethes (Progr.   Bromberg : 1884–87),
Die Metrik Lessings (Berlin : 1887).

See also, for tone and accent, Schneider's Darstellung d.
deutsch. Verskunst (Tübingen : 1861) ; Jessen's Grundzüge d.
altgermanisch. Metrik (Höpfner u. Zacher's *Zeitschrift*, II, 138);
Reichel's Von der deutschen Betonung (Dissert.   Jena : 1888);
Huss's Lehre vom Accent der deutschen Sprache ; and the articles by Paul, Sievers, Behaghel, and others, of which mention
is made in §§ 23, 25, 26.

On the opinions of Lachmann, Holtzmann, Zarncke, Bartsch,
and Fr. Pfeiffer, concerning the origin of the Nibelungenlied
and the nature of its strophe, see Werner Hahn's Das Nibelungenlied (Berl.–Stuttg.   Collection Speeman).   Pages 47–71
are devoted to an elaborate review of the theories of conflicting metrists, and will set upon the road any who desire to pursue investigation in this quarter.   On the Minnesinger, etc.,
the student must be referred to Weissenfels's Der daktylische

Rhythmus bei den Minnesängern, and in general to the histories
of German literature.

For the literature of German Alliterationspoesie, see Ferd.
Vetter's Zum Muspilli u. s. w. (Wien : 1872), pp. ix–x (Wacker-
nagel, W. Müller, Feussner, J. Grimm, Feifalik, Bartsch, Müllenhoff, Müllenhoff u. Scherer, Zarncke, Hofmann), and also pp.
1–3, where special reference is made to Schubert's excellent De
anglosaxonum arte metrica (Berlin : 1870), and to Vilmar-
Grein's Deutsche Grammatik.   On the same subject, see K. G.
Högelsberger, Alliteration u. Alliterationspoesie (Progr.   1857) ;
Loch, De alliteratione (Halle : 1876.   Dissert.) ; also Huemer's
Untersuchungen über die ältesten lat.-christ. Rhythm. (Wien :
1879), and Paul's Grundriss d. germ. Philol., Absch. IX,
p. 975, whence a full bibliography of the subject may be
extracted.

On rhyme, special reference should be made to Ferd. Wolf's
Ueber die Lais, Sequenzen u. Leiche, u. s. w. (Heidelberg :
1841), p. 161 *et seq.*, where further bibliography will be found ;
also to C. F. Meyer's Historische Studien (Mitau u. Leipz. :
1851) ; to W. Grimm's Geschichte d. Reims, p. 177 *et seq.*
(Berlin : 1852) ; to Mehring's Der Reim in seiner Entwickelung
und Fortbildung (Berlin : 1889); and to Kluge's article Zur
Geschichte des Reimes im Altgermanischen, in Paul u. Braune's
Beiträge, Bd. IX, p. 422.

On the German *vers libre* see A. Goldbeck-Loewe's Zur Geschichte d. freien Verse in d. deutschen Dichtung von Klopstock
bis Goethe (Diss.   Kiel : 1891).

8. ITALIAN VERSIFICATION. — The older treatises upon this
subject have been indicated above, pp. 445–448.   The following belong to the present century : J. u. M. Wiggers's Grammatik d. ital. Sprache, nebst Abriss d. ital. Metrik (Hamburg :
1859); G. Barengo's Della versificazione italiana (Venezia :
1854) ; E. Kurzweil's Traité de la prosodie de la langue ital.
(Paris : 1864) ; Zambaldi's Il ritmo dei versi ital. (Torino :

1875); A. Solerti's Manuale di metrica classica italiana ed
accento ritmico (Torino : 1886); R. Murari's Ritmica e metrica razionale italiana (Milano: 1891); Gius. Fracarroli,
D'una teoria razionale di metrica italiana (Torino: 1887);
Gius. Finzi, Principii di stilistica, versificazione e metrica
italiana, con un dizionarietto di modi errati (Torino : 1887).
For a concise scientific treatment of the subject, see G.
Körting's Encyklopaedie u. Method. d. rom. Philol., Theil 3,
pp. 663-675, or C. von Reinhardstöttner's Theoretisch-prak-
tische Grammatik d. ital. Sprache (2. Aufl. München: 1880).
An interesting chapter on the origin of rhyme may be found in
Tiraboschi's Storia della lett. ital., vol. III, p. 354 *et seq.* See
also Rob. Benzoni, Metrica e psicologia : frammento d'estetica
(Firenze : 1889); D. Guoli, *Nuova Antol.*, December, 1876 La
rima e la poesia italiana.

9. SPANISH AND PORTUGUESE VERSIFICATION.— (*a*) On *Spanish metres* the student may consult the Gramática castellana of
Don Vincente Salvá (Paris: 1872), pp. 390-434 Prosodia y
métrica. Salvá's history and rules of metric are drawn from
many sources, the most important of which will be found included in the following list : Marquis de Villena, El arte de
trobar (1433. See Ticknor's History of Spanish Lit., vol. I) ;
Rengifo, Arte poética española (1592) ; Carillo, Libro de
erudicion poética (1611); Cascáles, Tablas poéticas (1616),
Tabla Vᵃ ; Gomez Hermosilla, Arte de hablar en prosa y
verso, pt. II, lib. 1, cap. 1, 2 ; Luzan, Poética (1737), lib. 2,
cap. 22 ; Maury, Versificacion y elocucion (Paris: 1835), and
Espagne poétique, Prolog. to Tome I ; Masden, Arte poética,
dialogo 3°; A. L. Pinciano, Philosofia antigua poética (1596),
Epist. 6, 7 ; Martinez de la Rosa, Poética, Canto III, notas
1ᵃ, 2ᵃ ; Sicilia, Lecciones elementales de ortologia y prosodia
(Madrid), Tomo 2°; A. Tracia (Agustin Aicart), Diccionario de
la rima (Barcelona : 1858 ; Prolog. Elementos de poética, Sec.
II, cap. 3, §§ 1-3). The articles in *Romania* and other journals of

Romance philology are in the main of value only to specialists. Two articles of more general interest are Oservaciones sobre versificacion, by Cortoza, in *Rev. de Esp.*, vol. XCIII, p. 100; and Historia literaria del decasilabo y endecasilabo anapésticos, by Milá y Fontanals, in *Revista histórica-latina*, No. 7. For a treatise at once concise and comprehensive, see Körting's Encykl. u. Method. d. rom. Philol., Theil 3, pp. 527-553.

(*b*) For the principles of *Portuguese versification* reference may be made to Reinhardstöttner's Gramm. d. portug. Sprache (Strassb.: 1879), p. 374; to Körting's Encykl. u. Methode d. rom. Philol., Theil 3, pp. 583, 584; to José de Fonseca's Tratado de versificação port.; to A. F. de Castilho's Tratado de metrificação port. (Lisbon: 1851); and to F. Diez's Die erste Kunst- und Hofpoesie (Bonn : 1863).

10. Russian Versification. — A clear and simple presentation of Russian metric may be found in M. Brodovski's Manual of Versification (in Russian. St. Petersburg: 1887).

11. The peculiarities that obtain in the Versification of Northern Europe should not be overlooked in an attempt at inductive study. For the broadest statement of the characteristics of Old Northern metric, see Vigfusson and Powell's Corpus Poeticum Boreale (2 vols. Oxford: 1883). Vol. II, pp. 687, 688, gives a complete index to all that the two volumes contain on metre. Perhaps the most important reference in the Corpus Poeticum Boreale is to be found in vol. I, Excursus II, where are discussed the history, classification, and notation of Old Norse, German, and English metres. (See also vol. I, p. 458.) A valuable passage upon the subject will be found in Du Meril's Histoire de la poésie scandinave (Paris: 1839), pp. 63-72 De la versification scandinave. It is followed by an equally interesting chapter, De la traduction des poésies scandinaves. The footnotes in this volume will profit the bibliographer. For further information touching the history of Scandinavian forms in literature the student is referred to

Frederik Winkel Horn's Geschichte d. Lit. d. skandinavischen Nordens, von den ältesten Zeiten bis auf die Gegenwart (Leipz. : 1880), pp. 11–89 Die altnord. Lit., pp. 89–288 Dänemark und Norwegen, pp. 289–378 Schweden. Nearly all important authorities on Scandinavian poetry and versification are cited in the admirable Bibliographischer Anhang, pp. 378–399, which treats (1) of Die altnord.-isländisch. Lit., (2) of Dänemark u. Norwegen, (3) of Schweden, furnishing references not only to critical material but to the masterpieces themselves. The chapter on Altnordische Metrik in Paul's Grundriss d. germ. Philol., VIII. Abschnitt, pp. 876–888, by Sievers, gives in condensed form the researches of one of the highest authorities on the subject, and brings the bibliography up to date.

12. On the metrical systems of the LAPLANDERS, see the excellent and concise chapter Das Metrum, in O. Donner's Lieder d. Lappen (Uebers. aus d. fin. Zeitschrift Suomi 2. jakso xi osa. Helsingfors : 1876), pp. 29–36. See also G. von Düben's Lappland och Lapparne (Stockholm : 1873), where a chapter, pp. 318–347, is devoted to the much-neglected study of Lappish music and poetry. Much of von Düben's information is derived from the mouth of the famous Lapland scholar and pastor, A. Fjellner. Other authorities suggested by Donner are : J. A. Friis, Lappiske Sprogproever (Christiania : 1856); Scheffer, Lapponia (Frankf. : 1673), p. 282 ; J. A. Sjögren, Die Gemeinden in Kemi-Lappmark, vol. I, pp. 189, 440, 441 ; J. A. Friis, Lappisk Mythologi . . . (Christiania : 1871), p. 169 *et seq.;* Weatherby's transl. in Colburn's *New Monthly* of Bertram's arrangement of the Peivash Parneh, or Sons of the Sun-God (see also *London Acad.,* Jan. 17, 1874). Numerous other references, as well as original criticism, will be found in Donner's Lieder d. Lappen, *passim.*

13. ON FINNISH PROSODY, see also Donner, pp. 29–31, who refers with respect to Porthan's De Poesi Fennica (Åbo : 1766–68) ; to Lönnrot's Introd. to his first edition of the Kalevala

(1835); and to Aug. E. Ahlqvist's exhaustive treatment of
Finnish Metrik in his Suomalainen runous-oppi kielelliseltä kan-
nalta (Helsingissä: 1863), pp. 1–32. We have found of direct
service toward the history of this subject the An den Leser,
pp. v–x, of Hermann Paul's interesting verse-translation of
Finnish lyrics and ballads, entitled Kanteletar (Helsingf.:
1882). One of the most important authorities on Finnish
prosody is Comparetti, who in his Kalevala, German edition,
1892, p. 31, gives an account of parallelism in Finnish poetry.

14. The student of comparative versification will not stop
short with the metric of European tongues; he will examine
also such works on ORIENTAL POETICS as may be accessible and
within his comprehension.

15. ON INDIAN LITERATURE it is feasible here only to suggest consultation of the series, Sacred Books of the East, ed.
by Max Müller; prefaces to the various volumes (see especially Müller's Sacred Hymns of the Brahmans, and Hymns of
the Rig-Veda, Introd. to vol. I); Albrecht Weber's Indische
Studien, Indische Streifen, and the History of Indian Literature, transl. by Mann and Zachariae, pp. 182, 183, 232, 233 *et
passim* (Trübner's Orient. Series. Leipz.: 1878). In this work
of Weber's will be found many valuable references to bibliography. Also may be consulted J. Muir's Sanskrit Texts (5 vols.
2d ed. Lond.: 1868); his Metrical Translations from Sanskrit Writers (Trübner's); Monier Williams's Indian Epic Poetry
(1863); his Indian Wisdom (1875); and the preface to his
translation of the Nalopakhyanam; R. W. Cust's Linguistic and
Oriental Studies, pp. 60, 61; and his other works on Indian
literature and languages; and É. Lacereau's Groulabodha,
Traité de prosodie sanscrite, comp. par Kâledâsa (Paris: 1854).
In general, much is made accessible to the English reader by
Trübner's Oriental Series. More advanced students will of
course turn to the studies of Haug, Lassen, Burnouf, Roth,
Reinaud, Stenzler, Holtzmann, H. H. Wilson, Burnell, Bühler,

Colebrooke, Aufrecht, etc. H. H. Wilson's volumes on Hindoo
Dramatic Literature, while valuable in other respects, fail to
discuss the versification of the drama. His Essays, Analytical,
Critical, etc., may be consulted. See also W. D. Whitney,
Oriental and Linguistic Studies, p. 6 *et passim;* and Max
Müller, Chips from a German Workshop, vol. I, pp. 79-82.
There is an excellent treatise in the *Asiatic Journal,* N. S., 1837,
pp. 23-153, on the forms of Sanskrit metre. See also West-
phal's Metrik der indogermanischen Völker (Kühn's *Zeitschrift,*
9 : 437); his Allgemeine Metrik (§ **23**); and A. L. Chezy's
Théorie du Sloka ou mètre héroïque sanscrit (Paris : 1827).

16. A few of the most readily obtainable references on
HEBREW POETRY are Rob. Lowth's Lectures on Sacred Poetry of
the Hebrews (1770), transl. from the Latin by Greg, ed. by
C. E. Stone, Andover, 1829 (see chap. I); Jebb's Sacred Literature, p. 20; Philip Schaff's Introd. to Poetry of the Old Testament in the transl. of Lange's Commentary on Job (furnishes
an elaborate metrical scheme with illustrations); J. G. Herder's
Spirit of Hebrew Poetry (1782, transl. by J. Marsh, 1833),
vol. I, chap. XXVII; vol. II, chap. VIII; H. Ewald's Die
Dichter des alten Bundes, transl. by Kitto (1835-39), vol. I,
p. 83 (this is altogether the best article on the subject). The
most complete compendium of the various theories of Hebrew
verse with which we are acquainted is Saalschutz's Von der
Form der hebr. Poesie (Königsberg : 1825). See also the few
pages, 415-421, of Stevenson MacGill's Lectures on Rhetoric
and Criticism, introductory to study of Scriptures; Gesenius's
Lehrgebäude d. hebr. Sprache (ed. Rödiger, transl. Davies,
1869-76); and the works of Olshausen and Davidson. Schlottmann's Zur semitischen Epigraphie, V, VI, should not be overlooked.

17. ON EGYPTIAN VERSIFICATION, see the article by G. Ebers
on Rhyme and Alliteration in *Zeitschrift f. ägyptische Sprache
u. Alterthumsk.* 15 : 43.

18. On Chinese Versification the student is especially referred to Stanislas Julien's Hoeï-Lan-Ki, ou l'Histoire du cercle
de craie (Lond.: 1832), Preface, pp. xiii–xxix. The discussion
turns, however, rather upon Chinese imagery than upon metric.
For examples of balanced form in Chinese verse, see Julien's
L'Orphelin de la Chine (Paris: 1844), pp. 325–352. M. Bazin
(aîné), in the Introduction to his Théâtre chinoise (Paris: 1838),
traces the history of Chinese poetry, but devotes only pp. 37, 38
to the form of verse. Professor Douglas treats but meagerly of
the subject in his article on 'China' (Encycl. Brit.). Basil H.
Chamberlain, in his Classical Poetry of Japan (Trübner. Lond.:
1880), Introd., pp. 2–4, gives some definite information concerning rhyme, tone, and parallelism in Chinese verse. See also Dr.
James Legge's The Chinese Classics (Sacred Books of the East).
To these references may be added the following, kindly furnished
by Prof. John Fryer of the University of California:

Zottoli's Cursus Litteraturae Sinicae, vol. IV, pars Oratoria et
poetica (Shanghai: 1882); The T'u-shu-chi-ch'ing, or large Chi-
nese Encyclopaedia in 1639 volumes (Division V on poetry);
A. Wylie's Notes on Chinese Literature (Shanghai, Division IV,
Belles-lettres); Sir J. F. Davis's The Poetry of the Chinese;
Sir W. Medhurst, *The China Review*, 4: 46 Chinese Poetry;
Meadows's Desultory Notes on China (Lond.: 1847); C.
Gooderich, *Chinese Recorder*, vol. VIII, Chinese Hymnology;
The Shï-yün, or Dictionary of Rhymes (a Chinese native work);
J. Edkins, *China Review*, 17: 35 Poetry of Li-tai-po.

19. Japanese Metres. — Basil Hall Chamberlain's Japanese
Classical Poetry (Lond.: 1880), Introd., pp. 2–6, furnishes a
succinct account of the pillow-words, prefaces, and pivots of
Japanese verse; also of the principal stanzaic form, — the *uta*.
There is nothing new in the Encycl. Brit. article. A. Pfizmaier's
Die poetischen Ausdrücke der japanischen Sprache (Denk-
schrift d. Akad. d. Wiss., Philos.-Hist. Cl., Wien: 1873, p. 229;
1874, p. 341) may be mentioned at this point, though it does

not bear directly on the subject of metre.   Professor Fryer gives us the following :

Leon de Rosny's Anthologie Japonaise; R. Lange's Alt-japanische Frühlingslieder ; W. Aston's Grammar of the Japanese Written Language, p. 167 *et seq.;* Basil H. Chamberlain's Handbook of Colloquial Japanese ; and the article in *The Chinese Repository,* vol. X, p. 214 Poetry of the Japanese.

20. ARABIAN METRES are ably handled in H. Coupry's Traité de la versification arabe (Leipz. : 1875) ; in Guyard's Théorie nouvelle de la métrique arabe, précédée de considerations générales sur le rhythme naturel du langage; and in M. Hartmann's Metrum und Rhythmus : Die Entstehung der arab. Versmasse (Giessen: 1897).   Those who read Arabic may acquaint themselves with the extensive work on Arabian literature by L. Cheikhos, published at Beyrout in 1886.   The first volume contains the treatise on versification.   The Beiträge zur Kentniss d. Poesie d. alten Araber, by Theodor Nöldeke (Hannover : 1864), is suggested as a key to further bibliography and criticism in this direction.

21. TURKISH METRES. — See the article by W. J. Redhouse, on the History, System, and Varieties of Turkish Poetry, in *Trans. of the Royal Soc. of Lit.,* 2d Ser., 12 : 99.   It contains much translation.

APPENDIX.

A BIBLIOGRAPHY OF ARISTOTLE'S POETICS.[1]

GREEK.

Rhetores Graeci. Ven.: 1508. Aldus.

De rhetorica L. III. . . . De poetica liber unus. Graece. Ven.: 1536. In aed. Zanetti et dilig. Trincavelli.

Poetica, graece. Parisiis: 1541. Per Conr. Neobarium.

Rhetorica et poetica. Venet.: 1546. Jo. Gryphius.

Poetica cum Vinc. Madii et Barth. Lombardii comm. explan. Ven.: 1550.

De arte poetica liber graece, cum var. lect. Parisiis: 1555. Morel.

Poetica. Graece, cum P. Victorii comm. in librum primum. Florentiae: 1560. In off. Juntarum.

De arte poetica, graece, ad exemplar libri a P. Victorio correcti. Florentiae: 1564. Apud Juntas.

Greek text, ed. by I. Casaubon. Leyden: 1590.

Poetica. Heinsius recensuit. Lugd. Bat.: 1610.

Poetica cum animadv. Paccii et Riccoboni ac comm. P. Benii. Ven.: 1624.

Ἀριστοτέλους περὶ ποιητικῆς βιβλίον. Parisiis: 1630.

De poetica liber, ex vers. Th. Goulstoni perp. not. ill. acc. integrae notae Fr. Sylburg. et D. Heinsii, necnon selectae aliorum, quibus suas etiam immiscuit (J. Uptonus) editor. Cantabr.: 1696.

Ἀριστοτέλους περὶ ποιητικῆς (Lectiones variantes . . . et notae, etc.). Oxford: 1760.

[1] For the literature of the Aristotelian controversy concerning poetry, see vol. II of this work, especially under the *Epic* and *Tragedy*.

Aristotelis de poetica liber, textu goulstoniano; cum praelectione versione et notis editoris Guilielmi Cooke: accedit elegia grayiana, graece. Cantabr.: 1785. Typ. Acad.

De poetica. Rec. F. W. Reiz. Lipsiae: 1786.

Aristotelis de poetica liber, graece lectionem constituit, versionen refinxit, animadversionibus illustravit Th. Tyrwhitt. Oxonii 1794. Typ. Clarend. (Other editions in 1806, 1818, 1827.)

De poetica graece. Rec. J. Gl. Buhle. Gott.: 1794.

Aristotelis de poetica graece, cum notis ... edidit L. Sahl. Hauniae 1802. (With the Ars Poetica of Horace.)

Aristotelis de arte poetica librum denuo recensitum commentarii illustratum, recognitio Valettii, Hermanni, Tyrwhitti, Buhlii Harlesii, Castelvetri, Robortelli, aliorum editionibus edidit cun prolegominis, notitiis et indicibus Aug.-Guil. Graefenham. Lip siae: 1821.

Rhetorica et poetica ex rec. I. Bekkeri. Berol.: 1831.

Aristotelis rhetorica et poetica ab Immanuele Bekkero tertium editae Berol.: 1859.

Aristotelis de arte poetica liber. Recensuit J. Vahlen. Berol.: 1867

Aristotelis ars poetica ... edidit F. Ueberweg. Berol.: 1870.

Aristotelis de arte poetica liber: iterum recens. et adnot. crit. auxi J. Vahlen. Berol.: 1874.

Aristotelis de arte poetica (Vahlen's text): with notes by E. Moore Oxford: 1875.

Aristotelis ars poetica ... edidit F. Ueberweg. Lipsiae: 1875.

Aristotelis de arte poetica liber. Recensuit G. Christ. Lipsiae 1878; 1893.

De arte poetica liber. Recognovit brevique adnotatione critica in struxit I. Bywater. Oxford: 1898. Clarendon Press.

GREEK AND LATIN.

Poetica per Alex Paccium in latinum conversa; eadem graece Venet.: 1536. In aedibus haeredum Aldi. (Reprinted with slight changes at Basle: 1537; Paris: 1538; Leyden: 1549 Venice: 1572, 1600.)

Aristotelis de arte poetica, gr. et lat., cum Fr. Robortelli explica tionibus, accessere ejusd. Robortelli in Horatii artem poet. paraphrasis, et explicationes de satyra, epigrammate, comoedia, etc. (2 parts in 1 vol.) Florentiae: 1548. L. Torrentinus.

V. Madii et Bartholomaei in Aristotelis librum de poetica communes explicationes. (Text and Latin version by A. Paccius.) Venet.: 1550.

P. Victorii commentarii in primum librum Aristotelis de arte poetarum. In off. Juntarum. Florentiae: 1560. (2d ed., 1573.)

An edition by F. Sylburg, Frankfort: 1584, is noted by Blankenburg and others, but the exact title is wanting in these authorities.

Aristotelis de poetica liber; D. Heinsius recensuit . . . Latine vertit, notas addidit. Accedit ejusdem de tragica constitutione liber, pt. 2. Lugd. Bat.: 1610–11. Ap. Balduinum, prostat in bibliop. Elzevirii. (Republished in 1643.)

P. Benii in Aristotelis poeticam commentarii, etc. (Text, and Latin versions of Paccius and Riccobonus.) Patavii: 1613.

De poetica liber, gr. et lat., analytica methodo illustratus, a Theod. Goulston. Lond.: 1623. (Reëdited by J. Upton, Cambridge: 1696.)

De poetica, graece, cum versione Theod. Goulstoni et variantibus lectionibus. Glasguae: 1745. Rob. Foulis.

Aristotelis de poetica liber . . . cum notis. (Ed. by W. Parsons.) Oxonii: 1760.

Poetica, gr. et lat., ex versione Theod. Goulstoni: lectionis varietatem et observationes suas adjunxit Th. Winstanley. Oxonii: 1780. Typ. Clarend.

Aristotelis de poetica liber . . . ex recens. . . . T. C. Harles. Acc. not. F. Sylburgii. Lipsiae: 1780.

Aristotelis de poetica liber. Textu Goulstoniano; cum . . . notis ed. G. Cooke. Cantabr.: 1785. (Lond.: 1788.)

Aristotelis de poetica liber. Textum recens. . . . T. Tyrwhitt. Oxonii: 1794. (Also another edition, ed. by T. Burgess. 3d ed., 1806; 4th, 1817; 5th, 1827.)

De poetica liber, gr. et lat., cum commentar. Godofr. Hermanni. Lipsiae: 1802.

Poeticae Aristotelis nova versio, cum textu graeco haud paucis in locis emendato, auctore de Haus. Acc. app. duae de trag.

officio et de dram. poeseos apud Graecos origine. Panormi: 1815. Typ. reg.

De poetica gr. et lat. rec. et comm. ill. F. Ritter. Coloniae: 1839.

GREEK AND ENGLISH.

Aristotelis de arte poetica (Vahlen's Text): with translation by E. R. Wharton. Oxford: 1885. Parker.

The Poetics of Aristotle. Translated, with a critical Text, by S. H. Butcher. Lond.: 1895. Macmillan.

LATIN.

Rhetorica, ex arabico lat. reddita, interprete Alemanno, praemissa Alpharabii declaratione super eadem rhetorica. Excerptum ex Aristotelis poetica, ex recens. Lancilloti de Zerlis. Venet.: 1481. Per Philip. Venet.

Latin translation by G. Valla. Ven.: 1498.

Latin translation, with the summary of Averroes. Ven.: 1515. (This edition and the preceding are noted by Prickard.)

Aristotelis rhetorica ex arabico latine reddita, interprete Hermanno Alemanno. . . . Excerptum ex Aristotelis poetica per eundem Hermannum de Averrois textu arabico latine redditum. Basil: 1534.

Aristotelis poetica per A. Paccium in lat. conversa. Parisiis: 1542.

Ars rhet. gr. ab Ant. Riccobono Rhodigino lat. conv. . . . Ars poetica ab eodem in lat. ling. versa. Ven.: 1579.

Poet. Arist. ab A. Riccobono lat. conversa. Ven.: 1579; Patavii: 1587.

Aristotelis de poetica liber, latine conversus et . . . illustratus. (By T. Goulston.) Lond.: 1623.

ENGLISH.

Aristotle's Art of Poetry, trans. from the original Greek, with Dacier's notes. Lond.: 1705. (Republished 1709, 1714.)

Aristotle's Poetics, trans. from the Greek into English [by J. Willis]. Lond.: 1775.

Aristotle's Poetics, trans. from the Greek, with notes by H. J. Pye. Lond.: 1788. (2d ed., with commentary, 1792.)

Aristotle's Treatise on Poetry, trans.: with notes . . . and two dissertations . . . by T. Twining. Lond.: 1789. (2d ed. 1812. Another ed. with preface and notes by H. Hamilton, Dublin: 1851.)

Works of Aristotle, trans. from the Greek and ill. with copious elucidations from the commentators, by Thomas Taylor. 10 vols. Lond.: 1812. Vol. VII The Rhetoric and Poetic.

Rhetoric, Poetic and Nicomachaean Ethics, trans. by Thos. Taylor. Lond.: 1818.

FRENCH.

La poétique d'Aristote, trad. par Fr. Cassandre. Paris: 1654. (Republished 1675, 1685; Amst.: 1698, 1717; The Hague: 1718.)

La poétique d'Aristote, trad. du Grec par le Sieur de Norville. Paris: 1671.

La poétique d'Aristote, trad. du grec, avec des remarques, par And. Dacier. Paris: 1692. (Republished, Amst.: 1692, 1733.)

Les quatre poétiques d'Aristote, d'Horace, de Vida, de Despréaux, avec traductions et des remarques. Paris: 1771.

Chénier, M. J. de. Œuvres posthumes. Notice par Daunon. 3 vols. Paris: 1824-27. Vol. II La poétique d'Aristote, trad. en prose.

Racine, J. Œuvres complètes. 5e ed. par Aimé-Martin. 6 vols. Paris: 1844. Vol. V Fragments du premier livre de la poétique d'Aristote.

Egger, E. Essai sur l'histoire de la critique chez les Grecs, suivi de la poétique d'Aristote et d'extraits de ses problèmes, avec traduction française et commentaire. Paris: 1849.

Poétique d'Aristote, trad. en français et accompagnée de notes perpétuelles, par J. Barthélemy Saint-Hilaire. Paris: 1854.

GERMAN.

A German translation by Mich. Curtius (with commentary principally taken from Dacier), Hanover : 1753, is noted by Blankenburg, Zusätze I : 382.

Aristoteles über die Kunst der Poesie, aus d. Griech. übersetzt u. erläut. nebst Th. Twining's Abh. üb. d. poet. u. musikal. Nachahmung. Aus d. Engl. hrsg. von J. G. Buhle. Berlin : 1798.

Aristoteles von der Dichtkunst. Text mit Uebersetzung u. Anm. von C. H. Weise. Merseb. : 1824.

Ausgewählte Schriften des Aristoteles. Bd. I Die Poetik übersetzt von Chr. Walz. 2. Aufl. besorgt von Dr. K. Zell. Stuttgart : 1859.

Aristoteles Poetik übersetzt und erklärt von Adolf Stahr. Stuttgart : 1860.

Aristoteles über die Dichtkunst. Ins Deutsche übersetzt und mit . . . Anmerkungen . . . versehen von F. Ueberweg. Berlin : 1870.

Aristoteles über die Dichtkunst. Griechisch und Deutsch von M. Schmidt. Jena : 1875.

Aristoteles über die Dichtkunst. . . . Ins Deutsche übersetzt, mit kritischen Anmerkungen und . . . Commentare . . . von F. Brandscheid. Wiesbaden : 1882.

ITALIAN.

Rettorica e poetica d'Aristotile, tradotte di greco in lingua volgare da Bern. Segni. Firenze : 1549. Torrentino.

Poetica d'Aristotile vulgarizzata e sposta, per Lod. Castelvetro. Vienna d'Austria : 1570. Stainhofer. (Republished at Basil 1576, 1582 ; and, minus the commentary, Milan 1827 and 1831.)

Il libro della Poetica di Aristotile, tradotto di greca lingua in volgare, da M. Al. Piccolomini con una sua epistola a i lettori del modo del tradurre. Siena : 1572. Bonetti.

Annotationi di M. Al. Piccolomini nel libro della Poetica d'Aristotile, con la traduttione del medesimo libro, in lingua volgare. Vin. : 1575. Guarisco e comp.

La politica, la rettorica, la poetica ed i libri dell' anima, trad. dal Segni. Firenze: 1583. Marescotti.

Poetica d'Arist. tradotta dal Greco nell' Italiano da Ottav. Castelli Spoletino. Roma: 1642.

La Poetica d'Arist. trad. da Ann. Caro. Ven.: 1732.

Metastasio, P. Opere. 16 vols. Firenze: 1819. Vol. 13 Estratto dell' arte poetica d'Aristotile.

L' arte poetica, . . . tradotta sul testo di G. Vahlen da G. Barco. Torino: 1876.

MISCELLANEOUS TRANSLATIONS.

A translation of the Poetics into Spanish was made about the middle of the sixteenth century by Juan Paez de Castro. Other information concerning it is lacking.

Poetica dada a nuestra lengua castellana por Alonzo Ordoñez de Seijas y Tobar : añadese nuevamente el texto griego, la vers. lat. y notas de D. Heinsius y las de Batteux. Madrid: 1778. Sancha. (First ed., without the Greek, 1620.)

El arte poética de Aristoteles en castellano, por . . . Jos. Goya y Muniain. Madrid : 1798. Cano.

A poetica d'Arist. trag. em portugueza lengoa. Lisboa: 1779.

Aristoteles Verhandeling over de Dichtkunst, waar agter eenige Verhandeling over de Dichtkunst en het Toneel . . . door M. C. Curtis. Amsterdam : 1780.

Aristoteles om Digtekunsten, overs. af Busch. Copenhagen: 1780.

INDEX.

BOOKS ON ENGLISH LITERATURE

GINN & COMPANY, Publishers

| Boston | New York | Chicago | San Francisco |
| Atlanta | Dallas | Columbus | London |

THE ATHENAEUM PRESS SERIES

Issued under the general editorship of
Professor GEORGE LYMAN KITTREDGE, of Harvard University, and
Professor C. T. WINCHESTER, of Wesleyan University.

THE FOLLOWING VOLUMES ARE NOW READY:

Burke's Speech on Conciliation with America. Edited by Professor HAMMOND LAMONT, recently of Brown University. 50 cents.

Burns: Selections from. Edited by the late JOHN G. DOW, formerly of the University of Wisconsin. $1.10.

Carlyle's Heroes, Hero-Worship, and the Heroic in History. Edited by Professor ARCHIBALD MACMECHAN of Dalhousie College, Halifax, N.S. $1.25.

Carlyle's Sartor Resartus. Edited by Professor ARCHIBALD MACMECHAN of Dalhousie College, Halifax, N.S. $1.25.

Collins: Poems of. Edited by Professor WALTER C. BRONSON of Brown University. 90 cents.

Cowper: Selections from. Edited by the late Professor JAMES O. MURRAY, formerly of Princeton University. $1.00.

De Quincey: Selections from. Edited by Professor MILTON H. TURK of Hobart College.

Elizabethan Lyrics. Edited by Professor F. E. SCHELLING of the University of Pennsylvania. $1.12.

Gibbon's Memoirs. Edited by Professor OLIVER F. EMERSON of Western Reserve University. $1.10.

Gray: Selections from the Works of. Edited by Professor WM. L. PHELPS of Yale University. 90 cents.

Herrick: Selections from the Hesperides and the Noble Numbers. Edited by Professor E. E. HALE, Jr., of Union University. 90 cents.

Jeffrey: Selections from the Essays of. Edited by LEWIS E. GATES of Harvard University. 90 cents.

Jonson's Timber; or Discoveries. Edited by Professor F. E. SCHELLING of the University of Pennsylvania. 80 cents.

Keats: Selections from. Edited by Professor ARLO BATES of the Massachusetts Institute of Technology. $1.00.

Landor: Selections from. Edited by W. B. S. CLYMER, formerly of Harvard University. $1.00.

Malory's Morte Darthur, Selections from. Edited by Professor WILLIAM E. MEAD of Wesleyan University, Middletown, Conn. $1.00.

Old English Ballads. Edited by Professor F. B. GUMMERE of Haverford College. $1.25.

Pre-Shaksperean Drama, Specimens of. Edited by Professor JOHN M. MANLY of University of Chicago. In three volumes. Vols. I. and II. now ready. $1.25 each.

Seventeenth Century Lyrics. Edited by Professor F. E. SCHELLING of the University of Pennsylvania. $1.12.

Shelley: Selections from. Edited by W. J. ALEXANDER of the University of Toronto. $1.15.

Sidney's Defense of Poesy. Edited by Professor ALBERT S. COOK of Yale University. 80 cents.

Steele: Selections from. Edited by Professor GEORGE R. CARPENTER of Columbia University. 90 cents.

Wordsworth: Selections from. Edited by Professor EDWARD DOWDEN of the University of Dublin. $1.25.

GINN & COMPANY Publishers

GAYLEY'S CLASSIC MYTHS

THE CLASSIC MYTHS IN ENGLISH LITERATURE.

Based chiefly on Bulfinch's " Age of Fable " (1855). Accompanied by an Interpretative and Illustrative Commentary.

EDITED BY

CHARLES MILLS GAYLEY,

Professor of the English Language and Literature in the University of California.

12mo. Half leather. 540 pages. Fully illustrated, together with 16 full-page illustrations. For introduction, $1.50.

ATTENTION is called to these special features of this book :

An introduction on the indebtedness of English poetry to the literature of fable; and on methods of teaching mythology.

An elementary account of myth-making and of the principal poets of mythology, and of the beginnings of the world, of gods and of men among the Greeks.

A thorough revision and systematization of Bulfinch's Stories of Gods and Heroes : with additional stories, and with selections from English poems based upon the myths.

Illustrative cuts from Baumeister, Roscher, and other standard authorities on mythology.

Certain necessary modifications in Bulfinch's treatment of the mythology of nations other than the Greek and Roman.

Notes, following the text (as in the school editions of Latin and Greek authors), containing an historical and interpretative commentary upon certain myths, supplementary poetical citations, a list of the better known allusions to mythological fiction, references to works of art, and hints to teachers and students.

GINN & COMPANY, Publishers,

Boston.   New York.   Chicago.   Atlanta.   Dallas.

REFERENCE BOOKS ON POETRY

A Book of Elizabethan Lyrics. Selected and edited by FELIX E. SCHELLING, Professor of English Literature in the University of Pennsylvania. 327 pages. For introduction, $1.12.

Old English Ballads. Selected and edited by Professor F. B. GUMMERE of Haverford College. 380 pages. For introduction, $1.25.

Introduction to the Poetry of Robert Browning. By WILLIAM J. ALEXANDER, Professor of English, University College, Toronto. 212 pages. For introduction, $1.00.

Hudson's Text-Book of Poetry. By HENRY N. HUDSON. Selections from Wordsworth, Coleridge, Burns, Beattie, Goldsmith, and Thomson. With Lives and Notes. Cloth. 704 pages. For introduction, $1.25.

Sidney's Defense of Poesy. Edited by ALBERT S. COOK, Professor of the English Language and Literature in Yale University. 103 pages. For introduction, 80 cents.

Shelley's Defense of Poetry. Edited by Professor ALBERT S. COOK. 86 pages. For introduction, 50 cents.

Cardinal Newman's Essay on Poetry. With reference to Aristotle's Poetics. Edited by Professor ALBERT S. COOK. 36 pages. For introduction, 30 cents.

The Art of Poetry. The Poetical Treatises of Horace, Vida, and Boileau, with the translations by Howes, Pitt, and Soame. Edited by Professor ALBERT S. COOK. 214 pages. For introduction, $1.12.

Addison's Criticisms on Paradise Lost. Edited by Professor ALBERT S. COOK. 200 pages. For introduction, $1.00.

What is Poetry? By Leigh Hunt. Edited by Professor ALBERT S. COOK. 98 pages. For introduction, 50 cents.

A Primer of English Verse. By HIRAM CORSON, Professor of English Literature in Cornell University. 232 pages. For introduction, $1.00.

A Hand-Book of Poetics. By FRANCIS B. GUMMERE, Professor of English Literature in Haverford College. 250 pages. For introduction, $1.00.

Characteristics of the English Poets, from Chaucer to Shirley. By WILLIAM MINTO. For introduction, $1.50.

GINN & COMPANY, Publishers,

Boston.   New York.   Chicago.   Atlanta.   Dallas.

Outline of the Philosophy of English Literature

By GREENOUGH WHITE, A.M., B.D.,

Author of "A Sketch of the Philosophy of American Literature."

Part I: The Middle Ages.

12mo. Cloth. vi + 266 pages. Introduction price, $1.00.

THE motive of this treatise is to determine the bounds of the great historical divisions of English literature, to discover the salient features, the peculiar characteristics of each epoch, to trace the connection in thought between each, and to view all against a background of European history, literature, and art. It is believed that the causes of historic change, the principles that control the succession of ages, the revolutions of thought, sentiment, and action, are here clearly discriminated; so that in this little book, in a word, a sound philosophy of mediaeval history is suggested.

W. J. Courthope, *Professor of Poetry at the University of Oxford:* It would be quite impertinent in me to criticise the manner in which the work has been executed, but I may be allowed to express my admiration of the orderly manner in which its very diverse materials are arranged and of the agreeable style in which the narrative is conducted. To accomplish this result in so vast a subject as English literature as a whole is in itself a proof of the most skillful workmanship, and I cannot too strongly express my conviction that this comprehensive survey is based upon sound knowledge and just reasoning.

Edward Dowden, *Professor of English, Trinity College, Dublin:* It interested me much, and seemed to me something new and needful, — not merely a work of erudition, but a contribution towards interpreting the results of erudition — a book not merely of knowledge, but of ideas. . . . Especially on this ground — as an elucidation of knowledge — I value the work. The way in which it keeps the European movement present to the reader's mind, with England as having a part in it, is of great importance.

Edmund Gosse, *Author of a "History of English Literature in the Eighteenth Century," etc.:* I have read the book with pleasure. It appears to me to deal freshly and brilliantly with the old, worn lines of history.

Leslie Stephen, *Author of "Hours in a Library" etc.:* The design is good, the style is good, and the matter interesting.

Alois Brandl, *Professor of English at the University of Berlin:* Whites Buch voll allgemeiner Bildung sich zeigt — . . . drei Viertel [?] der Darstellung gelten politischen oder kontinentalen Verhältnissen. Gefallen hat mir eine Bemerkung über Chaucers 'gentle pite' und 'pitous joye' (S. 81–2).

GINN & COMPANY, Publishers, Boston, New York, Chicago, London.

STANDARD ENGLISH CLASSICS

Burke's Letter to a Noble Lord. Edited by ALBERT H. SMYTH, Professor of English Literature in the Central High School, Philadelphia. 30 cents.

Burke's Speech on Conciliation with America. Edited by HAMMOND LAMONT, recently Associate Professor of Rhetoric in Brown University. 30 cents.

Burns' Representative Poems, with Carlyle's Essay on Burns. Edited by CHARLES L. HANSON, Teacher of English in the Mechanic Arts High School, Boston, Mass. 30 cents.

Carlyle's Essay on Burns. Edited by CHARLES L. HANSON. 25 cents.

Coleridge's Ancient Mariner. Edited by L. R. GIBBS. 20 cents.

Cooper's Last of the Mohicans. Edited by JOHN B. DUNBAR, Instructor in English in the Boys' High School, Brooklyn, N.Y. 50 cents.

De Quincey's Revolt of the Tartars. Edited by W. E. SIMONDS, Professor of English Literature in Knox College, Galesburg, Ill. 25 cents.

Dryden's Palamon and Arcite. Edited by GEORGE E. ELIOT, JR., Instructor in English in Morgan School, Clinton, Conn. 25 cents.

George Eliot's Silas Marner. Edited by R. ADELAIDE WITHAM, Teacher of English in Latin High School, Somerville, Mass. 30 cents.

Goldsmith's Vicar of Wakefield. Edited by D. H. MONTGOMERY. 30 cents.

Irving's Sketch Book. (Complete.) Edited, with Introduction and Notes, by MARY E. LITCHFIELD. 60 cents.

Macaulay's Essay on Milton. Edited by HERBERT A. SMITH, Instructor in English in Yale University. 20 cents.

Macaulay's Essay on Addison. Edited by HERBERT A. SMITH. 25 cents.

Macaulay's Essays on Addison and Milton. (In one volume.) Edited by HERBERT A. SMITH. 30 cents.

Macaulay's Lays of Ancient Rome. Edited by M. GRANT DANIELL, recently Principal of Chauncy-Hall School. 35 cents.

Milton's L'Allegro, Il Penseroso, Comus, and Lycidas. Edited by TULEY F. HUNTINGTON, Instructor in English in the Leland Stanford Junior University. 25 cents.

Milton's Paradise Lost, Books I. and II., and Lycidas. Edited by HOMER B. SPRAGUE. 30 cents.

Pope's Translation of the Iliad. *Books I., VI., XXII., and XXIV.* Edited by WILLIAM TAPPAN. 25 cents.

Scott's Ivanhoe. Edited by CHARLOTTE M. YONGE. 60 cents.

Shakespeare's Macbeth. Edited by Rev. HENRY N. HUDSON. 35 cents.

Shakespeare's Merchant of Venice. Edited by Rev. HENRY N. HUDSON. 35 cents.

Sir Roger de Coverley Papers. From *The Spectator*. Edited by MARY E. LITCHFIELD. 30 cents.

Tennyson's The Princess. Edited by ALBERT S. COOK, Professor of English Literature in Yale University. 30 cents.

GINN & COMPANY PUBLISHERS

Boston   New York   Chicago   San Francisco
Atlanta   Dallas   Columbus   London

HUDSON'S SHAKESPEARE

For School and Home Use.

By HENRY N. HUDSON, LL.D.,

Author of "The Life, Art, and Characters of Shakespeare,"
Editor of "The Harvard Shakespeare," etc.

Revised and enlarged Editions of twenty-three Plays. Carefully expurgated, with explanatory Notes at the bottom of the page, and critical Notes at the end of each volume. One play in each volume.

Square 16mo. Varying in size from 128 to 253 pages. Mailing price of each: cloth, 50 cents; paper, 35 cents. Introduction price, cloth, 45 cents; paper, 30 cents. Per set (in box), $10.00.

Why is Hudson's Shakespeare the standard in a majority of the best schools where the greatest attention is paid to this subject? Because Dr. Hudson was the ablest Shakespearean scholar America has ever known. His introductions to the plays of Shakespeare are well worth the price of the volume. He makes the characters almost living flesh and blood, and creates a great interest on the part of the student and a love for Shakespeare's works, without which no special progress can be made. Whoever can command the interest of the pupil in a great author or his works is the person who renders the greatest service.

The list of plays in Hudson's School Shakespeare is as follows:

A Midsummer Night's Dream.	*Henry the Fourth, Part I.*	*Macbeth.*
The Merchant of Venice.	*Henry the Fourth, Part II.*	*Antony and Cleopatra.*
Much Ado about Nothing.	*Henry the Fifth.*	*Othello.*
As You Like It.	*Henry the Eighth.*	*Cymbeline.*
The Tempest.	*Romeo and Juliet.*	*Coriolanus.*
King John.	*Julius Cæsar.*	*Twelfth Night.*
Richard the Second.	*Hamlet.*	*The Winter's Tale.*
Richard the Third.	*King Lear.*	

C. T. Winchester, *Professor of English Literature, Wesleyan University:* The notes and comments in the school edition are admirably fitted to the need of the student, removing his difficulties by stimulating his interest and quickening his perception.

Hiram Corson, *Professor of English Literature, Cornell University:* I consider them altogether excellent. The notes give all the aid needed for an understanding of the text, without waste and distraction of the student's mind. The introductory matter to the several plays is especially worthy of approbation.

We invite correspondence with all who are interested in the study of Shakespeare in the class-room.

GINN & COMPANY, Publishers,

Boston.   **New York.**   **Chicago.**   **Atlanta.**   **Dallas.**

The Beginnings of the

English Romantic Movement

By WILLIAM LYON PHELPS, A.M. (Harvard), Ph.D. (Yale),
Instructor in English Literature at Yale University.

12mo. Cloth. viii + 192 pages. Introduction price, $1.00.

*T*HIS book is a study of the germs of English Romanticism between 1725 and 1765. No other work in this field has ever been published, hence the results given here are all the fruit of first-hand investigation. The book discusses, with abundant references and illustrations, the various causes that brought about the transitions of taste from Classicism to Romanticism — such as the Spenserian revival, the influence of Milton's minor poetry, the love of mediæval life, the revival of ballad literature, the study of Northern mythology, etc. It is believed that this book is a contribution to our knowledge of English literary history; and it will be especially valuable to advanced classes of students who are interested in the development of literature. The treatment is historical rather than argumentative.

GINN & COMPANY, Publishers,

Boston. New York. Chicago. Atlanta. Dallas.